Edison to Enron

To the Jack Bowen family

Edison to Enron

Energy Markets
and
Political Strategies

Robert L. Bradley Jr.

Scrivener

Co-published by John Wiley & Sons, Inc. Hoboken, New Jersey, and Scrivener Publishing LLC, Salem, Massachusetts.
Published simultaneously in Canada.

For general information on our other products and services or for technical support, please contact our Customer Care Department within the United States at (800) 762-2974, outside the United States at (317) 572-3993 or fax (317) 572-4002.

Wiley also publishes its books in a variety of electronic formats. Some content that appears in print may not be available in electronic formats. For more information about Wiley products, visit our web site at www.wiley.com.

For more information about Scrivener products please visit www.scrivenerpublishing.com.

Cover design by Russell Richardson

Library of Congress Cataloging-in-Publication Data:

ISBN 978-0-470-91736-7

Printed in the United States of America

10 9 8 7 6 5 4 3 2 1

Contents

"In a nation built so largely around the accomplishments and values of business, we should pay more attention to our business history."
— *R. Hal Williams*, 1986

Preface

KEN LAY ATTACHED A NOTE to a book he returned to me between the time of Enron's collapse and his fateful trial. *Insull* by Forrest McDonald (University of Chicago Press, 1962) was a masterful account about the towering rise and stunning fall of a business titan in the first third of the twentieth century. "I apologize I've not been able to read the book on Insll [sic]," Lay wrote. "There have just been too many demands on my time." And no doubt Ken Lay *was* working furiously, preparing for trial and running what he excitedly described as his three new businesses. He probably wrote the note well past a normal person's endurance point. He was always like that—almost superhuman in his work, doing the little extra to cover some base in his vast universe of possibility and ambition.

People had given Ken many books that he never opened, much less read. I know. I was his repository for such material during my sixteen years at Enron. But I told him that McDonald's biography was very relevant to his present predicament. Like him, Samuel Insull had been a Great Man of the energy industry, an icon of his city (Chicago), a Horatio Alger story. Insull, too, had gone from near-universal reverence to vilification, suddenly and completely. And, most important, Insull's defense strategy seemed to be one that Lay could employ effectively.

In the twilight of his life, Insull had put his five-decade career building America's electricity industry on trial, not just his last years with his bankrupt holding companies. He spoke matter-of-factly on the stand about his intentions and failures, knowing that honesty was his rock in thick or thin. The point, partly, was to ask the jury: *Why would I suddenly take up crime*? And to tell the jury: *You would have done about the same if you had been me*. The other part of Insull's strategy was to confess to overoptimism and an inability to heed caution. And he took full responsibility for the debacle, even apologizing to his subordinates.

In short, Insull humanized himself on the stand. The jury acquitted on the facts and in the face of such humility.

Ken Lay took a far different approach after his company's collapse. He did not flee to another country as had Insull, who feared for his personal safety and harbored pessimism about receiving a fair trial. Instead, Lay fled to another reality. With his legal advisors and number-two-man Jeff Skilling, Lay constructed an alternative universe, a strategy that was not discouraged by his inner circle, a story told in *Enron and Ken Lay: An American Tragedy* (Book 3 of this trilogy). Thus came the other worldly arguments: *Enron was a great company. Jeff Skilling and I were a great team. Enron would be thriving today if it were not for the criminal actions of a few employees, some short sellers, and a hostile press.* And then there was Lay's contempt at the whole proceedings, and even toward his own counsel on the stand.

The book that Lay did not find the time to read is an inspiration for this present work. The Insull saga, like the rise and fall of Lay himself, shows how unforgiving the market can be toward even the most powerful, particularly when they believe themselves to be insulated from the vicissitudes of capitalist commerce. Forsaken prudence applies to other individuals and their companies in our telling, beginning with Thomas Edison, the great inventor who founded the U.S. electricity industry, and continuing with John Henry Kirby, the founder of the company that over eighty years would metamorphose into Enron.

Edison came perilously close to financial ruin amid his feats of electrical invention, saved only by the best efforts of a whiz-kid named Samuel Insull. Kirby, offering many parallels to another seemingly invincible business leader and Mr. Houston, Ken Lay, suffered bankruptcy not once but twice and died under a financial cloud.

Edison summoned Insull from England to America in 1881, whereupon the two built the company that in 1892 became General Electric. Insull left Edison to father the modern integrated electricity industry in the next decades, achieving results as successful, orderly, and enduring as that done for petroleum by John D. Rockefeller.

Electricity, traditionally produced from either coal or white coal (hydropower), found a new primary energy source near the end of Insull's career when long-distance pipelines linked southwest natural gas fields to major population centers around the country. Costlier, dirtier manufactured (coal) gas was displaced, and natural gas went on to become the second leading option to generate electricity next to coal.

Long-distance transmission unleashed America's third great energy industry, natural gas. The history of gas pipelining is the prehistory of Enron, a company that began as a conglomeration of four Texas-sourced gas transmission systems. Ken Lay, Mr. Natural Gas, forged a career as a gas pipeliner before leaving Transco Energy in 1984 to head the company soon to become, through merger and acquisition, Enron. Thus the present book spans just over a century, the time from when Thomas Edison first focused on electricity (1878) to when Ken Lay became head of his own company (1984).

Countless books have been written on electricity and natural gas, but few attempt to cover the long, rich history upon which a number of today's notable companies and company divisions emerged. This book attempts to fill that gap for industry practitioners, energy historians, Enron aficionados, and other interested readers.

❧

Many generous, sharing people have brought this ambitious trilogy on political capitalism to life. My thanks begins with the board of directors of the Institute for Energy Research for their patience and support, as well as IER president Thomas J. Pyle.

As the history book of the trilogy, I respectfully acknowledge professor emeritus of history at my alma mater, Rollins College, Gary Williams, who first noticed my facility for summarizing data and opinions to get to the essence of things. He sought my contrary views in an open, fruitful manner in the classroom, providing an ideal of scholarship that is too often neglected today. And like a good professor, he made history fun and relevant.

Murray N. Rothbard (1926–1995) inspired my interest in the interdisciplinary approach to history that begins with economics but also relies on philosophy, political science, and other social-science disciplines. Rothbard, more than any other person, brought together the worldview known today as *the science of liberty*, and I will always be proud of having been his doctoral student for the degree of political economy.

Patient funding for this multi-year project has come from the late W. J. Bowen, Robert L. Bradley, the estate of Gordon A. Cain, Jeremy Davis, the late James A. Elkins Jr., Jerry Finger, the late Frank A. Liddell Jr., Leo Linbeck Jr., John H. Lindsey, W. R. Lloyd, Robert C. McNair, George Peterkin Jr., Doris Fondren Lummis, W. R. Lummis, Clive Runnells, Walter Negley, L. E. Simmons, David M. Smith, R. Graham Whaling, and Wallace Wilson. I also thank Douglas Wyatt for his friendship and support.

Other project support was received from the George R. Brown Foundation, Earhart Foundation, T. L. L. Temple Foundation, and Walter Looke Family Fund. Colloquia sponsored by Liberty Fund broadened my knowledge in the social sciences and the humanities in ways that improved this book.

Roger Donway provided invaluable research help, edited the entire volume, and helped write chapter 5. Richard Fulmer read many chapters for improvement. Jean Spitzner of R.R. Donnelley (Houston) provided the expert graphics herein.

Many provided material and/or critically reviewed one or more chapters in their area of expertise. For Part I, Robert Peltier read the chapters and provided detailed comments, and Forrest McDonald answered questions on the subject of his classic biography, *Insull*. For Part II: Philip Bee, Berry Bowen, Jack Bowen,

John Lollar, Brian O'Neil, and George Slocum provided constructive comments. Robert Murchison kindly shared his family archives and photos of his grandfather, Clint Murchison.

For Part III, the Houston Natural Gas story benefitted from conversations with members of Robert Herring family: his sons, the late Robert Jr. and the late Randolph Herring; daughter Diane Herring; sister Lonnelle Judson; and the late brother Charles Herring. The late Joe Foy, very central to the Houston Natural Gas story, provided materials and critically reviewed the manuscript. Jim Daniel, the late Barbara Daniel Hetherington, and Don Simecheck provided information on the little known lynchpin of the interstate natural gas pipeline industry, Ray Fish.

Archival research was facilitated by Kathy Young and Rebecca Hymen of the Loyola University of Chicago Archives Department; Dara Flinn and Lauren Meyers of the Rice University Woodson Research Center; and Angela Hermenitt of the Stephen F. Austin University East Texas Research Center. Linda Black of El Paso Corporation helped provide the final illustrations to complete the book.

I also thank my friends in the world of energy scholarship from whom I have learned much over the years. They include Robert Bryce, Richard Gordon, Ken Green, Kent Hawkins, Donald Hertzmark, Mary Hutzler, Marlo Lewis, Michael Lynch, Robert Michaels, Robert Murphy, Daniel Simmons, Vaclav Smil, and Tom Tanton. Jerry Taylor of the Cato Institute, the conscience of the free-market energy movement, deserves special acknowledgement in this regard. As with Book 1, footnotes have been kept to the minimum. Full reference information can be found online at www.politicalcapitalism.org. In addition, a complete bibliography and 74 appendices are provided online.

My publisher and friend Martin Scrivener aided the final product in numerous ways. My appreciation goes also to Scrivener Publishing and to John Wiley & Sons for their joint publication effort. Copy editor Evelyn Pyle made the final changes to make the book as good as it could be.

Any shortcomings, of course, are my responsibility alone.

Robert L. Bradley Jr.
June 2011

Introduction: Energy History in Rhyme

BOOK 1 OF THIS ENRON-INSPIRED TRILOGY on political capitalism[1] provided an overarching view of capitalism, the mixed economy, and energy markets. The present book (Book 2) covers the corporate and personal background leading up to the creation of Ken Lay's Enron. Book 3 will chronicle Enron's history and survey the post-Enron world.

Why three books? Why a theory volume and a background book rather than simply one integrated tome about Enron proper? The short answer is the necessity and challenge of properly understanding a complex and important subject, one that previous attempts have failed to adequately illuminate.

The rise and fall of Enron is a landmark in the annals of business, the history of energy markets, and applied political economy. Descriptions and interpretations of this iconic-to-disgraced corporation have produced a library of books and essays, inspired countless classroom discussions, and shaped many worldviews. Few if any business events have drawn more attention than that given to Enron, and it ranks as a notable event in the history of modern Western capitalism.

Reliable theory and accurate background must cut through the cacophony to capture the significance of and derive the proper lessons from Enron. Theory gives meaning to complex events that otherwise would be only an unintelligible conglomeration of data. But the theory must be sound, or the meaning it gives to history will be false. Hence the presentation of a multidisciplinary worldview in *Capitalism at Work: Business, Government, and Energy* (Book 1).

Background, or prehistory, is also necessary to understand events. Aristotle said: "He who thus considers things in their first growth and origin . . . will

---

1. Political capitalism is defined in Book 1 as "a variant of the mixed economy in which business interests routinely seek, obtain, and use government intervention for their own advantage, at the expense of consumers, taxpayers, and/or competitors."

1

obtain the clearest view of them." Alfred Chandler, the dean of business historians, wrote: "Most histories have to begin before the beginning." That is certainly
true for our subject. The Enron of the 1980s began as a group of natural
gas transmission companies dating back to the 1920s and the 1930s. Enron was
Ken Lay's third and final stop at a natural gas company. In addition, there is the
"historical continuum that connects [Samuel] Insull with Enron," a fascinating
linkage that ties the hubris of great men with the mixed economy (or the
smartest-guys-in-the-room and political capitalism). Hence this volume: *Edison
to Enron: Energy Markets and Political Strategies*.

Ultimately, though, the purpose of history lies beyond itself by usefully
informing current understanding. "The disadvantage of men not knowing the
past is that they do not know the present," G. K. Chesterton wrote in 1933. In
this regard, Enron serves as an infamous, riveting example of the whys and
wherefores of organizational failure and the perils attending the government
side of the mixed economy.

Enron's lessons, rightly understood, are timeless. But many conclusions
have been incomplete or misinformed, for no analysis of the company has
chronicled the company's quarter-by-quarter evolution to understand the
driving motivations of Ken Lay, Enron's board of directors, and other key
decision makers. Hence the series finale: *Enron and Ken Lay: An American Tragedy*
(Book 3), which builds upon the worldview of Book 1 and the background of
Book 2 to understand the company in you-are-there fashion.

᠅

The history of Enron's background brings to life the development of America's
electricity and gas industries, the patterns of which are germane to continuing
industry changes. "Anyone wishing to see what is to come should examine
what has been," observed philosopher Niccolò Machiavelli, "for all the affairs
of the world in every age have had their counterparts in ancient times." These
now-versus-then resemblances follow from the common motivations of money,
power, status, love, sex, and creed. They also follow economic law, where similar causes produce similar effects, other things being equal.

Yet history is not mere replication. Mark Twain allegedly said that "history
does not repeat itself; it rhymes." Similarities must be grasped, but literal
repetitions should not be expected. As Ludwig von Mises said: "The outstanding
fact about history is that it is a succession of events that nobody anticipated
before they occurred." Change and even surprise hallmark history.

The motivations of human action may be finite and eternal, but it cannot
be known which motivation will prevail. For example, men are tempted by
the acquisition of power, but they are also driven by the honors that history
bestows on high virtue. Thus, it cannot be known whether an unconstrained
vision of power will triumph over the goodness of discretion and humility.
George Washington sought honor and practiced prudence; Napoleon sought

power and did not. It was, in each case, a free choice that could not be anticipated from history alone. But what the study of the past does impart is this: *If* people replace prudence with hubris, *then* sooner or later there will be a price to pay. Such is the rhyme of history from Julius Caesar to Savonarola, to the Stuarts of England, to the Bourbons of France, to legions of others. And so too is it with three pivotal figures of this book: John Henry Kirby, Samuel Insull, and Ken Lay.

That is the sort of truth and wisdom imparted by good history. But what about *bad* history? What is it, and what are its effects?

The first sort of bad history is *irrelevant history,* which is devoid of real-world application. History that explains events by means of disembodied ideas or mysterious forces is counterfeit. Better a mere chronicle without explanation if effects cannot be traced back to causes. Humility in the search of historical causation at least avoids the appearance of certainty when there is little or none.

Far worse, though, is bad history that reaches *wrong conclusions* and imparts *false lessons.* Arthur Schlesinger Jr. asserted that "honest history is the weapon of freedom" (by *honest,* he presumably meant *objective*). Yet Schlesinger, one of the most revered historians of his generation, set back the cause of both freedom and history with a predetermined dogma of Progressivism, from which he shaped his evidentiary narrative.

Schlesinger's belief in activist government, or Progressivism, may have been sincere rather than cynical. But his history was nonetheless dishonest, being biased in motive, inaccurate in description, and mistaken in its teachings.[2] "Who does not know that the first law of historical writing is the truth," asked Cicero. Untruth has consequences: Arthur Schlesinger's misinterpretation of the Great Depression haunts our understanding of the cause and cure of today's Great Recession.

"The business historian hopes that by providing facts and generalization he will help political, social, and cultural historians to write more intelligently about business and business men as these touch their various fields," Henrietta Larson has stated. This is the public-spirited purpose of scholarship to better business, government, and civil society. To achieve this high purpose, however, academics and pundits, not only business participants, must develop and advance *good* history and discourage, discard, and correct bad.

⟡

Capitalism at Work presented a multidisciplinary framework to reinterpret the rise and fall of Enron. Its Epilogue foreshadowed the conclusion of Book 3— that Enron did not refute invisible-hand capitalism but rather was the perverted

---

2. See *Capitalism at Work: Business, Government, and Energy* (Book 1), pp. 142–43, 146–47, 166.

result of *political capitalism,* under which special government favor propels profit centers and can even define a whole company.

But *Capitalism at Work* went beyond political economy. Part I's Heroic Capitalism developed the theory of best practices behind personal and organizational success—and the opposite practices fostering failure. Adam Smith, in his early day, understood commercial success and failure in terms of prudence versus self-deceit, independence (authenticity) versus cronyism, and a natural order versus an imposed disorder. Smith's path from "over-weening conceit" to the "most humiliating calamity" of bankruptcy illuminates Enron as well as episodes in the present book, whose central figures scaled mountains only to precipitously fall, through some combination of personal folly and reversals in the general economy that left little room for error.

The enigmatic Ken Lay (1942–2006), in particular, was not an engineer, an accountant, a financier, or even a lawyer. Nor did he claw his way up the corporate ladder, apprenticing in the different core divisions. Lay was a Ph.D. economist interested in the ways and means of Washington, D.C., the place he knew intimately from his stints with the Navy, the Federal Power Commission, and the Department of Interior. So when Lay returned to the private sector, and when he got his own show at the company that would become Enron, he focused on regulated assets and sought regulatory opportunity. He got political to get government favor. In the jargon of economics, he was a *rent-seeker,* a master at positioning his company to receive a special tax provision, a regulatory nuance, or a check signed on the U.S. Treasury.[3]

But this master rent-seeker did not invent his trade. Political capitalism had a long history in the United States before Enron.[4] In particular, America's three major energy industries—electricity, oil, and natural gas—all had long, complicated legislative and regulatory histories that predated the career of Ken Lay. The preponderance of such interventionism had active, typically *crucial,* industry support. Whether the interventionism involved an import restriction, a public subsidy, an entry restriction, a tax code carveout, or a price or quantity control, a well-defined industry segment was politically at work. This regulatory inheritance is a focus of the present book.

⌐∞·

The background of Enron and Ken Lay unearths various links and parallels between individuals, events, and companies, along with dramatic examples of success/failure cycles. History meets itself coming and going in the Enron saga.

With Ken Lay and Enron atop the historical pyramid, its immediate parents are located in the 1970s and early 1980s, with the furthest ancestors reaching back in the early 1900s. Lay's pre-Enron career centered on Florida Gas

---

3. See *Capitalism at Work,* pp. 4–5, 8, 304–312.

4. See *Capitalism at Work,* pp. 130–34, 142–81.

Company and Continental Group (1974–81) and then Transco Energy Company (1981–84). Jack Bowen, who built Florida Gas (chapter 8) before leaving to head the soon-to-be-political Transco (chapter 9), hired Lay at both stops and became his business mentor.

The career of Jack Bowen (1922–2011) offers a window into the business and political sides of the natural gas industry. Despite supply challenges brought on by federal price controls, which became the law of the land in 1954 for gas sold in interstate commerce, Florida Gas Company innovatively matched supply and demand to make a viable project. Contracts were signed with Florida customers who were eager to replace coal, coal gas, and fuel oil with a cleaner, more economical alternative—natural gas.

But construction required a certificate of convenience and necessity from the Federal Power Commission (FPC) in Washington. (This agency, now the Federal Energy Regulatory Commission, was where Ken Lay worked shortly before joining Florida Gas.) A coalition made up of fuel-oil dealers and companies involved in carrying coal, organized as the high-sounding Florida Economic Advisory Council, opposed the project. After a 19-month cat fight between a hundred attorneys representing 41 parties, a 3–2 FPC decision cleared the way for the Sunshine State to receive natural gas service in 1959, one of the last regions of the country to so graduate.

Bowen's company became another bright light in the American gas industry. Even with its temperate climate limiting home heating, Florida was a good place for a desirable fuel for electrical generation. But interstate gas shortages from federal wellhead price controls caught up with Florida Gas in the late 1960s. Repositioning the company was a task that would go to talented, tough Selby Sullivan after Jack Bowen left Florida Gas to take over Transco Companies. Transco's major asset, Transcontinental Gas Pipe Line, was the leading gas wholesaler to New York City, Philadelphia, and Washington, D.C. (Transcontinental had been built in 1950 by Ray Fish, a major figure of this book.)

The pernicious consequences of federal wellhead price controls also caught up with Transcontinental, which had to impose severe curtailment on its customers for want of gas. Bowen aggressively addressed the problem, and played federal politics at every turn, but the solution turned into another problem when the company contracted for more gas than its customers could take. After Bowen brought Ken Lay to Transco as its president, resolving the gas surplus problem became Lay's task, and he was still working on it when he was hired away to run a large natural gas company down the street, Houston Natural Gas.

Bowen, who did not discourage Lay's departure, turned to George Slocum as the future of Transco, a decision that did not turn out well. The so-called take-or-pay problem of excess gas (really a can't-take-but-must-still-pay problem), coupled with other company missteps, some of these were regulatory and political, resulted in Transco's distress sale to Williams Companies, Inc., in 1994. Transco lost its independence just short of its 50th anniversary.

Jack Bowen was a talented engineer-turned-businessman and an inspirational leader. He built one company and revitalized another, at least temporarily. But in the end, he could not overcome federal price controls that left interstate pipelines hamstrung against their unregulated intrastate rivals (prominently including Houston Natural Gas) and the needs of the marketplace.

The ancestry of the Jack Bowen story brings the narrative to Clint Murchison (1895–1965), the man who hired Bowen in 1949 at Delhi Oil Corporation. A Midas-touch investor—and arguably the Warren Buffett of his day—Murchison loved the energy business and particularly natural gas pipelining (chapter 6). Along with his legendary sidekick Sid Richardson, Murchison was in the middle of the 1920s–1950s Southwest oil and gas boom.

Jack Bowen's mentor, and thus Lay's grandmentor, Clint Murchison was the quiet force behind Florida Gas Company. Murchison also fathered the gas-transmission systems of Southern Union Gas Company (now part of Southern Union Company) and Trans-Canada Pipe Lines (now part of Trans-Canada Corporation). In the 1920s, Southern Union piped natural gas to New Mexico cities and towns for the first time—a wholly market-based advance. But Trans-Canada, which entered service in 1958, was no free-market creation.

Late in his storied career, Murchison went political with his obsession to build an all-Canadian pipeline from gas-rich Alberta east to the population centers of Ontario and Quebec (chapter 7). Economics dictated a transnational approach instead, under which Canadian gas from Alberta would drop down to the U.S. Pacific Northwest and points south and east, while U.S. southwest gas would extend north to reach Ontario and Quebec.

But Murchison—finding a powerful political ally in C. D. Howe, Canada's "minister of everything"—went all-out to get the wrong pipeline built. Tepid support in Canada for a project sponsored by a fat-cat Texan created a political hurdle to join the sour economics of the north-of-the-border project. Still, Murchison and Howe—both in search of their monument, and finding themselves emotionally wed to a slippery slope—prevailed. Six years of toil climaxed in a vitriolic parliamentary debate that shook Canada and strained cross-border relations. The tawdry tale was out of character for Murchison, whose career was mostly about creating wealth through market entrepreneurship, not redistributing and destroying wealth via political entrepreneurship.

From Ken Lay back to Jack Bowen back to Clint Murchison; from Houston Natural Gas back to Transco Energy back to Florida Gas back to Trans-Canada back to Southern Union Gas. Part II covers this trigenerational journey into the U.S. natural gas industry, replete with grand moments of market-wealth creation and low episodes of political-wealth subtraction. Market entrepreneurship and political entrepreneurship in the natural gas business hardly began with Ken Lay and Enron.

Another sweep of energy history emanates from Houston Natural Gas Corporation (HNG), the company that hired Ken Lay less than three years after the death of its esteemed chairman, Robert Herring. As CEO from 1967 until his death in 1981, Herring built the modern HNG (chapter 13), which was primarily a Texas gas-transmission company. This mega-intrastate was about the same size as the mighty interstate Transco Energy, the company that Ken Lay left.

Herring had a mentor in Ray Fish (1902–62), the most notable builder of energy infrastructure in history (chapter 11), Among other projects, "Mr. Pipeliner" constructed four major interstates: Tennessee Gas Transmission (1943), Transcontinental Gas Pipe Line (1950), Texas-Illinois Natural Gas Pipeline (1951), and Pacific Northwest Pipeline (1956). Involved in this history were other major interstates, such as El Paso Natural Gas (serving California) and Texas Eastern Gas Transmission (serving the Northeast). Texas Eastern would itself own Transwestern Pipeline Company (1960), an interstate pipeline serving California that Lay's HNG bought in 1984. When one adds HNG's unrivaled intrastate system and Samuel Insull's Natural Gas Pipeline of America (1931), a goodly portion of the U.S. gas pipeline history falls within the scope of this book.

The entrepreneurs behind the above interstates would not take *no* for an answer from a regulatory system that was designed to block or delay entry and

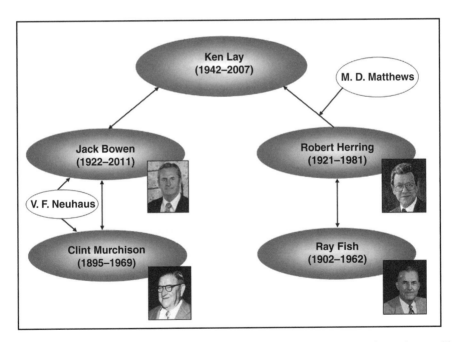

Figure I.1 Three generations of interstate gas pipeline executives are shown here, with Ken Lay (3rd generation) following Jack Bown and Robert Herring (2nd generation) and Clint Murchison and Ray Fish (1st generation). V. F. Neuhaus and M. D. Matthews linked the indicated individuals, as described in chapters 6 and 13, respectively.

to favor either entrenched fuels (coal and fuel oil) or, increasingly, the already existing interstate supplier.[5] The company builder behind El Paso was Paul Kayser; behind Tennessee Gas, Gardiner Symonds; behind Texas Eastern, Reginald Hargrove; and behind Transcontinental, Claude Williams. Clint Murchison also qualifies as a pipeline entrepreneur, although, like Ray Fish, he left the operations of the ensuing company to others. Jack Bowen, too, overcame regulatory hurdles and vested interests to displace manufactured gas with its superior natural alternative.

Houston Natural Gas was founded in 1925 as the natural gas spinoff of Houston Oil Company of Texas, itself founded in 1901 by John Henry Kirby. Initially capitalized at an unheard of $30 million, Houston Oil was a crude-oil driller that found large quantities of gas that it decided to market rather than flare or cap inside the well. Thus, Houston Oil created a wholly owned subsidiary, Houston Pipe Line Company (HPL), to pipe methane to Houston.

But when HPL reached the city limits and failed to win a wholesale contract with Houston's only retail distributor, Houston Natural Gas was created as a separate company to purchase gas from HPL for resale to residential and commercial customers. Chapter 12 describes this forward integration. One-on-one combat (sometimes literally) ensued as HNG wrestled the incumbent gas distributor in Houston for business. Such rivalry contradicted the textbook view that so-called natural monopolists cannot compete.

In 1957, HPL was purchased by Houston Natural Gas, achieving the wholesale-retail integration that would have occurred originally if not for the vagaries of Texas antitrust law. It was this surviving company that expanded its natural gas operations and diversified into other energy and nonenergy businesses in the next decades—and then became the foundation for acquisitions and mergers that resulted in Enron.

The background and history of Houston Natural Gas, spanning much of the twentieth century, is rich with lessons for the Enron story. The career of John Henry Kirby in the first decades of the century parallels that of Ken Lay in the last decades. In their prime, Kirby and Lay each sported grand businesses. Each became Mr. Houston, the city's go-to person for employment, civic projects, and political campaigns. Both men started modestly and reached the top, only to fail, fall, and become folklore.

It is difficult to overestimate just how towering Kirby was during a several-decade period in Houston and southeast Texas, if not swaths of the South. He was Texas's first great industrialist and inaugural multimillionaire, earning the moniker "father of industrial Texas." Kirby was the Prince of the Pines, the man

---

5. For further discussion of the politics behind the Natural Gas Act of 1938, see the Epilogue, pp. 503–505.

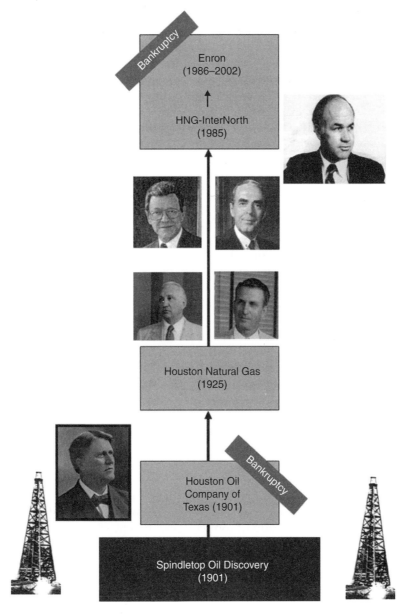

Figure I.2 Ken Lay began as CEO of Houston Natural Gas (HNG), which through merger and acquisition became Enron. The history of HNG can be traced back to John Henry Kirby's Houston Oil Company. The four leaders of HNG before Lay were (bottom left) Frank Smith (1933–55) and (bottom right) Bus Wimberly (1955–67), and (top left), Robert Herring (1967–81) and (top right) M. D. Matthews (1981–84).

with a million-dollar smile, and Lord Bountiful. Kirby embraced innumerable causes, private and political, making a difference in each. He was bigger than life, with towns, streets, and babies named for him.

But Kirby was also the Prince of Bankruptcy (chapter 10). Kirby's grand company went bankrupt three years after its founding in 1901, before reemerging five years later to achieve prosperity. But his fortunes reversed again during America's Great Depression, and Kirby's company went bust in 1934, with Kirby himself dying six years later. Lay's Enron collapsed after a 17-year run, and Lay died five years later. That Enron began as the legacy of John Henry Kirby is history in rhyme.

❧

The meteoric rise and fall of Enron and Ken Lay finds another powerful, fascinating precedent in energy history. Enter Samuel Insull, Mr. Electricity in the first third of the century, just as Ken Lay was Mr. Natural Gas later in the century. Insull (1859–1938) ingeniously developed and applied the right business model to accelerate the electricity business by years if not decades (chapters 2–4). Lay repositioned underperforming natural gas as a premium fuel for power generation across the United States and in Europe during his brief reign.

Each man built a company (in Insull's case, several companies) in his own image. Their transformations also involved trade association leadership, prolific speechmaking, and political activism. Such statesmanship, coupled with soaring company and personal wealth, gave each Great Man an aura of invincibility.

Yet both men failed to overcome success—spectacularly. Reaching too far, with grand ambitions unchecked, the energy titans quickly descended to depths that had scarcely been imaginable just a few years earlier. Few, if any, industries offer such compelling stories and such an intriguing parallel as that of Samuel Insull and Ken Lay. But it happened in the Edison-to-Enron world of energy.

Still, Samuel Insull's historical importance is much richer and deeper than that of Ken Lay. Whereas Lay rode political trends and played politics for much of his ascent, and spearheaded product development in government-created competitive space, Insull's half-century of work in electricity (1881–1932) was far grander. The Chief, as he came to be called, pioneered scale economies in production and consumption; matched the countryside to the city to increase load-factor efficiency and promote universal service; applied two-part rate making to solve the economic-calculation problem for a product that had to be instantaneously produced and consumed, not stored; and developed innovative financing techniques for a rapidly expanding industry. Insull also fathered statewide public utility regulation for his industry, trading (cost-based) rate regulation for franchise protection (territorial monopoly).

Insull, in short, did for electricity what John D. Rockefeller accomplished for petroleum. Many Americans put away their provisional candles when electricity became reliable. And Chicago—Insullopolis to some—emerged from Insull's business and civic leadership as the New York City of the Midwest, indeed as the Second City of the entire United States.

Insull's debt-burdened holding companies, however, controlling an eighth of the national power market, could not withstand the Great Depression. Insull's inability to turn down big new deals, even ones outside his expertise, based on a belief that promoting national recovery was both his opportunity and his duty, proved fatal. Middle West Utilities entered bankruptcy in 1932, as well as his new holding companies Insull Utility Investments and Corporation Securities Company of Chicago. More than a half million Americans lost most or all of their investment. Because company loans carried his personal guarantees, Insull's net worth, once as high as $150 million, went negative (chapter 5).

Facing Congressional critics and state and federal lawsuits after his bank-ruptcy, Insull pleaded innocent and strategically put his whole illustrious career on trial. In the end, he was acquitted. The jury saw a failed man more than a dishonest one. Insull's desperate actions to save his empire involved more philosophic fraud than prosecutable fraud. Good intentions, manipulated accounting, fruitless results. "If self-preservation is the first law of nature, we certainly were not interested, forgetting all about the morals of the case, in depreciating the value of the very securities that represented a lifetime of effort on our part," Insull testified. For his last several years, the faded icon lived abroad in modest and self-imposed exile, a titan disremembered.

Ken Lay, too, faced the wrath of a large constituency that had sung his praises and had invested much with him in heady times. But at trial, Lay misleadingly and tragically tied his legal case to Jeff Skilling's, his chief lieutenant, who had done so much, however inadvertently, to destroy Enron. With defiance and arrogance on the witness stand replacing humility, Lay's philosophic fraud could not be distinguished from prosecutable fraud. Lay was found guilty on all counts, just the opposite of Insull's verdict some 70 years before. The past can inform the present, and in Ken Lay's case, he ignored the lessons of history at great cost.

Fortunes, indeed, can change quickly and completely when consumers reject the bad and the not-good-enough. The case studies of Insull and Lay, not to mention that of John Henry Kirby, decades apart, show how unforgiving the market can be toward even the most powerful, particularly when they believe themselves to be insulated from capitalism's *perennial gale* of creative destru-ction, to use the term of economist Joseph Schumpeter.

Ken Lay banked on Enron's *unassailable competitive advantage*—what he also termed "house advantage." A century before, John Henry Kirby pronounced his Houston-based megacompany "one of the most meritorious enterprises ever organized." Two years later it was in receivership. Kirby's company would recover, but Mr. Houston went personally bankrupt in 1933, four years into the Great Depression (and one year after the Insull collapse).

The commonalities of John Henry Kirby and Ken Lay encompass more than personality, geography, and fate. As mentioned, Kirby's Houston Oil Company sired Houston Natural Gas, which became HNG/InterNorth in 1985 and Enron a year later.

History meets itself with Kirby, Insull, and Lay, all icons who failed in the end. But Shakespeare's "slings and arrows of outrageous fortune" also reached others in our chronicle. The Boss, as Jack Bowen came to be called, rose to the top and presided at two Fortune 500 companies, but federal price controls on wellhead natural gas in interstate commerce defeated his best-laid plans. Although he never went through personal or corporate insolvency, Bowen's multidecade career ended disappointingly.

Thomas Edison, genius inventor but haphazard businessman, dodged insolvency only with the mighty aid of boyish Samuel Insull, who, fresh from England, quickly assumed Edison's business affairs and kept the pieces together for what eleven years later became General Electric Company (chapter 1).

·◇·

Political business cycles and the fickle mistress of political entrepreneurship are major themes in the history of electricity and natural gas in the United States. Enron was a quintessentially political company, feasting on special government favor and gaming complex regulation. Without the noncapitalist side of the mixed economy, Ken Lay and Enron would be little known, perhaps unknown, to history.

The dizzying rise and precipitous fall of Insull's holding-company empire reflected the unintended consequences of government intervention, not only the tragic Napoleonic phase ending Insull's career. The expansionary finance of the Federal Reserve Bank (est. 1913) was Insull's play money to buy and pyramid in the Roaring Twenties. Insull was the bankers' Great Man and ensconced in industries that were protected by public utility regulation. The multistate holding company—and the numbing complexity and accounting legerdemain therein—was a device for utilities to navigate around the unwanted aspects of otherwise protective state regulation.

Insull's unhealthy proclivities were aided and abetted by post-Crash public policy. Herbert Hoover's normalcy campaign for business was the green light that Insull coveted to not pull back or turn away. Insull expanded for the common good, as he explained each step of the way, and utility stocks were advertised as depression-proof. Such investment, after all, was in protected monopoly space.

Insull's titanic fall was sealed by the repeated setbacks of the general economy. Little else could have been expected, in retrospect, with above-market wage guidelines, tariffs, tax increases, deficits, public works, codes of "fair competition", and other nostrums of Hoover, FDR, or both. What the federal referee in Insull's bankruptcy called "the tragedy of the century" was the failure of the New Deal to let market forces liquidate the malinvestments of the boom and build up from there.

◌

Whatever the level of regulatory constraint, there remain best business practices, including case studies of *failure* that help illuminate the prerequisites for *success*. The importance of general rules, as well as sound premises, humility, continual learning, and plan revision, are as true for productive organizations today as when Adam Smith and Samuel Smiles explored the interplay of capitalism and character in earlier times.

"In the last resort, sheer insight is the greatest asset of all," stated Herbert Butterfield. Business executives *should* become wiser as they live and learn history. But complacency, arrogance, and hubris have all too often displaced wisdom, in part from an underappreciation of how the mighty have fallen. The failure to overcome success, as it were, is a major theme of this trilogy. But how much of failure is due to external factors and how much to bad decision making?

Forrest McDonald fronted his biography *Insull* with Ecclesiastes 9:11: "I returned, and saw under the sun, that the race is not to the swift, nor the battle to the strong, neither yet bread to the wise, nor yet riches to men of understanding, nor yet favor to men of skill; but time and chance happeneth to them all." In McDonald's telling, happenstance brought down a good, talented, accomplished man. Insull, in this sense, hardly deserved his fate, and given a bit of historical twist, he could have gone out on top, or certainly wealthy and wise. (The same might be said for Ken Lay, who had planned to cede the reins to Richard Kinder instead of Jeff Skilling in 1997.)

Yet McDonald's opus explains how Insull lost his Smilesian prudence as his spellbinding career progressed, a turn that the Great Depression harshly exposed. External circumstances ruined Insull only because his decisions increasingly eroded his margin for error. Prudent men know when to temper ambition and throttle back, particularly later in their careers. Insull had his perfect exit in 1926, when he was honored with a request by Parliament to return to his homeland to revamp Britain's balkanized electricity grid. Instead, he imagined his empire to be under attack by enemies and layered unnecessary debt upon his fundamentally sound business. New projects were undertaken in the teeth of the Great Depression as if it were his calling. ("He took on greater and greater burdens until it appeared as if he were attempting to carry the entire American economy on his shoulders," McDonald lamented.)

The prudent man plans for storms in order to weather them. Did not Samuel Smiles tell Insull as much? "The uncertainty of life is a strong inducement to provide against the evil day," Smiles wrote in *Thrift*. To be prudent in good times and to prepare for bad "is a moral and social as well as religious duty."

The fable about the grasshopper and bees emphasized by Smiles went unheeded by the man who was arguably the most important practitioner, or advocate, of Smiles.[6]

Insull had brought this Smilesian message to his audiences. "I want to urge you," the Chief lectured employees in 1911, "to provide for a rainy day, to use your influence among your fellow-workers, so that they will provide for a rainy day." Such care, Insull explained, "is not only a benefit to you but a benefit to those who are dependent on you, who are family connections of yours, as nothing can so help a man to take a proper view of affairs in times of trouble as to feel that he is supported by a respectable bank account." Yes, Insull was selling something—company stock— to this audience, but it was generic advice too.

Believing that the October 1929 reversal was temporary, and acquiescing in Herbert Hoover's plea to practice business as usual (to act imprudently, in retrospect), Insull turned to debt time and again to steady his stocks and in hopes of bringing back prosperity. Out went the Smilesian virtues of thrift, forethought, and economy, leaving the necessary but insufficient attributes of perseverance, integrity, and sobriety to deal with a moribund economy. Insull had no reserve fund or contingency plan; he became intoxicated by success and blundered his way until he was "too broke to be bankrupt."

Prudence is tested not only by swings in the macroeconomy but also by the small fates of history. Jack Bowen's roller-coaster career would have been much steadier had President Eisenhower in 1956 stuck to his script to end federal price controls on wellhead natural gas. But with the bill on his desk, a surprise veto (owing to an industry lobbying impropriety) allowed regulatory promiscuity to survive, grow, and fester, resulting in debilitating natural gas shortages in the 1970s and, indirectly, problematic gas surpluses in the 1980s.

Ken Lay's career as a political entrepreneur owed much to public-utility regulation of natural gas and electricity, as well as to Eisenhower's reversal and the energy politicization that came from Richard Nixon's wage-and-price

---

6. Smiles fronted *Thrift* with this fable:

A grasshopper, half starved with cold and hunger, came to a well-stored bee-hive at the approach of winter, and humbly begged the bees to relieve his wants with a few drops of honey.

One of the bees asked him how he had spent his time all the summer, and why he had not laid up a store of food like them.

"Truly," said he, "I spent my time very merrily, in drinking, dancing, and singing, and never once thought of winter."

"Our plan is very different," said the bee: "we work hard in the summer to lay by a store of food against the season when we foresee we shall want it; but those who do nothing but drink, and dance, and sing in the summer must expect to starve in the winter."

control order of August 1971. Prudence in the mixed economy is different from prudence in the market economy if for no other reason than that the different vistas of opportunity and decision-making the two present and the different business leaders they require.

Such interventionist watersheds changed history for the worse. Yet an absence of best practices mattered too, for Kirby, Insull, and Lay's heady booms left little slack come adversity. Time and chance happeneth to all, but they work for the prepared and against the unprepared—and against those unschooled in history.

∽

The past is prologue when it comes to Enron. Not only have there been Enron-like organizational failures after the fall of Ken Lay's company, beginning with accounting firm Arthur Andersen, Enron's most important partner in misdirection. On the macroeconomic plane, there has also been the breakdown of Big Government à la political capitalism (Ken Lay's sandbox) wherein Business brought out the worst in Government, and Government brought out the worst in Business.

Enronish behavior in the private and public sectors seemingly resulted in the smartest guy in *every* room, leaving companies shattered and the economy sagging with malinvestments. But rather than liquidating the bad investments per Enron, a *new* New Deal by the party in power—Republican and then Democrat—chose to prop up malinvestments via deficit spending and other means. And so the recession turned into the Great Recession, just as government activism transformed a depression into the Great Depression eight decades before.

The Enron problem, in other words, transcends Enron. The smartest-guys-in-the-room phenomenon is an ideal type of personal and organizational failure.[7] It may be a wholly private-sector problem or, in its more pronounced cases, such as Enron itself, a private-public problem. The troubles of Arthur Andersen (which came into national prominence with Insull's troubles and died with Enron), AIG, and Lehman Brothers were analogous to Enron's modus operandi. One example reeks with irony. "Another lesson from Enron is that corporate behavior is fundamentally a product of the culture of the company," wrote Franklin D. Raines, CEO of Fannie Mae, in 2002. "At Fannie Mae we take pride in the tone we set at the top, in our risk management focus, in our commitment to integrity and intellectual honesty and in the values of our people."

---

7. The term is defined as follows: "An ideal type is formed by the one-sided accentuation of one or more points of view and by the synthesis of a great many diffuse, discrete, more or less present and occasionally absent concrete individual phenomena, which are arranged according to those onesidedly emphasized viewpoints into a unified analytical construct."

Yet Raines and Fannie Mae were all about an insular culture; accounting trickery; denial, arrogance, and hubris; and political capitalism. With liabilities parading as assets, it was bankruptcy walking. This and other examples led Bethany McLean and Peter Elkind to comment:

> Enron's bankruptcy seems not to have delivered this message, as the subsequent accounting scandals at AIG and Fannie Mae, which originated with the same please-the-Street impulses (but without such dire results), showed. But maybe, just maybe, a couple of decades in the slammer for Ken Lay and Jeff Skilling will send the message home.

But these authors missed the public-policy forest. The *message* is not so much pelting punishment for the failed and guilty. It is not throwing more regulation after bad. It is reforming a socioeconomic system that allows the worst to get on top.

The fall of Insull spawned the Securities Act of 1933, the Securities Exchange Act of 1934, and the Public Utility Holding Company Act of 1935, among other New Deal institutions. The fall of Lay inspired the Sarbanes-Oxley Act of 2002 and the Bipartisan Campaign Reform Act of 2002, and almost resulted in passage of the Financial Derivatives Act of 2002. But did New Deal reforms prevent or unintentionally enable Enron? Did post-Enron reforms prevent the financial tumult of 2008/2009 and afterward?

Less, not more, government intervention, removes false safe harbors, promotes prudence in place of opportunism, and checks artificial booms that must turn into corrective busts. This is the lesson of history that this book and trilogy points toward. Learning from Enron's background, its prehistory, to better guide the post-Enron world is the work of the chapters to follow—and energy history in rhyme.

Part I

The Chief: Samuel Insull

History has not dealt generously with Insull; the disastrous climax of his career burned itself into the public's memory. For newspapermen, politicians, and former competitors, Insull was a Depression scapegoat; the decades of [his] complex system-building were easier to ignore or forget—they involved difficult concepts, esoteric technology, uncommon economics, and sophisticated management.
—Thomas Hughes, *Networks of Power* (1983)

Introduction

"Light! Power!" So opens a history of Chicago's Commonwealth Edison Company. These "two of the most expressive words of human speech" can be expanded in the present history to four powerful ones: Edison Light! Insull Power!

Thomas Edison invented the common use of electricity, but Samuel Insull, more than anyone else, distributed it to the masses. Edison's genius is universally recognized and appreciated; lesser known is how Insull ingeniously developed the business model to affordably bring electricity into homes, stores, offices, and industry. Thomas Edison was the father of electricity; his protégé Insull was the father of the modern electricity industry.

In 1881, the 34-year-old Edison and the 21-year-old Insull came together and built the company that in 1892 would become General Electric (GE). But also in 1892, the 32-year-old Insull left GE and New York City for Chicago, with a grand plan of turning electricity from a luxury to a mass-produced, affordable necessity. It was there in Chicago that Insull applied his mentor's model of central-station generation, serving wide areas, instead of small, isolated plants serving a particular establishment or need. Don't self-generate, Insull insisted, backed by a sea of operational and financial statistics. Buy your electricity!

Scale economies from Insull-pushed engineering advances and Insull-led managerial innovations made Chicago "the electric city." From this base, Insull took his low-cost, high-volume model to the suburbs and then to the countryside, with his new companies combining long-reach transmission with central generation. "Insullization" became a noun in the burgeoning electricity business—now one of the nation's largest.

Before Insull was done, his electricity operations would be in 39 states. Insull's empire also spread from electricity to manufactured (coal) gas distribution, natural gas transmission, and urban transportation (a major user of power). In several decades, Insull became *the* leading figure in the field of energy, eclipsing the retired John D. Rockefeller. Insull was counted among the very top American business titans and as a friend of presidents.

The Great Man of energy and business, however, expanded his operations even as America shrank during the Great Depression; in the end, Insull's holdings became less than worthless. His last years were spent in exile, husbanding scarce dollars and thinking about a storybook career gone tragically wrong at its twilight. Still, there were flashes of thought about bettering the electricity industry. He died on July 16, 1938; when his estate was settled, creditors received one hundredth of a penny on the dollar. No businessman before or since had ever gone from such a high to such a low, nor has any since, possibly excepting Enron's Ken Lay, who was spared life in prison only by death.

.ᴏ.

The bankruptcy of mighty Enron and the disgrace of its once-esteemed chairman is eerily reminiscent of the fate of the mighty energy empire of Samuel Insull 70 years before. Insull was America's most powerful business-man in the 1920s and the most vilified in the 1930s; Lay was considered one of America's leading executives before becoming the most vilified following Enron's bankruptcy in late 2001.

Insull and Lay each qualified as a *Great Man* of industry, each having built his company from the ground up and becoming its public face. Enron was a *Great Company*—maybe even the *best* company. Insull was *Mr. Chicago* and Lay *Mr. Houston*—go-to leaders for civic projects, political campaigns, and instant credibility. Each left the scene with grand civic monuments to his credit—a skyscraper/opera house for Insull and a major-league baseball stadium for Lay.

Insull and Lay had Horatio Alger ascents. Fathers Samuel Insull Sr. and Omar Lay were perennially unsuccessful in business, but each, as a lay minister, could claim a higher calling. Young Samuel and Kenneth were smallish and hungry for *success* and *respectability*. Both had egos as big as their ambition, were optimistic to a fault, and hypersensitive to criticism.

Insull and Lay possessed a rare combination of intelligence, energy, and single-mindedness that set them apart even from their high-level peers. Both were benevolent leaders with high regard for the welfare of their employees and for the commoner. They were active philanthropists in public and private, often going beyond the call of duty. Both were revered in the workplace, in church, at society functions, around dinner tables.

Both rose to become leading voices for their profession, actively educating the public, employees, and legislators on energy and public-policy matters. Insull was Mr. Electricity in the first third of the twentieth century; Ken Lay was Mr. Natural Gas for much of the last quarter of the same century.

Insull and Lay were Schumpeterian entrepreneurs who *led* change rather than adapted to it. In today's parlance, they were *revolutionaries* rather than *incrementalists*. They created gales of competitive destruction for others, while being seemingly invincible themselves. Napoleonic, each sought new heights of greatness, but at the end, the *great* came at the expense of the good, even the viable. Both falls were sudden, stunning, and heard 'round the business world.

Insull and Lay were masters of their respective political universes. Through dedication, resources, and sheer skill, each gained ready access to governmental leaders at all levels. Ken Lay at the end of the century, in fact, labored to revamp the very system of public-utility regulation in electricity that Samuel Insull had fathered many decades before.

The accounting firm Arthur Andersen & Co. found itself in the middle of both high-profile bankruptcies—with quite opposite results. The fall of Insull's holdings companies and the demise of Enron seventy years later brought business before Congress and capitalism into disrepute. Insull and Lay, personally shamed, and their companies lost, could only retreat behind their lawyers and bear the hostility of the many constituencies they had so assiduously cultivated for so long.

But there was a fundamental, qualitative difference between Samuel Insull and Ken Lay. Insull understood the technology of energy and the technicalities of business in a way that Lay never could or would. Insull was little picture, big picture—the trees and forest both. Samuel Insull is rightly considered the father of the modern electricity industry for manifold contributions in generation, transmission, sales, corporate culture, and industry leadership that have stood the test of time.

The contributions of Lay and Enron to the physical and financial trading of natural gas and electricity were premised on a new regulatory regime—mandatory open access.[1] That new market, although created by *force*, would in all likelihood have developed earlier, absent regulation. Still, Enron can be credited with creating a portfolio of innovative products addressing price, reliability, regulatory compliance, and other needs of the marketplace.

Insull's career is left standing—the only one rivaling that of John D. Rockefeller in the mighty U.S. energy industry. Lay, his brush with greatness undermined, was, in comparison to Insull, more of a shooting star in a political sky than a great market entrepreneur.[2]

Insull, unlike Lay, was an intellectual, grounded in the classics and steeped in history. "The Chief," as Insull was called in his industry, needed no speech-writer—he lived his stories and mastered the details of his subjects. Lay had the academic pedigree—a Ph.D. in economics—but for him, knowledge was a convenience, a means to an end, not an end in itself as a pillar of greatness. The difference would matter.

Which bankruptcy, Insull's or Enron's, was bigger, more shocking, and more consequential? Each victimized more than a million investors, and both shared the ending: "Apparently, everyone had been duped." Perhaps there is not a right answer even after accounting for the differences in the purchasing power of money, the size of the national economy, and external circumstances. But understanding the fate of Samuel Insull's empire sheds much insight on the rise and fall of Enron.

---

1. Mandatory open access requires that natural gas pipelines and electric transmission be made available on equal, nondiscriminatory terms for sellers and buyers of the commodity itself. Producers and marketers that do not own pipelines or wires could thus reach customers, which created new competitive space for Enron and other marketers.

2. For my interpretation of Lay as a political capitalist first and free-market entrepreneur last, see *Capitalism at Work* (Book 1), pp. 3–9, 302, 306–312.

1

Building General Electric

THE DISCOVERY AND EARLY STUDY of electricity took place largely outside the United States. The commercialization of electric power, on the other hand, was the handiwork of "the most useful American," Thomas Edison, whose inventions, engineering, and entrepreneurship fashioned a whole new industry. His *killer app* was the incandescent light bulb, which was joined by a new distribution system that allowed single sources of generated electricity to serve whole geographical areas. "When Edison ... snatched up the spark of Prometheus in his little pear-shaped glass bulb," German historian Emil Ludwig observed, "it meant that fire had been discovered for the second time, that mankind had been delivered again from the curse of night." Other Americans, such as George Westinghouse, filled in the gaps to solidify Edison's revolution.[1]

The new industry, soon to be one of the world's largest, had capital requirements well beyond what could be mustered up from ordinary Americans. The wealthiest in the largest cities provided the capital that built the railroads—and now did the same for electricity. Much of that capital came from Wall Street and the era's greatest banker, J. P. Morgan. The mighty General Electric (GE) emerged from Edison's early inventions, and more than a century later, it would be none other than GE that, as buyer and financier, picked up pieces of bankrupt Enron.

Thomas Edison had to be not only an inventor but also a businessman for electricity. But he was an undisciplined, erratic entrepreneur, requiring a

---

1. The early history of electricity is surveyed in Internet appendix 1.1, "Electricity before Edison," at www.politicalcapitalism.org/Book2/Chapter1/Appendix1.html.

confidant to attend to all the details necessary for *profitably* and growth. Enter Samuel Insull, a young Brit, who was Edison's financial fulcrum for more than a decade, after which Insull would go out on his own to become *the* leading name of the electricity industry for 40 years, eclipsing many others, including Charles Coffin the heavyweight first head of General Electric Company.

Prodigy

Samuel Insull, the youngest of five children of Samuel and Emma Insull, was born in London on November 11, 1859, the annum in which Samuel Smiles published *Self-Help*, the most influential book of Insull's life. The year also witnessed the discovery of the world's first commercial oil well, inaugurating a new energy era. Coal was the energy mainstay for homes and factories on both sides of the Atlantic, and manufactured gas from coal provided lighting in privileged locales. Petroleum would bring illumination to the masses and, several decades later, fuel the transportation age. Electricity would also come to the masses in time—thanks in part to Insull.

The lower middle-class Insulls were descended from "'Children of the Soil,'" as Samuel himself would describe it. His mother, "one of the great influences in my life," was remembered as "a fine English matron whose main occupation in life was to keep 'the wolf away from the door.'" Samuel remembered his father as "a man whose ideals were more in his mind than his pocketbook." Both mother and father were leaders in England's temperance movement, a cause inspired by the demise of a family business from an ancestor's affinity for demon rum. Samuel himself would never take a drink, keeping a promise he made to his mother when he emigrated to the United States at age 21.

Samuel was very special. He inherited the best traits from both sides of his family: the toughness and discipline of his mother and the curiosity, imagination, and enthusiasm of his father. In his autobiography, Insull described himself as having a "combination of yeoman and 'white collar' blood" representative of the best of England—her middle class. He possessed a photographic memory and was barely aware that others might not have his capacity. ("Don't carry a notebook," he would say throughout his career. "Exercise your memory.")

Insull was a human dynamo. "He invariably awoke early, abruptly, completely, bursting with energy," wrote Forrest McDonald in his 1962 biography, *Insull*, "yet he gained momentum as the day wore on, and long into the night." Relaxation would never be easy, something Insull had to will himself into.

The temperance movement sent the family to Oxford, where Samuel received six years of private education from Oxford University students. He excelled at the practical things—basic mathematics, history, and political economy—but eschewed higher mathematics and philosophy. The classics interested him. This would be all the formal education that he would receive or need; a lifetime of dedicated self-study was ahead.

Samuel Insull developed a keen intuition of things and people. "Very early he learned to see to the heart of relations between things, or between men and things or men and men, and to grasp the underlying principles so clearly that he could perceive ways to shift them around a bit and make them work the better," McDonald wrote. Samuel could absorb and critically distill great amounts of information. His flexible, intuitive mind could bring order to virtually any task, small or large.

Figure 1.1 The Insulls circa 1866, with gleam-eyed young Samuel (far left). The prodigy applied boundless energy to his tasks, just one of his many positive traits. With parents Samuel Sr. and Emma (top) are, next to Samuel (left to right), Emma, Queenie, and Joseph. (Martin Insull was born four years later.)

Insull read inspirational books, particularly those by Samuel Smiles and took to heart the Victorian platitudes: *Idle hands are the devil's workshop. Things are simply "done" or "not done." An honest man is the noblest work of God. Time is money. Only that which is useful is good. Survival of the fittest and the devil take the hindmost. One never openly displays emotion, affection, or familiarity.* And so on. Insull's moral, utilitarian, pragmatic view of life would guide him all his days.

Insull entered the real world upon his family's return to London. With money scarce and his mother providing secret aid, the 15-year-old rejected his father's plea to enter the ministry and looked for work. A family friend, Thomas Cook, told him to wait a month to two for an opening at Thomas Cook & Sons, the tourist agency of international fame. But young Samuel wanted something immediately and found a position as office boy for a London auctioneer specializing in real estate. On July 1, 1874, the day after receiving the offer—five shillings per week— Insull began his 58-year business career, working from 9:30 a.m. until 6:00 p.m. weekdays and half Saturdays. His job? Licking stamps, delivering messages, and doing whatever other else an office clerk needed.

Insull survived some opening-day fisticuffs with an office bully (incidentally descended from the firm's founder),[2] and occasional boot kicks and "big black ruler" swats in the office basement, to steadily advance over the next four and a half years. "I learned very quickly how very little I knew," Insull remembered, so self-help off the job was the order of the day. First came plain writing, which led Insull to buy a copy book and spend evenings "writing pothooks and handles." Next was stenography (Pitman shorthand), which "opened up for me the possibility of a career." Bookkeeping, again at night with purchased books and lots of practice, would round out this business education.

Samuel's growing talent landed him a night job as stenographer for Thomas Bowles, the editor of *Vanity Fair,* a popular weekly that introduced the youngster to the fascinating world of people, politics, and connections. A very modest sleep requirement (four to five hours per night) left plenty of time for everything else in the day—which in his case was either skill-based learning or work.

No moment was wasted. Insull read the great books while going to and from his jobs. To stay abreast of current events, Samuel joined the Literary Society of Christ Church, where he authored papers and gave talks, the latter of which "laid the basis of my acquisition of the power to think and formulate speech while standing on my feet and facing an audience."

A highlight came when Samuel persuaded P. T. Barnum, visiting from America, to address the group on publicity and promotion, an event that introduced the 18-year-old to the power of public relations. (Insull himself a few

---

2. Recounting the incident 50 years later, Insull told a packed room of his employees: "Never provoke assault. But if you have to fight, hit hard and hit to finish it quickly. Apply it to your brain as well … to come out on top."

decades later would become "the link between P. T. Barnum and Madison Avenue" in his chosen industry.) When it came his turn to address the group, Insull happened upon a fascinating story in *Scribner's Monthly* about a rising American inventor who was the epitome of the self-made, practical man. The full story was found in the bookstores and libraries of London, and Samuel wrote an essay, "The American Inventor: Thomas Alva Edison."

Breakthrough!

Insull enjoyed these formative years despite an almost complete absence of leisure. Perseverance, broad skills, and innate smarts allowed Samuel to ace concurrent jobs and become the family breadwinner by the time he was 18. All his efforts, and his hard-earned skills in penmanship, shorthand, and bookkeeping, rewarded him well. Then his first setback came. At the conclusion of a positive year-end performance review, he was informed that his services at the auctioneer's would no longer be needed. A wealthy customer had arranged for his son to enter the business world and work for the experience, not salary. More than that, the blue blood would *pay* the firm handsomely. Insull's position was the one the articled clerk would take, notwithstanding Insull's four years of impeccable service at the firm.

The firing violated Insull's ego, which McDonald described as an "untouchable area," where "even a modest affront … was unforgivable and unforgettable."[3] But on this first Saturday of 1879, Insull saw a job posting in the *London Times* for a secretarial position with an American banker residing in London. Insull interviewed against dozens of other applicants and was hired for what was advertised (misleadingly, as it turned out) as a part-time position, to which he would add his two night jobs. He named his price too—50 percent more than he had been getting from the auctioneer.

On his first day at 6 Lombard Street, Insull received a second shock—this one of the best kind. George Gouraud was a banker as advertised, but *he was also the European representative of Thomas Alva Edison* of Menlo Park, New Jersey.

Before long, the 19-year-old became immersed in a race between the Edison Telephone Company and the Bell Telephone Company to introduce telephony in London. In a crisis moment, Edison became larger than life to the new hire. After Insull cabled the New York City home office that Bell was going to file a patent-infringement suit against Edison's telephone receiver, Thomas Edison replied that he would invent a new type of telephone receiver within 60 days. It was audacious, but Edison did just that. Insull now knew that he had to be at Edison's side and sought to learn everything he could about his hero.

---

3. Also see Internet Appendix 1.2, "Getting Fired: Never Letting Go," at www.political-capitalism.org/Book2/Chapter1/Appendix2.html.

Reviewing every document in the communication file in his spare time, Insull learned about the inventor's very promising electricity-lighting experiments in his Menlo Park laboratory, the very ones that had caused a "panic in gas shares" both in London and in Wall Street. Thomas Edison was a difference maker a world away.

At the same time, another letter of great import was being written, though one that Insull could know nothing about. In New York City, John Pierpont (J. P.) Morgan—assuming the mantle from his father, J. S. Morgan, as the world's leading investment banker—wrote a confidant about "a matter which is likely to prove most important to us all not only as regards its importance to the world at large but to us in particular in a pecuniary point of view ... Edison's Electric Light." Insull himself was just a few months away from seeing Edison's new light in a London basement. And the great J. P. Morgan would become a pivotal figure in not only Edison's but also Insull's future.[4]

⌒

Samuel Insull was at the right place at the right time, but he had made his own breaks by aggressively taking on new tasks and exceeding expectations. At his first job at the auctioneer, for example, Insull had become chief accountant, which included reconciling ledgers denominated in various currencies. In his new position, Insull soon found himself in meetings with London's finest businessmen and learning corporate finance, a brand new area.

But there was something else: Sundays and holidays spent with engineers at Edison Telephone Company on Victoria Street deciphering the technical side of Edison's operation and seeing "the first glimmer of an incandescent lamp, burning on about forty cells of Grove batteries." Insull, in fact, would be party to history as the operator for the first phone conversation outside the United States. Such was the 19-year-old's introduction to telephony, a new application of electrical engineering after the telegraph.

In the process, Insull befriended Edison's technical expert, Edward Johnson, by helping with experiments and by taking shorthand.[5] Before long, Johnson's weekly reports to Edison on the European telephone situation were being

---

4. J. P. Morgan was the son of Junius Spencer Morgan, judged "the best business man in Boston" and the "ablest American banker of his day." In 1854, J. S. Morgan moved his family to London upon becoming principal of George Peabody & Co., the world's premier investment banking house. When George Peabody retired ten years later, the firm became J. S. Morgan and Company. Young J. P. apprenticed at Peabody in 1856 before moving to New York City, where he spent the rest of his career.

5. Forty years later Insull remembered: "I was willing to work, unlike the average boy of my age who wanted to be off playing cricket or rowing on the River Thames ... for the enjoyment of the moment than for that greater enjoyment which comes with the acquisition of knowledge."

prepared by Insull himself. It was ideal positioning, for Insull saw his future as working alongside Edison. Johnson returned home to America and Edison with just this plan.

Samuel Insull so positioned himself that in February 1881, just two years after finding himself on the London end of Edison's activities, the 21-year-old got the call to come to America to be the inventor's private secretary. Johnson had come through, and Insull was ready for Edison in the flesh. Besides, as Insull recalled decades later, "Things American had always interested me."[6]

Insull's decision to steam 3,000 miles from Liverpool to New York City had risks. Edison had detractors, particularly among the top inventors in the electricity field. Untouched by his son's enthusiasm, Junius Morgan of J. S. Morgan & Co., the leading investment house in London, was skeptical about this new form of energy. Insull left a high-paying job and a wealth of connections in one of the world's two leading financial centers. He said goodbye to his roots—even his "'parental roof'"—not knowing when he would return. And now, with his reputation, Insull turned down another offer: to join Drexel, Morgan and Company in New York City.

The cable to come at once to America, sent by Edward Johnson, who had already returned home to the United States, did not include any explanation. An explanatory letter, it turned out, was delayed at sea. Yet Insull embarked on the 14-day, one-way voyage from Liverpool to New York. Said Forrest McDonald: "One of his most deep-rooted traits—one that derived perhaps from his energy, perhaps from his life history, possibly even from his body chemistry—was that he was absolutely unable, save on an abstract and purely intellectual level, to imagine the possibility of his own failure; he entirely lacked the sense of caution of those who doubt themselves." Insull, McDonald continued, "could take huge risks without even realizing that he was gambling."

But Edison needed Insull as much as Insull wanted Edison. Edison's personal and business affairs were unorganized, even chaotic.[7] The inventor's own ways of doing things included a bookkeeping system charitably described as "peculiar." Insull was ideally suited to bring a semblance of order, and the "private secretary and general business nursemaid" would not disappoint. Electricity was new, but

---

6. For Insull's readiness for his new challenge, see Internet appendix 1.3, "Gouraud to Edison on Insull: Letter of February 17, 1881, at www.politicalcapitalism.org/Book2/Chapter1/Appendix3.html.

7. Insull soon knew why: "Edison was a man who knew not the hour of the day or the day of the week. His one idea was to work and work, and then to work more, on and on, until accomplishment was achieved." Insull's workday often included a "midnight luncheon" with Edison to update the inventor on the business day's work. Fortunately, both Edison and Insull required only five hours, or less, sleep a night.

telephony was a good introduction, and Insull knew more than anyone else about Edison's European activities and how the inventor thought and worked. As Edison himself noted, Insull was as "tireless as the tides."

Thomas Edison

By the time Insull arrived, Thomas Edison (1847–1931), the eventual holder of 1,093 patents, had fathered the multiplex telegraph, stock ticker, talking machine (phonograph), improved telephone transmitter, and incandescent light. The photocopier, alkaline battery, and motion picture projector would come later. Creating an industry to commercialize electric lighting, his most challenging and (in retrospect) greatest endeavor, was under way. More was going on with Edison than anyone, even the inventor himself, and much less Insull, knew. "As he invented a system of electric lighting," one biographer wrote, "Edison was simultaneously reinventing the system of invention."

Edison saw electricity as his "field of fields," giving him the opportunity to "reorganize the life of the world." It began with his study of arc lighting and his review of the gaslight industry in 1877/78, whereupon Edison became confident that he could economically subdivide the great beams of arc light.[8] All this was scarcely work to the man who announced that he was taking a "long vacation in the matter of [electricity] inventions."

Edison would find many new uses for electricity in what he called "God Almighty's workshop," but it was never enough. "I am ashamed at the number of things around my house and shops that are done by ... human beings," Edison complained later in his career. "Hereafter a motor must do all the chores." But this required commercialization, commercialization required affordability, and affordability required efficiency. "Wherever man's power or horsepower can be eliminated," he would say, "speed, accuracy, and economy are the result."

Edison's range and quantity of discoveries set him apart from most other great inventors, such as James Watt (steam engine, 1769), Eli Whitney (cotton gin, 1793), Samuel Morse (telegraph, 1844), and Alexander Bell (telephone, 1876). Edison's genius combined theoretical comprehension, knowing what came before him, and intuiting from his special analogical powers—and old-fashioned hard work. Samuel Insull, who knew Edison better than anybody—and maybe better than Edison himself, at least when it came to electricity—remembered the

---

8. Pre-Edison arc lighting was inefficient and costly and produced uneven outdoor illumination. Edison's task was to discover how to subdivide light: as he said, "not to make a large light or a blinding light but a small light having the mildness of gas," as well as to create economical ways to produce and transmit electricity to displace coal gas, coal oil, and petroleum lighting.

inventor's tremendous enthusiasm for work, the brightness and magnetism of his eyes, his patient teaching, and kindness and simplicity of manner.

Edison, the man seemingly without a nervous system, could work around the clock in the heat of discovery.[9] "Putting off a thing until tomorrow was a practice unknown to Edison," remembered one of his lab assistants. Edison himself stated in an 1898 interview: "For fourteen years I have worked on an average of twenty hours a day." Edison defined genius as "1 percent inspiration and 99 percent perspiration," and he combined both with an ability to remember the thousands of things that did not work.

Innate intuition was a great part of it. Edison was not only a "marvelous experimenter," Insull explained, but also a "wonderful guesser." Insull never forgot how, during a tour of Chicago in the 1890s, Edison picked out what he thought should be the center of the city's electrical infrastructure. It turned out to be just that spot decades later.

Edison was neither a theoretician nor an ivory-tower experimenter. He was a *practical* inventor, a *homo economicus.* "I find out what the world needs, then I proceed to invent," he said. The market's verdict was taken as his own. "I measure everything I do by the size of a silver dollar," Edison said. "If it don't [sic] come up to that standard then I know it's no good." He once complained about an assistant's work at Menlo Park:

> *We can't be spending time that way!* We have got to keep working up things of commercial value—that is what this laboratory is for. We can't be like the old German professor who as long as he can get his black bread and beer is content to spend his whole life studying the fuzz on a bee!

Edison's utilitarianism made him the quintessential democratic, egalitarian capitalist inventor. But market verdicts would work against Edison too, something that tested his ego, a real problem area for him in his later career.

Money was a means and not an end for Edison during the fabled Gilded Age. Edison could not interrupt his work for leisurely pursuits; his (substantial) capital was for the next set of experiments or a machine for a new business. The newspapers described him as the "millionaire inventor"; Edison referred to himself as "machine-rich and cash-poor."

Edison was a realist in search of underlying causality. Self-educated, he had devoured the writings of Thomas Paine, whose *Age of Reason* (1795) proclaimed: "The most formidable weapon against errors of every kind is Reason. I have never used any other, and I trust I never will." Edison saw great possibility in science and discovery and, following Paine, one of America's founding fathers,

---

9. Edison, mostly deaf since childhood, said: "I have no doubt that my nerves are stronger and better today than they would have been if I had heard all the foolish conversations and other meaningless sounds that normal people heard. The things I have needed to hear I have heard."

had little time for the unknowable or chance.[10] "I never did anything worth doing by accident, nor did any of my inventions come indirectly through accident," the one exception being the phonograph earlier in his career.

◦

Edison paid little heed to his learned detractors, many of them university professors. Edison "was regarded by scientists as a sort of intruder, a revolutionist of an inferior stamp far below themselves," explained Francis Jehl. "He set the old school aghast by his methods of research wherein, instead of following the traditional technique, he went direct to Nature and asked her the questions he wanted to solve." The experts had determined that subdivided light was theoretically impossible, in fact, and the future was in arc lighting, pioneered by Charles Brush at home and Paul Jablochkoff abroad.

But these *smartest guys in the room* were lacking intuition, emotionally wed to their past work, and too focused on the impractical. This was a real loss, for Edison needed experiments, not verbal barbs. "All those who might have helped—the world's [electricity] experts, such men as Joseph Swan, Professor Henry Morton, Conrad Cooke, and W. E. Sawyer—were unavailable, for they were busily engaged in thinking up reasons why Edison's efforts were doomed to fail."

Mathematicians got Edison's goat, and those specialists on his staff were subjected to practical jokes to keep them grounded. "I can hire mathematicians, but they can't hire me," Edison would state. (Some years later, Henry Ford would say the same thing about professional historians.)

Edison had an intellectual side. He read newspapers and technical articles to stay abreast of new developments, part of his "voracious, even omnivorous, life-long" commitment to acquiring knowledge. Time was too scarce to read fiction. He did not talk about politics or religion, only business and technology—and briefly. Only in his moments of family time did he reveal his true spontaneity.

Edison cared little about appearances in his inventive prime. Louisville's finest once held a banquet in his honor where Edison went missing soon after his arrival. An electrical problem had been brought to his attention, and he disappeared into the basement as the event went on, and his food grew cold. His fine dress gathered grease and soot, but he fixed the problem. The other electricians thought it "wonderful" that such a man cared more for his trade than the "frills and fancies" of the evening.

---

10. Edison said of Thomas Paine (and really himself): "His Bible was the open face of nature, the broad skies, the green hills. He disbelieved the ancient myths and miracles taught by established creeds ... but atheist he was not." Edison himself would utter that "there's an engineer—somewhere" at the sound of weather events.

Edison personified Julian Simon's "ultimate resource" of human ingenuity. Edison captured the essence of mind over matter with the observation: "From his neck down a man is worth a couple of dollars a day, from his neck up he is worth anything that his brain can produce." The great inventor did more to make energy the "master resource" (another Simon term) than any other single person, excepting James Watt, whose steam engine put coal to its greatest use, speeding the Industrial Revolution.

Edison went from inventor to entrepreneur-industrialist in the quest to turn his patents into consumer goods. He was a free-market capitalist, financed by the private sector to meet consumer demand. Only occasionally did he turn to the political means to further his ambitions, and it proved to be a mistake.[11] Edison's tax-free earnings—at least until 1909, when the corporate levy began at 1 percent of earnings—allowed him to plow his profits back into his cash-needy lab and fledging manufacturing operations. His skin was always in the game, and he invested for the long term.

Edison was less an agent of "Darwinian harshness" than he was a wealth creator working amid the "perennial gale of creative destruction." He was a Schumpeterian entrepreneur who earned and lost fortunes over his six-decade career. Joseph Schumpeter's "capitalist reality" worked for and against him. Electricity displaced lighting from kerosene and particularly coal gas, the latter being described as "barbarous" and "wasteful" inasmuch as it shed "almost entirely heat and only incidentally a little light." Far better, Edison proved, was burning coal to generate electricity.

Electricity was not the total energy answer. A decade of toil by Edison to create a battery to make electric vehicles the transportation mode of choice was felled by Henry Ford's Model T with its self-starting internal combustion engine. To some, such "Darwinian harshness" was part of a flawed social system. Yet it was simply consumers rewarding good entrepreneurship and penalizing bad. Thomas Edison had himself to blame for his business failures, but overall, the Schumpeterian force that he released advantaged consumers and raised productivity for a rapidly increasing population.[12]

Edison's inspiring vision for the future made him an ambassador of the phenomenon of rising expectations. A popular song of the time jingled about an Edisonian future of electric horses, electric dinners, electric brooms, and police with "electric feet." Edison saw how new uses of energy—powering projectors, cars, or many other things—had made people restless with the status quo. Dissatisfied people invent progress, he explained.

---

11. See Internet appendix 1.4, "Edison and Politics," at www.politicalcapitalism.org/Book2/Chapter1/Appendix4.html.

12. Creative destruction as a driver of capitalist progress is discussed in *Capitalism at Work*, pp. 126–30.

Figure 1.2 Incandescent lighting began Thomas Edison's quest to invent a new industry (left panel). The drawing of the inventor at work is cornered by (clockwise from upper left) the darkness of the past, the light of the future, the spellcaster of old, and the gas-stock panic created by Edison's breakthrough.

Edison was a folk hero whose wisdom educated and delighted three generations of Americans. He gave capitalism its best face. Matthew Josephson's *Edison: A Biography* (1959) was as positive as his *Robber Barons* (1933) was negative. Part of it was the different subject matter; part was Josephson's own maturity, writing in a climate more favorable toward American enterprise.[13]

A poll by the *New York Times* in 1922 identified Thomas Edison as the greatest living American, ahead of industrialists Henry Ford and John D. Rockefeller,

---

13. For a critical review of Josephson as a muckraker historian, see *Capitalism at Work*, pp. 148–53.

politician Woodrow Wilson, and others. The same paper estimated that nearly $16 billion ($200 billion in today's dollars) of enterprise value came from Edison's inventions. *Life* magazine in 1997 chose Edison as "The Man of the Millennium," ahead of such icons as Christopher Columbus (#2), Martin Luther (#3), Isaac Newton (#5), Thomas Jefferson (#10), Albert Einstein (#21), and Adam Smith (#74). Such lists are open to debate, and higher weighting was probably deserved by the earlier giants who paved the way for so much that followed. Still, there can be little doubt: Young Samuel Insull had hitched his wagon to the star of stars.

"Financial Factotum"

Insull's arrival at New York harbor on February 28, 1881, was perfectly timed. Edison had completed his incandescent light at Menlo Park. Much work was under way with lamps and electric generators to offer a complete, affordable product to the marketplace. In 1878, New York financers had capitalized The Edison Light Company (Edison Light) at $300,000 to undertake these experiments in return for the right to own and license the resulting inventions for five years. The intent of Edison Light was not to commercialize the inventions but to collect royalties from others who did, in order to fund Edison's continuing laboratory work.

Just months before Insull arrived, the Edison Electric Illuminating Company of New York (New York Edison), the company now known as Consolidated Edison Company of New York, or ConEd, was created to underwrite the construction of a single station to generate electricity in bulk and serve a section of New York City. Edison and investors were confident that the facility would prove superior to both arc lighting and gas lighting.

Insull found Edison at his inventive best, which historians date from about 1873 to 1883, when Edison was age 26 to 36. Fifty-nine patents in 1880 would be followed by 259 in the next three years, almost all in electricity. Edison was also a gifted engineer, laboring to install his grand electrical system to show the world that gas lighting had been superseded by something much better.

Insull disembarked at dusk and went immediately to Edison's new offices at 65 Fifth Avenue, an address beautified by electricity. The first meeting was eye-opening for both. Edison was surprised at how young Insull was (21) and looked (younger)—all five feet eight inches, 117 pounds of him. Insull's "hero of my imagination" was disheveled and "looked nearer fifty than he did thirty-four… indicative of the work he had gone through in burning the midnight oil."[14]

---

14. Edison has been christened the "original nerd" for his "shabby appearance, strange sleep cycles, and bad eating habits." But there was also, Insull remembered, "the wonderful intelligence and magnetism of his expression, and the extreme brightness of his eyes."

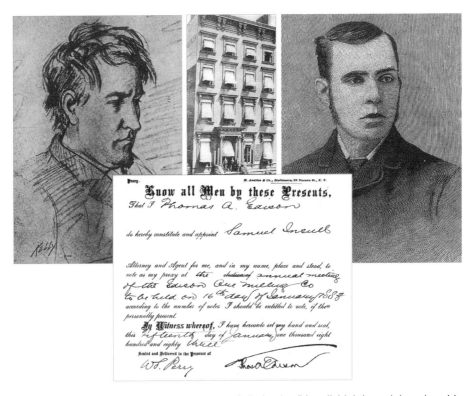

Figure 1.3 "I had expected to find a man of distinction," Insull (right) reminisced on his meeting with Edison (left) at the 65 Fifth Avenue building (center). Insull's surprise at the "careless" appearance of his new boss was matched by Edison's astonishment at the "boyish" look of his new private secretary. Nonetheless, Edison entrusted his business affairs to his protégé as indicated by this 1883 power of attorney.

But it was all business, exhilarating and nonstop, beginning with the first all-nighter. By morning, Edison himself was in awe of the youngster who had quickly sized up the prospects for raising $150,000 of European capital in such centers as Amsterdam, Berlin, Budapest, London, and Paris to help finance the commercialization of Edison's lighting experiments—a plan that Edward Johnson took to London and executed. "From that moment on," for 11 years at least, biographer McDonald noted, "Insull was Edison's financial factotum."[15]

Edison's battle cry was "factories or death!" Incandescent lighting and his early work on dynamos were one thing; inventing the components for an

---

15. "That was the condition during all the years that followed," Insull testified at trial 53 years later. "I found everybody in that business needed money."

integrated electricity system—boxes, cables, filaments, fuses, insulators, junction boxes, meters, regulators, sockets, switches, voltage regulators, wires— was quite another. Businesses needed to be created to manufacture, market, install, and service the new products. Customers had to buy them. His operating system, in short, had to be superior and affordable.

Capital was lacking. The half-million dollar—and growing—commitment to Edison Light and to New York Edison for experimentation and demonstration had not produced any profits (New York Edison gave away its electricity in its first months). The investors were wary of jumping into the more expensive manufacturing of products that had never before been seen, much less marketed. J. P. Morgan and his banking firm were in the habit of lending money against solid collateral, not anticipations. Edison and his top executives—such as Charles Batchelor, Edward Johnson, John Kruesi, Francis Upton, and Sigmund Bergmann—had to invest personally and retain profits to fund their operations. Permission from, and royalty payments to, Edison Light were required under a master contact that Edison called the "leaden collar."

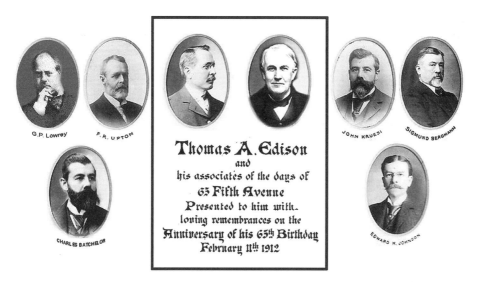

Figure 1.4 Thomas Edison's "star assistants," along with Samuel Insull (middle with Edison), included (clockwise from upper left): G. P. Lowrey, who brought Wall Street to Edison and later became the inventor's top legal representative; F. R. Upton, chief mathematician and head of Edison Lamp Company; John Kruesi, chief mechanic and head of Edison Electric Tube Company; Sigmund Bergmann, founder and head of Bergmann & Company; Edward Johnson: top engineer, European "prophet," and future president of Edison Light Company; and Charles Batchelor, head of Edison Machine Works before Insull.

That first night, Edison asked Insull something else: Did he know book-keeping, and could he set up an accounting system for Edison's new incandescent lamp factory at Menlo Park? Insull replied in the affirmative and did just that. Before long, Edison made Insull secretary for three new businesses: Edison Machine Works, which manufactured electricity-generation equipment; Edison Lamp Company, which produced and sold lamps; and Edison Electric Tube Company, which built and installed underground distribution facilities. Insull also had responsibilities for Bergmann & Company, one-third owned by Edison, which manufactured telephonic, telegraphic, and electricity devices.

Thomas Edison disliked board meetings; now, with Insull in charge, he no longer had to worry about attending them. The 22-year-old would soon be Edison's chief financial officer and given Edison's power of attorney. "He trusted me with his affairs when I was just a boy," Insull fondly recollected decades later. More than that, the great inventor personally trained his prodigy in science and engineering.

These aforementioned companies were "the acorn out of which the vast oak of the General Electric Company was to grow." The commercialization phase was next, and it would involve a second generation of Edison pioneers, including Samuel Insull.

Thomas Edison confidant Alfred Tate remembered his first impressions of the boy-man the boss fondly called *Sammy*:

> His mind was much older than his years would indicate…. He possessed unusual intuitive judgment in the affairs of business which compensated largely for his lack of experience…. He had a deeply sympathetic nature, but like all Englishmen did not wear his heart on his sleeve. His devotion to business almost constituted a religion. He permitted nothing to interfere with his duties toward the interest he was handling.

Insull's predecessor handled the mail and appointments; Insull redefined the position by taking charge of Edison's business side as well, not to mention aiding in experiments and troubleshooting in the field. Insull was agreeable, reserved, empathetic, and honorable—and focused, demanding, and addicted to work and strong coffee. Though always pleasant and appreciative of the rank and file, Insull was a tough taskmaster: He demanded attention to detail, execution, and all the other things behind maximum effectiveness. Insull fussed at sloppy work, as Alfred Tate, his successor as Edison's private secretary, would find out. Praise from Insull was not direct but disseminated from third parties. "[Insull] seemed to think that sustained criticism was the most effective spur towards efficiency," Tate recalled.

Insull was proper in all matters of appearance and manner and generous toward his friends. He was supremely loyal to Edison, developing a trust that permitted Edison to accept a systemization of his activities. Being the boss's favorite helped the smallish, funny-talking import to blend in with Edison's motley crew of scientists, technicians, engineers, mathematicians, and just plain tinkerers. So did Insull's work habits, his day spent on business and his night on engineering, often one-on-one with Edison himself. The crew also found out that Insull could play rough, a trait left over from his hard knocks as a London office boy.

Insull had endured seasickness on the boat and homesickness in America, but his confidence about making the right choice cured all. A letter sent home to London just two months after his arrival painted the following picture:

> His lamps last about 400 hours.... As for rivals, Edison has but little fear, *in fact*, none from them.... Menlo Park is practically abandoned.... We have large gangs of men wiring the houses [in Manhattan] in anticipation of the time when we can lay our mains, erect our dynamo machinery and light up....

> To carry out the gigantic undertaking of fighting the gas companies we have much to do. A great difficulty is to get our machinery manufactured. This Mr. Edison will attend to himself....

> I have gotten right in with Edison, sit in the same room with him, assist him in everything.... People say that he likes me very much; but time must be left to prove this. I am absolutely satisfied that I did the right thing in coming here.

The blossoming "wunderkind" exhibited other traits of note given his future career and ultimate fate. Insull seemed overly sure of himself at times. He was big on appearances, reflecting an "exaggerated sense of propriety" that stemmed in part from an ego that always remembered and never forgave. Insull welcomed debt as a means *and* an end, whether purchasing a machine for Edison or a business suit for himself. Alfred Tate noticed something else: how Insull "loved power and glorified in the exercise of authority."

J. P. Morgan

J. P. Morgan (1837–1913) was a towering figure in the formative period of American finance. Well descended, smart, in-the-know, decisive, and a master of the spoken and unspoken word, he seldom failed in money making or in negotiations to get to that point.[16]

Taking "to finance like a cat to cream," young J. P. apprenticed at his father's London firm, J. S. Morgan and Company, before moving to New York City and founding J. Pierpont Morgan and Company in 1862. A year later, a new partner changed the firm's name to Dabney, Morgan & Company. After a decade of strong money making and experiencing some health problems, the 34-year-old Morgan contemplated dissolving his firm and retiring. But an offer from Anthony Drexel of Philadelphia's prestigious Drexel & Company led to a new partnership in 1871: Drexel, Morgan, and Company. With the collapse of the

---

16. Also see Internet Appendix 1.5, "J. P. Morgan," at www.politicalcapitalism.org/Book2/Chapter1/Appendix5.html.

Philadelphia banking house Jay Cooke & Company two years later, Drexel Morgan became the preeminent investment banking house in the country.

J. P. Morgan & Co. was formed in 1895, two years after the death of Anthony Drexel. In its long and storied history as America's top banking firm, the so-called House of Morgan "spawned a thousand conspiracy theories and busied generations of muckrakers."

To his critics, Morgan was a quick-buck artist and the robber baron of finance. Did not President Theodore Roosevelt glare at Morgan while speaking of the "malefactors of great wealth"? But Morgan was a driver of capitalism, channeling scarce capital to its most highly valued uses at a time when the demand for scarce capital was unprecedented, and winning bets turned luxuries into necessities for ordinary Americans. Pragmatically making money off the government, Morgan was a political capitalist too.[17]

Morgan was neither a fool nor a short-termer. "Money men had learned that he was decisive, intelligent, and swift of action, and above all, he kept his word," stated one historian. He possessed an eagle eye for detail and prided himself on knowing everything about his business. Morgan was little interested in anything but results. If Morgan had been alive in our time, the post-1996 Enron would have been his least-favorite company. He would have been one of the few to say: *I cannot invest in a company I do not understand.*

⌒

Edison Light had been financed in 1878 by several top executives from Western Union Telegraph Company, a firm that knew Edison well from his inventions, as well as Drexel, Morgan and Company. William Vanderbilt, the world's richest man from his inheritance from father Cornelius, the steamship and railroad tycoon, was another early subscriber. Young Vanderbilt was the nation's leading investor in coal gas companies but saw great potential in Edison's light and wanted to hedge his bets. But J. P. Morgan was the invisible force, making sure that his company was both represented on the board and in charge of the banking business of the new company—and Edison personally. Drexel Morgan also secured rights to Edison's European patents by early 1879. It was unprecedented for an inventor to attract such a who's who of Wall Street, but Edison was no ordinary inventor.

In 1880, New York Edison was funded to generate electricity for lower Manhattan, including the offices of Drexel Morgan. Two years later, J. P. Morgan persuaded his father to have J. S. Morgan & Co. underwrite a similar Edison venture in London. By 1883, J. P. was hosting Edison Light board meetings in

---

17. See Internet appendix 1.6, "Morgan as Political Capitalist," at www.politicalcapitalism. org/Book2/Chapter1/Appendix6.html.

Figure 1.5 J. P. Morgan (left inset), the railroad industry's investment banker, was an early backer and publicist for Thomas Edison. Morgan's office on the third floor of the Drexel Morgan building at the corner of Broad and Wall in New York City (left) became the world's financial center. In 1892, Morgan engineered the merger that put Charles Coffin (right inset) in charge of the General Electric Company, headquartered in New York City (right).

his office and had a standing order at his firm to personally buy one share of Edison stock for every share sold to an outsider.

"Living well mattered to Morgan as much as doing well," a biographer wrote about the man who would define his era in American finance. One luxury J. P. could not do without was electric lighting. Morgan wired his Madison Avenue mansion with Edison's technology in mid-1882; for the fall social season, several hundred lights were on display for his many and honored guests.[18] Visitors reveled in the novelty, which outshone everyone else's lamps, whether they burned coal gas, coal oil, kerosene, as well as the traditional beeswax candles. Moreover, Morgan's superior light was both simpler to operate and without smoke or smell—at least in the house.

―――――――――

18. J. P. Morgan's residence was the first to sport electricity only because William Vanderbilt's wife, in Edison's words, "became hysterical" after learning that she was living above a boiler. The Vanderbilt's system was dismantled soon after it was operational.

Morgan installed lighting controls in each room and had a bedside master switch ready to spook an intruder. There would be no burglars, but there would be complaints from neighbors who chafed at the vibrations and racket from Morgan's coal-fired electricity generator and were downstream from its fumes and smoke. Electricity's first environmental problem was resolved when mats and sandbags stilled and quieted the machines and an exhaust line was built to the mansion's master chimney.

Morgan relished his electric light and worked to substitute electricity for coal gas at his business, his church, and a local school. "Pierpont sent [Edward] Johnson around with his mechanics and electricians, in the same way that he would send a basket of his best peaches or grapes," the financier's brother-in-law wrote. Edison's top publicist, however, was paying royally for his indulgence. An engineer had to be present whenever the home generator was on, and mishaps were likely to occur, none greater than a short circuit that set fire and ruined Morgan's library. Moreover, what Edison promised in "weeks" back in 1878—royalties from his inventions—took years, leaving Morgan without an appreciable return on his investment.

From Dynamo to Jumbo

Commercial electric lighting needed more than Edison's candle. Electricity itself had to become more affordable, which meant generating more electricity per horsepower input. Edison's crash effort to improve on-site electrical generators was largely accomplished by 1879, although it would be more than two years before the Edison Company for Isolated Lighting (Isolated Lighting) was formed to tap into the lucrative *dynamo* market. But this was not the answer, Edison felt. Something new was needed to "make electric light so cheap that only the rich will be able to burn candles."

Edison saw the future in *jumbo* generators (named for P. T. Barnum's circus elephant, Jumbo), as opposed to on-site dynamos, many of about eight horse-power. By wintertime 1880, his inaugural "Central Station" at Menlo Park (New Jersey) lit the laboratory and neighboring residences as well as powered the machines.

The construction of six-ton, 200-horsepower units came next at Pearl Street Station, located at 257 Peal Street in lower Manhattan. The first commercial electricity station, and the prototype for what would become the entire power-generation industry, began operation in September 1882. Each 100 kilowatt unit was capable of lighting 1,200 lamps versus the Menlo Park unit's 50.

One of Pearl Street's coal-fired units lit 900 dwellings in the First District of New York City, a one-square-mile area that included Wall Street and Drexel Morgan's 106 lamps. The newspapers pronounced Edison's grand demons-tration a success. "The dim flicker of gas, often subdued and debilitated by grim and uncleanly globes, was supplanted by a steady glare, bright and mellow,"

Figure 1.6 In 1886, Edison's transferred his major manufacturing operations from Goerch Street in New York City (top left and right) to Schenectady in upstate New York (bottom). Two hundred employees relocated along with Samuel Insull, and the great industrial facility would employ 6,000 by the time Insull resigned to form General Electric in 1892.

the *New York Herald* reported. The *New York Times*, lit by 52 Edison lamps, described electricity as "soft, mellow, grateful to the eye; it seemed almost like writing by daylight." Edison himself exclaimed, "I have accomplished all I promised." But this was a long four years after he had told the New York press, "I have it now!"

But as one historian put it: "Seldom has the dawn of an age been so well heralded, and seldom has the morning after been so anticlimatic." Applause aside, Edison was in the gales of his own creative destruction. Pearl Street, a technical marvel, had cost more than twice the amount estimated, not a good way to inaugurate a national sales effort. J. P. Morgan's house had needed a complete rewiring before his lights could be turned on. Outlays accumulating, Edison's backers favored incrementalism over revolution. Just as Edison rejected arc lighting, the first technology that introduced electricity to the public, he now tabled his new, improved dynamos despite a waiting market, committing fully to central stations. His board of directors, tiring of their recalcitrant genius, imposed a "go slow" policy for Edison Light "until [electricity's] practicability, economy, and profitableness had been fully established."

Edison could only complain about "the characteristic timidity of capital." After all, wasn't Morgan saying *no* to jumbo manufacture at the same time he was saying *yes* to bigger railroad projects? Yet other investors were not venturing in where Morgan was not, and Edison was dabbling in other ventures—unprofitably—when his full attention and dollars were needed in electricity.[19]

Still, few doubted that Edison had a good product. Pearl Street would turn profitable by 1884, and central stations in Appleton, Wisconsin, and Milan, Italy, proved economical too. Samuel Insull, in his later speeches, would marvel at how Edison's light was profitable in a few years compared to the decades it had taken coal gas.

Two Thomas Edisons were needed: one for incremental improvements and the other for revolutionary advances. After "tremendous pressure," Edison got his dynamo business turned around. Edison Light president S. B. Eaton, a Morgan confidant, proposed to buy out Edison during the "go slow" period, but the inventor refused and discussions ended in early 1883.

Edison Construction Department

With Pearl Street operational, Edison called on his own resources to create a new company to sell central stations to the market. In 1883, Edison tapped the 23-year-old Insull to run the Thomas A. Edison Construction Department. The business proposition was for cities and towns to commit between $50,000 and $250,000 for Edison Construction to install a jumbo to serve residences and businesses. Each of the local distribution companies (LDCs) would pay royalties to Edison Light and use the Edison name. The central-station proposition also benefitted from the inventor's new three-wire transmission system, which increased affordability and range by reducing copper requirements by two-thirds. What Edison called the pole-connected "village business" helped "place electrical service within the limit of every purse."

When Insull hit the road in 1883 with his turnkey proposition, there were precious few central stations compared to hundreds of dynamos (many of Edison origin) installed around the country. Insull's task involved not only economics but also politics. Regional lighting required a franchise from city fathers, and areas served by a gas company were difficult to legally penetrate. In virgin areas, special favors to politicians were often necessary for a permit.

Still, Insull was selling a good product. Jumbos built by Edison Machine Works and installed by Edison Construction Department created Edison LDCs in New York, Massachusetts, Ohio, and several other states. Profitability was in

---

19. See Internet appendix 1.7, "Edison versus Morgan," at www.politicalcapitalism.org/Book2/Chapter1/Appendix7.html.

sight. But off-the-top royalties were flowing to Edison Light at a time when every dollar was needed to expand production to meet demand. Quality control became a problem. "Trouble shooting without end" at some locations inspired customers to rename their contractor the "[Edison] Destruction Department." Many LDCs struggled with cash flow and had a problem servicing their notes to Edison. Taking payment in stock in the new companies left Edison Light Company with an illiquid asset in many cases. Cash-flow problems led Edison to liquidate Edison Construction in the spring of 1884, just short of its second anniversary.

Edison and Insull hit bottom. Personal resources depleted, badgered by overdue bills, and reduced to dining on credit at their beloved Delmonico's, Edison remarked to Insull late one evening: "This looks pretty bad. I do not know just how we are going to live. I think I could go back and earn my living as a telegraph operator. Do you think, Sammy, that you could go back to earn your living as a stenographer?" As Insull stated decades later: "That was the only time I ever saw that man lose courage."

A worse outcome for mankind, or a greater violation of the economic law of comparative advantage, could hardly be imagined! About then, however, with business improving and accounts receivables coming in, the crisis was weathered. Such a financial nadir, last experienced at Menlo Park years before when Edison had to bribe a sheriff to dodge a foreclosure order, would not be experienced again. Still, capitalization remained a problem in light of Edison's own foibles, as well as his refusal to merge Isolated Lighting, in whole or part, with Edison Light. Another problem was personal. The death of his wife, Mary Stilwell Edison, in August 1884 led to months of mourning and a loss of interest in his work in electricity, if not in invention itself.

Edison Light Company
It was Insull's job to oversee the operation of the companies and manage cash flow. A major issue was the six-year-old royalty/license arrangement with Edison Light Company, whereby different pricing and production strategies could advantage one Edison-related company at another's expense. Yet integration by merger was not an option. At Edison's instruction, Insull mined, and even gamed, the contracts to minimize payments—at least until Edison Light's Eaton dressed him down. Insull had not been this humbled since his sudden firing years before as a London lad, and such began his lifelong animosity toward New York City financers and the House of Morgan in particular, a row that would cost him dearly late in his career.

An upturn by mid-1884 led to a proposal by Charles Coster, the Morganite treasurer of Edison Light, to purchase 40 percent of Edison Machine Works, Edison Lamp Company, and Bergmann & Company on terms that one historian described as "to a large extent favorable to Edison and his manufacturing partners." Yet Edison, distraught over his wife's death, antagonistic toward his investors, and possessing an inflated vision of what could be accomplished on his own, refused to dilute his ownership. It then became Insull's job, once again at Edison's urging, even through "devious means," to accumulate enough proxies from the minority stakeholders to give Edison majority ownership and thus control.

Morgan, whose interest was now subordinate to Edison, quietly watched as a new team was installed, with Eaton demoted to corporate counsel. Insull gloated in a private letter, "There is no one more anxious after wealth than Samuel Insull, but there are times when revenge is sweeter than money." Perhaps Edison gave it to him, or perhaps it was inbred in his own sizeable ego, but Insull and Edison shared a common virus within their genius.

Royalty payments were now in the family with Edison Light in hand by the close of 1884. But the capitalization problem remained because the parent held illiquid and mostly non-cash-generating LDC stock. Antagonisms were created with Drexel Morgan, including Charles Coster, whose merger proposal had been rebuffed. Competition was also heating up, which led to a decision in 1885 to vigorously litigate to uphold Edison's patents. The "seven years' war" was now on.

The year 1886 was eventful for Edison and the burgeoning electric industry as a whole. Central-station electricity boomed. Jumbos, complemented by Edison's three-wire transmission, proved formidable to capture markets for entire square miles. Streetcars created a huge new daytime market for electricity, one that soon exceeded lighting demand. By 1889, some 180 electric-streetcar systems were operating or under construction across the United States, compared to fewer than 10 just 18 months before.

Edison himself worked on electric streetcars between 1879 and 1882, financed by railroad entrepreneur Henry Villard. Sensing opportunity, Edison Light purchased a one-twelfth interest in Sprague Electric Railway and Motor Company. The daytime-intensive traction demand was putting the generating plants to work during what had been the slowest hours of the day, improving central-station economics.

By 1886, Edison Light Company had a presence in major cities in the United States, Europe, South America, and Japan, with 500 dynamos and 330,000 lamps on the books. Jumbos had increased to 58 from a dozen in just two years. Total assets were $10 million (about $125 million today), and more profits were registered in this year than in all prior years combined.

But problems remained. The company was undercapitalized, and competition was accelerating. New entrants used alternating current (AC), which allowed central stations to serve a much broader area than did direct current (DC). AC was the first major electricity-related technology in a decade that Thomas Edison had not pioneered, and the once-progressive inventor put much of his operations at risk by not facing up to its commercial advantages.

Edison Machine Works

In 1886, Edison merged Edison Tube Works and Edison Shafting Company into Edison Machine Works. A piece of land was purchased in upstate New York and large buildings erected for 200 workers. But things were not going well, so Edison as 90 percent owner and Edward Johnson as head of Edison Machine Works jointly conferred and decided to put Insull on it.

"I [have] no authority," a surprised Insull told Edison when asked to go up to Schenectady.

"Well, that is up to you," Edison responded. "I don't want to interfere with the fellows up there. You just find some way of getting the work done. That is your job."

Insull commuted, studied, and reported back on the problems a month later. Edison knew who needed to be in charge. "Now, go back up there and run the institution," Edison demanded. "Whatever you do, Sammy, make either a brilliant success of it or a brilliant failure. Just do something. Make it go."

"That," Insull remembered, "was [my] first real independent opportunity in life." His initial position at Edison Machine Works as secretary-treasurer was upgraded within a year to general manager, the top position. Edison's other lieutenants had to adjust—though Kruesi cooperated with Insull more than did Batchelor—but there could be no doubt: Insull, just past his twenty-seventh birthday, was now Edison's top business executive.[20]

Edison Machine Works relocated to upstate New York to improve labor relations. At the new plant, production of dynamos, jumbos, Sprague motors, and their many components were scaled up. Insull found himself on a steep learning curve on how to improve operations at one of the largest manufacturing centers in the world. The operation was very profitable, and Insull received a new pay package that rescued him from his persistent financial worries. Such was the topsy-turvy life with Thomas Alva Edison.

A booming market masked two problems: Edison's central stations were wed to DC transmission technology, and Insull was struggling to fund Edison Light and the inventor's other businesses. Insull was constantly taking 180-mile train trips between Schenectady and New York City to juggle short-term loans and survive on cash reserves under $10,000. ("Raising money is the hardest battle," Insull would state throughout his career.) Forrest McDonald described Insull's relationship with Drexel Morgan as "frantic, nerve-racking, and disgusting." One loan for $20,000 came with a 20 percent rate, almost unheard of in its time. This only added to Insull's antagonism toward New York bankers, despite the true source of much of the problem: Edison himself and the rigors of managing a start-up megabusiness.

---

20. Also see Internet appendix 1.8, "Insull: Edison's Top Business Executive," at www. politicalcapitalism. org/Book2/Chapter1/Appendix8.html.

Figure 1.7 Dynamos dated from the 1830s, but Edison and others made them cheaper and more powerful. The first dynamo at Edison's research laboratory in Menlo Park (top) can be compared to a jumbo generator installed at Pearl Street in New York City two years later (below).

Competition Maximus

Artificial lighting was never a monopoly for any application or company. Coal-gas lighting was the first modern form of illumination in America, beginning in Baltimore in 1817 and extending to Boston, Brooklyn, New Orleans, and New York by 1835. By 1875, more than 400 gaslight companies blanketed urban America, whetting the peoples' appetite for more and better lighting.[21] Some of this appetite was met by kerosene lamps, which came of age in the 1860s with the rise of the commercial crude-oil industry. Coal oil also had a business—at least until petroleum came along.

The electricity age began with arc lighting. Brush Electric Company and American Electric Company, among others, introduced outdoor lighting in Cleveland, Niagara Falls, Philadelphia, and San Francisco by 1880. But the "blue moons" of arc lighting were no match for the "bottled sunlight" of incandescent bulbs, of which Edison was the inventor and first mover. "Edison's company is the only one actively in the field," it was reported in 1883. "It not only occupies the field, it comes near to filling it." Yet competitors were emerging, the first being United States Electric Lighting Company (est. 1878), which by 1885 had 80 stations versus Edison's 368. The upstart was not profitable and merged several years later into the company that would become Edison's most formidable rival, Westinghouse Electric.

In 1884, inventor George Westinghouse incorporated Westinghouse Electric & Manufacturing Company to pursue the incandescent-bulb market. Recapitalized at $1 million in January 1886, the renamed Westinghouse Electric Company began construction of central stations, using the AC transformers that he had helped perfect. Unlike DC, AC transformers could step up voltage to transmit power over greater distances with minimal losses yet also step down voltage to serve individual users. This allowed AC to bring electricity to a much larger population and at lower cost than to Edison's DC-based offering.[22]

Within a year, Pittsburg-based Westinghouse Electric had 68 AC stations built or under way. One Westinghouse station in New Orleans went head to head against Edison's DC station, an early instance of wire-on-wire competition. Thomas Edison himself alternately marveled and fussed at the "ubiquitous" Westinghouse and his products.

---

21. Coal-gas lamps were what electricity sought to displace. See Internet appendix 1.9, "Electricity versus Manufactured Gas," at www.politicalcapitalism.org/Book2/Chapter1/Appendix9.html.

22. At age 22, George Westinghouse (1846–1914) designed an air brake allowing train cars to stop simultaneously (or nearly so). In 1886, he secured American patent rights to a high-voltage transformer developed abroad, which he improved with the help of William Stanley. The AC system was first installed in 1886; two years later, he secured patent rights to an AC motor developed by Nikola Tesla, a Serbian-American inventor. Westinghouse would receive several hundred patents in fields as diverse as electric signaling, natural gas pipelining, metering, telephony, steam turbines, heat pumps, and shock absorbers. He was in a rarified league with Edison as an inventor and proved to be a better (although fallible) businessman.

Westinghouse had a formidable competitor using AC, which meant that Edison had two. Thomson-Houston Company of Lynn, Massachusetts (est. 1883), branched out from arc lighting to Westinghouse-licensed AC central stations, with 22 such projects completed or under way by late 1887. Thomson-Houston had three strengths that allowed it to expand quickly and profitably: an able marketing-oriented leader, Charles Coffin; strong financing from Boston-based Lee, Higginson & Company; and a stream of new technology from Elihu Thomson, who in a five-decade career would be awarded 696 patents, among the most awarded to one man in the United States.[23] Thomson-Houston also knew when to go to the outside, licensing Westinghouse's alternating current in 1887 and purchasing seven companies, including Brush Electric, between 1888 and 1891.

Westinghouse and Thomson-Houston together were catching up with the mighty Edison Machine Works, which claimed 121 DC-dedicated central stations, built or under contract at the time. Thomson-Houston focused on what Edison did not—arc lighting, alternating current, and product variety—and became more profitable than the industry leader. But with cause, Edison came down hard on the upstart for patent infringement.

The AC boom was not surprising. DC stations had to be situated in the middle of their service territory and reached less than a mile in each direction. Checkerboarding at the edges left customers unserved. Once such a unit was situated, changing market demographics might require a new generator. AC stations covered square miles, and upgrades could meet new demand in any direction. AC transmission also used significantly less copper than DC, a savings that was magnified with the metal's price spike in 1887/88. Also, the superior economics of AC was enhanced with a new motor invented in 1887 by Nikola Tesla, a "new titan" in the electricity field.

Edison resorted to a war of words, calling George Westinghouse a "shyster" and saying, "Tell Westinghouse to stick to air brakes." Edison called AC purveyors "the Apostles of Parsimony," a backhanded compliment. But the

----

23. At age 16, Elihu Thomson (1853–1937) was introduced to the new field of electricity by his high school teacher Edwin Houston, the man who later became Thompson's co-inventor and business partner. In 1878, they invented a rudimentary alternating-current system that attracted investors, and their future work together "helped convert electric lights, generators, and motors from lecture-hall curiosities in 1875 to commonplace products in 1900." Thomson was involved with three companies: American Electric Company (1880–83), Thompson-Houston Electric Company (1883–92), and, through merger, General Electric Company (est. 1892). Thompson was much more than "an excellent albeit not creative engineer" who positioned a "cowbird company, one that thrived upon the nests of others," as Forrest McDonald claimed. Thomson, one of America's great inventors, filled in gaps with electricity both during and after Edison's active period.

Figure 1.8 Competition from electricity disturbed the peace of the gaslight interests (bottom left), which meant working city hall to get permits and franchises, such as Thomas Edison's dinner for alderman (top left). By the 1880s, electricity competed vigorously with itself, creating "hideous masses of overhead wires" alongside telephone and telegraph wires (right).

market was speaking much louder than words, despite Edison's reputation. "The tide would not turn back at his frown," one historian noted.

Edison had one card to play: *safety*. AC voltage was more powerful and potentially lethal than DC. Edison also built his lines underground, a costly practice that gave his investors pause. Some high-publicity electrocutions from overhead AC gave Edison an opening to sway the public and, more important, the New York City Board of Electrical Control. Animals were "westinghoused" with lethal AC in public demonstrations at Edison's direction. The public relations department of Edison Electric Light wrote a law for New York to use electrocution for capital punishment to scare the public about Westinghouse's technology on the overhead wires. An elephant was electrocuted at Coney Island in 1903 for similar effect. But the effort to ban AC failed after it was documented that accidents with this technology were no more, and even less, than with DC, not to mention other public hazards. Similar efforts by Edison (and Insull) to ban AC were also turned back in Virginia and Ohio.[24]

Just about everyone but Thomas Edison knew that AC central stations were the future. The Edison organization passed up the chance to patent European AC technology back in 1885, a mistake George Westinghouse capitalized on. A study by Frank Sprague commissioned by Edward Johnson, the president of Edison Light Company, supported entry into high-voltage distribution. One of Edison's own, the inventive Nikola Tesla, quit and later sold his AC technology to Westinghouse.

Finally, with Westinghouse installing as much capacity in a month as Edison in a year, and with Insull pleading with other executives, Edison relented. Edison Machine Works entered the AC business by October 1890. The war of the currents was over.

The full shenanigans of Edison's futile crusade will never be known. Insull described the period as "hundreds of stories of happenings which occurred before there were such things as Rotary Clubs and business ethics codes." He thought it "best to let them die" to "avoid sullying Edison's memory." This early episode in the history of political electricity and, more broadly, political capitalism, would not be the last for Samuel Insull or for competing technologies.

Going Napoleonic

The Thomas Edison problem went beyond the battle of the currents. *The inventor extrordinaire was going Napoleonic.* Electric-train demonstrations in Menlo Park in 1880, 1882, and 1883, which Edison Light Company's investors refused to support, were technological successes but economic failures. A spirited return to phonograph experimentation, which hit full stride in 1886, was another distraction of mind and money. Edison's need for additional funding in this area led to a sequence of events that by 1888 caused "the first irreparable fissures in the proud, tightly knit Edison fraternity." The "phonograph fiasco" would stretch out 20 years.

Edison's "most consuming obsession" began in 1889 when he received a large payout from the new investors in Edison Light Company. His idea was to reduce the cost of iron via a separation process that could upgrade magnetic rock into high-grade iron ore, thus creating what he described as a "monopoly of one of the most valuable sources of national wealth in the U.S." Edison's iron-intensive inventions explained part of his interest. "This venture has all the elements of permanent success," the inventor exuded. "All the factors are known."

---

24. This foray of Edison and Insull into political capitalism is discussed in Internet appendix 1.10, "The 'Battle of the Currents' Revisited," at www.politicalcapitalism.org/ Book2/Chapter1/Appendix10.html.

"Edison's Folly" was a ten-year mistake. Expenses north of $2 million (about $50 million in 2008 dollars) ate up his wealth and misdirected his inventive and engineering skill. Four hundred men were misemployed and then unemployed. The venture depended on iron ore priced between $6.00 and $7.50 per ton, yet new high-grade discoveries kept prices well below this range.

After reading a dispatch in 1899 that iron ore prices had dropped to $2.65 a ton, Edison disbanded his vast New Jersey/Pennsylvania operation. His iron ore milling process was a *technological* success, but revenues below cost could not continue.

Edison could have advanced arc lighting as his investors wanted him to do. He was late creating a new subsidiary, Edison Company for Isolated Lighting, to tap into another ready, profitable market; after ramping up in 1882, more than a thousand dynamos were built and operating six years later. Edison was also late with his patent infringement litigation, which would bear fruit in the next decade.

Edison's Napoleon complex also worked against cost control. A new laboratory built in West Orange, New Jersey, capable of "build[ing] anything from a lady's watch to a Locomotive," was well over budget in 1887/88, which caused Insull to complain to the inventor's new private secretary, Alfred Tate:

> [Edison] wants a great deal more money than he at first anticipated, but this is simply a repetition of what has occurred so frequently before. The trouble is, that Mr. Edison does not have anyone with him who urges him to curtail his expenses on his new laboratory.

The good news was that Insull was now well away from the boss, affording him more managerial freedom to run Edison Machine Works. Edison was a micromanager, insisting on knowing minute details of his many enterprises before decisions were made. Edison for years spent too much time on trains going to his various enterprises, but the consolidation of 1886 and Edison's new ventures outside of electricity got him away to his lieutenants' benefit. Edison could have, should have, ceded greater control to his investors and concentrated on his strength: invention and engineering.

Thomas Edison's greatest foe was not J. P. Morgan, Wall Street, George Westinghouse, Elihu Thomson, or Charles Coffin. It was himself. Despite all the positives, Edison had become a burden to Samuel Insull and his whole organization ever since 1884, if not before.[25] Small wonder that Drexel Morgan and other potential investors declined to recapitalize the world's greatest commercial inventor. Small wonder that Insull was able to handle Edison and excel at running a company—and one of the world's largest manufacturing enterprises at that.

---

25. Also see Internet appendix 1.11, "Edison's Strengths and Weaknesses," at www. politicalcapitalism.org/Book2/Chapter1/Appendix11.html.

Edison General Electric Company: 1889–92

Enter Henry Villard, an up-and-down financer and backer of Edison's earlier work with electric railroads. Armed with European capital, Villard proposed to consolidate Edison Light and Edison's various shops manufacturing generators, lamps, and electrical devices. Sprague Electric Railway and Motor Company would become wholly owned, as would Edison's Canadian subsidiary. Eight entities were merged, with their separate identities set to end the next year. Villard's vision of creating a "world cartel" in electricity was exaggerated, but the benefits of consolidation, vertical integration, and scale economies were there. It would be a wise recapitalization/restructuring.

Insull favored the merger to address the capitalization problem. So did Edward Johnson, who told his boss, "We shall speedily have the biggest Edison organization in the world with abundant capital," after which it would be "goodbye Westinghouse et al." It was just enough to get Edison to go along.

J. P. Morgan set the terms, and Edison General Electric Company came into being in April 1889 with a par value of $12 million. Drexel Morgan placed the new stock with private investors, most going to Deutsche Bank because of Villard.

Edison General Electric earned $700,000 on sales of $7 million in its first reorganized year, a solid start. A good deal of potential earnings remained in stock held in and notes payable from LDCs serving Brooklyn, Boston, Chicago, Detroit, Philadelphia, and several dozen other cities.

Thomas Edison had his biggest career payday, receiving $1.75 million in stock (about $50 million today). "I have been under a desperate strain for money for 22 years," he allowed. It was time to "free my mind from financial stress and … go ahead in the technical field." Edward Johnson retired wealthy, and Sigmund Bergmann would parlay his share into greater success in Europe. The Morgan group emerged with a market value of $2.7 million, a 350 percent return on its original investment. An investment that never paid dividends in more than a decade was finally well worth it.

The recapitalization provided much needed funds for expansion, and the 29-year-old Insull himself, $75,000 richer (about $2 million today), was appointed vice president in charge of manufacturing and sales, while continuing as Thomas Edison's business manager. Villard was president, but Insull was to run the show—short of financing, which he did not want to do and probably could not humanly do. Both men were careful to consult with Thomas Edison on important business matters, yet the silent force was J. P. Morgan. He and Edison were still on top in their very different ways.

Back at the New York City headquarters, Insull had responsibilities for Edison Machine Works in Schenectady, Bergmann & Company in New York City, and Edison Lamp Company in Harrison, New Jersey. With virtually the whole organization beneath him, Insull centralized by creating seven regional sales offices: New England District (headquartered in Boston), Eastern District

(New York), Central District (Chicago), Southern District (New Orleans), Rocky Mountain District (Denver), Pacific District (San Francisco), and Canada (Toronto).[26] Insull also established a central intelligence group at the parent home office, the forerunner to the strategic-planning division of national organizations to come.

Each district was under one manager responsible for sales, installation, and service. Insull visited these offices twice yearly. "Out of their work," stated a history of General Electric Company published in 1941, "came principles of business administration and methods of financial accounting which persist today."

Insull embarked on an aggressive growth strategy, with all products priced to sell. He retained all earnings, sold stock, and borrowed to the hilt. "Never pay cash when you can give a note," Insull always said, "and then meet your notes promptly." The formula was to spread fixed costs over more and more units, allowing him to lower prices to maximize market penetration. Electric lamps that cost a dollar in 1886, for example, cost half as much four years later. As Insull (and Edison) suspected, increased volume made up for lower margins per sale. Sales also increased demand for the other side: more lamps, more demand for generators; more generators, more demand for lamps. In a major policy change, Edison General was put on a cash basis, which meant less business but more cash flow and liquidity.

Insull treated his workers well. Stung by labor problems that precipitated the move from Goerck Street to Schenectady and empathetic toward the little fellow, Insull implemented progressive labor policies that later in his career would inspire the term *Insullization*.

Challenges remained. Capitalization problems led Villard to approach Morgan for a loan of several million dollars. Villard was less interested in manufacturing than in owning and operating central stations and streetcars. He envisioned a future wherein a self-integrated company would manufacture only for itself, part of a grand vision of one dominant firm. But Villard's Morganesque view of consolidation over competition, not shared by Insull, compromised the company's real strength: manufacturing. Villard's policy of taking stock rather than bonds from LDCs meant less cash flow for Insull—hence the need for $3.5 million in new debt from Drexel Morgan. Edison General Electric was short of engineering talent, and Insull needed Edison working on arc lighting and streetcar systems, not phonograph improvements and iron ore milling. These problems could not be hidden in a market populated by formidable competitors, such as Thompson-Houston and Westinghouse.

---

26. As stated in Edison General Electric's 1890 annual report: "It was found practically impossible to exercise over so many distinct organizations the close supervision necessary to secure rigid accountability and conduct the business on an economical basis."

The Formation of General Electric Company (1892)

The early 1890s proved to be "the most competitive and tumultuous period in the history of the electrical manufacturing industry." In the autumn of 1890, London's Baring Brothers, the world's leading banking house, failed, tightening capital markets and depressing the value of the highly leveraged LDCs in which Edison General Electric had stock positions (totaling $6–$7 million in 45 to 50 firms). Internally, competition for the domestic central-station business was intense among the big three: Edison General Electric, Thomson-Houston Electric Company, and Westinghouse Electric. A dozen other companies had 20 or more central stations, and dozens more companies were advertising for the same business. This was quite different from a decade before, when Edison practically had the market to himself.

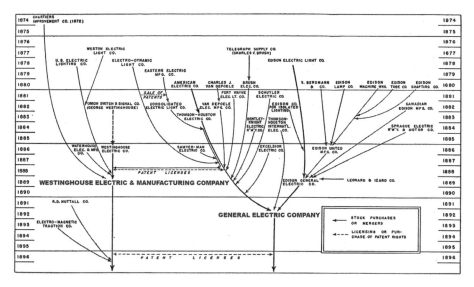

Figure 1.9 The growth of the Edison companies, consolidated as General Electric Company in 1892, is shown alongside the development of rival Westinghouse Electric & Manufacturing Company. In all, some 30 companies ended up as 2 over a quarter century.

Westinghouse, the most leveraged of the three and in the midst of an expansion, struggled to refinance its debt and faced the prospect of bankruptcy. George Westinghouse thought too little of Charles Coffin to merge with Thomson-Houston, which left Edison General Electric. As early as 1888–89, Villard, with Morgan's blessing, had been quietly talking to Westinghouse, considered a better merger candidate than Thomson-Houston because it was smaller and had AC patents.

The industry needed rationalization. Bids to install central stations were loss leaders, the builders betting on future parts business once their technology was locked in. Thomson-Houston, the most aggressive bidder, had more central stations by 1891 than Westinghouse and Edison combined. Thomson-Houston under Coffin was plenty profitable, one plum being a contract with the city of Boston to erect the world's largest generating plant (two megawatts). To Villard, this was "ruinous" competition. Morgan could not have agreed more.

Villard's hand was significantly strengthened when the courts ruled in favor of Edison's infringement suits in mid-1891. Edison's patents were set to expire in 1894, but the other companies could scarcely afford to stop manufacturing or pay high license fees during the interim. Consequently, Villard set his sights on the biggest prize, Thomson-Houston, in early 1892.

Villard traveled to Lynn for talks and took a tour but was told that Thomson-Houston was not for sale. A Morgan representative visited some months later and reported back that Thomson-Houston should be acquired. Soft business conditions in 1891 exposed excess industry capacity, suggesting a need for consolidation and cost cutting, and 60 patent suits between Edison and Thomson-Houston begged for a solution. Edison also needed the AC rights that Thomson-Houston possessed under its Westinghouse cross license. Edison General needed working capital as well.

As Morgan moved toward consolidation, Villard began to look shaky. The *New York Times* described Villard as "a strong talker" with "wonderful personal magnetism" but warned that "J. Pierpont Morgan ... is a hard man to dazzle." The planned takeover took a twist when Charles Coffin, perhaps bluffing, told Villard that he did not want to sell. "We don't think much of the way the Edison company has been managed," Coffin said, words intended to reach the kingmaker, J. P. Morgan. Morgan met with Coffin, who brought with him the financials for 1891, showing Thomson-Houston with a 26 percent return compared to Edison General's 11 percent. Part of the discrepancy was that Edison's LDC stocks were not generating income, whereas Thomson-Houston's LDC bonds were.

Without warning to Villard or anyone else on the Edison side, Morgan set the terms of the merger by valuing Thompson-Houston at $18 million and Edison at $15 million. He selected the board accordingly. Henry Villard was informed that his "courteous resignation would be courteously received," leaving Charles Coffin at the top of the merger that created General Electric Company. Edison had been "Morganized."

Edison's secretary, Alfred Tate, heard the news first and rushed to find his boss. When told, Edison turned "as white as his collar" before uttering, "Send for Insull." But nothing could be done.

Edison had himself to blame for the turn of events. Who had been in the New Jersey highlands for two years upgrading iron ore rather than tending to the (premerger) Edison Light? Who had reduced his ownership position and told Villard as far back as 1890, "I feel that it is about time to retire from the lighting business"? Edison had not attended meetings regarding the future of his namesake company; nor had he cultivated Wall Street and J. P. Morgan in years. Edison wanted glory in an industry that had now moved past him.

Insull professed complete surprise but supported the merger. No one knew more than he that capital was badly needed and that electricity was no longer Edison's passion. Emotionally wounded, hearing rumors that Insull somehow was in the know, and suspicious about an offer made to Insull to join the new company, Edison turned on his business chief. It was the first major disagreement between the two in their 11 years.

No evidence of a conspiracy within the Edison group emerged. Alfred Tate, in his Edison biography, opined, "To anyone who knew Insull's character as I did, that story is incredible." Villard had kept his negotiations quiet and got unexpectedly ousted in the end. But that did not keep some of Insull's enemies from starting rumors. Edison would back down from his accusation, but his spell over Insull was now broken.[27]

"Our orders were far in excess of our capital to handle the business, and both Mr. Insull and I were afraid we might get into trouble for lack of money," a subdued Edison remarked on the merger. "When Mr. Henry Villard and his syndicate offered to buy us out, we concluded it was better to be sure than sorry; so we sold out for a large sum." But the inventor's ego was apparent when he told the *New York Times*:

> I cannot waste my time over electric lighting matters, for they are old. I ceased to worry over those things ten years ago, and I have a lot more new material on which to work…. I simply want to get as large dividends as possible from such stock as I hold. I am not businessman enough to spend my time at that end of the concern. I think I was the first to urge the consolidation.

Edison boasted to friends that he was about to do something "so different and so much bigger … that people will forget my name ever was connected with anything electrical."

Villard, meanwhile, found a scapegoat for his ousting. "The impaired financial condition of the Edison Company, due to the extravagant management of Mr. Insull," he stated, "made the fusion imperative." Such was the indignity hurled at the man who had made Schenectady the most profitable part of Edison's whole operation. Insull could only remember it as "the first great crisis of my career in America."

·◌·

---

27. Insull's close friendship with Edison resumed and endured after the two broke off their business partnership in 1892. Insull gave many speeches on Edison, an excerpt of which is reproduced in Internet appendix 1.12, "Insull on Edison: Speech of March 14, 1926," at www.politicalcapitalism.org/Book2/Chapter1/Appendix12.html.

The $50 million General Electric Company came into being in April 1892. "Edison" was dropped from the corporate name at the inventor's request, and Edison began liquidating his interest in the new company—a payout that would total $5 million ($100-plus million today). Insull was offered the position of second vice president in charge of manufacturing and sales, the number-three position at the whole company, at the substantial salary of $36,000.

Insull accepted—but only to see the merger through. Coffin's decision to merge Thomson-Houston's network into Insull's seven-district organization required Insull's best efforts to help position his side's 6,000 workers in the new organization. Thus, it was really Insull, not Coffin, who was behind what business historian Alfred Chandler called General Electric's "standard way of organizing a modern integrated industrial enterprise." This belied Coffin's claim that Edison General Electric was not well managed, something that hardly sat well with Insull, who waited many years before saying how, "to put it politely, some people helped me get out [of General Electric]." It was less Coffin's fault, however, than the real decision maker: J. P. Morgan.[28]

General Electric Company under Charles Coffin would have a bumpy beginning before settling into the "center firm" known today as GE. After a solid 1892, when more than two million lamps were sold under the company's monopoly patents, the Panic of 1893 forced the firm to suspend its dividend and turn to Drexel Morgan for help. But by 1895, with more than 10,000 customers and more than 100,000 orders, GE was again profitable and well capitalized, and General Electric would never look back. Board members J. P. Morgan and Charles Coster (Morgan's chief lieutenant) could be proud of their new company. Naysayers who challenged the firm's finances and Coffin's integrity, and those who predicted failure for "the electrical trust," would be proven wrong.

Farewell, New York

Why did a 32-year-old with *future* written all over him resign from a top position at one of the world's greatest companies? The first reason was Insull's concern about working for someone (a fast-talking former shoe salesman, no less) who, he believed, knew less than he did about electricity.[29] Never mind that Charles Coffin was the president of General Electric and consequently *the* most powerful

---

28. "I guess [J. P. Morgan] thought that I was not sufficiently live enough kind of material to run the job, and so another man was made president," Insull would say decades later. Elsewhere, Insull allowed: "I really was one of the 'outs' in this new organization, and I made up my mind to branch out for myself, although it involved severing my personal [business] relations with Mr. Thomas A. Edison."

29. In his memoirs, Insull revealed how his early antagonism gave way to a close friendship with Coffin, a man whose "marvelous grasp of the business" propelled General Electric and the whole central-station business.

man in the industry—and someone Insull would come to regard as "a man of probably the greatest vision" of anyone in electricity manufacturing, excepting, of course, the industry's founder, Thomas Edison.

Second, leaving General Electric allowed Insull to break as cleanly as did Thomas Edison, his still-beloved mentor. (This also ruled out working for Westinghouse, the company that Thomas Edison so disliked in competitive battle.)

Third, Insull did not believe that General Electric was sufficiently focused on central stations as the future. Insull saw a better future in generation and distribution (the utility side) than in manufacturing, although he was not interested in the vice presidency of North American Company offered by Henry Villard. (Villard, who controlled the company that operated electric utilities in Milwaukee and Cincinnati, would apologize to Insull for his earlier criticism.)

Insull, in short, was ready for his own show—one that would be potentially bigger in scope than the business he was leaving, although still in the same industry. Moreover, he had an intriguing opportunity to pursue.

Chicago Edison Company, an upstart just two years into paying a dividend, needed a new president after the resignation of E. T. Watkins in 1891. Insull, who had handled its account for Edison General Electric, was asked by Edward Brewster and Byron Smith, two prominent members of Chicago Edison's strong board, for recommendations. The smallish company dared not ask Insull himself to take the position; with less than half of the embryonic lighting load in its city, Chicago Edison's capitalization of $883,000 was about 2 percent that of General Electric, where Insull was the number three. Moreover, the new president of Chicago Edison would command all of 300 men, whereas Insull had commanded 6,000 at Schenectady.

But Insull thought differently. Edison himself had identified Chicago as the ideal market in waiting, and Insull coveted the top job instead of a near-the-top job. It meant taking a self-imposed salary reduction and relocating to a city that was less to his liking. (He bound himself to a three-year contract—the only time he ever set a term—in order to not let himself venture back East.) It meant choosing generation/distribution over the (hitherto) more profitable manufac-turing side of the electricity business. But his visiting mother urged him to take it after he explained his options. So, on the same day that General Electric assigned him the number-three job, Insull wrote letters to Brewster and Smith offering his candidacy. The 32-year-old realized that he was taking over a small company, but he also knew how he could consolidate the Chicago electricity market as a platform for greater growth.

The Chicago Edison board was surprised and pleased. Little vetting was required. Thomas Edison's unreserved "yes" was about all the board needed.

So once Insull got his conditions from his new board—an increase in capital, construction of a large new generating plant, and the promise of ample capital to consolidate the Chicago market and internally expand—he was elected

THE ORGANIZATION OF THE GENERAL ELECTRIC COMPANY 1892

Executive Officers

Charles A. Coffin - President
Eugene Griffin - First Vice President
Samuel Insull - Second Vice President
Frederick P. Fish - General Counsel
E.I. Garfield - Secretary
Benjamin F. Peach, Jr. - Treasurer

Departments - General Managers

Lighting - S.Dana Greene
Railway - O.T. Crosby
Power - John R.McKee
Supply - Jesse R. Lovejoy

Board of Directors

H.M. Twombley - Chairman

F.L. Ames	Eugene Griffin
C.A. Coffin	F.S. Hastings
T.J. Coolidge, Jr.	H.L. Higginson
C.H. Coster	D.O. Mills
T.A. Edison	J.P. Morgan

Works Managers

Manager - Schenectady Works - John Kreusi
Manager - Harrison Works - Francis R. Upton
Manager - Lynn Works - George E. Emmons

* * *

Technical Director - Edwin W. Rice, Jr.

GENERAL ELECTRIC COMPANY.
SCHENECTADY N Y.

On July 8, 1892, the following resolution was passed by the Board of Directors of the General Electric Company:

"That the resignation of Mr. Insull of the office of Second Vice President of this Company be and hereby is accepted, to take effect August 1, 1892, and the Secretary is hereby directed to convey to Mr. Insull the thanks and appreciation of this Board for the efficient service rendered by him."

Mr. Insull of course has in his possession the letter of the Secretary written in compliance with the request contained in the above resolution.

Very truly yours,

HP/EMA

Figure 1.10 The new General Electric Company appointed the 32-year-old Samuel Insull as second vice president, the number three position at the company. Insull resigned from the great manufacturing concern to start anew in the distribution side of the business, leaving New York City for Chicago.

president of Chicago Edison on May 26, 1892, with a start date of July 1. His salary—determined by Insull himself—was $12,000, one-third of what he was making at General Electric.

A farewell dinner for Insull was held at Delmonico's, his favorite restaurant and New York City's finest—and the one that had let Edison and him run a tab in lean times. The merger completed, executives of General Electric hosted the event in honor of the departing dynamo. It was a sign of not only respect and goodwill but also client relations, given that Chicago Edison was a General Electric customer.

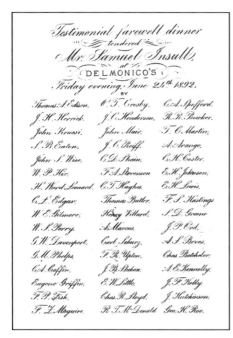

Figure 1.11 Insull, who resigned from General Electric in July 1892, was given a farewell dinner in New York City at his favorite restaurant, Delmonico's. The elaborate affair, hosted by Charles Coffin and General Electric, was attended by a who's who of the young industry.

The room was filled with "'intimate friends and intimate enemies,'" the former led by Thomas Edison and the latter including Henry Villard and Charles Coffin. Edward Johnson, Charles Batchelor, and John Kruesi from the old Edison ranks were present. J. P. Morgan, always the invisible force, was absent.

Speeches followed the repast, topped off with a resolution to the honoree and the presentation of a beautiful silver punch bowl. Insull then rose. He gave terse thanks and shared his goal and expectation: to make his new company bigger than the one he was leaving. *Chicago Edison bigger than General Electric? Insull besting Coffin? Chicago over New York City?* The prediction was audacious and even laughable—except for the fact that Samuel Insull, always serious, said it. Five days later, Insull was off to Chicago to make good for the fourth time in his life.

2

Dynamo at Chicago Edison: 1892–1907

L EAVING THE NEST OF GENERAL ELECTRIC and the comforts of New York City for a fledging enterprise in dingy Chicago was the second great gamble in Samuel Insull's young life. Not since he embarked from Liverpool to America on incomplete instructions 11 years before had he done something this bold. But Insull had to invent a company, not an industry; Thomas Edison had already done that. "Just imagine, if you can, that by the wave of your hand you could bring about such a condition of things that all the thousand and one articles used between the generator and the lamp were to disappear, and you had to start over again to create them," Insull would explain decades later. "Now that was the situation existing in the spring of 1881."[1]

So much had been done. The innumerable little things were joined by three major advances. A refined three-wire system was now doing the work of the bulky two-wire system with one-third of the copper requirement. Incandescent lamps had become more than twice as efficient. Alternating current expanded the reach of generators and improved scale economies. These things, in Insull's estimation, "made the central station business a certain financial success in cities of the first, second, and third rank." More engineering would come, but managerial breakthroughs were as needed as technical ones. In fact, one drove the other, as Insull would show the world.

---

1. "I arrived in this country at practically the birth of a great industry," Insull would later recall. "There were not more than three or four men in the world who had the slightest technical conception of the electric light and power system ... [and] there was only one man ... who had the slightest conception of the economics of the industry—that was Edison himself."

Samuel Insull was now his own man—and none too soon. Thomas Edison was a genius, caring mentor, and close friend, but his foibles nearly busted Insull as well as himself. "I fell a victim to [Edison's] spell at the first interview," Insull later admitted, a trance that would not be broken until the great inventor turned on him in the wake of the General Electric buyout. But it was probably too much to expect that someone at the beginning of his career could have done much more in helping Thomas Edison navigate what one historian called "the perilous journey between invention and commercial success." As it was, Edison was a positive force in electricity for the first several years and then a neutral or negative one for the last eight. Still, Insull would have nothing but praise for "the inventor of our industry" as the years and decades went by.

The spirit of Edison fueled Insull's quest to create *the* leading electricity enterprise. Insull saw the future in central stations generating more and more for less and less. It was none other than Thomas Edison who foreshadowed Insull's future when he remarked during a visit to Chicago: "You know, Sammy, this is one of the best cities in the world for our line of business."[2]

Hello, Chicago

The "windy city" was many other things when Insull arrived in the summer of 1892. It was the "lusty city," "shock city," and "wide-open city," a tough working-class town that exuded filth and vice. Also, "Chicago attracted writers, reformers, and social activists the way the saloons attracted the thirsty."

But make no mistake: Chicago, strategically located by land and by water (Lake Michigan, Chicago River, Illinois River), was the mecca of the American-based second Industrial Revolution, and a rival to London and Berlin on the world stage. The capital of the Midwest and "commercial New World crossroads" was the nation's hub for dozens of railroads, as well as for meatpacking and iron and steel manufacturing. Cheap, plentiful bituminous (soft) coal mined in Illinois and surrounds was behind much of this industrialization, making Chicago the first U.S. energy city.

Chicago's economic engine was evidenced by smoky air and "endless reaches of factories, marshaling yards, slaughterhouses, grain elevators, and iron mills, and slag heaps and coal piles." Legions of new workers fueled the boom. Hundreds of nouveau millionaires were at the apex of a material advance experienced by most residents. Chicago was the fastest-growing major city in the United States and world. Not even New York City—the only U.S. city with a larger population than Chicago's one million—could claim that.

Chicago was scarcely served by electricity when Samuel Insull arrived, presenting him with "the best opportunity I knew of in the United States to develop

---

2. See Internet appendix 2.1, "From Manufacturing to Integrated Distribution," at www. politicalcapitalism.org/Book2/Chapter2/Appendix1.html.

the business of the production and distribution of electrical energy." It was this opportunity that propelled the "man with electricity for a soul" and "genius of order and efficiency" to leave New York City. Thanks to Insull, Chicago would in time get its best moniker yet: "the electric city."

Chicago politics was wide open too. With franchises required to use city streets, incumbent firms greased palms at City Hall to stall interlopers who threatened them with competition.[3] Such was the case for gas, power, water, and streetcars only, however, leaving the rest of the economy "relatively free of conservative, or traditional, constraints." For the most part, Chicago was a get-it-done, "pliable" city, ripe for market entrepreneurship. Blue bloods need not apply.

·◈·

In 1878, electricity's arc lighting came to Chicago, offering a blaze of light far richer than that of coal gas. The *Chicago Times* announced the beginning of the end of Chicago's gas monopoly and foresaw a new era of lower rates and diminished politics.[4] Lower rates would come, but electricity franchises would add to, not subtract from, political involvement, leading to more formal regulation. Chicago, "not known for the efficiency and honesty of its government," as one historian charitably put it, would sink further into the abyss of political capitalism. "For the next thirty years," summarized historian Harold Platt, "franchise 'boodle,' bribery, and graft would become the order of the day from the neighborhood wards to the governor's mansion." The notion of rivalry, whereby franchises were automatically awarded upon a showing of viability, was not on the agenda; progressivism and municipal reform would lead only to more government and more concentration of power.

Electricity was catching on by the time Insull arrived. From its introduction in 1880, electricity demand grew until Chicago had more isolated plants per capita than any other city. Chicago Edison, serving Cook County (the heart of downtown) with a nonexclusive franchise awarded in 1887, erected the city's first central station under license from Edison Electric Light Company (Edison Light).[5] None other than Samuel Insull had been the "chief manufacturer" for

---

3. "The [Chicago] City Council, which would continue to lose members to the federal penitentiary as late as the 1970s and 1980s, reached its zenith of corruption during the late 19th century," one historian noted.

4. City Hall franchised two and only two gas companies: Peoples Gas Light and Coke Company for the West Side, and Chicago Gas Light and Coke Company on the South and North sides.

5. The forerunner to Chicago Edison was Western Edison Light Company, which was incorporated in 1882 with capital of $500,000 to negotiate with Edison Light to erect a central station and to sell Edison equipment (principally isolated stations). Chicago's city council granted Western Edison a 25-year franchise in 1887, whereupon a new firm, Chicago Edison

the steam-coal Adams Street Station. But its engineering plan did not come from New York; it came from Chicago Edison's consulting engineer, Frederick Sargent, who substituted his own for Edison Light's overengineered blueprint. Working at Chicago Edison alongside Insull, with whom he shared the same birth date (November 11, 1859), Sargent went on to "pioneer virtually every major advancement in central station development for 25 years."

When Insull arrived, Chicago sported approximately 30 companies operating 18 central stations and 500 isolated plants. Chicago Edison accounted for less than half this capacity. But Insull's company did not even possess a central-station monopoly on its home turf, which meant that duplicate facilities would be required, no small item given that underground cables were required. (Chicago's Board of Aldermen adopted this rule after the Great Fire of 1871 gutted the central business district.) But the requirement was also welcomed by gaslight interests, which desired increased costs for their energy rival.

Settling In

"By 1892, Chicago had set out to overthrow New York as master of the continent," Forrest McDonald wrote in *Insull*.[6] "Before it could do so, Chicago itself needed a master," McDonald continued. "He arrived on July 1."

The 32-year-old had his diploma from the "School of Experience," a title bestowed on him by Thomas Edison himself. Insull understood the technology of electricity better than did any other company head, even Charles Coffin of General Electric. Insull's years at Schenectady made him an expert in managerial economics—cost versus revenue per unit, work methods, and finance—not to mention the leadership skills necessary to inspire thousands.

Fearing the temptation to abandon his new "frontier town" for New York City, where he had many friends and enjoyed the cosmopolitan life, Insull had obligated himself to a three-year contract with his new company. His self-imposed salary cut of two-thirds ("It was all that so small a business could afford to pay") left him with "pretty hard [budgeting] work for a young man with many responsibilities." Insull was being strict, but his coming was really predicated on a financially strong board of directors' promise that he would

---

Company, received a charter from the Illinois secretary of state and assumed the franchise of Western Edison. The 1887 charter, purchased for $50,000, did not allow the company to impose infrastructure on property owners but permitted the city to require service so long as at least a 6 percent profit was made.

6. This 1962 biography remains definitive. John Wasik's more recent Insull biography, *The Merchant of Power* (2006), is less comprehensive and diminished by factual errors. See Internet appendix 2.2, "Some Discrepancies in Insull Historiography," at www.politicalcapitalism.org/Book2/Chapter2/Appendix2.html.

have ample capital for rapid expansion, freeing him to concentrate on every-thing else.

As part of this arrangement, the board authorized a $250,000 infusion, bring-ing Chicago Edison's capitalization past $1.1 million. This new stock, purchased by Insull himself at the market price as a company receivable, would fund the construction of a large central station to replace Adams Street. Looking ahead, the board approved Insull's plan to acquire rivals to rationalize the fragmented, underscaled industry. Such plans came as a "terrible shock" to employees who had never had a leader interested in expanding the way Insull immediately set out to do.

Insull, still a British citizen and unmarried, came alone. His private secretary lost out when he countered Insull's salary offer, believing that the difference would not be decisive. But Insull believed in betting big—hence his $250,000 stake in Chicago Edison's stock. Still, not wanting to be "embarrassed by going to the company which I was running for a loan," Insull persuaded Chicago business leader Marshall Field to make a personal note to remove the debt from Chicago Edison's books.

"Characteristically," noted biographer Forrest McDonald, "[Insull] began by gambling his whole financial future on the outcome of his efforts." The note to Field would be easily serviced and retired with the stock appreciation to come, but it also indicated Insull's supreme confidence in mastering his business and outdistancing his peers. He was a Great Man first and foremost to himself.

·◇·

Chicago had a gift in waiting for its newest émigré: the World's Columbian Exposition, better known as Chicago's World's Fair of 1893, commemorating the 400th anniversary of Christopher Columbus's discovery of the New World. Chicago, a 60-year-old city, bested New York City, Washington, D.C., and nearby St. Louis for the honor.

The 600-acre fairground at Jackson Park on Lake Michigan was beyond Chicago Edison's modest DC reach, but exhibitors of self-generated power—General Electric and Westinghouse—brought the present and future of elec-tricity to 22 million visitors for whom technology provided hope amid economic uncertainty and social change. "Sell the cook stove if necessary … and come," one enthralled visitor wrote to a relative. At least in this time and space, Chicago became the "White City," "Dream City," and "City of Light"—"the city of the future as a technological utopia."

One of the fair's goals of turning night into day represented, in Insull's esti-mation, "the first really successful effort in electric lighting of very large spaces." The fair successfully demonstrated elevated electric transportation (urban streetcars). Scalable power production was inaugurated with "marine type economical steam engines directly connected to large electric generators."

From the Electricity Building to the Machine Hall to the applications them-selves, electricity overshadowed just about everything else at the fair, which also exhibited architecture, art, and industry. Searchlights illuminated water foun-tains, motorized sidewalks moved thousands at a time, and electric gondolas traversed the waterways. There was the all-electric "servantless" kitchen, com-plete with such novelties as a thermostatically controlled oven, water heater, chafing dish, and coffee maker. Such items marked "the birth of home econom-ics," which early feminists associated with "liberation" and "modernity."

"Monumental, orderly, beautiful, and clean"—those words had never described Chicago until the exposition. Katharine Bates, a visiting English teacher from Wellesley College, was so moved by the fair that she wrote the words for the song that became *America the Beautiful* ("Thine alabaster cities gleam"). The Emerald City of the *Wizard of Oz* was similarly inspired. Chicago's showcase for America was what the Great Exhibition had been for Victorian England four decades earlier.

The six-month extravaganza propelled Samuel Insull and the nascent Chicago Edison. It introduced Insull to the important people he had not yet met in the industry. It whetted the public appetite for electrification—lighting now and appliances later. The World's Fair would put General Electric's 1,200-horsepower engine and two 800-kilowatt generators—the juice behind its 70-foot Tower of Light showcasing 2,500 different types of Edison incandescents—within Insull's reach. (Not to be outdone, Westinghouse exhibited 250,000 bulbs lit by a 15,000-horsepower engine.) General Electric's generator needed a home after the Exposition ended in October 1893, and, with a financial downturn, as well as a lull in the central-station business from General Electric's own policies favoring isolated plants, Insull bought the equipment for a fraction of its produc-tion cost. It would be housed at Chicago Edison's new Harrison Street station, the largest power complex in the world.

For industry executives, the "cultural significance of the World's Fair [was] a starting point in plotting new directions for their business enterprises." Indeed, the National Electric Light Association (NELA), founded in 1885 in Chicago, had meticulously planned the event, and the fair exceeded its high expectations.

✧

When Insull first took his chair at 139 Adams Street (at 7:45 every morning, set-ting the clock back for his hitherto 8:30 a.m. colleagues), Chicago had but 5,000 lighting customers with a peak load of around 4 megawatts (MW). The poten-tial market was pegged at 25,000, but Insull envisioned universal service for Chicagoans—now a million strong. Chicago Edison, although not the biggest fish in the pond, was well positioned with its Edison patent in the heart of downtown.

But Chicago Edison's power source was little more than 3.2 MW Adams Street, an overworked direct-current facility using Edison-patented machinery. Completed in August 1888, the "Dante's Inferno" was a disguised three-story office building adjoined to Chicago Edison's headquarters. But the heavy vibrations and smoke left few fooled. That it did not explode (there were periodic fires) was a tribute to chief engineer Frederick Sargent, who managed to quintuple its output in four years. But Insull knew that Chicago Edison had to start anew with something much bigger and expandable—hence the board's commitment to begin construction of a power station many times the size of Adams Street.

Figure 2.1 The 3.2 MW Adams Street Station, camouflaged as part of the Edison building, soon reached its limit under Insull's sell-sell-sell policy. A battery setup (middle right), helped to meet peak demand, but was prohibitively expensive for a scale-up.

Innovation Maximus

Chicago Edison's bold plan required the chicken and egg to both come first. Sales and generation had to simultaneously and economically surge, as lower rates were required to increase demand, and greater generation was necessary to lower costs and thus rates. Insull's solution put into play various components of his "largely theoretical" vision of how one firm could consolidate and modernize the electricity industry, creating *the new economics of mass-market electricity.*

"Cut-and-Try" Rates

Demand growth had to undergird the process, so Insull's sales group worked with customers to calculate what rates were necessary for electricity to back out gas, or specifically, the formidable Welsbach gas mantle. The top target was Great Northern Hotel, a luxury property then under construction for the World's Fair.

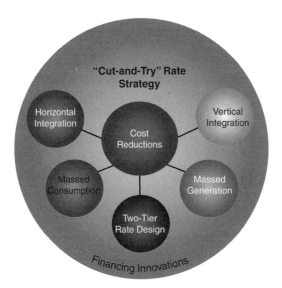

Figure 2.2 Chicago Edison's "ridiculously low" rates increased usage and improved the economics of electrical supply and demand. The drive for lower costs required a transformation of industry practices along the five lines diagramed above, all complemented by improved financing methods.

Chicago Edison's MIT-trained engineer, Louis Ferguson, ran the economics for wiring and lighting 4,100 bulbs. The necessary rate was below anything the electricity industry had ever quoted, but Insull signed a five-year contract with Great Northern to justify the capital costs. The industry derisively howled at what Insull himself called "ridiculously low" pricing, but it was part of his self-described "cut-and-try" strategy based on intuited scale economies.

His detractors, Insull later realized, "were unwilling to take risks in trying to develop a real knowledge of the economic conditions governing the business." Much innovation and creative destruction would be necessary—from organizational restructuring to infrastructure reengineering to rate redesign to debt-finance improvements—but Insull would prevail. As he would state in his memoirs, the Great Northern contract was "the first step in the direction of low prices for large users of energy" and "the forerunner of the vast wholesale supply of energy by the Chicago Edison Company and its successor companies."

Consolidation (Horizontal Integration)

Chicago's embryonic, sprawling electricity industry needed consolidation, which Insull's board had given its new hire the green light to accomplish.[7] So, just three weeks into the job, Insull purchased his second-largest competitor, Fort Wayne Electric Company, and moved its generators to Chicago Edison's new 27th Street (Harrison) station. Three months later, Insull set out after his larger rival: Chicago Arc Power and Light Company, the operator of the local Thomson-Houston central station.

The quest began when Chicago Arc's Norman Fay asked Insull to lunch in order to personally invite him to participate in a stock syndication that Arc was about to float. The conflict of interest of investing in a competitor was enough for Insull to demur, but the 32-year-old unsettled his host by declaring his intent that Chicago Edison should acquire Chicago Arc. Fay reminded his guest who had the bigger company, but Insull retorted that his had the better economics. "The relations at the end of the lunch were not quite as cordial as they were at the start," remembered Insull, "but it was the opening of a negotiation that finally ended in the Chicago Edison Company acquiring the stock of the Chicago Arc Light and Power Company ... in the Spring of 1893."

The $2.2 million acquisition was funded by Chicago Edison bonds paying 6 percent, which was below Insull's dividend rate. Fay got a 12.5 percent premium per share for his stockholders. More a promoter than an operator, Fay found his exit strategy, given that Insull was the future of the industry. Such would be the case almost a century later when Sam Segnar of InterNorth ceded control to a young Ken Lay in a merger with Houston Natural Gas, described in Book 3.

For both companies, consolidation was a cheaper alternative than constructing duplicate underground cables for load growth. Furthermore, Chicago Arc's alternating current allowed Insull to better match production to sales and retire uneconomic capacity.

---

7. Such horizontal integration would be joined in 1903 by vertical integration, whereby (after a labor strike) Insull purchased coal properties and related transportation to internalize risk. See pp. 97–98.

Chicago Edison's opening moves toward a "practical monopoly" in Chicago had another dimension. Before leaving New York, Insull received a promise from General Electric's Charles Coffin that only Chicago Edison could buy his equipment for Cook County. This blocked other companies from erecting the popular General Electric isolated plants and provided protection against new entrants with a nuisance franchise.[8] All this gave Insull more leverage with Chicago's politicos.

Chicago Edison continued by acquiring 14 companies between 1894 and 1898. A financial panic beginning in May 1893 was part of this story, lowering acquisition costs at a time when Insull's own stock price held its value. Even mighty General Electric was not spared amid the market tumult; its share price fell by three-fourths before J. P. Morgan stepped in. Chicago Edison's total outlay for the mostly mom-and-pop utilities was $511,000, about one-third for tangible assets and two-thirds for goodwill.

Goodwill, an accounting category for payment in excess of a company's book value, was not buyer charity. Such premiums typically reflected the value of the franchise rights to a customer base whose existing load and future growth reduced systemwide costs per unit of sales. Such payments, in Forrest McDonald's estimation, were also "good business ... [for] Insull recognized that while money may not buy friends it will keep many a man from becoming an enemy."

Samuel Insull was on his way to consolidating Chicago's central business district—not to raise electricity rates but to profitably lower them over a larger book of business. Still, much more was required to achieve his grand vision of elevating electricity from a niche, luxury product to one that everyone could afford.

Scaling Production/Distribution

"Insull brought to the job a comprehensive understanding of the industry second to none," noted historian Harold Platt in his retrospective of Chicago's energy history, *The Electric City*. Insull's technical intuition of what *could* be done versus the status quo was at its best regarding the scale-up of central stations. Insull drove not only Chicago Edison but also the biggest name in the business, General Electric. "Often in defiance of his own engineers and almost always over the protests of those at General Electric," Insull would demand and receive "generators two, three, and four times as large as any others in existence."

Adam Street was yesterday's state-of-the-art generation. To "inaugurat[e] a radical departure in power-house policy," Insull turned to Frederick Sargent, the man he would come to call "the greatest designer of power stations in his time."

---

8. A similar agreement between Insull and the German manufacturer Siemens & Halske left Cook County operators with only one option: Westinghouse Electric, a company that was just getting started in nearby Evanston.

A site was selected at Harrison Street on the western bank of the Chicago River, a natural terminus for rail and barge shipments of the hundreds of thousands of pounds of coal needed daily. This location also offered plenty of growing room, and river water cooled the high-pressure condenser generators that reduced coal use by more than half per unit of output (to about 4 pounds per kilowatt hour). These advantages easily outweighed the additional copper transmission line connecting Harrison to Adams Street's distribution network several blocks away. And who could complain that between 20 and 50 fewer tons of coal moved through Chicago's streets each day?

Completed in August 1894, Harrison was the largest and most efficient power plant in the world. Within two years, Harrison was operating at its full capacity of 6.4 MW (twice that of Adams Street), and expansions would be needed to keep up with Insull's aggressive sales campaign, as well to replace the Cook County isolated plants that Insull bought and retired.[9]

Figure 2.3 The 6.4 MW Harrison Street Station (1894), under the direction of Insull's ace engineer Frederick Sargent (inset), grew to 16.2 MW by 1902 to advance a low-rate/high-sales policy. Harrison Street became a reserve plant in 1910 and was razed in 1916 with the advent of newer, larger generating complexes.

Harrison was "Insull's first step toward mastering the complexity of central station economics," noted Forrest McDonald. It was also expand-and-try, for as Insull noted in his autobiography, "no one in the central station business at that time really understood its fundamental economics."

---

9. A small South Side generating station at 2640 South Wabash Avenue began service in April 1891. In 1907, the facility was converted to a substation called Twenty-seventh Street Station. A similar station to serve the North Side at 926 North Clark Street opened in 1893 and became a substation in 1909 for eight years. In 1900, a 2.4 MW station went into service at 56th and Wallace streets and was also used as a substation beginning in 1917.

Chicago Edison's supply radius, limited to two miles by its use of direct current, left Harrison unable to service outlying areas where the company was buying isolated plants for retirement. Constructing another central station could not be justified, and that created a bottleneck for Insull's grand plan of one company economically serving wide areas.

Technology rescued the situation. The World's Fair had shown some of the possibilities of a meshed AC/DC system, and in 1897, Louis Ferguson retrofitted Harrison with a newly commercialized rotary converter that stepped down high-voltage AC power for DC distribution to homes and businesses. With a new substation at 27th Street to perform the conversion, central stations could now reach across business districts, not just blocks.

Two-Part Rate Design

Lowering costs and rates to bring electricity into the mainstream was well and good, but a pricing problem plagued the whole industry. The issue was how to set rates for steady-use customers whose regular usage was near their peak demand (high-load-factor users) versus those with high momentary demand that used far less on average (low-load-factor users).

The problem was that distributors such as Chicago Edison did not measure load factors and charged rates solely on volume. Thus, low- and high-load-factor users paid the same rate, although their cost of service was vastly different because of the cost of the equipment that had to stand ready. The result was that steadier-use *good* customers cross-subsidized peak-prone *bad* users, and company decisions to expand to meet new demand could financially backfire.

The inadequacy of flat rates came from the unusual characteristics of electricity. Unlike other goods, electricity could not be economically stored for even short periods to allow steady generation. Electricity had to be produced the moment it was consumed, which required infrastructure to meet all momentary demand—or experience a brownout or blackout, as remains the case today. So a full-requirements system had large costs-to-revenue ratios attributable to low-load-factor users: the interest expense associated with capital-intensive generation and distribution equipment that had to be, as it were, profitably idle for part or much of the time. Other fixed costs that had to covered at any level of consumption were property taxes, insurance, and upkeep.

As it was, illumination customers paid about $0.20 per kilowatthour (kWh)—about $0.01 per 16-candlepower lamp hour. With volumetric discounts, so-called declining bloc rates, the charge fell to as low as $0.05 per kWh. Power (nonilluminate) rates were $0.10 per kWh—actually per estimated kWh, inasmuch as usage was estimated, not metered. Such rates were determined by Thomas Edison himself and were used from inception (1882) until about 1893. Special rates were negotiated to meet the competition, however, whether they were needed to forestall a proposed isolated plant or back out gas lighting. With the advent of electric motors to bring new customers with varying load profiles into play, the economic-calculation problem was magnified.

For two and a half years, Insull struggled to find his profit points under volumetric pricing. Opportunity-cost pricing to win the business and discounting to incite higher usage was one thing, but grasping the marginal-cost economics—the true extra cost for serving the extra customer—was another. Without a reliable compass, expanding to meet higher demand could be a siren song. Yet the problem had to be identified before it could be solved.

In late 1894, Insull serendipitously uncovered the secret of electricity—or non-storage—ratemaking while vacationing in England. Intrigued by the large number of well-illuminated shops he found at the seaside resort of Brighton, the visitor sought to understand why such usage was both profitable for the seller and affordable for the buyer. This led him to the head of the local municipal generating station, Arthur Wright, whose "demand meter" recorded not only total consumption but also *when* and *at what maximum* the electricity was used. From this a two-part rate was charged: a flat equipment charge for standing ready to serve a customer's peak demand and a volumetric rate for actual kilowatts used. So low-volume customers who put a strain on the system at particular times paid higher rates because their fixed, or demand, charge was spread over fewer units, which, in effect, acted as a surcharge to compensate the provider for keeping equipment idle for part or most of the time. High-volume users paid proportionally less with the same fixed charge because the charge was spread over more kilowatts. "The minimum interest cost is reached," explained Insull, "when the capacity of the whole system and the total units of output at maximum load are identical, although of course it will always be necessary to have a certain margin of capacity over possible output, as a factor of safety."

Now, different load-factor customers could pay their true costs, and each could be served simultaneously and profitably. With fixed costs so high in relation to usage costs, small users who did not add to peak load could be served at very low rates to improve the load factor for peak-prone users, who now paid their way. System expansions were now guided by fixed-charge subscriptions—an economic calculation made possible by two-part pricing. "I do not think it is any exaggeration to say that Mr. Wright first taught us how to sell electricity," Insull would later remark.

Returning to Chicago, Insull instructed Louis Ferguson to visit Brighton and figure out how to adapt Wright's demand meter to the far more complicated market of Chicago. The Wright meter would become standard equipment for Chicago Edison, and Insull brought the Englishman over to address the National Electric Light Association (of which Insull was the new president) to explain how to meter and charge economically rational rates. Ferguson also explained how "the intention is to give the low rate to the long-hour" now that the "short hour" (peak-prone) customer paid relatively more of the fixed costs. Thus, "we take any and every customer on the Wright demand meter basis."

With economic calculation, Insull honed in on the real challenge: maximizing the load factor, which meant minimizing the discrepancy between the average and maximum usage, over the market as a whole. "The nearer you can bring

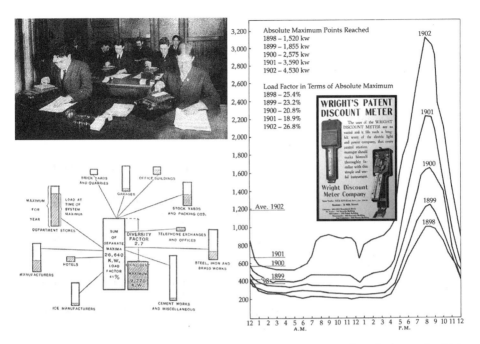

Figure 2.4 The Wright meter measured both average usage and peak demand, which permitted two-part rates capable of making each customer a profit center. Insull educated the industry on diversity factor, load-factor economics with the aid of his analytics department.

your average to the maximum load," in Insull's words, "the closer you approximate to the most economical condition of production, and the lower you can afford to sell your current."

Each of the two-part rates helped to even out the norm and peak: the demand charge by shaving the peak and the volumetric charge by rewarding higher usage. Still, day usage lagged far behind nighttime, when the lights were on. Thomas Edison had always fretted about daytime demand, and the advent of electric streetcars and elevators helped. The World's Fair told the future, but much work remained in the present to get there. Chicago Edison would be at the forefront.[10]

Financing

Insull's grand plan for rationalizing the electricity market required capital— hundreds of thousands of dollars now and tens of millions of dollars later.

---

10. Insull credited R. E. Bowker of Edison Electric Illuminating Company of New York with understanding the rudiments of rate design and implementing the first two-part rates in Brooklyn.

Chicago Edison's board had promised new capital, and the "LaSalle Street" bankers were won over by the company's profitable growth even during a recession. Insull's quarterly 2 percent dividend came without fail, and Chicago Edison's stock price held firm around $200 when about every other company's sagged.

But Insull got ahead of his board in 1895 when he asked for authorization to float $25 million or more in first-mortgage bonds. Over Insull's strong protest, the board approved $6 million—only $2 million of which was available for expansion—because of tight credit markets and concern that a larger bond issue would spook stockholders. (The board's Bryan Smith, for one, was the company's largest stockholder.) Worsening matters was the (William Jennings) "Bryan panic" of summer 1896, which unexpectedly prevented Chicago Edison from placing $1.2 million of the issue with London.

Help from Wall Street and J. P. Morgan seemed to be the next step—if Insull could swallow his distaste for that chapter of his life. But London was what interested Insull. Before crossing the Atlantic himself, Insull sent financial information to the bond syndicator Scottish American Trust, which was, in McDonald's estimation, "as disarmingly frank as it was overwhelmingly detailed." The proposal also offered bondholders a built-in depreciation reserve that improved upon the standard sinking-fund feature in terms of transparency and legal position.

Insull's entreaties did not begin well. But things turned around when he secured audiences with two real decision makers. One was sold by the fact that Insull's bonds had been endorsed by a mutual friend, a senior lawyer in Chicago. The other was wooed by Insull's story about how he had inspired him as a young man when working in Colonel Gouraud's office.

Such "salesmanship, Insull-style" was the margin of victory, and Insull steamed back to America just ahead of $800,000 in gold bullion that was part of a fully subscribed $1.2 million commitment. "This transaction opened up the London market for me and gave me an outlet for securities for upwards of twenty-five years," Insull would fondly remember. He also remembered it at his federal trial decades later as a brush with insolvency.

Insull's coup was big news in the United States, where credit markets were frozen. The financial press lauded his bond placement as "brilliant" and "astounding." Soon other Midwest financers would journey across the pond to present their case.

Chicago Leader, Industry Leader

A virtuous cycle between falling rates and increasing demand was under way. "With Wright's demand meter under one arm and Ferguson's rotary converter under the other," noted one historian, Insull "could push the company's sales effort as never before." Chicago Edison's Contract Department, founded in 1895, was selling wiring services, equipment, and appliances, not only illumination. The department's 25 "general contract agents" were increasingly marketing *power*—electricity for motors and appliances—rather than just illumination. And profit margins on appliances, Insull allowed, were more lucrative than on electricity sales.

Such economies of scope were creating economies of scale; electricity sales that quadrupled in Insull's first three years doubled in the next three and would continue to grow. What had been a parlor novelty was becoming a common luxury. But with only 16,000 customers at the turn of the century, Insull had plenty more market to win.

Now a U.S. citizen (he took the oath in 1896), Insull became interested in civic matters, for, as he put it, "The greater Chicago became, the greater the possibilities of the utility business within its gates."[11] Insull chose local trustees for Chicago Edison's bond offerings so that mostly locals clipped the coupons. A music lover, Insull soon found himself in the business circle covering the opera's perennial financial deficit. One thing he did not do was join a bank board. "I could not be a borrower and a lender at the same time," he explained, avoiding a conflict of interest that many others chose not to avoid. Insull held the same policy toward his company's suppliers, including General Electric, a plum directorship that was his for the taking.

Public relations became increasingly important. Municipalization had popular appeal and was stoked by gas companies that wanted to slow electricity's penetration and by electricity-equipment salesmen who envisioned an easier target for their wares. Insull's response was winning the public via lowering rates for new and existing customers (such as an across-the-board rate cut in 1898), publishing Chicago Edison's financial statements beginning in 1894, and keeping his own salary in check—despite presiding over a company with an appreciating stock price and 8 percent dividend.

Employees began receiving training in public relations in 1900, and Chicago Edison's advertising department morphed into something new: "one of the first full-fledged public relations departments in existence." Insull began making frequent public appearances to sell himself and his company to the public. It all worked, for Insull, "the personification of Chicago enterprise and persistence," as described in a *Sunday [Chicago] Chronicle* profile, "harmoniz(ed) the interests of Chicago so that differences can rarely arise."

Inside his company, Insull was a taskmaster. He set the example by early, late, and hard work. He practiced virtue and led by example. He offered few

---

11. Such "business ecology," as Forrest McDonald described this part of Insull's strategy, reflected a realization that "a development in any part of the organism must inevitably affect all other aspects and the whole."

compliments, but he set the tone for his whole organization by rewarding good behavior and removing those who blocked progress.[12]

·❖·

In 1897, Insull was elected head of the two major (and competing) industry trade associations. Just several years removed from being the number-three executive at General Electric, the 37-year-old was named president of the Association of Edison Illuminating Companies (AEIC),[13] which represented this company's license holders, who operated central stations in various U.S. cities. Insull was also elected head of the larger National Electric Light Association (NELA), which represented manufacturers, distributors, and just about every electricity enterprise in between. Removing frictions between the Edison and non-Edison licensees would be just one of his major accomplishments.

Both AEIC and NELA provided Insull with a platform to drive industry-wide reform, beginning with the Wright meter for two-part pricing and continuing with equipment standardization. Insull also had a political agenda to sell—something that recent events brought to his overall business strategy.

Insull's storied speechmaking, which would come to fill books, began with his AEIC presidential address in Niagara Falls, New York. He began by applauding the membership, whose $105 million investment was profitable "with hardly an exception," good news indeed coming out of a recession. Then Insull issued a call to action: scaling up generation and distribution to be able to serve more customers more cheaply. Taking on the (undersized) isolated plants was not to be feared given the "utmost permanency" of the "Edison system."

Insull's 1897 address also spoke to establishing a uniform system of financial accounts to allow benchmarking between companies, as well as creating a lamp-testing bureau to find the best designs for standardization. Another issue was helping General Electric defend its patents against rivals.

Insull did not have good news to report about battery storage—the industry's lacuna.[14] Accumulators (as they were then called) were grossly uneconomic except for very short time periods when there was a sharp disconnect between

---

12. See Internet appendix 2.3 "Corporate Culture," at www.politicalcapitalism.org/Book2/Chapter2/Appendix3.html.

13. AEIC, founded in 1885 by Thomas Edison to coordinate the activities between Edison Light Company and the central-station licensees, stands today as the oldest trade association in the electricity industry. Insull had been vice president before assuming AEIC's presidency in 1896/97.

14. As Insull would explain in an 1898 lecture at Purdue University, batteries not only were costly to manufacture and thus amortize but also released 30 percent less power than received. Also see Internet appendix 2.4, "Battery Storage for Central Stations," at www.politicalcapitalism.org/Book2/Chapter2/Appendix4.html.

demand and the capacity to serve it. Try as he might, Edison had not solved (and would not solve) the battery problem.[15] Two-part, load-factor rate making remained the way to go.

Insull's burgeoning responsibilities were part of his 16-hour workday, strenuous but not as bad as the Schenectady days, when he shuttled to New York City to keep Edison solvent. Ocean voyages back to his homeland restored his health when he needed it most. But Insull also needed more of a personal life, and that meant finding a lifemate, something that hitherto had been elusive for him. It would finally happen just short of his 40th birthday.

A Marriage of National Note

Insull was not all work, no play. The "Americanized Englishman" was "fond of society, a good clubman and 'good fellow' with his male friends as well as those of the gentler sex," as a newspaper described him. The confirmed (so it was thought) bachelor enjoyed a private life at home and at the Chicago Calumet Club, Chicago Athletic Club, Chicago University Club, and Washington Park Club. Entering his fifth decade, Insull had lady friends and even a rumored engagement with a local belle. But more was in store.

Insull had admired Margaret Anna Bird (aka Gladys Wallis) a star of the stage who performed in Chicago from time to time. On the way to lunch he sometimes saw her walking to the theater. An opportunity to meet her arose in February 1897 at a dinner party. Samuel quietly observed the person who was "the life of the evening"—and who 15 months later would be Mrs. Samuel Insull.

Gladys had many desirable qualities tucked into her petite (sub-five-feet, sub-90-pound) frame, and Insull, 17 years her senior, was soon conquered by her beauty, wit, charm, smarts, and, beneath it all, steely resolve. But she was independent, talented, and career driven—and not particularly prone to romance, despite having many suitors. The Danbury, Connecticut, girl who had debuted at age eight, and at age 14 starred as Shakespeare's 16-year-old Juliet, was no party girl. The banality of her mother's boarding house had taught her all she cared to know about liquor and sex.

So, in the spring of 1897, Samuel's mission was to win over Gladys, then touring with the prestigious William H. Crane Company.[16] It took hundreds of daily letters and occasional acts of divine intervention when Gladys needed it most, but in about one year's time, she consented. As it turned out, the 24-year-old was

---

15. See Internet appendix 2.5, "Edison, Ford, and the Electric Car," at www.political-capitalism.org/Book2/Chapter2/Appendix5.html.

16. Two papers, the *New York Evening World* and the *Buffalo Enquirer*, reported that Insull broke off another engagement to pursue Gladys, a fact otherwise not found in the Insull historiography.

looking for the father she had never had, and 41-year-old Insull was that. Samuel and Gladys were wed in May 1899.

Insull's friends and business associates were surprised at the sudden engagement news and actual wedding a week later—both announced in newspapers from coast to coast. It was news all around. "Half the chappies of America will be grief-stricken to learn that Gladys Wallis is to be married for she is one of the most charming, if not the most popular, of the ingénues," stated the *San Francisco Bulletin*. Announcing her permanent retirement from the stage, the *Detroit Free Press* lamented: "Once we are tarred with that stick, not all the multitudinous seas can make us clean." The *New York World* used the occasion to comment: "She has a voice of irresistibly sympathetic shading, her laughter is the jolliest, most musical ever heard; she romps and 'spoons' exactly as does the ingenue in real life and in expression of tender sentiment she is as alluring as a spring blossom." Other newspapers provided a short comment about how a stage talent had succumbed to the millionaire businessman, a not uncommon occurrence.

Figure 2.5 The union of Margaret Anna Bird ("Gladys Wallis") and Samuel Insull in 1899 was reported nationally despite the best efforts of the couple to stay out of the news. The couple would grow apart in the next decades, fueling rumors about marital woes.

A torrent of reminiscences and congratulations flowed to 49 Delaware Place, Insull's residence. One remarked on "the electrical swiftness with which you do most things." A colleague from the early Edison days thanked Insull for being "considerate and fair," although "disposed to be a little 'nasty' when 'crowded'.'" Thomas Edison himself reflected on "the many years we spent together, full of trials and disappointments 'spats etc.' but always neutralized by its moments of pleasure." The great inventor added before returning to congratulations, "it naturally does us good to feel that our efforts were not all in vain."

Old rivals were heard from, such as Henry Villard, who remarked that "your delay was wiser than my [marriage] ordeal." Charles Coster, the Morgan lieutenant to whom Insull had had to kowtow during trying times, wrote:

> During the last fifteen years you and I have had a good many important negotiations—oftentimes on the same side, often on opposite, or opposing sides. Even under the latter condition, the relations between us have always been pleasant .... (Incidentally I wonder what would have happened if I had not always let you have your own way, but on this point perhaps I shall be able to compare notes with Mrs. Insull later.)

Charles Coffin wrote: "You have always been thoroughly the whole of whatever you have been associated with, and beyond all question a most loyal, generous, and enthusiastic whole, and success and many friends have attended you." Speaking from experience that Insull did not have, the General Electric chief added: "Your sway and influence, thus divided [with Mrs. Insull], will be increased—the half greater than the whole, and the pleasure of being deprived of authority will be as delightful as it will be mysterious and unexplainable."

A Political Birth (Commonwealth Electric Company)

Samuel Insull was not naïve about Chicago's burly politics. He heard the stories, read the papers, and had a mentor on the subject—Frank Peabody, the founder of Peabody Coal Company, a "political" company that was part of the Chicago machine. "Sometime ward heeler, sometime sheriff, usually Democratic national committeeman from Illinois," Frank's knowledge could be as beneficial as his coal shipments for Insull's power plants. The two men's companies would grow together in "the city that coal built."

Insull's strategy was not about political shortcuts but self-help in the marketplace: entering into exclusivity agreements with equipment manufacturers and acquiring rival companies to rationalize markets. Insull was consolidating franchise rights as he went along, while lessening the value of nuisance franchises that might appear. Insull was much more a market entrepreneur than a political one in the wide-open competitive era.

The results were very positive all around. Chicago Edison's financial results proved Insull—"a thoroughgoing radical, but one who knew exactly what he was doing"—correct time and again. His technical intuition and financial sense were a powerful combination.

Things were different on the (manufactured) gas side. A fragmented, fragile industry was engaged in infighting—firm versus firm, technology versus technology. In Chicago, Peoples Gas Light and Coke Company, the city's first gas company, established in 1849, emerged victorious from the market and political fray, but the collateral damage was enough that most observers welcomed the advent of electricity to neuter the "gas monopoly."

Gas politics gave Insull "his initial bath of fire in Chicago's political inferno." But Insull's refusal to bribe and this strategy of self-help would leave him unsinged and even with a measure of political capital to spend. Such was the beginning for a man who in the next decades became "perhaps the most consistently successful and powerful political operator in American business."

In 1895, Chicago's gas politics reared its ugly head when the city granted a 50-year gas franchise to Ogden Gas Company, a dummy entity created to blackmail Peoples Gas into making nuisance payments. Eleven participants, including Chicago Mayor John Hopkins and emerging political boss Roger Sullivan, held shares in the new company. This franchise was then monetized—at about $650,000 apiece—when Peoples Gas purchased the paper company for $7.33 million (about $175 million today). No gas had been manufactured or sold for these millions. Such was "'the ethics of graft'" of the Ogden Gas Crowd, aka the Sullivan-Hopkins faction of the Democratic Party. (Republicans had their political packs too.)

This extracurricular success inspired a repeat by the organizers with Chicago Edison the target. What set the table for the legal extortionists was a political saga concerning Charles Tyson Yerkes, the unpopular streetcar magnate of Chicago.

Yerkes had ably electrified, modernized, and networked Chicago's transportation system. However, he had succumbed to franchise blackmail early— and thus often. As he consolidated the industry, his acquisitions had various franchise expirations. With a major renewal looming in 1903, Yerkes was having trouble floating long-term bonds. Thus, when the opportunity arose, Yerkes orchestrated an effort to get the Illinois legislature to enact a law whereby jurisdictions could award 50-year franchises (versus the then 20 years), and bipartisan state commissions would regulate such businesses as a public utility.

Chicago revolted against Yerkes's plan, now the Humphrey Bill. The press exposed his half-million-dollar slush fund to bribe state legislators, and the local city bosses feared a dilution of power. The public clamored for less private politics and more municipalization. In retreat, Yerkes was able to get the so-called Allen Law passed in May 1897 to up the franchise period to as many as 50 years.

Within a week of passage, a group of Chicago aldermen called the Gray Wolves visited Insull with their plan to create a new 50-year franchised electricity company in Chicago. A suitable payment in the hundreds of thousands of dollars would kill the idea, it was allowed. But Insull refused, which led the politicos to create the Commonwealth Electric Company. But Insull had protected himself. By having exclusive rights to virtually all the major electricity-generating equipment, Chicago Edison could keep Commonwealth at bay. With a stellar reputation, unlike Yerkes, Insull could not be bullied or shamed into extortion.

Four months later, Insull bought Commonwealth for $50,000—no high price for a one-of-a-kind 50-year franchise. The repeal of the Allen Law the next year by "as bizarre a collection of political bedfellows as Chicago had ever seen" still left Insull with a valuable right extending all the way to 1947—the only Illinois utility with such.[17]

But how could Chicago Edison reap Insull's windfall? Illinois law precluded one company owning stock in another, and a formal merger was too politically sensitive. Enter William G. "Billy" Beale, Insull's chief outside legal advisor, who devised an operating agreement between the two companies that awarded, in effect, the whole Chicago market to Insull.

Chicago Edison, which was still busy buying small operators on the fringes of its territory,[18] would stay confined to the inner loop, something that its DC transmission network required. Commonwealth Electric, whose franchise covered the rest of Chicago, it was decided, would utilize its AC reach.

·∽·

Insull needed major financing to enable Commonwealth Electric to serve the bulk of Chicago. Yet his board had sliced his $25 million request to $6 million, with only $2 million earmarked for expansion. Now $100 million was on his mind—a figure unheard of for any utility in any industry. But even this would not prove to be enough.

Insull's solution, drafted by Billy Beale, and effectuated with the help of new board member John Mitchell, the president of Illinois Trust and Savings, was the *open-ended mortgage*. A new wrinkle in utility finance, the general idea was that any amount for any term could be floated on the strength of a protective long-term franchise and collateralization (capped at 75 percent of plant investment). Thus, Chicago Edison's board did not have to set an upper limit on indebtedness, and Insull was free to get as much capital as his infrastructure could collateralize.

Insull's first bonds yielded 5.2 percent with an expiration date of 45 years. As before, English financiers proved more receptive to Chicago Edison's indentures

---

17. Yerkes failed to win a 50-year franchise from Chicago aldermen, whereupon he consolidated and sold his holdings, left Chicago for England in 1901, and went on to erect the London Underground.

18. Eight companies were purchased in 1897 for a total cost of just over $2.5 million.

than those at home. And as before, Insull did not bother to court New York, the financial capital of the world.

Insull's original vision of $100 million would turn into a half-billion dollars in the next years and decades. The open-ended mortgage became a popular tool throughout the industry and in other public-utility sectors. Insull had made a permanent mark in corporate finance.

A Call for Public-Utility Regulation

Insull swam with political sharks, and so far so good. But who knew what might lurk ahead? Long-term financing was needed more than ever, but Chicago Edison's franchises expired before the bonds would—a mismatch that complicated their placement. There was also the threat of municipalization. What was a pragmatist to do?

Insull needed what Yerkes had sought—and Commonwealth Edison fortuitously got in its short window of opportunity: a long-term franchise. Exclusivity was needed—one franchise and one only. But politicians would not just give this political plum away. There had to be a quid pro quo—regulatory oversight of the legal monopoly. Such a scheme, already in force in Great Britain, in the Bismarckian (German) tradition, and with support from academia,[19] captured Insull's imagination by the mid-1890s.

Insull had precedent for his crusade. Competitively stressed, the manufactured gas industry had already put itself in play for franchise protection in return for rate regulation. In 1885, the Massachusetts Board of Gas Commissioners formalized statewide public-utility regulation when complaints about market interlopers and price wars permeated the industry. In his 1890 presidential address to the American Gas Light Association (the forerunner of the American Gas Association), Emerson McMillin decried "raiders" with "processes that can make gas for almost nothing, and still have a valuable residual" who "do not seem to despair in their efforts to get a standing in cities already well supplied." He added: "If they were only modest enough to go to small towns not now supplied with gas, and demonstrate the value of the process there, they would merit the everlasting gratitude of existing companies."

But the electricity industry, amid an economy-of-scale boom and with a change agent (Insull) showing how self-help was the best help, was not yet in a protectionist mood. No state regulated electricity as a natural monopoly,

---

19. "It is everywhere acknowledged that the multiplication of wires overhead is a crying evil and danger," wrote Charles Baker in 1889. "Can there be any doubt that it is the height of folly to continue [competition], and that the only rational way of entrusting electric service to incorporated companies is to permit but a single company to operate in a district and control prices by some other means than competition?"

although some regulated railroads, and Massachusetts regulated manufactured gas in this way.

In 1898, Insull unveiled his controversial political program at the annual meeting of the National Electric Light Association in (where else?) Chicago.[20] Packaged as a middle way between "municipal socialism" and "acute competition," Insull sought exclusive franchise rights, with statewide regulation setting rates allowing for cost recovery and a guaranteed rate of return—public-utility, cost-of-service regulation.

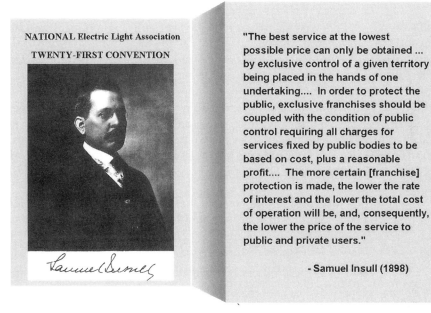

NATIONAL Electric Light Association

TWENTY-FIRST CONVENTION

"The best service at the lowest possible price can only be obtained ... by exclusive control of a given territory being placed in the hands of one undertaking.... In order to protect the public, exclusive franchises should be coupled with the condition of public control requiring all charges for services fixed by public bodies to be based on cost, plus a reasonable profit.... The more certain [franchise] protection is made, the lower the rate of interest and the lower the total cost of operation will be, and, consequently, the lower the price of the service to public and private users."

- Samuel Insull (1898)

Figure 2.6 Samuel Insull's call for public-utility regulation in 1898 before the National Electric Light Association (now Edison Electric Institute) set a new political agenda for one of America's largest emerging industries.

The competitive franchise, complained Insull, "frightens the investor, and compels corporations to pay a very high price for capital." The "inevitable" consolidation of companies leaves the survivor with duplicate facilities and high interest costs. The solution to avoid such waste is a quid pro quo: exclusive franchises for maximum rate regulation by an impartial agency. "The best

---

20. The NELA was founded in 1885 in Chicago, which was a hub city that industry executives could reach by rail. For much of its early history, the association (which in 1933 would become the Edison Electric Institute) focused on business and technical issues and only peripherally delved into political questions.

service at the lowest possible price can only be obtained ... by exclusive control of a given territory being placed in the hands of one undertaking," Insull opined. "In order to protect the public, exclusive franchises should be coupled with the condition of public control requiring all charges for services fixed by public bodies to be based on cost, plus a reasonable profit." The rationale was financial for both the company and consumers: "The more certain [franchise] protection is made, the lower the rate of interest and the lower the total cost of operation will be, and, consequently, the lower the price of the service to public and private users."

◇

Insull's proposal had a wrinkle intended to attract public and political support. In addition to rate, service, and entry regulation, the local municipality had the "right" to take over a private utility at a "fair" price. Insull did not preface municipalization on any underperformance measure, stipulating simply that the takeover could occur "whenever it is thought desirable" by the authorities.

But the majority of Insull's fellow executives favored the status quo of local regulation over public-utility regulation. Open competition created risks for established firms but a regulation that systemically governed rates and service was threatening as well. It would take a growing threat other than market competition—and a multifront public relations effort—to bring the majority of the industry to Insull's view.[21]

While putting his considerable weight behind public-utility regulation, Insull practiced self-help laissez-faire. He avoided bribery's slippery slope on which Yerkes had obligated himself. Insull made public-sector friendships and understood politics as a business dealing in the currency of public opinion and votes. Insull made campaign contributions to both sides and granted reasonable favors to politicos (such as "providing jobs—but never important ones, and always with the reservation that the jobs must be justified from a business point of view").

Insull was not against municipalization per se, peculiarly, although he ran an investor-owned utility. Indeed, such a threat would be an Insull card to gin up interest in statewide public-utility regulation. But for the present, "Insull was almost always able to obtain whatever his companies in Chicago needed (which most of the time was simply to be left alone), no matter how the political climate varied."

From Chicago Edison to Commonwealth Edison

"The prospects of the central station industry are certainly most dazzling," Samuel Insull lectured to the engineering department at Purdue University in

---

21. See chapter 3, pp. 121–26.

the spring of 1898. "I think it can be conservatively stated that we have scarcely entered upon the threshold of the development which may be expected in the future." Indeed, with electricity capturing just 20 percent of the illumination market and a power market emerging, a huge growth opportunity existed. But electricity needed to become more affordable for homeowners, shopkeepers, and industry to incite new applications—and outdistance manufactured gas for illumination (gas was ensconced for cooking and water heating). For Insull's business model, central-station electricity had to be cheaper than self-generated electricity (isolated plants). As for *political* risk, Insull had to win and retain public support to keep his investor-owned utility from being municipalized by local authorities.

The first five full years of Insull's Chicago Edison tenure (1892–97) would simply be a prelude to the next decade. This second growth spurt, which climaxed with the formation of Commonwealth Edison Company in 1907, advanced his existing initiatives and added new ones. Insull was bringing order to an emerging industry that was on its way to becoming one of America's very largest. He was acting as "an intelligent man … in an unintelligent world," in biographer Forrest McDonald's estimation, and not too far behind John D. Rockefeller's reshaping of the petroleum industry.

Insull's "mass consumption economics" brought together "the gospel of consumption" and "the massing of production." Consumption/sales required innovative advertising and marketing, as well as technological advances in electric motors. Production/generation required breakthroughs in scale economies—more kilowatt hours from material and fuel inputs—and large-scale financing. Vertical integration to reduce supply risk also became important. All this would create the platform from which "The Chief" (as Insull came to be called in his industry) became America's most revered businessman of the 1920s.

Selling Out Supply

By 1898, Chicago Edison's Contract Department was in full swing, selling electricity and related appliances and services. Salesmen with engineering skills performed feasibility studies, repaired equipment, and enhanced electricity displays. For John Gilchrist and staff, there were shopkeepers to convert, homebuilders and architects to court, and door-to-door sign-ups in the nicer neighborhoods. In return for sales contracts of one or two years, customers received free installation, at-cost retrofits, serviced equipment, and deferred payment plans. Displaced equipment was purchased for resale. Building owners were even commissioned to persuade their counterparts to convert to electricity—turning the formers' "cold indifference," in Gilchrist's words, into "interested friendliness." Collective agreements were negotiated with adjacent store owners to install electric lighting. Special rates—the cheapest being for daylight (off-peak) demand—were granted. There was even an across-the-board rate reduction in 1898.

In 1901, a "business getting" department was created within Chicago Edison to inform and entice homeowners, shopkeepers, and office managers. Newspaper advertisements began with pitches such as, "A Home Without ELECTRIC LIGHT is like a coat without a lining—unfinished, incomplete." In 1903, a glossy magazine published by Chicago Edison, *Electric City*, began publication, distributed by drugstores in exchange for free wiring and discounted electricity.

The marketing challenge was to sell more *daylight* electricity to better utilize its equipment. The gulf between average and peak usage, the load factor, had to be shrunk. The world's largest battery pack, installed at Adams Street in 1897/98, was capable of providing about 2 megawatt hours (MWh) for 90 minutes; was geared more for emergency service than for meeting that peak-of-peaks December evening; and was inefficient, expensive, and not scalable. Two-part rates got the economic signals right, but off-peak sales were still needed. Filling the valleys meant some combination of power sales for transportation, motors, and appliances.

Streetcar transportation was the elephant, using more electricity than did all the lights in Chicago. What had been animal-propelled in the early 1890s was electricity-driven by 1902. But all 15 area franchisees were off the grid, with all but one self-generating its power. Lake Street Elevated, buying surplus power from the others, became Chicago Edison's first customer in 1902.

≈

Electricity was the early front runner for horseless carriages, and Insull got out in front. In 1898, Chicago Edison opened battery-charging stations and offered promotional rates to jumpstart this market. "Load-leveling" rates meant cheap off-peak charging at wholesale to serve this embryonic market.

In 1899, Insull became president of the $25 million Illinois Electrical Vehicle Transportation Company, the western branch of the Columbia Automobile Company of New York, to market electric cabs and carriages in Chicago. The plan was to have 1,000 taxis and rental vehicles profitably operating in the city, which as a byproduct would create a steady, off-peak "typical long-hour load" for Commonwealth Edison—far better than business that might add to the peak. As compared to storing power itself, Commonwealth Edison could "shift the charge and discharge losses of about 20 to 30 percent to the customer, but also battery maintenance" to customers.

But electric vehicles as a "complement" to public transportation—such as (electric) cab rides for $0.15 from the home to the streetcar stop—would prove too optimistic. Profits were scarce, and Insull used the occasion of a March 1901 drivers' strike to liquidate Illinois Electrical. Other cities held on a little longer, but competition from horse-drawn vehicles and the emerging gasoline-powered car proved too much in view of the stubborn limits to battery technology. Indeed, the lead acid battery, which a 1898 issue of *Electrical World* complained "will sputter, fume, give out on the road, leak, buckle, disintegrate, corrode, short-circuit and do many other undesirable things under the severe pressure of automobile work," would never achieve the needed breakthroughs.

In 1900, Insull cofounded the Automobile Club of Chicago to sell the public on the new mode of transportation—and deal with the politics of a new entrant. The year before, for example, the city's South Park Board prohibited motor vehicles from using the boulevards and parks, leaving bicycles and horse carriages. This "unprogressive" ban would be overturned by Chicago's mayor.

Insull, "propelled by the vision of unified electric light, traction, and power distribution," was not done yet with electric vehicles. In 1903, Insull got involved with an electric-car maker, Walker Vehicle Company, a relationship that would continue into the 1920s despite limited success.

Outside of short-haul delivery trucks, this market for electricity would not take hold despite ongoing efforts by Insull and Chicago Edison. The reason was Henry Ford's gasoline-powered internal-combustion engine. Thomas Edison predicted as much in a conversation with Ford at the AEIC annual meeting in 1896, preserved for history by Samuel Insull himself. Edison labored to make batteries more economical for the transportation market, but the problem of weight/energy-density prevented both a *Ford Electric* market and a way to help meet peak load.[22]

·◇·

A better target was to be found right in Chicago's central business district (CBD), where building and business owners were self-generating their power for lighting, steam heat, and elevators. Isolated plants offered control and convenience for hotels, large department stores, and office buildings; in 1899–1900, no fewer than 241 such facilities entered service in Chicago alone.

Insull studied the situation and formed Illinois Maintenance Company to supply the one thing that he was missing to win this market: piped steam. This was an extension of his central-station strategy, and the new Chicago Edison subsidiary serviced and retrofitted existing equipment to ease the transition to such dual central service. But the real calling card was lower rates, particularly off-peak, from scale economies—something that isolated plants could not counter. Using the "one-two punch of rate cuts and special incentives," new isolated plants were on the wane by 1904. Self-generation would soon be the exception.

Elevators played to the strengths of central service, as did electric motors in general, perfected by the eccentric inventor Nikola Tesla in particular. Whereas electricity powered 3,000 horsepower of motors in 1895, the figure was 69,000 horsepower by 1905. Declining power rates also opened up new power applications in electrochemicals, electroplating, arc welding, and other processes used to mass produce bicycles and cars. By 1902, Chicago Edison's output was

---

22. See Internet appendix 2.5, "Edison, Ford, and the Electric Car," at www.politicalcapitalism. org/Book2/Chapter2/Appendix5.html.

one-third power and two-thirds illumination. Power demand was growing 50 percent faster than was the demand for lighting, offering hope for improving the load factor and increasing efficiency—and thus lowering overall rates.

Electrical appliances were another load builder for Chicago Edison. General Electric began running magazine ads for its hardware in 1898, and Chicago Edison made margins selling equipment and adding to off-peak power sales. The Electric Cottage, an electricity showroom on wheels featured all the latest gadgets, including lighting fixtures, and visited Chicago neighborhoods as part of this effort.

Insull's marketing success caught up with him by 1902. With many middle-class neighborhoods wired, but with two-thirds of the 170 square miles of the city still to reach, Chicago Edison found itself short of new electricity to sell. The workhorse Harrison Street Station was running at its expanded capacity of 14.5 MW to meet peak load. The North Side of the city reached its limit in early 1901, and the South Side soon followed. Despite Insull's best efforts, the peak/off-peak problem had deteriorated, with the load (average-use) factor dropping below 20 percent for the first time in 1901. Battery storage, extremely costly, was insurance against service interruptions, not a load smoother. Short of higher rates to moderate demand, at least in the short run, more electricity at the peak was needed.

Massing Production

A new generating station—no, a whole new generating *technology*—was needed for Chicago Edison to relaunch. Insull's goal of "massing production" entailed more than the "cautious experimentation" of traditional central-station design. So it was that a new technology—the reciprocating steam turbine, aka the turbogenerator—came into development. General Electric's in-house staff, led by William Emmet, was working on the concept with consulting engineer Charles Curtis.

European firms were pursuing the new approach, and Louis Ferguson and Fred Sargent ("the ablest central station designer of my acquaintance," Insull would say) were dispatched to investigate. Ferguson reported back that the new technology was cheaper, simpler, and had a low space requirement. Best of all, it worked.

General Electric built a half-megawatt prototype in 1900, about what was being readied abroad, but Insull decided that prime movers of 5 MW each were necessary for a 14-unit, 70 MW station. This was a grand leap from what had come before, and Insull wanted the first three units now in order to meet Chicago's growing demand.

The industry was abuzz. Ferguson and Sargent were not thinking this big. Westinghouse's biggest was 2.5 MW, Charles Coffin at General Electric suggested 3 MW, twice the size of his newest design. Insull, negotiating with his old company in New York, complained that such a size was a "step backward" from where the reciprocating engines were—at 5 or 6 MW but without much growth potential. Only when Insull threatened to let his order abroad did Coffin take on the manufacturing risk of a 5 MW turbine if Chicago Edison assumed the installation risk—really deinstallation cost if the unit had to be returned to Schenectady. It was no small gamble for Insull, who "staked his business reputation and designed his new station for it." The "great experiment," as Insull put it, began when the order was placed in late 1901.

Figure 2.7 Fisk Street Station, the first steam turbine station in America, entered service in October 1903 as the major electricity provider for Chicago. General Electric and Chicago Edison shared the risk for the unprecedented 5 MW turbogenerators (left), each of which would soon be retrofitted with larger units (right).

Chicago Edison's new facility would be located on the north bank of the Chicago River at Fisk Street. In 1903, Fisk Street Generating Station became operational when Unit 1's 5 MW, 11,000-horsepower coal-fired turbine was steamed up. Start-up problems in the first months, reflected in General Electric's (gyrating) stock price, got ironed out, and copy units were installed. But the first three 5 MW turbines did not pay for their higher capital costs compared to the state-of-the-art reciprocating units that had come before; it was with the fourth, improved unit—and the retrofit of the original three—that turbogeneration became a moneymaker and more.

By 1910, the station was at physical capacity with 14 turbines. The 5 MW units had been retrofitted to 9 MW and then 12 MW—and all, in Insull's words, "with the same building, the same number of boilers, the same grate surface, the same stack capacity, [and] practically the same amount of money

invested." Thus optimized, production costs were cut *by half*, opening up vast
new possibilities for Insull's business model.

Credit went to Insull's "daring engineering decision [made] by a man not an
engineer." Insull gave credit to his board of directors. All deserved credit, but
behind the success was the fact that the new technology had already been
proven at home and abroad—though at smaller scale. Sargent and Ferguson
verified that in Europe, and General Electric proved it at home. But the rapid
scale-up took courage and risktaking, which Insull had in abundance.

"The machines grew in efficiency beyond the rosiest dream," stated a history of General Electric. Insull called it "the greatest thing which has happened
in our business." So it would come to be that the shell of Fisk No. 1 ended up at
Schenectady as "a perpetual monument to an industrial victory."[23]

Fisk Street's turbines achieved 80 percent energy efficiency, double that of
Harrison Street's reciprocating units, whose belts transmitted energy from
one machine to the other. The turbos spun ten times faster than their predeces-
sors, were one-tenth the weight, yet required much less maintenance. A kilowatt hour that previously required seven pounds of coal now took less than
four, with proportional reductions in air emissions. Such technology-driven,
market-driven conservation needed no law. As Insull remarked in 1916, when
the Conservation Movement was in full swing:

> I think that while a great many of our well intentioned friends have been shouting
> about the conservation of natural resources, the steam-turbine inventors and the
> designing engineers of the great power companies using steam as a prime source
> of power have probably done more to conserve the natural resources of this
> country, in so far as fuel is concerned, than has been done by all the agitation that
> has taken place upon the general subject of conservation.

Fisk also allowed Commonwealth Edison to get ahead of the curve and
avoid accounting write-offs, the choice of other companies that stayed in the old
world too long. Obsolescence was avoided in real time by Insull's calculated
daring.

With supply aplenty, Chicago Edison was back in business; "from that moment
on," remarked Insull biographer John Wasik, "Chicago was on its way to becoming the most energy-intensive place in the world." But it was an industry-wide
triumph too. Insull's bold action on the generating front had accelerated the
moment when "the future of primary power arrived."

Chicago Edison's growing market required a network of high-voltage transmission lines and substations. Chicago Edison's substations, the first of which were

---

23. The history of the "super-slave" Fisk Unit 1 involved three men in addition to Insull
and Coffin: inventor Charles Curtis, designer William Emmet, and builder Billy Madigan.

built in 1897, numbered 22 with Fisk on tap. (Even mighty Harrison Street was destined to become a substation in the Fisk era.) A new position—the load dispatcher—had to instantaneously match supply and demand so that the generators produced just enough to keep the lights and machinery on. With storage a very expensive and limited option, there was little room for error. Running the Fisk Station and the new Quarry Station in parallel, for example, made sure that variation at one was made up by the other. Insull himself would make good use of the load curves and other graphic records in his speeches to come.

Sales Redux

With generation plentiful, it was back to "one part quality service, two parts hard selling, and three parts rates cuts." As before, the challenge was to manage the peak and fill the valleys via two-part rates: a fixed charge for standing ready to deliver power at all times (covering the interest charge for the equipment) and a usage charge covering the actual avoidable costs of providing service (mainly coal and manpower).

Off-peak rates were a bargain: The avoidance of new fixed costs meant that such business had to cover only variable costs, such as coal. Thus, the big users adding to peak—the "long-hour users" as Insull called them—subsidized the small on an average-cost basis. But the economics of such rate discrimination were sound, and city fathers had to be educated that rate ordinances flattening rates hurt the little guy, the household, and small shopkeeper. Such rate edicts were avoided, for what politician could fault the man who told audiences that "the avowed policy of the company is to do its small business at a loss and make its profits out of the big customers"?[24]

Streetcars and elevated trains ferrying commuters and shoppers was what the generators needed until the evening lights came on. Insull used "ridiculously low rates"—one-third of what other industrial users paid—to get the traction companies off self-generation. Long-term traction contracts, in turn, helped finance Fisk's expansions. "By 1908," added Harold Platt, "the transit business had built up and diversified the load sufficiently to trigger a self-perpetuating cycle of falling rates and rising demand." In fact, Insull's 30 percent of the transit market improved his load factor from 30 percent to 40 percent in a decade, a win-win for everyone.

Residences remained a central market. Middle-class electricity—complete with wall sockets—was a convenience right there with indoor plumbing. Chicago Edison advertised with a free monthly magazine, *Electric City*

---

24. As Insull explained, the most profitable customers were those with a 40 percent load factor and higher, equating to an average daily usage of nine and a half hours or more. Hotels were at the 40 percent mark, with traction companies higher. The small-hour users were small offices and residences (10 percent) and larger offices and residences (20 percent).

(1903), via direct mail (1904), and in newspaper buys (1906), using such messages as: "Make Your Wife Happy ... Electric Light in the Home Means Much to Women." As the magazine explained: "There is less cleaning and dusting to do. The air is pure, the light brilliant—turned on or off instantly with the turn of a switch." After this "opening wedge" came appliances, and none more popular than the electric steam iron, first introduced in 1905.

Electricity and entertainment were becoming synonymous. The first movie projector, introduced in Chicago in 1896, numbered 250 a decade later, making the 5¢ movie house a cultural phenomenon. Amusement parks, the first of which opened in Chicago in 1903, were an electrified "fantasy of romance and pleasure" for the young. Thousands of illuminated signs—Insull fingerprints were there too—made Chicago "the sign capital of urban America."

·◌·

Suburbia, itself enabled by affordable mass transit, created outlying markets for electrification. Insull's city-inward focus, however, left this market for others. In the 1880s and early 1890s, equipment salesmen from Thomson-Houston and Westinghouse, aided by their companies, started small utilities to provide electricity in townships, including those around Chicago. The business cycle took a toll on such underfinanced, underscaled operations, but by 1900, a new generation of inventors, investors, and entrepreneurs was bringing to the suburbs a level of electricity service comparable to that enjoyed in the city. Old companies were recapitalized, and consolidations improved economies, although not rivaling what Insull was able to do in his more concentrated market.

In 1901, with Fisk occupying most of this attention, Insull was persuaded to passively invest—on a personal basis—in two nearby undercapitalized suburban utilities, Highland Park and Evanston. But once committed, he got interested in a big way. In 1902, he profitably sold his companies to the newly created North Shore Electric Company, a Chicago Edison affiliate, which consolidated the suburban market with 11 purchases. In addition to North Shore, four other suburban companies were brought into the Insull fold to "form a defensive network around Chicago ... against predators."

Soon, high-voltage transmission created a "metropolitan web of energy." By 1907, with best-practice transfers from the parent, suburban electricity service was comparable to that in the city.

Insull had extended scale economies beyond the central business district in a way he had not thought possible when he had first invested six years before. It would be the beginning of a territorial expansion that would take Insull to the rest of the state and then to the whole Midwest, as described in the next chapter.

The entrepreneur whom Insull had to catch in the suburban market was one Charles Munroe, a highly ambitious youngster whose small hydro-generating plant and rural franchises had him on the verge of securing a major contract to supply all the power needs of a large traction company. Insull bought rather than fought, as was his style, and after a decade of training, Munroe "emerged as Insull's chief suburban lieutenant and, in many respects, his right arm as well"—and even "Insull himself in miniature."

Vertical Integration

A 1902 strike by the United Mine Workers of America in Pennsylvania's anthracite coal fields led Insull to expand his business model from horizontal integration (consolidation) to vertical (supplier) integration. Such risk management was necessary, for price spikes could put his fixed-price contracts under water, create ill will, and raise the specter of municipalization. So Insull sought to integrate backward, or, in his words, "arrange matters so that all of the operating companies, directly or indirectly, had an interest in the basic commodity they needed for their product."

Coal was the mother fuel for Chicago Edison, as it was for every other gas and electricity generator. For Insull, vertical integration meant taking an ownership position in coal properties, as well as in transportation to move the coal from the mine to the power plant. Such integration was insurance for what could not be done at arm's length. The price for coal and transportation was simply the going, or "spot," rate as determined by supply and demand. But Insull needed more assurance and stability, which necessitated owning the mines and mode of transportation, thus internalizing the cost components of the power sold at retail.

"The way to achieve the lowest cost of production of the product desired, and the means of obtaining supplies of absolutely necessary primary products when conditions are abnormal and prices are high, such as in times of war," Insull later explained, "is to own those basic products and the transportation facilities to insure their prompt and cheap delivery." This was true of large power companies and natural gas concerns, Insull added, "just as much as it is necessary for the United States Steel Corporation to own iron mines and railways; for the Ford Motor Company to own iron, rubber and steel plants, coal mines and railways; for a large retail dry goods establishment to be interested in cotton or silk mills; and for a manufacturer of farm machinery to own its own steel mills."[25] So in 1903, Chicago Edison integrated, first to the coal mines and then to coal-carrying railroads—all to ensure, in Insull's estimation, "a constant supply of fuel twenty-four hours a day and three hundred and sixty five days of the year."

Insull's coal strategy evolved from his relationship with Peabody Coal Company, the largest coal distributor in Chicago. Frank Peabody was interested in

---

25. Backward integration, business historian Alfred Chandler explained, was typically done to improve quality and delivery schedules, but Insull's interest was more about having first call on inputs in abnormal times.

integrating back to the mines and convinced Insull to stake Chicago Edison in the venture. Producing properties and coal acreage were purchased near Springfield, Illinois, with all operations assigned to Peabody and supply earmarked to Chicago Edison. Then Chicago Edison purchased a steam railroad moving coal from the mines to the Illinois River, where ships brought the supply to Insull's generation facilities.

Figure 2.8 Coal from the Midwest, and Illinois in particular, offered Insull a cost advantage with his major input. The advice of Frank Peabody (center), whose Chicago-based coal company supplied Commonwealth Edison, guided Insull, as would the advice of Peabody's son Jack (bottom right), after Frank's death in 1922.

Insull and Peabody would be two great names in Chicago history. "From the time I came to Chicago, up to the time of Mr. Frank S. Peabody's death," Insull recollected, "he was my chief advisor in connection with all matters that came up as to coal." Insull would turn to Frank's son, Jack Peabody, for the same counsel.

A New Name
In September 1907, Chicago Edison and its wholly owned affiliate, Commonwealth Electric, were merged to form Commonwealth Edison Company. Much political maneuvering preceded the merger, however. Two years earlier, a state

law empowered Chicago to set rates for any utility service, as well as to expand its lone isolated plant to take on Chicago Edison in some way. Insull, not wanting to tempt fate, asked the city council to sanction a merger in return for a general rate cut, one that would be on top of a similar cut effective July 1905. Insull won the council's vote, but Chicago's promunicipalization, antiutility mayor, Edward Dunne, vetoed. Insull then surprisingly announced that he would cut his rates anyway, which led a nonplussed Dunne to call in New York accountants to audit Chicago Edison for irregularities. Finding none, the politics grew quiet, and the merger was put up to a vote.

The merged company—a consolidation of about 20 companies from the time Insull began the process in 1892—was 60 times larger than the one Insull had inherited 15 years before. Such growth had not come at the expense of profits but was a source of it, as the company's steady 8 percent dividend attested. Stockholders were as happy as consumers were well served by the emerging titan of the electricity industry, now one of America's largest.

Fifteen Years of Progress

Lower rates and greater sales enabled by a new, aggressive, multi-faceted business model: That is what Insull spearheaded between the time he took his chair on Adams Street and the time when Chicago Edison became Commonwealth Edison. The original customer base of 4,000 now exceeded 100,000. Generation capacity of a lone megawatt was now hundreds of megawatts. At the same time, scores of isolated plants were bought and retired—"The junk pile is our most valuable asset," Insull would say.

Rates that averaged $0.20 per kWh in 1892 fell by half by 1897 before halving again to $0.05 per kWh in 1907. What Insull had called "ridiculously low" prices—in other words, the cheapest on earth—got more and more "ridiculous" as economies of scale and scope kicked in (and were "ridiculously" high in the rear-view mirror). Indeed, interplay of entrepreneurial drive and technological advancement was creating an invisible-hand result rivaling that accomplished with petroleum by John D. Rockefeller. Electricity needed Insull as much as the petroleum industry needed Rockefeller. (Manufactured gas had no such prime mover.) Little wonder that European electrical experts, eager to learn, went first to Chicago and the Fisk plant.

All this made for a better life for Chicagoans and neighboring suburbanites. "Trolleys running in the streets, electric cars rushing overhead, nickelodeons, well-illuminated shops with window displays, blinking signs, and ornamental streetlights brought high technology into the daily routines of ordinary people," energy historian Harold Platt explained. The silent, invisible, universal energy—*electricity*—was a "benevolent agent of moral uplift and democratic values" and the "ultimate symbol of progress." A good start had been made to reduce the drudgery that led Thomas Edison to remark as late as 1910: "I am ashamed at the number of things around my house and shops that are done by animals—human beings, I mean—and ought to be done by a motor without any sense of fatigue or pain."[26]

Such was the basis of Insull's gospel of mass consumption, the flip side of mass production. "The merchant of power" was on his way to transforming Chicago into the "electric city," a "networked city" where America's second-largest population center went "from death traps to places of convenience and luxury unparalleled in the rural heartland."

---

26. See Internet appendix 2.6, "The Utility of Electricity," at www.politicalcapitalism.org/Book2/Chapter2/Appendix6.html.

3

Expanding Horizons: 1907–1918

INSULL HAD DONE MUCH IN 15 YEARS atop Chicago Edison, not to mention his prior decade building the mighty General Electric. Chicago and surrounds were now *his* electricity market, and he was the undisputed leader of one of America's largest and fastest-growing industries.

His "gospel of consumption" was effectuated through "massed production." Insull-led managerial breakthroughs, and none greater than economic calculation via two-part rates—accompanied his engineering advances. He had deftly dodged political land mines to keep consumer economics front and center. Insull was educating the whole industry on technology, management, and politics via the National Electric Light Association (NELA, now the Edison Electric Institute).

Insull's self-described "experiments" included the discovery of a synergy between production and sales. "We came to the conclusion that the economical way to produce and distribute energy was to mass its production at a given point, convey energy by means of high-tension transmission lines to whatever subcenters of distribution we thought desirable, and then to distribute to possibly a lower pressure from those substations," Insull explained. Still, "we had hardly dreamed of the savings to be gained by massing diversified uses or diversified territories." Thus "the engineering of selling" gained its place alongside "the engineering of construction."

Thomas Edison was right about the promise of Chicago, "the market place of the richest producing valley in the world" in Insull's estimation. America's second most populous city was America's first energy city. (Houston would be second with the Spindletop oil gusher in 1901.) Chicago, the "electric city," was the most energy-intensive metropolis in the world, thanks to Insull and coal. And with Insull revitalizing the traction industry, Chicago was a world-class "networked city." All this was far better than the "preeminent 'shock city'" designation of earlier days.

Middle-Age Apex

"By 1907, at the age of forty-eight, Samuel Insull had achieved Success." Biographer Forrest McDonald continued:

> He had everything by which Success can be measured: the love of a beautiful wife, a healthy and intelligent son; a million dollars; the presidency of a huge business that he had created from almost nothing; the respect—and even affection—of his employees and associates; prestige in his community; international renown as the foremost leader in his industry.

Such was the result of "his own irresistible drive, his daring spirit of innovation, and his exhaustive attention to details, tempered by an ability to synthesize mountains of data into fundamental principles." And he had done it *his* way.

What was next? Would the wunderkind slow down or change directions, perhaps pursuing an avocation as his wife Gladys might have it? Twenty-six years in American business at Insull's pace constituted a lifetime, coming on top of seven years of nonstop labor back in England, beginning at age 14.

But there was so much left to do. Only 8 percent of Americans now lived in electric homes. The Panic of 1907, which jolted General Electric and put Westinghouse into receivership (Andrew Carnegie called George Westinghouse "a fine fellow and a genius, but a poor businessman"), presented challenges for Commonwealth Edison. However stellar the company's past, interrupted service or price jumps could inflame the public and bring municipalization to Insull's door.[1]

But the bold risk taker had checks and balances that worked well, beginning with his keen sense of intuition. Wife Gladys was an impartial observer in the Smithian tradition,[2] and able business lieutenants were emerging. Insull's Smilesian qualities—discipline, perseverance, attention to detail, judicious delegation, responsibility, authenticity, and humility—were in force.[3] Politicians had not been bribed, and conflicts-of-interest (the stock in trade of Ken Lay, the subject of Book 3) were minimized. Insull, in short, was not on a slippery slope—yet. In retrospect, the period under review was (per McDonald) the beginning of "the short, happy life of Samuel Insull."

---

1. A small book by Samuel Insull on municipalization issues published in 1899 was indicative of the importance of this subject.

2. See *Capitalism at Work*, pp. 25–26.

3. For Samuel Smiles's influence on Insull, see *Capitalism at Work*, p. 39.

Load Management

Profitability in such a capital-intensive business, Insull explained tirelessly, required diverse usage so that the (debt-financed) infrastructure produced revenue 'round the clock. Adding demand for its own sake could be a fool's errand if it added only to the peak; filling the valleys was the moneymaker. Increased load diversity—increasing the load factor between actual and maximum usage, or utilization percentage—meant more income from the same fixed assets (fixed costs), dollars that serviced the debt associated with the generators, substations, and wiring. Such fixed costs, or the capital invested, was a multiple of annual income—somewhere between five and seven times, in Insull's estimation. Debt intensity required the infrastructure to run for ever more hours and minutes each day, which required all work, no play on company time to service the debt. And so the Chief would tell the troops: "To you young men who have not been dealing with the problem of how to overcome interest quite as many years as I have." After all, Insull noted, "interest goes on 24 hours a day and 365 days a year."

Such was the challenge for a business that had to instantly provide a product that could not be economically stored.

·◇·

Massed production required the gospel of consumption. As explained in chapter 2, evening lighting had to be complemented by daytime load—the *power business*—to make the central-station business model robust. The sale of home appliances, a profit center from the mid-1890s for Insull, was part of this. The far bigger opportunity was wiring offices, hotels, and department stores for lighting, elevators, and winter heating.

One valley filler, electric railways, was so big that Insull would declare, "our business is decidedly a power business."[4] The streetcars and elevated trains that roared through Chicago's central business district and out to the suburbs had an early-morning and a late-afternoon commuter peak—and shopping load between. By pricing aggressively and engaging in one-on-one tutorials, Insull gradually weaned traction companies from self-generation to central service. Sometimes, it was an all-day affair; Insull would arrive at their office at 8:30 a.m., present loads of charts and statistics until noon, continue the tutorial over lunch at either the Chicago Club or the Union League, and continue negotiations in the afternoon.

"Sometimes he'd take us out to this house for the evening and draw more skeins for us," remembered one traction CEO. "I never knew a man who had a

---

4. By 1913, only 25 percent of Commonwealth Edison's sendout was for lighting, although this class accounted for nearly one-half of total revenue. Still, Insull called it "by itself … as poor a branch of business as any we take on our system" because of its low load factor.

head so full of crooked marks and straight thinking … and hang me if his own [economies] didn't always climb all over ours!" The cost implications of diversifying the load cinched the advantage of surface lines' buying power at wholesale and, however painful, scrapping their own generation plants.

By 1907, 56 percent of Commonwealth Edison's sendout went to transit, compared to less than 6 percent five years before. With only 30 percent of the total transit market served by Commonwealth Edison, Insull was looking for more. But just getting the business was not enough, given the political and managerial issues surrounding Chicago's transit industry. Insull would have to immerse himself in that business and would emerge by 1914 "as Chicago's leading traction magnate."

⟡

"Ace statistician" E. J. Fowler of Commonwealth Edison's research department quantified the diversity factor from various customer classes. Using the 30-minute readouts of the Wright wattmeters, 24-hour load averages for various classes were plotted for the days, months, seasons, and years. In a 1913 speech to a financial group in New York City, Insull explained how 11 customer classes created a whole of complementary parts.

Residential usage, with its heavy evening lighting peak, had a 20 percent load factor. Adding the stores down the street brought the overall load factor (utilization percentage) to 30 percent. A similar jump resulted with office buildings, hotels, and industry in the mix. Adding in the other customer classes and with valley filling in mind, the overall load factor rose from 42 percent in 1902 to 56 percent in 1912—a one-third increase in one decade.[5] This improvement to 13.5 hours of daily usage made rates more affordable for the "short hour consumer"—so long as a demand or reservation charge was paid for service at the ready.

Diversity also came from greater numbers within a class, Insull discovered. Analysis of 193 apartments in one city block revealed a group load factor several times greater than for the average individual unit, turning the losses from Insull's "ridiculously low" rates into a profit for Commonwealth Edison. Such load-factor economics, Insull explained, "is the fundamental basis of the profit-making of an energy-selling company" (read capital-intensive integrated electricity company).

---

5. Twelve classes were segregated in all: apartment buildings; department stores; public garages; office buildings; steel, iron, and brass works; manufacturing; stockyards and packing; telephone exchanges and offices; ice making; motels; brickyards and quarries; and cement works and miscellaneous.

Rural Electrification

"The way Insull's utility managed Chicago's power load," noted one technological historian, "is comparable to the historic managerial contributions made by railway men in the nineteenth century and is as interesting as the widely publicized managerial concepts and policies of John D. Rockefeller and Henry Ford." But beyond the city and the suburbs lay another frontier for the synergistic generation/distribution, adding yet more heft to Insull's "principle of concentration" and the virtuous cycle of more sales and lower rates.[6] Insull could only revel in "a business which affords so many remarkable surprises."

As described in chapter 2, North Shore Electric Company (North Shore), a Commonwealth Edison affiliate, conquered Chicago's suburbs.[7] This left the small farming communities, which had, at best, electric lights on their main streets. This sprawling market, covering most of America, was not in anyone's sights for electrification, much less from a network perspective. Still, farmers wanted energy, affordable energy, badly, just as city and suburban dwellers did; with the energy option, perhaps the advantage of lower land costs could spur rural industry.

In 1907, Insull purchased a farm near Libertyville, a country town where a small rickety generator lit the main street. He thought about installing his own generator to electrify his farm, but this was hardly consonant with the scale that he championed everywhere else. So Insull schemed. What about transmission to reach a properly scaled generator, which meant North Shore, six miles away? But the economics were daunting without a wider market to serve.

With Gladys and his infant son abroad on vacation in the summer of 1908, Insull bought a car and toured the countryside with more than pleasure in mind. Might there be a network of users in the hinterland? Insull commissioned a survey and talked up the idea of rural electrification. His colleagues were skeptical about profitably serving dispersed, poor farmers, but Insull envisioned production economies great enough to offset the transmission costs. A diversity gain could turn losses into systemwide benefits, and this market would only grow once the wires were in.

In 1910, North Shore wired 22 towns and 125 farms, serving 1,422 customers out of a total population of 23,000 in Lake County. For Insull, this pocket of northern Illinois was the "poorest territory" he had ever attempted to electrify. Ten isolated plants were purchased (most towns had no electricity), nine of which were scrapped. ("The junk pile is our most valuable asset," Insull would say.)

---

6. "[Edison's] gospel was the elimination of waste, the cheapening of production, and the enriching of public utilities and conveniences."

7. See pp. 96–97.

One plant serving several farms was upgraded as the central station from which substations were added. Transmission lines with improved reach (as much as 50–60 miles) completed the so-called Lake County Experiment.

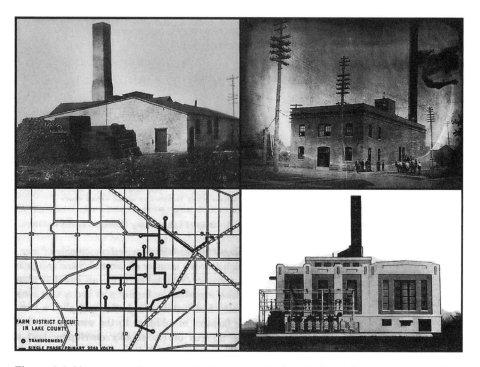

Figure 3.1 New-generation power plants accelerated rural electricity service, going from this circa-1890 model (upper left) to this North Shore Electric Company plant (upper right) and this Middle West Utilities plant (lower right). The Lake County map from 1910 shows the widening reach of transmission-rich rural service communities.

At the same time, Insull created the Committee on Electricity in Rural Districts within NELA to spur other experiments. There was derision within the ranks, however, with one prominent NELA utility executive calling rural marketing "a joke." Even farm groups were not inspired.

But good results began to emerge with each passing month; by 1912, the results were in: Lake County panned out spectacularly. The infrastructure makeover doubled the fixed cost per kWh, but amortization, lower fuel costs, growing usage, and improved load diversity kept rates down—and falling.

As Insull explained in a historic 1913 lecture to the Franklin Institute in Philadelphia, fuel costs fell 70 percent, and the load factor doubled to 29 percent (not too far behind that of a small city). Usage, meanwhile, jumped two-and-a-half-fold, with customer growth of 150 percent joining doubled usage per customer.

What was behind this success in a less-than-ideal market? Part of it was applying the knowledge and buying power of Commonwealth Edison to the experiment. Insull knew how to set rates and sell, sell, sell. But part of the success was a pleasant surprise, as E. J. Fowler documented: rural life's summer peak complementing the suburbs' winter peak, improving load diversity for North Shore as a whole. With electricity on tap, the farms used power to drain water and irrigate. Rural mining and manufacturing operations sprang up from affordable power too.

With the new investment amortized over many years and the economics of buying and selling exceeding expectations, sales growth brought revenue to the bottom line. With the load factor doubling in the first two years, partly from rate cuts that more than paid for themselves, the experiment was a resounding success.

The "new conception" of electricity service, as Insull called it, "exploded upon the industry." What his doubters missed, despite Insull's tireless education, was the importance of diversity, which flipped the economics. It was complicated and subtle, giving credence to those crediting Insull with accelerating the development of electricity industry by a decade or two or even a generation. "From being just a little shoestring business which no one would care to give any particular attention to," Insull explained to his brethren, rural electrification "grows to formidable proportions, is easily financed, and is put on a basis that is a credit alike to the owners and the users, and a great benefit to the territory that is served."

⋄

The industry got busy. "By 1914 lines had begun to emanate from cities all over the Middle West to electrify villages and hamlets in the surrounding countryside." The "systematization movement" was under way, one that "would dominate, and then carry, the American economy for better than a decade."[8] Insull described the benefits of enhanced rural life in terms of providing a better living and working environment:

> [The working man] will be able to establish himself under conditions where he can get healthful environment for his family. Instead of living in overheated, ill-ventilated, small tenements of the big city he will have the opportunity to establish himself practically amid the desirable conditions that those living in the country ordinarily enjoy.

---

8. Insull would later say: "I am not claiming any great originality for the Lake County Experiment. If I had not hit upon it somebody else would have, but it is rather an interesting sidelight that even the opponents of private ownership, such as the Tennessee Valley Authority, by their work have put the stamp of approval on such matters as the Lake County Experiment and the formation of the Public Service Company of Northern Illinois."

Electrification's "socioeconomic revolution" had reached its third market after the city and the suburbs. As with the other two, Insull was at the frontier.

The Gospel of Consumption

With abundant, expandable supply from the technological marvel of the Fisk Generation Station, Insull was back in full sales mode. In the city as in the suburbs, for homes and business, from illumination to traction: The recipe was low rates, aggressive advertising, and full service from wiring to appliance sales and installation. "Our experience is that the lower we set the price of energy, if we will get at our customers and educate them to the uses of electricity, the greater is the use, within certain limitations," Insull preached. Low rates "enable your customers to use the thousand and one devices that consume electricity at times other than the time that brings your maximum load," making "your properties of far greater value."

What a deal for consumers! A dollar in 1912 bought twice the electricity that it did five years before—and nine times more than a quarter century before. Further, this was after the government's tax take, which was more than a dime for every dollar of revenue received by Commonwealth Edison.

Such increases reflected efficiency improvements and economies of scale throughout the industry chain—and nowhere more than in Chicago, whose electricity rates were the lowest on either side of the Atlantic. The more mature New York City and London markets could not keep up with what their expatriate was doing in the Windy City.

Industry-wide developments were also part of the happy story. The same quantity of electricity was producing more energy services, not only more cheaply. The efficiency of electric lamps tripled between 1896 and 1913, pushed in part by the improved Welsbach gas burner.

Having low-cost power generation on tap was one thing; selling massive quantities of new supply to effectuate the mass economies of scale was another. As *McClure's* magazine documented: "Insull's achievements in Chicago deserve to be ranked among the great campaigns of business."

McClure's investigative reporter Edward Woolley, interviewing Insull's customers, rivals, and employees, got the lowdown. When Commonwealth Edison's Contract Department could not convince an important prospect, the man "know[ing] more about the habits of kilowatts than Edison himself" got involved, even if it required spending more time in their office than his own. "The 'old man' can sell more electricity in ten minutes than any of us fellows can dispose of in a day," one member of Insull's sales staff commented. "He got me all tangled up in his kilowatts," one department store executive pursued by Insull confessed. "He showed me how densely ignorant I was about kilowatt curves, load factors, and the cost of electrical output per unit; and he demonstrated ... that if

I ran my business on the same principle I followed in making my electricity, I would be out [a million dollars] at the end of the year."

So it was with traction companies on the one hand and manufacturers on the other: All the clients were persuaded to overcome their emotions, treat incurred costs as bygones, and scrap their plants for wholesale service. It took a lot of effort by the Chief himself, but the superior economics of central stations would win the day—one new customer at a time.

～

The home represented an untapped market that could help fill the valleys of demand. With wall sockets in waiting, plug-in appliances became the rage. Electric washing machines, toasters, and flatirons were commercialized in 1907, and the portable electric vacuum cleaner (invented by a Chicago janitor) came the next year. The electric range, refrigeration, and ice machines were introduced in 1910. All these appliances, as well as portable lamps and even coffee percolators, put "[Commonwealth] Edison's marketers ... on a roll." Moreover, such vertical integration was profitable.

The newfangled uses for electricity led Commonwealth Edison to open the Electric Shop in 1909 on the ground floor and basement of the Railway Exchange Building at South Michigan and East Jackson boulevards. The "high-class shop" was joined in 1915 by a downtown Electric Shop at the new headquarters of Commonwealth Edison on West Adams and South Clark streets—"the largest establishment of its kind in the world"—and other such shops opened in different parts of the city. The object was to increase the demand for electricity and the diversity of its uses, as well as to increase retail profits by selling not only electrical appliances and fixtures but also automobile accessories, lamps and shades, and kindred merchandize.

Commonwealth Edison's customer count soared from 15,000 at the turn of the century to more than 150,000 in 1911. What company was the national and world leader in electricity sendout? It was not in London, New York City, or Berlin. It was in Chicago. By 1912, in fact, Commonwealth Edison had more business than the electric utilities in New York, Brooklyn, and Boston combined.

Yet two-thirds of the available market had not yet been reached, in Insull's estimation. A $250 million investment was possible, compared to Commonwealth Edison's $75 million operation as of 1912. Such an investment, by bringing rates down for all, would benefit customers by 90–95 percent and reward investors by 5–10 percent, he calculated.

Then there was the Illinois market as a whole, that great expanse outside of Insull-controlled Chicago, the suburbs, and Lake County. Scattered isolated plants and unconnected distribution systems represented a $43 million investment, double the cost of a similarly sized centralized system. Demand of 225 MW and capacity of 437 MW was about 40 percent more than would be needed under Insull's centralized model, and the dispersed systems were burning three

to four times more coal than necessary. Thus, Insull formulated plans to conquer the rest of the Prairie State.

"Our business is really in its infancy," Insull told his audiences. Indeed, electricity was the youngest public utility, making marketing and public relations
vital. Insull embraced the adage "'Early to bed, and early to rise: work like Hades,
and advertise,'" and engaged in an aggressive print-advertising campaign where
potential customers phoned the company for service—a better proposition than
ringing doorbells that could have a one-in-ten payoff. To keep customers calling,
Commonwealth Edison began servicing lamps in 1907 and small appliances in
1910, filling a niche that independent companies would later fill.

·✑·

Traction was the great load builder, eclipsing lighting and also appliance
demand for electricity. Insull's aggressive rate policy spurred a sizeable
switchover from self-generation to utility purchases by streetcar firms, although
much remained for central-station service. Yet Commonwealth Edison's major
market was in financial trouble, and a badly needed consolidation of the El
surface and elevated lines required deft political maneuvering and $6 million.
The logical savior became Insull himself, given Commonwealth Edison's high
credit rating and interest in promoting its top customer class.

In 1911, with Insull's company guaranteeing the note, capital was raised to
form the Chicago Elevated Railways Collateral Trust pending political approval.
Commonwealth Edison took a call on the stock of the new organization should
the integration not be completed in three years.

With political permission proving elusive for the organizers, Commonwealth Edison took over the note in mid-1914 and supplied working capital,
giving Insull 80 percent of the El trust. Insull turned to Britton Budd, the head
of Metropolitan Elevated Railway, to secure the needed permissions from city
hall, integrate the companies, improve service, and turn a profit. Budd, who
would become one of the most able and reliable members of Insull's inner circle, did this and more. The "Moses for the tractions" cleaned up the stations,
instituted universal transfers, improved labor relations, and cut rates. Public
and political relations went from sour to pleasant. Chicago, long embittered
about its transportation system, rejoiced.

The next step of the reorganization was "acquiring, modernizing, and coor-
dinating the interurbans connecting Chicago with its suburbs." Akin to the
geographical economies that worked for electricity, this traction strategy was
executed during and after World War I by Budd, a gifted leader who some
considered Insull's best business disciple.

What about steam railroads? Could electrification replace coal and diesel
for both passenger and freight trains? "We have right within ourselves the
ability to get that business," Insull remarked at a 1910 dinner in Boston hosted
by General Electric, noting how the Atlantic seaboard had the population
density to support the requisite central stations every 50 to 75 miles. He

envisioned low rates and an improved diversity factor to make it work and questioned whether New York Edison Company and other utilities had done enough to interest New York Central and Pennsylvania Railroad in central-station power.

But converting railroads from steam to electricity, which was beyond what Insull's Illinois base of operation could do, would not take hold. Maybe it would have if Insull had been chief of New York Edison or Boston Edison. But maybe—like electric cars—it was just too efficient to have the power plant on board. Because coal-carrying railroads advantageously used the very fuel to which they were physically linked, natural economies favored steam power. Perhaps seeing the situation for what it really was, Insull rejected the "agitation to force the steam railroads in this country to electrify."

Figure 3.2 Commonwealth Edison's sales efforts included parade trucks advertising specials in bright light (upper right), while other company vehicles sold merchandise, such as GE flat irons in 1912 (lower left). *Electric City* magazine (lower right) was all about electrification for every need, while the Electric Cottage (1910) sported the latest in electric applications for residences (upper left).

What was happening in and near Chicago—and now across the nation, thanks to Insull's leadership—was part of the American dream. "Insull and his gospel of consumption epitomized contemporary aspirations to create a life-style of comfort, luxury, and leisure, a ubiquitous world of energy," noted Harold Platt. "The increase in the hours spent usefully or pleasantly by millions wherever electricity sheds its light is one of the greatest blessings of mankind," resource economist Erich Zimmermann wrote at midcentury. "If to this are added the endless hours of drudgery which electrically driven labor-saving devices spare housewives, farm families, and other workers, one gains some idea of the scope of this boon which has come to mankind from a force whose real nature remains a mystery." Insull's gospel of consumption glowed in countless directions.

More Massed Production

Commonwealth Edison's production growth curve had always been steep. The 3.2 MW Adams Street Station inherited by Insull in 1892 was joined two years later with the 6.4 MW Harrison Street Station, the very investment that Insull required from his suitors to come to Chicago. "Historic Fisk" inaugurated a new era in power generation in 1903, reaching 168 MW in 1910.

The Quarry Street Station was next, located across the street from Fisk to benefit from the same logistics. Composed of six 14 MW prime movers, it opened in 1908 and reached 84 MW in 1910.

Generation requirements mirrored Commonwealth Edison's peak load, which rose from 14 MW at the turn of the century to 185 MW a decade later. Surplus capacity and a host of auxiliary devices were designed to guard against generation problems to ensure, as Insull explained, "absolutely continuous and satisfactory service"—and particularly to avoid the "calamity" and "terror" of dark rooms, stuck elevators, paralyzed transportation, and a city immobilized.

Built to be run continuously, the generation fleet increased its average usage (capacity factor) to 41 percent from 29 percent in this period. Insull wanted more, of course, remembering his mentor. "A central station plant ought to be busy twenty-four hours," said Thomas Edison. "It doesn't have to sleep."

In 1912, a new generating station was opened on Northwest Street, housing two 20 MW units, four times the capacity with which Fisk had boldly experimented a decade before. In 1914, the world's largest turbine, a 30 MW General Electric turbogenerator, was installed there. Insull liked to lead, and it was no surprise that visitors from the European electricity industry traveled first to Chicago and to Fisk.

In 1913, the 14 MW Grove Street Station joined Fisk, Quarry, and Northwest as a result of Commonwealth Edison's purchase of Cosmopolitan Electric Company.

Figure 3.3 Northwest Street Station (top) continued the advance in turbogenerator technology inaugurated by Fisk. Beginning with 20 MW units in 1912, Insull again set the pace with a world-record 30 MW generator in 1914, the boiler room of which is shown (lower left). Landscaped grounds provided aesthetics to the public, as well as a meeting place for outdoor company events (lower right).

These completed the generation portfolio that would give Commonwealth Edison enough reserve margin to meet growing demand during World War I and reduce rates at a time of general inflation.

Earlier power plants had landscaping, but aesthetics reached a new level at Northwest, which was described as "a park-like estate of which any owner might be proud." Functionality, not only the company's image, was reason enough to preserve and add trees; plant lawns, bushes, and flower beds; and install driveways and walks. The finished product was the site of picnics where "employees from throughout the company flocked … for a day's outing that included foot races, baseball games, and pole climbing contests—even archery and trap shooting—and of course, plenty of refreshments." Such special occasions meant a five and a half day week instead of the customary six, with employees leaving work for Northwest on Saturday at noon.

"Massing of production" meant fewer stations and, as if led by an invisible hand, less power-plant sprawl. Isolated plants, Insull said in no uncertain terms, "must disappear ... be wiped out." Insull's "principle of concentration" was a good example of Joseph Schumpeter's *creative destruction* whereby the better replaces the good.[9]

In 1910, Insull reported that three stations were doing much more work than his nine stations did a decade before. Statewide, Insull reported that his original 63 units were halved by 1913, and fewer than ten superstations would likely stand when the consolidation was complete.

A sign of progress was the 1916 closure of the 16 MW Harrison Street Station, the flagship before Fisk. It had gone to standby six years before and was officially dismantled after a 22-year run. Only the 1,200-pound five-foot-diameter clock survived, finding a new home at the 72 West Adams Street headquarters. Fewer and bigger represented conservation and efficiency, getting more from less, and all in the name of profitability, reflecting economies of scale in production and in distribution. Insull had his valued junk pile.

Insull was clearly the driving force behind the engineering feats responsible for the massing of production. It was he who sent GE's Charles Coffin back to the drawing board and pushed his own Frederick Sargent to scale up from what had been thought possible. "You know I am not in the habit of paying compliments," Insull wrote to Sargent in 1914, "but ... I am not forgetful of the great assistance you have rendered me in my efforts to give cheap power to his community." He continued: "The great engineering ability which you have displayed in designing our power plants has placed us in the lead to such an extent that what has been accomplished is a matter of great satisfaction.... It gives me a confidence in the future which is very pleasant to contemplate."

Public Service Company of Northern Illinois (1911)

The ambition of Samuel Insull went beyond Chicago and even Illinois. As the Great Man of his industry and with a knack for righting underperforming assets, many propositions and opportunities came his way.

Insull backed inventors and magazines that personally appealed to him. He was a major investor of the Midwest traction holding company United Light and Railways Company and half-owner of a multifaceted Chicago-based utility consulting company, H. M. Byllesby. Insull had a large stake in General Incandescent Lamp Company, which was sold in 1903 for a quarter-million-dollar profit. He had stock positions in companies in which his reorganization had helped bring distressed properties back to life (bankers and others came begging with stock grants in tow). Not surprisingly, Insull held investor and board

---

9. On the concept of creative destruction, see *Capitalism at Work*, pp. 126–28.

of director relationships in electric utilities in California, Indiana, Kentucky, Louisiana, Pennsylvania, and Wisconsin.

In 1902, the same year as the formation of North Shore Electric, Insull bought a majority interest in an electric and gas utility in New Albany, Indiana, as well as an electric and traction company in nearby Jefferson. Samuel put his brother in charge, and by 1911, Martin Insull ably presided over a $5 million company sporting a street rail line between New Albany, Jefferson, and Louisville, as well as an electricity side poised to expand service to farming regions à la Lake County.

Insull's extracurricular activities doubled his salary and net worth from that attributable to Commonwealth Edison alone. In 1907, Insull's income neared $100,000 per annum, and his estate netted to approximately $1.5 million, which adjusted for inflation would be about $2 million and $30 million, respectively. He was a set man if, perish the thought, he wanted to be.

∾

In 1911, Samuel Insull acquired five companies and formed a new holding company, Public Service Company of Northern Illinois (Public Service). The $25 million organization gave him the electricity market surrounding Chicago and increased his territory from 1,250 to 4,300 square miles. Gas, interurban rail, and water properties were secured as well. And for the first time, Insull birthed a company.

Public Service was anchored by North Shore Electric, which had aggregated 14 companies from its formation in 1902. A star performer, North Shore's load factor was higher than Commonwealth Edison's. Economy Light and Power Company, centered on its Joliet operation, run by Insull protégé Charles Munroe, was purchased, as was Chicago Suburban Light and Power Company, an efficient operation by Insull (and North Shore) standards. Illinois Valley Gas and Electric Company and Kankakee Gas and Electric Company rounded out the now-affiliated group of suburban properties.

The 39-system, 50-community, 6,700-customer intrastate company was profitable from the start, confirming that Insull did not overpay and that the properties were sound. Within four years, spotty electricity service became reliable and 'round the clock. Rates fell by almost half, and the number of communities served tripled to 150—with a customer count of 65,000 for electricity and 56,000 for gas.

Lake County's beginning was now extending through the state, narrowing the gap between city conveniences and country life. Electricity meant more than lights and plugs for sundry conveniences; it vastly improved communication, sanitation, sewerage, and water and gas services. An energy-intensive lifestyle fostered suburbanization and industrial deconcentration, allowing "increasing numbers of the middle class ... an affordable means of escape from city neighborhoods to the relative safety of the suburbs."

By the Armistice, Public Service's $45 million of assets served approximately 90,000 electricity customers and 70,000 gas customers over 5,000 square miles. (Several thousand water and oil heat customers rounded out the company.)

A savings plan and retirement plan were in force to retain and energize human capital. ("We are vitally interested in your success," Insull told his 1,500 or so employees.) A major growth spurt was ahead.

Middle West Utilities (1912)

Networking the countryside was a bold application of Insull's principle of concentration, which had begun two decades earlier with the consolidation of Chicago, the place *Electric World* described as "in a class by itself" and "perhaps the most interesting city in the world." Lo and behold, the network was coming into its own when Commonwealth Edison could *import* low-cost electricity, such as hydropower from the Illinois River valley, to displace its own (higher-priced) coal-fired power.

The model proven, Insull needed new states and, indeed, whole new regions of the country. But his deep pockets could not keep up with (brother) Martin Insull's capital-needy southern Indiana properties, much less the expansion-minded Public Service Company of Northern Illinois. So in 1912, Samuel hatched a plan with financier Edward Russell of Russell, Brewster & Company of Chicago to form a holding company to buy both companies, issue stock to make Insull liquid (he would remain a large stockholder), and finance new projects.

The newly formed Middle West Utilities Company raised $4.5 million in a "relatively easy matter," reflecting Samuel Insull's great reputation on both sides of the Atlantic (New York not invited). The immediate challenge was to rationalize the isolated operations of a hundred small generators and several hundred miles of transmission line serving 173 communities, after which organic expansion and acquisitions would follow to achieve the scale economies needed for lower rates and 24-hour service.

Samuel Insull was named president, and Martin Insull relocated from New Albany to Chicago to become vice president of a company poised "to make the entire Midwest one large Lake County Experiment." Indeed, as Middle West would explain, the holding company was designed to provide "a continuous flow of capital" to erect the infrastructure for "bringing a high quality of electrical service at low cost to the small communities and the countryside, a field hitherto lagging far behind the metropolitan centers in electrical development."

The simple concept of a holding company, however, required "financial hocus-pocus" that "would forever leave accountants' heads spinning." Complex transactions with such ledger entries as *deferred assets*, *goodwill*, and *value as a going concern* were necessary to satisfy a regulatory requirement, later repealed, that stock be issued at par value instead of market value.[10]

---

10. Profit-maximization in the face of (artificial) regulatory constraints, also called *gaming*, is a major theme of political capitalism. See *Capitalism at Work*, pp. 10, 89, 112, 260–62, 292, 298, 303.

But Insull's business plan and intentions were not awry. His holding company was not about subterfuge and shady affiliate transactions; it was meant to be legal, transparent, and affiliate-neutral where subsidiaries dealt at arm's length. Such had been the case between physically interconnected North Shore and Commonwealth Edison, which shared common managers and owners. Only later would incentives under public-utility regulation bastardize holding-company behavior, so that the nonregulated side opportunistically captured profits denied to the regulated side.[11]

The 15 members of the board of the nation's leading rural electricity company were talented insiders ("those who ... have obtained their experience in one or another branch of the various organizations under my control") experienced in different aspects of the businesses of the holding company. They included B. E. Sunny, a veteran of various public-utility businesses in the state; L. E. Myers, whose large construction company specialized in electricity infrastructure; coal man Frank Peabody; brother Martin Insull of Public Service; Marshall Sampsell, a young, able promoter who would rise in the ranks to run a major Middle West subsidiary; trusted Commonwealth executive John Gilchrist; and Edward Russell, a major stockholder.

·◇·

Commonwealth Edison and the emerging Middle West gave Insull 10 percent of the $2.5 billion U.S. electricity market. He was recognized in the trade as "the most prominent figure in the public utility field." Was this the beginning of the end for a spectacular career? "In another eight or ten years he would be approaching retirement," explained biographer Forrest McDonald, "and already he was beginning to think of himself as the elder statesman, the grand old advisor of the electric industry." After all, had he not conquered his city, increasingly his whole state, and potentially the whole Midwest? Was not his empire bigger than General Electric, vindicating his bold toast at Delmonico's back in 1892? Were not his passive investments enough reason to travel the country and abroad? Was he not extremely wealthy? Had he not a beautiful wife and a son to nurture into manhood? Wasn't Hawthorn Farm, with its 4,000 acres, stately mansion, Suffolk horses, and gardens, beckoning?

But then came a "moment of corruption," in biographer McDonald's estimation, whereby no success would be enough for the titan of electricity. Ironically, and ultimately tragically, this moment came "out of love and the purest goodness, and ... because he was only a man."

Early in 1912, Samuel Jr., almost 12, contracted scarlet fever, a death sentence for most at the time. Gladys broke the quarantine to help the nurses, leaving Senior on the outside, receiving updates in the yard from an open second-story

---

11. The "regulatory gap" for gas and electricity is examined in the Epilogue, pp. 500–509 and 511–15 respectively.

window. The ordeal, stretching from weeks to months, broke the intimacy of the Insulls' marriage, already strained by a workaholic cohabitating with a prematurely retired star of the stage, one who had never been overwhelmed by the male of the species. So, after Junior cheated death to recover, two bedrooms replaced one, and the 52-year-old's need for physical intimacy went wanting.[12] Here he was, a powerful, admired man everywhere but in his own home.

From now on, business would come first, second, and third, with heightened ego and ambition straining his Smilesian qualities of prudence and humility. It would not be obvious at first, but a new path of ascent was created that would have more trajectory up—but also down.

Rapid growth was destined for Middle West's utilities, advancing the principle of concentration in Illinois and many states beyond. With this bold agenda and two large companies to run, not to mention wartime matters that would come to occupy nearly all his attention, Insull scaled back his passive investments. By 1917, he had resigned directorships at three out-of-state utilities and sold his interests in both United Light and Railways and H. M. Byllesby.

Middle West's first major acquisition was Central Illinois Public Service Company, which provided (sporadic) electricity to 15,000 users and ran streetcars and an interurban line. Central Illinois would become the major growth vehicle within the holding company, extending electric service to new regions and acquiring existing systems in southern-to-central Illinois. Within five years, this utility's 40,000 customers were buying reliable power at substantially lower rates, more than tripling usage.

Another Middle West company was busy in the state. In 1913, Public Service Company of Northern Illinois purchased Northwestern Gas Light and Coke Company to achieve "a complete monopoly of utility service in the suburbs."

Insull's drive to capture his home state met an obstacle in William McKinley, a businessman and congressman who controlled the electric and streetcar businesses in a number of cities downstate. McKinley criticized Insull's electrification program and also refused to sell or expand the scale of his own operations. This frustrated Insull no end ("That man is no good," he would say), and a new enemy joined the New York financiers on Insull's list. In the next decade, Insull and McKinley would clash again, with the stakes higher.

⟨∾⟩

---

12. Samuel overcame marital discord in 1909 with a second honeymoon for Gladys, but the friction between his work priorities and her aversion to physical intimacy remained. In the mid-1920s Insull described his inability to "shut my desk at a given hour. I was at it this morning at a quarter to seven and it will be after midnight before I get through tonight." It was also a time when he succumbed to having a mistress, a fact that came out after his death.

"Insull and his lieutenants appeared to be everywhere at once," noted John Hogan, "selling kilowatt-hours in Chicago and Chillicothe, expanding to Maine and Missouri, extending transmission lines across the Midwest, and peddling ice in downstate hamlets." By the eve of America's entry in World War I, Middle West was in 400 towns (farm villages, really) in 13 states with 131,000 electricity and 43,000 gas customers. Wartime conditions slowed growth, and pending rate increases at the public-utility commissions were a problem, but Middle West entered peacetime as growing (558 communities and counting) and profitable. Not many businesses could say that.

But such growth was not all good; some was even "irrational," according to McDonald. Electricity was one thing; water, gas, streetcars, and ice were another. It was not enough that these businesses were major power users and thus customers of the main business. These side enterprises had their own economics and issues and needed a different set of investors. In time, Insull would wise up to that fact.

Part of the problem was what came with the acquisition of coveted properties. Package deals got Middle West into far-flung places, such as northern New England (Maine, New Hampshire, and Vermont), and, closer to home, Missouri, Kentucky, Michigan, Nebraska, and Oklahoma. Core versus noncore thus involved geography, not just business lines. Part of this issue could be chalked up to Insull's "great many experiments," but part of it represented ego and power sneaking up on Smilesian prudence.

The holding company proved to be an effective financing vehicle that comforted investors with size and diversification, liquidity from an actively traded stock, and strong stock appreciation from underlying profits. Shareholders fared well: Lower financing costs improved margins, and Martin Insull ably consolidated production, upgraded service, lowered rates, and widened the service area via internal growth and acquisitions. But far greater opportunities—and challenges—lay ahead.

Peoples Gas Light and Coke Company (1913)

Samuel Insull's integrated, expansive business model for electricity led him to consolidate Chicago, extend from the city to the suburbs, form a new company to serve the countryside, and sell and service appliances. Then Insull changed industries—rationalizing the urban and suburban traction network with the creation of the Chicago Elevated Railway Collateral Trust. Traction was Commonwealth Edison's major growth market, and Insull had enough capital, civic pride, and ambition to take it on.

At about the same time, another home industry—and clumsy rival to electricity—was floundering: manufactured gas. Although Insull opined, "I am not in any sense a gas man," he would become board chairman of Chicago's Peoples Gas Light and Coke Company in 1913.

The gas industry needed its own Insull, although its managerial challenge was arguably tamer than for power, because more economical storage allowed less instantaneous gas production and consumption. Yet the gas industry fared poorly in Chicago between electricity on one side and petroleum on the other.

"The gas people have been asleep," Insull charged. Gas was still selling its product at flat rather than two-part rates, which created the potential problem of losing money by expanding to meet peak load. There was not the same generation and distribution push that Insull engineered for his commodity. Peoples Gas's 30 percent load factor was 50 percent below that of Commonwealth Edison. Insull publicly chided the underperformers:

> If they had been alive to their opportunities and the possibility of the diversity of business that could be created by a system of differential rates of one form or another, we would never have had the opportunity that we have had. Instead of taking twenty-five years to achieve what the electric companies have, it should have taken us nearly seventy years if the gas people had been alive to their opportunities.

Gas politics and public relations were a mess. Peoples Gas had won the consolidation war and held an exclusive franchise, but the gas monopoly inflamed the public with poor service (complaints were a hundred times greater for gas than for electricity) and chafed under a municipal rate cap. Peoples Gas had never recovered from a rate ceiling of $0.75 per thousand cubic feet, which was upheld by the U. S. Supreme Court in 1904.

In early 1913, Peoples Gas turned to the city's Great Man, offering its chairmanship to Samuel Insull for $50,000. The job was less about running the operation than righting local politics, something that Insull had done expertly for Commonwealth Edison. But gas was a rival to electricity, and Insull, mindful of conflicts of interest, balked at this peculiar arrangement.

Desperate to get their man the gas monopoly tried a different tack, an underhanded one that went beyond what Charles Munroe had done to get Insull's attention with suburban power some years before. Whether it was a "sophomoric stunt," "subterfuge," "hoax," "bluff," or "deception," it worked.

Insull was informed that Peoples Gas had developed a portable gas-fired motor that produced electricity cheaply enough to challenge central-station service. He was not allowed to inspect the "Rube Goldberg gas engine" but only to observe it from the ropes. This was not enough to see through the ruse, and Insull put himself into play. In September 1913, Peoples Gas had a new chairman of the board.

Why did such a careful man fall for the stunt, and why did he not reverse course when he found out about the subterfuge? John Hogan answered that Insull "relished a challenge" and felt empowered with his two hand-picked members on the five-member board: James Patten, a Chicago business leader, and John Mitchell, the president of Illinois Trust & Savings Bank.

Moreover, top management was the problem, not middle management, which was considered able.

Just months later, World War I introduced new priorities and constraints—and a price jump for the energies used for gasification—fuel oil, coke, and coal. The company found itself in a bind between (unregulated) costs and (regulated) rates that would require contested, protracted hearings before the Public Utility Commission of Illinois. Responding to public pressure, the city of Chicago argued that Peoples Gas's rate base was overvalued and that, therefore, the company was not entitled to higher rates even with its higher costs.

Insull argued for a 30 percent rate increase for "desperate" Peoples Gas and accused one Donald Richberg (a future foe as well) of being of "crooked mind" for his challenge to Peoples Gas's rate-base valuation. Richberg, special gas counsel for the city, a position he had received thanks to Insull (a power play that backfired, obviously), returned fire by calling Insull a "ring leader" of a "disreputable company" and a "gold plated anarchist." The man described as a "zealous, uncompromising idealist" added: "It is peculiarly offensive in this case where the gas company, under guise of seeking emergency relief from increasing costs, due to war conditions, seeks in fact to impose upon the public the burden of past corporate wrongdoing and present inefficiency of management."

Insull knew that his adopted company had troubles, but he did not know that it was the very antithesis of his carefully nurtured Commonwealth Edison. He could not speak ill of Peoples Gas in the political climate, but he knew that a house cleaning was needed. Despite his great reputation, Insull was no match for a populist when it came to the gas monopoly.

A wounded, teetering Peoples Gas would require wholehearted intervention by Samuel Insull in the postwar period, a "rehabilitation ... [that] was to be one of his most spectacular business achievements." Still, the experience revealed a self-deceit, as noted by McDonald, "that he could have the power without much attendant responsibility." That foreshadowed much bigger problems to come.

Road to Regulation

Insull's crusade for statewide public-utility regulation reflected a nuanced, pragmatic view of politics, regulation, and municipalization.[13] The industry icon walked a tightrope between undesired regulation on one side and municipalization on the other, while rejecting the free market's "regulation by competition." The end result—the Public Utility Commission of Illinois, as well as

---

13. Insull's public-policy position with electricity was also held for other public utilities—gas, telephones, telegraphs, local transportation, and railroads, not to mention water and sewage—that were municipally provided in Chicago.

similar state commissions before and after 1914—is part of Insull's legacy as father of the modern electric utility business.

On the one hand, Insull sported a desire to be left alone to apply best-business practices. "The one absolutely desirable thing to do is to be able to conduct your affairs without coming in contact with the government," he declared in 1908. His basic advice was to "keep out of politics all you possibly can."[14] After all, his principle of concentration was all about lowering rates, increasing sales, and bringing home sustainable profits. "Sell Your Product at a Price Which Will Enable You to Get a Monopoly," Insull titled one 1910 speech. But such natural monopoly (he used the term) did not mean that the company as sole seller would exploit consumers; there was simply too much potential market for electricity to attract and all-important public goodwill to husband.[15]

Yet ever since his historic NELA speech in 1898, described in the chapter 2, Insull tirelessly sought statewide public-utility regulation of entry, rates, and terms of service. "I am a very strong believer in regulation and control," he proudly stated in 1911. "In fact, I have been advocating it in my own line of business now for between fifteen and twenty years."

How did his affinity to be left alone square with his embrace of public-utility regulation? After all, Insull's *natural* monopoly did not need an exclusive government franchise, and regulation could introduce downside risk given *his* best-business practices.

Enter public opinion and real-world politics: specifically, the populist, unpredictable, and corrupt Chicago kind. Opportunism and extortion from home-rule regulation, which Insull reduced to "campaigns for the election of aldermen to the City Council," threatened even the best of companies. "While we are subject, and universally subject, to law, we are subject to a system of regulation [in Chicago] that is an absurdity," Insull complained. Arbitrary price edits from city council—always downward—were very different from cost-of-service rate making under public-utility textbook principles. "I would very much rather operate under a low rate and know that that rate had the endorsement of some administrative state body, and know exactly where I stand," Insull stated, "than to be harassed by, say, a board of aldermen, who are mainly governed by political considerations."

Insull had reason to feel insecure. In 1897, he had dodged an extortion attempt by the city of Chicago, adroitly turning a nuisance franchise into a

---

14. Insull made across-the-board political contributions and granted small favors to politicians, but he did not bribe public-sector decision makers, as did many others in Chicago.

15. "The possibilities of the next quarter of a century are far greater than those of the last quarter of a century," Insull said in 1911.

50-year license for Commonwealth Edison Company.[16] Peoples Gas in Chicago, far less expertly run than its energy sister, was hampered by punitive regulation.

And had not Westinghouse Electric in 1909 made a run at his traction business—"'butting in' and trying to disturb us in the enjoyment of a class of business which we have really created," as Insull complained to General Electric's Charles Coffin? Such was an example of what Insull decried as the "raiding promoter."

Still, Insull's view of public-utility regulation as nonpolitical was idealistic, if not naive. He had an idealistic view of government whereby "expert talent" using "scientific methods" selflessly administered "proper" "fair," "intelligent," "judicious," and "purely economic" regulation. His idealism carried over to business, characterizing those in the natural monopoly industry as "semi-public servants" with a "duty to the state"—even with a role akin to the "tax collector." But actual experience would give the crusader second thoughts over time.

◈

In a 1910 address, "The Obligations of Monopoly Must Be Accepted," Insull dismissed a colleague's plea to resist regulation in the name of liberty of action as impractical, although "laudable" in the abstract. "We cannot afford to place ourselves in opposition to public opinion," Insull charged, adding that regulation (now law in several states, including Wisconsin and New York) was "inevitable" for the Mississippi valley states. Effort was needed to shape regulation favorably for its "privileges," including the regulator's help to keep the price of debt "within proper limits."

How did Insull close this speech? "The surest way to build up your business and to serve your community … is to do everything you can to bring down the cost of production in your generating stations and so to serve the public and retain its good will," he said. "Do not run counter to the prejudices and opinions of the people, and keep out of politics all you possibly can."

Yet no person more than Samuel Insull made formal cost-of-service regulation "inevitable." Statewide regulation by a public-utility tribunal for electricity was not predestined; it was the result of a strategic, determined multiyear effort by Insull inside and outside of the industry and abetted by allies in academia and government. Insull had to convince the central-station industry that comprehensive regulation was preferable to the status quo of ad hoc intervention and creeping municipalization.

Alongside his 1898 address, Insull as NELA president created a Committee on Legislative Policy to sell his statewide regulation model. Joining Insull on

---

16. See chapter 2, pp. 84–85.

the committee were sympathetic utility heads serving Detroit, Cleveland, Atlanta, and Williamsport (Pennsylvania).

This committee failed to win a consensus within NELA in the next years, but the growth of municipalization would turn the tide. "In 1905 and 1906 the municipal ownership movement gained such momentum that it began to appear that regulation actually was the only way to stop it," noted Forrest McDonald. NELA's Committee on Municipal Ownership (1904) was renamed the Committee on Public Policy (1906) to promote NELA's new regulatory agenda.[17]

With Insull at the helm, CPP issued a report in 1907 warning that the self-preservation of private companies depended on replacing competition with regulation; if not, the wastes of competition would lead the public to demand municipalization. "Properly constituted general supervision and regulation of the electric light industry" required exclusive franchises, nondiscriminatory cost-based rates, uniform accounting, and full public disclosure. The report was adopted by the full association as the lesser evil, putting the industry four-square behind Insull at the very time, ironically, that the municipal bond market collapsed and government takeovers all but ceased.

The same year, the NELA study was joined by another study that reflected a business-wide consensus favoring state regulation. The National Civic Federation (NCF), a Chicago-rooted organization with Insull as president and representation from business, labor, and academia, published a three-volume report espousing "a system of legalized … monopoly … subject to public regulation and examination under a system of uniform records and accounts and full publicity." This position mirrored the NELA report—not surprising, since Insull directed both.

The momentum created by NELA and NCF translated into state action. Within months of the reports, New York reorganized its two-year-old Commission on Gas and Electricity as a full-scale Public Service Commission, and Wisconsin established a commission to regulate the entry, rates, and service of public utilities. The enabling legislation of the Wisconsin Public Service Commission was drafted by University of Wisconsin economist John Commons, who had worked closely with Insull on the NCF report. Commons's language would become a model for other states that followed the lead of New York and Wisconsin.

A follow-up report released by the NCF in 1913 was utilized by state legislatures considering statewide public-utility commissions. Ten states would establish such agencies regulating electricity in that year alone. The rationale of the state commissions over the piecemeal legislative approach was encapsulated by the Republican platform of one state: "We advocate a just, impartial, and unprejudiced control of public service corporations and public utilities

---

17. A similar strategy of rate-for-entry regulation by a statewide commission was being pursued in the telephone industry by Theodore Vail of AT&T.

generally in this state through incorruptible, enlightened, and non-partisan agencies; and we condemn any exemption from such supervision and control, and any other special favors to any particular enterprise or corporation.

By 1919, 36 states and the District of Columbia had adopted statewide utility regulation. But this was a beginning, not an end. As Insull would soon find out, regulation was a double-edged sword. The eschewed regulation by competition—needing and deserving its own educational campaign to thwart nuisance regulation by city fathers on one side and municipalization on the other—was now the neglected, unchampioned opportunity to the status quo.[18]

Insull's resolve against open competition went deep. He denied ever having a business reason to enter into an occupied market and decried "the desire of ... the raiding promoter ... to possess themselves of other men's property." Smaller operations were advised to "go into the consolidation and holding-company business on your own account." Insull saw the "concentrated production" of World War I directives of the Fuel Administration as a model for peacetime. As a second-best alternative, "if public regulation fails, public ownership should come," Insull concluded, rejecting the competitive path completely.

It was the empowered state commission, not open market, that Insull wanted to grade his report card. As he stated in 1916:

> If there is anything wrong with my business, I want to know it, and the best way for me to know it is to have a public official who has the right to look into my affairs so that he can employ the highest class of talent to help him come to a conclusion as to the right and wrong of the business he is passing judgment on.... I know of no better arrangement than a centralized regulating body covering the whole state.

Insull's belief that public-service commissions would be above city political machines and could objectively ascertain so-called just and reasonable prices characterized the honeymoon period of commission regulation. "The greatest event that has taken place in the last ten or fifteen years in the local public-utility business," Insull boasted in 1915, "is the transfer of control and regulation in most of the states from the state legislatures to state commissions which, besides exercising administrative powers, are also exercising semi-legislative and semi-judicial functions." He trumpeted the high approval of rate-increase applications by commissions around the country—about 90 percent in 1917.

But Insull's confident talk about *his* kind of regulation contained second thoughts as time went on. He worried about "the creeping of politics into commission affairs," an adversarial mentality between regulators and the regulated, and a lack of commission expertise. Most of all, Insull feared that regulated returns would be "destructive of the initiative of enterprise and the initiative of the inventor." Electricity was still a young industry that required

---

18. See chapter 4, pp. 172–76.

much innovation to succeed in the marketplace and against political forces, Insull emphasized. Yet "sometimes I wonder whether this regulation may not check enterprise and destroy individuality in management."

A much-discussed regulated return of 6 percent on invested capital, for example, was deemed by Insull as "somewhat unreasonable" as a "reward for private initiatives and private enterprise." Mediocre returns risked mediocre effort—a "paternalism which will end in our simply fulfilling our allotted task and being satisfied with just what we have today."

Insull had made his own bed—and that of his industry—and was in a tight spot. But he felt protected by a body of law restricting public-utility commissions from issuing arbitrary, punitive regulation that amounted to an uncompensated taking of private property. That, and franchise protection, were enough to accept rate regulation.

By 1919, things changed. Wartime inflation, labor shortages, and coal problems resulted in a backlog of rate requests before commissions. "Control of public utilities by means of state regulation is at a crisis in Illinois," Insull declared, a far cry from his happy talk two years prior. The problem behind coal was railroad regulation that left the industry sickly, not protected and strong. The coal problem became reason to extend federal control to energy, championed by none other than Samuel Insull.

Such reality contradicted the idyllic view of regulation held by Insull and within academia: the *dead* political science lambasted by Arthur Bentley and the *romantic* view of politics decried by political economists.[19] Bureaucrats are self-interested and fallible—in short, *political*. The market has an order and nonpolitical merit that cannot be replicated by coercive central planning, despite the best of intentions from reformers.

But also, there was an inescapable tension between Insull's fear of raiders and his concentration principle. A closer look at Insull's utility protectionism is undertaken in the Epilogue's look at the forest of regulation in the electricity and gas industries—a forest of trees planted and watered in large part by industry leaders themselves.[20]

A Silver Anniversary (1917)

In 1917, Samuel Insull reached his 25th year atop Commonwealth Edison, the largest, most successful, most admired electric utility in the world. Together

---

19. See *Capitalism at Work*, pp. 134, 139.

20. See the Epilogue for a reconsideration of the case for public utility regulation in the gas and electricity industries, pp. 509–511.

with the $400 million Middle West Utilities, Insull was responsible for approximately 15 percent of the national electricity market. No other figure was close enough to merit mention.

To commemorate his silver anniversary, the officers and directors of Commonwealth Edison held a gala for 1,000 employees in Customers Hall, the ground-floor business mart of the new Edison Building, 72 West Adams Street. Putting aside the world war that America was now involved in, the company went all out for its hero. Engraved invitations went out to 200 special guests, including members of the Insull family. The company's own symphony orchestra and choral society went into rehearsal. Commonwealth Edison's largest stockholder, J. Ogden Armour, filled the tables with beauty roses, and tree branches from the Northwest Station added to the decoration. A silver commemorative piece was inscribed to the honoree from the board and officers.

The evening began with the National Anthems of Allied Nations and, when Samuel Insull entered the room, "Hail to the Chief." William Beale, Insull's legal counsel and cherished friend,[21] served as master of ceremonies and introduced the honoree. Insull then arose to thunderous applause. Insull's voice cracked with emotion, but he steadied himself for the rest of his 35-minute address.

Insull spoke to the progress made since he took his chair on July 1, 1892. One statistic rang loud: a 70 percent drop in rates to less than $0.06 per kWh. Coupled with incandescent-lamp improvements, Insull calculated, consumers were receiving 14 times more lighting per dollar than a quarter century before.

Such progress centered on the power plant, Insull explained, where 10.5 pounds of steam produced a kilowatt hour of electricity that had required 70 pounds a quarter century before—reducing the coal requirement from 12 pounds to 2 pounds per kWh. Such economies propelled the top-sized generating unit to 35 MW, compared to a paltry 0.6 MW workhorse of 1892.

Insull lauded "the marvelous work of the scientists in the laboratory and by the engineers in the manufacturing establishments, who have supported so loyally the central-station business and have given us apparatus of higher and higher efficiency to enable us to meet the conditions presented in the great cities where we do our business." But it took *his* managerial acumen to drive technology and make it all profitable. A telegram for the celebration made the point that Insull would not dare make himself. "Insull is one of the greatest

---

21. Insull referred to Beale as "my close legal advisor and intimate friend, and to whom I have always felt under great obligations." As a brake to Insull's overambition, Beale's death in 1923 figured in Insull's problems to come.

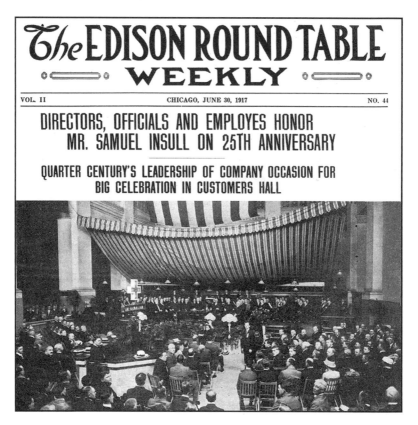

Figure 3.4 Samuel Insull's 25th year atop Commonwealth Edison was cause for celebration at Customers Hall, the ground floor of the new Commonwealth Edison building at 72 West Adams Street. Engraved invitations, symphonic music, roses and tree branch decorations, and tributes from family and friends filled the evening.

business men in the United States," wrote the 70-year-old Thomas Edison, "and as tireless as the tides."[22]

Smilesian wisdom came next. Acknowledging the sea of young faces before him, Insull spoke to their aspirations to excel, advance, and win riches—and the all-too-human trait to blame others for disappointment. The "'lucky' man" who sits atop a great company like Commonwealth Edison, Insull explained, was

22. Another telegram of congratulations was read from Electra, the organization of female employees at Commonwealth Edison, indicative of the in-place male audience and male-dominated corporate culture.

not simply the product of fortune or even smarts.[23] He was many things: wise, alert, and diligent; physically fit with great powers of concentration and capacity for work; and a "straight and true" thinker who was "ready when opportunity knocked." Insull singled out "the cultivation of a memory" as particularly important to workplace success.

"Captains of industry 25 years hence," Insull predicted, "will be looking for the young men with vigorous constitutions, alert minds, capable of working not merely by the clock, but as long as there is work to do; and the remuneration and reward for that class of service will be in proportion to the demand made for it by capital and great business organizations." Insull was speaking for the future, sharing the characteristics that he himself possessed and wanted everyone to have.

Insull cautioned the rank and file against discouragement by those who possessed a college degree: "Bear in mind that in most cases where men have had great advantages of education they have lacked the incentive of personal necessity to achieve success."[24] (Similarly, Enron would confront its own smartest-guys-in-the-room problem generations later.)

◦〜◦

This was not the first time that his employees had heard the Victorian platitudes from their leader. In "Opportunity for Advancement" (1911), Insull lectured about "ambition," "'sticktoitiveness'," "plenty of hard work," and "taking hard knocks." He described how John Gilchrist, an office boy at the old Chicago Edison, was now vice-president of Commonwealth Edison and president of the National Electric Light Association, adding:

> There is no reason whatever why many of you in this room, relatively young, relatively occupying minor and obscure positions in the company's service, with really far greater opportunity for success than that afforded to Mr. Gilchrist— there is no reason why you should not succeed as he has succeeded, and reach the goal which he has reached.

The good news was that economic growth meant more opportunity for all. "The capital of the country flows so much easier today than it did twenty years ago, or fifteen years ago, or ten years ago," Insull noted in 1911.

In a "confidential and very personal talk" given at Orchestra Hall in 1912, commemorating Commonwealth Edison's silver anniversary (1887–1912),

---

23. Insull's use of gender in his speeches reflected the fact that only men were in his audience. Gender segregation changed during and after World War I, when Insull publicly referred to "an Edison man or an Edison woman" (1918) and "the young man and the young women" (1922).

24. Insull elsewhere warned against "men who have very superior intelligence [who] are sometimes very erratic and very hard to deal with, and they do not all do very good teamwork" versus "ordinary, average intelligence, backed by an indomitable will."

Insull spoke about the company's mission to foster a resourceful, self-reliant workforce. "The company does everything it can for you," Insull stated, pointing out Commonwealth Edison's new employee savings and retirement programs, very progressive for its day.

In this address, Insull boasted of internal advancement ("I do not know of any case where a man of considerable position has come into our office from the outside") and characterized Commonwealth Edison as a meritocracy, where "ninety-nine chances [in a hundred] that the reason you stand still and do not go ahead is because there is something lacking inside of you." Favoritism was the exception, he opined, adding, "There are very few men in Chicago who have been born with silver spoons in their mouths," citing the self-made examples of Marshall Field and George Pullman. And he reminded his awed listeners that "it is not so many years ago that I used to lick stamps in an office in London."

Intellectual capital was becoming more important: "The price that will be paid for brains will be greater than ever," Insull remarked. Such capital was doer-determined, not a reward for pedigrees, for was not "the inventor of our industry," Thomas Edison, "without education," the greatest inventor of all time?

In two 1915 talks—"Service," to students of the Chicago Central Station Institute, and "Can a Ten-Thousand Dollar Man Be Made?" to his employees—Insull returned to old themes and added vignettes to his recipe for business success. "Punctuality," "honesty," "exactness," "quick decisions," and "firmness of action" were prerequisite. There needed to be *optimism*—"[our] business … has no place for pessimists" —as well as "absolutely good health" to afford balanced, rational decision-making.

Extraordinary accomplishment required another ingredient: "imagination." Insull pointed to railroad pioneer James J. Hill as the epitome of both optimism and imagination "to picture what would take place after twenty or thirty years' work."

With such attributes, he concluded, "it will not be so very long before you will be a successful candidate for a ten-thousand-dollar job [about $250,000 today], and possibly a job paying a much higher basis of remuneration." And not to despair: while the top might appear crowded, "the fact is that the top has so few that it is almost lonely."

Corporate Culture

"Our policy is to sell the greatest amount of energy at the lowest possible prices consistent with a reasonable return on the investment, and we invite you to join us in carrying that policy to fruition." Behind Insull's charge was a culture that not only stressed hard work and teamwork but also a sharp focus on customer service, which he called "the fundamental cornerstone of the policy of every public-service utility." As Commonwealth Edison's *Employee Handbook* made clear: "The ideal which the company aims to achieve throughout its whole organization is courtesy to the public and best possible service."

Insull feared arrogance, by which "the attitude of the employee is one of superiority to the common individual." Arrogance was worrisome because, in the absence of competition through which the disgruntled could patronize another provider, discontent would result in "general hostility to the large corporations," which was one step away from a hostile city council, punitive regulation, and even a death spiral to municipalization.

Thus, "your main motto in life" should be "the very best service to the public." The reward, Insull continued, would be "positions in life not only of honor, but positions that carry with them the usual emoluments that go to the successful man."

Hard work and public service were two sides of the same coin. Six-day workweeks with Sunday rest, the norm for business in general, prevailed. On company time, Insull asked the troops to "put most of your small affairs of amusement to one side" to work diligently. But in a Smilesian vein, Insull saw work and living as more than toil.[25] "There is a great deal to be gotten out of our business beyond the mere humdrum of work," he allowed. Moreover, "I do not mean to say that you should forego all pleasure by any means." Such balance required "look[ing] after your body as well as our mind."

Wellness included workplace sanitation and safety, where the dollars spent—about $2 million annually for the industry's 200,000 workers—were "dividends [for] physical, mental, and moral health—very valuable assets in any community and in any country."

Insull looked for respect from the top down and for loyalty from the bottom up—and a culture of give-and-take between. Each employee must have the "courage" to "stand up against a rebuff," and every manager must "overcome any feeling of jealousy" and "give a 'leg up' to the fellow under you." Such teamwork would inspire "loyal support of your subordinates" in place of contempt.

Insull warned that the jealous would extinguish themselves "because I do not care to have them around me." As for himself: "There is nothing that I like to see so much as the progress of my own people; it does not matter whether it is in my own personal office or whether it is in the organization." Such, indeed, was a hallmark of Commonwealth Edison as summarized by company historian Forrest Crissey:

> Employees are encouraged to enter the Commonwealth Edison service as a career. They are told that the highest offices in the organization are not beyond the reach of their ambition.... [For example], the president was a shorthand

---

25. See *Capitalism at Work*, pp. 54–55.

writer who became secretary and man of affairs to Thomas A. Edison; one vice-president, an engineer, started by testing underground "Edison tubes" in the streets, another began as an office boy, a third as a stenographer, and still another as a bookkeeper. It has been the general policy rule that the business shall be developed by the brains within the organization, and such financial arrangements, have been made that it is believed that no faithful employee who spends his working years in the service need feel the dread of coming to want in his old age.

Insull believed in hierarchy and formality, hardly unusual for the day. "I am looked upon as a martinet," he admitted, "a great believer in following orders."

Figure 3.5 Samuel Insull brought the teachings of Samuel Smiles to his thousands of employees and, really, a new generation in America. Perseverance, thrift, attention to detail, and other attributes peppered Insull's speeches, all harking back to the Victorian platitudes of self-help.

"Corporations today spend money to *elevate* their employees and cultivate their minds in a way that never existed when I was of your age," Insull wistfully observed. "The only inspiration that we used to get when I started work upwards of 43 years ago was from the books of such men as Samuel Smiles, who wrote *Self-Help* and *Lives of the Engineers* and books of that character, together with the inspiration of the literary and debating societies and the associations that one made in such company."

On-the-job education was emphasized, prominently including trade association memberships and meetings. Insull urged his people of rank to join the National Electric Light Association. NELA's annual conference proceedings were the "textbooks of our business, as they deal with every branch of the industry, whether it be commercial or technical."

In 1909, a company magazine, *Edison Round Table*, began publication. The monthly was not only "received with great interest by employees high and low" but also eagerly read throughout the industry, even abroad.

In the same year, Commonwealth Edison funded 28 scholarships to night school for technical training. The need for more formalized, specific training led to the creation of the Chicago Central Station Institute in 1913, a company school that would continue until the Great Depression.

⟨~⟩

Also in the name of "good business policy," Commonwealth Edison introduced employee benefit programs that had not been dreamt about in the past. "The company does everything it can in the way of helping you to save your money, putting you in the way of making money, and in return all we ask you to do is to do all you can for yourselves," Insull remarked in 1912. Commonwealth Edison's employee savings plan (established in 1909) was intended to "reward steady, constant attention to work in performance of service [to] enable a man, in addition to his own efforts in the direction of saving, to look forward to having a competence in old age as the result of the service that he has rendered to the corporation." "A respectable bank account," explained Insull, "help[s] a man to take a proper view of affairs in times of trouble."

Both before and after the introduction of the Employee Thrift Plan, Insull promoted thrift by exhorting employees to own stock in Commonwealth Edison. "I am particularly anxious to see the largest possible ownership in the company for which we work held by our people who contribute toward the results achieved by the enterprise," said Insull. "And it is for that reason that I refer almost on every occasion when I have the privilege of addressing you to the subject the savings fund." Some years later, with coal prices surging during America's neutral period, prior to World War I, and Commonwealth Edison's stock under pressure, Insull implored his employees to buy this stock, with its dividend being as secure as their salary, and in fact, the second-most secure security next to U.S. bonds.

Insull's determined effort to sell his workers—and later, just about everyone else—on holding his stock would have unintended consequences. The same would be true for Ken Lay at Enron in a cycle of boom and bust.

In 1912, Commonwealth Edison introduced an employee pension plan, Service Annuity System, that provided an annual stipend for employees reaching 55 years of age with 30 years of service, or 60 years of age with 15 years of service.

With a floor of $240, the annual payment was computed by multiplying 2 percent of recent-year pay by the number of years employed. A retiree having made $2,500 per year in salary with 20 years of service, for example, would be eligible for a $1,000 annual stipend. By 1919, some 26 employees were receiving $38.25 per month under the program, and many times more would become eligible in the 1920s.

Other initiatives in the period contributed to a unique, progressive corporate culture. An Employee Suggestion Plan was introduced in 1910 whereby small cash awards were given for money-saving, efficiency-enhancing ideas. In 1913, a service badge program was inaugurated, whereby a gold pin was awarded for five years of service, with each subsequent five years (until 50 years) memorialized with stars and jewels. Both programs, remarked employee and historian H. A. Seymour, "have done much to stimulate that loyalty and esprit de corps for which the organization of this company has always been noted, and which has been referred to as 'Edison Spirit'."

⌒⌒

Insull was *authentic*. This Smilesian walked the talk to magnify his message. He avoided conflicts of interest and political traps. He worked hard and possessed, in his words, "no great reputation for leniency." This leader was at his desk each workday morning at 7:30 to read mail and newspaper articles prepared by his (earlier rising) staff so that by 9:00, the desk was clear, and he was ready for meetings and the matters of the day.[26]

Insull was *hands on*. His speeches, sometimes peppered with "curve sheets and tables," were self-written or extemporaneous. He did not allow subordinates to ghostwrite his articles. "I do not want any responsibility, whatever, with relation to any article written for publication by … anybody else," he informed one solicitous financial magazine editor in 1917. "It is not a question of my not having the time to prepare such an article—I make it a practice of not writing for publication or expressing my views that way, irrespective of whether I have the time or not." Every man would write under his own name, per Insull policy, if he chose to write at all.[27]

Insull was *realistic*. "The very best investment that you can possibly make is to find out just where you stand," Insull commented at a NELA session on

---

26. At Insull's weekly staff meeting (President's Conference), held at 9:00 Monday mornings, his direct reports and guests were expected to "discuss freely [their] problems" to get opinions and "consensus" from the group.

27. Insull's policy was just the opposite of that of Ken Lay of Enron, who had a speechwriter/ghostwriter on tap (the present author) to maximize his persona. Both Insull and Lay depended on internal research departments for factual material, however.

appraising public-utility properties. In the case of Commonwealth Edison, this meant not relying on company engineers, auditors, or department heads but instead hiring outside experts "to tell me exactly the value of the property I am operating." Such a "proper appraisal," while "not … cheap," is "the very best investment that you can possibly make."

Insull was *fair*. Had he not come unaided to Chicago Edison Company, a fact remembered by those at the company who wondered what their fate would be under the wunderkind. "He gave us all a chance to show what we could do," remembered John Gilchrist of the 1892 days. "He came alone and he never put anybody in at the top over the other people." And "whenever anybody was put into the service they were put in at the bottom and made to work up through the organization."

Insull was *empathic*, albeit a legendary taskmaster. He was a philanthropist known as the grand patron of Chicago opera and leader in other civic matters. But he was an unknown benefactor too. "I specialize in individual cases," he once said, underscoring a soft touch for those who wrote him personal letters of their plight and need. This "country gentleman" would end up having a long list of dependents, beginning with family, which aggregated some $50,000 per year.

Insull was a *builder* perhaps most of all, growing his businesses in a sustainable, farsighted way. "The greatest pleasure I find is the pleasure of achievement—of doing things and building up—of creating something constructive." Advancing the whole required advancing the parts, which began with each employee.

Insull was a *leader* to admire and trust—and emulate. And so it was: thousands of employees of Commonwealth Edison held company stock just as the Chief implored them to do.

But Insull could not be *too* empathetic and loved as a tough-love practitioner of creative destruction. Early in his Chicago career, *McClure's* magazine described "a bachelor … in his early thirties with a keen and often unfriendly cast in his eyes, except when he was looking for kilowatts." The "liveliest young Englishman that Chicago had ever seen" had "dead loads of business enemies." One acquaintance described Insull as "a diplomat when he finds it necessary, but an autocrat always." Insull's frank, direct approach was also insightful, "saying many interesting things in few words."

The great producer and seller of kilowatts, a $100,000-a-year man, tops in Chicago, "remained in the deepest of shadows." The low-profile Insull "was willing that anyone else should have the credit; he dodged photographers with amazing success; he did not see reporters." But the next years and two decades would witness a more senior, reflective Great Man working hard to befriend his tens of thousands of employees, not only the general public that bought his goods and held his stock.

World War I

The 51 months from the onset of European hostilities in August 1914 through the Armistice of November 1918 were significant for Samuel Insull and his enterprises. His business ambitions became subservient to his mission to save his homeland, which meant drawing America into the war and then helping the Allies win. Insull engaged in secretive, even illegal, propagandist work during America's neutral period. After the United States declared war, in April 1917, he became Illinois's top wartime bureaucrat and a force for unprecedented federal wartime regulation—not unlike his earlier efforts with public utility regulation.

Despite their leader's being in absentia for much of 1917/18, Commonwealth Edison did well and Middle West Utilities reasonably so, weathering the coal crisis that engulfed much of the industry, including Peoples Gas. Insull's traction properties suffered from manpower problems and other wartime ills. "The trouble Insull's companies had in surviving the war and postwar crises depended on how long they had been Insull's companies," noted McDonald.

·◌·

Just weeks after the outbreak of World War I, speculation that America would abandon the gold standard triggered a gold drain and collapse of the dollar. Treasury Secretary William McAdoo closed Wall Street in an attempt to prevent stock sellers, many from England, from demanding bullion. Money hoarding in the United States worsened matters.

"The stock exchanges are closed, the banks are all on a clearing house certificate basis, and no gold is paid out or shipped which can possibly be avoided," a nervous Insull wrote in mid-September to Billy Beale, urging his trusted aide to scurry home from London. Interest rates doubled to between 6 and 7 percent, Insull reported, and some holders of Commonwealth's Edison bonds were demanding gold as their coupons came due.

Facing "the most tremendous crisis in business that I have known since I first went into business," Insull reduced Commonwealth Edison's payroll by 1,000 employees (about 15 percent). "Everyone is putting the best face on possible," Insull reported, with the only consolation being "that practically everybody is about in the same boat."[28]

Cost cutting at Commonwealth Edison began "the Monday morning after hostilities" and would continue unabated for the three-year neutral period. "Many unnecessary expenditures," even "some extravagances," were pruned. Employees were ordered by Insull to "guard zealously the pennies" and warned

---

28. Insull's rare concern is provided in a letter to his financial advisor. See Internet appendix 3.1, "Insull and the Financial Crisis of 1914: Letter to William Beale," at www.politicalcapitalism. org/Book2/Chapter3/Appendix1.html.

"not to be carried away by the speculation and inflation that is going on." Samuel Smiles would not have said it any differently.

"We have little to fear," Insull told a packed house of Commonwealth Edison employees in his first wartime speech, adding that it was "a little ridiculous" that the company's stock price was sagging over concerns about coal supply and retail rates. "The best securities, next to the bonds of the United States Government are the securities of the company you are working for." This was comforting for employees, a majority of whom were also stockholders.

Insull's indebted enterprises were now swimming in uncharted waters. But Insull had to be sure that America joined the conflict on the side of the Allies— and sooner rather than later. He was sickened by the stories of deprivation back home and worried greatly about his parents. So, as Forrest McDonald noted, "Insull went to war when Great Britain did," which was a month before President Wilson's neutrality speech. Few would do as much as Insull in the 32-month neutral period. "Had he been found out, he might have gone to jail," McDonald posited.[29]

Insull's first priority—making the U.S. press (as McDonald says) "a propaganda agency for the British government"—involved a personal donation of $250,000 and sending prowar material to 360 outlets that did not subscribe to wire services. Insull, by his own admission, "ran the underground railroad during the early days of the World War which permitted men from all over the United States to get to Canada and enlist under British colors." Chicago's business titan also fronted charity events through which medicine, food, and other goods were supplied to Britain, and he sent cash to the UK home front to try to alleviate shortages of food and other essentials.[30]

Two thousand Commonwealth Edison employees took time off in 1916 to participate in a "preparedness parade" in Chicago, part of the 130,000-person event. This was remarkable for a city that had deep German roots and sympathies—testament to Insull's quiet leadership. "The last thing I want to be guilty of is to hurt in any way the feelings of American citizens of German birth," Insull stated, only to add: "The German viewpoint is entirely wrong." He held no quarter for the Bismarckian "policy of blood and iron" intended to "supplant

---

29. "Not one thing was done to compromise American neutrality," Insull would later claim. He referred to himself as just one of "all Englishmen in America" who worked to "arrange that England should be assured of a benevolent American neutrality." Insull also allowed: "I did nothing hostile to America but much for England."

30. Biographer Forrest McDonald cracked Insull's "secretive" activities by probing into "mysterious expenditures … extensive travels … certain [letter] references … and occasional absences from board meetings."

democracy in Europe with military state socialism, another name for sublimated feudalism."[31]

That year, Britain's number-one American patriot—and the man *The Times of London* would call "the best and most successful Englishman in the United States"—was elected an honorary member of the Royal Institute of London. The first U.S. citizen so honored, Insull would not disappoint.

Figure 3.6 The tireless, risky work of Samuel Insull (inset) on behalf of the Allies in World War I was fundamentally on behalf of his homeland and family in the United Kingdom. This family picture shows his beloved mother Emma. Samuel Insull's work was recognized in the proclamation of the State Council for Defense of Illinois.

On April 6, 1917, the United States entered the war against the Central Powers. Within a week, Insull was appointed by the governor, Frank Lowden, as head of the State Council of Defense of Illinois (SCDI), the first such state organization in the country. Chafing over CNDI's assigned role as little more than a domestic surveillance group, Insull set out to get the region fully behind the

---

31. In September 1918, Insull narrowly escaped a bomb explosion at the entrance of the federal building on West Adams Street. Four were killed and 30 wounded in what was believed to be a terrorist act by a German sympathizer or I.W.W. radical.

war and into a war-production mode. It made Illinois a model for the rest of the country—and Insull a wartime economic czar.

As a full-time volunteer bureaucrat, Insull delegated his businesses to subordinates. Needing office space for his new organization, Insull had Commonwealth Edison donate the recently vacated six-story Chicago Edison building at 120 West Adams Street (formerly 139 West Adams Street). This in-kind contribution of rent, maintenance, and utilities would continue until peacetime.

"Our first duty is to follow the instructions of the Council of National Defense at Washington," Insull explained, referring to the newly created cabinet agency composed of the secretaries of war, navy, agriculture, commerce, interior, and labor. But Insull did not wait for orders, and "one the first things our Council did ... was to call upon the Federal Government to take control of the production, distribution and prices of all food, fuel, and other basic commodities, realizing that as a state body we could do very little to regulate prices of our own accord."[32]

The result was the Food and Fuel Control Act of August 1917 (Lever Act), the stated purpose of which was to "provide for the national security and defense by encouraging the production, conserving the supply, and controlling the distribution of food production and fuel [coal and fuel oil]," and to "prevent, locally or generally, scarcity, monopolization, hoarding, injurious speculation, manipulations, and private controls, affecting such supply."

Insull's push for federal control of energy did not come out of the blue. Coal problems began in August 1916 from a combination of growing demand set against insufficient transportation (take-away) capacity to get supply to markets. America's entry into the war exacerbated the mismatch, sending prices to record highs. Worse was feared come winter, raising the prospects of a dangerous lack of heating, not to mention the shutdown, on businesses, schools, and wartime manufacturing.

Coal-producing, coal-dependent Illinois was at the center of things, and a failed voluntary price cap schema brokered by Frank Peabody led to the exercise of federal authority to regulate prices under the Lever Act. As the nation's top energy executive and now one of the most influential bureaucrats in the country, Samuel Insull was instrumental in the new, unprecedented federal authority over energy.

The United States had never experienced a food or fuel crisis, but state and federal price and service controls on railroads turned ample supplies of food and fuel at the source into a shortage at delivery points. "The coal

---

32. For more detail about regulation, the coal crisis, and further regulation, see Internet appendix 3.2, "World War I's Coal Transportation Crisis," at www.politicalcapitalism.org/Book2/Chapter3/Appendix2.html. Insull's concern over rising fuel prices also included coke and fuel oil, key inputs for manufacturing coal at Peoples Gas.

problem is a railroad problem," concluded one expert. "The railroad owners, operating officials, and regulatory commissions, state and federal, are
dramatis personae in the tragedy of coal." The "great [rail] car shortage" and
"breakdown" of train transportation did not lead to deregulation, however,
but to nationalization of the industry in late 1917 with the United States
Railroad Administration in charge.

Amid transportation bottlenecks (Illinois's coal mines were operating at
60 percent of capacity at one point because of a lack of rail cars), coal prices
doubled and tripled after America's entry into war. The electricity industry
groaned as state commissions could not keep up with numerous utility filings to raise cost-of-service rates. In response, Insull-qua-bureaucrat
denounced coal profiteering and asked the federal government for authority
to seize Illinois's coal mines.

Things would get worse with the unusually harsh winter of 1917/18. With
shortages came government-directed conservation, or *conservationism*.[33] Stating
that "in time of war personal convenience must give way to public necessity,"
Insull championed federal edicts restricting daytime lighting displays and other
end uses deemed nonessential to the war effort. Businesses deemed nonessential were closed, and heatless/lightless Mondays were ordered amid the worst
cold of early 1918. Appeals were made to limit maximum temperatures in the
home at 68 degrees Fahrenheit as well.

From an economic view, electricity rates were *too low*, which encouraged
business as usual, as though there were no war conditions. Price regulation
immobilized the invisible hand, and the visible hand of government intervention allocated coal in the name of addressing shortages. One regulation led to
another, a major theme of political economy during World War I, not unlike
public-utility regulation of gas and electricity at the state and federal levels over
a century of time.[34]

·◇·

Commonwealth Edison was well insulated from the coal problem. Unlike other
companies, Insull's mine-to-furnace integration strategy left two-thirds of the
company's supply secure and internally priced. Cost-plus contracts with the
traction load, however, representing 55 percent of total sendout, proved inadequate when the companies (some owned by Insull), lacking rate relief under
city contracts, could not pay.

---

33. See *Capitalism at Work*, pp. 187, 242. The World War I experience would be repeated in
World War II and during the 1970s, both as a result of price controls and physical shortages.

34. The dynamics of gas and electricity regulation, beginning on the local level and expanding
to the state and then federal levels, is described in the Epilogue, pp. 500–509, 511–15.

Commonwealth Edison's improved efficiencies for all its noncoal costs—84 percent of the total—prevented rate hikes, unlike so many other companies. Existing surplus production capacity became better utilized, and 200 MW of new capacity added between 1917 and 1919 averaged down coal usage per kilowatt and reduced total unit costs. Behind this happy story was a 45 percent increase in load, and thus improved load diversity factor, as electricity (mechanization) substituted for the manpower lost to the war.

All told, Commonwealth Edison *reduced* rates during the war, continuing a trend that began at the very beginning of Insull's tenure in 1892. The company's dividend remained at its customary 8 percent, also impressive for wartime.

Insull's soul remained at 72 West Adams, although he worked down the street. Six months into his new job, he addressed "my own people" at Commonwealth Edison, reveling in his newfound ability to "address you as belonging to a nation that has at last joined in the great struggle for the world's freedom."[35] Insull warned the ranks about the "stern realities" of "increased taxation, higher cost of the necessities of life and regulations that some of us will be inclined to resent." His speech continued: "We all, whether we are young enough to go to the front or so old that we have to stay at home, must … [make] the sacrifices that are always necessary where there is anything worth winning." Indeed, Commonwealth Edison would send 1,377 to the war, some to never return.

For the "war-worn" company veterans visiting home, there was always a personal visit with the chairman—and a job waiting. "When any former employee of the company appears with his service discharge," Insull instructed, "put him on the payroll at once—and find a job for him later." As part of Insull's policy, each veteran was given "a little time with his folks and his friends before going to work … on our time while we are placing him."

Self-help during wartime benefitted Commonwealth Edison. With expansion capital scarce, the company turned to its own employees to retail stock to friends, family, and, most of all, customers. "During the war … we had to go to the customers of our properties to take our junior securities, and it was the very best thing that ever happened to us." Postwar, Insull would take this model to new heights with all his companies, thus not only raising capital but also aligning the interests of the customer with the company to create political goodwill.[36]

~

The State Council of Defense of Illinois was composed of 35,000 volunteer "men and women who are," Insull explained, "giving up their leisure, their recreation,

---

35. For Insull's rationale for America's entry into World War I, see Internet appendix 3.3, www.politicalcapitalism.org/Book2/Chapter3/Appendix3.html.

36. See chapter 4, pp. 159–60.

and their loafing time to do their war work." Beneath them were thousands more volunteers operating at every jurisdictional and organizational level imaginable. Patriotism and teamwork minimized friction and complaints, but one exception was the head of one neighborhood committee, Harold Ickes, who had failed to secure a desired appointment to the state committee. Ickes would turn that setback into "a lifelong enmity for which Insull would one day pay dearly."

Civic leaders, ministers, newspaper editorialists, publicists, and labor leaders exhorted a "'proper war spirit'" at thousands of events, even to the point of "infusing the people of Illinois with a zeal that many thought excessive." By war's end, some 2,000 speakers in the state (part of 75,000 nationwide) were exhorting victory at all costs to millions in a variety of venues.

Behind closed doors, Insull got done what he felt was needed for the war effort. SCDI had room to roam and run. "Both duties and power are set forth in broad and very general terms," Insull explained. "We didn't know then, and we don't know yet, all the duties we may be called upon to perform ... and ... the limits of our powers." Food and fuel were the two most active areas for SCDI czarism, but Insull got involved in virtually all things economic and urged greater powers, such as a licensing system for construction equipment.

Such power, used and requested, was viewed as self-evident and was confidently wielded. "There is no politics in the Council at all," Insull maintained.

In the 18 months of declared war, Illinois sent 314,504 men to war. Insull's organization raised $42 million for war relief, sold $1.3 billion in Liberty Bonds (50 percent above the national per capita average), and accelerated the shift of the state's industries into war mode. When it came to the Illinois economy, "Insull and the council simultaneously stimulated it, drove it, and streamlined it." Illinois's war leader went interstate as needed, forming a 13-state group to better deal with federal contracting problems and bottlenecks. Such centralization was how things got done in the absence of price, profit signals, and competition.

Wartime scarcities made Insull's principle of concentration official policy. Insull's powerful one-off influence was part of this. SCDI's own fuel administrator, John Williams, worked with U.S. fuel czar Harry Garfield. Insull only wished he had the same influence with the federal food czar, Herbert Hoover of the U.S. Food Administration.

"On just one page," noted Insull, the U.S. Fuel Administration ordered "the production of energy be massed; also that isolated plants should be dispensed with as much as possible, and that large distribution systems should be connected up so as to get whatever advantage there is from the differences in diversity of load between one system and the other." With Secretary Garfield withholding fuel from isolated plants, self-generation by industrials became virtually nonexistent by 1919. Such scale economies and single-purpose drive gave Insull the central-planner bug. "If we could achieve this unity of thought and purpose under stress of war," he asked, "why can't we do it in times of peace?"

⌀·

Insull's wartime work put him "in the public eye as a miracle worker with a Midas touch." While Commonwealth Edison was keeping ratepayers and investors content, the populist planner exited the public stage as a decorated hero after the signing of the Armistice, which coincided with his 59th birthday. The workhorse of the nation's first, largest, and most active state council and its "unpaid army" had really erected another company, albeit temporary.

In the winter of 1918/19, it was time for SCDI to unwind and pass bouquets. The highest praise went to Chairman Insull, as stated in this proclamation from his colleagues:

> With zeal and unselfishness he employed his great talent for business organization in the service of the State during the entire period of the War. He met the new and difficult problems which the combat presented, with distinguished success. Under his guidance the State Council of Defense became, as we believe, and competent critics beyond the borders of our State concede, the premier body of its kind in the United States. He coordinated the multifarious, and sometimes conflicting, interests of the Commonwealth so effectively—that Illinois stood forth in all her majesty and might, a pillar of strength to the authorities charged with the responsibility of carrying on the War to Victory.

A New Path

A quarter century had made the Electric City's per capita usage more than double the national average. Residents paid the lowest rates in the world, and theirs held steady or fell in periods when just about everyone else's rose. With the invested dollar producing one-third more electricity in Chicago than elsewhere, power demand soared in peacetime and wartime. Thomas Edison had surmised great potential for what now was the nation's second-largest metropolis, and his protégé made it reality.

Samuel Insull was also responsible for manufactured gas and traction in his adopted city. Add in his many civic and philanthropic endeavors, and Mr. Chicago was without peer in any other major U.S.—if not world—city.

Between 1907 and 1918, Insull's new world of electricity expanded from what he called the "hub of the wheel" (Chicago) to the suburbs, then to the countryside, and then to neighboring Indiana. While these two states were moving toward an interconnected grid, Middle West Utilities was going national with the principle of concentration.

"Picture to yourself what must take place in this country, certainly east of the Mississippi River, from the development of general systems of energy distribution," Insull challenged his audiences. Imagine "a network of lines for transporting electrical energy"—"great truck lines of transportation"—in place of isolated systems. Imagine electricity "in every hamlet and along at least the more important highways."

An interconnected coast-to-coast, border-to-border *supergrid* would emerge in fits and starts over the next decades in the hands of a new generation of utility executives and regulators. It all started with Edison and Insull.

The *Insullization* of companies and regions was Adam Smith's invisible hand in action. Falling costs, declining rates, expanding markets, and reliable service spoke for itself. But behind the success was a remarkable suite of business advances accompanying—and driving—technological progress. Insull's business model was all about getting more from less, or as he would put it, "making two blades of grass grow where one grew before." Within his companies, Insull was turning Smilesian wisdom into a can-do corporate culture in which his thousands, ladies included, felt appreciated, rewarded, and empowered.

The private and public good blended well. The industry's "constructive possibilities," Insull noted, were about more than rewarding investors and helping one's associates win in business and life. Electricity work was also about "contributing something to the progress of the country in which he lives and of the people among whom he has his abiding place."

Conservation, a hot political topic, was well within Insull's invisible hand. "While a great many of our well intentioned friends have been shouting about the conservation of natural resources," Insull stated in 1916, "the steam-turbine inventors and the designing engineers of the great power companies using steam as a prime source of power have probably done more to conserve the natural resources of this country, in so far as fuel is concerned, than has been done by all the agitation that has taken place upon the general subject of con-servation." Such business ecology would be noticed. "Today the conservation movement is led by sober business men and is based on the cold calculations of the engineers," noted Erich Zimmermann in 1933. "Conservation, no longer viewed as a political issue, has become a business proposition." Still, as W. S. (William Stanley) Jevons had explained some decades before, greater economy in the parts did not reduce overall usage but, in fact, increased it via mass affordability.[37]

Rural electrification, fathered by Insull, was no less than a *socioeconomic revo-lution*. "If power is made cheap everywhere, or nearly everywhere, by means of the co-operation of the scientist, the inventor, the capitalist, the enterpriser and the engineer," stated Insull, "then it may be possible perhaps to do away in great measure with overcrowding—or one may say with the slums—of great indus-trial cities." Generations later, environmentalists would decry urbanization. But

---

37. The Jevons Paradox is discussed in *Capitalism at Work*, p. 197.

for those involved, adding conveniences formerly available only in the city gave country life the best of all worlds.

"How did anybody ever get along without electric light, rapid transportation, the telephone, the automobile, the radio," the *Chicago Daily News* asked. Just decades before, "the city by night was dimly illuminated by flickering gas jets." Horse and buggy and dawdling wood-powered trains moved people and goods, including the mail.

Now, with all the spectacular progress and another burst of practical inventions in sight, the newspaper wondered whether "we will grumble about too much speed, and ask what are our young folks coming to, anyhow?" But the public would never tire of such progress, all to make life easier, more pleasant, more interesting, safer, and longer.

⌁

Insull was electricity's new icon, rising to take his place in history next to the aging Edison. "By 1910," remarked McDonald, "all men in the business walked in his shadow." With war ceding to peace, Insull was ready for new and higher orbits. Forrest McDonald noted the process that was taking the nation's leading energy icon into the rarified air of a very top national business titan:

> It was not that he launched a campaign to increase his power. Each step toward it was taken separately and each was dictated by circumstances, the kind of circumstances that push a successful man around. Each seemed the only sensible thing to do in response to the demand of immediate conditions, of responsibility, to family or friends or community or nation. Each was taken because there seemed to be no one else able and willing to assume the responsibility. Yet all, from 1912 to 1919, pointed in the same direction, and that direction was increased power. For Insull, in his great ego, now was certain of something he had once only suspected: that in public and in private matters, he was power's safest repository.

A colossal boom—and bust—lay ahead.

4

Peak and Peril: 1919–1929

S AMUEL INSULL ENTERED THE POSTWAR PERIOD with 34 formal business associations: 10 as chairman of the board and director; 11 as president and director; 10 directorships only; and 1 each as chairman of the executive committee, member of the executive committee, and receiver. The energetic 60-year-old started each morning before eight and worked into the evenings. Having aged noticeably during wartime, when he shuttled between three offices as Illinois's top wartime planner and top businessman, the now grandfatherly figure faced serious challenges with his companies. Insull responded the only way he knew how: "My sermon, all the time, is work, work, and work some more."[1]

This was a tonic for domestic estrangement. "Insull found himself increasingly alone on the home front," noted biographer Forrest McDonald, so "he turned to what Gladys always regarded as her one rival, Commonwealth Edison Company." But Commonwealth Edison had rivals too, as Insull took on resuscitating Peoples Gas Light and Coke Company and overseeing the burgeoning multistate Middle West Utilities Company. And then there was Public Service Company of Northern Illinois, the growing company he had started from scratch.

---

1. In 1922, the 63-year-old Insull suffered a nervous breakdown (one of three in his career) and voyaged to Europe to recuperate. Others in his inner circle would not be so fortunate; the postwar period proved to be a "man-killing ordeal" for ace powerplant engineer Fred Sargent, super accountant Arthur Young, innovative lawyer Billy Beale, political operative Roger Sullivan, coal confidant Frank Peabody; and rural electrification expert Frank Baker.

Together, those Big Four were on their way to a ten-figure capitalization by the early 1930s. Annual earnings in the tens of millions of dollars made Insull a rarified six-figure-salary man by the mid-1920s. But it was earned largely from consumers in the market rather than from cronyism or political spoils, the public-utility covenant notwithstanding. Insull was a Schumpeterian entrepreneur, leading change to turn the good into the better.

Insull was also Chicago's "civic helper" and "burden bearer." "It is not too much to say that he saved Grand Opera for Chicago," the chairman of Illinois Bell Telephone Company remarked in 1926. Insull was also instrumental in opening a special community center in 1922 that became the South Side Boys' Club for Negroes the next year. Insull's lead donation of land and money resulted in the Condell Memorial Hospital in Libertyville in 1928. These were only the biggest things.

Such was the man atop his city, his state, and his industry—a man who was ascending to the top echelon of all American commerce. A rare combination of talent and energy abounded in him. "One can pick up Insull's trail anywhere, and move along it in any direction," explained McDonald, "and find a sensible, sometimes surprisingly sensible, anticipation of future needs."

Insull remained the great teacher to those in his companies and in his industries. "I am not coming here to give you a lot of theories," Insull explained in one of his many speeches. "I am here to speak as a man who started at the bottom rung of the ladder and, by hard work and great sacrifice, and with the assistance of many loyal friends, has managed to mount step by step." His utilitarian talks—some technical and some Smilesian wisdom—were signposts to personal and organizational success.[2]

By 1923, Insull would be back on top with his various companies after almost a decade of diversion. Boom years would follow as Insull extended his tried-and-true business model. But by decade-end, problems would emerge, beginning with the onset of America's Great Depression and continuing with Insull's perilous, high-stakes decisions as the economy failed to recover. The result, described in chapter 5, was tragic.

Commonwealth Edison: At the Core

Insull had done much in the prewar period to maximize sales, diversify load, and minimize costs and rates at ground zero: Chicago. He convinced department

---

2. Insull's speeches and public persona were guided by his staffer and public relations pioneer, Bernard "Barney" Mullaney. Insull's political fights necessitated Mullaney, described as "a publicity wizard [for] … Insull's … many propaganda efforts." But outside of politics, Insull's public-relations efforts were wholesome and helpful to promote best business practices and self-help.

stores, manufacturers, traction companies, and towns to scrap their inefficient isolated plants, often in one-on-one technical presentations at which some of his subjects "suffered from mental astigmatism." It took five stenographers and draftsmen to put together his diagrams "that looked, inside, like a railroad map of the freight yards in South Chicago, multiplied by a thousand, [with] hundreds of laciniated and crooked lines crossed and crisscrossed one another." But Insull's analysis was sound and convincing. There would be few regrets by buyer or seller.

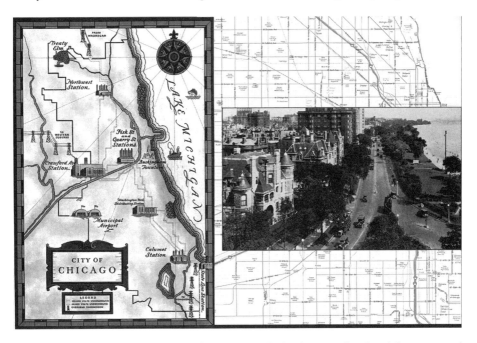

Figure 4.1 Chicago was home to Samuel Insull's businesses in electricity, gas, and traction. The City of Chicago map highlights Commonwealth Edison's major assets; the Gold Coast photo shows the city as it was in 1926.

In the 1920s, Insull resumed his business strategy of load growth and diversification plus cost and rate reduction. His compass was unchanged: "Gain in … the central station business can only be obtained by reducing costs to a minimum, and increasing the value of energy to such a point that its use is almost universal, and consequently the density of production and distribution is very great as compared with the dollar needed to be invested in the plant."

This lowered rates and improved reliability. The cost economies of his turbogenerators more than offset the higher transmission costs (including energy line losses) needed to displace self-generation. Mass conversion and scale economies created a virtuous cycle of electricity improvement for all.

Massed Production

Taking the reins from the reciprocating engine, which had reached its practical limits at century end, the steam turbine revolution began with Fisk Street Station's 5 MW vertical-shaft, 500-revolution-per-minute machine in 1903. Within ten years, 20 MW machines were being installed that required 40 percent less coal than first-generation models. By 1924, 75 MW generators were available; five years later, a 208 MW unit set the standard. The seven pounds of coal that the old reciprocating engine burned to produce a kilowatt hour of power would fall to less than two pounds in the 1920s and only a half-pound in the next decade.[3]

Commonwealth Edison was at the turbogenerator forefront. Central-station complexes Fisk Street (1903), Quarry Street (1908), Northwest Street (1912), and Grove Street (purchased in 1913) were joined by the mega-complexes Calumet River (1921) and Crawford Avenue (1924).

Compared to Fisk's 5 MW prime movers, Calumet and Crawford units came in at 30 MW and 50 MW, respectively. Design and scale improvements demonstrated that Insull's central-station model remained robust. Thomas Edison, although no longer active with electricity in the 1920s, was very proud of his vision, his pupil, and his industry.[4]

Scale economies with turbogeneration would continue, but Commonwealth Edison was done with new power-plant complexes after 1924. Industrial-zoning regulation by the city was only secondary to two other disincentives. First, planned growth came from adding new generators at existing sites. By 1928, Crawford became the largest generation complex in the world, with 424 MW of installed capacity and the potential to reach 1,000 MW. It was the most efficient power station anywhere, averaging less than two pounds of coal per kWh.

Second, supergrid interconnections meant more service for the same level of electricity generation. Interchange agreements and capacity-rights purchases were part of the new network economics. In 1929, Commonwealth Edison announced "the beginning of a new epoch in power production," in which purchased power substituted for self-generation.

But something else came into play that halted the happy-decade expansion. The advent of the Great Depression in late 1929, an economic malaise that

---

3. The U.S. fuel mix for electricity generation in the early 1920s was 62 percent fossil fuels (primarily coal) and 38 percent water power, also called *white coal*. Insull noted that hydro was dependent to one degree or another on steam plants, given the occurrence of drought.

4. Thomas Edison died in 1931 at age 84, just six months before Insull's collapse. Samuel stayed in close touch with his mentor and visited him on his deathbed, concluding a very close relationship that he modestly described as follows: "He was my employer, but he was more: he was my inspiration and my guide and, I believe I can say, my friend."

Figure 4.2 Completed in 1923, the six-unit, 190 MW Calumet Station of Commonwealth Edison had prime movers as large as 35 MW, compared to Fisk Street's 5 MW experimental units 20 years before. Shown on the bottom are coal-fired Calumet's boiler room (left) and turbo-generator room (right).

scarcely abated as the 1930s wore on, caused Commonwealth Edison to slam on the brakes, as it did other utilities across the country. Mighty Calumet went idle in the summer of 1932 and served intermittently thereafter. That had not been the plan.

Still, what had been done in the Insull era was historic. The original prime mover behind Commonwealth Edison's prime movers was a gifted engineer whom Insull had happily inherited with his new job. "Personally, I owe a great debt of gratitude to Fred Sargent," Insull remarked four years after the world's foremost power-plant engineer died in 1919.

> We were born on the same day of the same year, within a couple of hundred miles of each other. Each of us, unknown to the other, went four thousand miles from home to make careers in this country…. We can well say that Fred Sargent contributed perhaps more than any other one man toward … the great central stations that we have here in and near Chicago.

In this case, *Chicago* also meant *the world*.

Massed Consumption

Insull's superior economics persuaded customers to purchase at wholesale rather than to self-generate. Supply drove demand, just as demand drove supply in his central-station model.[5] Without sales, the turbogeneration revolution could not happen. "It was a realization of the true engineering of selling, the true engineering of distribution, that brought the demand for very large prime movers in our stations, and that forced the rapid development of the steam turbine," Insull explained.

Chicago was Insull's sales laboratory. As discussed in chapter 3, Commonwealth Edison opened electric shops peddling the latest gadgetry, almost all manufactured by General Electric. The display at downtown headquarters was the largest in the world. This multipronged sales effort inspired a moniker, "the gospel of consumption," and made Chicago "the electric city."

The marketing department, which would be reorganized in 1925 with a vice president for Sales of Electric Light and Power, was certainly creative. One "crazy" publicity play was delivering a large electrical appliance by plane. More down to earth, parade trucks would tour Chicago filled with electric appliances and with banners advertising "free demonstration" and "sold on time payments." Door-to-door solicitation resulted in appliance orders and a new line item on the monthly electric bill. Additionally, there were advertising campaigns such as "Give Something Electrical for Christmas."

One provocative advertisement became a classic in the field. "How long should a wife live?" the headline blared to the husbands. This full-page spread showed a woman with child in her lap, basking in the light of a floor lamp, her time freed by home mechanization. "The home of the future," the ad read, "will lay all of its tiresome, routine burdens on the shoulders of electrical machines, freeing mothers for their real work, which is motherhood." And more: "The mothers of the future will live to a good old age and keep their youth and beauty to the end."

The new world of electricity was now more than the fantasy model electric kitchen of the 1893 World's Fair. In addition to lamps and fans, there were toasters, coffee percolators, clothing irons, curling irons, corn poppers, chafing dishes, grills, sewing machines, heating pads, and vibrators. In 1925 alone, Commonwealth Edison sold 111,000 appliances led by clothing irons (39 percent) and curling irons, heaters, and coffee pots at 9 percent each. By 1926, virtually every Chicagoan had electric light, almost nine in ten had an electric iron, and

---

5. Demand drives supply ("The sole end and purpose of production is consumption," said one economist). But supply creates its own demand (Say's Law) in that inventory must be sold at some price, even unprofitably. With Insull's business model, supply and demand were two blades of the same pair of scissors.

Figure 4.3 Insull's gospel of consumption took to the sky, the streets, and the printed page. The first delivery of an electric appliance by plane (upper left) went from downtown to Evanston in 1919. A parade truck (lower left) roamed working-class neighborhoods in 1923. Bruce Barton's 1925 advertisement for Insull (right) remains a classic in the field. The Electricity Shop (center) was the place to buy just about any appliance on the market.

seven in ten had a vacuum cleaner. Four in ten had a washing machine but just one in a hundred a refrigerator.[6] Seven hundred electrical conveniences were counted in the catalogues and on the show floors. Electric *power* predominated what had once been only electric *illumination*.

"Do it electrically" was code for not only "remaking leisure" but also sanitation, nutrition, and child care—essential elements of human progress. At the forefront was Samuel Insull, "an icon of a higher standard of living," whose positive message was entirely new for a public that had grown up mostly with the image of business titans robber barons.

---

6. The vacuum cleaner was commercialized prior to World War I, the washing machine, in the postwar period. The refrigerator got a foothold in the Roaring Twenties before the Great Depression sent consumers to the sidelines.

"Electricity has become the household servant and has rendered life back of the dining room a great deal more tolerable," Insull noted in one 1927 address. In addition to "radical" changes in public and home lighting, the invisible energy meant refrigeration, air conditioning, and new means of urban transportation and communication. "I think we people in the electric business are very fortunate in having been able to take part in the development that has brought such wonderful results of improved living conditions, increased wealth, and increased happiness to our people," he told his employees.

"What electricity has meant in terms of national wealth," the president of the National Electric Light Association stated in 1926, was "motors throughout the country [that] are doing every day as much work as could be accomplished by 170 million men." Such man-work was greater than the population of the United States by 50 million plus.

Electricity consumerism had some growing pains. Nonstandardized wall plugs slowed dissemination. Repairing defects that came with new products could be frustrating. Critics of the monied class noted that only the affluent could buy new appliances. But the early adopters began the long process of funding greater production for mass consumption. All this was little different from any other good in the life cycle as luxuries became more affordable and performance and repair improved under the discipline of a competitive profit-and-loss economy.[7]

When electricity did not serve needs relative to other alternatives, consumers balked. "No amount of promotion could get Chicagoans to buy electric cars, despite Insull's best efforts," noted Harold Platt. "From the early days of the automobile, consumers preferred the peppy gasoline engine over the heavy storage battery, which weighed 2,000 pounds or more."[8] Electric locomotives stayed with coal and then diesel despite the best and multiyear efforts of Samuel Insull. Still, the "thousand and one articles" using electricity created more of a round-the-clock load than ever before, although still with peaks and valleys.

Beyond the city, rural electrification meant "amusement and education have been brought within the reach of the loneliest dweller in the prairie and in the desert." Public Service of Northern Illinois headed this effort in the state, and Middle West Utilities took the model to new state after new state.

---

7. These problems, addressed by profit-and-loss entrepreneurship, hardly make a case against the electrification of the home. See Internet appendix 4.1, "Antielectricity, Anticapitalism," at www.politicalcapitalism.org/Book2/Chapter4/Appendix1.html.

8. Also see Internet appendix 4.2, "Insull and Electric Vehicles," at www.politicalcapitalism. org/Book2/Chapter4/Appendix2.html.

The engineering of selling was encapsulated by Middle West in its 1926 annual report, which spoke of "the constant expansion of the business by development of old and new service opportunities and the constant efforts of the investment company's staff, in co-operation with the local operating organization, to discover and promote new types of service and methods of developing older types."

The power of power also meant higher productivity—and thus rising wages. All this was a boon for mankind, providing a new energy frontier that could not even be envisioned by W. S. (William Stanley) Jevons in his the first treatise on energy, *The Coal Question* (1865).

World Leader

"There is no institution that I work for that is so close to my heart as the Commonwealth Edison Company," Samuel Insull remarked in 1926. He did not found this company as he had Public Service Company of Northern Illinois and then Middle West Utilities. Neither was this story a turnaround job as with Peoples Gas. But turning modest Chicago Edison Company into the preeminent national and international company for electricity generation and distribution was Insull's signature success.

"Chicago is today the first electrical city of America by reason of the almost perfect team-work of these two constructive forces: superior engineering supported by equally able, economical and constructive business administration," wrote company historian Forrest Crissey. "The neighborhood in which we live is known the world over as the greatest field of electrical power in existence," added Insull. The city's three million inhabitants used half again as much power as the average American and paid the cheapest rates for its 96 percent coal-generated electricity.

Commonwealth Edison grew impressively in the 1920s, with a doubled customer base of 930,000 by 1928. Per capita usage in Chicago more than doubled between 1919 and 1929, continuing a prewar pace that had also been part of Insull's gospel of consumption. Monthly bills rose far less than consumption, however, although appliance purchase often swelled the total.

If Chicago were considered as one of the states (excluding Illinois), its electricity consumption would rank fifth. On a per capita basis, usage increased from 16 kWh in 1885 to 255 kWh in 1910 and 936 kWh in 1925, and peaked near 1,100 kWh in 1929 (about one-tenth of today's usage). But higher sendout was about more than maximization for its own sake; two-part rates improved load diversity to better utilize debt-financed equipment. "The greater demand and the better distribution of demand over the twenty-four hours of the day has effects in operating economies peculiar to the nature of the electric industry," a Middle West Utilities annual report explained. Chicago's capacity factor (also called noncoincident demand), which stood at 12.5 percent in 1896, improved to 33 percent in 1920 and reached 50 percent by decade end. Commonwealth

Edison had "the largest maximum load of any company in the world" and annual output "exceeded only by the electricity supply undertakings around Niagara Falls."[9]

Unsurprisingly, the center of the U.S. electricity market was near the capital of the Midwest: in 1907, 45 miles northeast of Chicago; in 1917, 65 miles northwest of Chicago, and in 1926, 55 miles southwest of Chicago. "Chicago is the hub of the wheel that extends out northward and westward and southward," Insull explained.

Resuscitating Peoples Gas

Samuel Insull liked challenges and exuded civic pride. Chicago was his home and the rival of New York City—the place of Morgan, General Electric, and all the things he had left behind with some bitterness. What was good for Chicago was good for his businesses and psyche. So when Insull confronted his major problem in the postwar period—Peoples Gas, which he had nominally headed since 1913—he had to fish or cut bait. But disengagement was not part of his character. His confidant and Peoples Gas director John Mitchell pleaded, "Sam, do you realize what a black eye it will be for Chicago if we let a utility of this size go under?" So Insull put gas rather than electricity at the center of his workday.

Peoples Gas was a turnaround challenge not experienced since the time, 33 years before, when Thomas Edison had sent him to right Edison Machine Works (the core of what became General Electric). The industry switch was ironic. "For a good many years Insull was not loved by the Peoples Gas Light and Coke Company, for every day he cut off a big slice of that concern's business."

"Peoples Gas," as Forrest McDonald explained, "was so ill-prepared and so badly managed that its history could well serve as a manual on how not to run a utility company." The un-Insull-like company had the wrong political footing and chafed under regulatory constraints. The business model was staid. Management was little match for its predicament. Employees were demoralized and customers discontent. Still, Peoples Gas had a territorial monopoly and a niche product to compete against kerosene on one side and (Insull's) electricity on the other.

Before the war, Insull, as chairman of Peoples Gas, had tweaked management, improved financing methods, and begun to resolve a $10 million rate case that had been in dispute since 1911. But the war came, and the company was back on its own. Wartime cost increases for coal and oil eroded the profit margins on manufactured gas, and the company suspended its dividend in 1917. With unpaid taxes and irate customers, receivership was possible, if not inevitable.

---

9. Commonwealth Edison lagged other utilities spread out over more area in average load, such as Pacific Gas & Electric, Southern California Edison, and closer to home, Philadelphia Electric and Detroit Edison.

So, in early 1919, Insull sent a four-man team from Commonwealth Edison down the street to Peoples Gas. In addition to his private secretary, George Mitchell, Insull engaged his top engineer, Fred Sargent; his troubleshooter, Charles Munroe; and his public-relations ace, Bernard Mullaney. Mullaney's first message to the downtrodden employees was that the Great Man was about to arrive.

Job one was to ditch the status quo. Insull halved his salary and reduced pay for the others at the top. An *Insullization* program commenced. Management responsibilities were streamlined toward relatively strong middle management. Renegotiated contracts cut operating expenses. New financing strategies were implemented, and a public-relations drive began to rebrand "probably the least popular utility in the state." Last but not least, the $1 million tax bill was magically tabled after, in a colleague's words, "Mr. Insull spoke to some of his political friends."

In 1919, Peoples Gas broke even for the first time in three years, the result of $2 million in increased revenue and $1 million in reduced cost from the prior year. But the company was losing money on both appliance sales and office rentals, and sustained profitability required a fundamental shift toward lower-cost (manufactured) gas.

A Fisk Station for gas was badly needed long term. Short term, a solution to rising production costs was found in the Chicago sky, which was illuminated at night by flared industrial waste gases. Dump gas could be captured and sold cheaply, so Insull and Charles Munroe entered into purchase contracts with Wisconsin Steel Company, Mark Manufacturing Company, and Inland Steel by pipeline. Substituting away from higher-priced internally generated gas with the formerly waste gas was enough to make Peoples Gas profitable in 1920 and again in 1921.

The second breakthrough came with a $20 million state-of-the-art gas-manufacturing plant completed in 1922. Bank negotiations for financing failed, but Insull got an audience in Pittsburg with Andrew Mellon, whose riches from both Gulf Oil and Aluminum Corporation of America enabled him to personally commit $13 million to launch the project. The new plant brought the latest technology and scale economies into play, and a six-year payout left the plant as wholly owned property of Peoples Gas. Insull in later years gave special thanks to the man whose large bet had "made it possible for me to reorganize"—Andrew Mellon, now secretary of the treasury.

By 1922, sales and revenues had increased one-third and 80 percent, respectively, from prewar 1914. Lower costs and rates kept profits steady and customers content. A "courtesy campaign" improved public relations too. On all fronts, Insullization had made the jump from electricity to gas.

Employee perquisites pioneered at Commonwealth Edison were put in place at Peoples Gas. The Peoples Gas Club mirrored the Edison Club. Employees of both companies enjoyed the same spacious lunchroom downtown. Insull would describe the esprit de corps at Peoples Gas as the best; after all, this company's workforce knew what it was like to be at the bottom, unlike their counterparts at Insull's other companies.

In 1926, Insull described a company that was profitable enough to reinstate the dividend. In two years, the payout was raised to 8 percent, an all-time high. Progress continued "towards putting this property into a very substantial and conservative position." Insull was applauded for the "long hours" and for the "great genius for small details and great essentials" that had turned the company around.

Figure 4.4 Samuel Insull's prewar work with Peoples Gas Light & Coke Company turned into a full effort to save the company after World War I. By 1926, the company's stock dividend had been restored, and Peoples Gas was a healthy manufacturer and distributor of coal gas.

In his 1928 address to stockholders, Insull spoke triumphantly: "Our institution has regained its credit," he boasted. "It has reestablished itself as one of the leading gas companies in the country." And perhaps the best of all, "our

name has altogether disappeared from the front page of the newspapers."
Customer complaints against Peoples Gas were no longer newsworthy!

Stockholders who paid $29 per share for Peoples Gas near the bottom saw
their investment soar into the hundreds before the Roaring Twenties played
out. Even when the stock collapsed in mid-1932, it was still more than double
the price at which Insull began the rescue.

·∾·

While righting his company, Insull labored to right the industry. In a 1921 key-
note to the American Gas Association in 1921 in Chicago, Insull challenged his
new industry to upgrade to electricity's engineering and managerial standards.
"The electric men have beaten you in the race for brains," Insull stated. "We
need a decided improvement in engineering," whereby scaled-up plants would
give gas a "first class scrap pile."

Unsophisticated flat rates had to be replaced by two-part rates reflecting
customer usage between peak and average demand—what he had gotten the
electricity industry to do a quarter century before. "Unfair" flat rates created an
"economic absurdity" that hurt both the seller and the buyer. "Fair" rates would
"square the rights of the public with those of the stockholder."

New thinking and proper execution promised lower costs and steady
rates—and less political fighting. The future of the industry lay in lower, not
higher, rates, Insull intoned. All this was part of a new philosophy about
public-utility service, under which one needed to scrap not only equipment but
also "obsolete ideas."

The new thinking needed to be imparted throughout the company. "Our
first duty is to see to it that everybody in our organizations, from the man at the
top to the girl at the cash window or the boy who delivers the bills, is so educated
in the fundamentals of our business that he will carry a message of good will ...
to the whole of our respective communities." Insull offered the ambassadors a
slogan: "You can do it better with gas."

Addressing the AGA in Chicago again in 1927, the emerging Great Man of
gas cautioned his brethren about the work remaining before manufactured gas
could justify its self-proclaimed status as the *ultimate* and *universal* fuel. The
kitchen stove and home water heater, responsible for much of the
half-trillion-cubic-foot annual market, hardly constituted a universal fuel. Gas
from coal needed to replace straight coal burning in heating and industrial
markets—no small task. The answer would come in *natural* gas, something that
Insull did not envision.[10] In fact, Insull saw natural gas as but a bridge to

---

10. "It is estimated that eventually a large portion of the natural gas will be replaced by
manufactured gas, as the natural gas fields become depleted," Insull stated in his 1927
address.

manufactured gas, given the relative plentifulness of coal. In fact, natural gas would prove superabundant under market incentives.

Public Service Northern Illinois: Measured Progress

Public Service Company of Northern Illinois, formed in 1911 to power the countryside in response to Samuel Insull's phenomenally successful Lake County Experiment, emerged intact from World War I. By 1923, the year in which Britton Budd became president and Insull chairman of the board, Public Service with its 150,000-plus electricity customers, was entering a rarified realm: superpower. Public Service also distributed manufactured gas to 87,000 customers.

Compared to a decade earlier (1914), revenue in 1923 was $16 million (versus $6 million); peak load, 110 MW (31 MW); sendout, 350 million kWh (versus 120 million kWh); and total customers from all business lines, 255,000 (versus 112,000). Public Service had 3,764 employees and 18,889 stockholders compared to fewer than two thousand of each a decade earlier.

Public Service's area—6,000 square miles—encompassed 195 communities, about 11 percent of Illinois. The company's four modern steam coal plants replaced 60 isolated plants, 5 of which survived only in standby mode. Twelve pounds of coal per kWh in the shuttered plants now averaged 2.5 pounds. Sendout was mainly for lighting and concentrated between the hours of 5 p.m. and 11 p.m.

Samuel Insull was fond of speaking at Public Service gatherings. "I look forward year after year to these meetings," he allowed. "They are a matter of great pride to me, that my associates and myself should have been able to create this great business in which so many people are so happily engaged." Employees were content and energized by a series of perquisites that Insull had pioneered at Commonwealth Edison. A group insurance plan came first, followed by a savings fund and a pension plan. An Employee Benefit Program allowed dues-paying members to receive disability protection and purchase company stock at a discount. Social and athletic programs (including a Rod & Gun Club) were part of company life too.

Company ownership by employees was only the start. When Insull tabled a request for needed capital because of borrowing constraints, his Joliet district manager secured permission to sell Public Service preferred stock to his customers. Its successful placement was the beginning of "a major innovation in corporate finance" as Insull took note and set up securities marketing divisions at Public Service and his other companies.[11] Thousands

---

11. In 1928, a new corporation, Utility Securities Company, consolidated the operations of the served companies.

Figure 4.5 Public Service Company of Northern Illinois, founded in 1911 to serve rural areas in the state, was the one company Insull started from scratch. In the 1920s, it offered its 6,000-square-mile territory city-like electricity services.

of new employee owners enlisted tens of thousands of customer owners during the 1920s. "By 1930, a million people would own the Insull companies," McDonald noted.

Networked Power

Insull's central-station model began in Chicago's Inner Loop and spread throughout the city. The suburbs followed. Rural electrification came next, abutting the city-and-suburb network with farm-and-village service. By 1921, 10,000 Illinois farms had the electricity services hitherto enjoyed only by city dwellers, bringing 87 percent of the state's generating capacity under "group management." In so doing, Commonwealth Edison's 200-mile system directly or indirectly linked with most of the 8,800 miles of electrified area in Illinois.

Central electricity service also predominated in Indiana (83 percent), Michigan (78 percent), Ohio (88 percent), and Wisconsin (86 percent). The five states'

Figure 4.6 Interconnected grids (lower left and right) in Illinois and surrounding areas were a further advance of the Edison/Insull central-station model. Higher transmission costs (as with the 132,000-volt line shown bottom center) were more than offset by lower generation costs from scale economics and an improved load factor from greater usage diversity.

85 percent put the region's electrification well above average for a nation that in the early 1920s was just one-third electrified (6.3 million of 20.5 million dwellings served).

With the cities served and farm villages consolidating around a central plant and transmission system, it was only a matter of time until the properties began to interconnect. The Insull-pioneered Big Company, also known as the *super-power*, or *superutility*, led the way.[12] Insull's holdings in Illinois and Indiana became the nation's first integrated supergrid, or what was called the "gridironed" system by Charles Steinmetz, the German-American electricity inventor who foresaw an ocean-to-ocean power network.

---

12. Insull defined "the Superpower idea" (which he dated to about 1911) as "the transfer of loads from small uneconomical industrial plants and by the development of large, modern, highly efficient steam-turbine stations and the large development of waterpower by the central-station companies."

Chicago was "the center of a great 'pool of power,' with large and economical electric generation stations [in] a 'Superpower Ring'." The nexus was a 132,000-volt line connecting Chicago Edison Company to Public Service Company of Northern Illinois. An Interchange Energy Contract between these two companies and Northern Indiana Gas and Electric Corporation allowed each superutility to maintain a smaller reserve margin (surplus of standby generation to sendout) than would otherwise be the case.[13]

The "electric belt" reduced costs while improving reliability. Generation outages in one area could be made up by another. Power could be purchased rather than generated at any point on the system according to momentary advantage. More connections improved rates and service for all—the phenomenon of network economies.

A nearly 50 percent drop in investment per maximum load between 1908 and 1920 was due to higher volume, an improved diversity factor, and system integration. Insull wanted more. "No doubt the day is not far distant when this business of electric distribution will be just as much a universal business as the telephone business is today."

With his companies reaching into 15 states, Insull envisioned an *Atlantic Coast Superpower* that could apply the Illinois/Indiana model to the well-populated eastern seaboard. He envisioned hundreds of millions of dollars of annual savings from network economies whereby more efficient generation, requiring less coal input and less capital investment, could follow a larger, more diverse load. One central plant with state-of-the-art transmission could reach almost 200 communities, providing service to clusters of 50 dwellings here or 100 there—a major advance from the early years, when an electrical system served one square mile. "Nature takes no account of political barriers or imaginary lines," Insull noted, and technology was now nature.

"We are now getting well into the third stage of public-utility development, which is marked by still further concentration in production and still wider distribution," Insull announced in 1921. Such was the new world of electricity that Samuel Insull was accelerating through his companies—and industry-wide through his trade association activities.

The superpower network was anchored on hard assets, fundamental economics, and consumer preference. It was substance first, far different from the vaporous claims of an integrated natural gas-and-electricity network made eight decades later by a New Economy energy company: Enron (1986–2001).

---

13. The annual report explained: "By means of this contract, the systems of the three companies are operated to some extent in conjunction, so that the reserve capacity in any one station … can be made available to relieve a lack of capacity in any other station, while, during certain hours, the load of less efficient stations can be transferred to stations having a higher efficiency."

The latter, a self-styled "logistics company," was playing a regulatory high card via government-directed access to interstate gas transportation and electricity transmission.[14] Mandatory open access created new competitive space for independent (non-transmission-owning) companies to buy and sell the commodity unbundled from transportation. The spot market revolution with gas and electricity was the result.

Middle West Utilities: Going National

Middle West Utilities Company was established in 1912 to bring electricity to rural America outside the territory served by Public Service Company of Northern Illinois. Samuel Insull's Lake County experiment demonstrated how scale economies could profitably replace isolated town-sized plants with long-distance transmission from massed production. Two new holding companies were the result.

By World War I, Middle West operated in 13 Midwest and New England states. With brother Martin Insull ably in charge,[15] the geographically diversified holding company attracted capital for consolidation and expansion that otherwise would have been absent—or certainly slower in coming. The enterprise was profitable, and country life was enhanced with citylike electricity.

Middle West grew rapidly after the war as the result of property purchases, extending distribution from existing properties, and increasing sendout to existing customers. By 1924, the company had more than doubled its size and sales from five years earlier, with earnings increasing to $41 million from $15 million. The company touted its "stability of earnings due to the widely diversified business served by the companies." Electricity was foremost, but gas was important, followed by smaller water, streetcar, and ice service. These sidelines were not particularly profitable, however.

By 1924, Middle West's network covered "virtually a third of the states of the Union, reaching from New England across the Middle West into the valley of the Platte and from Canada's door on the North to the meeting place of new and old civilizations at the Mexico border."[16] "Superpower plans" began to emerge from the "knitting together of the companies' production and

---

14. Mandatory open access as a regulatory program is described in chapter 9, p. 347, and placed in historical context in the Epilogue, pp. 508–509.

15. Martin Insull, the "driving force" behind Middle West, was also described by Forrest McDonald as "long on enthusiasm and imagination and short on practicality and toughmindedness," although in his brother's eyes, he "could do no wrong."

16. The states were Illinois, Indiana, Kentucky, Maine, Michigan, Missouri, Nebraska, New Hampshire, New York, Oklahoma, Tennessee, Texas, Vermont, Virginia, and Wisconsin. Four states—Arkansas, Kansas, Louisiana, and Mississippi—would join the fold a year later.

transmission systems and similar projects of other companies on every side." Huge 33,000-volt and 66,000-volt steel towers, part of $27 million in new construction for 1924 alone, interconnected Middle West's 915 areas to 290 outside communities.

In 1924, a Public Relations Department was founded to educate and inspire employees and better communicate with the company's half-million customers. Community relations were vital, since Middle West's subsidiaries were, in Insull's words, "largely non-competitive and subject to public regulation," necessitating "an intelligent, friendly, well-informed public opinion." Federal regulation of the interstate company would come later.

A Women's Public Information Committee was formed the same year at Middle West to better serve the interests of a burgeoning female workforce. The perquisites enjoyed by employees at Insull's other companies were adopted, such as a retirement annuity program in 1925.

·◌·

Rapid growth in the next years integrated small towns "frequently handicapped by the absence of a diversified demand and by inability to meet the service requirement of the larger industrial users." The success of Insull's massing model was evidenced by a growing junk pile (as Insull liked to characterize it) of 350 isolated plants. Increased sales and a better matching of demand to capacity (an increased load factor) brought overall rates down.

Such economies also brought into play the latest in generation technology, which reduced coal usage per kWh, such as a one-third-pound drop in 1927 from the year before. A bigger electricity family was a more efficient, prosperous one.

In 1925, purchases of several multistate companies brought the state count to 19, with a 50 percent jump in communities served, reaching almost 1,500. No cities were in this mix; the niche continued to be "the average electrical customers in the average American community."

In 1927, Middle West reached 2,000 communities and surpassed one million customers. "Instead of the user coming to the power, the power must seek out the user," Middle West's annual report explained. The company's Industrial Development Department marketed "the advantage of breaking away from congested centers into smaller communities where living costs, land cost and production costs can be considerably reduced." Attracting industrial demand to complement residential/farm usage set the "groundwork ... for an equalization of the industrial possibility of city and country."

The year 1928 marked the most growth of all. Capacity of 1,153 MW generated 1,153 billion kWh sent over 27,751 miles of transmission lines to 1,587,907 customers in 3,679 communities in 29 states (ten more than just two years earlier). Aggressive investment and falling rates (8.3 cents per kWh, 15 percent below that in 1922) accompanied and, indeed, contributed to this growth.

Profits in 1928 reached $150 million, almost three-fourths of which was attributable to electricity. (The balance came from manufactured gas, transportation, ice, and water services.) Middle West's 263,000 owners benefitted from appreciating stock and a dividend increase to $7 a share. The 1928 annual report envisioned universal electric service for the countryside, which "may fairly be called one of the turning points of American economic development."

There would be one more expansion year, in 1929, before growth slowed and then ceased during America's Great Depression. But what a run it had been: from 600 miles of transmission at the beginning to 40,000 miles—"one and one-half times the circumference of the earth." The private sector's push for rural electrification would be forgotten as electrifying the countryside became a political issue during the New Deal, specifically with the creation of the Rural Electrification Administration in 1935.

Still, a boom had occurred in rural electrification from profitable private activity at no cost or risk to taxpayers. Middle West acknowledged the social good following the private good ("such accomplishments invite the most attractive prophecies of future social effects," noted Insull). The Great Depression—which became Great as the 1930s wore on, due to unprecedented government intervention—not only arrested the progress of self-interested rural power service but also would prove to be the undoing of Samuel Insull himself, the story of the next chapter.

From Edison Spirit to Welfare Capitalism

Commonwealth Edison's workplace progressivism is noteworthy in the annals of American business. Insull's *Edison spirit* evolved into a multidimensional, perquisite-rich corporate culture that set a standard for its day and exemplified "welfare capitalism."[17]

There is little evidence that Insull's largesse came at the expense of profits. Insull's corporate programs "resulted in important economies in the cost of employee turnover, and in a higher efficiency of the working force by virtue of increased average length of training and experience," noted one historian of Commonwealth Edison. This company was regarded as the premium employer in Chicago and in the industry. Insull's innovation, experimentation, and one-upmanship also gave allure to Public Service Company of Northern Illinois and, as the 1920s went on, Peoples Gas.

Insull's workplace in the first decades of the century presaged what Ken Lay championed in Enron's heyday later in the century. But Lay was never in a league with Samuel Insull, despite their notable parallels, including both men's role advancing the socioeconomic system of political capitalism.

Samuel Insull was the great corporate doer and communicator. The Edison of the business side of electricity inspired his own thousands. His teachings

---

17. Insull's *Edison spirit* is also discussed in chapter 3, pp. 130–34. *Welfare capitalism* refers to the strategy of business leaders to offer employees fringe benefits to increase loyalty, improve productivity, and discourage unionism.

reached the whole industry via the National Electric Light Association and through Commonwealth Edison's popular magazine, *Edison Round Table*. The Great Man's oeuvre about business and life reached the wider public with his speeches to financial groups, local Chicago organizations, colleges and universities, and even high schools. The educator, master motivator, and perquisite pioneer sought no less than to revolutionize his industries—first electricity and then gas. Every citizen was a customer, after all, and every industry member a potential employee. All were potential stockholders.

Smilesian/Insullian Man

Insull "set out to create a new kind of employee, a kind that would be styled the organization man." Insullian man began with Samuel Smiles, the self-help missionary whose books exhorted diligence, perseverance, and other Victorian principles as the foundation of workplace success.[18] Insull sought to remake employees in his own image. Time and again, he shared his example of starting on the bottom, encountering hard knocks, learning new skills, seizing opportunities, and, in the end, "making two blades of grass grow where one grew before." And work? It was nothing for the Great Man to give talks and preside over stockholder meetings at three companies in the same day.

Insull was the quintessential self-made man. "Horatio Alger, discoverer of the most respected American pattern, would not have changed a word in the autobiographical sketch that Samuel Insull presents now and then to his intimate audiences," a 1926 profile concluded in the *New York Times Magazine*. "The Insull story and the Alger formula agree precisely: Lowly beginning, painstaking devotion to humble tasks, promotion, fidelity to the boss, and success."

For Insull, self-education and practical training trumped formalities. He found it "pathetic" that "the young man or young woman, thirsting to improve himself or herself, should fill the classes of educational institutions which can give them only a purely academic education." Insull warned his flock not to be intimidated by degreed colleagues or those sporting superior intelligence. "The men I know who have gone ahead faster have been just normal fellows," Insull opined. "Near-geniuses have a way of getting tangled up in the special limitations which brilliant people so often seem to have." Echoing the verdict of his mentor Thomas Edison, Insull went a step further: "My experience is that most of the men in our organization who have 'superior intelligence' are a confounded nuisance." All this was in Smiles, for whom perseverance trumped genius and luck.[19]

---

18. For Samuel Smiles's influence on Insull, see *Capitalism at Work*, p. 39.

19. For more of Insull's views on education and other areas such as government, thrift, and work, see Internet appendix 4.3, "Insull's Views: Some Quotations" at www.politicalcapitalism. org/Book2/Chapter4/Appendix3.html.

Figure 4.7 In his many lectures (most collected and reprinted in book form), Insull spoke the Victorian platitudes about character and success, while also presenting technical diagrams about supply, demand, and efficiency in the electricity business.

A close cousin to genius was arrogance, which Insull saw as a threat to a company's hard-earned good public standing. Insull knew that bad service or bad relations in a monopoly industry such as his would translate into consumer-qua-voter unrest—and troublesome politics. Insull feared what in the post-Enron vernacular would be called the *smartest-guys-in-the-room* problem. "It is a very mistaken idea to imagine for one moment that simply because you are working for a big corporation you can afford to boss it over the rest of the community," he explained. "Exaggerated ego" had to be replaced by a customer-first, respectful mentality.

Employees revered their no-nonsense boss, who arrived early, left late, and could dismiss a worker who failed to properly greet him or who was not punctual ("I had to fire that boy," he once said of an assistant who violated this 100 percent rule). Although formal, polite, and empathetic, Insull was also nervous, hurried, and impatient—even brusque, blunt, and demanding. It came with the superhuman pace that Insull subjected himself to—and thrived under.

But Insull's empathetic side grew over time, in part because of age; he entered his seventh decade the day the armistice ending World War I was signed. His evolution also reflected his 21 months running the State Council of Defense of Illinois, where all were equal in cause (the war) and in pay (nothing). Formalities and hierarchy meant little to his unpaid army, the guts and glory of winning the war on Illinois's home front.

"After the war [Insull] began to exhibit a new kind of paternal attitude toward his employees," noted McDonald. Insull's "strictly business" approach had excluded almost all personal communication beneath his direct reports. This changed as "his employees were as much as part of his family as his brothers and sisters had been, as important to him as his wife and son."

Insull's speeches increasingly pivoted to the big picture. "We have got something beyond the mere question of money making," Insull intoned to his employees. "We have helped to point the way to supply humanity with a product that will add to their comfort, lessen the cost of the things that they consume, and make life on the whole happier than it was at the start." His message for all: "My greatest ambition is to see everybody connected with me get a real chance in life." Little wonder that Insull would be credited with "develop[ing] more successful executives than any other man in this country."

Perquisites

Commonwealth Edison had set the pace by introducing an Employee Thrift Plan in 1909 and a Service Annuity System (aka retirement, or pension, plan) three years later. In the postwar period, the Commonwealth Edison Mutual Benefit Association offered death and disability benefits for its several thousand members, which was about half of the workforce. Group rates reduced coverage costs at more than threefold compared to retail policies, as the company found out on a smaller scale when employees were offered life insurance in lieu of their traditional holiday turkey. It was not until 1921, a year after the Association was formed, that employees voted out turkeys in favor of coverage between $500 and $1,500, depending on length of service. This annual perk could accumulate to make the surviving family "pretty independent" and "a long way from the poorhouse," Insull estimated. He considered at least $8,000 respectable in this regard.

Savings, retirement income, and insurance all promoted the Smilesian virtues of thrift and prudence—and the freedom of action and peace of mind that came with financial security. "I do not know why it is, but I seldom get on my feet on an occasion of this kind without talking about saving money," Insull remarked once to his employees. The answer was that he knew that Smiles was right.

·◌·

In 1919, Commonwealth Edison founded the Edison Club "to create a feeling of good fellowship among its members and to promote a spirit of loyalty toward the company." The club's several thousand members enjoyed dances and other social outings, a guest speaker program on electricity, and educational classes.

In 1921, the club began interdepartmental competitions, replete with handsome trophies, in golf, tennis, bowling, and riflery either during the evening or on Saturday afternoon.

In 1923, Commonwealth Edison, Public Service, and Peoples Gas Light jointly refurbished a lakeside Wisconsin resort about a hundred miles northwest of Chicago. At nominal charge, employees could get, per Insull, "a little country air at a time of their annual vacation." The Lake Delavan Resort's hotel, cottages, and swimming, boating, fishing, and camping facilities (capacity: 400) were for all employees and their relatives. "We want the girls to go there," Insull explained, and "want to get as near a family affair as we possibly can."

Figure 4.8 Social activities at Insull's companies set the standard for the day, whether baseball at Commonwealth Edison (upper left); activity at Lake Delavan (upper right); or a social night at Chicago's Medinah Temple (center). Dean of Women Helen Norris (lower left) regulated the interaction between the sexes in the workplace. The Insull Medal (lower right) was awarded to industry workers who brought back to life those who had been electrocuted.

The owners described the purchase to shareholders as providing "healthy recreation [for employees] at comparatively small cost." In one speech, "Just as One Friend to Another," Insull explained the vacation experience as a means to "build up your health resources" and as "a help in building up the acquaintanceship, friendship, and fellowship of our institutions."

Another perk saved time and improved communications for employees: a company cafeteria (called self-serve restaurant) in the Edison building. Such was another pillar of what Forrest McDonald called Insull's "group consciousness."

Insull-style corporate culture included the fine arts. "I am a great believer in the general cultural development of our people," he stated in a 1926 address. "[I] try to inculcate into [our people's] minds a love of good music, a love of the good things of life." Commonwealth Edison sponsored employee plays ("dramatic entertainments") and musical productions. The Edison Symphony Orchestra "made for itself a distinct place in the musical world of Chicago." As inspiration for these amateurs and all employees, Insull "democratize[d] opera in Chicago" by hosting Sunday night performances at nominal charge.

⌁

Employee empowerment was part of Insull's postwar drive to break down hierarchy and improve worker satisfaction and productivity. Insull's open-door policy had practical limitations, so a Department of Industrial Relations was established in 1920 to promote "harmonious relations between the employees and the management of the company." Staffed by labor professionals, the department issued an Employee Representation Plan the next year "to insure fairness and justice to the employees, the management, the stockholders, and the public." Grievances went through a committee process, with the final court of appeals being Samuel Insull himself.

Employee input on major labor and management issues led to a reduction in the formal workweek by two and one-half hours, "a change that was joyfully received by the employees." But this was afforded by the increasing productivity of a workforce empowered by increasing investment, not the simple act of the request itself.

The Department of Industrial Relations was a center for other employee programs and initiatives. An "Americanization program" at the Fisk Street Station helped employees achieve U.S. citizenship (as Insull himself had in 1896), which was a requirement to receive company benefits, with certain exceptions. Insull urged employees to use the department to team together to reduce the cost of home ownership. He also asked employees to keep their homes tidy to help impress the neighbors and public about the company they worked for. ("I am a great believer in smartness of appearance," he would say. "Your mental attitude toward our customers will be reflected in your mental attitude when you get home with the family and among your friends and acquaintances.")

An Employee Suggestion Plan (1910), which awarded small cash prizes for money-saving, efficiency-enhancing ideas, continued in the 1920s. "If every employee will think of the problems encountered in his work, analyze the conditions and make concrete and constructive suggestions, it will be a great help to the management of the company in the conduct of its affairs and will give the employees a chance to present their plans to the management."

Women in Commonwealth Edison's workforce quintupled during World War I. After the war, with the men back, many ladies reverted to homemaker, as was customary. But a barrier had been broken (as with black employees during wartime), and single women in entry-level positions became a rite of passage to marriage and homemaking, a strategy that Insull fondly spoke to in his speeches.[20]

The growing importance of women was reflected in the new department whose a Dean of Women reported to the Manager of Industrial Relations. In the same period, the Woman's Public Information Committee was formed for Commonwealth Edison's thousand female workers, and a woman employee society, Electra, was organized. A special lounge area was set aside for women, a far cry from just years before when the 18-story Edison headquarters had just one ladies room.

Vocational training was integral to Insull's view of self-help. The Chicago Central Station Institute, founded by Commonwealth Edison in 1913, offered 27 courses utilized by hundreds of employees. Commonwealth Edison's library and reading room contained 3,500 books and 80 periodicals. Essay contests with prizes were held. Americanization classes helped make English a second language for some employees.

Health and safety were another part of Insull's self-interested progressivism. "The greatest nuisance is the sick employee," Insull complained. (Insull himself was rarely ill but took trips abroad to fight exhaustion.) "The first thing is to take care of your health," Insull implored employees, adding: "Sickness as a rule in probably 90 percent of the cases is avoidable if a man will learn how to take care of himself." An on-site medical department and a visiting nurse reduced lost work time by employees at Commonwealth Edison.

Company safety was emphasized. Insull protégé Britton Budd said it best to his employees at Public Service: "No organization that has unsafe practices, unsafe methods, which resulted in accidents, and maybe in loss of life, or the crippling of some of the employees, is efficient."

In 1922, at Insull's suggestion and with his funding, NELA began awarding the Insull Medal for Resuscitation to industry employees who saved electric-shock victims. As part of this effort, an industry-wide campaign taught the prone-pressure method of resuscitation. By 1932, some 400 "meritorious cases" were documented for the award. The Insull Medal was the second such initiative by the Great Man of his industry, the first being the 1914 Franklin Medal, awarded

---

20. In one 1923 talk to employees, Insull implored the ladies to marry a man "inside of the building" rather than outside because "the fellows inside are a better class." On another occasion, Insull spoke about "the opportunities for every young man and every young woman … whether you look at it from a business or domestic point of view."

annually by Philadelphia's Franklin Institute to the researcher who had done the most to advance knowledge in the fields of physical science or technology.

✧

As elsewhere, Insull set the pace. Only occasionally did he have to catch up to another company's initiative (which he did quickly). Such competition made other companies both inside and outside the public-utility field uncomfortable. "Insull's employee relations program—prewar and postwar—was ill-designed to win him imitators and admirers amongst the moneyed," Forrest McDonald. "Most frowned upon such innovations as too generous, too personal, or simply dangerous."

But impressing and rewarding the workforce were handmaidens to capitalist progress, resulting from firms that competed against each other for the best employees. If higher costs could be offset with greater output—as was the case at Insull's enterprises—there could be little doubt that Insull's progressivism benefitted company owners too.

Showered with perquisites, including incentives to own shares in their own company, "Insull men developed an *esprit de corps* seldom equaled in modern industrial history." But an obligation came with it. Setting the example, Insull expected employees to perform community service on their own time. "No top-ranking employee was safe in his job unless he was actively and conspicuously engaged in such work," Forrest McDonald noted.[21] After all, they "worked for the best public service organization in the world." As Insull made clear, they were in the public-utility business—and thus were quasi–public servants whose goodwill in the community meant better relations with local government and at the public-utility commission.

Decades later, Ken Lay at Enron would impose the same obligations on his executives in return for showering them with financial incentives and perks. This quid pro quo was seen as mutually reinforcing, with external goodwill translating into internal success. But at Enron, it would turn out to be unsustainable without the business profitability behind it.

Managing Regulation

The father of modern electricity was also the father of public-utility regulation of the industry. Samuel Insull's 1898 speech before the NELA began a successful multidecade crusade to convince the industry to accept rate regulation in return for franchise protection. It worked, as state after state replaced local regulation with statewide public utility control.

---

21. "Throughout the twenties Insull men were in the center or at the top of virtually every important community service activity in Chicago, and they continued to be so long after Insull was gone."

In 1914, "one of [Insull's] greatest political accomplishments" came into being: the Illinois Public Utility Commission (now the Illinois Commerce Commission). Formal public-utility regulation voided a pernicious Chicago city rate ordinance passed the prior year, which itself had replaced a 1908 city ordinance. It was the threat of arbitrary edicts from lower political jurisdictions that drove Insull to champion statewide cost-of-service regulation.

In the 1920s, Insull continued to push tirelessly his four interrelated political and regulatory themes: the capriciousness of local regulation, the inefficacy of municipalization, the inadvisability of open free-market competition ("regulation by competition"), and the desirability of state-level public-utility regulation. In the same period, federal authorities became interested in industry affairs, creating another political front for Insull.

Home-rule regulation was the least-liked policy alternative. With hundreds of political jurisdictions within his service territories, Insull faced death by a thousand cuts. "The demagogue plays upon the prejudices and weaknesses of the unthinking," Insull complained, resulting "if unchecked … [in] hostile legislation or unfair regulatory restrictions."

The imposition of arbitrary rate ceilings by city authorities was a thorn in the side of Commonwealth Edison despite its history of rate reductions. The proposals "become more of an absurdity day by day," Insull complained, the untruths, half-truths, and divisive rhetoric coming from "people who are … in the business of tearing down what others construct and adapt the 'holier-than-thou' attitude toward all the rest of the world."

Municipalization, while not rejected per se (Insull favored this alternative over pure competition), was an increasing threat to the investor-owned utilities, including Insull's own. But the Chief employed a counterstrategy to beat the socialists at their own game: employee and customer stock ownership. Mass ownership was explained strategically:

> What I am deliberately after is public ownership. Not municipal ownership, but public ownership, that will result in a vast army of stockholders … to stand guard over their own property. When the junior securities of all these local public utilities are owned by the people themselves, as individuals, you will hear less about attacks upon public utility interests, and you will find that the senior securities we have put out will be very desirable collateral.

So if the Public Ownership League of America threatened to municipalize an Insull property in such a way as to eviscerate value, an army of stockholders would have to be placated. If the Illinois Commerce Commission deviated from allowing the recovery of prudent costs and a reasonable rate of return, Insull had the takings clause (Fifth Amendment) of the Constitution for legal redress, as well as self-interested public opinion favoring fairness.

What about the *nonregulated* alternative whereby terms of service and entry were determined by the market? "No monopoly should be trusted to run itself," claimed Insull, drawing upon the textbook view that natural monopolies are inefficient in the short run and exploitive in the longer run. Unfettered competition was seen as economically irrational: "I know of no greater financial crime than to spread along the streets of any city … investment duplicated to afford exactly the same class of service," he opined.

A tension, even contradiction, resided in Insull's rejection of free-market competition. His business model—consolidating the industry and preventing duplicate facilities—was the antithesis of natural monopoly. (Insull called natural concentration "economic law.") There was no *long run* where rates were jacked up by the *natural monopolist*. The Insullian central-station model and his business philosophy of more sales, greater diversity, less cost, and lower rates precluded irrationality, although market entry might seem that way to an entrenched monopolist.[22]

The tension between Insull in theory and in practice was one argument in favor of free-market electricity provision. Another problem was his naïveté that public-service commissions would be apolitical and able to objectively ascertain just-and-reasonable rates.

As early as 1915, Insull worried about the "new element" of politics. "Laws are getting more strict, and regulation is getting closer," he warned, which might "check enterprise and destroy individuality in management." Might "we … [drift] to a species of paternalism which will end in our simply fulfilling our allotted task and being satisfied with just what we have today, forgetful of the fact that the electricity-supply business is relatively a new industry?" During World War I, in fact, state commissions fell behind in their duties and caused severe financial problems for electric utilities, which led Insull to declare: "Control of public utilities by means of state regulation is at a crisis in Illinois."

Future decades would give credence to Insull's early fears that his vision of "calm, scientific, and just regulation" would distort incentives. But more than that, state regulation would increasingly turn on politics in unintended ways, as he would unpleasantly discover. Insull's "oaks-from-acorn affair" involved one Frank L. Smith, the chairman of the Illinois Commerce Commission, who ran against incumbent William McKinley for an Illinois Senate seat in 1926.[23]

Insull, who spread his bets with campaign contributions to different and sometimes opposing candidates, went "overboard" with a generous six-figure donation to Smith. This was not because the commissioner had done any special regulatory

---

22. Also see the Epilogue's discussion of Insull's antimarket political program, pp. 499–500.

23. The complicated politics resulting in the Smith imbroglio, which required 15 pages of explanation by Insull biographer Forrest McDonald, is only sketched here.

favors for the giver; he had not. The largesse came from Insull's animosity toward McKinley, the fellow who had irrationally blocked Public Service's consolidation drive some years before. Insull simply did not forget or forgive his opponents.

McKinley charged Insull with conspiring with Smith for out-of-sight favors for his regulated companies, an allegation that caught fire politically. A hearing in Chicago in the summer of 1926 found Insull on the defensive as the U.S. Senate probed into all his contributions. No smoking gun would be found, but the air of suspicion was red meat for "throngs of Democratic and Progressive politicians ... to reap their share of the political hay."

Smith would prevail in the election, but an inflamed U.S. Senate refused to seat him amid more charges and investigation about how the "power trust" corrupted the election process. "God only knows how many Senatorial campaigns Mr. Insull has financed," said Nebraska Senator George Norris.

So the carefully cultivated image of a business titan working for the common good was now undone as federal politics joined and even overtook local and state politics. But the worst was yet to come.

·❦·

Federal regulation of electricity did not exist in Insull's day, although industry issues from public power to interstate transmission piqued the interest of Washington, D.C. In 1920, with wartime shortages still remembered, the U.S. Geological Survey conducted a Super Power Survey with an eye to creating an integrated grid for the industrial Northeast from Boston to Washington, D.C. An advisory board of industry and government officials went so far as to recommend creating a Federal Super Power Corporation, which was opposed by the electricity industry when fully aired. With natural economics dictating interconnections, such as those pioneered by Insull's companies, central-government direction was superfluous at best—although it was natural for politicians to want cheaper power for all. The plan died in 1921.

In 1923, Secretary of Commerce Herbert Hoover resurrected a scaled-back version of Super Power, under which the government would provide expertise, leaving all business to the private sector. A Northeast Superpower Commission was established, and an engineering subcommittee mapped out a grand plan of new generating plants and new interconnections within the zone. Hoover's "voluntarism" or "associationalism" approach, the opposite of the government-centered Giant Power plan for Pennsylvania,[24] proved superfluous, given what firms were naturally doing and faded away.

---

24. A Giant Power interconnection plan for Pennsylvania was proposed in 1924 by Governor Gifford Pinchot and engineer Morris Cook whereby the state's Public Service Commission and a new Giant Power Board would direct the investment blueprint. The plan was rejected by the Pennsylvania legislature in 1926 and not resurrected in this state or elsewhere.

In 1925, interest in regulating the power industry began with a Senate Resolution, sponsored by Thomas Walsh, instructing the Federal Trade Commission (FTC) "to investigate ... and to report to the Senate the manner in which the General Electric Company has acquired and maintained such monopoly or exercises such control in restraint of trade or commerce and in violation of law." The first comprehensive government study of the U.S. electric industry, released two years later as a 272-page report, compared the entire investor-owned and municipal industry to the financial performance of General Electric. This company's 8 percent profit margin was not found to be particularly excessive, and the report did not reach any major policy conclusions.

In 1928, Senate Resolution No. 83 instructed the FTC to undertake a thorough study of the nation's gas and electric holding companies and draw conclusions for public policy.[25] Seven years and 101 volumes of testimony later, the verdict was in. Although some "real public benefits" of the holding-company structure and ownership concentration were cited—capital attraction, territorial diversification, economies of operation, rapid implementation of technological improvements, and timely service extensions—the alleged disadvantages carried the day, not only in the report but also in the popular press. The negatives included "excessive construction and management fees," "intercompany profits on transfers of properties or securities," "write-up's, improperly capitalized in-tangibles and inflation," "manipulation of stock-market prices," and "pyramiding in holding-company groups." The study concluded:

> The cumulative effect of some of these abuses undoubtedly resulted in the maintenance of higher than reasonable rates to the consumer and unfavorably affected the value of the securities in the hands of many investors. For these conditions the Commission concludes that a thoroughgoing reform is necessary in the intercorporate relations within the holding-company groups, in corporate and financial structure, in accounting practice, and in the extent and methods of public regulation.

This opened up a new front for hitherto local- and state-regulated electric utilities, and after 1928, Insull and the rest of the industry responded the only way they knew how: redoubling their public-education efforts on the home front and setting up shop in the nation's capital. Federal politics would be here to stay.

Leveraging Success

In 1926, British Prime Minister Stanley Baldwin invited Samuel Insull to return home as electricity czar to consolidate Britain's grid. Insull had long advocated

---

25. For the wording of the 1928 resolution, see Internet appendix 4.4, "Federal Trade Commission Investigation," at www.politicalcapitalism.org/Book2/Chapter4/Appendix4.html.

his massing model for the balkanized system, and the homecoming promised a grand finale for the 66-year-old. But Insull decided to stay put, in part to ensure that Samuel Jr., the rising star of his empire, could take over where he left off.

"I think I'm going to establish a dynasty, and thereby render myself immortal," Insull confided to a friend, and who was to caution the Great Man? Six individuals who "Insull had made a part of himself" and had served "not as brakes but as regulators" were no longer. Billy Beale, his legal eagle and chief protector, the "one man who could say no and make it stick," had died in 1923. Wife Gladys, once so important, was estranged from Samuel. Her absent affections, in fact, made his business ambitions that much more unquenchable. Accountant Arthur Young, the man who transformed Insull's complexity into balanced books, was dead, as were political operative Roger Sullivan, coal man Frank Peabody, and rural-electrification expert Frank Baker.

Some remained, such as the "banker's banker" John Mitchell, Chicago's best, and second only to Beale as an Insull confidant. But the new talent, a generation below the Great Man, was deferential. None emerged as the *impartial observer* that Adam Smith identified as crucial to help the successful man stay that way.

So Insull responded imprudently, if not recklessly, when a challenger to his grand plan emerged in the Roaring Twenties. His name was Cyrus Eaton, a successful operator of electric utilities whose accumulated properties put him in the rarified billion-dollar club. In addition to Eaton's holding company, Continental Gas and Electric, the "man of vast ambition and wily talent" started an investment trust, Continental Shares Limited, offering wealthy investors a higher-risk, higher-return alternative to bonds.

In 1927/28, Eaton began buying large blocks of common stock in the Big Four: Commonwealth Edison, Peoples Gas, Public Service, and Middle West. By mid-1928, Eaton's holdings were several times Insull's. Although not alarmed, Insull could not help but wonder whether a hostile takeover, aided or not by New York and J. P. Morgan & Company, might be in the offing.

Late in the summer of 1928, Insull got word that Eaton was increasing his holdings to 80,000 shares of Commonwealth Edison. Although Eaton said nothing when the two returned from Europe together on an ocean liner, Insull was sure that a raid was imminent.[26] So before the year was out, Insull founded Insull Utility Investments Company (IUI) "to perpetuate ... the existing management of the Insull group of utilities." The goal was for Samuel Insull and allies—led by wife Gladys, son Samuel, and brother Martin, bringing the all-in-the family stake to nearly $10 million—to buy enough shares via IUI to retain control of his operating companies. The Chief was

---

26. See Internet appendix 4.5, "Was Cyrus Eaton a Threat to Insull's Empire," at www.politicalcapitalism.org/Book2/Chapter4/Appendix5.html.

nearing 70; all knew that the "Insull group" was about Samuel Insull Jr., with some brother Martin thrown in.

Insull and friends traded their interests in the Big Four for IUI stock, which came to a book value of $7.54 per share. Market value, what forward-looking investors would pay for ISI common, included a goodwill premium for the Insull association. Also buoyed by the speculative fever of the day, par was $12 per share, a 60 percent premium to book.

Insull was not fond of speculative booms. "I want to see public-utility stocks sell on a fair investment basis," he had said in response to one bubble in his securities several years before, not on "the foolish predictions made recently by those interested in speculation." But he could only watch and wonder as the price of IUI common soared, peaking at $147 in August 1929. This made Insull a billionaire in today's dollars. But it complicated his antitakeover strategy by pricing out small investors who diversified and expanded IUI's capital base. At such a high share price, buyers were the investment-trust managers that Insull was trying to neutralize, including Cyrus Eaton.

Share values of the operating companies were also soaring, which meant higher costs for increased IUI ownership. But getting that money faced a legal quirk under Illinois law. Rather than selling more shares and cashing in on its own escalating stock price, IUI's charter required that new shares be sold first to existing shareholders at par.[27] This not only limited new capital but also opened the door for Eaton to buy preemptive rights at par to control IUI common.

Insull's solution was to start *another* investment company, one whose shares would be unrestricted and thus the vehicle for retaining Insull-led ownership of the three operating companies, holding-company Middle West Utilities, and IUI. Corporation Securities Company of Chicago (CSCC), also referred to as New Corp or just Corp, was formed on October 4, 1929. As before, Halsey, Stuart & Company, Chicago's premier investment banker, provided the services and participated in the investment.

⌁

"As the fall of 1929 approached, Insull's self-confidence was matched only by his strength and prestige," remarked biographer Forrest McDonald. Facing another difficulty in the summer of 1929 (just months before the market crash), Insull moved aggressively with more indebtedness.

Middle West Utilities, a holding company for numerous small utilities located throughout the United States, had been financed in the early 1920s

---

27. Insull himself referred to this feature of the stock as simply *pre-emptive rights*, saying: "Corporation Securities Company of Chicago was formed without pre-emptive rights." If the stockholders' rights were a matter of Illinois law, it is not clear how creating CSCC would have solved the problem.

when interest rates were high and preferred stocks had to pay a high dividend. Now, interest rates were low (reflecting the Federal Reserve Bank's expansionary monetary policy, a driver of speculation), and preferred stock was paying lower dividends. It was time for a thorough refinancing of Middle West, one that ended up making the holding company debt free.

Current shareholders were given the right to buy a new share at $200, which would then be split 10 for 1 to help common people become capitalists behind his empire. But Middle West was selling at $170, making the right to buy a new share at $200 noncompetitive.

To make a market, the investment bank Halsey Stuart began buying Middle West stock in mid-1929 for its own account and for the Insulls. By the end of July, the price of the stock was up to $310, whereupon Halsey Stuart ceased buying. By late September, Middle West reached $500 per share, seemingly reconfirming that all things Insull were golden. And that was not the only good news. The launch of CSCC was oversubscribed by 125,000 units (about 15 percent) at the opening per share price of $75. Salesmen pitches of "fine," "good," "safe," "sound" and "interest paying" resonated with the feverish public, as well as officers and salesmen of Halsey Stuart.

At the Peak

Samuel Insull in the 1920s "became the Babe Ruth, the Jack Dempsey, the Red Grange of the business world." Chicago's business titan became a national figure by dominating one of the very top U.S. industries, electricity, making a splash in gas, and participating in other public-utility fields. His magnanimity added to his stature, and his business and political expertise were welcomed by American presidents.

Despite his aversion to newspapers, interviews, and photographers, Insull was positively profiled in such national publications as *Financial World*, *New York Times Magazine*, *Saturday Evening Post*, and *McClure's*. "He has changed the light-and-power map of America," said one article, "and has made vital electrical history in this country." Chicago's "depository of power," said another, was all about creative construction, supersalesmanship, loyalty, and honesty— not selfishness and moneymaking for its own sake. Another described the "vivid career" of a man spanning public utilities, opera, politics, and farming.

Coverage of Insull in Chicago's multiple newspapers, however, was less cordial. Populism was at work, with big business and corporate titans portrayed as ipso facto adverse to the commoner. Insull lost his hope and patience with the local press and was quick to anger, thus adding to the friction.[28]

---

28. "The newspapers as a general thing, dislike Insull, chiefly because Insull dislikes them: on a number of conspicuous occasions he has been very sharp to the news and camera men," one profile noted. "He refuses to be interviewed and hates to be photographed."

Figure 4.9 This 1927 caricature captures the public's fascination with Samuel Insull's multifaceted empire and the power of just one man.

Entering the 1930s, the Insull holding companies, serving 4.5 million customers, had a market value estimated at $2.5 billion (nearly $30 billion today). Insull's stake of around $150 million made him a billionaire in today's dollars, a sizeable American fortune. Atop the pyramid were two holding companies: Insull Utility Investments, Inc., which was controlled by Insull and his family members and the hometown investment firm, Halsey, Stuart & Co.; and Corporation Securities Company of Chicago, which owned an interest in Insull Utility Investments. These two, in addition to having an interest in each other, owned: Middle West Utilities, which held 111 subsidiaries; Peoples Gas Light & Coke, with eight subsidiaries; Commonwealth Edison Company, with six subsidiaries; and Public Service Company of Northern Illinois. Midland United Company, finally, owned by those four entities, had thirty subsidiaries.

Figure 4.10 Completed at the tail end of the Roaring Twenties, "Insull's Throne" was a 42-story office building housing the Chicago Civic Opera Company on the ground level. Insull is shown with civic leader Stanley Field at the opening performance on November 4, 1929.

Insull even got his monument—but at a dark turn of history. Insull conceived and financed a $20 million, 42-story office building, the base of which was the new home of the Chicago Civil Opera and other city musical activities, "making Chicago the music capital of the world." "Insull's throne" was shaped as a chair with the view out to the west. To some, this was Insull's way of thumbing his nose at the East: in particular, the New York bankers who had taken Edison General Electric away from him and Thomas Edison.

The opening opera was held November 4, 1929. But the first-nighters could not entirely enjoy the show. The week before, a stock panic left the Dow Jones Industrial Average 40 percent below its all-time peak high reached just the month before. Insull's monument, in a sense, would be what Enron Field became to Ken Lay 72 years later.

5

Plummet and Ruin: 1930–1938

S AMUEL INSULL HAD EMBARKED upon establishing a family "dynasty" to make himself "immortal" when the Crash of 1929 hit. The Great Man of Chicago, electricity, and the utility sector (he had interests in gas and street-cars too)—and arguably the most powerful businessman in America—aimed to perpetuate and leverage his empire through two new investment-holdings companies that would leave brother Martin and son Samuel Jr. in charge.

Formerly, Insull had been a "thoroughgoing radical, but one who knew exactly what he was about." Now, he was in perilous waters. In his seventies, Samuel Insull would prove no match for an economic contraction that would feast on every government intervention meant to ameliorate it. The über-optimistic, work-aholic Insull would expand and borrow as the economy contracted. "He took on greater and greater burdens until it appeared as if he were attempting to carry the entire American economy on his shoulders," Forrest McDonald concluded.

The result would be bankruptcy for Middle West Utilities Company and his two interrelated pyramid investment structures in 1932; an ignominious end to a half-century atop American business; personal bankruptcy; and a final leg of life on the run, in the courtroom, and in humbled exile. Insull would die in Paris on July 16, 1938, at age 78. His bankrupt estate would be probated two years later, with creditors receiving one hundredth of a penny on the dollar.

The greatest of all business collapses since the collapse of Jay Cooke's banking house in 1873[1] was global news—and a rhyme of history for what

---

1. Following Cooke's collapse, "panic swept Wall Street, where banks and brokerage houses . . . failed by the dozens and the New York Stock Exchange was forced to close down for ten ten days. . . . A deep depression stalked the land for the next six years."

would happen to Enron and Ken Lay 70 years later. The similarities between Insull and Enron are striking, although commentators have erroneously linked both debacles to underregulation and free-market incentives rather than to the government side of political capitalism.[2]

Foibles and Flaws

Insull was little deterred by the numbing business reversal of fourth-quarter 1929. The downturns of 1893, 1896, 1902, and 1907, he lectured, had been temporary, as had another panic that he weathered in 1920/21. In November 1929, had he not attended the White House, where his fellow utility executives announced $1.4 billion in business-as-usual investment for 1930? Had not President Hoover asked business leaders to talk-and-walk normalcy to make it happen? Like other things New Deal, FDR's "the only thing we have to fear is fear itself" began with Herbert Hoover.

Insull stood tall at the White House that day. "I was rather proud of the fact that the institutions it is my privilege to preside over showed an amount representing 15 per cent of the total that is going to be expended [by utilities in] the whole country," Insull shared. Comparable to prior years, some $200 million was budgeted for 1930, almost all of which would be expended by his Big Four companies.[3]

Back home, Insull told Public Service Company of Northern Illinois: "I, myself, do not think [the crash] is going to affect things at all." As for Middle West Utilities: "Its possibilities are brighter today than they have ever been in the past." And for all of his companies: "Irrespective of the price registered on the Stock Exchange, our business goes on just the same." Not to fear: "We are in a business [electricity] that has not, so far, reached the point of saturation." Newspaper headlines flashed Insull's swell news too.

Insull assigned his public relations ace Bernard Mullaney to "an 'everything is normal' campaign." The "brilliant" revolutionist of public imaging, whose work on behalf of World War I patriotism and on public utility regulation was

---

2. "Seventy years [after Insull's collapse], Enron's embrace of free markets and deregulation can be viewed as a brilliant public relations tactic to secure new laws and regulations that worked to its own advantage" concluded an influential essay in the *Energy Law Journal*. The "new laws and regulations" sported by Enron had less to do with free markets than with rent-seeking and regulatory change, as the introduction to *Capitalism at Work* (Book 1) concludes and *Enron and Ken Lay* (Book 3) will exhaustively document.

3. For Insull's conviction of normalcy and coming recovery, see Internet appendix 5.1, "Insull's Blind Spot: Business as Usual," at www.politicalcapitalism.org/Book2/Chapter5/ Appendix1.html.

for the textbooks, now had to convince America to hold Insull stock as a sound investment and as part of the national recovery.[4]

Insull's brave face ("I have every confidence in the outlook for business") was tauter behind the scenes. Even before the Crash, Insull was battling against sell orders ("Your friends making great mistake in selling Middle West Common at this time," one cable to London said. "I speak with more knowledge of subject than average investor.") After October 1929, it would be topsy-turvy, with partial recovery in stock prices giving way to a demoralizing reversal.

Insull saw the Washington problem. "Business will never get anywhere whilst our leaders there are trying to promote prosperity at one end of Pennsylvania Avenue when destructive criticism goes on at the other end." Insull warned: "Neither will we establish a sound basis of prosperity throughout the country by trying to give something more to the farmer which must be taken away from the manufacturers, or vice-versa. To rob Peter to pay Paul will be no great help to the general purse."

Figure 5.1 Samuel Insull was little changed when the Roaring Twenties reversed into macroeconomic peril. His business-as-usual approach continued through 1931. This picture of Insull is among his last happy, top-of-the-world moments.

---

4. Mullaney was at the center of a 25-million-piece literature blitz by the gas and electric utility industries in the 1920s to gain public goodwill and achieve favorable state regulation instead of municipalization.

Insull's worry about government was on the mark. A raft of new interventions and tax hikes by Hoover, populist words against business by Roosevelt, and FDR's New Deal itself led to "regime uncertainty" under which private-sector investment was stymied. The Great Contraction turned into the Great Duration, a downturn that would far outlast all the total time of all aforementioned crises (during which government practiced laissez-faire).

·◊·

The Insull of the late 1920s and early 1930s was not the Insull of old. For most of his career, great moments of prudence had saved him from pitfalls on his fast, high-risk track to success. In business and in politics, Insull had assiduously avoided conflicts of interest.[5] that brought down others (such as Chicago traction king Charles Tyson Yerkes). Insull decried speculation that unduly inflated the stock of his own companies, while calling out corporations that played to the moment. "No little damage has been done to the corporate interests of this country by the action of some officials of corporations," he lamented in 1915, "who seem to have had much concern for the profit of the moment and little or no concern for the permanency of their investment in the future."

Insull had even been critical of the very pyramid trusts that he now fathered. Would the Insull of old have entertained the rationales he now was uttering— that investment holding companies were fashionable? That his investment trusts were a "rallying point of ownership and friendship in connection with … the name of Insull"?[5] Would he even have bought his ultimate argument—to "protect the interests of stockholders by easing the market by taking securities from time to time as they were offered"? This hints at speculation given the bet on future prices, what Insull insisted was not the purpose of the new entity.

Insull had been a Smilean in thought and action except when it came to indebtedness. "Never pay cash when you can give a note," Insull insisted. His days with Thomas Edison were lived on the edge. From 1892 forward, Insull deftly financed a consolidation and expansion of the capital-intensive electricity generation and distribution business, even fathering new financial instruments to do so.

But Insull had foibles, faults, and blind spots that grew and converged as his career went on. His "exaggerated sense of propriety," as McDonald put it, which made Insull feared by his employees, did moderate over time. But his unbroken success—"since his humiliation at the hands of Coffin and Morgan in 1892, he had been undefeated, untied, unscored-upon"—bred overconfidence. Great risk taking, beginning with his maiden voyage to America, reflected a belief in his own infallibility.

---

5. Some 4,000 utilities had come under holding-company control in the decade prior to Insull's decision to create the same. In an era of easy-money debt-finance and rising stock prices, such pyramids, particularly with leverage, could and did report fantastic appreciation.

Far worse was a streak of *arrogance*. Even with J. Pierpont Morgan (d. 1913) long gone and with General Electric his powerhouse partner, Insull's animosity toward New York continued. *Why not embrace the world's leading financial center for whatever might lie ahead?* Insull acknowledged that Morgan had done far more good than bad for Edison's pioneering work, and Charles Coffin had certainly worked out well for General Electric, the progeny of Edison and Insull. And hadn't Insull gone on to master the less developed side of the electricity business? It should have been: All's well that ends well.[6]

That there were too few *impartial observers*—confidants who could swing Insull to *no* or *go-slow*—was also responsible for Insull roaring his engines at the moment of greatest needed restraint. Gladys was no longer a brake. Insull's checks-and-balances team had been racked by death and inadequately replaced. It was father, son, and brother as triumvirate, not enough others.

Having foregone a grand opportunity to exit the public stage as England's electricity czar in 1926, estranged from his own wife and keeping a mistress, Insull was a changed man. Back around Insull's 50th birthday, biographer Forrest McDonald surmised, the Great Man started to become too great in his own mind. "Before, he had pursued Success with a single-minded determination and firmly adhered to a maxim he liked to quote, 'shoemaker, stick to your last,' meaning limit yourself to those activities that you know best." Now, McDonald wrote, "he was driven by a craving for power, and he expanded his activities into fields barely related to electric power supply." The debt finance he used so deftly at the core began to be employed for wholly new purposes.

Fatal Attractions

Sixteen-hour workdays remained common. "You can't work for 50 odd years and then drop it and feel very comfortable," Insull told a woman's group in early 1929. "I always feel I am playing truant." Hawthorn Farm was nearby for escape, but it was not the lifestyle of ocean voyages, European excursions, and hobbying that most others in his situation would seek.

Maybe Insull was one soul mate away from this road not taken, but there was ever more to do in business. His hundreds of companies were investing in *just about anything and everything*. One real estate venture in Texas alone involved a port, citrus crops, and a town site. There were home, car, and truck manufacturing businesses; hotels; oil plays; mining ventures; dairy investments; and other excursions "bearing no visible relation to the operation of utilities."

In the early months and first years of the Great Depression, Insull made bet after bet that he could help distressed individuals, companies, and government to survive. His first act was to collateralize employees whose stock purchases

---

6. Also see Internet appendix 5.2. "Insull Confessions," at www.politicalcapitalism.org/ Book2/Chapter5/Appendix2.html.

on credit encountered margin calls. Insull had enticed hundreds, if not thousands, into their sudden predicament—he could not abandon them now. Besides, there surely were more company stock-sale programs ahead.

The $197 million Big Four investment in 1930 represented business as usual. With equity markets paralyzed, each company's indebtedness (in the form of secured bonds or unsecured debentures) grew 10 percent.

In October, Insull reported another business-as-usual year. "It has been easy enough to raise money for capital expenditures this year," he said, "and we believe it will be the same for the expenditures we expect to make next year [1931]." The Insull companies were spending in 29 states.

Bull strategies for 1931 encountered a roadblock. "For the first time, I think, on record," Insull reported to stockholders in first-quarter 1931, "we have had a decrease in customers in the Commonwealth Edison Company." Sure enough: The 115 MW Waukegan Station came on line right when overall electricity demand at the company fell 4 percent, a decline that was similar in the rest of the nation.

Insull also went debt-heavy with his holding companies during 1931. Insull Utility Investments (IUI) issued $60 million in debentures, and Corporation Securities Company of Chicago (CSCC) issued $30 million in serial gold notes (numbered debt obligations that must be redeemed in gold, in numeric order). Such leverage was not about making a killing in a growth market but rather shoring up a sagging portfolio to meet margin calls and to create buy orders. The Insulls were going all out.

In 1929, Middle West head Martin Insull took imprudence to a new level with a $50 million issue of serial gold notes that had a $10 million annual redemption. Worse, the monies were not for core utility purposes; they were first-aid for failing textile and shipbuilding businesses in Maine, North Carolina, and other states—on the rationale that saving the business would save the utility. Would Samuel Insull, who was abroad at the time, have passed on this customer bailout that, as it turned out, "undid most of the good accomplished in Middle West's 1929 refinancing"?

Insull played aggressively on the gas side too. After integrating the Peoples Gas pipeline system with suburban Public Service Company's, he debt-financed a quarter of the $80 million Natural Gas Pipe Line of America project. Upon completion in October 1931, the 980-mile line from the Texas Panhandle to Chicago (supplied by the multistate Hugoton field) displaced manufactured gas with its cheaper, cleaner substitute.

Insull took on indebtedness and collateralization in the teeth of the Great Depression in other ways. The city of Chicago turned to him in early 1930 for more than $50 million to meet its payroll for policemen, firemen, and teachers. Several months later, Insull's traction companies fronted a $500 million modernization of the city's transportation network. Not all this was Insull, but his leadership and some millions got the deals done.

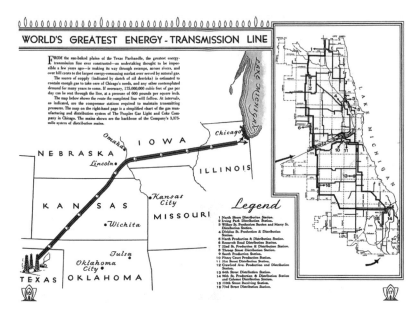

Figure 5.2 The "world's greatest energy transmission line," spanning the distance from a Texas gas field to Chicago, was the greatest interstate gas line of its time. Upon the project's completion in 1931, natural gas made costlier, more polluting gas manufactured from coal a thing of the past.

There was also Insull's unabated philanthropy, such as a $660,000 donation from the Insull Group (and $60,000 from Samuel personally) to aid the unemployed in Cook County in 1930, and a $160,000 donation from Samuel to a hospital in England in honor of his late parents. America's good-guy, white-horse financier was committed to saving individuals and organizations in America's desperate hour. Such action was not so much about financial gain: "Money ceased to be important to him; henceforth, he gave it away almost as fast as he earned it," biographer McDonald noted. It was about empathy-and-duty turned power-and-prestige—or, in McDonald's words, "delusions of grandeur." Insull would end up in the textbooks—but as villain, not savior.

Pyramiding Gyrations

The "throne room of the Insull empire," Insull Utility Investments Corporation (formed January 1929) and Corporation Securities Company of Chicago (formed October 1929), was designed to prevent an involuntary ouster such as Samuel Insull had experienced at Edison General Electric 37 years before. By buying and holding large minority positions in the Big Four and enticing others to do so too at the pyramid level, Samuel, Samuel Jr., and Martin could remain in control.

The holding companies were created near the end of the greatest bull market in U.S. history. Continental Illinois and other lenders repeatedly pushed easy credit Insull's way. In retrospect, inflationary monetary policy by the U.S. Federal Reserve Bank was fueling an artificial boom that would require liquidation of malinvestments—if and when government anti-Depression policies would allow it.

The trusts did start well. At IUI's first stockholders meeting, Insull reported a $10 million profit for 1929 and a small appreciation in the market value of the securities held. A $26 million appreciation in the first 45 days of 1930, creating a hold value of $170 million, was even better news for 35,000-plus stockholders. Looking forward, Insull admitted to "the same confidence that I have had" about "reasonably good" conditions.

At the end of this meeting, Insull received a question from the floor. "I can't see the object of the two [investment] organizations," asked one Maggie Gray. "What is the difference in the objects of the two?"

"They are about the same," responded Insull.

"Why is it necessary to have two?" she then asked.

"Because we needed some more money," said Insull, evoking laughter. "You need more than one string in your bow when you are playing with such big chips."

Cyrus Eaton, whose uninvited stock positions prompted the pyramiding strategy, went unmentioned. "I naturally became quite alarmed," Insull later recollected in his memoirs about Eaton's growing presence, which in retrospect was exaggerated. Insull, too, was blind to the sensibility that investors should be welcomed, not feared, to increase enterprise value in a competitive (and certainly depressed) economy.[7]

As it turned out, Insull changed his mind and bought out Eaton in mid-1930 for $56 million, $48 million in cash (debt financed) and the balance at the going price of IUI and CSCC stock. The cash portion was at a 15 percent premium to market, not unreasonable given the very large size of the purchase.

Continental Illinois had led Insull to believe that it could finance all his deals, including an Eaton buyout.[8] But the deal required Insull to borrow $5 million from General Electric with personal collateral and close with $20 million from New York banks. The latter were tied to the House of Morgan, an ominous development given Insull's ill-will, including an "incendiary blast" not yet a

---

7. Also see Internet appendix 5.3, "Why Pyramiding?" at www.politicalcapitalism.org/Book2/Chapter5/Appendix3.html.

8. Insull's buyout came after Eaton had offered to merge his interests on friendly terms. The foregone alternative would have avoided debt, but Insull could not accept the risk of a potential power struggle against a strong rival in the future.

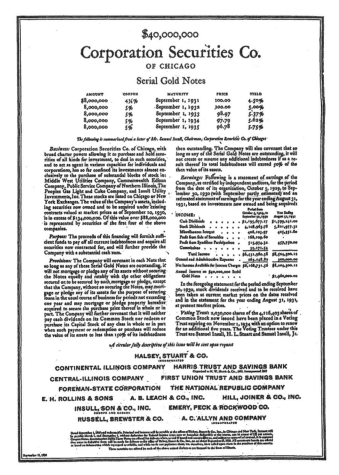

Figure 5.3 This five-year, $40 million gold-note offering by Corporation Securities Company of Chicago, issued in September 1930, was entirely underwritten by Chicago-based firms, leaving New York banks on the sidelines.

year old. Now Morgan was the tail that wagged the dog. Insull, ironically, was losing control while trying to ensure control.

A Final Celebration

On Saturday evening February 28, 1931, Samuel Insull's friends and associates commemorated the fiftieth anniversary of his arrival in America. Organized and hosted by Samuel Insull Jr., with Insull's securities salesman John Gilchrist as master of ceremonies, an elaborate dinner was held at the Palmer House in Chcago, beginning with caviar and ending, for dessert, with Bombe Middlewest.

A scroll was presented to the honoree, highlighting his half century in the United States and particularly his nearly four full decades in Chicago.

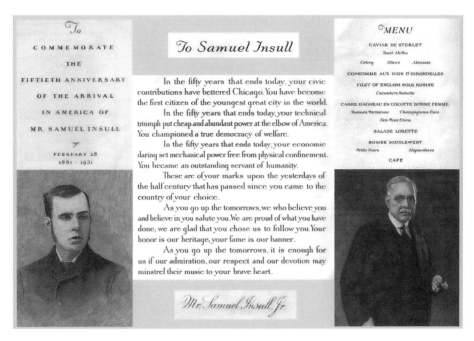

Figure 5.4 The half-century career of Insull in America was celebrated in one of the greatest parties held during the Great Depression. Bankruptcy for Insull's holding companies would come the next year.

A booklet for the evening chronicled 17 Insull enterprises, whose capitalization of $2.2 billion in 1930 represented 12 percent of national utility investment. That contrasted with $1.1 million, or less than 1 percent, in 1892. Earnings in the 38 years had gone from less than a million dollars to several hundred million; stockholders, from 50 to approximately a half million. The customer count exceeded 4.5 million compared to several thousand in 1892, a period during which the total number of employees rose to 72,800 from 400. An empire had sprouted from one man's direction.

Heartfelt tributes were shared from business associates and titans across America, beginning with Gilchrist's description of Insull's half century

> of vision; of planning; of labor; of fruition … of action; of courage; of battling with conditions; of overcoming difficulties; of close mingling with his fellow men; of progress and accomplishment; of human sympathy; of rare sentiment; of great kindness; of truth, honor and justice; of patriotism; of wise foresight; of discipline; of education and culture; of marvelous balance and common sense; of vigorous, red-blooded life.

The supersalesman of Commonwealth Edison added: "When the biography of Mr. Insull is written, it will be the history of more than the first half century of the electric utility business of the world."[9]

Heartfelt tributes were read from business associates and from leaders of industry. Owen Young, the successor to Charles Coffin at General Electric, acknowledged the "obligations which the electrical manufacturing industry owe you." U.S. Treasury Secretary Andrew Mellon pointed to Insull's "constructive way in increasing the prosperity and welfare of this country." U.S. Steel's James Farrell spoke to Insull's nearly half-century experience in leading an industry. Even New York was well represented, with read telegrams from J. P. Morgan & Company, Chase National Bank, and New York Central Lines.

The finale tribute of the evening came right on cue. Insull's beloved mentor, in the last year of his life, called from his home in Florida. With the phone line connected to a loudspeaker, Thomas Edison recounted his first encounter with "Sammy" 50 years to the day. "His youthful appearance daunted me, and I wondered whether my choice was a wise one," he confessed to the sea of listeners. But "no mistake had been made," Edison remembered about that first night, which got right down to crucial business. "He had a mature and thoughtful mind, a mastery of detail and a prodigious capacity for work." Edison added: "Insull was one of the few men of those early days who soon acquired a comprehensive knowledge of my Central Station idea, and he has amplified his knowledge through the succeeding years."

Insull rose to give the last word. He gave thanks all around and then recounted his long business road, beginning at age 14, seven years before coming to America. Special tribute was reserved for Thomas Edison: "I have endeavored to fulfill my duty as I have seen it," Insull stated. "The figures that you have heard are the results of the work of no one man; they are the results of the work of a great organization, of which, by accident, I happened to be the leader." Near the end of his remarks: "I am rather proud of the fact that over a period of 52 years I have had the opportunity to follow the banner of Edison. It has been a great inspiration to me."

The occasion was fortuitously timed. A rebound in stock prices was reversing most of the numbing losses of late 1930. Still, Insull's investment trusts were barely above water, and his creations were at the mercy of a precarious market and of New York. Who could have known that Samuel Insull would be broke and banished from his companies within 16 months?

---

9. Insull's half century is the history of electricity covered in this book. The natural gas industry is traced herein from its 1920 maturation through the 1980s.

Collapse and Resignations

The Insull-related stock rebound of late winter/early spring 1931 was not acci-dental. The Big Four reported strong earnings, and thousands of Insull employees were peddling stock with every incentive and sales tip that the Great Man could concoct. CSCC was in positive territory and paying its regular dividend. One Fred Scheel skillfully worked the floor of the Chicago Stock Exchange and the New York Stock Exchange to make markets on Insull's behalf. Still, it was a titanic clash between "all of the forces of the Depression … and the popularity of the securities and the repeatedly proved earning power of the Insull operating companies."

Enter New York and, specifically, the House of Morgan, which Insull had publically criticized since his departure for Chicago in 1892. In addition to having very close ties with the banks that had become friendly with Insull, the invest-ment house's 32 NYSE traders had "all of the weapons of the bear raid … at their disposal: short selling, tape advertising, wash and matched sales, life or death power over the liquidation of brokerage accounts, and the deadliest weapon of all, the Wall Street rumor." Morgan had its own utility holding company, United Corporation, and few good feelings about Mr. Chicago.

By mid-1931, Scheel was losing against the macroeconomy and the tuggings of Morgan. IUI and CSCC were $100 million under water with debt coming due. Insull turned to personal guarantees to meet margin calls. One New York bank that wanted less exposure required Insull to borrow $1 million from General Electric on a personal basis, which was done by pledging $1.25 million of CSCC securities. By year-end, CSCC was down to $2.25 per share, but its liquidation value was nil. Insull *finally* realized that he was in trouble.

The New Year brought no reprieve. The holding companies (Middle West, IUI, and CSCC) suspended dividends, and Arthur Andersen & Company (replacing longtime auditor Arthur E. Young & Company) was brought in by the creditors to reaudit the company, overhaul the accounting systems, and manage the cash function. The up-and-coming accountant, Arthur E. Andersen, would become a leading light of his profession on the strength of this prominent job, leading in time to a major national practice.

Investor lawsuits in April 1932 asked for receivership for all three. Mercy rounds followed with New York and Chicago banks for standstill agreements to let troubled loans ride on their present terms. The head of both General Electric and the New York Federal Reserve Bank, Owen Young, who had lavishly praised Insull just the year before, found himself in precarious negotiations between the Great Man and New York (Morgan).

What to do? Insull vetoed as "immoral" a proposal by Scheel to sell short the stocks of the Big Four in order to hedge against the price declines that Morgan brokers seemed determined to cause.[10] Thousands of Insull's employees, after

---

10. See Internet appendix 5.4, "The 'Morgan Conspiracy' Theory," at www.politicalcapitalism. org/Book2/Chapter5/Appendix4.html.

all, were selling stock to customers, neighbors, friends, and family on the pitch of price strength, not decline.

The beginning of the end was under way in September 1931 when the market broke and Insull's one-week $150 million loss put the bears in firm control. Insull pledged the last of his personal assets. "Pathetically futile" intercompany transactions from stronger to weaker parts of the empire were made that ended up just spreading the failure.

"The kill took about six months," said McDonald, "for though the House of Morgan could be devastatingly predatory, it was never impatient and it was never messy." The decisive blow came on April 8, 1932, when the banks, led by New York, chose not to renew a $10 million note of Middle West Utilities.

"Does this mean a receivership?" asked Insull.

"It looks that way," responded Owen Young. Indeed. Middle West Utilities had lost more than 99 percent of its value from its 1929 high of more than $500 per share.

Insull returned to Chicago and entertained grandiose thoughts about counterattacking from the court of public opinion. Harold Stuart, head of the securities firm that had been so active with Insull all the way—$2 billion in all—suggested renting Chicago Stadium, where tens of thousands of Insull employees, Insull stockholders, and Chicago citizens could rally against the big bad banks. Insull thought about it, but he was tired. He declined his populist opportunity. "Aw, hell," he muttered. "Somebody would just shoot me."

∾

IUI and CSCC were liabilities parading as assets; bankruptcy was declared for each two days after Middle West entered receivership. Their aggregate loss of $330 million reflected the decline in stock value of each of the Big Four. From the peak in 1929, the stock of Commonwealth Edison was off 89 percent; Peoples Gas, 88 percent; Public Service, 91 percent; and Middle West, 99 percent. Insull's fortune, estimated at its peak to be $150 million, was gone. The goodwill value of the Insull brand was nil.

The next blows came after Insull returned to Chicago from New York. Stanley Field, a personal friend and a director of Commonwealth Edison, one whose Marshall Field & Company was an early convert of Insull/Chicago Edison Company to central service, broke the news. "Mr. Insull, we want your resignations, and we want them now."

A letter of resignation, dated June 4 (Saturday), was addressed to the board of Commonwealth Edison. On Monday, June 6, 1932, Samuel Insull resigned from all his corporate posts—62 in all—in a marathon meeting in his offices.[11] Insull left the meeting and told the press: "Well, gentlemen, here I am, after forty years a man without a job."

---

11. Insull's biography is reproduced in Internet appendix 5.5, at www.politicalcapitalism.org/Book2/Chapter5/Appendix5.html.

James Simpson, chief operating officer of the Marshall Field department stores and a member of the Commonwealth Edison board, was appointed successor at Commonwealth Edison, Peoples Gas, and Public Service of Northern Illinois. (Middle West Utilities, in receivership, removed Insull as well.) At the insistence of creditors, Samuel Insull Jr. continued as vice chairman, joining Simpson at the three companies.

"If I had a man like you around me ten years ago who would tell me 'No!' I wouldn't be here now," Insull confided to one of Middle West Utilities' receivers, Charlie McCullough, during the cab ride home. But Insull could not tell himself no or decline many pleas for help that came from friends, employees, customers, investors, family, charities, towns and cities, and government.

"Due regard for my health necessitates my retirement from the business responsibilities I have been carrying," Insull wrote in a short statement. Said a joint statement from the three companies: "Mr. Insull's resignations bring to a close his long association with these Companies during which he has brought them into an outstanding position in the utility field."

Behind closed doors, the directors of Commonwealth Edison gave thanks to Insull for his 40 years. Insull returned the thanks, expressed his sorrow about the events of the last months, and praised the prospects of a company that was managing to add more business than it was losing. "I could say a great deal more, but I cannot trust myself any longer," Insull closed. "Gentlemen, I thank you, and officially I bid you goodbye."

In reverence to their fallen leader, the companies sweetened Insull's pension to $50,000 a year, and Gladys's widow pension to $25,000 (in 2009 dollars, this was, respectively, more than $750,000 and $375,000 per year). The dethroned would not be a pauper, at least as things currently stood. Otherwise without assets, Insull was not so sure. "I have gone from the bottom to the top and now to the bottom again," Insull told the press. "I only hope to be able to keep a roof over my head and care for my wife."

Insull's many business ties came into view on this fateful Monday. His chairmanship resignations included Peabody Coal Company; Chicago Rapid Transit Company; Chicago, Aurora & Elgin Railroad; Indiana Natural Gas and Oil Company; Michigan & Adams Safety Deposit Vaults, Incorporated; and Metropolitan Real Estate Improvement Corporation. There were the presidencies of Chicago Civic Opera Company, the Opera Shops Building Corporation, and Utilities Finance Corporation, among others.

There were directorships at Electrical Testing Laboratories, Walker Vehicle Company, and Commercial National Safe Deposit Company. He also relinquished his voting trustee rights at various companies. Socially, Insull resigned from 12 clubs on June 9, including the Metropolitan Club of Washington, D.C., and the New York Yacht Club.

～

"The collapse of these companies has hurt our city more than did the great fire," lamented one Chicago banker. Actually, it was the Great Depression and the misguided public policies therein that were victimizing Chicagoans and virtually all Americans otherwise. Insull was more an effect than a cause of the recovery that would not stick.

Letters of condolence came in from friends and strangers. A farmer outside of Chicago reminded Insull to think of past achievements. Another missive expressed "shock" and added: "I wish you were a bit younger ... to reestablish your business on its old footing."

Joseph Tumulty, a friend of Insull's for six years, penned a small booklet, *A Plea for Fairness,* in which he asked all to remember the fallen titan's past accomplishments. "Perhaps the aid he offered his country in this grave crisis was foolish, but it was the foolishness of the optimist, the dreamer and lover of his country," Tumulty said. "Perhaps he stands alone, deserted by those who were lifted to power, and wealth, on those venerable shoulders now weary with almost unbearable burdens, but there are those in Chicago and elsewhere, like myself, through whom the electric current of his life and affection passed, who remain loyal to him in their friendship." Tumulty quoted from an article in the *New York Times* describing the other Insull: the system builder and philanthropist, the man whose optimism turned out to be his undoing.

"Nervous, exhausted, and at wit's end," Insull spent his first jobless days sequestered in his mansion in Chicago's Gold Coast, also home to "Insull banks, Insull schools, Insull country clubs, and an Insull electric suburban railroad." There was not much left for the fallen titan to do except to receive visits from a number of disgruntled former subordinates who wanted help in the reorganization. But those days were over for Insull.

After a week, and knowing that the three operating companies did not need his distraction, Insull quietly escaped Chicago by train to Montreal, from which he went to Quebec to board the *Empress of Britain,* bound for Cherbourg. Insull received many urgings to resettle in London, but Gladys preferred Paris, where they soon took up residence in an apartment hotel.

"To go for several days and have only hotel clerks and writers to speak to is not very exciting," Samuel wrote to Junior ("Chappie"). There was some business, such as September meetings in London with James Simpson, his replacement at the Big Three. But mostly it was walking the city and keeping up with the U.S. news, which was not at all encouraging about a return to Chicago.

"[J.] Odgen [Ketting] says I am an entirely different looking man to what I was when he left Chicago—I certainly feel very different," another communication to Junior read. There was also hope: "Should business start to improve Andersons (sic) write offs will look absurd." And there were pangs of conscience:

> I am very sorry indeed that you are in Chicago and have to bear the burden of being in the midst of all this trouble. I feel like a loafer and slacker being over here and out of the immediate troubles whatever the future might have in store for me in the way of trouble. I of course feel quite depressed ....

Although rumored to have sequestered as much as $10 million, Insull was in fact $16 million in the hole. He had avoided personal bankruptcy only because he had pledged (and now lost) everything to his creditors. Gladys, better situated under the laws of Illinois, had assets of a million dollars (about $15 million today)—including the right to half the couple's former country estate. The pension was the lifeline in any case—but one that would not be as secure as thought.

Political Scapegoat

Labor Day 1932 began the political hunting season. With so many victimized from his three fallen holdings companies, public opinion was running hard against Samuel Insull. He was the prime quarry on both the Illinois and the federal levels for the November 8 election ahead.

The opening salvo came from the state's attorney for Cook County, John Swanson, a Republican running for reelection in what promised to be a Democratic year. Swanson was strongly advised to go after Insull but initially balked. "Sam Insull is the greatest man I've ever known," he confided to his son-in-law, Russell Olson. "No one has done more for Chicago, and I know he has never taken a dishonest dollar."

Politics won, and the investigation was announced September 15. "Insull knows politics, and he will understand," Swanson told Olson.

Franklin Roosevelt, challenging Herbert Hoover in the 1932 election, was campaigning against Insull coast to coast. FDR had tangled with public utilities as governor of New York, and Insull enemies, the progressive Chicago lawyers Harold Ickes and Donald Richberg, were atop the Roosevelt campaign.[12] Worse yet for Insull, his brother Martin had forcefully rebutted FDR, pointing out that America consumed one-half of the world's electricity with one-seventeenth of global population and observing quite rightly: "Every foreign commission that has come here to find the reason for America's industrial supremacy has included in its report that an important explanation is 'cheap electric power, anywhere and everywhere'." Martin added that half the country's 21 million users paid a nickel a day for their power (about the price of a pack of gum), and the other half paid eleven cents (about the price of a pack of cigarettes).

But truth mattered not to the politicians. In a September 21, 1932, speech in Portland, Oregon, Roosevelt attacked the power industry as inadequately providing for America. "Electricity … can relieve the drudgery of the housewife

---

12. After Roosevelt won, Ickes would become the longest-serving Secretary of the Interior ever, holding that post through Roosevelt's entire 13-year administration; Richberg would be named to head up so many so-called emergency posts that he actually had power over the Cabinet, which led to his being dubbed "the assistant president."

and lift the great burden off the shoulders of the hardworking farmer," FDR intoned. But too many areas were backward.

> What prevents our American people from taking full advantage of this great economic and human agency? .... The reason is frankly and definitely that many selfish interests in control of light and power industries have not been sufficiently far-sighted to establish rates low enough to encourage widespread public use.

Then FDR shifted the argument to the scapegoat numero uno:

> The crash of the Insull empire has given excellent point to the truth of what I have been arguing for four long years. The great "Insull monstrosity" . . . had distributed securities among hundreds of thousands of investors, and had taken their money to an amount running over one and a half billions of dollars—not millions, but billions!

Two days later in San Francisco, Roosevelt opined that a person's "right to his own property," meant "to the fullest extent ... the safety of his savings," and thus "restrict[ing] the operations of the speculator, the manipulator, even the financier ... [was] not to hamper individualism but to protect it." He spoke of a new role for "formal government—political government"—and again brought in numero uno:

> Whenever in the pursuit of this objective the lone wolf, the unethical competitor, the reckless promoter, the Ishmael or Insull whose hand is against every man's, declines to join in achieving an end recognized as being for the public welfare, and threatens to drag the industry back to a state of anarchy, the government may properly be asked to apply restraint.

Following FDR's lead, Democrats everywhere—prominently including the Illinois Democratic candidate for governor, Henry Horner—raised a hue and cry against unchecked financial capitalism. But Swanson was out front, with the *Chicago Tribune* reporting in sensational fashion his findings that "favored buyers" of Insull Utility Investments paid $12 per share, while it was selling on the market for $27 per share.

Two days later, the *Tribune* blared: "List 205 Insull 'Insiders'" with the subtitle, "Given the right to buy stock at half price." The first paragraph read: "A list of 205 of Samuel Insull's 'favored investors' who were permitted to subscribe to common stock of Insull Utility Investments, Inc., at less than one half of the initial market price was made public yesterday by State's Attorney John Swanson."

Yet this was no smoking gun. The book, or liquidation, value of IUI common (which the government would later insist was a stock's only true value) was $7.45 at the time of assignment, meaning that "insiders" had if anything overpaid for their shares. In keeping with Insull's desire for long-term investors, the subscribers contractually agreed to not sell their stock for two and a half years (at which time, it turned out, the stock was worthless).

But amid a bull market, perhaps the greatest in U.S. history, the stock opened at $25 and quickly reached $30 per share. Insull publicly denounced these values as unwarranted, as they would later turn out to be. But the market was what it was.

So, the half-price accusation was a half-truth at best. Insull believed in January 1929 that IUI common had a solid future, and he wanted a substantial amount of it to be held for at least a couple years by friends, not enemies or speculators. (His friends ranged from Owen Young and Gerard Swope of General Electric to Insull's valet T. W. Obee to the opera diva Rosa Raisa.) But such context was ignored amid the political witchhunt that followed his collapse in mid-1932.

·◌·

The national GOP followed Illinois's Republican Party and Swanson in the anti-Insull crusade. The day after Insull's "insiders" list appeared in the *Chicago Tribune*, the progressive Republican Peter Norbeck, chairman of the Senate Banking Committee, announced that he was going to launch an investigation into the Insull empire. The following day, U.S. Attorney Dwight "Pete" Green, representing the Hoover administration, announced that the Department of Justice was launching its own investigation.

In the *Tribune*'s front page story concerning Green's announcement, the lead paragraph breathlessly proclaimed: "A sweeping federal investigation to bring out the real facts behind the 2 billion dollar crash of the Insull Utilities empire will be launched tomorrow morning, with every resource of the government thrown behind the inquiry."

But if the Hoover administration thought that it could take the leadership of the anti-Insull forces, they reckoned without the wiles of Cook County's state attorney, John Swanson, who had started it all. On September 29, he released a second list, of 318 names, and this time they included officials and politicians at the city, state, and national levels. On the list was none other than Chicago's Democratic mayor, Anton Cermak. But then so was Republican David Shanahan, speaker of the Illinois House of Representatives. Frank L. Smith, a Republican national commiteeman, was on the list—but so too was a Democratic national committeeman, Michael L. Igoe. A former U.S. Senator from Illinois, Republican William Lorimer, was listed. But so was Joseph P. Tumulty, White House chief of staff under Woodrow Wilson, the last Democratic president.

Roosevelt's special train stopped in Chicago on October 1. Armed and ready to denounce the Insull empire at a dinner for 3,000, FDR had a last-minute change in plans. The heterogeneity of the list forced FDR to new messages rather than railing against the "Insull monstrosity" and "the Ishmael or Insull whose hand is against every man's," was thrown off message by the list.

But if the immediate partisan advantage of denouncing Insull had been removed, there was political advantage in playing an avenging angel for little-guy stockholders. On October 4, one month ahead of the election, state's attorney Swanson secured indictments against Samuel and Martin Insull for

Figure 5.5 State and federal investigations of Insull were headline news in Chicago and elsewhere. Such negative publicity soured Insull on Chicago (the city which he fathered in important ways) in favor of various European locales.

embezzlement. The amount that the Insulls were accused of thieving from their $2 billion empire was an improbable $66,000.

"Rumors in La Salle Street [Chicago's financial district] were to the effect that both Samuel and Martin Insull would resist to the utmost any efforts to return them to Chicago," the *Tribune* reported. Swanson asked Illinois governor Louis Emmerson to initiate extradition proceedings. Samuel Insull, a fallen business titan, was about to be a fugitive from justice.

On the Run

"When he was on top, almost everyone who counted had been on Insull's side, and out of fear, those who were not had held their peace," Forrest McDonald summarized. "Then as the war drums began to roll and the battle sharpened up, there were two sides…. Then Insull lost, and there was just one side again."

The critics were legion. Hundreds of thousands of investors felt duped. Politicians of both parties used Insull to score points. Intellectuals decried capitalism, and the *Chicago Daily News*, for one, editorialized for municipalization to atone for the sins of Insull. Little wonder that Europe had beckoned.

In September 1932, Samuel and Gladys received their son in Paris. Junior was bringing sorely needed cash, but his visit also involved telling dad about a pension cutback to the earned amount of $21,500 per year. At the same time, the news came from Cook County that Insull would be indicted, which meant extradition. That was very bad news. Not only was a fair trial considered improbable, but also the strain would be great for a man whose 74th birthday was just ahead.

Where to go? Insull and his son decided on Athens on the advice of former Judge George Cooke, inasmuch as Greece did not have an extradition treaty with the United States. (Martin Insull, also indicted, was living in Canada, but as a British subject, he could not be extradited easily.) Leaving Gladys in Paris, father and son took boat, plane (his first), and train to get to their new destination. Junior departed with just enough money to return to Chicago, which left Senior with $3,000 and the promise of future pension checks. Far gone were the days when the Great Man would crack open the office safe to dole out tens of thousands of dollars on the spot.

November 1926

November 1932

Figure 5.6 Two *Time* magazine cover pictures, six years apart, showed one Insull in prosperity (left) and one in ruin (right).

"It is quite a possibility I will ... [take] up some business here," Insull wrote Junior in February 1933. "I understand the government would like me to take up the Power and Traction situation, the lignite (fuel) questions, possibly the telephone situation, and possibly the question of sewage and drainage in and around Athens." Not much would come of this, but the 18 months in Greece proved to be a much-needed safe harbor at a perilous time.

In late 1933, more bad news came. As Insull was a fugitive from justice, his pension was revoked by Commonwealth Edison, Peoples Gas, and Public Service, effective January 1, 1934.

"What do you think of an appeal to the various men in the industry to do something for me?" Senior hurriedly wrote Junior. "There is no doubt of my being a pauper.... I do wish it were over." The letter ended: "I am so sorry for you that you have all this trouble on my account—It breaks my heart when I think of it."

Meanwhile, under pressure from the U.S. government, Greece passed an extradition treaty, but deportation was limited to actions that were crimes under Greek law. In protest, the Roosevelt administration revoked the money-transfer privileges of the Greek-American Merchants Association, which pressured Greece to ask Insull to leave the country. This was a step short of deportation, however, and the original January 1, 1934, deadline for Insull was extended for medical reasons until March 15.

FDR's extralegal actions made Insull more wary about the prospects of receiving a fair trial in the United States. So, borrowing money from friends in London, he chartered the *S.S. Maiotis* to cruise the eastern Mediterranean in search of refuge, perhaps in Romania or a Middle Eastern country.

On March 22, the House and Senate rushed through a bill authorizing the State Department to arrest an American citizen in any country where the United States had extraterritorial rights. *Time* magazine pronounced it a "Great Day" for FDR and called Insull a "sniveling old man." The new legal authority came into play when Insull sailed in Turkish waters. On March 29, as the *Maiotis* passed through the Bosporus toward the Black Sea, the ship was halted and commandeered to Istanbul. American Ambassador Robert Skinner persuaded the Turkish government to seize Insull, and the fugitive was detained in a small jail cell.

On April 2, Turkey denied Insull's appeal to stay extradition, and Insull was transported under guard to Smyrna (modern Izmir), on the Aegean coast. The next week, President Roosevelt and Secretary of State Cordell Hull signed a warrant authorizing the third secretary of the American embassy, Burton Berry, to bring Insull home.

On April 13, the two men boarded the SS *Exilona* to begin the 24-day journey back. Relieved to be out of jail, Insull greeted Berry with a jovial handshake, saying "So you, young man, are my custodian." But as the journey progressed, depression set in. Insull confided his thoughts of suicide to Berry, but his sympathetic 33-year-old guardian convinced him that such an action would be taken as an admission of guilt and would forever disgrace not only his name but also his family's.

Figure 5.7 Insull's life on the run ended with his extradition in 1934. *Left:* reading about his extradition in the *New York Daily News. Right:* spending a day in a Chicago jail after his arrival in Chicago.

There was one person whom Insull truly needed to fight for the future: his son. Thus, when Samuel Insull Jr. unexpectedly boarded the *Exilona* as it approached New York, the old man got a shot of adrenalin for his prepared statement for the press. "I have erred," he said. "But my greatest error was in underestimating the effect of the financial panic on American securities and particularly on the companies I was working so hard to build." Insull continued:

> I worked with all my energy to save those companies. I made mistakes, but they were honest mistakes. They were errors in judgment but not dishonest manipulations. …. You only know the charges of the prosecution. Not one word has been uttered in even a feeble defense of me. And it must be obvious that there also is my side of the story. When it is told in court, my judgment may be discredited, but certainly my honesty will be vindicated.

These words had come pro bono from Steve Hannagan, who would go on to become one of the notable twentieth-century practitioners of public relations. The transformation of Samuel Insull from a New Deal villain to an industrialist-victim of the Depression would prove to be one of Hannagan's greatest accomplishments.

On May 9, after "one of the most bizarre international legal fiascoes in history," Insull arrived with federal agents in Chicago. Junior had arranged to pay the expected $100,000 bail, but the court required $200,000. Floyd Thompson, a former Illinois Supreme Court justice whom Insull Jr. had hired on the advice of Insull's regular lawyer, George Cooke, offered to make bail, but Insull wanted to spend the night in jail to make a case for the government's overzealousness.

It was just this spirit that Thompson wanted in his client. "Both men recognized that, whatever the legal trappings with which the case would be surrounded, in large measure Insull would be tried at the bar of public opinion." Continued McDonald:

> The publicity attending the bail and jailing incident was the first step in transforming the popular image of Insull from that of an evil manipulator and swindler, brought back to face justice, into an infirm and aged sometime public benefactor persecuted for the sins of his generation. And on that issue— prosecution versus persecution—the defense was to rest.

The Trial of Samuel Insull

On May 11, Samuel Insull was released from jail and began preparing for trial, which was set for October 2. He took up residence at the once-stately Seneca Hotel, which was not only within his budget but also in keeping with a man down on his luck. Such an image, moreover, could only help Insull win in the court of public opinion and in a court of law.

While his lawyers prepared, Insull dictated his memoirs. He wanted to leave behind a record, whether or not it could generate income to defray his legal bills.[13] But most of all, Insull needed to recall his long career in order to execute his defense. That was the strategy of his lead attorney, Floyd Thompson, who would ask (in the words of Forrest McDonald): "Could the jury take seriously a charge that this man—rich, powerful, respected, idolized after a distinguished career spanning five decades—decided to take up crime in 1929?"

The federal fraud trial was the first and greatest Insull trial (of three). Insull and 16 others were charged with selling to the public stock that they knew, or should have known, to be worth far less than they claimed in 1929 and in 1930. Illinois attorney general John Swanson's charge that Samuel and Martin Insull embezzled $66,000 was all but forgotten, given the $100 million stakes of the federal case.

The Participants

The scale of the federal fraud trial seemed congruent with the magnitude of Insull's collapse. The prosecution had the full resources of the U.S. government, beginning with the attention of President Franklin Roosevelt. Alongside FDR was U.S. Attorney General Homer S. Cummings, who would later engineer the president's unsuccessful Court-packing scheme.

---

13. In fact, Insull's book-length memoir did not appear to be marketable in its time and would not be published until 1992.

The man on the scene was Dwight "Pete" Green, the U.S. attorney for the Northern District of Illinois. Green's strategy, perfected against bootlegger Al Capone, was to target his victim and then nail him in any way possible. Ironically, the judge who had overseen Green's successful Capone case was the same judge who would oversee Green's case against Insull: James Herbert Wilkerson.

Green's capable assistant, Leo Hassenauer, had practiced law with Insull's notorious Chicago foes, Harold Ickes and Donald Richberg, early tutors of FDR in hatred of Insull. Green and Hassenauer were "aided by scores of brilliant investigators, sent from Washington by the Justice and Treasury departments, and these experts worked full time for more than two years to get the case ready."

Yet Green called for more help, and the Justice Department sent Forest Harness, the special assistant the U.S. attorney general had sent to Greece to argue for Insull's extradition. Harness worked furiously during the summer to prepare the case and organize the prosecution.

Nevertheless, shortly before trial, Green asked and got still more help from Washington, in the person of Leslie Salter, reputedly "the hottest special prosecutor he had in New York and probably the best in the country." Like Green in Chicago, Salter had worked in New York as a federal prosecutor, focusing on Prohibition.

Of the 17 defendants, the big four were Samuel Insull; Samuel Jr.; Harold Stuart, president of Halsey, Stuart & Company; and Charles Stuart, Harold's brother and a vice president of Halsey, Stuart. Also charged was Edward Doyle, president of the Commonwealth Edison Company and a director of Corporation Securities Company of Chicago, as was, somewhat ironically, Stanley Field, who had forced Insull out of his companies. Field was chairman of the board of the Continental Illinois Bank and Trust Company, as well as a director of Commonwealth Edison. One defendant was a public accountant responsible for the audits and financial statements of CSCC, but the remaining ten were merely officers and directors of the Insull companies and/or Halsey, Stuart.[14]

The defendants could hardly match the resources that the U.S. Government had poured into the case. But lead attorney Floyd Thompson was formidable. After coming up the old-fashioned way, by studying law on his own rather than in school, Thompson had spent nine years (1919–28) on the Illinois Supreme

---

14. Although he had been indicted with the others, Martin Insull was not on trial. He had been extradited from Canada on Swanson's state charges and therefore could not be tried on federal charges unless he returned to Canada and was extradited again. Martin's absence probably aided Samuel, for Martin had been behind some of the Insulls' most ruinous actions, and he was disliked in Chicago as a British snob and dandy.

Figure 5.8 Scenes from the Insulls' trials: (top left, left to right) mail-fraud-trial defendants Harold Stuart, Waldo Tobey, Samuel Insull, and Fred Sheel; (right) federal attorneys Dwight Green, Forrest Harness, and Leslie Salter; (bottom left) cover of Insull's memoirs; (center) state-trial participants Samuel Insull Jr., Martin Insull, defense attorney Jonathan Northrup, and Samuel Insull; (right) Samuel Insull.

Court, including a three-year term as chief justice, before unsuccessfully pursuing a political career.

On neither side, supposedly, was the judge, James Herbert Wilkerson. Yet his role in the Insull trial had come about through a series of incidents that, in retrospect, may have worked for the defendants.[15] Alongside Judge Wilkerson was the jury: 12 good men and true. Two alternatives were picked for a trial expected to last as long as four months.

The Prosecution

The government's case was straightforward: In 1929, Samuel Insull realized that he did not control enough stock in his operating companies to prevent a

---

15. See Internet appendix 5.6, " Insull, the New Deal, and Judge Wilkerson" at www.political capitalism.org/Book2/Chapter5/Appendix6.html.

takeover that might oust him and his son. In October 1929, therefore, he created Corporation Securities Company of Chicago, a holding company that he and his close associates could control and that would, in turn, control the Insull utilities—if enough common stock in them (or in IUI, which held such stocks) could be purchased.

CSCC's large capital needs required the organizers (now the defendants) to advertise their new entity as an investment company specializing in public-utility stocks. Under this ruse, as the prosecutors portrayed it, the public was told that an investment in CSCC was essentially failure-proof. The schemers went on to nefariously maintain the price of the offered stock, after which they cooked the books to sustain the illusion of profitability. By 1932, however, the shares of CSCC had lost their value. The purchasers had been utterly defrauded, losing $100 million.

The case was simple in one way but very difficult in another. The prosecutors could parade small, hapless witnesses who had lost their life's savings by succumbing to the blandishments of CSCC salesmen. But it was quite another to show that the losses involved fraud—and not merely the truth that a fool and his money are soon parted. To prove deceit, the prosecutors had to show that the defendants withheld or falsified material information.

On October 4, after U.S. Attorney Pete Green had finished his opening statement to the jury, Judge Wilkerson delivered the first of his four prodefense rulings. Declaring that the government's statement was so sweeping and so vague that the defense had no idea what it would have to prove, the Insulls' attorney therefore asked that defense statements to the jury be postponed until after the government had presented its whole case. Judge Wilkerson obliged. This gave the defense two opportunities to rebut: once immediately after the prosecution had finished its entire case and then again at the end of the trial.

On October 10, Salter presented one of the major pieces of evidence against the Insulls. CSCC's inaugural 1929 annual report had been rewritten seven times, turning an original loss of $174,000 into a $630,000 profit. This was accomplished by charging organization expenses to a capital account rather than as an expense against income and by recording dividends received in the form of stock as income at the stock's current value. So, accounting elasticity had been employed to paint a different, happy picture.

On Friday, October 12, two victims testified for the prosecution. One recollected how he had been told that the $75 units were being offered to "a few select persons," and how a hard-charging salesman then doubled his subscription from 10 to 20 shares. Prosecutors also documented an agreement among nine stockbrokers to "take care of the market" for 60 days after the sale of the stock.

At the end of the second week, however, two crucial events occurred that would affect the outcome of the trial. One was a comment by a juror, a former sheriff, to his colleagues: He said that he never knew of crooks who kept such complete, meticulous records as those under examination. Second, sensing that the jurors were being numbed by accounting minutiae, the prosecution decided to simplify and shorten the case. With 2,500 account books lodged in the courtroom and a projected four-month trial, Salter persuaded the U.S. attorney to focus only on essentials.

The parade of victims would continue, each testifying to having been taken in by seductive sales pitches. But that did not prove fraud, short of a finding of deceit authorized by the defendants. The prosecution still needed to cinch its case.

During the third week, the prosecution introduced sales documents that had described CSCC stock purchases as "the opportunities of a lifetime." But on cross-examination, the witness involved admitted that "so far as his knowledge went there was nothing misleading in the advertisements." A day later, more little guys told their sad stories, two of the witnesses (coincidentally?) living not far from two jurors.

In week four, Salter called on Harold Huling, a Justice Department expert accountant who had spent two years going over the books of the Insull companies. He now had only a few days, not weeks, to summarize his case. Nevertheless, Huling ably testified that CSCC's first annual report had wrongly "charged expenses against capital and credited stock dividends as income."

On Monday, October 29, U.S. Attorney Green rose and dramatically read the April 16, 1932, minutes of the CSCC board meeting, when the directors were informed that a certain Frank B. Schoeneman, holder of $5,000 of serial gold notes, had filed a petition for receivership. According to the minutes, the board authorized Insull "to answer the bill and admit the allegations and consent to the appointment of a receiver." With that, the government rested its case, stunning the defendants and their lawyers by its swift conclusion. "We've been double-crossed," Thompson thundered to reporters in the corridor. But Judge Wilkerson ordered the defense to begin its case after allowing only a recess.

As a formality, all the defendants except the Insulls requested a directed verdict of not guilty. According to one source (whose account of the trial McDonald described as "excellent and impartial"), the government "had made a strong prima facie case—a stronger case, indeed, than many of the so-called mail fraud cases to be found in the Federal reports in which convictions have been sustained."

Judge Wilkerson concurred. "I have examined the record carefully and have considered the able and earnest arguments of counsel, and am constrained to say that at this point in the case I cannot hold that from the circumstances proved by the United States, uncontradicted and unexplained, a reasonable man might not draw the inference of knowledge of the scheme and participation in it by such defendants," he stated. "As to the scheme itself, it does not seem open to serious debate, that at this point in the case, the question of its fraudulent character is clearly one for the jury."

The Defense

On October 31, the defense cashed in on Judge Wilkerson's decision to permit addressing   the jury after the government rested its case. Thompson briefly described Insull's career and then turned to the accounting issues, to the purchase of Cyrus Eaton's stock, and to Insull's determination to sustain IUI and CSCC in the face of the Depression. "Based on his 40 years' experience in operating public utilities and his knowledge of the values of the properties under his management," Thompson stated, "Mr. Insull believed implicitly in the intrinsic value of securities held by Utility Investments and Corporation Securities."

The defense proper came next. At 10:00 a.m., November 1, Samuel Insull was called to the witness stand. The lifelong salesman now had to sell the jury on one thing: his unimpeachable character, despite all the years in which political demagogues and their echo-chamber media had sullied his name.

After settling comfortably in his chair and turning slightly to the jury, Insull embarked on his long history. With just a few Thompson interjections, Insull began recounting his career in spellbinding terms. Witnessing the powerful effect that Insull's rags-to-riches story was having on the jury, Salter objected: "I have been hoping all afternoon that counsel would get down to the issues in this case, which is false representation of values to the public." To which Thompson replied heatedly: "Perhaps counsel cannot see the purpose of it, but the strongest test I know of a man's actions in the later years of life is the character in him during the time he is building his life, and his experience."

At this moment, Judge Wilkerson could have sustained the prosecutor's objection by reminding Thompson that his client's character could be attested by character witnesses, not by a full autobiographical retelling. But in his second major prodefense decision, Wilkerson overruled the prosecution's objection and allowed Insull to continue.

Insull went on to describe his arrival in Chicago, the growth of Chicago Edison, and the formation of Commonwealth Edison. Then he told of the spread of electricity to the suburbs and the countryside, the formation of the Public Service Company of Northern Illinois, the birth of Middle West Utilities, and his assumption of the responsibility for Peoples Gas Light and Coke Company.

After a brief recess, Thompson had Insull tell of the services he had rendered to his adopted land during the Great War. In the course of that narrative, even Thompson warned his witness that he was straying far afield, but Thompson was overruled—by Insull! "It is a little matter of personal pride," said the defendant, "and I'm sure the prosecution will bear with me."

In his discussion of the postwar years, Insull told how he had mentored young men just as Edison had mentored him. Insull also emphasized how he wished to take responsibility for his actions and even apologized to several of his codefendants. "I feel some embarrassment at my position sitting in this chair; I feel it infinitely greater on account of those young men who had no responsibility in this situation."

Insull next recalled the little-known story of his invitation to return to England to "do in the country of my birth what I had done in the country of my adoption." He had refused out of a sense of obligation to the security holders who had entrusted their money to him to develop the great utility businesses of the Middle West. It was after that that he became concerned about the possibility of "interests not connected with Chicago" accumulating large blocks of stock in his businesses.

The witness then described the formation IUI and CSCC and the complications arising from the Crash in October 1929. "The general attitude was that it was a stock market episode, serious in its character, but could not have any decided effect upon the business of country." That, he admitted, had turned out wrong. Yet his most crucial error, he averred, was not having developed friendly banking relationships with New York and Philadelphia.

The Cross-Examination

By November 1, Samuel Insull had successfully sold his character to the jury. "That man could have sold me anything," one person was overheard saying in the courtroom. The remaining question of the trial was whether Leslie Salter could reverse Insull's sale. Thus, on November 2, according to the *Chicago Tribune*, "[Insull] passed from the quiet sea of direct examination … into the barbarous and uncivilized climate of the government cross-examination."

Prosecutor Salter asked Insull about CSCC's initial annual report (covering October–December 1929): Why had it gone through eight drafts? Wasn't it because the first draft correctly showed that the company had sustained a deficit that Insull needed to reverse in order to facilitate the 1930 sale of 1,250,000 shares of common stock? The exchange went as follows:

> Q. You were planning to sell more stock that year to the public?
> A. Yes....
> Q. If this [taking dividends at market price] had been eliminated there never would have been any profit, would there?
> A. There is just as much reason to exclude interest and other items.
> Q. Why not answer my question?
> A. Because it is misleading.
> Q. You were trying to mislead the public?
> A. No sir, no sir. We were not.

Salter also questioned the charging of organization expenses to a capital account rather than to current expenses, which likewise allowed the company to show a profit. Insull answered: "I can't conceive anybody making up an income account and charging the organization expenses of an institution of this kind against the first three months of operation."

Salter asked about the accuracy of a sales flyer declaring that CSCC had $80 million in assets. "What you meant here was, when you made this statement to the public, 'Dear Investor, if you buy all these units we are offering, at the price we are offering, then we will have 80 million in cash and assets." Pounding his knee, Insull replied: "No sir, no sir. I didn't mean any such thing." He then tried in a few words to summarize the process of underwriting securities, whereby wealthy individuals guaranteed the sale of certain quantities of stock. But Salter appeared baffled.

Turning to the question of motive, Salter, at the urging of Huling, went through each of Insull's numerous salaries and then asked the witness about his total income:

> Q. For the year 1930, $434,413.45, and for the year 1931, $485,767? I've taken the totals from your personal income tax return.
> A. Yes.
> Q. To that extent, at least you had some personal motive in wanting to see the control of these companies kept by you and your associates.
> A. You may think that is the motive. I don't.

Thompson later rejoined with the fact that, in many years, Insull's charitable contributions exceeded his income. Salter, taken by surprise, admonished Huling in a voice just loud enough to be heard by the jury: "You son of a bitch. Why didn't you tell me that was in there, too?"

Following Insull's testimony, the defense continued with technical and legal presentations from defendants and witnesses, some being accounting experts. Much of their testimony was devoted to persuading the jury that the market value of a security is its true value—not a popular idea following the Crash of 1929 and the resulting demagogy. They would also clear up an issue that Insull had not been able to explain: Halsey, Stuart's support for CSCC stock during the sales campaign. Insull had said: "I haven't any recollection of discussing it at the time." Pressed again on the matter, he answered: "I said I didn't know anything about it at the time."

This left the market-rigging accusation unrefuted. But Clarence MacNeille, vice president and secretary-treasurer of Halsey, Stuart, answered the charge adroitly. "Are you at all familiar with stock transactions, Mr. Salter? ... You can't just sell and step out from under. There is a lot of responsibility connected with this business." Throughout his exchanges with Salter, MacNeille handled himself so well that he gave Insull a rare chance to laugh at his tormenters.

Summation to Verdict

"In view of the complicated and technical nature of the evidence, which has been largely a matter of book accounts and opposing theories of accounting, the summations of the attorneys are regarded as of unusual importance," the *Chicago Tribune* previewed on November 20, 1934. "They will bring the case to a focus, each from his own point of view," the newspaper added. "The charge of the court, which is expected to include comment on the evidence, is also awaited with unusual interest."

The summations were broader than simply accounting, however. Forest Harness, who had pursued Insull across continents, did boil his case down to three financial issues: (1) The defendants had misrepresented the assets held by CSCC at the time that the stock was sold. (2) They had rigged the market in CSCC stock to preserve the illusion of value. (3) They had engaged in accounting fraud for the same purpose.

In response, though, Floyd Thompson turned to oratory. "At times he would lean over the rail and talk to [the jurors] in an intimate conversational way, in so low a tone that he could not be heard ten feet away," the *Chicago Tribune* reported. "At other times he became vehement in denunciation of some suspicion that the government had cast upon his clients, the elder Insull and his son, Samuel Jr., and shouted in a voice to be heard a block away." And what an effect Thompson had! "He told stories to make them laugh and drew comparisons to make them weep."

Thompson's arguments were basic and not too technical. First, he argued that there was no fraud, because neither a misappropriation of money nor a covering up of misappropriation was present. Even more important, he returned to the fundamental defense: Insull and son were of a character that made it impossible to believe that they had committed fraud. "Consider their lives," Thompson implored. "We have laid them bare, so that you will know what was built here. Men do not lead honorable lives for three score and ten years and turn crook overnight." Tellingly, the Insulls were the only defendants not to call character witnesses. It was as if to say: No one could lend us the prestige of his character, for no one has a character higher than ours.

Prosecutor Salter had a definite problem when it came time for rebuttal. The central pillar of the defendants' case was their personal character. Perhaps for that reason, he chose to attack the defendants' character and even their use of character witnesses. But here he had to deal with the Insulls' striking refusal to call any character witnesses. Backed into a corner, he was forced to *praise* Insull's action. "You've got to admire him for it," Salter said. "He could have brought in millions to testify for him."

In the same way, Salter had to acknowledge Insull's industrial achievement and yet convince the jury that he was capable of turning to fraud at age 70. According to the *Chicago Tribune* reporter: "He [Salter] divined the mind of Insull here as swept by an overweening and sweeping ambition of wealth and power, torn away from the safe old moorings, much as the character of Napoleon the great overreached his capacities after his early victories."

When the two sides finished summation, Judge Wilkerson instructed the jury. He explained that the fraud statute includes any scheme to obtain money from another by the means of "false and fraudulent pretenses, representations, or promises." A person, he said, "has a right not to be subjected to a risk which the other party to the transaction fraudulently induces him to believe does not exist." It does not matter if the deceiver himself has great expectations for the plan and intends that the person deceived shall lose nothing by the fraud. "The confident hope and belief of ultimate success of the enterprise, enthusiasm and optimism does not justify or excuse the employment of false and fraudulent pretenses, representations or promises as a means of obtaining the money of others for the enterprise." Likewise, a person cannot use false representations to obtain another's money "even though he himself at the same time risked his own money in the enterprise."

This last point told heavily against the defense, given its argument, made time and again, that the defendants obviously did not intend to carry out a fraud, because they had lost huge sums in the deal—and in some cases lost everything. However, the judge ameliorated this consideration by adding: "The investment of his own money may be considered on the question of knowledge and intent in making the representations which it is charged were false."

Judge Wilkerson's next instruction was his third declaration in favor of the defense: A person may not be convicted of fraud simply because his business judgment was bad. "There must be the underlying purpose and intent to deceive and defraud," he said. "The Government must prove beyond a reasonable doubt not only that the statement was false in a material respect, but that the defendant knew it was false and made it with the intent to obtain money or property by inducing [others] to believe that statement was true."

In his last major action favoring the defense, Judge Wilkerson told the jury that a company was permitted to use any valid accounting procedure. Experts had testified that the CSCC's annual reports had followed a valid procedure, so this instruction weighted mightily.

The jury retired on November 24 at 2:20 p.m. What then happened in the jury room? According to a contemporary account, the jury was evenly split but soon came around to acquittal. According to McDonald, however, the not-guilty decision was immediate. The story also exists that the jurors purposefully delayed their quick decision to avoid any appearance of impropriety. Learning that it was the birthday of one juror, they sent out for cake and had a birthday party to kill time.

The jury returned to the courtroom at 4:23 p.m. "'Have you reached a verdict, Mr. Foreman?'

"'We have,' said Mr. Lent, fingering the papers in his lap. 'Hand it to the clerk,' he was instructed. Clerk Joseph O'Sullivan took the fateful paper and read in a loud, clear voice the simple sentence: 'We, the jury, find the defendants not guilty.'"

U.S. Attorney Pete Green said only, "We all gave the best we had in us." The defendants basked in relief and joy.

Final Years

"I sincerely appreciate the vindication of the motives of myself and my associates," Insull told the press upon his acquittal in the federal mail-fraud case.

Congratulations followed, none more passionate than that from the Friends of Insull in America, an organization formed ahead of the trial for "the purpose of Insuring Fair Play and Justice for Samuel and Martin J. Insull and Associates."

The open letter congratulated Insull for having defeated "outrageous, unmerited, and trumped up charges" to regain "your honor, prestige, and reputation, which are all unimpaired and unsullied." Insull was then called upon to return to the public stage to fight against FDR's crusade for public power and demonization of private power (including "Insull, whose hand is against every man's"). The letter urged a new beginning, "a program of sane, clear thinking and determined opposition to the wild vaporings and insane activities of the Washington group of long-haired men and short-haired women and miscellaneous borderline cases that go to make up the so-called 'Brain Trust'."

But Insull was not unsullied. Nor could he be a voice for his industry. He was beyond broke and still facing civil suits, which Junior would handle from Chicago. Although sympathetic to the trial's verdict, hundreds of thousands were still licking their financial wounds. Nor was Insull young and spirited for the big stage. That is why he had resigned all his posts without a fight and left Chicago a few years before.

There was post-Insull cleanup too. James Simpson, Insull's successor, would pare the number of companies within Commonwealth Edison from 77 to 12 in his first seven years, disposing of real estate, manufacturing ventures, and even a radio station, among other things. This left, in Simpson's words, "investments properly related to a public utility, thus enabling the management to center its full attention upon the company's fundamental business of supplying electricity." The esprit de corps needed some work too, with the Edison Club and Electra having been "temporarily deactivated" in Insull's final year.

Samuel Insull Jr. worked under Simpson to implement the restructuring as vice chairman. In late 1938, the two would part ways, with Junior entering into the insurance business. Overall, Junior was a respected executive in the utility industry—and more so than uncle Martin Insull of Middle West Utilities (until he resigned in 1932), who came under fire for spending "too much time on Pullman trains, expanding into all parts of the country, instead of studying the books."

⌒

With the not-guilty verdict, Insull's old companies reinstated his annual pension of $21,000. This was a huge relief, but the lifeline could not erase a long list of creditors that Insull chose not to discharge by declaring personal bankruptcy. Still, the pleas for repayment came in, to one of which Junior responded as follows:

> Both my father and I are broke—he for several million dollars, and myself for about $750,000. He has pensions paid to him by the companies for which he worked…. I have a job with a salary attached to it. He supports himself and my mother from his pension. From my salary I support my own family and some other relatives who were wiped out along with us in 1932.

Then there was the overhang of legal matters: "Although all criminal phases of our legal difficulties have been over for some time," Samuel Jr. continued, "we are still under considerable legal expense for civil proceedings which will undoubtedly go on for some time." This would not change in his father's lifetime.

Samuel Insull left his accounts open with the hope of achieving one last business victory. His first opportunity came right after the trial when Nikola Tesla asked him to help commercialize his Tele-Geodynamic scheme to transmit electricity without wires. "You could regain your old place of wealth and power while remaining perfectly independent," the inventor wrote. Insull was interested and capital was raised, but Tesla's technology proved noncommercial. The venture soon died.

In 1936, Insull and Junior embarked on a plan to form a radio network in the U.S. Midwest. Stations were bought, but insufficient advertising revenue and other problems ended the effort within a year. (This was still the Great Depression.) This would be Insull's last business foray.

Chicago remained unattractive to Samuel and Gladys, so it was back to Europe after the trial. Samuel loved London; Gladys, Paris. Paris won out, if for no other reason than that England's income tax limited stays to less than half the year.

Insull feared isolation but coveted Europe's relative privacy from the press and gawkers. ("It is such a relief not to be stared at," Insull commented.) Insull visited England as much as possible. "I am a 'has been' in Chicago but I am 'someone' here," one of his letters from London read. He elaborated:

> This man gives a dinner for me, that man gives a luncheon for me, another man (he runs the British end of the General Electric Co) takes me to "staff" luncheon.... Another instance the Chairman of the Central Electricity Board (the Grid) told me he is very anxious to have the advantage of my advice.... No wonder I feel happier over here [than in Chicago].

Even Cyrus Eaton, the man who had panicked Insull into his great blunders, visited Insull for advice about opening a London investment office.

In early 1938, Insull was approached about making a movie about his life. Not interested! "All publicity is bad, even good publicity," he wrote to Junior, adding: "If the work that I did during over half a century of active business is not a monument sufficient of my accomplishments, it is better that Samuel Insull and his work be forgotten."

In New York City, this rejection left a 22-scene play showing, *Power*, which was anything but sympathetic to Insull and private power. Produced by the Works Progress Administration, a New Deal entity that employed 12,000 in theater alone, Insull, according to one reviewer, "was shown swindling America's Little Man."

Insull's energy and active mind were tested by periods without visits from industry figures or worldly company. Sometimes he took to pen, as when he wrote a white paper: "Possibilities of Greek Trade Development," explaining why low-cost power was "the only obstacle in the way of Greece becoming great in manufacturing as she already is great in commerce and maritime transportation."

Lectures were virtually a thing of the past for the speaker whose addresses between 1897 and 1923 had filled 900 pages in two volumes. His last public address, "The Life and Works of Edison," was in Chicago in February 1937. The master of ceremonies described Edison as the man who "relegated the kerosene lamp to the antique shop, and put the windmill out of business." The 78-year-old guest speaker was then introduced as in the same league as the greatest American. "Edison invented the incandescent lamp, but Insull sold it to the world."

Insull went on to describe his mentor in colorful detail, while parenthetically noting how happy he was to speak other than "when Uncle Sam and the sovereign State of Illinois compelled my appearance under less pleasant conditions."

⌁

"I am fit as a fiddle," Insull wrote from London in summer 1937. Actually, Insull had a heart condition and took medicine for his nerves—and was a very old man for the day. The end came in Paris on July 16, 1938, at age 78. "An unidentified man was found in a state of collapse on the platform of the Tuileries subway station near the Place de la Concorde," the police report read. "He was neatly dressed in a gray suit with red strip, wore a brown felt hat and had [85 cents] in his pocket."

The white-haired man had no identification papers. But the initials S.I. were found on his clothing. Doubtless thieves had lifted Insull's wallet, but the story developed that the once titan had died penniless in a Paris subway. "And so in his death, as in his life," Forrest McDonald ended his biography, "Samuel Insull was robbed, and nobody got the story straight."

Condolences and tributes came from some former companies and organizations that Insull had built up in his prime. There was silence from other quarters, with memories green and the Great Depression worsening. Insull's estate would be settled two years later, with assets of $9,091 applied against $4.1 million in liabilities—a small fraction of a penny on the dollar for creditors.

Depression Scapegoat

"The collapse of the great Insull holding companies has tended to discredit all holding companies, especially utility holding companies," wrote one expert of the day. Concentrated in the public-utility-regulated sector and riding high on the belief that legally protected businesses were depression-proof, these entities seemed to represent capitalism rather than its bastardized political makeover.

The boom and bust of such holding companies was also a legacy of expansionary monetary policy by the Federal Reserve Bank, which was established in 1913 at the behest of leading businessmen to "furnish an elastic currency." Monetary expansion and artificially low interest rates, however, proved to be a short-term drug that had hangover effects—unsustainable, for short. Speculative fever, ironically, turned out to be bad for business and for the public's perception of the same.

Like Hoover, FDR had himself to blame for turning a needed contraction into the direful Great Depression. FDR pinned blame on Insull, a political ploy that became official dogma via Arthur Schlesinger Jr., the most revered historian of his generation. In *Crisis of the Old Order*, Insull got the FDR treatment:

> The Insull group … expressed the unlimited ambition of its founder, Samuel Insull of Chicago. Insull's talent was partly his superior knowledge and daring, party his astute use of the devices of incorporation, partly his ruthless managerial skill. Once when asked on the witness stand whether more humane policies in his gas plant might not result in greater efficiency, Insull characteristically replied, "My experience is that the greatest aid to efficiency of labor is a long line of men waiting at the gate."

Insull was hardly a foe of efficiency or his workforce; quite the opposite. It was he that brought power to the masses at declining rates and busily electrified the countryside—all New Deal aspirations.[16] Insull also was a progenitor of welfare capitalism, having turned holiday turkeys for each employee into life insurance policies and having implemented company-subsidized savings plans, pension plans, education programs, service awards, and recreational opportunities. Insull was no more a robber baron than John D. Rockefeller, the architect of efficiency on the petroleum side. Schlesinger did not bother to research the Insull record before jumping to his preordained Progressive conclusion.[17]

"A further charm of the holding company lay in its immunity to regulation," Schlesinger complained. "'A Holding Company,' said Will Rogers, 'is a thing where you hand an accomplice the goods while the policeman searches you'." Schlesinger went on to conclude:

> As the utility empires grew in complexity, they grew in irresponsibility. The first effect of the corporate sleight of hand was to disenfranchise the already bewildered stockholders…. In the end, only sheer momentum—or the will of a dominant personality—could hold the structure together.

---

16. As opposed to Insull's "essential principle of ever widening private monopoly," FDR promoted the "essential principle of all the public power and all the control measures that may be needed to make the people the masters of their own electrical destiny."

17. See also *Capitalism at Work*, pp. 146–47, 166.

Schlesinger's indictment of holding companies failed to examine the economies behind the creation of, say, Middle West Utilities (1912) or to differentiate
between earlier sound and later unsound structures. (One study put the demar-
cation line around 1922.) He failed to note how incentives created by regulation
spawned a new generation of utility holding companies, and no blame was
assigned to expansionary credit by the Federal Reserve Bank, the government
monopoly over money and credit.

More Government

The Insull collapse, according to a popular book of the day, "had shaken capitalism, in a period of poverty, hardship and nerve-shattering strain when capitalism
was in poor shape to stand shaking." But the *government* side of the mixed economy was attacking and weakening capitalism in its desperate hour, with Insull as
much a victim of failed public policy (in both the boom and the bust) as he was
an instigator. The recovery that never came prevented Insull's holding-company
investments from escaping from the deep red.[18]

With the misdiagnosis of Insull came more government, not less. "It is no
exaggeration to see in the legislative innovations of the New Deal a phoenix
arising from the ashes of the Insull empire," one retrospective concluded. Insull
was found *politically guilty* by the New Dealers, his trial verdicts notwithstanding. "The New Deal legislation that passed on the heels of the Insull debacle
proceeded on the assumption that Insull and other high-profile promoters and
utility magnates had swindled the American people," Richard Cudahy and
William Henderson noted. Ironically, "seventy years later, the collapse of the
Enron Corporation was employed in a similar way to push through 'the most
far-reaching reforms of American business practices since the time of Franklin
Delano Roosevelt'."

A failed Insull became the argument for more social control, not less. Insull-
inspired New Deal regulation (Insull's failure being the largest and the setup
for FDR's first hundred days) included the Securities Act of 1933 and the Securities Exchange Act of 1934. Quite apart from the common law's prohibition
against misrepresentation and fraud, these laws sought to prevent unscrupu-
lous activity, while not unduly discouraging stock offerings by public companies. It was a balancing act that, like other new regulation, failed to foster
recovery in the 1930s.

Federal public-utility regulation was next. The Federal Trade Commission's seven-year (1928–35) investigation of the electricity industry, published

---

18. Regarding the severe downturn in 1937, which exposed FDR's government-led recovery program as misguided, Insull wrote from London: "The great drop in the American market must have caused lots of trouble for a great many people. I am really glad to be out of it
but cannot believe it is more than a temporary situation." Insull was too optimistic on this
count as well, as the Roosevelt Recession stretched into 1938.

in 84 volumes, painted Insull and his industry unfavorably. Pundits had a field day; John Flynn wrote in the *Nation* that Insull was "the most arrogant, insolvent and unsocial of all of the power barons." But Insull was so much more than that—if Flynn and Schlesinger had done their homework. Such was the fashion: to superficially blame business, not the failed activist government policies that, time and again, defeated business recovery.

The Public Utility Holding Company Act of 1935 (PUHCA) required covered entities to divest properties to operate in a single state. This law was Insull's legacy too. Section 11's "death sentence" required large companies to be dismembered, removing what FDR characterized as "private socialism of concentrated private power."[19]

Arthur Schlesinger gave an academic imprimatur to the breakups:

> To replace Samuel Insull by that which would make Insull's return impossible would be to grant Insull the greatest privilege one generation could grant another—the kingly privilege of fixing the succession to the throne. "If only an iron tombstone will keep Mr. Insull from rising then it is Mr. Insull who has designed the iron tombstone."

Retrospect

The "Depression scapegoat" was the forgotten master of "complex system-building" and "difficult concepts, esoteric technology, uncommon economics, and sophisticated management." Technology historian Thomas Hughes continued: "On a highly abstract level [Insull was] … a systems conceptualizer comparable to Edison," and his business acumen was "comparable to the historic managerial contributions made by railway men in the nineteenth century and is as interesting as the widely publicized managerial concepts and polities of John D. Rockefeller and Henry Ford."

Such is the historical verdict based on Insull's half-century career. But what about the tragic 1929–32 era when his business judgment faltered and his desperate acts only made things worse? Did they transgress into real crimes? The judge and jury resoundingly rejected the prosecution's claim of fraud. Insull, they found, was overoptimistic and all too human on the way down, as he was on the way up. That was tragic but not criminal.

Frank Tate, a student of Insull in the Thomas Edison years, opined:

> However much his judgment may have erred, there is one thing of which I am certain and that is that Samuel Insull was incapable of the performance of a dishonest or a dishonorable act. I think the situation brought about by the collapse of his empire in the whirlpool of national disaster was most intelligently and justly

---

19. PUHCA, "the most bitter legislative battle of Roosevelt's first term," took 31 days of hearings versus 3 days for the National Industrial Recovery Act of 1933 (NIRA), the mother legislation of much of FDR's early New Deal.

summed up by [General Electric head] Mr. Owen D. Young when he described it as "too much confidence in the future of the country." But hadn't we all?

Samuel Insull himself stated before the trial:

Not one dishonest dollar has ever passed through these hands. For years I … ran my business with a corporation lawyer at my elbow. But when I was fighting for my life—for the money that each of my stockholders had invested with me—I didn't, I couldn't take that precaution! That is why I am under arrest now. If I had taken the time to save myself, if I had not fought so much for my stockholders, they could not hang a criminal charge on me today. I am not sure that they can anyway. The points they are basing their case on are before the courts for the first time.

Insull did not duck blame, but he could not help but wonder about his ultimate fate if recovery had come as promised by the politician-in-chief:

I often wonder how much of my failure can be traced to following the policies of Herbert Hoover. Understand, I am not blaming him. His policies happened to be my policies and so I acted upon them. If he advocated something different I would have been likely to have followed my own judgment. My troubles came from overestimating the capacity of the United States to come back after the first blow of the depression. When in 1931 the tide seemed to have turned, I thought recovery had set in. In that I was fooled—and so was the President. I—my companies—spent money as though things were all right. We believed that they were becoming all right. We increased our floating debt and this eventually brought about our bankruptcy. That was the penalty that I paid for helping with recovery and following the advice of the President, but, as I said before, the policies that I followed were my policies.

Insull's final thoughts presaged his witness-stand demeanor that would aid in his acquittal:

When I think of what I am facing I am simply overwhelmed. I do not lose my courage but I realize that I am the administration's most prominent sacrifice upon the altar of depression. What can I do? How can I fight against this? Don't you see the horror or it? I have devoted my life to making gas and electricity available for everyone. In doing this I prospered during the good times, and I lost what I had made during the first years of the depression. But today the benefits of my labor are going on—my dream of cheaper and available gas and electricity for the masses is realized—but I am crucified. Where is the justice in this?

Insull was hardly a lone agent in the great demise. An example of history in rhyme, there were parties aplenty—as there would be with the Enron debacle eight decades later. "When the parts played by directors, lawyers, bankers, utility commissioners, his industry, investor, and the public are considered, Insull's melodrama becomes easier to understand," wrote one observer. "Almost everybody joined gleefully in paying out an abundance of economic rope with which he might, and did, hang himself."

The man described in one recent biography as a "classic American enigma" was an all-too-human man who failed to overcome success and failed alongside government policy.[20] That he pioneered a major expansion of government in his own way earlier in his career is an ironic reminder that the state power is a two-edged sword.

20. Internet appendix 5.7, "Government Depression and Antidrpression Policy and Insull's Colapse" at www.politicalcapitalism.org/Book2/Chapter5/Appendix7.html.

Part II

The Boss: Jack Bowen

Jack Bowen was a wonderful promoter and probably the best
salesman you will ever meet. He liked to be called
"the boss" and was just an unusual, dynamic man.
—Selby Sullivan, 2006

Clint Murchison was my role model.
—Jack Bowen, 2007

Introduction

William Jackson "Jack" Bowen, reverently called Boss by his associates, is an important figure in the history of the natural gas industry.[1] In the 1950s, he built small pipelines in South Texas, part of an energy education that included engineering work at oil and gas wells, a gas-liquids plant, and an oil refinery. Bowen then constructed a major segment of the first pipeline to bring natural gas to Florida and went on to become CEO of the resultant Florida Gas Company. Finally, Bowen became CEO of Transco Energy Company, the parent of the largest interstate gas pipeline in America, where he worked until retiring in 1992 at age 70.

Jack Bowen's career bridged those of two leading figures in the gas pipeline industry: Clint Murchison and Ken Lay. Bowen went to work for Murchison in 1949; Lay went to work for Bowen at Florida Gas in 1974 and again at Transco in 1981. Ken Lay left Transco in 1984 to head the company that, through acquisition and merger, became Enron.

The next four chapters describe three eras of the interstate gas industry and its politics. Southern Union Company and Trans-Canada Corporation, both founded by Murchison and still leading companies today, are described in chapters 6 and 7, respectively. Murchison also conceived Florida Gas Company to deliver natural gas from Texas to Florida, and he put Jack Bowen in charge, the story of chapter 8. After 14 years as CEO of Florida Gas, Bowen accepted the challenge of turning around the ailing giant of the interstate industry, Transco. A turnaround was achieved but not sustained, as recounted in chapter 9, a saga that involved Ken Lay and others.

In the early 1970s, Lay spent two and a half years in Washington as an energy bureaucrat, then made two business stops at companies whose major assets he had previously regulated: Florida Gas Transmission (headquartered in Winter Park, Florida) and Transcontinental Gas Pipe Line (of Houston). At Florida Gas (1974–81) and then Transco (1981–84), Lay became the natural gas industry's bright young star. It was the ups and downs of these companies—and the political turbulence within the gas industry generally—that shaped Lay's business persona for his fateful 17 years at Enron.

Given his regulatory background, it was not surprising that one of Lay's first acts as CEO of Enron's predecessor company, Houston Natural Gas Corporation, was to buy Florida Gas Company for its valuable interstate pipeline, as well as for its executive talent. He also purchased another regulated interstate, Transwestern

---

1. Bowen's career, and that of his mentor Clint Murchison, was mostly in the midstream pipeline segment between upstream natural gas production and downstream gas distribution.

Pipeline Company, from Texas Eastern Corporation. He then merged his now federally regulated company with InterNorth Inc., whose major asset was the (regulated) Midwest interstate giant, Northern Natural Gas Pipeline. In a single year, the company to be known as Enron was transformed. Ken Lay liked the complexity and tumult of regulated assets.[2]

·◇·

Part II's pipeline adventures are case studies of political capitalism. Government franchises, whether required at the local or the federal level, put politics up front. Southern Union in the 1920s and Florida Gas in the 1950s had to overcome coal interests and fuel oil interests to effectuate contracts between waiting gas customers and ready gas producers.

During the Great Depression, El Paso Natural Gas helped its gas-hungry smelting customers secure copper tariffs in order to increase domestic prices for the metal and thus keep the fires lit. Government-built and -owned pipelines constructed during World War II would lead to postwar political debate about privatization and the auction process used to choose a winner (Texas Eastern Transmission, which beat Transco and Tennessee Gas Transmission Company).

In the biggest political fight in the history of the North American gas industry, Trans-Canada Pipe Lines used brute political force to fend off the will of the marketplace. All manner of government obstruction was employed against viable binational gas pipeline projects, while sizeable government subsidies got the all-Canada project constructed. The most uneconomic project won, leaving practically everyone a loser—except for a bruised Clint Murchison.

Pipeline politics was exacerbated by natural gas shortages in U.S. interstate markets in the 1970s, deficits that were the product of federal price controls on the wellhead price of gas. Although shortages resulting from price ceilings are no mystery to economists, government policy at the time was less about deregulation than about gapism, or ameliorative regulation that tries to bring supply and demand together by increasing the former and decreasing the latter.[3]

This policy of gapism added regulatory waste to regulatory waste. But it was here that engineer Jack Bowen found common cause with America's engineer-president Jimmy Carter and his National Energy Plan of 1977, which sought to use the levers of government to supplement supply (productionism)

---

2. Ken Lay's business persona as a Washington–savvy Ph.D. economist is described in *Capitalism at Work*, pp. 3–4, 306–12.

3. Gapism is defined and applied to energy regulation in *Capitalism at Work*, pp. 266–67.

and moderate demand (conservationism).[4] The epilogue of this book examines the dynamics and distortions of natural gas regulation that began in the nineteenth century and culminated in the 1970s and led to the open-access era of gas transmission the next decade.

Jack Bowen was an engineer with a degree; Clint Murchison was an engineer without one. Both learned business on the go: Murchison as a child and Bowen as an adult. It is said that an engineer can learn business far more easily than a businessman can learn engineering. Jack Bowen did learn business, for the most part, and Clint never needed to. Ken Lay, despite his brilliance, drive, and endearing personality, proved to be neither a competent businessman nor an intuitive engineer, although he thought that he and his team were the masters of the energy universe.

⌒

This book and this trilogy on political capitalism revolve around different episodes of boom and bust for companies and individuals. Part of the cycle is the nature of politics in an industry in which special government favor is temporary and fleeting. But part of the instability comes wholly from outside government. The *creative destruction* of the marketplace is where changes in technology and consumer preference reverse business fortunes for established firms and even for whole legacy industries. Particularly in those circumstances, success, particularly great success, can lead to the bad practices and arrogant behaviors that result in failure.

And thus Ken Lay's Enron and Samuel Insull's utility empire went from dizzying triumph to stunning failure. (John Henry Kirby of Part III"s chapter 10 also had pronounced ups and downs that were brought about by his own failings and, late in life, also by the Great Depression.) As summarized in an Internet appendix to chapter 7, Clint Murchison Jr. squandered much of his father's empire and good name—another case study of success falling victim to arrogance and worse.[5] Biographer Jane Wolfe noted the intergenerational legacy of the Murchisons:

> The Murchison story is an important part of American history. From Clint Murchison Sr.'s early play in the great Texas oil boom [and the Southwest gas boom] to his son John's powerful takeover of the giant Allegheny Corporation and Clint Jr.'s founding of the Dallas Cowboys, the Murchisons serve as a paradigm of Texas and America. The family rose with the oil [and natural gas] boom and with the country, and fell with the [1980s] oil bust and the national economic decline.

---

4. Conservationism is government-directed demand reduction and stands in contrast to market-driven conservation. The concept is applied to energy regulation in *Capitalism at Work*, pp. 187, 218, 242. Productionism is the corollary on the supply side and stands in contrast to consumer-driven free-market production.

5. See Internet appendix 7.6, "The Rise and Fall of Clint Murchison Jr." at www.political-capitalism.org/Book2/Chapter7/Appendix6.html.

Families—not only individuals, companies, and industries—must carefully navi-gate the vicissitudes of the creatively shifting marketplace. The perils are even greater in the mixed economy whereby artificial booms and corrective busts from government intervention supplement the market's creative destruction.

6

Meadows to Murchison

I T WAS NOT THE ENCOUNTER that William Jackson Bowen (b. 1922) could have wanted, but it would change his life for the better. Early one Saturday in the spring of 1941 Annah Bowen traveled from Waco to pay a surprise visit to her son, who had entered the University of Texas at Austin that year as a junior. Jack's grades were poor, and she wanted to find out why.

Arriving at Jack's apartment, Annah was greeted by a dark-skinned lad of 14 years dressed in a white dinner jacket.

"Who are you?" she asked.

"I'm Meadows, Mr. Bowen's valet."

"I am looking for Mr. Bowen" retorted Annah. "Where is he?"

"He's gone to San Antonio with Miss Annis for the Fiesta of Flowers parade and will be back tomorrow," Meadows explained.

"Well Mr. Meadows, you tell him that he better call me!"

It was small relief when Annah heard Jack's explanation that Annis Hilty, a charismatic beauty who hailed from a nice Houston family, required his best social efforts. Jack's absence was part of a wider problem, something that Annah thought had been addressed when she postponed Jack's entry to UT by sending him to junior college at the New Mexico Military Institute in Roswell. The idea was to instill in Jack the discipline that his late father never quite had. Berry Bowen, weakened by alcoholism, died of pneumonia in 1928 at age 40 when Jack was 6. So Annah supported herself and her two children—Jack and Joanne—by managing the drugstore chain that her late husband had built up.

Annah returned to Waco thinking about what might be necessary for her son, who had so many good qualities, to get over the top. Her encounter with Meadows, coupled with the attack on Pearl Harbor later that year, led her to secure an appointment for Jack in a far stricter environment—the United States Military Academy at West Point, New York.

That change proved to be very wise. Graduating in the top quartile with an engineering degree, and now having a more disciplined outlook on life, Jack Bowen embarked on a career path that would give the United States one of its top natural gas executives—and a worthy mentor for a young industry executive named Kenneth Lee Lay.

Discovering Energy—and Clint Murchison

Jack married Annis the day after graduation and began training as a pilot in the U.S. Army Air Forces. With the end of hostilities, Jack transferred to the Army Corps of Engineers, flying cargo planes in the Pacific before returning to the United States.

A career in the military seemed like a good plan. There would be many interesting places to visit and friendly people to meet. The necessities would be taken care of, and a military pension offered security. Jack and Annis were too young, healthy, and in love to desire much more. The thought was to retire from the army and live in Winter Park, Florida, an idyllic lake-studded suburb they discovered while stationed in adjacent Orlando. Winter Park would be in the Bowens' future—but in a way quite unlike what they had imagined.

·◌·

In mid-1949, the couple visited South Texas, staying at the home of Annis's uncle, prominent businessman Vernon F. "Doc" Neuhaus (1901–82). Doc was an early riser, and Jack woke up at dawn in order to chat with him over coffee. Bowen soon discovered Doc's ritual: early-morning phone calls discussing banking, real estate, and oil and gas deals with such luminaries as Clint Murchison (who arose at 5 AM daily) and Sid Richardson (who phoned Clint every day at 6 AM sharp).[1]

Overhearing these conversations gave Jack an epiphany. What if he returned to civilian life for a career in this exciting energy business? He was sure that he could learn what he needed to know given his smarts and his bachelor of science degree in general engineering from West Point (the first engineering school in the country). This plan could bring him back to Texas and might be financially rewarding. It was peacetime anyway, and military promotions would be slow.

---

1. Sid Williams Richardson (1891–1959) grew up in Athens, Texas, where he and Clint traded cattle as teenagers. Sid would make and lose several fortunes before major natural gas finds in West Texas put him over the top. By the mid-1950s, Richardson had a reputed net worth of $1.25 billion (almost $10 billion in today's dollars), making him "the first billionaire west of the Mississippi." The hydrocarbon reserves of the reclusive bachelor were greater than those of any other independent, including J. Paul Getty and H. L. Hunt.

Annis liked the idea, so Jack wrote Doc a letter of inquiry. Doc told Murchison about his niece's personable husband, who had done well at West Point and had some worldly experience.

Murchison arranged for an interview at his new company, Delhi Oil Corporation, which was engaged in exploration and production projects, with plans to build pipelines and other energy infrastructure. Jack met with head geologist Frank Schultz and accepted a position as a junior engineer, working with Delhi's two senior engineers. Many projects were on tap, and Jack's starting salary—$400 per month—was a nice bump up from military pay. Bowen secured his release from the army, gathered his few possessions, and drove to Dallas with his wife and infant daughter to start his new career in the fall of 1949.

Figure 6.1 Bowen's military career began upon graduation from West Point in 1946 and ended after a 1949 visit to South Texas, where Annis's uncle, Doc Neuhaus, interested him in the energy industry.

Little did the 54-year-old Murchison and the 27-year-old Bowen know that two generations of leadership in the natural gas pipeline business—one present and one future—were joined. A quarter century later, a third generation joined the chain—a bright, young Ph.D. economist leaving government service, Ken Lay.

◦◦◦

Clinton Williams Murchison (1895–1969), known simply as Clint, was a legendary Texas oil and gas man, venture capitalist, and investor whose visage graced the cover of national publications in the 1950s and 1960s. Born into a prominent East Texas family, Clint eschewed a college education to get on with his first love, deal making.[2] Clint's higher education would consist of voracious reading of practical and learned books, studying the dictionary, seeking advice from professionals in different fields ("listen to the doctor," he would say), and baptism by doing. Clint would invest in a panoply of businesses in his half-century career but always considered himself "a pipeliner at heart."

Murchison traded horses and livestock as a boy before learning the oil business from his childhood friend, Sid Richardson. Both had gifted minds for numbers and trusty intuition that enabled them to more than hold their own amid "adventurers, gamblers, 'blue skiers,' and assorted fortune hunters." Clint and Sid mastered the art of finding out about discoveries and dry holes before others, in order to capitalize on volatile lease values. ("To some extent we lived off rumors," Clint remembered, "and sometimes our own rumors.") The pair's greatest deal was quadrupling $50,000 in one 24-hour period by getting ahead of the news of an oil gusher in north Texas.

Clint's first oil company, Murchison–Fain, traded leases and drilled wells. With the aid of a new breed of professional, the geologist, the company was not only lucky but also good. In 1925, Murchison–Fain was dissolved between the partners, with Clint receiving $1.6 million in cash and a group of oil properties.

Murchison Oil Company was now the center of activity. Joining Clint in the venture were his brother Frank, who left the banking business, and a gifted geologist who once worked for Gulf Oil, Ernest Closuit. Geologists were new to the industry, and Clint felt that they could pay their way by siting discovery wells and interpreting oil sands for in-field drilling. A bonus, as Clint would soon appreciate, was estimating proved reserves to determine the feasibility of building long-lived pipelines.

Doc Neuhaus was active in Clint's ventures at the time, although he was not employed by Murchison Oil. Clint and Doc would remain close friends and business associates for life.[3]

---

2. Clint was two weeks into college life at Trinity University, a Presbyterian school in San Antonio, when he got in trouble with the dean over a craps game. Rather than turn in the names of his friends who were at the table, he returned to Athens to work at his father's bank, ending his formal education and beginning a full-time business career.

3. Late in life, Clint sent Doc a photograph with the inscription, "The seeds of our friendship have long been sown into the fertile soil of mutual affection and have blossomed into love and admiration."

Southern Union to Delhi Oil

Murchison Oil began as a petroleum company. This changed in 1927, when an oil prospect in the Permian Basin of West Texas turned out to be a major natural gas find. An oil pipeline under construction was reengineered for gas and routed to Wink, Texas, where several hundred homeowners and dozens of businesses signed up for gas at a flat monthly fee—no meter needed. Lines were laid to other nearby West Texas and eastern New Mexico towns, and similar field-to-town projects followed in South Texas and southern Oklahoma.

Water-distribution opportunities became part of the pipeline play. In 1929 Clint formed Southern Union Gas Company to handle his gas production, transmission, and distribution properties, as well as to house Cities Water Company of Texas. Seventy-five years later, Southern Union would become part of the Enron story by purchasing the bankrupt company's remaining interstate pipelines.[4]

The next step for Southern Union came when a vacationing Clint Murchison discovered that Santa Fe, Albuquerque, and Farmington, New Mexico, did not have natural gas service. Closuit calculated that the nearby Kutz Canyon field in the emerging San Juan Basin had ample reserves to anchor a pipeline network.[5] But while franchises for Santa Fe and Farmington were granted to Murchison without opposition, Albuquerque was another matter. The state's largest market was already served by manufactured gas (coal gas), and two other groups aspired to the same legal monopoly as did Southern Union. An auction was held, and only Clint's hand was raised when the ante reached $100,000 (about $1 million today). His check was drawn on First National Bank in Dallas, and after the meeting, Clint outraced his hot check to Dallas and talked the bank into a loan.

With the Santa Fe–Albuquerque–Farmington market secured, Murchison entered into contracts to build a 150-mile gas line from Kutz Canyon (near the four-corners area of Arizona, Colorado, New Mexico, and Utah) east over the Continental Divide. The project's first months went like clockwork, but the best-laid plans were disrupted by the stock market crash in October 1929. Monetary deflation made the project's fixed borrowing costs more expensive relative to the customers' eroded purchasing power. Pipe and other equipment were arriving daily, interim financing was expiring, and Frank Murchison, Clint's brother, was unable to float bonds or stock in Chicago to refinance the venture. The project continued on a pay-as-you-go basis on the strength of

---

4. Southern Union Gas Company, now Southern Union Gas Services, is part of Southern Union Company, a member of the New York Stock Exchange and one of the larger gas distribution holding companies in the country. Southern Union's early customers are now served by New Mexico Gas Company, a separately traded entity.

5. The San Juan basin, still a major gas-producing area, stretches from northwestern New Mexico to southwestern Colorado.

Murchison's reputation and the fact that most everyone was in the same predicament. Clint needed all his business skills and optimism, and he kept his
humor by answering the telephone, "the check's in the mail."

Clint began on the oil side but was now a natural gas man. Gas was a different business proposition and not for everyone. But it would be a good fit for
Murchison. Explained one Murchison associate:

> Many oilmen won't drill for gas because you have to wait for the returns. After
> you find the gas, it's another two years getting a pipeline built and another two
> years before you start seeing income, whereas in oil the payoff is so much faster.
> But the gas business was perfect for Clint because he wanted the long-term
> payoff. He always went for the big killing years down the road.

⌖

In October 1930, with the final segment of the pipeline completed, thanks in
part to financial aid from the city of Albuquerque, gas and dollars began flowing. Still, Southern Union was deep in arrears and Murchison Oil at a standstill.
Another desperate hour was at hand—and one that would again turn into one
of Clint's finest. Hearing about some major oil discoveries in East Texas, Clint
sent his ace geologist to the scene. Ernest Closuit talked to his counterparts at
Humble Oil & Refining Company and Gulf Oil, mapped the likely field, and
reported back to Clint that the oil play was for real.

East Texas was for real—and much more! Wells spaced many miles apart had
tapped into what was a 211-square-mile contiguous reservoir of shallow, high-
quality crude. America's largest oil field was in the making, but nothing was
known for sure at the time. Still, Clint recognized that any surge of crude production needed pipeline transportation and refining capacity to reach market.

Murchison went to see the Oil Well Supply Company in Dallas with a plan
to build a 30-mile crude pipeline to the refining and railroad center of Tyler,
Texas. Clint knew the "center of East Texas" well. He was born and raised 35
miles away in Athens, and Tyler was where he had married in 1920.

Clint's infrastructure would have to be financed on credit and backed only
by a business plan, but Oil Well Supply had a special incentive to make the deal
work. Its parent, U.S. Steel, owned the pipe-manufacturing company to which
Southern Union was heavily indebted. Clint's numbers showed that a crude
line supplied by his leases, and supplying his new joint-ventured refinery, could
service its debt and retire that of Southern Union as well.

Murchison received financing to build the Tyler Pipe Line, and his new
company, American Liberty Oil Company, was on its way. Although the crude
from other discovery wells encountered transportation bottlenecks, American
Liberty's oil had a path to market. Large profits retired both notes according to
plan and financed new drilling by Clint in East Texas.

Although Sid Richardson stayed away because he felt that East Texas was too
crowded, Clint Murchison and H. L. Hunt became the two leading independents

in what was now the world's most prolific oil field.[6] It was here that Clint perfected "financin' by finaglin'"—trading partial interest in some assets to buy into others, such as oil rigs. The biggest player in East Texas was Humble Oil, half owned by Standard Oil of New Jersey (now Exxon Mobil). It was Humble Oil, the prince of all energy companies headquartered in Houston, Texas, that several decades later would be the first stop for an economics graduate from the University of Missouri, Ken Lay.

Clint's early-in, integrated strategy in East Texas helped save the day for the natural gas side of his small empire. The strategy also allowed American Liberty to survive the price wars that resulted from East Texas's prolific output and that ruined many other producers. Oil fell to a dime a barrel (about the cost of a bowl of chili in Tyler) before state and federal regulators limited production to reduce "waste"—and achieve "dollar oil" as important segments in the politically active industry wanted. Never again would Clint Murchison depend on one side of his business rescuing another, but there would be only one Great Depression and East Texas field in his or any other lifetime.

·≈·

By 1931, Southern Union had 17 divisions serving 19,500 customers in 43 towns, each of which considered the introduction of natural gas service as a proud civic moment. Clint Murchison, as a first-generation pipeliner, shared in this pride. Profitability finally arrived for Southern Union in 1933, proving that a market niche was being filled by Clint's young team ("there wasn't a man in it over forty years old"). Their strategy was to move the "wonder fuel" to homeowners and commercial establishments (in franchise-protected areas) upgrading from more expensive (and dirtier) coal, coal gas, or fuel oil. Only "superstition and lack of knowledge" could keep the "high heat content, cleanliness, convenience, efficiency, and low cost" of natural gas from winning the day, Southern Union advertised.

Southern Union found itself in the gas-appliance business as well. Increasing gas demand, called "load building" in the trade, required gas-run heaters, stoves, and ranges in homes and businesses, and Southern Union's district offices sponsored appliance sales contests with one another with the losers preparing meals for the winners. Revenue from appliance sales provided a Christmas bonus for every Southern Union employee.

Natural gas proved to be the right business once the transition got beyond some obstructionist tactics employed by coal interests in parts of New Mexico. But even the most economical fuel choice could not hide from the Great

---

6. Part of Murchison's success came from using an invention of his own: the *reversionary-interest agreement* under which leases were sold at nominal prices in return for a royalty interest that reverted to the seller after certain production and financial goals were met.

Depression.[7] Scarce cash forced Southern Union to barter its gas for the goods it needed at hardware stores and gasoline service stations, requiring an extra bookkeeper. Scrip became a second currency as Southern Union and other firms issued promissory notes in lieu of cash to service their obligations too. It would not be until the next decade that good times would return to the economy and survival was assured for even franchise-protected companies.

Figure 6.2 The various faces of Southern Union: clockwise from left, Clint Murchison; Southern Union trucks peddling gas appliances; Frank Murchison; and Wink, Texas, an oil boomtown that received early gas service.

The gas utility business was not well suited for Clint Murchison. Public-utility regulation made the business more a matter for lawyers than for risk takers. The federal Public Utility Holding Company Act of 1935 required Southern Union, and all other multistate gas and electric utilities, to divest its physically nonconnected assets in all but one state in order to atone for the pyramiding sins of utility magnate Samuel Insull.[8] Political dealmaking was also distracting for Clint, although his East Texas investments required him to take sides in the debate over government regulation of wellhead production with other oilmen,

7. The Great Depression got its name from its unprecedented duration, not the severity of the original downturn. See Internet appendix 6.1, "The Great Depression (1929–38)," at www. politicalcapitalism.org/Book2/Chapter6/Appendix1.html.

8. Chapter 5 describes the demise of Insull's natural gas and electric holding-company empire in the early 1930s and related congressional investigations and regulation.

such as the president of Sunray Oil Company (later Sun Oil), J. Edgar Pew.[9] Years later, the Sun Oil fortune would fund the Pew Charitable Trusts, a philanthropy that turned against the oil and coal industries and promoted Enron's natural gas strategy, discussed in Book 3.

Clint retired from the active affairs of Southern Union in 1934 to concentrate on his other projects, most of which were conducted within American Liberty. A 200-mile oil pipeline from East Texas to the Gulf Coast provided a delivery point for tankers departing for refineries in the U.S. Northeast and Europe. Locally, a refinery specializing in high-octane gasoline was built to meet wartime aviation needs.

But American Liberty's expansion halted when Toddie Lee Wynne, Murchison's partner in the company, experienced health problems and wanted to dissolve the partnership. It was then that Clint took inventory and learned about Wynne's secret side deals, which was that much more reason to part company.

A valuation dispute between the two led to a coin flip to decide who would get the company and who would be bought out. Clint lost and received the money. It was 1947 and time to start anew.

In nearly a quarter century, Clint Murchison had made many more fortunes than he had lost and gained valuable experience in the energy corridors of Texas and New Mexico. He had experience in all sectors of the natural gas and oil business except for gasoline retailing, which he shunned as a notoriously low-margin business.

What now? After some time off, Murchison turned to a production subsidiary that Southern Union had spun off, Delhi Oil Company. The Delhi story is one of the most important chapters in Clint's career—and Jack Bowen's as well.

While Clint was busy with American Liberty, the wartime excess-profits tax burdened Southern Union with a 91 percent marginal tax rate for its 1944 income. As the company's largest stockholder, Clint convinced the board to take advantage of a drilling provision that reduced the tax liability dollar for dollar. Even dry holes and a complete write-off would leave the company no worse off than simply paying tax. Any dollar earned from exploration was a gain because Uncle Sam was, in effect, paying for the wells.

Southern Union entered into a contract instructing American Liberty to acquire and drill acreage in northern Louisiana. The results could not have been better. A major oil strike in the Delhi field increased the value of the parent stock many times over, and a new subsidiary was created within Southern

---

9. Wellhead proration by state authorities and Murchison's alleged role with illegally produced "hot oil" are discussed in Internet appendix 6.2, "Clint Murchison and Oil Regulation," at www.politicalcapitalism.org/Book2/Chapter6/Appendix2.html.

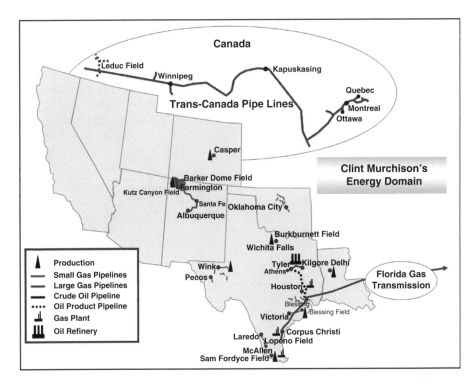

Figure 6.3 Clint Murchison's energy adventure began in North Texas in the 1920s and continued in West Texas, New Mexico, southern Oklahoma, East Texas, Louisiana, Arkansas, and Canada in the next decades.

Union Production—appropriately named Delhi Oil. The newfound profits gave Southern Union capital to expand the utility side of its business by year-end 1945. Murchison's American Liberty had done it again for Southern Union.

Southern Union Production Company had another crown jewel. In 1942, shallow gas was found in the Barker Dome field on the northern side of the San Juan Basin. Several years later, a nearby deeper, richer gas vein was discovered, and Barker Dome Oil and Gas was created as a separate subsidiary.

In mid-1946, Southern Union spun off Delhi Oil to shareholders, and early the next year, Southern Union sold Barker Dome to the now-independent Delhi. These production properties became the basis for Murchison's new company.

Barker Dome was strategically positioned. It not only supplied the growing Southern Union system but also was ideally located to serve the burgeoning California gas market. Enter Paul Kayser and El Paso Natural Gas Company.

El Paso Natural Gas Company

Paul Kayser (1887–1980) shared similarities with Clint Murchison. Kayser began life eight years earlier than Clint in a small town near Tyler, Texas, and was destined to be a natural gas pipeliner. But unlike Clint, Kayser was formally educated, with an undergraduate degree from Baylor and a law degree from the University of Texas.

After several years representing a small gas utility, Kayser founded El Paso Gas Utilities Corporation in 1928 to serve the last remaining city in Texas without natural gas service. The city of El Paso received its gas from the company's 200-mile pipeline system, which originated from five wells in southeast New Mexico. Service began in mid-1929, just months before the onset of the Great Depression and a year ahead of the aforementioned New Mexico pipeline project, which became the core of Southern Union Company.

In 1932 Paul Kayser persuaded a group of southwestern copper smelters to substitute natural gas for manufactured (coal) gas, the long-term contracts of which anchored a $6 million, 290-mile expansion of the renamed El Paso Natural Gas Company (EPNG) into Arizona and Mexico. But soon after the natural gas began to flow, the smelters faced copper selling prices that were below production cost. Uneconomic smelting put the gas contracts in jeopardy. Without this revenue, EPNG would not be able to service its debt.

Kayser exercised political entrepreneurship. The domestic oil industry, battling cheap imports, was in the process of securing a tariff, and Kayser got Phelps Dodge and other smelters to lobby the Department of the Interior for similar relief. The result was a sizeable copper tariff—four cents a pound added to the going price of five cents—to turn back supply from Africa and other low-cost copper-producing countries.

Signed by Herbert Hoover, the Internal Revenue Act of 1932, described as "one of the greatest increases in taxation ever enacted in the United States in peacetime," increased the domestic price of copper to nine cents a pound. Still, depressed demand left the smelters operating at low capacity. EPNG responded by expanding its reach to more stable markets in Tucson and Phoenix the next year, a strategy that found Kayser turning to the political means once more.

Scarce credit during the Great Depression brought Kayser to the door of his former legal client, Houstonian Jesse Jones, now ensconced in Washington, D.C., as head of the Reconstruction Finance Corporation (RFC), a major federal lending agency established by Herbert Hoover as a business-recovery program. Kayser argued that a $2.2 million loan would get many able-bodied men off government welfare and back to work and paying taxes. EPNG received the loan in 1933 on the condition that the pipeline trenching operation would forgo machinery for picks and shovels to create as many local jobs as possible.

This practice was certainly not as useless as digging ditches just to fill them back up, a strategy notoriously sanctified by economist John Maynard Keynes as a recovery measure. But using more resources than necessary to perform a given task was hardly what Adam Smith, or virtually any economist today, would call wealthcreating. As it was, the *Tucson Daily Star* summarized the EPNG/RFC project as "a huge private enterprise [that] became, in effect, a relief agency for the many communities along its route."

The expansion proved profitable despite the featherbedding. In 1936, with natural gas demand strong, EPNG was able to refinance its debt, retire the government loan, and become listed on the New York Stock Exchange. El Paso Natural Gas was finally, Kayser exclaimed, a *Company*.

·❧·

EPNG entered the big time when surging demand for natural gas in California began to overtake in-state supply. As far back as 1938, Kayser had eyed the state and Southern California Gas Company, the local distribution company serving Los Angeles and surrounding areas, answered Kayser's call in 1945. EPNG had to acquire a certificate of public convenience and necessity from the Federal Power Commission (FPC) to expand to the California border,[10] which did not prove difficult for several reasons. First, there was a bona fide need for out-of-state gas to serve a state that was a major consumer market and national-defense manufacturer. Only 2 percent of the state's associated gas was not going into a pipeline, and even this amount was "rapidly dwindling," noted the FPC. Second, coal and fuel-oil interests did not contest the application, owing to their limited operations in the state (something that Jack Bowen did not enjoy when he introduced peninsular Florida to gas in the next decade). Third, state and federal authorities welcomed the fact that much of El Paso Natural Gas's supply would come from waste gas associated with oil production. The Texas Railroad Commission had helped matters by issuing so-called conservation orders, forcing oil producers to stop flaring residue gas. This was part of the late 1940s "gas war" politics, whereby pipelines teamed with regulators to force producers to sell rather than flare their gas to serve new markets.

EPNG's need for long-term gas supplies to serve California brought Paul Kayser and Clint Murchison together in 1950. Delhi's Barker Dome gas was particularly coveted. Clint's first thought was to parlay a gas-sales contract into an ownership interest in Kayser's company, but Delhi Oil's sales would then become subject to federal regulation as an affiliate transaction with an interstate pipeline. The prospect of a 6 percent maximum profit, the FPC-sanctioned rate of return, was not lucrative enough to justify the high risks of exploration and production.

---

10. The federal Natural Gas Act of 1938 began the certification process, one that EPNG and Southern Union did not have to go through with their earlier interstate pipeline projects. EPNG's extension stopped at the California border to avoid the jurisdiction of the California Public Utilities Commission, which regulated the rates of Southern California Gas and Pacific Gas & Electric as in-state distribution companies.

Figure 6.4 Clockwise from upper left: advertisement of natural gas to the El Paso area; Paul Kayser, the founder and company builder of El Paso Natural Gas; and system map of EPNG in 1954.

Rather than sell the gas under an ordinary gas-sales contract subject to federal regulation, however, Delhi decided to sell its producing properties to El Paso for a combination of cash and a royalty on every cubic foot of gas produced.[11] Clint also negotiated a price-escalation clause to protect his long-term royalties against inflation. He also figured that natural gas was underpriced relative to oil and coal on an energy-equivalent basis and saw the price gap narrowing in the future.

This left the sales price of the lease to be determined. After negotiations with Kayser at Clint's Hacienda Acuña ranch in eastern Mexico reached an impasse, a coin toss was decided upon. (Clint was prone to use this form of a tie breaker.) Kayser won the $500,000 flip, but Murchison was satisfied that more business with the rapidly expanding interstate was in Delhi's future.

Paul Kayser's long career at EPNG would make him, by some estimates, "the best known and most highly respected man internationally in the gas industry." Like Clint, Kayser was a first-generation pipeliner, and like his fellow company builders Gardiner Symonds of Tennessee Gas Transmission and Reginald Hargrove of Texas Eastern, Kayser was tenacious when push came to shove in the regulatory and political arenas. El Paso had the California market all to itself until the entry of Transwestern Pipeline in 1960 to southern California and Pacific Gas Transmission in 1962 to northern California. Transwestern would go through ownership changes and become one of Enron's core interstate lines beginning in 1985.[12]

Inside Delhi Oil

By 1950, Clint had sold his quarter interest in Southern Union with thoughts of making Delhi Oil "the biggest independent oil company in the world." It was this spirit that Jack Bowen had begun to assimilate when he joined the company the year before. Bowen was fortunate; few firms in any business were as poised for growth and personal advancement as Delhi Oil.

Delhi Oil's small staff reflected a corporate culture that started at the top. Clint chose his "brains" carefully and delegated well. He summarily forgave mistakes so long as they were not repeated. He was a noted practitioner of handshake integrity—not only as an end in itself but also as a means to win repeat business.[13]

---

11. Creeping regulation of gas production dedicated to interstate commerce began in 1940 when the FPC issued field orders regulating transactions between a pipeline and its affiliated production company. Comprehensive wellhead price regulation of interstate gas would start in 1954 with the Supreme Court's *Phillips* decision.

12. Transwestern's purchase by Enron from Texas Eastern Corporation is discussed in *Enron and Ken Lay: An American Tragedy* (Book 3), chapter 1.

13. See Internet appendix 6.3, "Murchison and Handshake Integrity," at www.political capitalism.org/Book2/Chapter6/Appendix3.html.

Clint was a patient investor who enjoyed buying much more than selling. He believed that each side, not just one side, should win at a deal. He was attracted to projects that could create value over the long run—hence his great interest in pipelines. He eschewed dividends in favor of retained earnings and stock appreciation. For tax purposes, he structured his deals for capital gains rather than ordinary income.

Clint drew great satisfaction in making his senior executives wealthy and the rest of his employees secure. Stock options were key. When Delhi Oil was spun off from Southern Union in 1945, Murchison gave his top five partners—a geologist, an accountant, a petroleum engineer, a pipeline engineer, and a manager—stock options that increased in value a hundredfold when Delhi Oil went public two years later. Dozens more of Murchison's business associates would become millionaires. And being a millionaire in the 1950s was both rare and a badge of honor, even in top social circles.

Clint dressed casually, put people at ease, and served lunch gratis to all his employees in a spacious dining room at the Dallas headquarters. Drinking, gambling, cursing, and off-color jokes were verboten on company time or property. One could walk down the street to the Dallas Petroleum Club for that. Extramarital affairs could be career limiting in his employ. Discrimination not based on merit was out of place simply because Clint did not make such arbitrary distinctions himself.

Murchison did not seek attention if he could help it, nor did he rationalize self-publicity as a company builder. His charity was conducted personally and discreetly. Clint was too busy *doing* to focus on Dallas boosterism, unlike some of his fellow city luminaries. He loved the great outdoors and was a conscientious steward of his far-flung properties. His views and practices did not reflect any advertised beliefs, religious or otherwise, but simply what he felt was honest, fair, decent, and practical.

"In the order named," Murchison stated, "I consider that honesty, personality, courage, and an indomitable will to succeed (which means to the point that there is no time to watch the clock) are the most important elements in business success." He was influenced by leading industrialists in U.S. history, particularly the work ethic and acumen of oil titan John D. Rockefeller.

Murchison once put his business philosophy to verse:

With dreams, musings, and ideas combined
With men, money, and materials
Vast projects can be started and completed,
Provided management is not deleted nor depleted.

Murchison was an intellectual, his abbreviated formal education notwithstanding. He read the classics and often consulted the dictionary to learn new words and settle bets with friends who challenged his word usage. (He made money at this too.) He was fascinated with science and technology and searched for related business angles. He could trade thoughts on the classics or impart a learned worldview with friend or foe.

Most of his voluminous letter traffic consisted of one-sentence missives, but some contained poetry and heartfelt philosophy. Clint's definition of education was learning about "one's own experiences and observations, and the other fellow's record of his thoughts." His text was a little black book filled with his own personal observations.

All this came from an unassuming, pudgy, soft-spoken man standing five feet six inches tall.

Clint Murchison was in many ways a role model in a rough-and-tumble industry and volatile business era. No one doubted his character, integrity, and ability to get things done. He navigated the ravines of debt financing to make his career much more successful than it could have been otherwise. Murchison adroitly mixed business and pleasure.

But one mighty episode, described in the next chapter, mars his legacy. It concerns Murchison's dogged, at-all-cost effort over seven years to finance and construct the Trans-Canada Pipe Line over the will of the marketplace. This episode is illustrative of the perils of egotism (versus rational egoism) and the *political means* (versus economic means) for business success.[14] Murchison's folly was neither the first nor the last, as this book's account of Samuel Insull and Ken Lay will attest.

·❧·

Such was Jack Bowen's company and leader. Jack's career at Delhi Oil began in late 1949 with an orientation period at the Dallas headquarters, home to fewer than ten employees. The two company engineers were his mentors, along with chief geologist Frank Schultz. But as a small company, everyone worked with and learned from everyone.

Bowen's first field assignment was working with Delhi's gas wells in the San Juan Basin in northwest New Mexico. Bowen was then transferred to Wyoming where Delhi was drilling and completing oil wells north of Casper. "Drilling was 24 hours a day 7 days a week so I was constantly on call," Bowen remembers. After completing about 15 wells, Bowen was transferred back to Farmington, New Mexico, to resume his San Juan Basin work.

The next summer, Bowen spent two weeks in southeast Canada to gauge customer interest in buying natural gas from a proposed all-Canadian pipeline, Trans-Canada Pipe Lines, a new Delhi/Murchison project, that proposed to bring gas from Alberta to the consuming provinces Ontario and Quebec. Bowen

---

14. See Internet appendix 6.4, "Other Murchison Political Involvement," at www.political capitalism.org/Book2/Chapter6/Appendix4.html.

would take a return trip to Canada the next year to assess Delhi's gas reserves in Alberta that would anchor the project.

Jack spent most of the first 18 months staying in small-town hotels or sleeping in the car while working the wells, so it was a relief when he was summoned back to Dallas in late 1951. Jack had had his baptism of derrick and dust, and his Canadian work introduced him to a megaproject in which gas reserves, pipeline engineering, and finance had to come together to convince customers to sign long-term contracts. Natural gas pipeline projects in South Texas would be next.

7

A Monumental Mistake

G AS POLITICS HAS A LONG HISTORY in the United States. It began in the nineteenth century when city officials entered into street-lighting contracts and issued franchises with manufactured-gas distributors. Gas distribution then came under statewide public-utility regulation, which set maximum rates and established terms of service, including the right to enter or exit a market.

In the 1930s, such retail regulation by local and state authorities was joined by wholesale public-utility regulation by the Federal Power Commission (FPC) for interstate pipelines. (In 1977, the FPC was reorganized as the Federal Energy Regulatory Commission.) Each of Enron's four interstate natural gas pipelines had a political persona stemming from decades of rate and entry regulation under the Natural Gas Act of 1938. Ken Lay, a third-generation pipeline executive, knew the political side of his business very well by the time he left Transco Energy Company to join Houston Natural Gas Corporation in 1984.

Interstate gas pipeline executives were market and political entrepreneurs. Paul Kayser saved El Paso Natural Gas in the 1930s with his Washington, D.C., work. Political maneuvering was also integral for other big-name first-generation pipeliners—Gardiner Symonds of Tennessee Gas Transmission Company, Reginald Hargrove of Texas Eastern Transmission Company, Burt Bay and John Merriam of Northern Natural Gas Company, and Clint Murchison of Trans-Canada Pipe Lines (the company known today as TransCanada Pipelines Ltd.). Three of these four were involved in one of the biggest events in the history of the North America energy market—the entry of Canadian gas into the United States.

Murchison at Twilight

Clint Murchison was a driven entrepreneur who took sizeable risks—mostly with other people's money—and won many more times than he lost. In the first half of his career, he survived oil price collapses and the Great Depression because his creditors knew that Clint was their best bet in bad times as well as good. Without his integrity, smarts, and drive, there would have been one less legend in the U.S. oil and gas industry.

The second half of Murchison's career, which began after World War II, was smoother sailing. Regulation firmed up domestic oil prices just as the domestic industry intended. Improvements in pipeline technology made natural gas, once an unwanted byproduct of crude oil production, an attractive option for homes, businesses, and electricity generation. The general business climate was stable: There were periodic recessions but never a depression.

Clint played the inflation game in this period, knowing that dollars repaid had less purchasing power than dollars borrowed and invested. His affinity for debt was memorialized by his declaration that the promissory note was mankind's greatest invention.

After his disassociation from American Liberty, Murchison had more time to dabble in new businesses. "If you trade in peanuts you can trade in watermelons too," he found. His favorite deal was "the next one." Hundreds of proposals flowed to 1201 Main Street because Clint could like what the banks did not. The dealoholic also enjoyed, in his words, helping the "'little fellow' make money."

By the mid-1950s, this "incurable venture capitalist" had stakes in such diverse industries as chemicals, banking, insurance, cattle, transportation, publishing, water, building materials, and homebuilding. "The first of a brand-new breed of Texas oilmen," *Time* magazine told the nation, was now "the biggest wheeler-dealer of them all." *Time* counted in Clint's portfolio 48 companies employing 50,000 people. *Fortune* counted more than 100 small and large ownership interests. Almost all were profitable, qualifying Clint as the Warren Buffett of his day.

Clint was more than halfway to being a billionaire when billionaires scarcely existed. Dozens of other Athens-born men became millionaires, some via Clint himself. Some of Murchison's top partners went their own way, but Doc Neuhaus and Sid Richardson would remain close to Clint and his many and varied deals.

Although Murchison preached a good sermon on self-reliance and free enterprise as a member of the rugged-individualist oil and gas fraternity, he was politically pragmatic when enough dollars were on the line. Murchison's positions, like those of his industry brethren, were driven more by the wallet than by a principled belief in free-market capitalism. He opposed—and with a vengeance—government activism where it hurt. But he welcomed intervention that helped.

Figure 7.1 Clint Murchison was a nationally recognized oil and gas entrepreneur and venture capitalist in the 1950s. Murchison's stature was akin to today's legendary investor Warren Buffett.

This pragmatism was crucial when late in his career, Murchison decided to play a political high card in pursuit of what he considered the biggest prize of all. It was his greatest mistake. The financial loss to himself and Delhi Oil's stockholders was modest, although it could have been much worse. The greater damage was to an integrated North American gas market, the Canadian parliamentary system, and cross-border relations between the United States and Canada.

Canadian Pipe Dreams

The discovery of oil and gas in the Leduc field south of Edmonton in 1947 put the Canadian province of Alberta on the energy map. Murchison scouted the "Texas of the North," incorporated Canadian Delhi Oil Limited within Delhi Oil Company, and embarked on a major exploration and production program. Natural gas was of particular interest. Murchison believed that Alberta could supply all Canada's needs if a major pipeline network could be built.[1] It was almost like 1927 again. But instead of 4-inch pipe skimming just beneath the

---

1. Canadian natural gas production in 1950 amounted to only 1 percent of U.S. output because of a lack of pipeline outlets. Coal, manufactured (coal) gas, and fuel oil were used in the Toronto, Montreal, Ottawa, Vancouver, and other Canadian markets until gas exports from the United States. Canadian gas arrived later in the decade.

West Texas sand, this would be a 36-inch, high-compression line traversing 2,100 often rugged miles from central and southwestern Alberta to the population centers of eastern Ontario and southern Quebec.

Canada's population and industry were centered in the southeast. Toronto and Montreal watched as the northeastern United States converted from manufactured to natural gas with the entry of Tennessee Gas Transmission (1944), Texas Eastern Transmission (1946), and Transcontinental Gas Pipe Line (1951). The three Ts, bringing gas up from the southwestern United States, whetted the appetite of such utilities as Consumers' Gas Company, of Toronto, which in 1947/48 postponed building another coke-oven plant in order to pursue natural gas delivered from an extension of Tennessee Gas. That was the only alternative; Alberta gas had no way to get to eastern Ontario and Quebec or even to Vancouver in western British Columbia.

An all-Canadian natural gas line would be the largest in the world and a feat for the engineering textbooks. It would not be a career builder for the "pipeliner at heart"—Murchison was well beyond that—but a capstone to his 35 years in energy. The $300 million project (more than $2 billion today) was also a step toward Murchison's goal of making Delhi Oil "the biggest independent oil company in the world."

Figure 7.2 Canadian "Minister of Everything" C. D. Howe (left) and powerful American entrepreneur Clint Murchison (right) and the were a formidable pair in transnational affairs, as the trans-Canadian gas pipeline would prove.

Canadian Delhi was formed in August 1950 as an oil and gas exploration and production subsidiary. Delhi Oil was not in the long-haul gas pipeline business—at least not until early 1951. That was when Clint fêted C. D. Howe, the Canadian minister of trade and commerce in the Liberal government of Canadian Prime Minister Louis St. Laurent, at Hacienda Acuña, Murchison's six-ranch, 75,000-acre spread in Mexico's Sierra Madre. Between hunts, cards, food, drink, and worldly discussion ("I never enjoyed a week more," Howe said), the two set a new course for the Canadian gas market, signaled by Canadian Delhi's incorporation of Trans-Canada Pipe Lines Limited in April 1951.

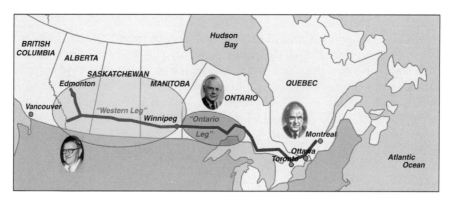

Figure 7.3 A meeting in early 1951 joined Clint Murchison (left) and C. D. Howe (right) on a mission to construct an all-Canadian, west-to-east pipeline. Ontario prime minister Leslie Frost (center) would ally himself with them, to do by the political means what could not be done by market means alone.

Murchison and Howe, who had met once back in 1939, greatly respected each other's stature. Murchison presented Howe with something as big and bold as each man's reputation—the construction of a Canadian line using Canadian gas to upgrade and expand the country's heating capacity. Having postponed his retirement from politics ("Where else could I get so big a job?"), Howe, in his seventieth year, overcame his initial concerns to think majestically: *An all-Canadian pipeline could be the most important national project materially and spiritually since the building of the Canadian Pacific Railway in the last century.* For Howe, a U.S. native and MIT-trained engineer, and the man most responsible for the Crown's Trans-Canada Airlines ("*my* airline"), this would not be a job but a mission and the capstone to *his* career.[2]

---

2. Clarence Decatur Howe (1886–1960) left a successful career in engineering and construction in 1935 to become a federal minister representing Ontario in Parliament's House of Commons. He became minister of transport a year later and never looked back. In World War II, he created 28 Crown corporations as the minister of defense production. He continued

Murchison and Howe faced a daunting problem. Their project was wildly uneconomic because of its route. An all-Canadian line had to traverse the Rocky Mountains and Laurentian Shield in Ontario—the latter a formidable stretch of lakes, rock, and bog with virtually no gas market. Energy observers wondered why Trans-Canada did not at a minimum follow the route of the Interprovincial Pipe Line Company, which moved crude oil from Alberta some 1,100 miles to the U.S. Midwest.

◁∾▷

Murchison's idea was also a day late and a dollar short. A half-dozen gas-export incorporations has taken place after enactment of Canada's Pipe Lines Act of 1949,[3] and four serious paper pipelines emerged. Each proposed to transport Canadian gas to markets in Canada and the United States and avoid the Laurentian Shield. Sending Canadian gas south would push the flow of U.S. gas eastward to markets abutting the major Canadian population centers. There was good reason why an all-Canadian line never made it beyond paper—at least until Clint Murchison came along.

The first serious proposal came in the summer of 1947 from Faison Dixon, principal of a New York engineering firm. He proposed a 950-mile line that would bring gas from southern Alberta down to major cities in the U.S. Pacific Northwest and come up to terminate in Vancouver, the third-largest Canadian market. Northwest Natural Pipeline Company, with strong backing, started the clock ticking on customer contracts and financing—as well as regulatory delay.

Two years after Dixon's, a dual-transmission plan was championed by "Mr. Pipeliner" Ray Fish. Fish, head of his own Houston-based energy engineering and construction company, was nearing completion of the then-largest pipeline in the world, Transcontinental Gas, stretching 1,850 miles from southern Texas to New York City.[4] Fish Engineering Corporation proposed a Canadian system from Alberta to Ontario, but the line dipped into the United States near Emerson, Manitoba, and continued on the U.S. side of the Great Lakes before terminating near Quebec's southern markets. The other half of Fish's ambitious proposal was

---

as economic czar in peacetime as minister of trade and commerce, a position he held until the Liberal Party's defeat in 1957. Howe's demeanor and ambition evoked such descriptions as "swarthy, impatient, sometimes testy," even "a Fascist, but a nice Fascist."

3. The 1949 law established a licensing procedure for pipelines exporting gas across Canadian provinces and/or the international border to the United States. It put the Canadian Ministry of Trade and Commerce, headed by C. D. Howe, in charge. Already, the Electricity and Fluids Exportation Act of 1907, originally enacted to regulate hydroelectric sales to the United States, required companies to obtain export authorization for international sales.

4. Transcontinental Pipe Line Company (Transco) and other Fish projects are described in chapter 9, pp. 317, 318–319.

a pipeline running from the San Juan Basin in the American Southwest up to the Pacific Northwest, where it would receive Alberta's gas through Pacific North-west Pipeline, a sister line running down from the North.

A third proposal—a 1,200-mile pipeline from gas fields in the Peace River area of northern Alberta and British Columbia to Vancouver and the U.S. Pacific Northwest—was backed by Alberta oilman Frank McMahon. Westcoast Trans-mission was designed to market the gas associated with McMahon's oil produc-tion that would otherwise be flared. This project also left open the possibility of an Alberta-sourced pipeline moving east-southeast to serve the U.S. Midwest and central and eastern Canada.

The fourth serious plan was Western Pipe Lines Limited (Western Pipe), backed by three Canadian investment houses. It proposed to pipe gas 750 miles from southern Alberta through Saskatchewan to Winnipeg, Manitoba, before dropping down to an export point near Emerson to serve the U.S. Midwest. The proposal, finalized in early 1950, was backed by a feasibility study from the "conservative and widely respected" engineering company Stone & Webster.

The same study dissuaded Western Pipe from pursuing an all-Canadian route, because of its unfavorable economics. The head of Western Pipe was H. R. "Ray" Milner, known as "Mr. Alberta" because of his extensive hydro-carbon and cattle holdings in the province. With customer interest, Western Pipe applied to the Alberta Conservation Board for a long-term export license in early 1950. Milner and his colleague, Allan Williamson, had another asset of note—a good relationship with C. D. Howe.

Not all these competing proposals could be undertaken, but separately and together they made Murchison's idea "a pipedream, not a pipeline." Economics favored an integrated North American market wherein Alberta and British Columbia gas would drop down to serve northwestern and central markets in the United States, and gas from the U.S. Southwest would continue north on the three Ts to serve Canada's southeastern population centers. Western Pipe could be expanded eastward to Montreal if gas markets along the way developed sufficiently. As it would turn out, pieces of a binational market would emerge during the multiyear delay engineered by Howe and Trans-Canada.[5]

A binational approach was attractive to most parties in the debate—although not, as it turned out, to the most politically powerful. In addition to the juggernaut Howe, Trans-Canada was strongly supported by the province of Ontario, which welcomed the idea of natural gas service to its sparsely populated areas. But unlike Ontarians, everyone else was part of the alternative

----

5. Dixon's Northwest Natural proposal would fight an unsuccessful five-year battle with regulators. Fish's Pacific Northwest Pipeline and McMahan's Westcoast Transmission would enter service in 1956 and 1957, respectively, and link to serve a binational western gas market. Trans-Canada would either incorporate or crowd out the other proposals.

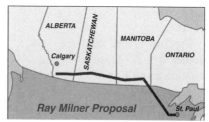

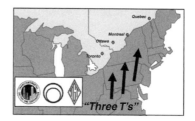

Figure 7.4 Between 1947 and 1951, four pipelines were proposed to export gas from gas fields in Alberta and British Columbia to western or central U.S. markets. The international gas exchange would have redirected southwestern U.S. gas (via Tennessee Gas Transmission, Texas Eastern Transmission, and Transcontinental Pipe Line) to southeastern Canadian population centers.

proposals, with prices and profits being the motivations. Lower transportation costs meant higher netbacks for producers—including the province of Alberta as the predominant royalty owner. Lower transportation costs meant lower rates for consumers on each side of the border. An international approach was a win for producers and consumers in both countries. What was good for Alberta was also good for Texas and Louisiana, *Delhi included;* what was good for Vancouver and Seattle was also good for Toronto and Montreal.

High-volume Canadian gas exports to the United States and U.S. gas exports to Canada would create mutual strategic dependence, which was favored by the U.S. Federal Power Commission and Canada's two energy agencies—the Alberta Conservation Board and the federal Ministry of Trade and Commerce. Pro-supply policies would be politically supported by each country and protectionism self-defeating. A fluid North American gas market and the wider promotion of economic relations between the two neighbors were what the market wanted.

Getting Political

Meanwhile, an absence of producer, customer, and financing contracts by Trans-Canada was creating regulatory delay and skepticism on both sides of the border. As much as Murchison tried, salesmen for Trans-Canada in the early 1950s, Jack Bowen included, were not producing the contracts necessary for financing.

Producers and customers *feared* Trans-Canada's rates and *lobbied against* the project. The best that Trans-Canada could do was to stymie competing projects, insist on an all-Canadian line with Howe setting the rules, and hope that growing gas demand would ripen the pipeline's economics—or have the government step in to make up the difference. Howe was the kingmaker who could make or break the project; Murchison knew this and deftly kept Howe at his side.[6]

In the fall of 1951, Western Pipe became the front-runner when it finalized a sales contract for 150 MMcf/d at the Emerson, Manitoba, border point with Northern Natural Gas, a large Midwest gas distributor eager to diversify from its U.S. sources. Northern Natural proposed to build a 409-mile line to the border to bring Alberta gas down to Minneapolis–St. Paul and serve northern Wisconsin as well. Western Pipe had something else going for it—a proposed transportation rate to Winnipeg (about 80 miles due north of Emerson) that was 40 percent below that projected by Trans-Canada. With regulatory approval from both sides of the border, the project could be operational in 1953, and the international strategy would be on its way.

Murchison "immediately became a fierce competitor" of Western Pipe. The Canada-first gas-export policy (1949) already tilted the rules toward Trans-Canada, but more was needed. Murchison deftly played the nationalism card by befriending the prime minister of Ontario, Leslie Frost. Frost threw his support to Howe, and in March 1953, the minister of trade and commerce announced a "Canada always" policy toward gas pipelines and exports. Quebec *and* Ontario had to be served before gas could be exported, Howe informed the prime minister of Alberta, Ernest Manning, whose stranded supply needed markets.

Still, Western Pipe remained in the fight. Two of its executives had a special relationship with Howe, and the proposed line was amended to add a second phase from Winnipeg to Ontario and Quebec when the markets matured. Murchison, though disappointed, had no choice but to acquiesce when Howe brokered a 50–50 "shotgun marriage" between Trans-Canada and Western Pipe in early 1954 in order to keep the *nearly* all-Canadian project on track.[7]

With gas exports to the United States now part of the plan, Howe announced a new export policy to incite greater Alberta production and improve

---

6. The extent of the Murchison-Howe relationship is documented in their exchange of letters that discuss, among other things, vacations for Howe to warm climes, influencing U.S. legislation favored by Canada, blocking a U.S. gas project in the Pacific Northwest to help a Canadian project favored by Howe, and reelection help. See Internet appendix 7.1, "Lobbying Howe," at www.politicalcapitalism.org/Book2/Chapter7/Appendix1.html.

7. Murchison sought for Western Pipe a one-eleventh interest in Trans-Canada, corresponding to the size of Canada's capital market compared to that of the United States. Western Pipe sought one-half ownership of the project and prevailed.

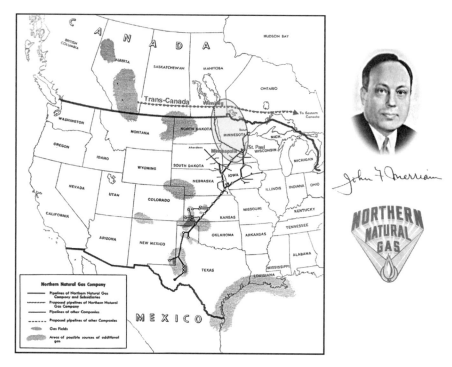

Figure 7.5 An interconnect agreement between Western Pipe Lines—soon to be part of Trans-Canada Pipe Lines—and Northern Natural Gas Company gave Trans-Canada an early dose of reality. Northern Natural, headed by John Merriam, needed gas to meet demand growth in its Midwest territory, and an Alberta supply was a nice diversification from the company's domestic sources.

Trans-Canada's economics—as if these benefits had not existed since exportable quantities of gas were first available in 1947.

⋄

Murchison's Canadian Delhi lost half of its project, but that was the price he had to pay to become the front-runner. Yet there was trouble nipping at Trans-Canada's other foot. In early 1953, Toronto's Consumers' Gas Company announced plans to build an 80-mile line to Niagara to receive Louisiana gas delivered to the border by Tennessee Gas Transmission. Tennessee Gas, one of the giants of the transmission industry and led by its strong-willed founder, Gardiner Symonds,[8] had just been certificated by the FPC after a protracted

---

8. H. Gardiner Symonds (1903–71) founded Tennessee Gas and Transmission Company in 1943. The pipeline received a wartime loan from Jesse Jones's Reconstruction Finance Corporation to begin operations in October 1944. The renamed Tennessee Gas Transmission

fight to serve New York City and other Northeast destinations. Tennessee Gas's 80-mile extension to the Niagara River improved the economics for all and portended greater binational business for the future. Displacement of Trans-Canada's most uneconomic and vulnerable segment—the northern Ontario route—was in the making.

Tennessee Gas's entry into the area that Trans-Canada was unable to finance reconfirmed the superiority of the original route by Western Pipe, a project that was really all that Canada needed to move Alberta gas for the time being. This strongly suggests that Trans-Canada should have merged with the Western Pipe proposal rather than the other way around to provide a market solution by 1953. But a stubborn mix of ego, false pride, and politics between a Great Man of industry and Economic Czar of government would drag the issue on for four more years.

Trans-Canada embarked on a two-front battle against the Niagara proposal. Murchison lobbied against an export license for Tennessee Gas at the FPC on grounds that Trans-Canada's eastern leg would serve the same market. Murchison also lobbied the Eisenhower administration.

Meanwhile, lawyers for Trans-Canada, with Howe's aid, found an obscure way to delay the interconnection by using Canada's Navigable Waters Protection Act. It wasn't much, but the *Maid of the Mist*, a pleasure boat that brought tourists to the edge of the roiling waters at the bottom of Niagara Falls, was deemed navigation that a pipeline crossing the river could *conceivably* impact. Just putting the legal issue into play bought time for Howe to gin up legislation requiring importers to acquire a federal license from the Board of Transport Commissioners, which was desperately needed to delay the project further.

But Gardiner Symonds, too, was adept at political hardball. His lobbyists were able to link Tennessee Gas's export application at the FPC to an import license needed by Westcoast Transmission. Westcoast was planning to pipe gas from fields in British Columbia to Vancouver. For the economics to work, however, the pipeline had to dip south, crossing the border to serve gas markets in the United States, and then reenter Canada for its final discharge in Vancouver. Westcoast had received Canada's first export license in 1952 and needed an import license from the FPC to complete the deal.

Howe and Murchison had to back down. Obstructionism at Niagara, already hurting Toronto, now put Vancouver at risk. Tennessee Gas received export authorization from the FPC in August 1953, and Howe 11 months later

---

would become one of the nation's two largest interstate gas pipeline companies during Symonds's long tenure, which ended with his death. Symonds was called "the real doer of the American gas industry—he has never lost a major battle before [the Federal Power Commission]." In 1964, Tennessee Gas purchased Delhi-Taylor Oil Corporation to bring Symonds's association with Clint Murchison full circle.

authorized Trans-Canada to build and lease the new line (stretching between Tennessee Gas's terminus at the border and Consumers' Gas system) to Consumers' Gas. Tennessee Gas began exports from its own pipeline extension to the international border on November 1, 1954.

But company-builder Symonds had bigger plans. In the spring of 1955, he proposed a 2,067-mile line from Tennessee to the Minnesota/Manitoba border. Midwestern Gas Transmission, a wholly owned subsidiary of Tennessee Gas, would receive half of its 400 MMcf/d from Trans-Canada at Emerson, Manitoba, and bring the rest up from the South. Better yet, as far as transportation efficiencies went, the received Canadian gas was redelivered by Tennessee Gas using Southwest gas at Niagara to serve Ontario and Quebec. The exchange would expire when Trans-Canada physically connected to Montreal, whereupon the Niagara line would be reversed to flow surplus Canadian gas to Tennessee Gas for delivery to New York.

This intricate arrangement gave Tennessee Gas and Trans-Canada the best of all worlds given the refusal of Howe, in cahoots with Murchison, to allow market forces to kill the Ontario leg of the Canadian line. Trans-Canada could placate part of its eastern market before it was physically connected, and Tennessee Gas would be smack dab in the gas-hungry Midwest, competing with both Northern Natural Gas and two gas lines built from Texas to Chicago by Natural Gas Pipeline of America in 1931 and 1951.

Although Northern Natural's contract with Western Pipe was stymied by the FPC,[9] Tennessee Gas went to work with its own proposal. During a chance encounter in the lobby of the Mayflower Hotel in Washington, Gardiner Symonds informed Northern Natural's CEO John Merriam that Tennessee Gas was taking over Northern Natural's Canadian contract. Merriam threatened Trans-Canada with legal action, but the contract had expired by that time, and the threat not carried out.

Midwestern's certificate application, filed at the FPC in October 1955, attracted motions to intervene by 125 parties, led by incumbent pipelines as well as area coal interests. In a controversial decision, the application was rejected three years later, in October 1958, the very month that Trans-Canada finally began service. A bitter Symonds, who argued that the Natural Gas Act favored gas-on-gas competition rather than territorial protection, immediately filed an amended application at the FPC—and an antitrust suit against his rivals. A resurrected Midwestern received approval, with more support from industry parties, and began serving Chicago in 1959 and importing gas from the

---

9. Northern signed a new contract with Trans-Canada in September 1954 after the Western Pipe merger. The FPC, as before, denied certification on grounds that the Alberta reserves behind the agreement were less than a 20-year supply, which was a standard requirement to receive a certificate of public convenience and necessity.

international border the next year. Thus ended a five-year regulatory effort before the FPC and Canada's newly established National Energy Board, a monument to politicization that was part of the legacy of Murchison's fateful meeting with C. D. Howe back in 1951.

Dodging Failure

In late 1954, Trans-Canada, now merged with Western Pipe, still could not live up to the Murchison magic of old. Toronto was served by a spur line off Tennessee Gas, but Winnipeg still had only a paper pipeline after four years of promises. Winnipeg's gas distributor, Central Gas Company, warned Howe that it could not continue to "keep our utility alive by continuing our coke oven operation and . . . supply[ing] propane as an interim substitute." Alberta producers also were still waiting.

In search of a "bold coup" to break the impasse with producers, consumers, and financiers, Trans-Canada asked Stone & Webster to reassess the viability of its route. It had been five years since the respected engineering and consulting firm rendered a verdict supporting Western Pipe's route over Trans-Canada's. This time would be no different. Central Canadian markets, Stone & Webster explained, had simply not grown enough in the interim to reexamine the issue. Once again, it appeared, the wrong company was on top of the merger.

By 1955, it appeared that the bell would toll for Trans-Canada. Neither Alberta producers nor utilities from Ontario and Quebec utilities were signing enough contracts to permit financing. Construction costs were escalating, and a threatened steel strike clouded timely construction even if everything else went right. "Most people in the gas business were simply waiting for the Trans-Canada scheme to collapse; the logic of north-south patterns would then reassert itself," two historians wrote. Howe warned that any failure could make an east-west line "a dead issue for all time."

In January 1955, Trans-Canada first inquired about government assistance to commence construction come spring: an 80 percent taxpayer guarantee of the total construction cost of $350 million. This opened new fronts. The socialists in Parliament called for a Crown corporation to take over the entire project. Alberta producers hinted that they expected better terms with public involvement. Canadian Gulf, the largest potential gas supplier to Trans-Canada, had to wrestle with its internal policy prohibiting long-term contracts with a government entity. Westcoast Transmission and B.C. Hydro would be put in a position of pressing for tax breaks or government favors based on a Trans-Canada precedent. But most of all, a major fight loomed in Parliament over whatever federal aid was needed in addition to that already promised by the provinces.

Despite the Tennessee Gas exchange contract and some progress with government financing, Trans-Canada did not have enough credit to place the $40 million order that was required for timely construction. Murchison went to work. He first approached his business partner and Acuña buddy, Paul Kayser.

But El Paso Natural Gas Company had its hands full with its California ventures, so Murchison had to turn to "the ablest and the toughest operator in the whole business"—Gardiner Symonds. Tennessee's push to break into the Midwest with Trans-Canada's exports made for a natural partner, but Symonds was no crony of Murchison or anybody else. He and his stockholders would have to be well served by any deal.

Symonds was interested, and Murchison thought he had a deal whereby Tennessee Gas would take a minority interest in a partnership designed for Trans-Canada's construction phase only. But wanting to lay off some of his risk, Symonds also brought in the Alberta producers Canadian Gulf (Gulf Oil Company) and Bay Oil and Gas Company (majority-owned by Continental Oil Company) for a 51 percent stake of 17 percent each. Suddenly, Murchison lost control of his project.

Humbled and hurt, the fabled entrepreneur had only himself to blame. Symonds and partners were providing the $40 million guarantee to U.S. Steel, whereas Murchison was following his policy of using other people's capital instead of his own. Without Symonds, Trans-Canada might have died a natural death. In any case, Canadian Delhi's interest was now subordinate to that of Tennessee Gas, Canadian Gulf, and Continental Oil, bad cosmetics for Murchison and Howe's patriotism strategy.

As 1955 wore on, C. D. Howe's nationalist strategy was under siege from all quarters. "All-Canadian Line Fades," "Continental Policy Likely for Natural Gas," the newspaper headlines read. A discouraged Murchison, just one month shy of his sixtieth birthday, wrote Howe a lengthy letter recapping the history of the project and suggesting new ideas for going forward.

Canadian Delhi had put $10 million into drilling, he calculated, and the pipeline group had spent $6 million with another $500,000 dollars accruing per month. Murchison wrote how he had "conceived the idea of an all-Canadian pipeline knowing in the beginning that anyone would take the routes into Minneapolis and Chicago as being much more remunerative and easier to finance." Nonetheless, it was his "feeling that the Canadian citizens were of such patriotism that they wanted a fuel system within the confines of their own boundaries." Apologizing to Howe for all the trouble that the project had caused, Murchison stated that it was his "rare honor" to be involved with a project akin to the great east-west railroad of Canada's past. And as for this great national project, Murchison added, government credit would be necessary.

Two weeks later, Murchison again wrote Howe: "I know I have taxed your patience . . . but I beg of you to be lenient with me as I have set the completion of this pipeline as my definite goal of achievement before I retire to the sunny valleys of Mexico." Such prose was intended for Howe and just about everyone else in this highly public and scrutinized matter. Murchison had reason to reminisce and rationalize. Heady thoughts and optimism at the beginning had turned into a slippery slope. Trans-Canada "was pouring money into staff, survey, and

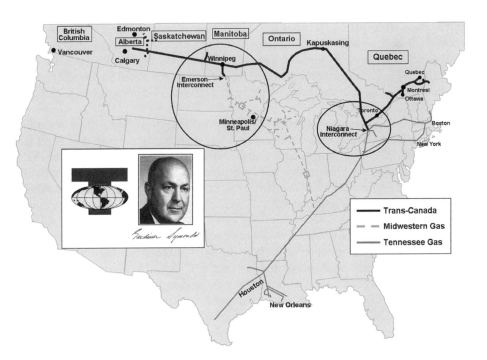

Figure 7.6 Tennessee Gas reconfigured Trans-Canada into a dual domestic/export pipeline in 1954 and took majority control of the project the next year. Gardiner Symonds (inset) was as tough as C. D. Howe and as calculating as Clint Murchison.

right-of-way costs" to help things politically. If the project did not prevail, millions of dollars in development costs would have to be written off. But if Trans-Canada prevailed, Delhi and the other investors were entitled to full recovery of their accrued expenses as well as a return (around 8 percent) on capital invested under Canada's public-utility regulation. By the time Trans-Canada's gas began to flow some three years later, the prepayments recoupable from consumers amounted to more than $15 million ($100 million in today's dollars).

Trans-Canada needed much public-sector help, and in the fall of 1955, Howe worked to get it. The Northern Ontario Pipe Line Crown Corporation was created to finance the most expensive and uneconomic leg—some 675 miles from the Manitoba/Ontario border east to Kapuskasing, Ontario. The $118 million price tag would be as much as 90 percent taxpayer funded, with the federal government paying two-thirds and Ontario one-third. Trans-Canada promised to turn its lease of this stretch of the pipeline into a purchase in the fifth year of full operation.

The western leg presented issues too. Trans-Canada ran into financing troubles when the FPC held up its 200 MMcf/d agreement with Tennessee Gas's

Midwestern. As before, Trans-Canada's troubles attracted competition, this time in the person of Frank McMahon, head of Westcoast Transmission, which had proposed the aforementioned pipeline running from Alberta to the American Midwest to central and eastern Canada. In the spring of 1956, just as his company began exporting Alberta gas to the Pacific Northwest, he sent a certified letter to Howe containing a startling proposition: "I am prepared to undertake a Canadian-owned, privately financed project to construct an economically feasible gas pipeline from Alberta to Montreal, if Trans-Canada is not immediately available to present a suitable proposal." The project was heavily dependent on gas sales to the United States, however, and McMahon's group included several U.S. pipelines that were contesting the Trans-Canada/Tennessee exchange.

Howe kept this incendiary development from Parliament—not his first liberty with the truth about Trans-Canada when dealing with Canada's highest body. But as the contents of the letter seeped out, the red-faced Howe had to back down. The public, the press, and the Conservative Party now had more ammunition for the looming parliamentary fight over federal aid to Trans-Canada.

Parliament's Bailout

It had been *nine years* since Faison Dixon's proposal had put Alberta's natural gas into play and Consumers' Gas asked for natural gas for Ontario. It had been *five years* since Trans-Canada arose phoenixlike to challenge the front-runners. Much had changed. Elements of an international exchange had watered down the once all-Canadian proposal. Delhi Canada (Murchison) and Western Pipe (Milner) were minority partners to Gardiner Symonds's group, and the project was 83 percent American owned. Now on the table was a serious offer that promised to do Trans-Canada's work without federal subsidy.

The mood of Parliament, the public, and the press was scarcely favorable toward bailing out Trans-Canada's western—and supposedly economic—leg, never mind the rest of the project. The fires of nationalism that Murchison and Howe stoked had now turned against their project.

C. D. Howe introduced the bailout bill on May 14, 1956, with a speech called by his biographers "probably the best of his career." The bill was read in the House of Commons the next day and enacted several weeks later. What happened in between "shattered a quarter century of political quiet" by creating "the stormiest episode in Canadian parliamentary history." Black Friday, as the June 1 finale was called, "was a day at whose end no Member of the House of Commons could go to his bed with much pride in what he had done." What began as a pipeline debate degenerated into questions of morality and "the dignity of Parliament itself."

Two sparks ignited the "grand national steamletting." First was the unpleasant fact of Canadian taxpayers "bailing out an American-controlled company which has among its shareholders some of the richest oil companies in the country." Second was Howe's "incredible audacity" invoking cloture when the debate was ready to begin, a rarity that Canadian Prime Minister Louis St. Laurent, another Trans-Canada ally, could only meekly condone. Howe had done some controversial things in his public life (just a year before, he had tried to make his wartime emergency powers permanent), but this was worse. He simply decided to let nothing stand in his way to ensure that Trans-Canada was able to begin construction of its western leg by July 1 in order to save the fragile contracts.

In shouting sessions, the bailout was described as "a Colombo plan for Texas tycoons"; Parliament was called "the old German Reichstag"; and Howe's procedural tactics (aided by Speaker of the House Louis-René Beaudoin) was denounced as "the rape of our liberties by the government." The press was no kinder to Howe and the behind-the-scenes force, Clint Murchison.

In the end, Howe had just enough support in Parliament to ram through a two-prong bailout of Trans-Canada. One prong authorized construction of the federal portion of the government-owned northern Ontario leg (the portion that could not be privately funded). The second was authority for Canada's Industrial Development Bank to lend up to $72 million (more than $450 million in today's dollars) to build the western leg. This interim loan was necessary

Figure 7.7 The great pipeline debate brought ridicule to Howe, the Liberal Party, and Texas oil tycoon Clint Murchison, who did not dare show his face in Canada.

because Trans-Canada's private financing could not proceed until the FPC approved Trans-Canada's contract with Tennessee Gas. Various tax breaks were also part of the deal.

Subsidies secured, Trans-Canada construction began concurrently in late 1956 on the western prairie leg and the treacherous Ontario leg through the Laurentian Shield. Permanent financing retired the federal interim loan of $50 million as scheduled in February 1957, and the pipeline became fully operational in October 1958. It had been more than a decade since the first proposals to export Alberta's gas had surfaced, and more than seven years of that time was attributable to a combination of regulatory delay and political obstruction.

Collateral Damage

Years of delay extracted a high price. Exploration in Alberta made in the expectation of a major pipeline outlet had resulted in capped wells, sometimes for years. Canadian Gulf, which was in the midst of a ten-year, $350 million drilling

Figure 7.8 Howe won his prize of an all-Canadian line, but his hard-fought victory on behalf of his close friend Clint Murchison stained the legacy of both men. Aiding Howe in Parliament was Canadian Prime Minister Louis St. Laurent. (top right). Howe and Vermont Governor W. H. Willis (lower right) weld the pipe at the international border.

program, was particularly victimized. The supply concern of Canadian export regulators was partially self-fulfilling given that politics discouraged reserve development. Alberta's oil had been developed in a timely manner with the completion of two international petroleum pipelines in 1955 and 1956, but the gas associated with oil was simply flared, at an estimated loss of $50,000 per day. Dirtier and costlier fuel oil and coal, and more expensive propane, were burned instead.

And last but not least, the winning pipeline project (Trans-Canada) piled up unnecessary costs that consumers had to pay under the rules of public-utility regulation. There were very few winners in the grand political game that structured Canada's gas market.

Steps toward a binational exchange improved a bad situation. Louisiana gas transported by Tennessee Gas began to be exported at Niagara in late 1954, although the second part of the company's Canadian strategy, importing gas at

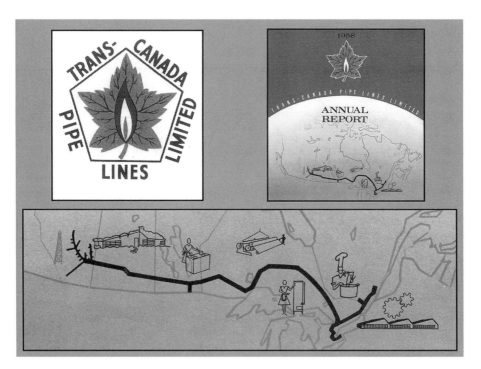

Figure 7.9 The 2,290-mile, $378 million Trans-Canada line had an initial capacity of 300 MMcf/d, two-thirds of which was for export to the United States at Emerson and Niagara. Added compression and other improvements would increase the capacity to 780 MMcf/d in the next years.

Emerson for Midwest delivery, was delayed until 1960.[10] In 1956, Ray Fish and his "right hand man," Robert Herring, the future leader of Houston Natural Gas (the predecessor to Enron), completed a 1,500-mile line that brought gas from the San Juan Basin to major utilities in Washington, Oregon, and Idaho. Pacific Northwest Pipe Line took away a natural market for Alberta gas, although Westcoast—Canada's first export pipeline—would begin feeding the project with Canadian supply the next year.

The six-year delay caused Trans-Canada's construction costs to jump by nearly half, well above inflation that was averaging 1 percent per annum. The opening estimate of $250 million increased to $300 million, then $350 million, and finally $378 million (more than $2 billion today). About $40–$50 million of the final tally represented the cost of building north rather than south of the Great Lakes. The project was still not viable even after sponsorship upgrades and rival projects were blocked. An eleventh-hour proposal to displace Trans-Canada without federal taxpayer financing added controversy to controversy.

"Anti-Canadian Pipe Lines Limited," also nicknamed "Howe's folly," was hardly comparable to the nation's other major nation-spanning projects. The government-financed Canadian Pacific Railway, completed in 1885, brought British Columbia into the Union and linked the country for the first time. The Crown's Trans-Canada Air Lines cut the time of cross-country air travel by more than 80 percent, to 16 hours from 4 days when service began in 1937. Trans-Canada Pipe Lines had simply been one alternative among several—and the one that took the longest and cost the most. The question was never whether Canadian producers would find buyers and Canadian consumers find supply, but rather from whom and at what price.

᠂ᢀ᠂

Howe, oblivious to the fact that his political career was ruined, remarked in his victory moment that he "enjoyed the battle," and "the end will justify the means." It had been the most difficult task in his life, but he was now nearer what he had penned in a note to his friend Murchison—"a normal life, after which I will be camping on your doorstep." Acuña was the stuff of dreams.

For his part, Murchison wrote in his last communication to Howe, "I intend to have a statue dedicated to your honor before I lose control of Trans-Canada." But it was not to be. Parliament's "wild and violent" debate, which ruined the health of several Parliamentarians, was harsh to Howe too. In the elections held

---

10. The import certificate of Tennessee Gas's Midwestern Gas Transmission Company encountered a 48-month delay before the FPC and another 6-month delay before the Canada's National Energy Board for its export license. The pipeline itself was constructed in 3 months, which meant *that the regulatory delay was 18 times greater than actual construction.*

a month after the Trans-Canada bailout, the Conservative Party, led by populist John Diefenbaker, defeated the Liberal Party for the first time in more than 20 years. Howe's two-decade career as minister of trade and commerce was over— in large part due to his role with "the greatest pipeline project ever undertaken anywhere in the world." The end for Howe himself came before he could enjoy his earthly reward with Clint. He died instantly of heart failure on New Year's Eve 1960, at age 74.[11]

For Murchison, his monument turned out quite differently from what he envisioned. The problematic project required repeated compromises before significant government involvement cinched it. There had been a forced merger so that Trans-Canada could integrate Western Pipe's superior export plan, which ended the all-Canadian veneer. Then Gardiner Symonds's Tennessee Gas teamed up with two major Alberta producers to exploit Murchison's shaky position.

Another new risk opened up when Parliament, dealing with an unpopular prospect of a government bailout for the besmirched Texan and other Americans, debated the idea of the Trans-Canada project becoming a Crown (government) corporation. Not only could Murchison have been left with some or all of his costs to eat, but also he would have been responsible for a bit of that so-called creeping socialism that Texas oilmen so opposed—at least in speech. The final insult was the actual government bailout and media field day depicting fat-cat Murchison exploiting the poor Canadian taxpayer.[12] It was a steep fall from rugged individualism for the otherwise lionized deal maker.[13]

With all the power of his reputation and purse, and with Howe after the same monument, Murchison strong-armed a political assumption (Canadians want an all-Canadian pipeline) into a project. In truth, *Trans-Canada was less the result of nationalism and anti-Americanism than the cause of it.*[14]

---

11. The career of the speaker of the Canadian House of Commons, Louis-René Beaudoin, a rising star before accommodating Howe by choking off parliamentary debate on Black Friday, was also ruined. After retiring from Canadian politics in disgrace, he failed in an attempt to receive a doctorate at Columbia University and worked menial jobs (including serving beer at a saloon) before dying in 1970 at age 57.

12. One cartoon depicted the greed of the pudgy, short, superrich Murchison, cigar in hand, looting the Canadian taxpayer with the caption, "Now is there anything else we can give you, *Mr. Murchison?*"

13. There were other examples of Murchison's pragmatism trumping competition. One was his investment in a Dallas taxicab company that enjoyed an exclusive franchise from City Hall. Dallas was the largest metropolitan area with such an arrangement, and not surprisingly, Murchison made "good money in an exclusive situation."

14. See Internet appendix 7.2, "Nationalist Arguments for Trans-Canada," at www. politicalcapitalism.org/Book2/Chapter7/Appendix2.html.

Clint's was a peculiar victory that went against usually reliable business judgment. Murchison almost always evaluated his projects, and even his hobbies, on their economic viability. Yet Delhi Oil surrendered an undetermined amount of revenue by leaving a trillion cubic feet of Alberta gas reserves without a pipeline connection. Delhi Oil struggled to recoup its investment in Trans-Canada, and as Murchison himself admitted, he never "received one penny for my time or efforts" with the project.

The Trans-Canada Pipe Lines may have become a positive part of Murchison and Howe's legacy in the official lore, but historical revisionism is called for. *Trans-Canada should not have been built—at least in the lifetimes of its two fathers and probably well thereafter.*[15]

Epilogue

Trans-Canada turned a profit in 1961, its third year of full operation. The company purchased Northern Ontario Pipe Line Crown Corporation from its government sponsors the next year. Much damage had been done, however, and Trans-Canada as the only game in town operating under public-utility regulation was wired for profitability.

The legacy of Murchison-Howe was a *thoroughly politicized Canadian/United States gas market.* The Alberta Conservation Board and U.S. Federal Power Commission were given new sets of litigants to bring out the worst in the regulatory process. Parliament spewed anti-Americanism. Ex post, a government audit of the new pipeline was undertaken, in part to quell a public outcry against the lucrative stock options of Trans-Canada's management.[16] The study recommended a federal energy-planning agency. What became the National Energy Board was proposed on the very day that Alberta gas first arrived in Montreal. The political created the political.

It did not have to be this way. Murchison and Howe could have left Trans-Canada unhatched and directed their considerable energies toward expediting the most viable projects—north-south and/or east-west—through the approval process. Canadian gas would have secured markets much sooner, and cash flow

---

15. Also see Internet appendix 7.3, "Would Trans-Canada Have Been Built?" at www. politicalcapitalism.org/Book2/Chapter7/Appendix3.html.

16. Trans-Canada executives received options at a strike price of $8 per share in 1954. The public offering in early 1957 was at $10 per share, and the price peaked at $38 per share in the fall of 1958. The Canadian head of Trans-Canada, Eldon Tanner, a political operative whose major contribution to the company was his "quiet diplomacy," was cut in at $1 per share when he joined in 1954. He resigned from Trans-Canada in late 1958, exercised his options, and moved to Salt Lake City, where he joined the Council of Twelve Apostles and became General Authority of the Mormon Church. Noted a fellow pipeline executive on Tanner's odyssey, "I like to think all pipeliners go to heaven, but the rest of us have to wait until we die."

would have triggered new rounds of development in Alberta and British Columbia. Canadian Delhi would have been a major beneficiary.

There *was* political work to be done circa 1950 to effectuate any finalized commercial agreements. Greater market reliance, not new layers of intervention, was needed. The Alberta Conservation Board was slow to estimate new gas reserves and unnecessarily required 30 years (or more) of gas reserves behind each export contract.[17] Coal interests had to be overcome in the United States, as did rival gas projects that found the FPC's lengthy certification process a weapon to block competition. The FPC's caution against gas exports was another political challenge. And creeping wellhead price controls in the United States created an interstate natural gas problem than was also, inter alia, a North American gas problem.[18]

Another item that promised greater pipeline capacity *sooner* to belea-guered producers was not on anyone's agenda—simultaneously removing rate-of-return regulation and franchise protection given interfuel competition and emerging gas-on-gas rivalry. The roots of political capitalism in the gas market, prominently including public utility regulation, were strong.

Private contracts—which courts of law on both sides of the border could be expected to uphold—offered a near-painless alternative to politics and obstruc-tionism. Canada and the United States were peaceful neighbors, and mutually advantageous economics promoted open borders. Indeed, two major inter-national oil pipelines—that of Interprovincial Pipe Line Company from central Alberta to the U.S. Midwest (completed in 1950) and that of Trans Mountain Oil Pipe Line Company from Alberta to the U.S. Pacific Northwest and Vancouver (1953)—were the product of natural economics. While Canadian crude was exported daily to the United States, Montreal refineries welcomed crude from Venezuela and other nations—a cost-minimizing arrangement. Trans-Canada was an *exception* to the trend of U.S. investment "forc[ing] a realignment of the [Canadian] economy away from its historic east-west axis.

Amid the wreckage of international gas relations from Trans-Canada, a blue-ribbon group of businessmen, labor leaders, and academicians from both sides of the border championed a fresh start. The Canadian-American Committee complained about how "narrow national considerations . . . [such] as self-suffi-ciency and self-determination" hampered "a more rational development of our natural resources."

---

17. The Alberta Conservation Board's first estimate of proved gas reserves of 4.6 trillion cubic feet for year-end 1950 would balloon to 14 TCF four years later.

18. See Internet appendix 7.4, "Trans-Canada and U.S. Wellhead Price Controls," at www. politicalcapitalism.org/Book2/Chapter7/Appendix4.html.

The committee favored greater gas exchange and an import-export network to minimize transportation costs, lower prices for consumers, improve reliability, and encourage "fresh reserves." "For the sake of the long-term interests of both of our countries," the report concluded, "unduly rigid regulatory concepts must not be allowed to stultify the healthy growth of gas transfers." And as it would turn out, Canadian gas exports would find their niche.[19]

Such foundations for a North American market could have been cemented a decade before, but wellhead regulation of natural gas in the United States, another political blind spot, would become an issue in the 1960s and a crisis by the 1970s. Cumulative politicization and energy nationalism would highlight the next chapter in United States–Canada gas relations.

⋄

Murchison was a *doer*. A liberalization strategy to enhance Canadian Delhi's burgeoning production would have been a smaller mountain than the summit he chose to climb. Howe, the "Minister of Everything," was a powerful force. Although Murchison and Howe did not think in such terms, a legacy to open borders would have been a far greater monument than approval of an uneconomic project that required government bullying against almost everyone.[20]

What "became for its backers a matter of pride and honour beyond all rational economic sense" was the greatest mistake of Murchison's career, although it did not rock him economically.[21] Murchison's folly was a saga of human fallibility, not dishonesty or a deep-seated character flaw. (The story would be different for Clint, Jr.[22]) A combination of intellectual error and hubris blinded him to the democratic function of *market signals*—the collective reflection of self-interested producers, consumers, and financiers in two countries. And once on a slippery slope of his own doing, Murchison found himself an instigator and accomplice to greater and greater machinations that were really not in his character—at least as represented by his long, storied past.

---

19. Also see Internet appendix 7.5, "Canadian Gas Export Policy," at www.politicalcapitalism. org/Book2/Chapter7/Appendix5.html.

20. As it would turn out, Canadian gas exports to the United States exceeded domestic deliveries beginning in 1993, the year after the North American Free Trade Agreement was enacted to create a free-trade zone.

21. Two other late-life grandiose schemes of Murchison—creating the world's largest life insurance company via acquisition and dying with more cattle than anyone else—were never achieved but did not create major problems in the effort either.

22. Also see Internet appendix 7.6, "The Rise and Fall of Clint Murchison Jr." at www.political-capitalism.org/Book2/Chapter7/Appendix6.html.

Two generations later, the pursuit of business objectives through political power and egotistical monuments would fate another Great Man of the industry, Enron architect Ken Lay. Other greats in our story—Samuel Insull, and before him, Thomas Edison and John Henry Kirby—were humbled by egotistical forays after great triumph. And as politicization begets politicization, a bit of the Lay/Enron story was foreshadowed, even predestined, by the events that produced Trans-Canada Pipe Lines Company.

8

Florida Gas Company

CLINT MURCHISON LOVED THE PIPELINE BUSINESS. It might not have been as exciting as exploration and production, but it was a money maker. The Southern Union Gas Company, which he founded in the late 1920s, had successfully piped natural gas from remote fields to towns and cities in New Mexico. Oil pipelining had proved to be Clint's ticket in East Texas. And in the 1950s, Murchison would push, at the highest levels of government, an all-Canadian line that would move natural gas (including his own) from Alberta to the population centers of Ontario and Quebec.

So, when his brother Frank Murchison and close friend Doc Neuhaus apprised him of an opportunity to supply natural gas to two South Texas power plants, Murchison created a new Delhi Oil Company subsidiary—Delhi Pipe Line Company—to build the lines. Murchison's chief engineer, Joe Bartlett, was put in charge. It was Bartlett who had recently brought his protégé, Jack Bowen, back to company headquarters in Dallas.

Since joining Murchison in 1949, Bowen had built small gas-gathering lines in the San Juan Basin and scoped the route of a major interstate transmission line from the San Juan Basin to Salt Lake City. The interstate was never built, but the paper line had given gas-producer Murchison a card to play in his negotiations with Paul Kayser, who was looking to buy wellhead gas to support an expansion of El Paso Natural Gas Company to California. Now that Central Power and Light of Corpus Christi needed gas for two large steam turbine units in South Texas, Bartlett tasked Bowen with building a 60-mile line from the Lopeno field to Laredo and with assisting in the construction of a shorter line from the Blessing field to Victoria.

The projects taught Bowen the ins and outs of the pipeline business: surveying routes; securing rights-of-way from landowners; letting and managing

271

equipment contracts; and trenching, welding, caulking, and testing the lines. When the two projects were completed in 1952, Jack Bowen was a bona fide pipeline engineer.

From Coastal Transmission to Houston Corporation

Deals poured in to Clint Murchison "like flies to a light," but some of his best ones were his own. A good one later in his career—and one that would to an extent offset the Trans-Canada Pipe Lines folly—began as a plan to gather and transport gas from South Texas to Louisiana for sale and redelivery to large northeastern markets. Majors such as Sun Oil, and independents such as Oscar Wyatt's Wymore Oil Company, were rapidly developing natural gas reserves in South Texas, and Murchison was optimistic about his own gas properties near McAllen. The pipeline would eventually start from there, although Delhi Oil's reserves would turn out to be much less than thought.

Murchison's idea of a Gulf Coast interstate had a second inspiration. Interstate pipelines buying gas in South Texas were reluctant to pay more for new supply because they would then be required to pay the higher price for the gas already being purchased.[1] The overall price increase would require contentious hearings at the Federal Power Commission (FPC) and could be rolled back, contracts notwithstanding. This contractual/regulatory quirk provided an opportunity for Delhi Oil to pay a higher price for new supply, transport the gas to the Baton Rouge hub, and resell the gas there. That way, the interstates could buy the gas as needed without triggering price escalations back in the field.

Delhi Oil created Coastal Transmission Company to build the pipeline—but only if the new entity could profitably buy gas on one end and sell it on the other. Jack Bowen, assistant chief engineer of Delhi Oil, was promoted to vice president of Coastal with responsibilities for engineering and gas supply.

Bowen was ready. The 33-year-old had wellhead and pipeline experience and negotiated with customers for Trans-Canada. Following his Texas pipeline projects, Bowen's stints at the 90,000-barrel-per-day Taylor refinery in Corpus Christi and a gas-liquids plant in the McAllen field introduced him to a wide slate of hydrocarbon products.[2] Night courses in petroleum geology and corporate finance at Southern Methodist University had filled in some gaps in his

---

1. These so-called most-favored-nation contract clauses were designed to allow producers to keep up with inflation and capitalize on the higher value of natural gas over the life of their long-term (often 20-year) contracts. In his San Juan Basin contracts with El Paso Natural Gas, Clint Murchison had been one of the first to require the clause.

2. Effective January 1, 1955, Clint Murchison bought Taylor Refining Company to make Delhi Oil a wholly owned subsidiary of Delhi-Taylor Oil Company.

knowledge. Now, Jack Bowen was in charge of a project budgeted in the tens of millions of dollars—very big money for the day.

Working from Corpus Christi but traveling by car to Houston, New Orleans, and other places, Bowen had secured 250 MMcf/d of gas for the project. But with his new responsibilities, Bowen relocated to the energy capital of Houston in 1957 and began hiring an engineering staff to scope the pipeline. Bowen reported to Joe Bartlett as before, but his big boss was Philip Bee, executive vice president of Delhi at Dallas headquarters. Before long, Bowen would be promoted to president of Coastal Transmission.

The project started slowly. Skeptics renamed it "Ghostal Transmission" after Transcontinental Gas Pipe Line Company and Texas Eastern Transmission Company backed away from their early interest in buying gas at Baton Rouge. But this setback led to a major development. In 1954, the Houston Texas Gas and Oil Corporation approached Murchison about buying Coastal's gas at Baton Rouge for redelivery to Florida via a second pipeline. Murchison was interested, and Houston Texas interested Tulsa gas-industry veteran and pipeline builder Floyd Stanley in heading up the Florida leg. With Ray Fish and Robert Herring having reached the Pacific Northwest with gas supply from the San Juan Basin (as discussed in chapter 11), the Florida peninsula remained *the* last major American market without natural gas.[3]

Florida did not have interstate gas for a reason—the state's semitropical climate offered little market for space heating. The Florida State Chamber of Commerce had put out the welcome mat for natural gas in 1949, but only now were the state's electric utilities seriously interested in generating power with natural gas instead of burning fuel oil or coal. Florida was a tourist state, and air quality in Tampa, Fort Lauderdale, and Palm Beach was an issue.[4] But most of all, power plants, like industrial users in the state, sought gas as a cheaper and higher-quality alternative. On the residential side, gas manufactured from coal, increasingly anachronistic, was a money loser for Florida Gas & Light and other distribution companies that sold the product for cooking, water heating, and space heating.

From a business perspective, there were many unanswered questions about building an interstate pipeline. Would producers dedicate their gas reserves under long-term contracts, given FPC regulation of the price of gas sold in interstate commerce? Would end users enter into long-term contracts

---

3. A spur of United Gas Pipe Line Company served Pensacola and Tallahassee in northwest Florida, but natural gas was not available east to Jacksonville and in the peninsula, because of a lack of in-state production.

4. The environmental advantages did not translate into pricing advantages for gas, however, as discussed in Internet appendix 8.1, "Natural Gas and Florida Environmental Issues," at www.politicalcapitalism.org/Book2/Chapter8/Appendix1.html.

with producers and two pipelines to get the gas to Florida? Could gas interests overcome entrenched fuels and their carriers to receive an FPC certificate of convenience and necessity to proceed? A letter of intent between Delhi-Taylor Oil Company and Houston Texas Corporation in February 1955 began the process of finding out.

The Texas-to-Florida proposal was anchored by a contractual arrangement that avoided wellhead price controls, the law of the land for interstate gas supply since a 1954 Supreme Court decision. The federal law applied to sales-for-resale (gas sold interstate to a utility or municipality for resale to end users). Producers, however, could sell supply directly to large customers at the wellhead (an intrastate transaction) at an unregulated price and pay the interstate pipeline a federally regulated transmission fee. Such direct-sale gas and transportation gas, just out of reach of the Natural Gas Act of 1938, gave Coastal Transmission the wherewithal to attract gas supply that otherwise might stay in unregulated home-state markets.[5]

The anchor of the 282 MMcf/d conjoined pipelines was 150 MMcf/d sold by Sun Oil and Pure Oil at the wellhead in South Texas to Miami's Florida Power & Light Company and St. Petersburg's Florida Power Corporation—all for electricity generation. Thus, some 90 percent of the capacity of the line was under transportation contracts with the final user. Only 20 MMcf/d was (regulated) sales-for-resale supply, virtually all of it replacing manufactured gas or liquefied petroleum gas used by homes and small businesses.

With contracts in hand, Coastal Transmission and Houston Texas jointly applied for certification at the FPC. The hearings were acrimonious despite the fact that long-term contracts for natural gas had been signed with customers seeking to displace inferior alternatives, a conversion completed almost everywhere else in the United States. Nevertheless, the burden of proof was on this project as being in the public convenience and necessity. Bowen, who was named president of Coastal before the proceeding, had some learning to do. "I thought [the FPC] Staff was here to help us," Bowen whispered to his lead attorney, Leon Payne, during a tense moment during a hearing, which evoked the rebuke, "*What did you say?*"

One especially contentious matter was whether a negotiated contract between a construction company owned by Floyd Stanley and Houston Texas (of which Stanley was chairman) was just and reasonable, in FPC parlance. Bowen's leg had been competitively bid in an arm's-length transaction, but Stanley had, in effect, negotiated with himself. Regulators worried about this as a regulatory gap whereby profits denied to a regulated pipeline could be

---

5. The complicated federal-gas regulation nuances that were crucial to the development of a project are discussed further in Internet appendix 8.2, "Wellhead Gas Price Regulation," at www.politicalcapitalism.org/Book2/Chapter8/Appendix2.html.

captured by the construction company through a nonbid contract.[6] It seemed not to matter that consumers were willing to pay the rates that resulted from the total cost of the project even before the project was built.

In late 1956, Coastal Transmission and Houston Texas survived a scare when the five-member FPC narrowly approved the project. The 3–2 victory for natural gas was a defeat for the Florida Economic Advisory Council, a high-sounding name for a group of area fuel-oil dealers, coal-carrying barges and trucks, and two coal carriers—the Atlantic Coast Line Railway Company and the Louisville and Nashville Railroad Company. The 19-month certification process involved 41 parties and more than 100 attorneys—creating costs for both taxpayers and gas ratepayers. In the end, the FPC supported gas service for a "fuel have-not area" that was "almost entirely dependent on imported energy . . . vulnerable to interruption." Leon Payne, who had successfully navigated Pacific Northwest Pipe Line through the FPC for Ray Fish and Robert Herring a few years before, had now prevailed in a much tougher fight.

Financing negotiations began while the ruling was on appeal. To simplify matters, Coastal Transmission and Houston Texas merged in March 1957, with Stanley as chairman and president and Bowen as senior vice president of the renamed the Houston Corporation (and president of Coastal). In May 1958, the FPC decision was upheld without further appeal, but even so the process had added another 17 months of delay to a project that had been hatched back in 1954. Interim bank financing was replaced with $107 million of 20-year first-mortgage bonds placed with approximately 40 insurance companies. Stock and short-term bonds funded the rest of the $164 million project (about $1.2 billion today). Bowen's first experience with Wall Street ended with a master agreement in July 1958.

This achievement resulted in Jack Bowen's first big payday. When he became president of Coastal Transmission, he received a 3 percent interest in the company and the right to buy up to $250,000 of stock at $10 per share. This required a bank loan, a bank loan required a guaranty, and a guaranty required Clint Murchison. After the Houston Corporation went public, Bowen sold enough stock at $22 to retire the loan, leaving him with a good deal of free-and-clear stock. Bowen also received a missive from Clint congratulating him for the project and mentioning that this was the first time anyone had paid off a loan ahead of time to relieve him of his guaranty.

Construction was next. Bowen's job was to build a 561-mile line from McAllen, Texas, to Baton Rouge, which was accomplished in nine months for $60 million, as planned. But Stanley's 915-mile leg from Baton Rouge to Miami did not go as

---

6. Gaming, or superfluous entrepreneurship, is a political-economy term that refers to opportunistic business strategies that seek to overcome, to one extent or the other, the intended effects of regulation. See *Capitalism at Work*, pp. 10, 89, 112, 260–62, 292, 298, 303.

well. It was completed on schedule, but a major capital cost had been left out of the FPC-approved rate base—*the cost of freight to move the pipe from the mills to the site*. The error left the project 5 percent above budget and underfinanced—at least until the $8.5 million cost could be authorized by the FPC in a future rate-case hearing and the debt reworked.[7] And business revenues could not yet help. Only two customers were hooked up to the system, and both were taking just a fraction of their anticipated quantity. Nonetheless, at the Brooker compressor station in Brooker, Florida, on June 1, 1959, it was all smiles at the valve-opening ceremony, which was followed by a celebratory dinner for 500 guests in Jacksonville, with Stanley as master of ceremonies.

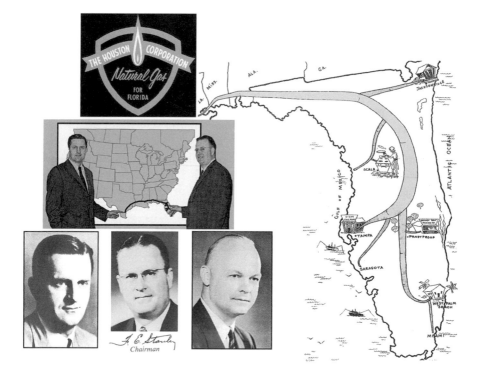

Figure 8.1 Organizers Jack Bowen (center left and lower left) and Floyd Stanley (center right and lower center) and attorney Leon Payne (lower right), were key figures in bringing natural gas to Florida, allowing the state to no longer use more expensive, dirtier manufactured gas.

---

7. This rate-base deficiency at an FPC-authorized 6 percent rate of return reduced income by $500,000 per year, but the immediate problem was paying the freight bill in addition to other costs without adequate financing.

A New CEO

Stanley's failure to add in the cost of moving pipe and his consequent inability to recover full costs required new short-term financing and restructured long-term debt. The existing long-term debt holders held a first mortgage on the facilities, and the banks refused to get back into the picture on an unsecured basis. After negotiations with the bluebloods of the New York investment banking community reached a stalemate, Clint Murchison (Delhi-Taylor was the largest shareholder of the Houston Corporation) and fellow board member Doc Neuhaus personally guaranteed a $6 million bank loan (about $45 million in today's dollars) on one condition: a change of management. No other change was required, not even with the seven-person board of directors. The lenders were pleasantly surprised; guarantors usually required a stock override or warrant for their trouble.

Jack Bowen was named acting president and CEO of Houston Corporation, effective July 1, 1960, and took up residence in St. Petersburg, Florida, the company headquarters. Stanley, nominally continuing as chairman of the board, announced a search for a new president and quietly moved back to Tulsa to his construction business. It was a vote of confidence for the 38-year-old Bowen, whose skill set now encompassed all aspects of the pipeline business.

Bowen had much to do while the search committee did its work. With the 282 MMcf/d mainline completed, large staff reductions (from 1,100 to 650) were necessary. The Houston Corporation's long-term debt with the insurance companies (the first-mortgage bondholders) had to be restructured, which was done with the help of a Stone & Webster study showing profitability under a range of realistic scenarios, including FPC-allowed recovery of the higher incurred costs. The key was fixed customer monthly payments based on their contractual gas quantity, which had to be paid whether actual gas was taken or not. Such demand charges, also called reservation charges, amortized the fixed costs of the project, as opposed to volumetric charges that were incurred with actual gas takes.

Planned projects had to be postponed to preserve cash flow given early losses. Florida's modest heating load required an aggressive effort to sell gas appliances—sales that would reduce everyone's rates when the pipeline's fixed costs were spread over more volume. (Appliance sales also generated unregulated profit, although margins were small.) There was another incentive: an FPC-approved rate design allowing the company to pocket extra profits if its throughput was higher than assumed in the rate case, as well as higher margins from sales-for-resale gas than from interruptible transportation.[8] With empty

---

8. The at-risk portion of pipeline throughput is discussed in Internet appendix 8.3, "Revenue Risk at Florida Gas Transmission," at www.politicalcapitalism.org/Book2/Chapter8/Appendix3.html.

pipeline space on all but the coldest days, Bowen called the marketing effort "fundamental ... to the realization of our tremendous potential."

A big problem for the new company was converting gas-distribution properties from manufactured to natural gas. The Florida Development Commission described the state's manufactured-gas-and-propane distribution systems as "antiquated, high cost, poor service, and unprofitable." Florida Power & Light had owned some of the biggest systems, including one serving Miami, that was sold to the Houston Corporation as a condition for entering into its transportation contract.

The Houston Corporation purchased manufactured-gas distribution systems for conversion in Miami, Orlando, Daytona Beach, Lakeland, and the triangle cities of Eustis, Mount Dora, and Umatilla. Each had a monopoly franchise for its territory and was regulated by the Florida Railroad and Public Utilities Commission, soon to be renamed the Florida Public Utilities Commission. Florida Gas's purchase and conversion budget was $23 million, which covered most of the state's 32 distributions systems (municipal and for-profit) that converted to natural gas in year-one. After early losses on the retail side, double-digit annual sales growth for Florida Gas would make for a happy ending, augmented by the later purchase of Jacksonville Gas Company (1962) and the municipal system of St. Petersburg (1968).

Florida's residential gas rates were much lower than electricity rates on an energy-equivalent basis but still were the highest in the country, given the amortization of brand-new infrastructure. The rates and proposed increases for sale-for-resale gas sparked protests and hearings across the state. At one point, Miami refused to grant a franchise to the Houston Corporation until some customer charges were lowered. Little-guy politics was in play. The pipeline and distribution facilities, once in the ground, were captive to the regulatory process on the federal *and* state levels.

But the new system proved operationally sound. A cold snap created a peak-day volume of 321 MMcf/d on January 20, 1960, 15 percent above the pipeline's design capacity. A press release trumpeted, "Natural gas has once again proved to be the ideal fuel for heating, as well as for all household and commercial uses, just as it has been for the past 143 years." The alluded-to history concerned *manufactured* gas for street lighting that began in 1817—about the only use of gas in that early day. This was not the first time—nor would it be the last—that a little hyperbole was used to enhance the image of natural gas.

The Houston Corporation's loss of $3.4 million for the first three quarters of 1960 followed 1959's deficit of $4.2 million. This occurred *despite* an FPC-approved rate structure that allowed the company to make a 6 percent return on a $164 million capital investment—all because of a cost deficiency that began with Stanley's error and continued with the project's regulatory delays during inflationary times.[9] The purchase and conversion of money-losing gas-distribution properties around the state was a drain. Still, natural gas demand was increasing nicely.

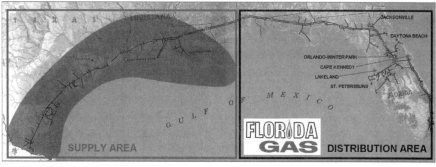

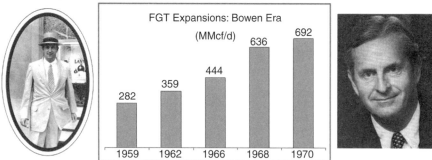

Figure 8.2 The 2,592-mile system (about the distance from Los Angeles to Jacksonville) consisted of 1,476 miles of mainline, 414 miles of gas-field supply laterals, and 702 miles of end-user distribution laterals crossing five states and 25 rivers. The Houston Corporation's gas-distribution properties are shown to the right. High gas demand led to four expansions in the Bowen era before gas-supply problems intervened.

In December 1960, the Houston Corporation recorded its first monthly profit. An appreciative board ended its search by appointing Jack Bowen president and chief operating officer. The *New York Times* ran Bowen's picture in the business

9. Under public-utility regulation, the cost could be recouped in future rates if the higher-than-anticipated costs were found just and reasonable by the FPC. This would turn out to be the case. The corrected cost of the pipeline was 14 percent above that originally presented and approved, most of the cost being due to escalating labor and steel costs resulting from regulatory delay.

section alongside the story, "Houston Corp. Picks President, Revises Debt, Maps Expansion." It was hard to believe that just a decade before, Jack Bowen had been a rookie in the energy industry.

Mr. Natural Gas

In early 1961, Bowen moved his family from Houston to St. Petersburg, which was located on the Gulf (west) side of the state. St. Pete was already the home of Florida Power & Light, and the Houston Corporation was not a very neighborly name. Before long, Bowen chose a new name, Florida Gas Company, and a new home, Winter Park, a picturesque lake-studded suburb of Orlando in central Florida ("a little 'Shangri La'"). Jack and Annis Bowen found themselves in the very spot where, years ago, they had thought they would retire after Jack's career in the military.

Once in place, Bowen had fires to extinguish and growth to manage. There were FPC hearings over rate changes and a proposed expansion of the main-line. Rate disputes with the Florida Public Utilities Commission and city commissions added problems on the distribution (retail) side. The good news was that Florida Gas Transmission (FGT), which represented almost 90 percent of the assets of its parent, Florida Gas Company, had an "excellent" supply position and "market demand … exceed[ing] the capacity of the pipeline," Bowen reported to shareholders in 1963. Half of the nation's gas was being produced within FGT's far-reaching supply territory, and the pipeline was running at 99 percent of capacity year-round.

Electricity demand was growing with the state's economy, which was expanding at three times the national average. As predicted by the Florida Development Commission back in 1957, the availability of natural gas was encouraging new investment in the chemical, stone, clay, and glass industries. The Florida Development Council began a national advertising campaign in the *Wall Street Journal* and other publications, touting the state's new industry and natural gas service.

Jack Bowen became Mr. Natural Gas in the state. There were many interviews and speeches extolling the virtues of the new energy choice for Florida. The story of Florida Gas was a good one for the industry—a can-do company with a can-do fuel. Bowen was elected a director of the American Gas Association and, in 1969, would serve as president of the Interstate Natural Gas Association of America.

The Bowen home in Winter Park sported a variety of gas appliances to set the example. There was the usual—gas for water heating, cooking, washing and drying. There were gas lights outside the house—sporty and used. A gas lighter for the fireplace was functional though doomed to infrequent use. A gas refrigerator was novel but workable; a gas-fired incinerator, esoteric and of limited utility. Still another use was downright problematic. Florida Gas tirelessly promoted gas air conditioning as the regional equivalent to space heating up north, but "repairmen seemed to always be at the house to fix it," Jack Bowen remembered.

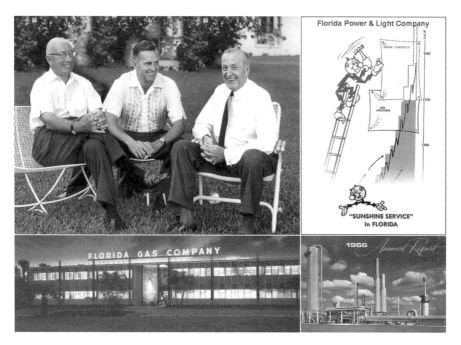

Figure 8.3 (Clockwise from upper left) Jack Bowen (center), Florida Gas Company chairman J. French Robinson (left) and director V. F. "Doc" Neuhaus (right) at a board meeting in 1965; "Ready Kilowatt" showing electricity growth in Florida; the gasoline-extraction plant at Brooker, Florida, a successful diversification for Florida Gas; and the original home of Florida Gas Company in Winter Park.

A Problem in Paradise

In the 1960s, Florida Gas Transmission expanded three times to keep up with surging gas usage in the state. After the third expansion, in 1968, the year Florida Gas Company became listed on the New York Stock Exchange, the company faced its first real constraint. The problem was not market demand for gas on a pipeline that had more than doubled in size in its first decade; it was attracting enough gas to the pipeline to meet that demand.

Supplies for transportation gas were not the problem for FGT. Indeed, there was plenty of unregulated gas for buyers in Texas and Louisiana, including from Houston Natural Gas Corporation's Houston Pipe Line. But gas was short for distribution customers (gas utilities) and direct-sale customers (industries). Fifteen years of price controls on sales-for-resale gas were coming home to roost. Bowen reported to shareholders in 1970 that "uncommitted proven gas reserves are in very short supply," and so-called *supplemental gas*—"synthetic gas from coal and liquefied natural gas imported by ocean tankers"—was being

seriously considered as the way out. Synthetic gas—wasn't that what natural
gas had displaced around the country and finally in Florida itself?

Jack Bowen had been introduced to exploration and production in his early
Delhi Oil days, and in 1969, he revved up Florida Gas's nascent activity into
exploration and production. Coastal Production Company, which was formed
in 1963 and participated in its first drilling syndicate two years later, was
enlarged by the purchase of a Louisiana exploration company. Southeastern
Exploration Company was formed to act as general partner for drilling in FGT's
gas-supply area. Monies dedicated to exploration and production would double year to year, as Bowen and Florida Gas got to know the business.

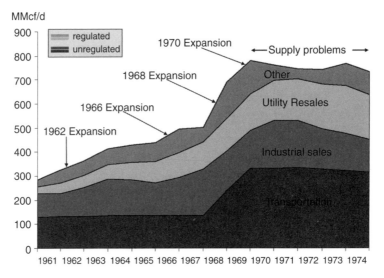

Figure 8.4 FGT throughput in the Bowen era was primarily for power plants (transportation gas) and industrial customers (direct sales). Regulated sale-for-resale gas, going to
small residential and commercial customers, grew rapidly in the 1960s before price controls stymied growth. FGT expanded to 700 MMcf/d before gas-supply problems set in.
("Other" gas is compression fuel, leakage, and off-system sales.)

Coastal Production Company, soon to become Florida Gas Exploration
Company, had a particular angle—partnering with large gas users that
intended to transport their finds on FGT for their own use. The transaction
allowed the partners to obtain scarce gas and, ideally, make a profit to benefit
shareholders (industrials) or ratepayers (electric utilities). For Florida Gas
Company, this backward integration was necessary to attract the gas that the
pipeline needed but—given federal price regulation— could no longer depend
on drillers to provide.

Diversification

Florida Gas was very much a regulated company, with its pipeline profits set by federal authorities at 6 percent, and its distribution profits set a bit higher by state regulators. Wall Street was looking for something extra to boost the stock price, something more substantial than could be provided by the company's three nonregulated energy units: Florida Hydrocarbons Company (1962), which extracted propane, butane, and natural gasoline from rich natural gas off the mainline near Gainesville; Florida Liquid Gas Company (1962), which retailed bottled gas to customers beyond the reach of the natural gas distribution system; and Coastal Production Company. So, in 1966, the Florida Gas Company announced a diversification program outside of energy.

In 1965, tens of thousands of acres of undeveloped land, mostly swamp, was being purchased just south of Orlando. Speculation grew that the many buyers were a front for just one. Was Howard Hughes buying land in the middle of nowhere, as he had done on the outskirts of Las Vegas? Was a large manufacturer, such as Boeing, looking for a new site? The answer came in February 1967 when Walt Disney Company announced plans to build a vacation kingdom that would be five times larger than Disneyland in southern California. The project would include not only the theme park but also industrial parks and planned communities.

Eager to diversify into a business with unregulated returns, Jack Bowen in 1969 purchased 4,500 acres at $1,700 per acre between Orlando and the planned park. A new division, Florida Land Company, was formed to develop residential subdivisions and apartments and sell undeveloped tracts, such as a 125-acre patch tendered to Sea World for a theme park in 1972. Thousands more acres in or near Orlando would be purchased and developed or resold during the next years by Florida Land Company. Behind this activity was the thought, shared by Bowen with analysts, that land development could become the largest division of Florida Gas Company.

Bowen expected land values to rise from a tourist boom in central Florida, and he rationalized some value to stocking the new construction with gas appliances. The latter was penny ante, however, and raw land was not an income generator. The nonenergy, nonregulated diversification play needed something more.

Citing a need for low-cost housing, Florida Gas built a 120,000-square-foot manufacturing facility south of Orlando in 1970 to construct modular homes. The three-bedroom units were functional and durable. There were buyers at $20,000 each. But try as the company might, the units could not be profitably manufactured. The last house, languishing in inventory, was purchased by Bowen and his new president, Selby Sullivan, and plopped on a sand dune at New Smyrna Beach, an hour's ride from Orlando.

The house was a place for the family to go, but it was also a reminder, in Bowen's words, to "stay out of things we don't know anything about." Bowen did take away one positive when his NYSE-listed stock rose after he announced that the division, Contemporary Building Systems, was being closed and a write-off taken.

"Cut your losses, and let bygones be bygones," Jack Bowen said. The company's outside auditor since 1963, Arthur Andersen & Co., could also feel vindicated for its advice in the matter.[10] And if it was any consolation, noncore diversification by other energy companies on a much grander scale in the 1970s fared little better.

Grandeur for Gas

Jack Bowen had a hobby that grew to a passion—art. Drawing classes from his Delhi Oil days in Dallas graduated to weekend lessons in water coloring while at Florida Gas. Bowen's skills grew, and his drive could keep him painting for five hours at a sitting. He would paint for the rest of his life, have one-man shows across the country, and collect art for both himself and his companies. He drew inspiration from another part-time artist, Winston Churchill, who said: "Painting is a friend who makes no undue demands, excites no exhausting pursuits, keeps faithful pace with feeble steps, and holds her canvas as a screen between us and the envious eyes of Time and the surly advance of decrepitude."

Bowen's aesthetic interests came into play when Florida Gas Company needed a bigger building to consolidate its scattered employees. Bowen instructed the architects to "come up with a building that will be strikingly handsome—a work of art in itself." The result in 1970 was the seven-story stone-and-glass Florida Gas Building, called by the *Orlando Sentinel* "a stunning addition to the Central Florida skyline."

The building was the embodiment of Bowen's vocation and avocation. All energy came from a gas-fired Total Energy System housed in the basement, entirely displacing electricity purchases from Florida Power & Light. One hundred and fifty pieces of original art were purchased for the award-winning building. A 15,000-foot underground floor housed a company cafeteria, lounge, and auditorium capable of holding all 300 employees. The décor was modernistic and, in places, artsy.

Samuel Insull had the ultimate company cafeteria in downtown Chicago back in the 1920s, Clint Murchison set a standard for his employees at Delhi's Dallas headquarters in the 1950s, and Bowen set a marker in central Florida. Bowen would do so again in grander fashion a decade later as head of Transco Energy—as would his protégé-to-be, Ken Lay, as CEO of Enron Corp. Natural gas, long oil's poor cousin, now had grandeur.

---

10. Another noncore diversification, Florida Computer Systems Company, founded in 1968 to perform data processing for companies, was brought in-house after several years of performing outside work and did not affect earnings appreciably.

Figure 8.5 Completed in 1970, the seven-story Florida Gas Building in Winter Park, Florida, had a landscaped parking lot, night lighting, modern décor, pop art, a gas-fired energy system, a gas-control room, and much more.

The Energy Crisis

In his *1971 Annual Report*, Jack Bowen identified long-term gas supply as "the most critical problem confronting the company." Reserves attached to the system were down 20 percent in three years, and further declines were imminent. Florida Gas began a moratorium on new service to industrial customers served by utility companies, husbanding sale-for-resale gas for the residential and commercial markets. It was frustrating: After finally getting demand up to 99 percent of the line's capacity, the problem came at the other end of the pipe.

Bowen blamed falling supply on "insufficient incentives," not "inadequate resources." He quoted from the FPC's acknowledgment of clear evidence that there was "a worsening gap between supply and demand, and that price must have a major responsibility for eliciting new supplies." Opinion 598 of July 1971, a mea culpa for the commission's price-control policy, was partly the handiwork at the FPC of a young Ph.D. economist, Ken Lay, who would become part of the Florida Gas story several years later.

Florida Gas Company calculated that the alternatives to natural gas—imported LNG, petroleum liquids, or gasifying solid fuels—would cost around

$1 per Mcf compared to their average cost of $0.21 per Mcf. Should large capital outlays be committed for such supplemental supply projects, particularly in light of the artificial situation created by government intervention in the market? Or should capital be directed toward drilling in the vicinity of the pipeline? Fortunately, the latter strategy was chosen rather than building a synthetic-fuels plant to gasify coal or building a liquefied natural gas (LNG) plant to receive and regasify the liquid at Jacksonville.[11]

The gas problem became a national crisis in the winter of 1971/72, when interstate pipelines curtailed deliveries to their highest-priority customers in many markets around the country. "Interruptible" industrial customers, with alternative-fuel capacity, were routinely cut off as wintertime space-heating load soared. But "human need" customers—households and small businesses— did not have ready alternatives and were under priority contracts *not* to be curtailed. But they were. There was pipeline space and withdrawal capability from storage—but no gas! Florida, with its small heating load, was in far better shape than the rest of the interstate industry, including Transco Companies, a company soon to be in Jack Bowen's future.

Bowen used every forum at his disposal to call for legislative and regulatory change to address the gas crisis. His 1972 annual report called for a

> comprehensive national energy program; realistic environmental and health standards; accelerated leasing of public lands for exploration and development; continued tax incentives to encourage discovery and development of energy supplies; maintenance of oil and uranium import controls; relaxing of natural gas price controls at the wellhead; and reliance on private enterprise as the least expensive and best method of providing energy needs.

A "massive" commitment to coal gasification and shale-oil research was advised. On the demand side, Bowen called for "the intelligent use of resources and careful conservation."

One simple and profound word was absent from the preceding public-policy lexicon—*deregulation*. Bowen's framework was to bring supply and demand together *given* a regulated price. Such an attempt to fill in the gaps, a second-best approach compared to ending price controls, was pragmatic.[12] Existing sale-for-resale customers benefited from wellhead regulation that kept prices below free-market levels. Deregulation would mean rate hikes and contentious hearings in Tallahassee. What Bowen wanted, and what the interstate gas-pipeline industry desired, were *continued price ceilings for existing production* and *free-market incentives for new production*. Florida Gas Company was drilling for *new* production; tax

---

11. Bowen's ill-fated decision to build a coal-gasification plant as head of Transco Energy Company is discussed in chapter 9, pp. 333–34.

12. "Gapism" as a second-best approach compared to deregulation is described in *Capitalism at Work*, pp. 266–67.

breaks and expanded federal leasing in offshore waters would make that activity all the more lucrative. Mandatory conservation was a more complicated public-policy stance for the gas industry, but it was certainly politically correct and consonant with Bowen's engineering mentality.

The changed energy equation between supply and demand created another headache for the company. The price of unregulated gas sold by Florida Gas to a variety of industrial and power-plant users was tied to (nonregulated) residual fuel-oil prices. When oil prices began to rise in spring 1970, lawsuits were filed by a group of Florida cities. The municipalities persuaded the attorney general of Florida to join in as well. Settlements in 1971/72 required Florida Gas to make partial refunds and limit future increases in gas prices to a regulated percentage. Thus, a lightly regulated portion of the company's business—gas sales to municipal electric companies—came under more formal regulation.

For private-sector buyers, industrials and utility power plants, on the other hand, a contract remained a contract; they paid floating prices for their gas, depending on the price of their closest fuel substitute, which was fuel oil.

More Diversification

Florida Gas Company was redefining itself in the face of regulatory distortion. Bowen told stockholders in March 1974:

> As the energy picture has changed, the Company has changed. Five years ago, we were strictly a gas transmission, extraction, and distribution company. We now have developed substantial organizations in oil and gas exploration and land development, and we are planning to enter into the transmission of petroleum products for the first time.

In 1973 Florida Gas announced its intention to convert part of its natural gas mainline to petroleum products, offering common-carrier services (per federal regulation) for gasoline, heating oil, and jet fuel. The natural gas volumes needed to support FGT's 700 MMcf/d line were at risk, and an oil-product pipeline could displace more expensive marine transportation along the Gulf Coast. Moreover, federal regulation of interstate oil pipeline rates by the Interstate Commerce Commission (ICC) was less stringent than FPC regulation of interstate gas pipelines, offering greater profitability.[13]

But Transgulf Pipeline Company, organized in 1974 as a wholly owned subsidiary of Florida Gas, could not get its project off the ground. This was despite the best efforts of Gus Maciula, an executive brought in from Williams Pipeline Company, which operated the nation's largest oil pipeline, and a new young face at Florida Gas, Ken Lay. Integrated oil companies were hesitant to enter into long-term contracts given the short-term nature of buying and selling crude

---

13. ICC regulation is discussed in Internet appendix 8.4, "Transgulf Pipeline and Federal Rate Regulation," at www.politicalcapitalism.org/Book2/Chapter8/Appendix4.html.

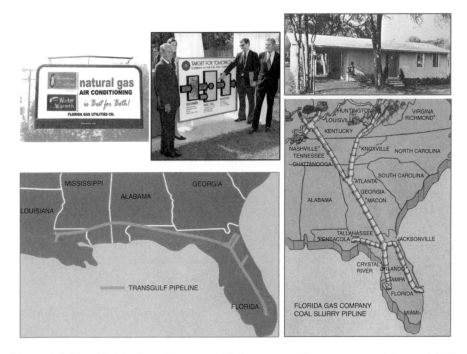

Figure 8.6 Five Florida Gas Company initiatives were either unsuccessful or not built. Unsuccessful were (clockwise from upper left) natural gas air conditioning in the early 1960s, natural gas fuel cells at Walt Disney World in 1972–73, and modular home construction in 1970–71. A proposed coal-slurry pipeline and a proposed gas-pipeline conversion to petroleum products were not built.

oil and petroleum products, and they were not quite ready to build a pipeline themselves. Regulatory uncertainties also hung over the project. By the time Transgulf received final approval from regulatory authorities and the courts in the next decade (competing forms of oil transportation used these forums for delay), oil markets would change, and the project would be canceled.

A second pipeline diversification would be proposed by Florida Gas in 1978: construction of a 1,500-mile coal-slurry pipeline from coal fields in Kentucky to power plants and industrial customers in Georgia and Florida. The $2 billion project, named Concoal Pipeline Company in a 1981 employee naming contest, would deliver 40 million tons of coal per year at a projected savings of billions of dollars compared to the cost of status quo train and barge shipments.[14] Concurrently,

_____

14. Pipeline-quality coal required that virgin coal be ground down to the consistency of sugar and mixed with water for movement. Upon delivery, the stew would be dried and

Florida Gas Company lobbied for a federal eminent-domain law to ensure that a pipeline right-of-way could be sited affordably—and not obstructed at railroad crossings by the coal carriers themselves. Ken Lay would spearhead this project for Florida Gas and later serve as president of the Coal Slurry Pipe Line Association.

Power-plant customers in Florida were very supportive of underground coal transport. The project sponsors, however, were unable to persuade Congress to enact a federal eminent-domain law to overcome right-of-way blockage. The railroads adamantly protected what one industry executive described as "our great black hope," effectively killing the project.[15]

Management Changes

Wellhead price regulation was profoundly influencing Florida Gas Company. Jack Bowen found himself in the middle of the nation's top domestic issue: energy policy. He increasingly became Mr. Outside for the company, dealing with regulators and legislators in Washington and state regulators in Tallahassee, in addition to his work with producers, customers, and investors. Energy education and the need for a comprehensive energy policy became his passion. At the same time, new talent coming into the Florida Gas Company presaged a new chapter in Bowen's career.

Nominally, Jack Bowen had a boss after Floyd Stanley was eased out in the early 1960s. J. French Robinson, a respected gas-industry veteran who had retired to the Sunshine State after heading Consolidated Gas Company of New York City, became board chairman of Florida Gas in 1960. His presence lent credibility to the young company. Robinson accompanied Bowen to important meetings but did not spend the day at the office. During this time, and after Robinson stepped down in May 1968, Bowen was CEO, with division heads reporting directly to him. The most important of these was fellow West Pointer H. L. "Smokey" Wilhite, who ran Florida Gas Transmission.

Bowen also had "the best lawyer I have ever known": Leon Payne. A partner in Andrews, Kurth, Campbell, and Bradley (now Andrews & Kurth) in Houston, Payne held the title of secretary and general counsel of Florida Gas.[16] Payne had two offices: one at the law firm and one in Winter Park.

---

burned at the power plant. Transportation by pipeline was quieter, more reliable, and less labor intensive than railroad carriage.

15. Another coal-slurry project, Energy Transportation System, Inc. (ETSI), would file an antitrust suit against the railroads for concerted access blockage, resulting in settlements of $100 million to Ken Lay's future company, Enron Corp., between 1987 and 1990.

16. Bowen originally contacted Jack Head of Vinson & Elkins to represent Coastal Transmission. But because of a conflict of interest with another client, the firm referred Bowen to

In May 1972, Payne, age 56, was felled by heart failure. Selby Sullivan, who had worked on Florida Gas Company matters under Payne for nearly a decade, was elected secretary and general counsel. Two months later, Sullivan resigned from Andrews & Kurth and moved to Winter Park as vice president, legal.

The quick-minded, quick-tempered, no-nonsense Sullivan advanced rapidly. In November 1973, Bowen was elected chairman and CEO and Sullivan president. For the first time, there was a real number one and a real number two at Florida Gas Company.

Figure 8.7 Chairman and CEO Jack Bowen with President Selby Sullivan. Upon Bowen's departure, Sullivan became CEO in October 1974 and led the company through its acquisition by Continental Group in 1979. His four chief lieutenants would be (bottom left to right) Kenneth L. Lay, J. Ronald Knorpp, R. Philip Silver, and T. P. McConn.

Bowen and Sullivan reported net income of nearly $17 million for Florida Gas in 1973 (about $85 million in today's dollars), led by steady pipeline and distribution earnings, real estate sales and development, and higher gas-liquids

---

Leon Payne at Andrews & Kurth, who had just completed an FPC certificate application for Pacific Northwest Pipeline Company.

income. The environment for energy companies was improving, thanks to rising commodity prices. FGT's utilization percentage was slipping, however, and more declines were expected. There was simply not enough price-regulated gas available for distribution and utility customers.

A Doctor for Natural Gas

The price-induced shortage of natural gas during the winter of 1971/72 was joined by spot shortages of petroleum products in 1972. The energy crisis was on. As with natural gas, crude oil and oil products were price controlled, and federal lawmakers and President Nixon looked for quick fixes short of politically volatile decontrol. One action was for the Department of the Interior to offer new tracts for oil and gas development in federal waters.

In 1973, a 1.4-million-acre lease sale was proposed for offshore areas adjacent to Mississippi, Alabama, and Florida—all within reach of Florida Gas Transmission. More than 300 parties submitted oral or written testimony, followed by three days of public hearings in the Florida capital of Tallahassee. The Interior Department official in charge, visiting from Washington, D.C., was Ken Lay, deputy undersecretary of energy behind Secretary Rogers Morton and Undersecretary John Whitaker (Lay's boss). It was at this hearing that Ken met Jack Bowen.

The 30-year-old already had a full résumé. At the University of Missouri, Lay was elected president of school's largest fraternity, Beta Theta Pi, and graduated Phi Beta Kappa with two degrees in economics. After receiving his master's, Lay's first job was corporate economist at Humble Oil & Refining Company, the nation's largest producer, refiner, and marketer of petroleum products. His starting salary of $13,000 per annum (about $85,000 today) was more money that he had ever seen. With this stability came the decision to settle down. In June 1966, a year after joining Humble Oil, Ken married his college sweetheart, Judith (Judie) Ayers, in her hometown of Jefferson City, Missouri.

Among other tasks, Lay wrote speeches for M. A. "Mike" Wright, Humble Oil's CEO, who was acting president of the U.S. Chamber of Commerce for 1967. Lay's literary work became essays in a book published under Wright's name by McGraw-Hill, *The Business of Business: Private Enterprise and Public Affairs*.[17]

At the same time, Lay was working toward his Ph.D. in economics at the University of Houston.[18] "He was taking a five-course load in evening classes,

---

17. See *Capitalism at Work*, pp. 172–74.

18. Lay was accepted for the Ph.D. economics programs at the University of California at Berkeley, University of Michigan, Princeton University, and the University of Wisconsin. He was most interested in Michigan but chose to pursue his doctorate at the University of Houston, which had an evening curriculum that allowed him to continue working. Humble Oil not only

which he said was easy, and jogging a number of miles after work too," Professor Henry Steele remembered. "I was quite taken by his energy, to say the least."

With a military obligation to discharge during the Vietnam War, Lay took a leave of absence from Humble Oil in 1967 to join the navy. After graduating from the U.S. Navy's Officer Candidate School in Newport, Rhode Island, uniquely academically credentialed Ensign Lay secured an analytical position at the Pentagon with the help of his former employer.

Winning the support of some senior officials, Lay developed a mathematical model and obtained interdivisional data estimating the economic impact of reduced military spending come peacetime. The project formed the basis of his dissertation for a Ph.D. in economics, awarded by the University of Houston in 1970. Professor Steele remembered how Lay would periodically visit the campus to update his dissertation committee on his progress. Each time the professors asked for more, wanting a "landmark dissertation, perfecting all the intricate details of the analyses which academicians find so fascinating." Steele continued:

> Ken went along with this until one day when, in front of the entire committee, he asked the chairman, "Look, stop hazing me, will you? Haven't I done enough to join your fraternity now?" We all laughed, and the chairman conceded that while he was trying to get a superior dissertation out of a superior student, what Ken had done was more than enough to fulfill the department's requirements for a dissertation.

"Never before or since," Steele added, "have I seen a Ph.D. candidate take so confidently independent a stance in front of his entire committee."

Lay planned to resume his career at Humble Oil after leaving the navy. It was a top company and one that for three years had paid him the difference between his navy pay and last company salary under its military leave-of-absence policy. As Lay's tour of duty was wrapping up, his mentor from the University of Missouri, Dr. Pinkney Walker, a newly appointed FPC commissioner and public-utility specialist, asked Ken to become his deputy technical assistant. Pinkney knew that Ken, his prize student and graduate assistant, could dissect archaic regulations using economic principles and build a consensus for reform. Charls Walker, deputy secretary of the Treasury Department, and later an Enron director (1985–99), also lobbied Lieutenant Lay on behalf of his brother, Pinkney.

Ken told Pinkney about his obligation to return to Humble Oil, soon to become the core of Exxon USA. Pinkney almost gave up but asked Ken a question. Could he (Pinkney) call Humble's Mike Wright about it? Intrigued about being the top

---

offered a good paycheck, but also was able to secure Lay a Critical Employment Deferment from the State of Texas Draft Board during the height of the Vietnam War.

aide to the vice chairman of one of the most powerful regulatory agencies in Washington, Ken consented.

"I knew I had Kenneth because the president of Exxon is not going to offend a new member of the Federal Power Commission," Pinkney Walker would later recall. Sure enough, Wright could only mutter, "Hell, that will be fine," after hearing Walker explain how much the FPC (read: America) needed Lay at this critical juncture and how such Washington experience would be good for Ken when he returned to the company. So, victory went to the FPC, which, after all, regulated most of the gas bought and sold in the country, including that of Humble Oil, the nation's largest gas producer.

But Lay would never return to Humble/Exxon. During the next 15 years, the Ph.D. economist would cut a path in the highly regulated midstream of the natural gas industry, then head a company that became, by his measure, *the world's first natural gas major* and then *the world's leading energy company.* Enron would be in businesses different from Exxon's, but the venerable oil major would always be in the back of Ken Lay's mind. Exxon was the path not taken. Exxon was also a company that represented the energy past, whereas Enron represented the energy future—or so Lay thought.

Walker and Lay were the highest-ranking economists in the FPC's lawyer- and engineer-dominated history.[19] With Walker preoccupied with his ailing wife, Lay became a commissioner de facto, handling all matters for his boss.[20] To supplement his government pay (he no longer received a corporate stipend from Humble Oil), Lay taught graduate-level courses in macroeconomics, microeconomics, and government-business relations at George Washington University. The assistant professor's favorite text was Peter Drucker's *The Age of Discontinuity,* which described a "new economic reality" in which *knowledge* trumped *experience,* and the managerial role was ceding ground to the entrepreneurial function.[21] The Age of Continuity, Drucker explained, was being overthrown by rapidly improving knowledge, disruptive technology, and the

---

19. The Federal Power Commission, founded in 1920 to regulate hydroelectricity, greatly expanded its jurisdiction with the passage of the Federal Power Act of 1935, the Natural Gas Act of 1938, and administratively regulating wellhead prices for gas moving interstate beginning in the 1940s.

20. Pinkney Walker recalled, "Helen, my then wife, was getting into a very serious Alzheimer's situation, which meant that Kenneth was doing all the work at the office. He thus became a *de facto* member of the Federal Power Commission."

21. In Drucker's words: "Equally important and equally new is the fact that every one of the new emerging industries is squarely based on knowledge. Not a single one is based on experience."

diffusion of new products. This was heady stuff, and Lay, ever impatient with the status quo, took it to heart.[22]

Lay worked on electricity and, particularly, gas issues in what turned out to be only 18 months at the FPC. The commission was under pressure to relax wellhead gas-price ceilings in light of the shortages in (regulated) interstate markets and surpluses in (unregulated) intrastate markets. Walker and Lay had a lot of work to do given a mindset at the commission that low prices *increased* supply by creating new markets for gas. Whatever modicum of applicability this had, prices needed to rise to induce producers to find new gas and to ration demand to available supply. If prices could not go up, producers needed other incentives to bring more gas to market, such as allowing interstate pipelines to finance drilling programs whereby the associated costs could be recovered in the pipeline's rate base. Such second-best strategies were endorsed by Walker and Lay—and embraced by the pipeline industry.

Setting maximum rates at the average cost of production was recognized by the two as particularly distorting. Average-cost pricing worked for pipelines in a monopoly position but could not work for producers in a competitive environment. Those with higher-than-average costs would be forced out of the market, a cycle that would repeat itself with each recalculation of average cost for federal rate setting. Basic microeconomics explained why the marginal cost of average-cost pricing was too low and a recipe for steadily declining supply. Walker and Lay so persuaded Commissioner John Carver, the author of FPC Opinion 598 (July 1971), which forthrightly described the need to conform to market realities to better deal with the wellhead gas imbroglio. It was this mea culpa that Jack Bowen shared with his stockholders.

Walker and Lay also favored incremental (marginal) over rolled-in (average) pricing to set the prices at which interstate pipelines bought and sold gas. The economists were instrumental in defeating a proposal by some interstate pipelines to average down the cost of much more expensive liquefied natural gas (LNG) by rolling it in with their price-controlled supply.[23] Some of the nation's biggest pipelines, including Transcontinental Gas Pipe Line Company, poised to invest hundreds of millions of dollars in LNG facilities, were stymied by the requirement for stand-alone pricing of LNG sales.[24]

⋅∽⋅

---

22. The influence of another business-change guru on Lay, Gary Hamel, is discussed in *Capitalism at Work*, pp. 83–85, 101–103, 265.

23. For further discussion about rolled-in versus incremental LNG pricing, see in Internet appendix 8.5, "Ken Lay and LNG Pricing," at www.politicalcapitalism.org/Book2/Chapter8/Appendix5.html.

24. Lay-qua-regulator favored incremental pricing, but Lay-the-businessman would plead for the opposite to save the economics of Transco's coal gasification plant, described in chapter 9, p. 344.

Regulating major parts of two of the America's largest industries (gas and electricity) was heady stuff, but Lay longed to return to the industry. He had a family of four to support and looked forward to the fast pace and value creation of the marketplace. But this was not to be, just yet. Lay's White House connections knew his intentions and put his name into play to join the Department of the Interior, which was looking to upgrade its analytical capacity. Once a backwater bureaucracy dealing with federal land management, including oil and gas leasing, Interior was suddenly the lead agency dealing with oil issues that were becoming the top domestic priority of the Nixon administration.

Interior Secretary Rogers Morton obtained an exemption from the U.S. Civil Service rules to be able to offer Lay a premium salary, and the 30-year-old joined Interior as deputy undersecretary of energy in October 1972. Eleven months later, Ken Lay was in Tallahassee overseeing the hearing at which he and Bowen, wearing different hats, testified in favor of drilling in federal waters off the coast of Florida to help meet the area's growing energy needs.

The hearing was in response to President Nixon's energy message to Congress on April 18, 1973, which directed the Department of the Interior to triple the annual acreage leased on the Outer Continental Shelf (OCS) by 1979. Nixon's was the first-ever presidential speech to Congress on energy, and Lay knew it intimately. He had cancelled his Christmas vacation to begin working on it and by the end could claim to be its chief analytical architect.

Untapped areas in the Gulf of Mexico were a good place to start leasing. Environmental groups, such as the Florida Audubon Society, Natural Resources Defense Council, and Sierra Club mobilized to slow the process. But the arguments from government and industry for greater supply in a time of crisis won out. Federal leases off Florida were granted, although major discoveries would not be forthcoming.

A few days after the hearing was completed, Jack Bowen received a letter from Ken Lay mentioning his desire to return to industry after two and a half years in government. "I would be most interested in being considered for possible job opportunities with Florida Gas Company," the letter said. "The natural gas industry, obviously, faces some very difficult challenges in the months and years ahead, and I would like to be in a position in industry to help meet these challenges." A bountiful résumé was attached, but what Bowen liked best was the way Ken had managed the hearing.

"I was very glad to get your letter this morning," Bowen shot back. "You are certainly right in that the natural gas industry faces some very difficult challenges. We at Florida Gas are investigating a lot of different ways to meet the problems of gas supply as well as continuing the growth of the company."

Jack arranged for a lunch meeting in Washington a few weeks later and Ken arrived in an official car with a driver. "Not too bad," thought Bowen.

Ken and his wife of seven years, Judie, visited Winter Park. They were instantly attracted to the area's beauty and climate, as compared to wintertime up north. Ken's interviews, mostly perfunctory and deferential, went well. After all, this polite young man had stellar credentials and Bowen's imprimatur.

But one of the interviews was unexpectedly rigorous. It was with Bowen's understudy, Florida Gas president Selby Sullivan. Lay found Selby "prickly"; Sullivan remembered Lay as "just a kid who wanted to be called Dr. Lay, and who was seemingly over-impressed with his title as deputy under secretary of energy, which he must have repeated four or five times." Still, Lay liked the people, location, and opportunities better at Florida Gas than at his other serious suitors—ARCO, Westinghouse Electric Company, and Columbia Gas Company.

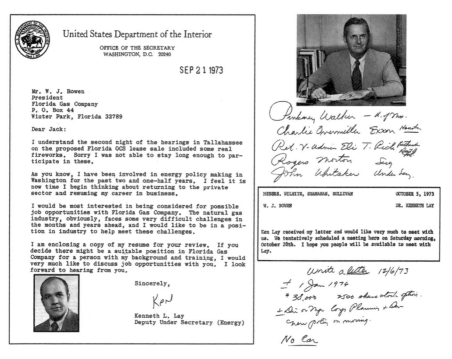

Figure 8.8 Ken Lay's inquiry on Interior Department letterhead led to interviews and a job offer from Florida Gas, which Lay accepted over his other suitors.

Sullivan posed no objections to hiring the "nice, bright young man." "If Jack wanted to bring him in," Selby recollected, "that was Jack's call." Bowen ran the traps with Ken's references, all previous bosses: Charles Overmiller (Exxon USA): "good worker, very smart, lots of imagination … (maybe too ambitious)." George Kinnear (Navy): "tops! never had a better man technically…. can get along with people very well." John Whitaker (Interior): "terrific, no reservations … good speaker … innovative—a self-starter." Pinkney Walker (FPC): "extremely able, dedicated, loyal, sharp, practical, hard worker … Stands out in a crowd."

Bowen negotiated with Lay and scribbled down the outlines of the deal: $38,000, moving expenses, stock options for 2,500 shares subject to board approval, *"No Car."* January 1, 1974. Director or Manager of Corporate Planning.

This position was a new one. "We wanted someone to be our individual think tank and come up with new ideas on this or that," Bowen recollected.

The Pride and Pleasure of **WINTER PARK, FLORIDA**

Figure 8.9 Winter Park in central Florida was an ideal place to work and raise a family. Many houses, including those of Jack Bowen and Ken Lay, were located on lakes offering boating and a beautiful vista.

Sullivan, taskmaster extraordinaire, wrote a two-page memorandum to Jack Bowen and other senior staff outlining Ken Lay's initial responsibilities. Lay was Bowen's direct report, but he would be working closely with Selby. It was time to test the kid's mettle, thought Sullivan. The New Year's Eve memo was just in time for Ken's first day, 48 hours away.

In that memo, Selby gave Ken six days—calendar, not working—to "become intimately familiar with the Company, its history, its present activities and its goals." Ken was to read everything important about the company—from annual reports to exploration and production agreements. For January 9–25, Ken was to rotate between divisions, beginning with Land and ending with Distribution.

He was to help finalize the company's strategy and "be responsible for determining the return on investment, present and projected, for our exploration efforts."

After this "initial introductory phase," Ken was to manage an industry-wide effort in Washington against proposed legislation that would restrict the use of natural gas as a boiler fuel. Such legislation, intended to redirect supply to the residential market, had the potential to take away FGT's major growth markets. Ken was also instructed to undertake a feasibility study for purchasing undeveloped coal reserves or an operating coal company and to recommend avenues for diversification, preferably within the energy sector. "At the end of January," Sullivan concluded, "Ken's activities will be reviewed and his responsibilities as Director of Corporate Planning will be further defined."

And then Selby Sullivan brought in the New Year.

Ken Lay first reported for duty on Wednesday, January 2, 1974, a week removed as one of Washington's top hands-on energy officials. It had been Lay who helped coordinate the federal government's response to growing oil shortages created by its own regulation—a thankless task.[25] And now he was learning everything important about a 15-year-old company in very short order.

Lay flew through Selby's itinerary and immersed himself in the task of recommending how the company should respond to all the propositions streaming in the door. Some were in real estate, but most were energy related. There were start-up opportunities in oil gasification, coal gasification, and ethane recovery. There was a proposal to build a natural gas pipeline between Venezuela and the United States. There were opportunities to buy coal reserves, uranium reserves, and a coal company. The price was too high for a coal acquisition, Lay concluded in one memo, although "coal will inevitably be a growth business over the next two decades despite itself, and a well-rounded energy company should attempt to gain a position in it."

All the proposals were tabled for further evaluation.

The best opportunity to Sullivan was the one announced prior to Lay's arrival: the proposed conversion of part of the mainline to petroleum products. Converting or purchasing existing assets was preferable to building a new business from the ground up, Selby thought. This led to Lay's promotion to vice president, Transgulf Pipeline Company in September 1974, nine months after joining Florida Gas, while continuing as director of corporate development for the parent. Transgulf, designed to carry gasoline, jet fuel, heating oil, diesel oil, and kerosene from Baton Rouge to Fort Lauderdale, was scheduled to begin operations in 1977 if the requisite contracts could be secured.

It was not to be. In three years, oil supplies would become scarce and the project canceled—and Sullivan would be the head of Florida Gas.

---

25. Lay's work at the U.S. Department of the Interior is also reviewed in *Capitalism at Work*, pp. 3–4, 242.

Bigger Things for Bowen

Jack Bowen's success building Florida Gas Company had made him very well known and respected in the industry. Back in 1971, the board of directors of Transco Companies, Inc., approached him about joining the Houston-based firm as chief executive officer. Transco was ailing. The interstate gas-transmission company, stretching from South Texas to New York City, was short of gas. And the problem was worsening. Transco's high-priority customers were being curtailed when they needed gas the most—during winter cold snaps. The directors wanted Jack Bowen to come and do for Transco what he had done for Florida Gas: secure enough gas to meet almost all customer demands.

Transco was a top-tier interstate compared to midsized Florida Gas Company, but Bowen politely declined. There was much to do at the company he had nurtured from the ground up. Winter Park was perfect for raising a family. So, Transco ended up hiring as its new CEO a consultant, G. Montgomery Mitchell, from the New York office of Stone & Webster. An engineer by training (like Bowen), Mitchell knew Transco well as a client and had big plans to get the gas Transco badly needed.

In the summer of 1974, Transco contacted Bowen again. Mitchell's supply strategy, long on supplemental gas and short on drilling near the pipeline, was in tatters. The Arab Oil Embargo doomed the type of projects that Mitchell had been counting on, as explained in the next chapter. Bowen was doing things differently from Transco with better results. "While we are investigating possible alternative sources of supply, including synthetic natural gas," Bowen told his Florida Gas stockholders in the *1971 Annual Report*, "we are convinced that the best solution for our Company is a very active oil and gas exploration program in the Gulf Coast in the vicinity of our pipeline." Transco needed that in 1971 and needed it more now.

By 1974, Jack felt differently about an offer to move. He had been CEO at Florida Gas for nearly 15 years and was feeling stale. The operating results were decent, but the stock price was discouraging. Central Florida was in a recession, and FGT faced a throughput decline because of federal gas policies. Bowen had a good number-two man in Selby Sullivan, who was laser focused on the company's challenges. A stable core of senior executives was behind Sullivan, as well as Ken Lay, the newest vice president of the company.

Winter Park was a hard place to leave. "On reflection," Jack would state in his autobiography, "Annis and I believe the … twelve years in Winter Park were the best years in our lives." But the children were growing up, and Transco offered a fresh start and a real challenge. Transco was in *the* energy city, Houston, Texas, a city where Jack once lived and liked. He agreed to an incentive-laced package to become president and CEO of Transco effective October 1, 1974.

Bowen broke the news to Sullivan, who, Jack recalled, had the look "of an undertaker at a $25,000 funeral, trying to look sad but inside, so happy!" Sullivan, age 40, became CEO to go along with his existing title of president. Ken Lay—a rising talent with a keenly analytical mind, a large capacity for work, a worldview on economics and politics and, compared to Sullivan, a rosy, affable demeanor—was now a step closer to the top.

There were parties and tears as the Bowens got ready to move. Annis Bowen would later wonder how she could have ever told her husband, "Okay, let's go back to Texas." Winter Park's greenery, lakes, and mild winters were special. But business is business.

Stan Horton, a young Florida Gas talent who would later head Enron's interstate pipeline group, never forgot the words he heard in a jam-packed auditorium one September morning in 1974. "A CEO can stay in one place too long," Bowen told the employees. "I believe I have been here long enough. I have accepted a job to become the CEO of Transco."

The surprise, though, did not unsettle investors. Raymond, James & Associates released a report in November 1974 rating Florida Gas "an attractive speculation," noting:

> Although Florida Gas' former chairman and chief executive officer recently departed to join another utility, we feel the remaining management has more than adequate depth. Clearly, at no recent time has Florida Gas in any way resembled a one-man operation.

Jack Bowen left as a fatherly hero. The company had gone from nothing to a regional powerhouse. He was a demanding boss in some ways but very loyal and empathetic in other ways. He had many friends and maybe a few cronies in the wide organization. But the stock was underperforming in a down market. The Dow Jones Industrial Average (DJIA) was off 40 percent (from 1,020 to 616) between the end of 1972 and the end of 1974, and Florida Gas (FLG) was off 60 percent ($21.50 to $8.375). Selby Sullivan, with an early vote of confidence from Wall Street, had some serious work to do.

Oil and Vinegar

Selby Sullivan inherited a company with problems and opportunities, evidenced by a stock price that had slipped below $8 dollars per share. Oil-price spikes after the Arab Oil Embargo had flattened Florida's tourism industry, and Florida Land Company was caught in a badly overbuilt market. Florida Gas Transmission was losing ground because of gas-supply problems—hence the plan to convert part of the mainline to petroleum products. The rich BTU gas that Florida Hydrocarbons Company made money from was about to disappear as producers were building the facilities to extract the liquids themselves.[26] A three-year, $12 million drilling program of which Florida Gas Exploration Company (FGE) was the managing partner was not structured to be a profit center but of help for pipeline throughput. Sullivan had to correct this and do something about real estate. Bowen's dream of the land division becoming the largest part of the company was history.

In the 1974 annual report, his first as CEO, Sullivan announced records for revenue, net income, and earnings per share, helped by tripled earnings from gas-liquid extraction at the Brooker plant. The company was coping well with interest rates that had doubled in the last few years and an economic slowdown in its market area. Still, the stock price indicated a lack of perceived upside. And FGT, which for many years had been at full capacity, was running at 90 percent and falling.

Sullivan's major priority was to realign FGE's production contracts. It was well and good that the discovered volumes would go to FGT, thus increasing pipeline revenue. But as structured, FGE sales to FGT could receive only the federal maximum price of $0.26/Mcf, not the unregulated intrastate price of $1/Mcf. It was a no-risk deal for the partners, who did not put up the initial drilling capital but repaid FGE upon production. But FGE was losing money and would continue to do so under the multiyear deal.

The solution was to have FGT relinquish its rights to the gas, allowing higher-priced intrastate sales from which both parties could share. Future drilling costs had to be shared up front as well.

Sullivan also had to convince gas users hitherto receiving the cheap gas that only higher gas prices would allow FGE to have a viable drilling program in the vicinity of the pipeline, thus providing gas for the future. Spending the majority of his time on the upstream problem in his first year as CEO, Sullivan was able to renegotiate the contracts to allow Florida Gas to begin afresh in exploration and production.[27]

The new CEO purged many things Bowen, including the Stuart Beach Fish Camp, which was sold to Bowen's new company, Transco. New aims and more accountability were needed. Peter Drucker's "management by objectives" was adopted to set specific goals and have regular reviews. Andrews & Kurth, Selby's former employer and legal counsel to Florida Gas since the beginning, was replaced. The eventual successor to the position held by Leon Payne and then Selby himself would be Harry Reasoner of Vinson & Elkins, who had made partner in only five years and was a longtime friend of Sullivan's.

---

26. Hydrocarbon earnings before interest and taxes (EBIT) in 1974 of $12.4 million would fall by half in 1975 and by half again the year after.

27. Ken Lay recalled: "There were some serious problems with Florida Gas that had to be solved, and that is where Selby really dug into it early after Jack's departure."

Reasoner earned his spurs by winning a major lawsuit for Florida Gas against a group of municipalities alleging underdeliveries of gas, and he was named chief outside counsel and a member of Florida Gas's board of directors in 1977.

After a net income decline for 1975 compared to a year earlier, things improved. Earnings increased 13 percent in 1976 and 38 percent in 1977, a major reason being the new profit center of exploration and production. Thus, it was little surprise when Selby Sullivan was elected chairman of Florida Gas Company in July 1977, adding to his titles of president and CEO. The board was pleased because investors were; the stock of Florida Gas Company (FLG) had recovered from a low of $7.75 per share to more than $20 per share. This 150 percent increase outperformed the DJIA, which had risen by a third.

·◦·

Selby Sullivan had smarts, energy, and ambition. He knew the law, understood numbers, and attacked problems. He was the negotiator you wanted on your side. He saw things quickly and was prone to micromanage. He knew that stockholders came first and got results.

But patience and tact were not his forte. Stan Horton described Sullivan as "the greatest manager by fear that I have ever seen." Jim Barnhart, another Florida Gas employee who, like Horton, is also part of the Enron story to come, had a code name for the Sullivan era: "ROT—reign of terror!" "He embarrassed me many times," recalled Barnhart. "Every time I deserved it, but I didn't deserve the crowd!" A staff meeting with Sullivan could be very unpleasant if an error was revealed or the news was bad. The dreaded sentence at Florida Gas was, "Mr. Sullivan wants to see you." It could get icy at 1560 Orange Avenue when Selby's secretary escorted the summoned to his office and closed the door.

Lay was unsure about his staying power with Sullivan given their mercurial post-Bowen relationship. Why, Lay sometimes wondered, hadn't Bowen asked him to go to Transco? Sullivan, for his part, viewed Lay as an "unwilling student" who was too confident about where markets were headed.[28] Lay remembered Sullivan as "a perfectionist for whom nothing was ever good enough." With Sullivan, Lay recalled, you got one mistake, and few if any employees were indispensable.

There were fireworks. Selby exploded at Lay, and Lay returned fire. Ken was willing to go to the mat with Selby, maybe just because he was not afraid of leaving the company. Other firms had courted him when he left government, and Bowen might well want him in Houston. But Sullivan needed Lay's skills inside and particularly outside the company, and Lay, even if he did not realize

---

28. Sullivan remembered how Lay cited his connections with the U.S. ambassador to Saudi Arabia to try to convince Bowen and Sullivan that Florida Gas should plan on oil, then priced at $6 per barrel, returning to $3 per barrel. Just the opposite proved true, with an explosion of gas prices in the next years.

it, needed Sullivan's iron discipline.[29] The two men, talented different ways, were complements. After months of civil war, a truce emerged. By the close of 1975, in fact, Lay's promotions—first to vice president of corporate development and then to senior vice president of Florida Gas Transmission with responsibilities for engineering and gas supply—made the 33-year old the youngest senior executive of the company.

Sullivan, now chairman, president, and CEO, would never appoint a number two as president, but Lay was number two judged by his compensation package in 1978 of approximately $200,000 (more than a half-million dollars today). Lay, a people person, found out just how to deal with Sullivan on the sensitive issues, a strategy that was less sinister than strategic. Lay explained:

> Selby exploded every few days where he beat the bejesus out of somebody. And then, within three, four, five hours, he would feel really sorry about it. I found this aftermath ... to be an awfully good time to sit down with Selby and get some decision-making. So, I let decisions stack up on my desk until I found the right time, then would walk in there and get three, four, five, six key decisions made and then move ahead.

Sullivan, for the record, disputes the frequency of these episodes and Ken's modus operandi. Still, there was battle going on, one that Ken would not otherwise experience in his business and government career until the fateful end of Enron. But more than he ever knew, Ken Lay needed a hard-nosed, nondeferential boss.

·◌·

Lay created a quite different impression around the company than the big boss. Stan Horton remembers Lay as "a buffer and a good one between his employees and Selby." Lay was approachable, tactful, and forgiving. Whereas a wanting proposal could bring a personal rebuke from Sullivan, Lay would say something like, "Why don't you go back and massage it?" Lay dealt directly with employees at all levels who were involved in the matter at hand. Horton remembers how a "very people-oriented" Ken Lay broke down a "very hierarchal" Florida Gas Company with phone calls, visits, and conversation in the halls. Lay had something extra. "He would always remember your name, your wife's name, and ask how things were," remembered Horton.

Lay's presence meant something more. Not only did he personally bring "a new perspective to the business," but also he brought in new employees "that were not from the traditional regulated energy structure." Some of Lay's hires

---

29. Sullivan would later say, "If Ken were to say that I was the most domineering man he worked with, it might relate to the fact that I am probably the only one, looking at his career, that ever told him 'no' because basically he only worked for the government, he worked for me, he worked for Bowen, who probably never told him no, and then he was on his own."

between 1974 and 1980— Joe Hillings, Robert Kelly, Richard Kinder, William Morgan, Harry Stout, John Wing, and Ross Workman—who would later join Enron. Kelly and Wing held advanced degrees from Harvard, a Ph.D. in economics and MBA, respectively. Kinder and Morgan would leave Enron to form Kinder-Morgan, Inc., a phenomenally successful company in the years before and after Enron's bankruptcy and one that will forever be a reminder of what Ken Lay's company might have been.

Ken Lay became the youngest president of a major interstate pipeline when he was named president of Florida Gas Transmission in September 1976, just two and a half years after he joined the company. His predecessor, Smokey Wilhite, began his transition to retirement after 20 years at the company. Just a couple of months later, Lay's old boss at Interior, Rogers Morton, now in private industry, was elected to the board of directors. Morton was the first Washington insider on Florida Gas's board. The company had important Washington issues, and Ken Lay was instrumental in Morton's appointment.

Ken hardly surprised himself with his rapid progress. It just continued his life story. He had always taken the initiative, gotten things done, and organized others for success, whether it was getting a group together for summer work as a teenager or leading the Beta Theta Pi, the largest fraternity at Missouri, as president. Ron Knorpp, whom Selby Sullivan hired at Florida Gas the year before Lay came, remembers how Ken audaciously told him of his career goal to reach the very top. "There was no equivocation about it," remembered Knorpp.

> Here was this 30-year-old, without experience other than briefly working for the president of Humble Oil and two jobs as an energy regulator. He didn't have industry experience in corporate finance, capital budgeting, stockholder relations, or operations. Yet he told me as if it was written in stone: *I am going to be the CEO of a major energy company.*

In the *1976 Annual Report*, Wilhite and Lay described a pipeline that was profitable but operating at about 85 percent of capacity because of inadequate gas supply. Company-related production was helping, but reserves connected to the system were half of their 1960s peak. An FPC order in July 1976 increased the price ceiling for newly discovered gas to $1.42/MMBtu from $0.52/MMBtu, but this was *still* below what unregulated gas was selling for within Texas, Louisiana, and other gas-producing states.

Lay had to deal with market, legal, and regulatory issues on both ends of the pipe. FGT's largest supply source was a 20-year, fixed-priced contract with Amoco, gas that became more and more underpriced as prices rose in the 1970s. It was Lay's job to require performance under the terms of the agreement, even as Amoco wanted out and was finding ways to underdeliver gas.[30] Finding new

---

30. Also, the FPC, renamed in October 1977 the Federal Energy Regulatory Commission (FERC), wanted to abrogate the previously certificated contract between Amoco and Florida

Figure 8.10 H. L. "Smokey" Wilhite (left), the longtime head of Florida Gas Transmission, handed the reins in 1976 to Ken Lay (center), whose main task was to attach gas to the pipeline. The gas crisis would ease and pipeline volumes increase before Lay left in April 1981, whereupon William Morgan (right) took over.

gas in the face of federal wellhead price controls and placating customers who wanted more gas and were paying higher prices for the gas they did receive was a full-time job.

Things were looking up with a 15 percent jump in pipeline throughput in 1977, the first year-to-year increase since 1973. But overall reserves attached to the system were declining, and a major gas supply and transportation contract with Petróleos Mexicanos (Pemex), Mexico's hydrocarbon company, was blocked by U.S. authorities because the negotiated price of $2.60/MMBtu (about $8/MMBtu today) was deemed too high.

In a 1978 quarterly report to shareholders, Selby Sullivan complained about "unnecessary and serious obstacles from various government bodies." The energy bill under debate was far too timid to solve the gas crisis, he added. Congress had refused to enact the eminent-domain bill needed to site and build a coal-slurry pipeline. FERC had not ruled on Transgulf, the project that would convert part of the mainline to carrying petroleum products. The departments of Energy and State were blocking the Pemex contract, according to which FGT would receive gas from the Reforma and Gulf of Campeche areas.

Gas Company to free up scarce wellhead gas to serve residential/commercial users, instead of Florida Power & Light's power plants.

Sullivan urged his stockholders to take action to "begin to reverse some of these unresponsive and irresponsible government actions, though the effort will take many years."

Continental Resources Company

Florida Gas Exploration, with offices in Houston, Midland, Jackson, Denver, and New Orleans, was now profitable and accumulating quality reserves. The supply picture was improving for Florida Gas Transmission. Better yet, FGT did not have the liabilities associated with so-called take-or-pay provisions in its supply contracts, as did other interstates.[31] (Such contracts obligated a pipeline to pay for gas whether or not it was needed and taken.) The proposed oil-product pipeline and coal-slurry pipeline offered upside. Real estate in central Florida was valuable. And Selby Sullivan was a tough, reality-focused chief executive who was moving the company with a good team, *his* team, including Ron Knorpp (finance), Phil Silver (real estate), and Tim McConn (exploration).

In early 1979, Sullivan proposed a new company name, TRENEX CORPO-RATION. The work of Lippincott & Margulies, a New York firm specializing in corporate image and branding, TRENEX spliced together TR for transportation, EN for energy, and EX for exploration and production. The new name would signal a new era for a now mature, profitable company whose stock price was above $20 per share with good upside. Selby Sullivan exuded confidence to Wall Street analysts—a first for him.

◇

By the late 1970s, Florida Gas was a valuable company, and energy assets were prized as oil and gas prices reached new heights. Energy companies were attractive takeover candidates. The common wisdom was that depletable resources, such as oil, gas, and coal, would only appreciate in value.[32] One company particularly interested in entering energy was the Continental Group, which had participated in exploration syndicates led by Florida Gas. Originally Continental Can Company, Continental Group was the world's largest manufacturer of packaging products and had recently diversified into forestry and

---

31. Sullivan resisted entering into take-or-pay obligations and remembered, "Even in 1979, which was the end of my time at Florida Gas, I had to tell Ken [Lay] 'no' as he tried to argue many times that we had to give 'take-or-pay' contracts to the producers if we wanted to buy any more gas."

32. The fallacy of the fixity-depletion view of minerals (including oil, gas, and coal) from a business/economic viewpoint is discussed in *Capitalism at Work*, pp. 272–78.

financial services. Continental was still searching for "good balance," as its CEO, Robert Hatfield, put it. And energy was *the* hot area.

Jim Glanville of the investment banking firm Lazard Frères in New York City was an old friend of Selby Sullivan's from their undergraduate days at Rice University. They kept in touch and played golf occasionally. One day on the course, Jim asked Selby, "Would you ever be willing to sell the company?" Sullivan answered, "Well, not really. We have built it up to where we have a great team and a good future for ourselves."

Glanville said, "Well, you know, there has got to be some price at which you would sell." Sullivan answered, "Well, yes, from the shareholders' standpoint, there would have to be some price we would have to consider." Glanville, knowing that Florida Gas was selling for about $23 a share, had a number in mind. "Well, what about $50 a share?"

"Well, I would have to consider an offer like that because as much as I love Florida Gas, I guess shareholders could take their money and put it somewhere else," Sullivan responded. "However, I would have to be convinced that it would be a good fit and was good for the employees and customers."

Continental Group was the suitor behind Glanville's overture. The conglomerate was looking for new assets to help its lethargic stock price. Hatfield, near retirement, was looking for new management to help run a conglomerate that was selling more than 1,000 different products.

Continental contacted Florida Gas in February 1979 about merging at $50 per share. Rumors began, and on the eve of an announcement about merger discussions (March 21), Florida Gas's stock price had risen near $29 per share. A tentative agreement was announced in May, and the acquisition was consummated in August 1979 for $351 million (about $900 million today), comparable to the $50 per share price that was proposed at the outset.[33]

The "New Continental" now labeled itself "Packaging, Natural Resources, Financial Services." Selby Sullivan had hit quite a home run, increasing the stock price sixfold in his six years as CEO. Energy and Florida had proved to be the right product and the right place, but Sullivan had done much to capitalize on the potential.

The mood was upbeat at Continental. The acquisition represented "a new economic sector, the entire energy field, not just natural gas," CEO Hatfield told the press. A management team had also been acquired, for 15 top Florida Gas

---

33. Terms set in June exchanged a share of Florida Gas common stock for $32.50 in cash, plus 0.35 share of a new series of Continental cumulative preferred stock entitled to an annual dividend of $4.50 per share. This summed to exactly $50 per share; however, in the months after closing, the value of Continental stock fell because of general market conditions and other factors.

Figure 8.11 Selby Sullivan (upper left) and Continental Group CEO Robert Hatfield (lower right) address employees of Florida Gas Company on August 28, 1979, on the merger. The "New Continental" was highly diversified, with only 11 percent of its assets in resources (energy). The renamed Continental Resources Company would be run by Ken Lay (lower left).

executives had signed contracts to stay with the company for a minimum of 18 months. "Before we made the bid for Florida Gas, we had a pretty good estimate of [Selby Sullivan's] capacity—which we judged superior," Hatfield told the *New York Times*. "Furthermore, Selby had gathered around himself a very capable group of managers."

When asked about his success at Florida Gas by Continental's *Insight* magazine, Sullivan attributed it to "being able to enjoy working a little harder than the next guy" and "bringing in good people and providing an environment where they are not only financially rewarded but also find their work stimulating and the achievement of their goals satisfying." He added:

> One thing we do here that's maybe a little unusual, and sometimes very difficult—we ask some very hard questions of each other. Sometimes if you're very sensitive, you don't last very long. The end result, though, is that the remaining people—the people you really want as part of the company—stay, and find it a very rewarding environment.

Such a challenge culture was congruent with what would be codified into a *science of success.*[34]

Selby Sullivan was promoted to executive vice president and chief financial and administrative officer of the parent, as well as a member of the board of directors. The plan was to make Sullivan president and COO when Hatfield retired and make Smart CEO. Sullivan moved to Stamford, Connecticut, as would his protégés Ron Knorpp and Philip Silver. Ken Lay was promoted to president, Continental Resources Company—the renamed Florida Gas Company.

Sullivan also considered Knorpp and Silver for his successor. He did not feel that Lay necessarily had the best business judgment of the three, but the 38-year-old was a great communicator with employees, regulators, and Wall Street. Sullivan also had no doubt that Lay was "extremely honest and always on top of the facts in which he was involved." But there was a downside. "Ken's problem was that he liked to focus on the big picture, deal with people at the top, and not get involved with details," Sullivan remembered. Still, "if he were involved, he would know the facts."

Effective August 1979, Ken Lay was heading a company with divisions in oil and gas exploration and production, natural gas transmission, gas processing, and real estate. Missing from the list was gas distribution, a division that was sold to Peoples Gas System (not affiliated with Peoples Gas Company of Chicago) a month before the merger because of an Insull-inspired law—the Public Utility Holding Company Act of 1935. PUHCA required a utility to be headquartered in the state in which it operated, which would have required Continental Group to reincorporate in Florida short of divesting gas distribution.

There was excitement in the halls when Lay took Selby's office atop the Winter Park building. "People wanted to work with Ken because of his attitude," remembered Jim Barnhart. He noted something else about the new boss. "Once you earned his trust, he believed in you come hell or high water."

Lay himself remembered a "great big sigh of relief" in the ranks. It *was* time to exhale. But everyone was a little richer because of Selby Sullivan, and Lay inherited a shipshape company, enjoying "the easiest transition I have ever had in my whole career." Ken impressed the new brass in Connecticut too; in November 1979, just three months into his new job, he was elected to the additional position of executive vice president, Continental Group.

Continental's purchase of Florida Gas Company looked smart as energy prices soared. FGT volumes rose in 1980 and again the next year as company production attached to the pipeline increased. There was a gas drilling boom,

---

34. Sullivan's penchant for micromanaging and his personal style, however, offer tensions to the business principles of, Market-Based Management®. See *Capitalism at Work*, pp. 314–17.

and the Natural Gas Policy Act of 1978 had changed the rules so that interstate pipelines were no longer disadvantaged relative to intrastate buyers. Lay continued to pursue the Transgulf project, as well as the renamed coal-slurry project, Concoal Pipeline Company, now a $3 billion proposal. But things would change in the next years. Energy markets would turn south, and Tom Rollins, not Ken Lay, would have to deal with it as head of Continental Resources Company.

Ken Lay Moves On

Things were changing in Ken Lay's personal life too. In 1976, Linda Ann Phillips Herrold, an attractive divorcée with three children, became his secretary. Linda had been the office manager of a Winter Park insurance office when she joined Florida Gas as a senior legal secretary. When Ken's assistant returned to school, he talked Linda into joining him on the promise that she would handle important projects, something she was eager and able to do.

Linda discharged her responsibilities well, impressing Ken. He was also very empathetic to her situation as a single mother. One year together turned into two and then three, and Linda and Ken became intimate. Compared to what he was otherwise used to at the office and at home, Ken became *enthralled*.

Linda was more than just smart. She had grace and ambition. She had not been in a position to acquire his level of education (or Judie's for that matter) or achieve his business stardom, but she was a starter and finisher.[35] This single mother seemed to be able to do everything asked of her, something that Mrs. Kenneth Lay could not do in far better circumstances. Linda also understood her boss inside and out, becoming Ken's trusted person, by whom he judged his actions and strategies at the end of the day.

On paper, though, Judith Ayers Lay seemed a good match for Ken—with nothing to fear from Linda. Judie was tall and attractive. She came from a college-educated family that had economic stability, unlike Omer Lay's. She was a sorority girl at the University of Missouri, where she graduated with a journalism degree. Judie had been plenty popular through school. But she had a bit of an unpredictable, dark side. Still, nothing romantic had happened to Ken in his first year at Humble Oil, and he was lonely despite his very full schedule of work and school.

Ken and Judie were married in the summer of 1966, right after her graduation. Things went reasonably well in the first years despite the regular relocations. Then Mark (1968) and Elizabeth (1971) brought the stress of parenting. Things were financially tight (both she and Ken brought virtually no assets into the marriage), and Ken was almost always working.

Then, too, Judie was just not organized and reliable enough to manage the home. Ken, as busy as he was, found himself cleaning up inside the house in

---

35. Linda Phillips married at age 19 and had her first child nine months later. She was married eight years, divorcing approximately two years after her third child.

addition to his therapeutic yard work. Maids and yardmen would come into play in the late 1970s when his salary jumped, but even then, things were not quite right domestically.

Judie was not very interested in church. She liked to drink and had an impulsive side. At social events, she could even get aggressive and embarrass Ken in front of his colleagues. They sometimes argued in public. This was hardly what Ken Lay wanted. He needed and expected a responsible corporate wife who could grow with him—and also aspire to reach the top of the business world.

Judie's affectionate side went downhill in the late 1970s. Some of it was just the way she was. But some of it was a growing indifference by her husband, who was finding love outside of the home—emotionally and physically.

Sometime in 1979/80, Ken Lay's marriage entered into a death spiral. Time with Linda grew. Judie, feeling isolated, began drinking heavily. Ken first broached the subject of divorce in October 1980. This was certainly not a good thing for Mark (now age 12) and Elizabeth (age 9), but love is love. And Linda badly wanted this man for herself and her children: Robyn (15), Todd David (11), and Robert Beau (9).

Ken Lay was not a mean person—quite the opposite—suggesting that he would have stuck it out. But Linda had so much of what Judie did not. And Ken Lay was too ambitious to lower his expectations in the name of holy matrimony. His life was at the office, leading many hundreds of people and making enough money to become the rock of his whole, big family. He needed a significant other who could help, not hinder, his ascent.

Linda and Ken were a *team*. Every one of his promotions was hers too—literally and figuratively. And now he was running one of the largest enterprises in the state and was a leading man of the energy industry, as evidenced by his directorships at the American Gas Association, Gas Research Institute, Interstate Natural Gas Association of America, and Southern Gas Association. Lay also chaired the Slurry Transport Association, representing a cutting-edge energy-transportation alternative for the nation's most abundant fuel, coal. He was also a community leader as director of Sun Banks of Florida, a member of the Florida Council of 100, and a person known for his charity work with the Central Florida Capital Funds Drive and Winter Park Hospital.

In January 1981, Ken moved from his house at 641 Via Lugano in Winter Park to the Langford Hotel. This was a separation, but Ken knew that the marriage was over. So did Linda, who knew that her future would be with Ken, hopefully sooner rather than later.

It was around this time that Lay contacted Jack Bowen at Transco about his unease about working for a conglomerate where energy wasn't the primary focus—and his openness to new opportunities, such as accepting an important energy job in Houston. Indeed, Lay missed dealing directly with investors and the board. He was uncharacteristically removed from the action, sometimes having to call Ron Knorpp to find out what was going on at headquarters. And what he was hearing about Connecticut was not reassuring. The unwieldy conglomerate had its share and more of internal politicking and uncertainty. Who knew what the company would look like in the future? Amid all this, Selby Sullivan, who had been slated to become president, bailed and was back in central Florida practicing law and weighing his next move. Part of it was Selby's decision, but the old brass at Continental was not endeared by Sullivan's brusque style.

Effective September 1, 1980, Bruce Smart, age 57, became Continental's new CEO. With Sullivan out of the picture, Smart talked to Ken about moving to Connecticut with the idea of becoming, if all went well, his successor. The president's slot was open with just Smart as chairman and Donald Donahue, age 55, as vice chairman. There was a lot of upside with the parent if Lay really wanted it.

But Bowen had taken note of Lay's concerns and called a few weeks later to ask about his interest in moving to Houston to become Transco's president. As much as Jack liked to promote from within, he was now 58 and had not found a number two at Transco. Lay, 20 years his junior, fit the bill well.

Ken called back a week later. He expressed interest but confided about his personal problem. He was heading for a divorce with Judie. Jack expressed his regret but said that Transco was hiring him, not her.

It was time to work on the details. Transco's board, deferential to Bowen, and apprised of Lay's stellar reputation, worked quickly to land their star. There would be no long-term contract—everyone worked for Jack on a day-to-day basis—and the salary bump would not be that great. But it was a fresh start for Ken in *the* energy city. The top job with a Fortune 500 company was now in clear sight, for everyone knew that Jack had all but chosen his successor. And for Ken, there would be competition from other energy giants in the neighborhood should Transco not work out. This was what he saw for himself all along.

On April 9, 1981, Jack Bowen announced that Ken Lay was joining Transco Companies imminently as president and chief operating officer.

Lay filed for divorce just days before leaving Winter Park for Houston. He cashed out of his Continental Group stock options, realizing $101,000 to help address the challenges ahead. Linda got a transfer to Continental Resources' Houston office to be near Ken. Being his secretary at Transco was not possible given their not-so-secret affair.

Judie, devastated, turned to pills and alcohol and experienced a psychotic episode in June, leading to involuntary commitment at mental health facilities that summer. She had lost her rock, the man she married for his "maturity and dependability," among other traits. Yet she had gone backward while Ken had gone forward. It was all very complicated, but Ken Lay, highly ambitious and resolute, was trading up personally and professionally. The substitution—ambitious Linda for small-world Judie—would have far-reaching consequences.

Transco was coming off of a strong year when Lay arrived in early May 1981. Still, as in 1974, when Selby Sullivan took over Florida Gas Company, there were problems beneath the surface requiring new thinking and strategies. Ken Lay would soon prove to be just the executive that Transco needed.

9

Transco Energy Company

THE COMPANY KNOWN FOR MOST of its life simply as Transco lost its independence just short of its fiftieth anniversary. Incorporated in 1946 and acquired in distress by Williams Companies in 1995, the nation's longest interstate natural gas pipeline was supposed to lead a predictable, peaceful life as a regulated public utility. Its first decades were just that way. But when federal authorities extended such cost-of-service regulation to gas production sold in interstate commerce in 1954, little did they know that they were seeding the demise of a healthy company—and weakening an industry.

With price controls drying up supply, Transco would embark on ill-fated supplemental-gas projects and had to curtail gas utilities serving millions of residential and commercial users in its major Northeast markets. The troubled 1970s inspired company strategies that appeared prudent but turned out badly. The roller-coaster of distorted gas markets from regulation and then risky business strategies undertaken to undo that distortion, ultimately ended Transco as a thriving Fortune 500 company.

The Transco story reveals political capitalism to be a two-edged sword. Yes, public-utility regulation tamed industry-feared cutthroat competition and sanctioned a means for automatically passing through increased costs to captive consumers. But regulators could and did change the rules of the game, applying unprecedented regulation that would sever and distort industry relationships, leaving the nonintegrated pipeline with unrecoverable costs.

⌥

Transco Companies needed new leadership years before Jack Bowen arrived from Florida Gas Company in 1974. Transcontinental Gas Pipe Line (TGPL), extending from South Texas to New York City, was severely short of gas. Florida Gas

Transmission had escaped the problem by carrying unregulated (and thus available) *transportation* gas—gas that an end user could buy at the wellhead and pay to ship as a (nonfederal) intrastate transaction. But TGPL's throughput was bought on one end of the pipe and resold on the other, which gave the Federal Power Commission (FPC) jurisdiction to regulate the wellhead gas price. Such regulation created a shortage of sale-for-resale gas because producers in Texas (as in other gas-rich states) avoided regulated sales. The prodcuers preferred an unregulated, higher price from an in-state carrier such as Houston Pipe Line Company (the subsidiary of Houston Natural Gas Corporation, or HNG), or from an end user buying gas at the wellhead, such as Florida Power & Light using FGPL.[1] It was complicated and quirky, but federal regulation created two very different markets. Pinkney Walker and Ken Lay had worked to relax wellhead price regulation at the FPC in the early 1970s, but their efforts were scarcely enough.

Wellhead price controls by Washington bureaucrats also meant that some gas was not produced at all. Capital and entrepreneurship that would have gone into exploration and production went elsewhere in the multitrillion-dollar U.S. economy. Forgone supply was an unintended consequence of federal regulators' setting so-called just-and-reasonable prices for natural gas bought and sold in interstate commerce.

Transco was in the middle of a public-policy crisis created in Washington, D.C. Without a production affiliate, the company could not self-produce the supply its customers needed. Yet that was really the only answer in the heavily regulated 1970s. That is why Transco's board of directors reached out to the man who had created a supply affiliate at his previous company, and that is why Jack Bowen left beautiful Winter Park, Florida for bustling Houston to tackle the biggest challenge of his business life.

To the Northeast

The Transco story began during World War II, when Claude Williams, an East Texas attorney working as a Washington lobbyist, heard about the government's plan to sell its surplus wartime assets. His entrepreneurial spirit kicked

---

1. TGPL was not certificated to accept transportation gas (a regulatory category, not a simple descriptor)—gas that industrial or power-plant customers bought in the field (an *intrastate* transaction) to escape federal price controls. The pipeline's major contracts were with distribution companies that served not only industry but also thousands of commercial establishments and millions of residences with gas purchased and resold in interstate commerce. FGT was set up as a transportation pipeline to attract supply in an era of price controls, which was possible since its throughput was mostly for large users (power plants in particular), not for small-customer heating load.

in—the same spirit that had him, as a child, selling peaches and peanuts through train windows to afford to start a hamburger stand.

The asset Williams coveted was the War Emergency Pipelines—the Big Inch and Little Big Inch lines that transported crude oil and petroleum products, respectively, from East Texas to New Jersey. Both lines had been built to escape the German U-boat threat to oil tankers traveling from the Gulf Coast up the East Coast. But there had not been a market need for petroleum pipelines before the war; after the war, the highest and best use for the carriers was in debate.

Claude Williams knew that plenty of wellhead gas being flared in the Southwest could displace manufactured gas in the Northeast—if it could get there. Tennessee Gas and Transmission Company, a natural gas pipeline completed in 1944, had barely begun the Northeast's conversion process. So, with the help of his uncle Rogers Lacy, an oil and gas producer in Longview, Texas, Williams put together a consortium to buy the War Emergency Pipelines or, failing that, build a new natural gas line from Texas to the world's biggest market, New York City.

Williams's new creation, Trans-Continental Gas Pipeline Company, incorporated in February 1946, applied for an FPC certificate a month later to keep all options open. The regulatory initiative would prove to be a very smart move.

Soon after incorporation, Trans-Continental submitted a $40 million offer to the War Assets Board to try to seal a deal. Another $40 million was readied to convert the line to natural gas. This bold action quickly moved sentiment toward having an open-bid process to privatize the pipelines.

After advertizing in 34 newspapers and 5 trade magazines, a federal auction took place in summer 1946. Trans-Continental submitted the high bid of $85 million, but the War Assets Administration called for a rebid, this time with a specific methodology for determining financial value to better assess the competing proposals.[2]

For the second and final bid, Trans-Continental readied a $148-million offer. However, a major lender got cold feet, and $131 million was bid instead. Still, that amount was substantially more than any of the 16 bids that had been submitted just seven months before.

The paper corporation Texas Eastern Transmission Corporation *increased* its bid at the last minute and won with $143.1 million (about $1.7 billion today). Trans-Continental came in second and Tennessee Gas third. It was a major disappointment for Tennessee Gas's Gardiner Symonds, whose company was operating both oil lines under a government lease and had plans to convert

---

2. Political questions surrounding Texas Eastern's winning bid and contract work with Brown & Root are discussed in Internet appendix 9.1, "Politics and the Origins of Texas Eastern Transmission Corporation," at www.politicalcapitalism.org/Book2/Chapter9/Appendix1.html.

them to natural gas. Now, there would be *two* gas-pipeline companies for the Northeast from the Southwest. The competition was on.

Texas Eastern's aggressive tack turned out to be quite prudent. The purchase price became the rate base upon which the regulated rate of return was applied. So the higher bid would translate into higher profits if two conditions were met. One, borrowing costs had to be less than the FPC's authorized rate of return (they were). Second, the delivered cost of natural gas had to be far enough below the cost of manufactured gas for the utilities to convert and write off the book value of their manufactured-gas assets over a period of years. Such write-offs, in the hundreds of millions of dollars for New York City alone, were blessed by state regulators as being in the public interest and thus did not dilute authorized earnings.

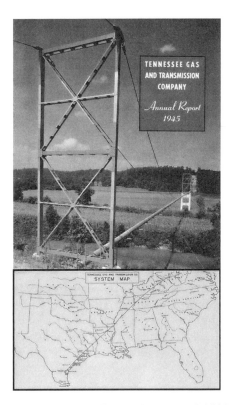

Figure 9.1 Texas Eastern's successful bid to privatize the War Emergency Pipelines created a second natural gas line to that of Tennessee Gas to serve the Northeast. The strong-willed CEOs went head to head but fought a common enemy at the FPC: the solid-fuels industry.

Leveraged financing and strong prospects gave Texas Eastern's 28 stock-holders a big payday at the November 1947 closing. A $143-million pipeline purchased with only $150,000 of equity (the rest was debt) now had an equity value of nearly $10 million—a return exceeding 6,500 percent in less than a year![3] The biggest winners were George and Herman Brown personally—and their construction company. The brothers each owned 14.25 percent of the project, and Brown & Root would do more than a billion dollars worth of projects for Texas Eastern in the next decades.[4]

⌒

Claude Williams and Trans-Continental regrouped and brought in a strong new partner, Ray "Mr. Pipeliner" Fish. The affable Fish, along with Richard Ricketts, had designed Tennessee Gas and now headed his own engineering company in Houston: Fish Engineering. A new subsidiary, Fish Contractors, was created to build Trans-Continental and take an ownership position as well. In fact, for many years, Fish would be *the* largest stockholder in the new company.

New York City was a tremendous potential market for natural gas. The consumer of more than one-third of the nation's manufactured gas was ready for a cheaper, cleaner, and more reliable substitute.[5] The head of Texas Eastern, Reginald Hargrove, was interested in expanding his converted gas line to New York City, but he left it to the utilities to determine the best route and how to secure enough steel for the project. Properly, this was work for a for-profit pipeline, not for its customers, but Texas Eastern had a full plate serving gas-short Appalachia and hooking up Philadelphia, which was abandoning manufactured gas. The Northeast market thus remained ripe for a third pipeline, one with New York City specifically in mind.

Trans-Continental's application to the FPC for a certificate of public convenience and necessity faced stiff opposition from both Tennessee Gas and Texas

---

3. The size of this gain led to a debate in the *Harvard Business Review* in 1948 over the fairness of "promoters' profit."

4. The irascible Symonds questioned the validity of Texas Eastern's winning bid and, alongside coal interests, lobbied the FPC to require a formal hearing on the temporary certificate allowing the company to engage in natural gas service. After this failed, Symonds met with Texas Eastern and, after promising to use all legal means to protect his territory from a second pipeline, proposed dividing up the Northeast market between them. This did not fly either, but Symonds's efforts are an example of how political settings can result in unsavory business dealings.

5. Coal strikes were always a problem for manufactured (coal) gas, and, in fact, saber rattling by John Lewis of the United Mine Workers Association persuaded the War Assets Administration to hold a rebid, with the conversion of the Big Inch and Little Big Inch to natural gas in mind.

Eastern, each of which wanted to serve the same region in due time. Another interstate, Southern Natural Gas Company, opposed having competition from Trans-Continental in the South. A slew of interventions—all opposed to Transco—came from the coal side: the United Mine Workers of America (aka United Mine Workers Association), National Coal Association, Anthracite Institute, and a group of 23 coal- and coke-hauling railroads, as well as 4,900 solid-fuel retailers. Naked politics based on self-interest was business-as-usual political capitalism.

On the other hand, would-be natural gas utilities and state utility commissions supported Trans-Continental's application. They represented not only existing customers who wanted a fuel upgrade but also waiting consumers who were otherwise unorganized. FPC staff also favored, rightly, competition between fuels and between pipelines.

Trans-Continental received its certificate in May 1948 after a nine-month hearing involving 125 witnesses, 10,000 pages of testimony, and more than 1,000 exhibits. "Increasing the use of natural gas is the quickest and cheapest method immediately available to reduce domestic consumption of petroleum," the decision read, noting that 629 million gallons of fuel oil would be saved annually. The commission rejected Texas Eastern's attempt "to obtain a monopoly of the natural gas markets in the Middle Atlantic Seaboard area."

This victory for the applicant cost $500,000 (and almost ten times more in today's dollars) to get the same verdict from regulators that it had already received from customers whose own businesses were on the line. Indeed, gas distributors estimated $35 million in annual savings, and they were not about to retrofit their systems to take natural gas if they did not think that long-term supply was forthcoming. And how could Transco attract financing if the throughput was not locked in also?

Gas supply was the most contentious issue at the hearing. Shortages during World War II and during the winter of 1947/48 in areas served by Tennessee Gas put the onus on Trans-Continental to present regulators with detailed reserve data showing that, in Claude Williams's words, "the country is not running out of natural gas." This was accomplished to the satisfaction of regulators.

As it turned out, a gas-drilling boom was getting under way. When Trans-Continental began flowing gas, the nation's proven gas reserves were nearly 200 trillion cubic feet compared to 180 trillion in 1949, despite record consumption. Additions would continue to outpace through the 1950s and well into the 1960s. Gas that once had been flared from oil wells was now a *premium fuel*, giving consumers a superior deal on an energy-equivalent (BTU) basis.

⌒

Ray Fish jumped for joy in his Houston office when he heard that Trans-Continental had received certification from the FPC. That was Ray. The salesman and engineer/entrepreneur relished the challenge of constructing the world's largest pipeline. Work began in May 1949, and with a last-minute expansion from the original 340 MMcf/d for an extra $49 million, the renamed Transcontinental Gas Pipe Line Company (TGPL) began delivering 505 MMcf/d of South Texas gas to the world's largest metropolitan area in early 1951.

The $240-million, 1,840-mile, 18-month project was the business creation of Claude Williams and the engineering feat of Fish and Richard Ricketts. "Another bright chapter in this ever building free America had been written," one account of the opening noted. "Thousands of people, including investors, engineers, right-of-way buyers, brush gangs, and brawny pipeliners, had brought natural gas to Manhattan."

Figure 9.2 Claude Williams (left) and Ray Fish (right) stand by a map of TGPL. Below, the original stockholders opening the valves in New York City: (from left) Clyde Alexander of Dallas; Norman Kinsey of Carthage, Texas; Alfred Glassell of Shreveport, Louisiana; and Ray Fish of Houston. The (windowless) Transco building in downtown Houston was fronted by a bas-relief, "The Rider of the Elements," signifying the mastery of energy by man to serve the cities.

Transcontinental's terminus was the center of the cultural and business universe, replete with eight million inhabitants. *Transgas*, the company magazine, turned to a leading man of American letters, E. B. White, for description:

> New York [City] is the concentration of art and commerce and sport and religion and entertainment and finance, bringing to a single compact arena the gladiator, the evangelist, the promoter, the actor, the trader and the merchant. It carries on

its lapel the unexpungeable odor of the long past, so that no matter where you sit
… you feel the vibrations of great times and tall deeds.

At the one-year mark, President Williams reported that the foundation for
future growth had been set for the infant company. Additional compressor stations would soon increase system capacity to 555 MMcf/d. Group insurance
covering illness and death, a pension program, Christmas bonuses, and a credit
union were delivering benefits to 1,400 employees. "We are happy that these
programs could be instituted so early in the life of the company," Williams said.

TGPL's first business challenge was regulatory. The company needed to
increase its cost of service above that anticipated in its original rate case in order
to make its revenue requirement—a must, given stockholder expectations.
(Pursuant to FPC policy, this revenue requirement was the sum of the company's *prudent* costs and a *reasonable* rate of return on invested capital.) Gas costs
were rising as more pipelines courted producers. Federal income taxes were
edging up, and the Federal Reserve Bank's expansionary monetary policy was
causing a general inflation.

In just its second year, Transcontinental described its new challenge, one
very different from the engineering/construction risk of before:

> Increased costs have made the rates now charged to our customers for gas
> insufficient to meet operating cost and pay an adequate rate of return on the
> capital invested in the Company. We are vigorously prosecuting a rate increase
> application before the Federal Power Commission. The procedure is slow and, at
> times, disheartening but … a fair rate will be obtained eventually.

But as long as the higher costs were arm's length and not due to negligence
on the part of the company, customer rates could be increased because the regulated utility's revenue requirement was the law of the land. There were lags in
the process, but undercollection in one period could be made up in the next
(generally every three years). By avoiding extravagance that would run afoul of
regulators, Transcontinental was on solid ground as a predictable cash
generator.

This left another challenge that all interstate gas pipelines faced. Theoretically, the company's regulated profit—determined by multiplying the allowed
rate of return by the book value of the pipeline—would decline as the system
depreciated.[6] Therefore, without further capital investment, the rate base would
vanish—and so too a company's profit, although it would continue to recover
its cost of service.

However, the pipeline's rate base could be preserved and even increased by
maintaining and expanding the system. The name of the game was to keep

---

6. Book value is the original cost of the pipeline minus accelerated depreciation, as reported
for tax purposes.

growing by investing—and borrowing money at less than the FPC-authorized rate of return. "In general, you run like hell to keep even in a regulated industry," as Gardiner Symonds of Tennessee Gas liked to say.

·᠍᠍

Transcontinental was headquartered in a large windowless building in downtown Houston, the oil capital and now becoming the natural gas capital of America as well. Transcontinental's workforce melded expertise in "engineering, organization, financial planning, marketing, advertising, public relations, political schmoozing, legal maneuvering and community psychology." Between a gas-drilling boom and a gas-hungry market, Transcontinental increased its certificated capacity to 1 Bcf/d in 1958—double its initial throughput of seven years before—and 2.3 Bcf/d a decade later.

Along the way, the pipeline was the first to use 36-inch-diameter pipe (1954) and 42-inch pipe (1965). Major investments in storage capacity allowed the company to inject gas when demand was low for withdrawal during the winter space-heating peak. A small liquefied natural gas (LNG) storage facility would be completed in New Jersey in 1970, one of the first in the United States. Market-area storage would later be joined by supply-area storage to ensure steady supply should gas wells be temporarily disabled from a hard freeze or hurricane.

After Ray Fish had completed the project and joined TGPL's board, Claude Williams named Clyde McGraw vice president of operations. McGraw would rise to the presidency in 1957 and hold that position for a decade before becoming chairman. After overseeing the next three company presidents, McGraw finally retired in 1976, with his title going to Jack Bowen.

In 1963, Transcontinental Gas Pipe Line Corporation shortened its name to Transco Corporation, although it was still was a nonintegrated, nondiversified pipeline company. "We decided to let the investors diversify on their own," McGraw told *Forbes*. If another business had been joined, it would have been exploration and production. But the FPC discriminated against affiliated transactions whereby, theoretically, the unregulated (producer) side could determine the price that the regulated (transmission) side would pay, a regulatory gap.[7] So, Transco stood pat, and its stock price moved with the general stock market, though not much more.

Transco's earnings set yearly highs in the 1950s and 1960s. Some of this was just keeping up with inflation, which regulators permitted. But the bigger reason was strong markets that drove the company to expand its rate base. Investing

---

7. What the FPC called a "gap in effective regulation of the natural gas industry" led to price regulation in certain fields in the 1940s and universal regulation of sale-for-resale gas in interstate commerce a decade later. FPC staff swelled from 48 in 1930 to 653 in 1954 with its expanding jurisdiction: first over interstate gas pipelines and then over gas production sold in interstate commerce.

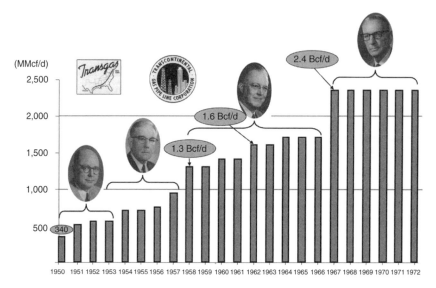

Figure 9.3 Transcontinental's expansions in the 1950s and 1960s are shown along-side the company presidents Claude Williams (1948–53), Tom Walker (1953–58), E. Clyde McGraw (1958–67), and James Henderson (1967–72). Gas-supply problems from federal wellhead price controls would end the expansion boom in the late 1960s.

was good business, given an authorized rate of return of around 6 percent ver-sus borrowing costs between 4 and 5 percent. The company also avoided major cost disallowances by not provoking regulators with extraneous costs, impor-tant because the FPC was "an intrusive and powerful referee." With a debt-to-capital ratio of 60–65 percent, each dollar from shareholders was producing income of three.

"Even a monkey could run Transco" went a quip about the era when growing gas supply and demand and friendly customer relations left little more than engineering and facile marketing to do. But a major government intervention would disrupt Transco's sweet spot. In 1954, the U.S. Supreme Court gave the FPC authority to determine a maximum price for gas sold by a producer to a pipeline for resale in interstate commerce. This was practically all the compa-ny's gas, and Transco president Tom Walker warned in 1956 that price controls threatened the producers' "ability and willingness to perform." In response, Transco tried to circumvent price controls by allowing end users to buy gas directly at the wellhead (an unregulated intrastate transaction) and providing the buyers transportation service only. But the FPC squashed that idea in 1961, leaving the pipeline at the mercy of federal regulation that might or might not give producers enough incentive to meet Transco's gas needs.

A Gas-Supply Problem

Transco reported record earnings in 1969 for the seventeenth consecutive year. Gross plant investment, the all-important rate base upon which earnings were calculated, was growing nicely. Deliveries for the year neared one trillion cubic feet, above 5 percent of national consumption. No other natural gas pipeline in America was this big. With the addition of storage capacity, Transco's peak-day deliveries were able to exceed 4 Bcf/d—a lifeline to the Northeast each winter when the Arctic storms came. But one statistic boded ill: In 1969, reserves dedicated to Transco declined for the first time in the pipeline's history. The outlook was for more deterioration, due in large part to the cumulative effect of federal price controls on wellhead gas sold in interstate commerce during the previous two decades.

The changing supply environment was not lost on management. Transco CEO James Henderson (1967–72) embarked on a new program to cofinance dozens of wells in collaboration with companies such as Boone Pickens's Mesa Petroleum. With the blessing of the FPC, whose own regulations were causing the problem, Transco got first call on all discovered gas in return for its interest-free loan to drillers. Better yet for Transco, the FPC allowed the company's drilling investment to be placed in the rate base for a rate of return, and any earnings deficit (cost in excess of revenue) was recoupable as a customer charge. Regulators, in a very convoluted way, were giving back some of what they had taken away.

In 1971, with the winter peak approaching, Transco received FPC approval to make emergency gas purchases above the regulated wellhead price, in order to replace supply lost to two hurricanes and an offshore platform mishap. Transco also began evaluating manufactured gas (called synthetic natural gas, or SNG) and purchasing additional LNG. The delivered cost of so-called supplemental gas was around $1 per thousand cubic feet, more than double the cost of the system's supply from the field.

Henderson's program was barely under way when an abnormally cold winter in 1971/72 forced Transco to impose a severe curtailment on its utility customers, who in turn rationed gas to several million end users. Transco simply did not have the pipeline flow or storage gas to meet peak demand. Neither did its distribution companies have the flexibility to increase rates to ration demand to available supply in the short run. Scarcity pricing was precluded by the method of determining rates under public-utility regulation. Instead, the New York Public Service Commission (NYPSC) ordered utilities in the state to get into the conservation business with programs such as Save-A-Watt.

It was one thing to cut off deliveries to low-priority interruptible customers, generally those with alternative fuel capability who would not face a crisis. Such interruptions were contractually permitted and not unusual come winter. But the winter curtailment of 1971/72 was to high-priority (so-called firm) users who were contractually entitled to supply.[8] Factories shut down, schools and businesses closed, and residents were forced to leave their homes or stay near the fireplace. Such was the result, though hardly the intent, of the FPC's just-and-reasonable pricing, as stated in the Natural Gas Act. Transco, meanwhile, escaped major financial consequences by rolling uncollected demand charges from curtailed firm customers into future rates for all customers to pay. Although federal policy caused Transco's gas shortages on the front end, federal policy also protected Transco as a public utility on the back end.[9] In fact, Transco's earnings were actually *higher* in 1971, and again in 1972, despite a decline in delivered volumes.

Other interstate pipelines were in the same predicament as Transco. Fourteen were purchasing emergency gas, and 26 had curtailment plans on file with the FPC. Federal policy notwithstanding, whole new ways of doing business had to be devised. Transco's sinking stock price indicated as much. Without enough gas to serve existing markets, the prospects for rate-base expansions were dim, which meant falling earnings with equipment depreciation. President James Henderson, who had been with the company since 1949, took early retirement, and for the first time in its history, the Transco board looked externally for a new president.

Their first choice was Robert Herring, the CEO of Houston Natural Gas Corporation (HNG), the nation's largest intrastate gas pipeline and industrial gas supplier. Alfred Glassell, one of Transco's seven founding board members and a friend of Herring's, made the pitch. Herring declined and would stay at HNG until his untimely death from cancer in 1981.[10]

The search broadened, and the next choice was Jack Bowen, the CEO of Florida Gas Company. Florida households had not been curtailed, although there was a moratorium on gas service to new industrial users because of tight supply. But Bowen had proactively begun cofunding drilling in the vicinity of the pipeline. As chairman of the Interstate Natural Gas Association of America (INGAA), the interstate pipeline trade group, Jack Bowen was well known and respected. In fact, Transco's in-house magazine, *Transgas*, had published a speech by him to the Southern Gas Association, in which he outlined a strategy to address the industry's "serious" gas supply situation. Transco needed just that strategy.

---

8. Firm customers paid a flat monthly *demand charge*, in addition to a *volumetric charge* for the gas they used, to ensure that they would not be interrupted.

9. Rationing priorities are discussed in Internet appendix 9.2, "FPC Curtailment Policy," at www.politicalcapitalism.org/Book2/Chapter9/Appendix2.html.

10. Herring's death began a series of events that would bring Transco's young president, Kenneth L. Lay, to HNG in 1984. See chapter 13, pp. 475–78.

Transco had two and a half times the assets as Florida Gas, but Bowen was not ready to leave the company that he had built from the ground up. Nor was his family of six interested in leaving Winter Park. So Transco's board turned instead to G. Montgomery Mitchell, 42, vice president and head of the New York City office of Stone & Webster Management Consultants.

Monty Mitchell was a wellhead engineer who had worked with Continental Oil Company (Conoco) and Consolidated Natural Gas before joining Stone & Webster. Transco was his biggest account, so he knew the company well. Mitchell moved to Houston in September 1971 to join Transco as executive vice president and was elected president and CEO early the next year.

Just two months into his reign, Mitchell announced a bold plan to increase the gas supply available to his pipeline by 1.1 Bcf/d between 1974 and 1977. Given what he described as "the demise of low cost supplies of natural gas," Mitchell's business plan was all about supplemental, or nontraditional, gas. Transco planned to build facilities near its Northeast customers to gasify crude oil, gasify naphtha, and regasify liquefied natural gas from Algeria (that is, from Sonatrach, the state-owned oil and gas company). Supplemental gas was forecast to cost $1.25 per thousand cubic feet (Mcf), which compared poorly with wellhead natural gas purchased at a then-regulated price of $0.25 per Mcf. But these were extraordinary times. With regulatory approval and some fancy technology, Transco could reward investors by refilling its pipeline *and* expanding the rate base with the capital-intensive SNG/LNG investments.[11]

Transco took another step toward remaking its supply base via a September 1973 agreement with the Iranian government to convert 750 MMcf/d of the country's flared gas into methanol for delivery and gasification in New Jersey.[12] An international solution was needed, given the hamstrung domestic energy supply.

The Iranian initiative and Monty Mitchell's other supplemental-supply projects were jolted by the Arab oil embargo, announced in October 1973. Naphtha prices skyrocketed, ruining the economics of gasification compared to other alternatives. Iran decided to reinject its gas to increase oil production. The Algerian LNG project, headed by El Paso Natural Gas, was hung up at the FPC—thanks in part to the incremental pricing policy championed by Pinkney Walker

---

11. Transco's proposal was one of 30 synthetic natural gas projects proposed or under construction in mid-1972, a monument to FPC regulation of natural gas prices at the wellhead.

12. *Transgas* profiled Transco's country partner with information provided by the Iranian government: "The Shah contributes to the stability and operation of the government through the traditional esteem in which he is held by the public as head of the national family and purveyor of justice.... Iranians today are living with one of the most stable governments on earth." In early 1979, the Shah was ousted in the Iranian Revolution.

and Ken Lay[13]—and canceled by Sonatrach. All Transco's big supply deals were suddenly dormant, if not dead.

Closer to home, Transco entered into options to construct a coal-gasification plant at the Powder River Basin in northwest Wyoming. "Coal gasification seems certain, long range, to be one of the most important methods of supplying gas for the nation's energy needs," Mitchell said. Transco was also one of 26 companies of the Arctic Gas Project that planned to transport gas from the North Slope of Alaska and northwest Canada to the U.S. and eastern Canadian markets. But these projects, capital intensive and requiring a long construction period, would never come to fruition, leaving Mitchell with little more than an expanded version of Henderson's advance-payment drilling program. And even there, a nine-month delay with a federal offshore-lease sale dampened prospects.

On the home front, all was brave and happy. Transco employees moved into the new 25-story Transco Tower (with windows!), in Houston's Galleria area. Mitchell gave the company a new name and logo with the message, "Our old, familiar trademark now gives way to new conditions and new situations, heralding an era of progress for Transco Companies Inc. and its subsidiaries."

But cosmetics could not change the fact that Transco needed gas badly and soon. Curtailments amounting to 8 percent of total contract demand in 1972 grew to 13 percent in 1973 and 25 percent a year later. Pipeline throughput declined from 2.6 Bcf/d to 2.2 Bcf/d in these three years. Customers were going without gas when they needed it the most, a public relations disaster given the millions of meters served by Transco's gas-short distribution customers. Another problem was how to recover increased costs given President Nixon's price freeze of August 1971. Not only the FPC but also the White House Cost of Living Council had to be assuaged in difficult times.

Year-to-year declines in quarterly earnings began in 1974, another first for the quarter-century-old company. A slumping stock price—from $17 to under $10 per share during Mitchell's tenure—reflected Transco's woes. Transco's board grew restless, and Jack Bowen was approached again in the summer of 1974. This time, Bowen said yes, and before long he was in Houston meeting with Mitchell and getting the lay of the company and its problems.[14]

When the time came, Mitchell graciously told employees: "In the face of [supply-side] frustrations, when the opportunity arose to engage Mr. Bowen, your board of directors, including myself, felt it would be a prudent choice."

---

13. The Ph.D. economists persuaded the commission to price LNG separately rather than to roll in (average) the price of the high-cost gas with the price of cheaper supplies and charge all users the same price. See chapter 8, p. 294.

14. Bowen's departure from Florida Gas Company is described in chapter 8, pp. 299–300.

Figure 9.4 The signing of a 750 MMcf/d gas-supply contract with Iranian officials (bottom) would be the last of four megaprojects of CEO Monty Mitchell, each of which would fall victim to a changing world energy market. Mitchell joined the company in 1971 at age 42 (top left) and was forced to resign three years later, just months after addressing investors for the last time (top right).

Mitchell opened a Houston office for Stone & Webster and would not be actively involved with Transco again.

Jack Bowen Arrives

Bowen found his challenge after he began at Transco on October 1, 1974, as president and CEO (Clyde McGraw remained as chairman, a position he held until 1976 when Bowen assumed the title.) The stock price continued to drop and reached an all-time low below $5 per share. Winter gas curtailments were expected to worsen in the company's Philadelphia–New Jersey–New York City market. Transco's exploration and production staff was a fraction the size of that at the much smaller company that Bowen had left. The organization chart was in total disarray, and the board of directors was awkwardly involved in day-to-day decisions. A rare reduction in force was necessary. Early retirements were necessary, and new talent was needed. The stock dividend had to be eliminated to save cash. Enthusiasm, not only gas, was in short supply.

Bowen held four (at capacity) employee meetings to reach everyone with his message of change and hope:

> You're not a pipeline company anymore. You're an energy-supply company.... We're going to get as big as we can in domestic oil and gas exploration in the Gulf Coast, onshore and offshore, using our money and other people's money.... I'll work with you in coming up with our plans and in putting them into action.... I'm very confident or I would not be here today, that Transco is going to be ... a strong, healthy company, making a significant contribution to the supply of energy to the country.

"Jack," as he asked to be called, promised open communication and asked for a renewed effort from everyone to do their jobs well. It was a fresh beginning. A Houston newspaper likened Bowen to actor George C. Scott of *Patton* fame, while an employee described Bowen's arrival as "MacArthur returning to the Philippines." A quarter century removed from his military days, Jack Bowen had that type of presence: tall, handsome, confident, articulate, and trustworthy.

Business Week described Bowen's back-to-the-basics plan for gas supply and quoted a rival pipeline executive who opined, "Transco just hasn't fought hard enough in rate cases." In fact, new executives were needed in Rates and Legal. A young lawyer from Andrews & Kurth, Brian O'Neill, was chosen as general counsel over more experienced outside candidates. O'Neill would have a long history with Transco in ways no one could imagine.

Bowen's first Transco annual report announced earnings of $12 million in 1974, down from $44 million the year before, primarily as a result of a $21.5 million after-tax charge for discontinued gas-supply projects that could not be recouped in customer rates. Shell Oil Company had made some hits with Transco's money in the Gulf—Mitchell's lone success—but exploration in Alberta, British Columbia, and Nova Scotia, as well as in Alabama, Mississippi, and New York were dusters. The company was unlucky too when its gas purchases in the Gulf of Mexico were disrupted by Hurricane Carmen, lowering pipeline throughput that could not be made up. There was simply no room for bad luck or operational error.

Transco had no excuse for making only $12 million, even in an off year. Over at Florida Gas in the same year, Selby Sullivan reported record earnings of $18 million in his first annual report as CEO. And his company was a third the size of mighty Transco, one of the three Ts serving the Northeast, the world's most concentrated market for natural gas. (The other two were Tenneco, the renamed Tennessee Gas Transmission Company, and Texas Eastern Transmission.)

Bowen had little to talk about apart from his underperforming pipeline, so his first stockholders report indicted federal energy policy. The federal price ceiling for new wellhead gas, $0.50 per Mcf, compared with unregulated (intrastate) prices that were several times as high. Bowen's public-policy message was unchanged from his Florida Gas days: *deregulate the price of new gas*

Figure 9.5 Bowen (left) is shown alongside Monty Mitchell (right), speaking to employees, and outlining offshore gas prospects. Transco as Jack Bowen found it: an 1,800-mile, 2.9 Bcf/d system purchasing gas from onshore and offshore in Texas and Louisiana for resale to 69 customers in 11 states extending from Mississippi to New York. Working storage of 90 Bcf allowed peak-day deliveries of 4.6 Bcf/d.

(not old gas that was under contract with the pipeline); *accelerate offshore leasing* (the Gulf of Mexico was in Transco's supply bed); *expedite certification* for new-supply infrastructure (new offshore laterals and terminals were needed to get gas to shore); and *promote conservation* (to reduce gas demand to meet available supply).

"To revitalize the growth potential of the Company," Bowen told shareholders, "we are seeking to develop new profit centers by diversifying into related areas of our basic role as a supplier and transporter of energy." It would require new ways of doing things *and* government support. "Energy independence requires a total effort in research and development to create new ways of making energy, including converting coal into non-polluting gas and liquid fuels," he said.

"Transco has a critical gas shortage," Bowen warned the ranks, that "must be overcome if we Transcoers are to keep our jobs." Transco's exploration staff often, a sixth the size of Florida Gas's, had to be greatly expanded. Enter Transco Gas Supply Company, Bowen's new vehicle to finance producers. By year-end 1975, more than $200 million was advanced to producers by the new subsidiary, and more would follow. Per FPC approval, this money became part of the capital (rate base) on which Transco was entitled to collect a reasonable rate of return.

In the same period, an unregulated and thus at-risk subsidiary, Transco Exploration Company (TXC), was founded with $150 million of capital (about half a billion dollars today) to drill for and produce oil and gas in the Gulf of Mexico. It was the first real diversification in company history. One of the TXC-financed drillers was McMoRan Exploration Company, an independent off-shore company, run by Jim Bob Moffett, that specialized in high-risk, wildcat commercial wells.[15] Another independent in Transco's fold was Mosbacher Exploration, owned and operated by Robert Mosbacher, later a member of the Reagan administration. Unlike Monty Mitchell, who combed the continent and world for gas supply, Bowen focused on Transco's backyard. This backyard, however, did not include onshore prospects, because of stricter gas-price ceilings under federal regulation. Offshore Gulf of Mexico was Transco's frontier—and a good one, as studies by the Department of the Interior indicated.

◦

"Our Company's level of activity in Washington is on the increase with no relief in sight," Bowen informed his board of directors in mid-1975. Federal work had become too much for the D.C. branch of Transco's outside law firm and its consulting company, (Andrews & Kurth and Zinder & Associates, respectively). Transco needed its own office in the nation's capital. The company had issues before the FPC (curtailment plans, rate cases, gas-supply incentive programs), Federal Energy Office, Department of the Interior, Securities and Exchange Commission, and congressional subcommittees. A Washington government-affairs office was needed "to assist the Company in administrative details of getting in and out of Washington, rooms, appearances, getting copies of various documents, but most important … persuad[ing] various members of Congress, or their administrative staffs, of Transco's position." Bowen also had some proactive proposals for the nation's capital that were not about simple deregulation.[16]

A hotel suite of two bedrooms and living room was recommended. "Nearly all the pipelines have established hotel suites, and most of them have offices in Washington," Bowen closed. "We have so much at stake, we feel it is necessary

---

15. Moffett's drilling skills were complemented by an engaging, optimistic personality. "He can almost make you feel good about a dry hole," Bowen once said. The drilling efforts for Transco by Moffett and Mosbacher would not be everything that was hoped, but it was a better option than Transco's trying to quickly rev up to undertake the same activities in-house.

16. See Internet appendix 9.3, "Jack Bowen as Political Capitalist," at www.politicalcapitalism. org/Book2/Chapter9/Appendix3.html.

to be as efficient as we can in going about our business in Washington." Bowen was tight when it came to spending, but he also knew that prudently incurred government-affairs costs would ultimately be borne by ratepayers, not shareholders.

Transco's financial department also needed beefing up. "Our basic problem is money supply rather than gas supply since, given enough money, we believe we can solve our gas supply shortage," Bowen reasoned. The FPC, indeed, was allowing back-door incentives for new supply that lenders could finance. New positions in Corporate Finance and Financial Relations would result.

A year into his new job, Bowen had one more message for his board: "Tonight, for the first time, some of my watercolors are going to be put on the market." He had 22 paintings to sell in a showing at the Meredith Long Gallery of Houston. "If the public demands that I cast aside my career as an oil and gas man and do nothing but paint," he said, "I may have to follow that call." Everyone smiled at that one. Bowen sold many paintings that night to business associates and some friends, but no career change would be forthcoming.

⟨∽⟩

Earnings recovered in 1975 despite higher curtailments, thanks to a tracking account that ensured that Transco received its full demand-charge payments from customers. In other words, uncollected demand charges in the current period (from curtailments) were recorded for future recovery. Reserves attached to the system increased for the first time in seven years in 1976. The abnormally cold winter of 1976/77, which saw curtailments peak near 50 percent of demand, hurt consumers more than it did Transco, which continued to be protected because the company's gas-supply policy was not found imprudent by federal regulators. Indeed, Bowen and Transco were aggressively entering into take-or-pay contracts obligating takes at the 80, 90, even 100 percent level, assuring producers that Transco would pay for most or all of the presented volume, whether the supply was needed by the market or not.[17] (Of course it would be needed, the company thought!) A force majeure clause protected the pipeline should a so-called Act of God, such as a pipeline rupture or hurricane, prevent the company from taking the gas, but Transco was obligated to take much or all of what a producer could muster.

Transco's all-important rate case went well. An approved filing in 1975 gave Transco a 10 percent return on the pipeline rate base, equating (thanks to debt leveraging) to a 17 percent after-tax return on shareholder equity. The regulated pipeline was a cash cow.

---

17. When an Andrews & Kurth attorney asked what the company would do if there was too much gas compared to market demand, the Transco executive chuckled and said, "If we ever have that problem, that will be a happy day for us. Too much gas."

By 1978, big slugs of gas were coming on stream from the $353 million High Island Offshore System (HIOS), a Transco-led consortium that built and operated a 125-mile, 1-Bcf/d transmission system in the Gulf of Mexico. Onshore, Transco entered into its largest supply contracts since 1967, thanks to the Natural Gas Policy Act of 1978 (NGPA), which evened the playing field by applying the same pricing to intrastate gas as to interstate gas—and providing higher prices for newly discovered gas. No longer could intrastates, such as Houston Pipe Line, outbid their interstate brethren for much-needed gas supply.[18]

Transco's success showed at the other end of the pipe. TGPL's average deliveries in 1978 of 2.3 Bcf/d were 13 percent higher than the year before, the first increase since 1970. A third of this volume was *transportation gas*, the result of an FPC ruling in August 1975 allowing large industrial users to contract directly with producers to escape federal price controls. Florida Gas had been conceived around FPC-blessed transportation gas; TGPL, having suffered a commission refusal in the 1960s, was now, finally, allowed to employ the same tactic.

Record-high energy prices in the late 1970s created a boom throughout the energy industry, and Transco was no exception. The pipeline was in full recovery, and the exploration and production unit, TXC, was becoming more valuable with every uptick in oil and gas prices. Transco's stock, which was first listed on the New York Stock Exchange in April 1975 at $8.875 per share, broke $60 in late 1980. The company was getting big too—so much so that it had outgrown the 25-story Transco Tower, the one that had opened in 1973 with the company occupying just 8 floors. So Jack Bowen proudly announced plans to build a significantly larger skyscraper—the largest anywhere outside of a downtown district—and charged the developers to design "the most beautiful building in America."

Earnings in 1980 broke $100 million for the first time on record revenues of $2.6 billion. TXC, now profitable, was stepping out from offshore Texas and Louisiana to onshore U.S. basins with NGPA-pricing incentives. Curtailments were a thing of the past as customers received full requirements on the coldest days. Transco was in the sweet spot, with much credit due to its new NYSE-listed affiliate, which was supplying much of the gas behind TGPL's 25 percent sales increase. Jack Bowen had replaced Monty Mitchell's supplemental-gas projects with offshore drilling and was rewarded geologically and financially. Bowen's triumph enhanced his stature as a top executive, maybe *the* top executive, in the interstate gas-pipeline business.

But years of curtailment and rising prices had bred pessimism that the gas resource base was tiring, and this mentality did not fade with the end of curtailments. Despite the Mitchell experience, supplemental gas was on Jack Bowen's mind—as it had been back in his days at Florida Gas Company.

---

18. See chapter 13, pp. 457–58.

Figure 9.6 Jack Bowen's interest in supplemental-gas projects back at Florida Gas Company was rekindled in the wake of the severe winter of 1976/77, which saw curtailments in many places, including New York City (upper). In response, Transco led a consortium to build the Great Plains Coal Gasification Plant (lower), the economics of which would be ruined by declining gas prices.

Predicting $7 per Mcf gas for the mid-1980s, Transco and three industry partners—American Natural Resources (ANR), Peoples Gas Company (of Samuel Insull import), and Tennessee Gas Pipeline (wholly owned by Tenneco)—announced plans in 1978 to build the nation's first commercial-scale coal-gasification plant, to be located in Mercer County, North Dakota. In 1980, the Federal Energy Regulatory Commission (FERC), successor to the FPC, approved the Great Plains Coal Gasification Project, which aimed to produce pipeline-quality gas at the rate of 125 MMcf/d. In 1981, the Reagan administration, with the president overruling his budget director, David Stockman, approved a $2.02 billion federal loan guarantee for the project.

What its sponsors had called the "Great Plains" or "Great Pains" project could finally enter construction. The FERC-approved sales rate for the coal-gas was put in the NGPA new-gas price category for January 1981, which was $6.75 per Mcf, plus a monthly escalation. Like the aggressive take-or-pay contracts executed with natural gas producers, Great Plains would ensure plenty of gas for TGPL well into the future. But transforming 14,000 tons of lignite into 125 MMcf of gas each day was an elaborate and expensive process compared to finding gas in its natural state—and uneconomical should gas prices head south.

Bowen was committed to synthetic fuels despite a turn of events that was considered an anomaly, not a sea change. Buried in the back of Transco's *1979 Annual Report* was this paragraph under "Commitments and Contingencies":

> Higher than anticipated production rates offshore have resulted in full use of the existing delivery capacity in the High Island Offshore and the U-T Offshore systems.... If Pipe Line is unable to obtain modification of these [take-or-pay] contractual provisions, the amount of gas that it may initially be required to pay without being able to take may be substantial, which would result in substantial additional financing requirements and costs to Pipe Line.

The winter of 1976/77 had been the worst curtailment experience ever. Now Transco had just turned the corner on gas supply. But was the company going too long on supply? It would take a fresh face at Transco to better recognize and deal with a new, entirely unanticipated problem.

Another Doctor Call

In the fall of 1980, Ken Lay, now head of Continental Resources Company (the renamed Florida Gas Company), invited Jack and Annis Bowen to Winter Park for a homecoming. Jack had visited the company when Florida Gas was sold to Continental Group the year before, but this was different. There was a buffet lunch with employees and a speech. Lay was good about keeping up relationships, and he and Jack were very interested in each other's progress.

Ken called Jack about his interest in pursuing new opportunities (Ken, in fact, was disappointed that Jack had not already called him about leaving Selby Sullivan for Transco). So at an American Gas Association meeting in Washington several months later, Lay explained his unease about working for a conglomerate with only a tenth of its assets in energy. As much as he enjoyed Winter Park and running the energy subsidiary, he felt removed from the action. Ken, in short, wanted to stick to (regulated) energy and not be tasked with managing an amalgamation of businesses.[19] But he wanted a bigger energy stage—one that Transco could provide.

Bowen took note of Ken's situation with interest. In his six years at Transco, no obvious number two or potential successor had emerged. He was now 58; Ken, not quite 38. Jack informed his board of the opportunity and described the man who many thought was the brightest young executive in the natural gas

---

19. Also see chapter 8, pp. 311–12.

industry. The light was green, so Jack called Ken and popped the question: Would he be interested in moving to Houston to become president and chief operating officer of Transco? If all went well, Jack explained, he would be Jack's successor as CEO.

With assets of $3.4 billion and 3,300 employees, Transco was much bigger than Continental Resources Company. Working with Jack Bowen would be much better than dealing with the brass in Connecticut. Houston was the right place to be for any up-and-comer in energy. Ken explained to Jack his complicated marital situation, accepted the job, and worked to get temporary custody of his two children.[20] Linda Herrold, his secretary but much more, was also in his future plans. She was fine with Houston.

·◌·

"We've got a lot to do in the '80s, and it will take our best effort," Bowen told his senior managers upon breaking the news that Ken Lay would arrive as Transco's president and chief operating officer effective May 1, 1981. "This addition gives us more depth in the company." The plan was for Bowen to spend more time on Transco Exploration Company and energy policy in Washington. The COO, just as the title implied, would be hands-on and focused on company details.

Lay was the second major outside addition to the executive suite. George Slocum, vice president and senior credit officer of Citibank, N.A., in New York City, and manager of Transco's account, had been hired to head Transco's corporate finance department in 1978. Slocum was promoted to chief financial officer shortly before Lay joined Transco. Nominally the number-three man, Slocum would have a faster track to the top of Transco than he could know or even imagine.

HotTap, the renamed in-house company magazine, profiled Transco's new president for the employees. The article reviewed the interesting journey "of a boy from Missouri who made good" and then let Lay share his management philosophy: "I like people who can get things done—can take information, analyze it and come up with solutions or better ways to accomplish goals." He elaborated:

> Over the years, I've been surprised at how many people in all kinds of organizations just can't do this. A lot of people are good at an activity, but can't take whole projects or even a single problem and do anything with it. The best people are those who understand a situation thoroughly and then take action. The most dangerous are those who don't take time to understand, but take action anyway. I make it a point to understand the system, learn the results from past experience, and consider the opinions of the people who are actually involved in the work before making a decision.

---

20. Lay's personal situation is described in chapter 8, pp. 310–12.

Lay described his management style of open communication and a nonhierarchal work structure where formalities gave way to teamwork:

> I value the contributions of people at all levels of the organization. There are some managers who believe that only a few key individuals are important and who try to rely on only those people. I'm not that kind of manager; I believe people at all levels can and do make significant contributions.

"Most of all," he added, "I like to have fun doing what I do, and I like for the people around me to have fun too because when people are having fun, they tend to be more productive."

The interview mentioned Ken's hobbies (a bit of tennis and golf, avid jogging) and modes of relaxation (music, books, the beach). The profile ended with Ken speaking of his will to succeed. "I want to be the best I can be at whatever I'm doing," he said. "I have worked hard, I have had a lot of good support, and I've been lucky."

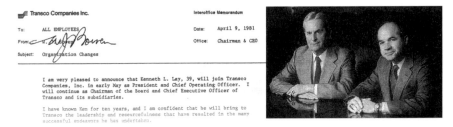

KEN LAY   *Transco's new president*   **HotTap**
Vol. 28, No. 6, June 1981

"The best people [in an organization] are those who understand a situation thoroughly and then take action. The most dangerous are those who don't take time to understand, but take action anyway."

"I make it a point to understand the system, learn the results from past experience, and consider the opinions of [others]."

Figure 9.7 Ken Lay joined Transco in May 1981 and immediately set a company-wide tone of innovation, teamwork, respect, and friendliness.

The Transco that Ken Lay found was coming off its best year in history and was still in the midst of a price-propelled boom. Lay, once settled, did what all good chief operating officers do: find the problems, particularly the big hidden ones. Lay knew about Transco's aggressive producer contracts (while at CRC, he competed against them for gas) and dove in, only to find a real problem: insufficient takes under the pipeline's aggressive take-or-pay contracts. Transco's offshore take-or-pay problem involved a potential liability of $108 million in 1980 alone—a fact again buried in the back of the annual report.[21]

Transco had not faced up to this problem and, in fact, the excess of supply over demand was expected to be gone by winter. "We still have a long-term need for [gas] reserves," stated one Transco executive just weeks after Lay arrived. But the problem was growing worse, not better. Soon, Lay took on an additional title: president, TGPL. The former head, Jack Earnest, responsible for the pipeline-producer contracts in question, was gone.

Excess deliverability under contract was not only a Transco problem. FERC began receiving filings in 1980–81 from other interstates trying to dispose of gas they could not sell but were obligated to buy under take-or-pay contracts. It was a strange situation that no one, least of all regulators, had anticipated. Price ceilings intended to protect gas consumers from rising prices had instead become price *floors* (contractual minimums) as prices fell, leaving gas unsold, helping virtually no one. Prices had to fall, yet prices were fixed by law, and private contracts were worded to accept the (higher) government price, not the (lower) market price.

In response, FERC began allowing pipelines to dump system supply in other markets. ("The industry may not need all the regulation we are giving it," quipped one commissioner.) Spot sales between new gas-marketing companies introduced gas-on-gas and pipeline-on-pipeline competition, something never seen before under the Natural Gas Act of 1938. Regulatory balkanization was giving way to entrepreneurial responses. Transco would need to get in front of the problem and fast.

◦◦◦

It was happy times at the annual meeting of the New York Society of Security Analysts in September 1981. "Transco has successfully evolved from a pipeline/utility company into a diversified domestic energy company with substantial investments in oil and gas exploration and production," Bowen announced. In fact, Transco Companies would be changing its name to Transco Energy Inc. for this reason. Bowen added that Transco Exploration Company, six years old and producing 250 MMcf/d of gas and 14,000 barrels per day of oil and condensate, was a star contributor to earnings and the largest gas source for TGPL. Lay told analysts how gas reserves attached to the pipeline had increased more than 10 percent between 1978 and 1980 despite an increase in

---

21. Transco's practice of entering into high take-or-pay producer contracts began with offshore production associated with its advanced payment program. It reached onshore production after 1978's NGPA allowed interstates to compete head to head with intrastate pipelines for new gas supply.

system takes. By middecade, he added, major new supplies for the pipeline would come from Canada and the Great Plains Coal Gasification Project.

Strong cash flow presented Transco with new opportunities. George Slocum told analysts about a $284 million investment in TGPL, its first sizeable upgrade on its flagship asset since the late 1960s. Slocum also allowed that Transco was primed to add a third division to the company—coal. In fact, ongoing negotiations would conclude just a few months later when Transco purchased two coal properties for $75 million. Back in 1975, Ken Lay had told Selby Sullivan at Florida Gas that coal should be a part of any well-rounded energy company, and Transco was now that.

Transco was not quite ready to own up to a long-lived gas surplus. Jack Bowen, cognizant of his company's $100 million investment in the Great Plains Coal Gasification Project, told security analysts that "domestic oil and gas will never be in an oversupply position."

But TGPL was living near the edge. Take-or-pay liabilities were sizeable and growing. The pipeline's cost of gas had tripled in the previous three years, and industrial users and power plants with dual-fuel capability were switching to fuel oil—utilizing the very equipment they had installed in response to gas curtailments. Fully one-third of Transco's market was alternative-fuel capable, making the company's throughput very sensitive to rising prices. The nation was showing signs of entering a recession, in part from record-high fuel costs. By early 1982, it was an open secret: Transco was seriously long on gas relative to consumer demand on its system.

In spring 1982, TGPL became the first interstate to exercise its market-out provision in producer contracts, a clause that allowed the pipeline to lower its purchase price if the gas could not be sold at the contract price. The company's most predominant gas type under NGPA regulation—Section 107 gas that was priced at $7.50/MMBtu—was cut back to $5/MMBtu (more than $11/MMBtu in today's dollars).[22]

Transco had little choice. Contractual gas prices were increasing monthly by NGPA formula, whereas the market price for gas was eroding owing to weakening oil prices, the recession, and mild winters. The offshore gas from Transco's suppliers was roaring in to take advantage of the overpriced situation. Producers found new ways to maximize deliverability from a given quantity of reserves—drilling more wells, completing wells differently, and increasing tubing. A gas reservoir that used to be produced over seven or eight years could now be drained in two. As Transco would lament to Congress (as part of its effort to

---

22. The NGPA, called by two attorneys "the most complicated and ambiguous statute ever enacted," contained 8 major pricing categories and more than 20 subcategories for natural gas, depending on location and vintage (when discovered). Section 107 high-cost gas had one of the highest legal maximum prices, which was more than the market could bear.

find a legislative solution), deliveries under its take-or-pay contracts increased 140 percent in the five years ending in 1983, whereas proven reserves attached to the system barely rose. Brian O'Neill, who succeeded Lay as president of TGPL, and the chief legal officer who signed off on the deals in the first place, described this development to lawmakers as "completely unprecedented and … [un]predicted by pipelines and probably also producers back in 1978." A death spiral could develop if rising prices reduced gas sales, for that would leave the same level of fixed costs to be recovered over fewer sales, necessitating an increase in rates (which would further lower demand) in the next period. The problem could not solve itself but only get worse if left to its own devices, given the nature of public-utility regulation.

Bowen had to acknowledge that contractual rigidities had caused supply to get out of whack with demand. Just a year after telling analysts that an over-supply of oil or gas would not occur, Bowen predicted a two-year surplus after which "we'll be scrambling for gas again." Others were more pessimistic about the supply overhang. Sam Segnar, CEO of InterNorth, the parent of Northern Natural Pipeline Company, stated: "I had felt in 1980 that it would take 3–5 years to work through the so-called gas bubble, and I think I'd have to say [in 1982] that we're still looking at 3–5 years."[23]

Transco's clampdown on wellhead contracts was not enough. Stuck between non-market-responsive producer contracts and teetering markets, TGPL still faced an insufficient market for gas that it was obligated to take. Such unmarketable gas was estimated at 600 MMcf/d, about the amount that would fill a smaller pipeline, such as Florida Gas Transmission.

In a cab-ride discussion in late 1982, Ken Lay, Brian O'Neill, and another new executive, Hal Miller, produced the genesis of a plan to address the conundrum. The Industrial Sales Program (ISP), approved by FERC as part of Transco's rate-case settlement the next year, allowed TGPL's gas suppliers, otherwise facing the prospect of having shut-in gas, to agree to sell to Transco discounted spot gas, which then could be resold to customers who would otherwise switch to oil. The price and volume would be determined midmonth by Transco and posted for the next month's business.

Another so-called special marketing program (SMP) sold discounted pipeline-system gas (as opposed to the released spot gas) to retain markets and undercut rival pipelines competing in Transco's market. This initiative allowed Transco to double its share of the Washington, D.C., market at the expense of Columbia Gas Transmission Corp., a pipeline that would struggle and finally declare bankruptcy in 1991. A third FERC-approved initiative

---

23. In 1985, Segnar's InterNorth would purchase Ken Lay's Houston Natural Gas, creating the company that would become Enron.

allowed TGPL to reprice gas sold to distributors in order to stay competitive during the winter heating season.

By year-end 1983, one-third of TGPL's throughput was being sold at market-responsive rates, quite a jump from the 5 percent recorded the year before. Transco's stock price, which began the year at around $23 per share, closed the year near $38.

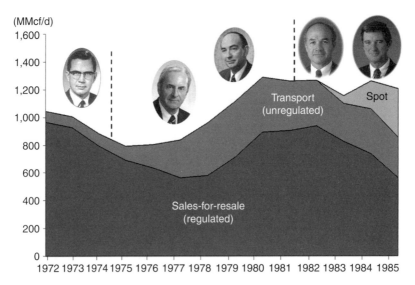

Figure 9.8 Transco successfully addressed its gas-supply deficiency in the mid-1970s to boost gas throughput, but overpriced supply in the early 1980s required new programs to boost sales and reduce take-or-pay liabilities with producers. Ken Lay and then Brian O'Neill would deal with these problems, trying to turn challenges into opportunities.

Transco's burst of innovation came because, in Jack Bowen's words, "we were first in the hospital." But problems do not automatically produce solutions, and Transco benefited from a marketing department whose expertise went beyond traditional customer relations. The head of marketing, Hal Miller—an engineer, MBA, and adjunct professor with Ph.D. aspirations—had come to Transco in 1973. Claude Mullendore (Miller's boss) and John Esslinger (a street-smart salesman) were talents who would be heard from again in the restructured gas industry (working, in fact, for Ken Lay at Enron). And the arrival of Ken Lay in 1981 came just in time to help Transco master the economics of gas supply and demand—and sell the company's innovative proposals in Washington.[24]

_____

24. For a free-market interpretation of business strategies in the face of regulatory distortions in the late 1970s/early 1980s natural gas market, see Internet appendix 9.4,

The natural-monopoly days when gas sold itself at average system cost were over. Monkeys need not apply to run Transco. As did much of the industry, TGPL faced the possibility of a death spiral between rising rates and falling demand that had to be creatively defused. The lesson learned was that buying and selling gas had financial downside and no upside, and transportation-only service (versus buying/selling the gas commodity in a bundled product) was the real business to be in for a pipeline. Ken Lay would remember this, post-Transco.

·◇·

Ken Lay was busy, productive, and settled. Except for one incident, his personal life stabilized when his divorce became final.[25] Linda Herrold was now Linda Lay. He had five children in one happy house—his two and Linda's three. Ken joined River Oaks Country Club and otherwise became ensconced atop Houston society.

Ken reported positive news about TGPL to employees in his year-1981 review. Deliveries were the highest in more than a decade, and customer and regulatory relations were improving. "We added a lot of new well-educated people to our staff," he added, a timely development given the number of imminent retirements coming at a company in its thirty-third year. One addition was Ph.D. economist Grant Sims, who had followed one of his Texas A&M professors, Dr. Philip Gramm, from College Station to Washington. On the recommendation of Rep. Gramm (R-TX), Lay hired Sims, who had worked on what became the Gramm-Rudman-Hollings budget resolution. Sims, in turn, would hire another Ph.D. economist he had known from the A&M days, Jay Lukens, a young analyst who previously had been figuring things out for partially deregulated AT&T. Natural gas was no longer an industry for engineers and lawyers only.

Lay's 1982 year-in-review reported that TGPL increased sales, whereas the interstate industry as a whole lost ground. Still, hard times required belt-tightening, even under the cost-plus ratemaking of public-utility regulation. (After all, *earning* its legally maximum rate was not automatic in a competitive market.) "We made a lot of progress throughout the company in the area of cost consciousness," Lay allowed. "We've trimmed costs by several million dollars just by looking at how we've been doing our business." Looking longer term, he predicted: "In the late '80s, energy supplies will again be short. Prices again will

---

"Reconstructing Markets under Natural Gas Price Controls," at www.politicalcapitalism. org/Book2/Chapter9/Appendix4.html.

25. Just months after joining Transco, Lay had to jet to a North Carolina mental hospital to deal with Judie (Ayers) Lay, who experienced what doctors described as a psychotic episode resulting from a manic-depressive disorder, coupled with the stress of her impending divorce from Ken.

increase in real terms. In the long term, the nation has a need for synfuels and alternative fuels."

Was Lay, like Bowen, a resource pessimist? If so, he was hardly different from the many prognosticators, including many leading energy economists, not to mention leading lights in industry and government. But Lay was also a company man, seconding Jack Bowen's faith in synthetic gas. Talking up prices was important for a company that was still increasing its bet that energy prices would rise in the future.

Public-Policy Activism

No natural gas or energy company was more active on the public-policy front than Transco. Jack Bowen, now a father figure in the industry, spoke forcefully about the need for a national energy policy, a *comprehensive* energy policy, favoring domestic fuels, including synthetics, over oil imports. Government correction of markets—and sometimes its own regulation—was what Bowen sought.

Bowen got interested in national energy policy in the late 1960s when gas supply became the dominant issue at Florida Gas Company. This interest, or really concern, carried over to Transco. Wellhead price ceilings had put the interstate gas industry on its back, and policy reform was necessary. Bowen had never taken an economics class or otherwise studied the subject (out-of-office time was for family, painting, recreation, and socializing), but his engineering mind told him that supply and demand could be balanced by activist government policy, not only (partially immobilized) impersonal market forces.

With backing from all the gas-industry trade associations—from the wellhead (Natural Gas Supply Association) to the burner tip (American Gas Association)—and with the support of the Interstate Natural Gas Pipeline Association of America, Jack Bowen spearheaded the creation of the Gas Research Institute (GRI) in 1976. Appropriately, he became the first chairman the next year.

A technical organization, GRI would fund research and development projects to (in Bowen's words) "develop urgently needed supplemental supplies, to find means of conservation, and to contribute to the more efficient use of gaseous energy." Funding came from an FPC-approved surcharge on all deliveries made through interstate gas pipelines, and the federal government matched the private funds by half again (contributing in a ratio of 1.5 to 1). Fittingly, Bowen was elected the first board chairman of the Chicago-based nonprofit.

Jimmy Carter's National Energy Plan, televised in prime time in April 1977, was bullish on conservation and bearish toward supply, not all bad according to Transco's chief. Although concerned that Carter's proposed increase in the federal price ceiling for gas, to $1.75 per MMBtu, would not be enough, Bowen applauded the potential equalization of intrastate and interstate gas prices and welcomed energy-use mandates as "the cheapest way to conserve fuel" and "something the nation must do." Bowen was pleased that "the President has made this effort to convince the American people that there is an energy crisis which is real, worldwide, and won't go away." Coming out of a severe curtailment in the winter of 1976/77, Bowen had reason to be conciliatory toward conservationism.

In the Reagan era, and with the production of synthetic gas on his mind, Bowen pushed hard for federal legislation to expedite (fast-track) permission for major non-nuclear energy projects. A cabinet-level Council on Energy Mobilization, the centerpiece of the proposed Energy Mobilization Act of 1981, would determine qualifying projects. The Transco-backed initiative—intended to help Bowen's synthetic-gas projects—died in committee, however.

Ken Lay, who knew the ways of Washington well, focused on natural gas policy reform after becoming Transco's president. In congressional hearings in September 1982, Lay testified in favor of the complete decontrol of wellhead prices. "Transco believes immediate decontrol would lead to many benefits," the former FPC staffer, Interior Department official, and economics professor said. The NGPA had done its job, he explained, and it was time to unwind the convoluted price tiers and get to a free market in gas. But there was a catch. Transco's definition of *free market* was not only unregulated pricing but also *abrogating producer contracts that were not price competitive in the market*. (Ken Lay would prove adept at using free-market rhetoric to describe government activism at Enron also.)

In fact, Transco's producer-reformation efforts were falling short.[26] Producers were not following Transco's example of having its production side tear up its take-or-pay contracts with the pipeline. The company desperately needed to start anew, creating on its pipeline a market that would have the pricing freedom to avoid both shortages and surpluses.

Lay argued that the problems created by preexisting regulation required a regulated transition:

> The lack of immediate success in [our] renegotiation efforts should not be construed to mean that the industry cannot function free of government control; Transco maintains that the industry can function in a free market to the ultimate benefit of all involved. There are, nonetheless, difficulties in correcting problems within the same regulated environment which led to the problems initially. Until such time as the industry is allowed to function in a deregulated environment, and the rigidities of thirty years of regulation are removed, attempts to solve market ordering problems will continue to be difficult, if not impossible.

---

26. For example, Transco in November 1982 invited 80 of its producer-suppliers to discuss contract reformation. Sixty-five attended the meeting where Transco proposed substituting a new contract provision allowing the company to prospectively apportion takes based on the size of the market. Of the 65 attendees, 38 were open to contract renegotiation, but only 2 accepted something close to Transco's proposal.

Transco's policy proposal toward oil was quite different from its proposal for natural gas. Ronald Reagan decontrolled petroleum in January 1981, and falling oil prices were hurting Transco every which way. A direct downside was less income for Transco Exploration Company's oil properties—and a lesser valuation for its oil reserves. An indirect result was lower natural gas prices for TXC from greater competition in dual-fuel markets. Taken together, the subsidiary that had first turned profitable in August 1980 and accounted for nearly one-third of Transco's consolidated earnings in 1981 was back in the red in the second half of 1982. "This company has invested $2 billion in its exploration effort," TXC's new chief John Lollar fretted, "and it's the exploration subsidiary that ought to be reporting profits." In fact, Transco's finding costs were high by industry standards, and the price environment was no longer forgiving.[27]

Transco's $113 million equity interest in the Great Plains Coal Gasification Project was in trouble even with most of its construction cost underwritten by taxpayers. Spot-gas prices were less than half the maximum price that the coal-gas was authorized to receive by FERC. No one, including TGPL, which was committed to buy a fourth of the project's output, wanted gas at that price. Government price guarantees and rolled-in pricing—under which the cost of Great Plains gas would be averaged down by all the other gas in a pipeline's mix—were now necessary for the project to be completed. Perhaps Ken Lay had conveniently forgotten about it, but his incremental-pricing initiative back at the FPC was exactly what Great Plains had to avoid![28]

Transco's long bet on commodity prices hurt in other ways. Falling fuel-oil prices made gas-price renegotiations harder for TGPL's special marketing programs. Transco's coal market investment was also on the wrong end of price trends.

Energy and politics were tied at the hip, and it was a small step for Jack Bowen to embrace a quick fix to the predicament that was not of the free-market variety. Lay, schooled in pragmatic politics, wholeheartedly agreed. In Transco's *1982 Annual Report,* the two advocated a stiff federal tax on imported oil as "consistent with the nation's policy of reducing dependence on foreign energy supplies and encouraging further development of our domestic resources." Getting oil prices back up and keeping them up was required to aid Great Plains, a project whose economics required 30 years of high gas prices. "Transco urges that

---

27. Gamble Baldwin, energy specialist at First Boston Corp., rated Transco Energy's stock a "weak hold" in the fall of 1982 when it was priced at $35 per share, down from a high of $64¼ in November 1980. One of his concerns was TXC's production costs. "It cost them a great deal of money to find reserves quickly, and their finding costs are very high compared to what they get for their gas and oil," Baldwin said. And, in fact, without new investment, TXC was self-liquidating, with its high production rates and natural reservoir decline.

28. See chapter 8, p. 294.

we not lose sight, in this short-term period of apparent surplus of oil and natural gas, of the long-term need for synthetic fuels to replace our diminishing domestic supplies," Bowen and Lay said. "Only with the use of our abundant coal, peat, and oil shale resources can we be assured that we will not have to return to a dangerous reliance on imported energy."[29]

The three pillars of Transco's national energy policy were natural gas price decontrol with contract abrogation, oil tariffs, and synfuel price guarantees. Few companies had embraced so much government intervention, but then few were tied in so many ways to the need for higher energy prices. Transco's stock price was off by half since its late-1980s peak, and there was no way out without a price recovery. The good news was that Transco's innovative gas-marketing programs were buoying pipeline throughput, and the pipeline was the cash cow of the corporation.

Looking Ahead

The early 1980s were a happy time at Transco, with good financial results, a dream team at the top (Bowen and Lay), and the completion of a beautiful new headquarters building for 1,500 area employees. Constructed next to the first Transco Tower, five miles west of downtown Houston in the Galleria area, the 64-story, 901-foot, glass-and-anodized-aluminum Transco Tower was designed by Philip Johnson and John Burgee, masters of their field.[30]

Bowen's Florida Gas Company Building was a thing of beauty for 1970s suburbia; the Transco Tower was a building for the ages. The art deco recreation was as big a monument as ever created in the energy industry—and one reflecting the persona of an artistically inclined chairman.[31] The Empire State Building of the south, the Transco Tower's open house in April 1983 for a crowd of 2,000 included a visit from a costumed King Kong himself.

The 1984 stockholders' meeting was held May 9 at the spacious new Transco auditorium. Jack Bowen reported the company's financial position as "the

---

29. Transco's coal-gasification project and purchase of coal properties had the full support of Ken Lay, who was concerned about the adequacy of the natural gas resource base. See Internet appendix 9.5, "Ken Lay on Coal and Coal Gasification," at www.politicalcapitalism. org/Book2/Chapter9/Appendix5.html.

30. "The dean of American architects," Johnson had an avant-garde architectural style that influenced Frank Gehry, whose "complex, seemingly irrational" architecture would be part of an Enron publicity campaign in 2000–2001.

31. *Architecture* magazine described the exterior of the new Houston landmark as follows: "Through a number of sleight of hand tricks … [the structure] continually confounds its viewers with the seemingly opposite qualities of transparency and opaqueness…. The glass enables the building to change colors almost instantly. Depending on the light, at one moment it will be blue or green, at another gray or black. At sunset … it resembles a 'gold ingot.'"

Figure 9.9 Artistic Jack Bowen built a monument to his company and himself in the $200-million, 64-story Transco Tower, located in the Galleria area of Houston. The art deco building, codesigned by Philip Johnson (upper right), stands as one of America's beautiful skyscrapers and the largest outside of a central business district.

strongest in history." Ken Lay, the future of the company, spoke of exciting days ahead. "Transco will be looking into new projects, such as gas-fired cogeneration and carbon dioxide transportation," he said. "We might also look into acquiring other companies in 1984, searching for a good strategic fit with other exploration, production or pipeline operations." Indeed, mergers were reshaping the industry, and Ken Lay, an innovator at heart, was ready to reshape the company.

On the marketing front, Ken Lay and Transco were driving the pipeline side of what would become the U.S. Natural Gas Clearinghouse (NGC), a spot-gas brokering company. In late 1983, discussions began with the concept's originators, the New York investment banking firm of Morgan Stanley & Company and the Washington law firm of Akin, Gump, Strauss, Hauer & Feld. The next spring, Lay hosted his pipeline counterparts in the Transco boardroom in hopes of getting the brokerage house off the ground. Transco was not the only carrier needing to have more competitively priced gas bought and sold on its system, and the more pipelines that were in the program, the better it would be for each participant as co-owner.

There was particular reason for Transco to get out front, just as it had by creating the nation's first special marketing program some months before. Transco had severe take-or-pay problems and more contracted gas than a market for that gas. Thus the company was interested in new ways to increase sales. But there was also defense: Transco feared open-access rules, which might allow spot gas to overtake its system on someone else's terms.

"We're not in it for the money," said Brian O'Neill of the new initiative. "We are in it to prove a point." The point was that the industry could voluntarily create a national pipeline grid short of being forced to do so under FERC action. The goal was to get spot-gas deals done in less than one week! And even if Transco did not make money off the transaction, it could save money by avoiding take-or-pay.

As it turned out, Transco would become the first of six pipeline member/ owners to join Morgan Stanley and Akin, Gump, followed by Colorado Interstate Gas, Columbia Gas Transmission, El Paso Natural Gas, United Gas Pipeline, and Houston Natural Gas. NGC opened for business in July 1984 on Transco's 40th floor with employees borrowed from its eight member/owners. After reorganizing in late 1985, the company that would be renamed Dynegy 13 years later became a force in natural gas marketing alongside the spot-gas affiliates of pipeline companies and a few other independents.[32]

Take-or-pay was a big and growing company problem, but Lay was getting his hands around that, too. He began by having Transco's senior vice president of gas supply and regulatory affairs, Claude Mullendore, lay out the specifics of the problem. Marketing, legal, and finance then fashioned the boundaries of an acceptable settlement, whereupon Lay took over, personally calling on the production company's top executive to put negotiations on a fast track.

There was reason to be proactive. Producers needed cash flow, not nonpayment and litigation; Transco needed to eliminate uncertainty for its stockholders. A charge to earnings would clear the decks and increase Transco's ability to market price-competitive gas. Public-utility regulation would allow at least some cost recovery in rates, another negotiation that Lay could handle.

Lay knew something else. The problem would not go away, and it could grow worse, especially since the untaken gas would keep coming back to TGPL for more claims.

Transco's 1984 First-Quarter Report announced resolution of several hundred million dollars of potential producer claims, including one settlement for $140 million. "Negotiations continue with producers to resolve remaining

---

32. John Barr of Morgan Stanley and Jim Rogers of Akin Gump originated the idea of a national spot-gas marketing entity, but Ken Lay can be considered the third founder because of his work with pipelines. NGC is further described in chapter 1 of *Enron and Ken Lay: An American Tragedy* (Book 3).

Figure 9.10 Ken Lay, who increasingly assumed day-to-day operations in his three years at Transco, was a compelling communicator to employees and Wall Street. Resolving take-or-pay problems and creating spot markets for gas off of TGPL were his two top priorities.

take-or-pay obligations," the interim report said, and a further adverse material impact was not expected. This encouraging message was different from what Lay (hat in hand) had told Congress two years before in support of a legislative fix.

Another agreement with Superior Oil Company (Lay worked directly with Finis Martin, Superior's president) was all but signed. On the table were other offers whereby the producers would take cash and release their supply into Transco's special marketing programs.

Lay Leaves Transco

It had been an interesting and productive three years at Transco for Ken Lay. He had run the nation's largest gas pipeline expertly. He had overseen the formation of special marketing programs, including the nation's very first spot-market program for gas. Take-or-pay settlements were promising, although much was left to do. Ken was as well liked as Jack Bowen inside the company and highly respected by Wall Street. A rebounding stock price from a 1982 low was attributed in part to "Lay's credibility and his bold and unique accomplishments." Bowen and Lay were the most revered top-management team in the interstate gas business. And last but not least, certainly for a highly regulated company, FERC saw him as one of their number who had graduated to the top.

Lay relished the big leagues. Transco's stock symbol—"E" as in Energy—said it all. The Transco Tower, adjoined by a 3-acre grass park, jogging track,

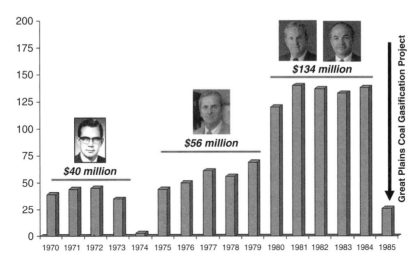

Figure 9.11 Jack Bowen, and then Bowen and Ken Lay, led Transco's financial turnaround between 1975 and 1984. Transco's income would plunge in 1985 because of a write-off of the company's equity in the Great Plains Coal Gasification Project.

64 -foot Water Wall, and 7,000-watt rotating beacon light visible from as far as 30 miles away, was the talk of the town. The resplendent structure created a corporate culture of its own, complete with an exercise facility and locker rooms (a perk pioneered by Tenneco in downtown Houston some years before), a health center with a corporate nurse, a 370-seat cafeteria, and multiple private dining rooms. There was a large employee lounge and an education center. There were skywalks to the garage and neighboring Galleria shopping mall. Transco's beautiful lobby boasted an art gallery hosting regular exhibits. The corporate offices and boardroom were luxurious, a real eye-opener for visitors. And Transco's just-off-the-assembly-line Lear Jets made travel easy—as did the helipad that ferried executives from the top of the garage to the airport.

Such an environment was reminiscent of what Samuel Insull, some decades before, had fashioned for his workforce at Commonwealth Edison, Peoples Gas, and Public Service Company of Northern Illinois. And it would be the corporate culture that would sparkle at Enron some years later.

The company was setting a new standard in the once-staid natural gas pipeline business, and Ken Lay was in the middle of it. It was fun being successful—and bringing success and satisfaction to thousands of energized employees. The stock price surge was certainly helping Lay financially, although Bowen's compensation structure was not all that aggressive. Still, Lay was happy and not looking for a professional change. It would just happen.

∽

In January 1984, Oscar Wyatt's Coastal Corporation made an unsolicited bid for Houston Natural Gas Corporation (HNG), a major event that is described in greater detail in chapter 13. Coastal was headquartered between Transco and HNG in Houston's Greenway Plaza. Wyatt was an industry maverick and persona non grata to M. D. "Bill" Matthews, CEO of HNG, and to Jack Bowen as well. Consequently, Transco was approached by HNG to be a white knight, whereupon Ken Lay became his company's representative with HNG's board of directors.

John Duncan, the chair of HNG's executive committee, thought highly of Ken from their charity work together. And the rest of the board soon came to be impressed by the 42-year-old's affable, efficient style, not to mention his Horatio Alger–like life story and stellar industry reputation.

By contrast, Matthews's nondescript tenure as CEO at HNG was put under severe strain by Coastal's hostile offer, which itself could have been avoided if Matthews had seriously entertained a prior merger overture from El Paso Natural Gas. After an expensive standstill agreement was signed with Coastal, the subject of chapter 13, Duncan called Jack Bowen, explaining the desire of HNG's board to replace Matthews as chairman and chief executive officer. Could he speak to Ken Lay about the position? Things proceeded quickly, and Ken Lay's last day at Transco and first day at HNG was Friday, June 8, 1984.

"If I were 42, I would probably do the same thing," Jack Bowen told the press, which was curious about how Transco could lose such a rising star just a few years before Bowen was scheduled to relinquish the CEO title. "I think he's a great guy, and I wish him every success," Bowen continued. "After all, I've trained him twice."

It was a smiles-all-around, somewhat strange because HNG was gaining what Transco was losing, which was a lot by all indications.

Transco's stock price on Lay's last day was $38\frac{1}{8}$, compared to $43\frac{3}{4}$ on his first. In real terms, it had fallen 10 percent more. Yet this was a pretty good performance considering that oil prices had fallen by almost a third when adjusted for inflation in the 37-month period, and the gas pipeline industry was in turmoil.

The good news was that Transco's debt-to-capitalization was below 50 percent for the first time in its history, and the company's credit rating had been upgraded to "A" by Moody's and by Standard and Poor's. A letter-of-intent signed with the Department of Energy would provide up to $790 million in price supports for the coal-gas produced by the nearly completed Great Plains project.

In short, Transco had held up well in a very tough market, and Lay as COO could take credit for Transco's reputation as *the* most innovative pipeline company in the industry. His Industrial Sales Program (1983) began a series of innovative spot-gas programs. Lay's hires were working out well: John Lollar, exploration and production; Grant Sims, spot-gas marketing; and Jim Wise and

John Clark, finance. Still, Jack Bowen was not ready to retain Lay if it meant accelerating his own retirement by several years and redoing Lay's remuneration package, which would also mean redoing the packages of his other senior executives. So, he let his protégé go.

George Slocum Takes Over

Jack Bowen quickly moved on Lay's replacement. Given his age (62), Bowen felt that he could not leave the presidency open. Wall Street needed to be reassured with a confident move. Bowen had two internal candidates: George Slocum (43) from finance and Brian O'Neill (48) from the legal/pipeline side. To some on Transco's board, neither candidate was so self-evidently stellar as to preclude an external search. But Bowen, forceful and beloved, did not want to disturb morale by searching externally. O'Neill was a good lawyer but not financially savvy like a Selby Sullivan, Bowen thought. So his choice was George Slocum, which meant a promotion for others.

Transco's board of directors immediately named Slocum president and chief operating officer, effective June 9, 1984, the very first day that Lay was not on the payroll. Bowen remained chairman and CEO, and Brian O'Neill, who had joined Transco back in 1975, was elected president of TGPL and a member of the board of directors. Jim Wise was promoted to replace Slocum as CFO.

Bowen praised the new team:

> We are proud of the quality and depth of the management team at Transco, and with these new management appointments, we will be continuing a strong management effort. Ken Lay is recognized as one of the outstanding leaders in the natural gas industry. He has made a significant contribution in his three years at Transco, and we wish him the best in his new endeavors.

The quick action surprised many inside the company, beginning with Slocum himself. He had not envisioned himself as a president and CEO-in-waiting of a company like Transco. But he was delighted with the promotion, at ease working with Jack Bowen, and confident about the health of the company. It was not wholly different from the sudden promotion of HNG's Bill Matthews three years before.

For his part, Lay expected Bowen to reassume the president's title and give some time to the selection of Lay's successor, who, after all, would really be Transco's next CEO. Brian O'Neill, more surprised than disappointed at the choice of Slocum, had plenty to do after his promotion. Still, there were rumblings inside the Transco Tower. Everyone knew, or just about everyone except Bowen, that George Slocum was no Ken Lay. Slocum certainly was untested.

The stock price firmed through the brief management transfer and jumped by one-fourth several weeks later. The surge in "E" reflected a new dividend policy, which was in the works before Lay left. Transco Energy shareholders were given shares of Transco Exploration Partners (TXP), a master limited partnership that had assumed the assets of TXC the year before.[33] This one-sixteenth allocation (about 5 percent of the company's value) increased the dividend payout to $7 from $2 per share. It was a great start for a rookie president, and Slocum vowed to communicate effectively Transco's "innovative trendsetter" story to stakeholders for continued momentum.

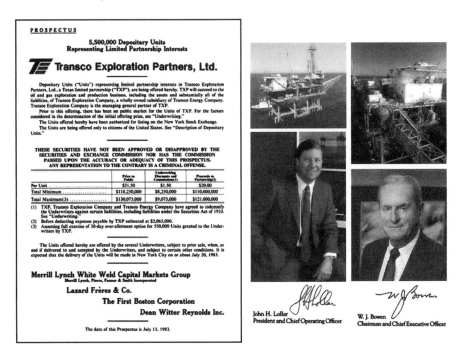

Figure 9.12 Transco Exploration Company (TXC) transferred its growing assets in 1983 to a newly formed Master Limited Partnership, Transco Exploration Partners (TXP), which enjoyed success under CEO John Lollar before energy prices collapsed in 1986. TXP was liquidated by 1992, whereupon a small subsidiary, Transco Exploration and Production Company (TEPCO), would produce modest amounts of oil and gas in the Gulf of Mexico.

But things changed quietly yet unmistakably with Lay's departure. Claude Mullendore, the point man for producer-contract problems, was instructed to disengage. The new take-or-pay strategy was litigation, in which Transco would plead commercial impracticability under the Uniform Commercial Code. The

---

33. The special dividend came from Transco Energy's 89 percent holding of the NYMEX-listed TXP, with 11 percent already distributed in an initial public offering. TXC was the managing general partner of TXP, which held Transco Energy's majority interest.

unspoken reason was a belief at the top that supply would tighten and prices rise to alleviate the problem. Or a legislative solution might emerge. It was the easy thing for Slocum to do given all the legal talent he had on tap that welcomed business-by-litigation. And Bowen above him and O'Neill below him obviously did not disagree.

The Lay-led Superior Oil agreement did not receive final signatures, and Superior soon filed a $61 million damage suit against Transco for breach of contract. Other active take-or-pay negotiations quieted.[34] Disillusioned, Mullendore, an 18-year company veteran, took early retirement from Transco and moved to Dallas to work with a new company. But as it would turn out, there would be future take-or-pay work for him with Ken Lay at Enron.

∾

After pipeline-led earnings produced a solid 1984, Transco bit the bullet by writing off its entire equity investment in Great Plains. There was little choice, inasmuch as natural gas was selling at half the cost of what it took to manufacture coal-gas. The $92 million after-tax charge left 1985's net income at $18 million, which was 1974 redux for Jack Bowen. Supplemental gas failed back then, and it failed now. The charge to earnings would have been bigger had take-or-pay problems been addressed (companies usually like to clean house at one time), but Transco was embarking on a new bet—that the gas surplus, or bubble, would moderate, and settlements, somehow, someway, would be less in the future than they would be now.

In their first stockholders letter, Bowen and Slocum promised that Transco's superior talent would turn challenge into opportunity, just as it had in the recent past. There was no Ken Lay to lead this time around, but the stock price was strong. In fact, with merger fever in the midstream gas industry, Transco's stock reached $61.25 per share in early 1986. The rumor was that Wagner & Brown, a Midland-based oil and gas producer that had earlier bid on Midcon Corporation, was interested. Other large producers, such as Exxon, Shell, and Amoco, were reputedly on the hunt. In response, Transco fortified its antitakeover defenses. Some combination of overconfidence, even arrogance, was at work. And Bowen, in retrospect, was missing his big chance to go out on top.

Transco's best efforts in 1986 were no match for the nearly one-half plunge of crude oil prices (from a 1985's $24 per barrel to 1986's $12.50 per barrel[35]) that brought natural gas and coal prices down as well. Transco's unregulated

---

34. Brian O'Neill told Congress in November 1985 (about 17 months after Lay's departure) that Transco's strategy was "not to pay out dollars," because the amount was too big to absorb, and if it was allowed pass-through, the resulting rates would be so high as to ruin markets, creating a death spiral.

35. In today's dollars, the fall in crude prices was from about $50 to $26 per barrel.

gas-trading subsidiary, Transco Energy Marketing Company (TEMCO), actively bought and sold 30-day spot gas under the new FERC transportation rules to keep TGPL deliveries competitive with fuel oil in dual-fuel markets. But in about every other way, the company was losing. Bowen could do little more than extol protectionism as the missing cornerstone of an effective national energy policy. He proposed a variable oil-import fee that would set a floor price of $25 per barrel, twice the price of crude in 1986 but about the average price in 1985.

Taking the argument to Capitol Hill, president George Slocum described how fuel-oil cargoes in Transco's market were selling for $15 per barrel (about $30 per barrel today), equating to a gas price of $2.50/MMBtu at the burner tip and below $2.00/MMBtu at the wellhead. "I think anybody that has been in the E&P [exploration and production] business knows that you have to be superexplorer over time to be able to find, develop, and get a satisfactory return on your investment at [that price]," he told a Senate subcommittee as part of Transco's testimony espousing an oil-import fee.

Things got no better in 1987. TGPL had not put its take-or-pay liabilities to bed in the 19 months since Lay's departure. Now the problem was much worse. In 1987, an $81 million write-off relating to producer settlements and litigation costs resulted in the largest quarterly loss in company history and brought the cumulative payouts to $688 million. But that was not all. Cash flow fell farther when TGPL, nominally an open-access transporter under a new FERC regulation (Order 436), suspended transportation to reduce its growing take-or-pay liabilities, preferring to operate as a merchant pipeline, a complicated strategy.[36] Closing TGPL to outside transportation ten months after opening for such service pursuant to FERC Order 436 reduced throughput and inconvenienced customers, although those that did buy gas paid higher rates to nominally help Transco with its wellhead obligations.

The news just got worse. A $75.5 million loss in 1987 necessitated cutting the dividend by half and paring capital expenditures by one-third. Transco's stock price dipped below $20 per share for the first time in nearly a decade. And the write-off did not end the problem as most write-offs do.

⋗◌⋖

Transco took time from its troubles to celebrate the passing of the CEO baton from 65-year-old Jack Bowen to George Slocum, 46, effective June 1, 1987. Expressing confidence in Transco's leadership ("I couldn't be more confident

---

36. The regulatory-driven difference between a *merchant* interstate pipeline that buys and sells gas as system supply and an *open-access* pipeline (pursuant to Order 436) that transports gas bought and sold by others (producers, marketers, or endusers) is explained in Internet appendix 1.4 to *Enron and Ken Lay: An American Tragedy* (Book 3), at www.politicalcapitalism. org/Book3/Chapter1/Appendix4.html.

that I'm leaving the company in the hands of the best management team in our industry"), Bowen, still chairman, planned to spend a third of his time working on company business—specifically, energy issues in Washington and Transco's charity work (as chairman of the United Way's annual Houston campaign).

The celebration included a look back at Bowen's life and career in *HotTap*. The retrospective included a comment from "Dr. Kenneth Lay, a close friend who worked for Jack as president and chief operating officer before becoming chairman of Enron Corp. in 1984." Lay said: "It's easier to *be* chairman than it is to *work* for the chairman." Bowen chuckled at that one. But no reader could have known the full meaning of those words for Lay's ultimate fate. Ken Lay, under a strong chairman, knew his business and exercised financial discipline. He had to.

Things were so different and positive at Enron, which also had interstate pipelines and exploration/production. Lay's team, which now included Claude Mullendore, was resolving Enron's take-or-pay problem once and for all. Enron made itself much less sensitive than Transco to commodity prices by creating the deepest and most profitable natural gas marketing company in the industry, something Lay's early work at Transco had portended. Ex-Transco marketer John Esslinger was leading Enron's charge. Another new profit center for Enron—building and operating gas-fired cogeneration plants—was something Lay was working on before he left Transco.[37] Such was the tale of two companies, or really two leaders, George Slocum and Ken Lay.

·◌·

Things were coming unglued at Transco. Brian O'Neill, a board director and nominally number three at the company (as head of Transco Gas Company, the parent of TGPL, TEMCO, and Transco Gas Gathering Company), resigned in November 1987. The month before, in a move that admittedly made him "toast," O'Neill had met with the board, sans Slocum, to urge a change at the top. Jack Bowen was there, dutifully listening as O'Neill outlined the reasons why Transco needed to tap the outside market for new leadership. It had been an excruciating two and a half years for O'Neill after Lay departed. Slocum had torpedoed some of O'Neill's carefully vetted plans, sometimes arbitrarily and to the surprise of just about everyone. Transco was headed in the wrong direction, although the status quo–oriented board was not going to rock the boat—at least not until Jack Bowen concurred. O'Neill knew he had lost when a board member asked, "Brian, can't you just be loyal to George?" To which O'Neill

---

37. Cogeneration used less energy to produce the same quantity of steam and power compared to prior technologies. Thus it became politically favored under the Public Utility Regulatory Policies Act of 1978 (PURPA), a federal law requiring utilities to buy a "qualifying" plant's output at a state-hearing-determined "avoided cost." See Internet appendix 1.1 (Book 3), at www.politicalcapitalism.org/Book3/Chapter1/Appendix1.html.

replied, "I have no case against George personally, but as Directors our obligation is to shareholders and not to individuals."

The news of O'Neill's departure rocked the industry. He was one of the most respected names in the business, personally and professionally. Had he not been recently elected chairman of the Interstate Natural Gas Association of America, the pipeline trade association? O'Neill resigned his position at INGAA at the same time that he was dismissed from Transco. Hal Miller, who had been a very high profile member of Transco's FERC strategy, and an ally of O'Neill, was purged too. Grant Sims, who had also been in the O'Neill/Miller camp urging the ouster of Slocum, bailed out of the coup attempt and was rewarded in the ensuing restructuring, reporting straight to Slocum with O'Neill gone.

It was dramatic corporate politics—and not good for Transco, no matter how powerful Jack Bowen's words on behalf of his CEO. Transco needed talent, and some of Transco's best were now gone, including some who were working for Ken Lay at Enron.

More Problems

In 1988, Transco remained in the red with what it described as "higher than anticipated [take-or-pay] settlement costs and management's assessment of the status of [future claims from ongoing] negotiations." Transco Exploration Partners, having become a top-20 U.S. oil and gas producer, was now executing an exit strategy. The white flag at TXP had been raised in the face of a 50 percent plunge in oil and gas prices since 1983. "Despite efforts to significantly reduce costs, persistently low oil and gas prices have resulted in continuing losses and sharply reduced cash flow from operations," TXP CEO John Lollar explained. One-fourth of its properties were sold and the rest put up for sale. A fourth of Transco coal properties were sold, and Petro Source, an oil and liquids marketer purchased from Enron three years before, was sold at a loss.

But Transco was not yet ready to completely exit the exploration and production business. With TXP winding down, Transco Exploration and Production Company (TEPCO) was formed to explore in the Gulf of Mexico, with John Lollar as president and CEO. However, a brand new find in West Chalkley, Louisiana, a farm-out to Exxon USA, would keep TXP alive until August 1992.[38]

With capital to redeploy, Transco in late 1988 agreed to acquire Texas Gas Transmission Corporation (TGTC), a 6,000-mile interstate pipeline to the north of Transco's southern system. Bowen and Slocum called the $853 million purchase "an excellent strategic fit with Transco's existing pipeline businesses." Industry analyst John Olson of Drexel Burnham Lambert was pleased. "I think that

---

38. TXP would make liquidating distributions of $9.50 per share in 1989 and $1.06 per share in 1992, the former funded by property sales to Amerada Hess for $902 million, and the latter funded by the $82 million sale of the West Chalkley field.

Transco has pulled a rabbit out of the hat," he said, citing his expectation for a net increase in earnings and cash flow, and the prospect for growing gas demand in TGT's rust-belt markets. However, he noted, "Transco's balance sheet gets a lot more leverage," and "Wall Street and the banks do not like leverage."

The acquisition could not be a company savior. With a regulated rate of return, seller and buyer knew what the asset was worth. Still, it was a predictable income generator, which made it safe and probably the best move of the Slocum/Bowen era.

Figure 9.13 Transco's purchase of Texas Gas Transmission in 1988 was a safe, lateral integration. Texas Gas, headquartered in Owensboro, Kentucky, extended from the Louisiana Gulf to Indiana and Ohio. The 6,000-mile pipeline is shown next to TGPL's 10,000-mile system.

Transco was "predominantly a natural gas services company," the *1988 Annual Report* stated. Ninety-two percent of the company's capital expenditures were gas related. "Natural gas is the fuel of choice," the annual report announced. "A solid foundation for future growth and profitability has been laid." But all this seemed a far cry from what Ken Lay and Enron were doing with their natural gas strategy.

In 1989, Transco reported earnings of $89 million, its first profit in three years. "Restructuring completed, 1989 goals accomplished," the annual report gushed. It was the first light since Slocum had taken Ken Lay's chair five and a half years before. But at the core, things were badly awry. A complicated, multi-issue rate-case agreement between TGPL and its customers, implemented April 1, blew up. Customer agreement was very important and could be counted on to carry great weight at FERC. But regulators had to approve any settlement before it could be implemented. Yet Transco made fundamental business changes pursuant to the customer agreement three days before making its interim settlement filing at FERC—in violation of the Natural Gas Act. FERC Commissioner Elizabeth Moler called Transco's action "outrageous"; fellow commissioner Martha Hesse called it "arrogant." Ever jealous of their statutory authority, Moler called Transco's unilateral action "a cynical, premeditated attempt to evade our regulation under the gas act and the NGPA. The fact that it was implemented on April Fool's Day is fitting."

The Commission came down hard, citing numerous violations of federal law and issuing a cease-and-desist order. The July order, quickly accepted by Transco, forced the company to return to its pre-April practices. "FERC Scrambles Transco; Customers Eye $50 Million Cost," *Natural Gas Week* reported. Slocum could only meekly tell his employees, "Members of the commission seemed to have been upset that TGPL implemented the settlement before they had a chance to review it."

That would have never happened under Brian O'Neill.

Another problem made Transco the dunce of the industry to regulators—and just about everyone else. At about the same time as the April Fool's flap, FERC issued a show-cause order citing "at least 22 separate violations of the Commission's regulations" with regard to construction of a 123-mile gas line in Alabama. Transco had not received federal authority for the Mobile Bay Pipeline despite offering jurisdictional transportation services. Nor had Transco complied with FERC policy regarding the excavation of archeological sites. A $37 million fine was levied, which would be settled along with other FERC enforcement actions in 1991 for approximately $35 million—the largest fine ever levied by FERC and one of the largest by any federal agency. As part of one settlement, the 100 employees of Transco's spot-gas subsidiary, Transco Energy Marketing Company (TEMCO), were ordered out of the Transco Tower into a separate building to avoid violations of Order 497, the marketing-affiliate rule.

⌖

The rate-case debacle was the beginning of the end for George Slocum. His major fault was his indecisiveness. He was "too nice a guy," one board member remembered, prone to accept what others wanted him to do rather than reach consensus with his managers and order what *he* wanted done. The strategy among his subordinates in either-or situations was to "get to him last." Factionalism was rampant. A skilled CEO would have also known the minutiae of the gas business—including the all-important winds at FERC—in order to lead and win rather than be led and victimized.

In March 1991, time ran out on George Slocum. Take-or-pay settlements aggregating $1.1 billion—the FERC-approved ceiling for partial recovery—had not put the company into the clear. Ten claims totaling more than a half-billion dollars from gas producers were outstanding without prospect for partial recovery in rates. The company faced a $140 million potential cost disallowance from FERC, as well as a $170 million lawsuit filed by the state of Alabama over the Mobile Bay indiscretions. A coalbed methane project in Alabama's Black Warrior Basin, the project of Sandy McCormick of McCormick Oil & Gas Company, was a technical failure and financial headache. Income from the nonregulated (nonpipeline) gas activities was lackluster because of declining sales and squeezed margins. Transco's capital expenditures were down to the company's meager cash flow, and $1.8 billion of total company debt, figuring to a debt-to-capital ratio of 67 percent, was burdensome. Stockholders equity in the last six years had fallen by almost half. A stock that had rebounded to $50 per share in 1989 had dropped by half and was sinking fast.

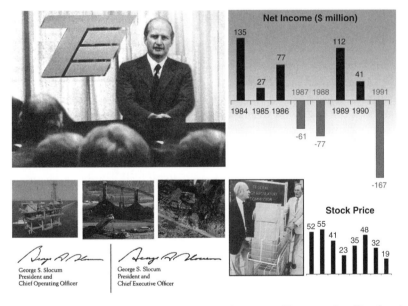

Figure 9.14 George Slocum, Jack Bowen's choice to run Transco after Ken Lay left in mid-1984, was brought down by a collapse in energy prices and managerial failings. Take-or-pay liabilities; soured ventures in oil and gas production, coal mining, and coal seam gas; and TGPL's regulatory problems severely depressed earnings and the parent's stock price.

Jack Bowen broke the news to his protégé. Slocum's firing was a defeat for both men. Bowen had hand-picked Slocum as president, believing that Transco would not miss a beat after Ken Lay left for Houston Natural Gas. Bowen had given his CEO title to Slocum three years later, believing that things were getting back on track. George was a dear friend. So was his wife, Priscilla, an expert swimmer who had come to Jack's rescue when the tides rushed in during a beach walk on the Isle of Guernsey. But this ignoble end for George Slocum should have come sooner. It had been more than three years since Brian O'Neill bet and lost his job over the performance of an able, decent man who had been promoted one time too many, not unlike Monty Mitchell before at Transco just two CEOs before him, and not unlike Bill Matthews down the street at Houston Natural Gas, the man whose firing was the catalyst for HNG's hiring Ken Lay to give Slocum his chance at the big time in 1984.

New Leadership

George Slocum resigned effective March 22, 1991, thanking everyone for his 12 years at Transco, as well as his "splendid opportunity" as CEO during the last four.[39] Calling George "one of the best young men that I've ever known," Bowen, still chairman, jumped back in as interim CEO. The board embarked on the course it should have taken seven years before: conducting an external search for the next president and CEO.

There was plenty of blame to go around. Fossil-fuel prices had fallen nearly 50 percent during his reign as markets adjusted to artificially high energy prices globally (oil prices) and in North America (natural gas and coal prices).[40] In fact, when Slocum resigned, oil, gas, and coal prices were at about the level, adjusted for inflation, they had been when Bowen joined the company in 1974.

Bowen had made most of the big bets on the future strength of commodity prices. Transco director Henry Groppe, the founding principal of Groppe, Long & Littell, industry consultants, had provided the forecasts that the gas glut was going away and that energy prices would firm. Still, the buck stopped with

---

39. As commonly happens in the corporate world, the firing was presented as a personal, voluntary decision. Slocum characterized the decision as his own and "an extremely difficult one." Bowen for his part told the press that he "personally regretted, but understood, Slocum's decision."

40. The unprecedented rise in world oil prices between 1973 and 1981 resulted from political control of oil production in the Middle East, not from free-market forces. Such prices allowed (competing) natural gas prices to rise as well in North America. The unintended consequences of federal price controls on energy—a fall in drilling activity, reserves, and deliverability—also caused prices to rise. Without international politics and domestic regulation, energy prices would have been flatter, creating a much better climate for business decisions.

Slocum. He could not or would not step into Lay's shoes and aggressively settle take-or-pay claims with Claude Mullendore at his side. The liability problem worsened with falling gas prices, and untaken gas just kept coming back for more claims, claims that held up in court.[41] Transco had repeatedly run afoul of regulators in a variety of ways, triggering myriad lawsuits. The company doubled its bet on coal at an inopportune time. Factionalism ran rampant. It all pointed to one thing: George Slocum was not CEO timber for a company of Transco's size and complexity.

Bowen promised a turnaround with "a little help from the weather, energy prices and some favorable decisions from Washington." He assured employees that the board would "select the best possible person to lead this company through the 1990s." Bowen reminded the troops that Transco was the "low-cost supplier to the eastern half of the United States," and gas was the fuel of the future. But when could Transco return to a nine-figure annual net income, which was easily within its allowed rate of return on invested capital under FERC guidelines? The years of rebound (1975–79) and prosperity (1980–84) seemed like an eternity ago.

·◇·

Transco found its new president and CEO in an interstate petroleum pipeline veteran who had most recently headed a NYSE-listed company, Los Angeles–based Santa Fe Pacific Pipelines. John DesBarres, 52, began at Transco on October 1, 1991, 17 years to the day after Jack Bowen arrived to revitalize the company. What greeted DesBarres was near chaos. In the last weeks of September, a double whammy sent Transco's stock price down almost 30 percent.

The first setback was an aborted sale of TXP's last major asset in the Chalkley field in Louisiana. In response, Standard & Poor's downgraded Transco's credit rating to BB+ from BBB, and the company released an advisory that it "is neither experiencing or [sic] expecting to experience any inability to fund its ongoing capital needs."

A week later, FERC ordered a $50 million customer refund because of its earlier rate-case-implementation snafu. With debt of $2 billion, Transco had a debt-to-capital ratio of 68.5 percent, and the common-equity value was just $590 million. (Enron, by comparison, valued about the same as Transco when Ken Lay took over, was now worth several times more.)

Transco could barely afford such judgments. One FERC commissioner fretted about forcing Transco into bankruptcy, and another commissioner assigned FERC's chief accountant to evaluate the company's condition.

---

41. As summarized in a history of Andrews & Kurth, Transco's outside legal counsel, "in those cases where settlement was not reached and the case was tried, the producers [almost] always won."

"We are in a serious situation," DesBarres told employees on his first day. "Currently, there is too much debt, too many non-performing assets, and not enough earnings." With the new leadership came the resignations of two executives closely aligned with George Slocum: David Mackie, the replacement for Brian O'Neill as head of Transco Gas Company, and Jim Wise, chief financial officer.

A record net loss of $193 million was taken in 1991 to close out the Slocum/Bowen era. The regulated pipelines were money makers, something public-utility regulation not only allowed but also facilitated. But a $213 million multiyear write-off was recorded for the company's failed coalbed methane project,[42] regulatory and legal costs, and restructuring expenses. Transco stock, which had been at $29 per share when Slocum resigned, was falling toward single digits, a "precipitous decline" (DesBarres said) requiring major corrective action if the company were to be kept afloat. The dividend and capital expenditures were slashed by half, and 500 positions were eliminated. Enron, meanwhile, reporting "exceptional" operating and shareholder results, split its stock, and increased its dividend in 1991.

The "new Transco" was defined as pipelines, gas marketing, and power generation. Exit strategies were planned for most everything else—exploration and production, coal, liquids processing, and gas gathering. It was almost back to the James Henderson era but with two flagship pipelines instead of one—and a lot more debt left from failed ventures. The hope was a new beginning.

Bowen, reaching the mandatory retirement age of 70, stepped down in May 1992 to leave DesBarres as chairman, president, and CEO. It was not the exit that Bowen had imagined. A quarter century of success had been marred by the post-1984 swoon. Many could not help imagining how different it might have been if Bowen had accelerated the CEO handoff back in 1984 in order to keep Ken Lay.

Bowen had one last interaction with Transco when he and John Lollar submitted a bid to take Transco Exploration and Production Company private. Formed in 1989 alongside the decision to liquidate TXP, TEPCO had had some success securing blocks and drilling in the Gulf of Mexico. The Bowen/Lollar bid was in the ballpark, but DesBarres sold the company in July 1992 for $45 million to Forrest Oil, a company that had been turned around by Enron financing. For Bowen, it was "the worst business day of my life." The new owner dismissed the entire staff and integrated the operation into its

---

42. A $64 million charge concerned Transco's Alabama coalbed methane venture begun in 1989. A 500-well drilling program resulted in 150 costly, low-volume wells and a badly over-sized pipeline built to move the gas. Even with a generous federal (Section 29) tax credit for coalbed methane production, the 1991 charge of $97 million would be followed by a $70 million charge the next year.

Figure 9.15 Transco's turmoil, which began in 1985, led to new leadership in 1991. John DesBarres, age 52, whose expansion options were very limited owing to the company's debt overhang, would find an ideal merger partner and make a personal exit four years later.

own; Bowen and Lollar had planned to keep the company intact. It was a bitter end to the Transco chapter for Bowen and also for Lollar, whose ten years with Transco were now over.

DesBarres had little better to report for 1992. A net loss of $75 million was incurred from more take-or-pay settlements, coal-seam write-offs, and losses in gas marketing and in Transco's residual coal- and gas-gathering operations. An across-the-board credit downgrade by Standard & Poor's increased Transco's borrowing costs. The stock price bottomed out at $9.50 per share in the second quarter before ending the year at $14.25.

In what amounted to progress for Transco, 1993 neared breakeven with a net loss of $4 million. The stock price stabilized, trading in a range between $13 and $18 per share. The crisis was over, but Transco was hamstrung with debt service that largely offset its large pipeline earnings.

In what would be Transco's last year as an independent company, 1994's net income turned positive for the first time in four years. Volumes on TGPL (1.4 Tcf) and Texas Gas (0.8 Tcf) accounted for 10 percent of national gas usage. But Transco, with its 4,500 employees and $4 billion in assets, was a mighty big operation to simply break even.

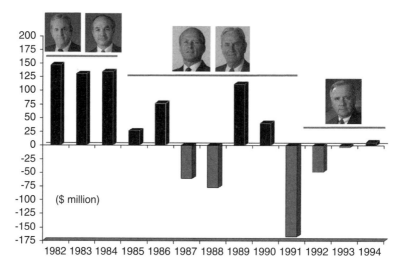

Figure 9.16 Transco's modest profitability in the mid-1980s turned negative, yielding profit in only two years between 1987 and 1994. The company's pipeline rate base was entitled to several hundred million dollars of annual profit, but write-offs, losses, and high debt service drove the final result in net income (net loss).

Transco was back to being an interstate pipeline company but without its best pipeline executive, Brian O'Neill, who was now running the interstate pipeline group of the Williams Companies in Tulsa, Oklahoma. O'Neill, in fact, managed the largest pipeline system in the country next to Enron's. Williams's interstates were

- Northwest Pipeline, the Ray Fish/Robert Herring creation, now a 3,900-mile, 2.5 Bcf/d system;
- Williams Natural Gas, a 6,000-mile, 2.2 Bcf/d system serving five states in the central United States; and
- Kern River Transmission, a new 900-mile, 700 MMcf/d system running from Wyoming to central California.

Little did Brian O'Neill know that his portfolio would soon become the largest in the country with the addition of two pipelines that he knew very well.

Williams Companies

Transco was out of danger, but tough industry conditions and its debt load precluded an expansion strategy. "Operating on a very narrow margin, Transco was vulnerable," a company history related. Transco's stock was lackluster, and the board was weighing its limited alternatives when Williams expressed interest in buying the company.

Williams Companies was flush with cash thanks to a recent agreement to sell for $2.5 billion the voice network service operations of its wholly owned subsidiary, Williams Telecommunications (WilTel), to LDDS Communications. WilTel was a key supplier to LDDS, a company founded in 1983 as Long Distance Discount Services, Inc. Williams had not been looking to sell, but LDDS's chairman, Bernard "Bernie" Ebbers, made an offer. Sensing his eagerness, Williams asked for $500 million more and asked that WilTel be able to retain parts of the business. Ebbers agreed to both conditions, and Williams's CEO, Keith Bailey, announced a sale made at a price reflecting "a substantial strategic premium—by any measure." In fact, it was a good deal for both parties, although later acquisitions by Ebbers and the company soon to be WorldCom would become problematic.[43]

Two factors made the deal particularly attractive for Williams. One was Transco's woeful stock price and the fact that new investment was needed with the pipelines, which represented rate base. Second, Transco's tax-loss carryforwards could offset the extraordinary gain from WilTel's sale to LDDS. From Transco's perspective, any premium to the going stock price was a plus, as was a proven, successful pipeline operator with the means to make pipeline reinvestments.

John DesBarres negotiated with Williams CEO Keith Bailey in the fall of 1994. A deal was struck whereby Williams would purchase Transco's common stock for $17.50 per share, a one-third premium to Transco's recent price of $13 per share. The total acquisition cost, $3.1 billion, comprised equity of $800 million and the assumption of $2.3 billion in debt and preferred stock. The two pipelines—TGPL and Texas Gas—were desired; Williams would sell the coal mining, coalbed methane, and methane extraction assets.

DesBarres and Bailey walked through the merger terms at an all-employee meeting at the Transco Tower on December 12, 1994. Transco veterans were

---

43. The Ebbers/WorldCom saga, which eclipsed Enron's bankruptcy filing as the largest in U.S. history at the time, had some similarities to the rise and fall of Ken Lay/Enron. Both companies had a strong period before overexpanding and failing to make midcourse corrections to get back on track. WorldCom, however, was about pure accounting fraud compared to more accounting legerdemain at Enron. Bernie Ebbers described his experience as "fifteen unbelievable years and two very challenging years." In a similar vein, the perennial optimist Ken Lay might have called his tenure 16 good years and 1 bad.

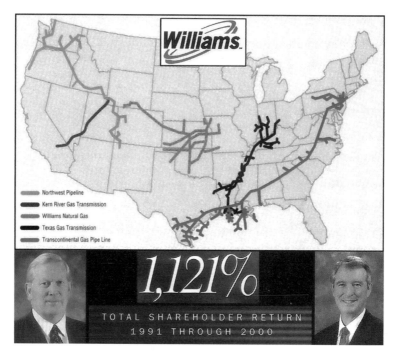

Figure 9.17 Transco's weak balance sheet presented a good purchase opportunity for cash-rich Williams Companies, headed by Keith Bailey (left). After the Transco purchase was consummated in early 1995, ex-Transcoer Brian O'Neill (right) ran TPGL and Texas Gas as head of Williams's Interstate Gas Pipeline Group.

saddened by the loss of Transco's independence just before the company's half-century anniversary (1996), but Williams was an industry leader with a future. Williams's stock had gone up 30 percent in the 1990s, while Transco's was down 65 percent. It was time to change horses—and to a good one at that.

DesBarres praised the "powerful combination," creating a company with five major interstates going "from corner to corner and across the country." Enron was standing pat with its interstate network, bidding on but failing to acquire new gas systems, given its strategy of emphasizing asset-light, unregulated energy trading over regulated iron. Thus, Williams replaced mighty Enron as the new mileage leader.

Bailey lauded the "powerful engine" provided by TGPL and Texas Gas. But the capital-constrained engine was having "trouble doing what it once did best—build, innovate, and serve." Williams announced a $950 million recapitalization program and plans to reenter the nonregulated markets off the two pipelines. It was a good move all around, contributing to a record-setting year at Williams in 1995, one that saw its stock appreciate by 75 percent—from 25⅛ to 43⅞. Transco employees could now share in some success.

Transco was steady on its feet for the first time in a decade. Brian O'Neill, back in the saddle, moved the pipeline group from Tulsa to Houston and the renamed Williams Tower. DesBarres, mission accomplished, took a nice payout and moved back to California.

Retrospective

Transco was victimized by federal price controls that left its nonintegrated pipe-line system imperiled for want of gas in the 1970s, at the same time creating the conditions for what in retrospect was a costly overcorrection. Jack Bowen got Transco out of one ditch (gas shortages) but overaccelerated and put the com-pany into another (gas surpluses).[44] There were periods of glory, as when Bowen was named outstanding chief executive in the natural gas industry (*Financial World*, 1977) and the pipeline industry (*Financial World*, 1980, 1981), and when he was named Man of the Year by the American Gas Association (1982). But 1984 was really the last strong year the company had as an independent entity.[45]

The Bowen/Lay team at Transco was considered the industry's finest for its short duration (1981–84). There was also talent behind them, and some of that talent would later join Ken Lay at Enron.

Bowen wished that he had been smart enough to have added just one more clause in his problematic 1970s gas-purchase contracts: *in no event will the buyer be required to take more gas than the originally estimated recoverable reserves.* If so, Transco would have had to pay only *once* for the gas it was obligated to take, and the gas not taken would have been *prepaid* for future delivery. As it was, Transco accrued liabilities for the same gas just because it could not be taken— again and again. And producers had every incentive to spend extra money to rev up deliveries to a pipeline that was receiving market signals to lower takes. Ken Lay was willing to bite the bullet and get the contracts reformed, but Transco's new leadership postponed and hoped—a decision that turned out to be wrong.

Jack Bowen, a great man of his industry for more than two decades, left wounded. An industry that once was really *too easy* given public-utility regula-tion became *too hard* because of the distortions created by wellhead price con-trols and a boom/bust gas price cycle. Transco, and much of the industry, simply did not have the talent base to overcome it—except for one shining period that ended with the departure of Ken Lay.

---

44. Trying to put the best face on a failed strategy, a 78-page in-house Transco history released in 1995 called the company's coal-gasification effort and other ill-fated energy-supply diversification ventures "noble errors" and America-first: "For Bowen, the matter had always been not just about supply but patriotism: a pioneering effort to rid America of dependence on foreign oil."

45. In his last years at Transco and after retirement, Bowen was elected vice chairman of the World Energy Council (1990) and chairman of the United States Energy Association (1992).

What if Lay had stayed on? What if Jack Bowen had ceded the CEO title three years earlier to retain his real protégé? Bowen told his board at Florida Gas that he was leaving for Transco because ten years as CEO "is a good target, and I have been at it for nearly fifteen." Bowen's tenth year at Transco was about the time that Lay was offered the CEO position at Houston Natural Gas. With Lay at the helm, more or most of Transco's take-or-pay problem would have been addressed earlier (as Lay did at Enron), and mergers and acquisitions would have led the company in new directions. Just where Transco would have ultimately ended up under a Ken Lay regime will never be known, but the latter 1980s and early 1990s would have been, in all likelihood, better.[46]

---

46. Ken Lay inherited some problems at Houston Natural Gas Corporation (HNG) and created a few himself, such as having InterNorth overpay for HNG in a reverse merger in 1985, and failing to heed an oil-trading scandal that threatened the combined company in 1987. See *Enron and Ken Lay: An American Tragedy* (Book 3), chapters 2 and 3, respectively.

Part III

Houston Natural Gas Corporation

There is no locality in the world today so interesting as Southeast Texas.
Our magnificent timber forests would make us great, and when you
add to these the greatest oil field in the whole world, you
present opportunities that simply bewilder imagination.
—Houston Oil Founder John Henry Kirby (1902)

What a land—what an empire—is this favored region—the Coastal
Plain of Texas! The bases of natural vegetation and crop production
at the surface; the geological materials beneath it: all at the
seaside, with the world at our door! With utter confidence in
Nature's pledge of our region's brilliant future, let us make the
most of our great advantages and put their fruit to the best uses!
—Houston Natural Gas President Frank Smith (1937)

Introduction

A major oversimplification of the Enron story is that founder and CEO Ken Lay transformed a sleepy, obscure Texas-based natural gas pipeline company into an international corporate colossus.[1] In fact, Houston Natural Gas Corporation (HNG) that Lay took over in mid-1984 was as sizeable as the Fortune 500 firm he had just left, Transco Energy Company. HNG's core asset was the largest intrastate gas pipeline network in the United States. The company also produced oil, gas, and coal; manufactured petrochemicals; and engaged in marine transportation and construction.

HNG, like Transco, was falling on hard times after energy prices peaked in 1981. Still, the 59-year old company had been a top performer on the New York Stock Exchange in the 1970s and remained a favorite son of Houston, Texas, the energy capital of the world. This company was always profitable and, outside of a lone incident in the 1930s, scandal-free. HNG was the *forgotten company* of the Enron era and is virtually unknown today.

The modern Houston Natural Gas was built by Robert Herring, its CEO from 1967 until his death in 1981. As documented in chapter 13, it was Herring, not Lay, who transformed a one-dimensional pipeline company into a large, diversified energy conglomerate. HNG's robust cash flow quadrupled the company's assets in the 1970s. Herring's run was helped by an unprecedented commodity boom in energy markets, not to mention federal regulation that advantaged the largely unregulated Texas natural gas market.

The Natural Gas Policy Act of 1978 removed this intrastate advantage, however, and falling oil and gas prices several years later created a very tough business environment for oil, gas, and coal companies. HNG's margins were squeezed across the board. Herring's death from cancer in October 1981 began a series of events that would put the company and its challenges into the lap of Ken Lay less than three years later.

◇

Flash back to John Henry Kirby, one of the most colorful characters in Texas business history. As described in chapter 10, Kirby founded Houston Oil Company in 1901, a company that emerged from its bankruptcy (1904–09) to become profitable in exploration and production. In the mid-1920s, Houston Oil discovered two major gas fields that needed a market. Houston, 200 miles away, needed natural gas, and Houston Pipe Line Company was formed as a

---

1. See Internet appendix 13.7, "HNG as a Fortune 500 Company," at www.political-capitalism.org/Book2/Chapter13/Appendix7.html.

wholly owned subsidiary to get it there. This subsidiary became an independent company, Houston Natural Gas, the subject of chapter 12.

Robert Herring, like Jack Bowen at Transco, was a second-generation pipeline executive standing upon the shoulders of such luminaries as Clint Murchison, Paul Kayser, Gardiner Symonds, and Ray Fish. Herring and Bowen, born a year apart, paved the way for a key third-generation pipeliner, Ken Lay.

Robert Herring's mentor was Ray Fish, the man who engineered the construction of Tennessee Gas Transmission (1943), Transcontinental Gas Pipe Line Company (1951), Texas-Illinois Natural Gas Pipeline (1951), and Pacific Northwest Pipeline Company (1956). Little wonder that Fish became known as Mr. Pipeliner during the postwar natural gas boom, the subject of chapter 11.

These four chapters on the prehistory of Enron and Ken Lay focus on HNG and Robert Herring in particular. HNG made as much or more annual net income as Enron ever did. In important ways, Herring was the energy executive Lay turned out not to be.

What if Robert Herring had lived another decade and Ken Lay had stayed at Transco? How would their companies have fared? Transco surely would have enjoyed much of the hard-earned prosperity that Enron did in the 1980s and into the 1990s. Herring would have had to reshape HNG, even undoing his prior diversification program—a sea change for an executive spoiled by a commodity-price boom. This hypothetical question can never be answered. Still, understanding what did happen can provide reasoned speculation about what might have transpired with a different turn of history.[2]

---

2. For interesting parallels between the two CEOs, see Internet appendix 13.8, "Robert Herring and Ken Lay: Parallels" at www.politicalcapitalism.org/Book2/Chapter13/Appendix8.html.

10

The Prince of Bankruptcy: John Henry Kirby

"WHAT'S PAST IS PROLOGUE." Shakespeare's words are relevant to the role of Houston Natural Gas Corporation (HNG) in the Enron story. Enron Corporation began as HNG, which was formed in 1925 as the natural gas side of Houston Oil Company. Like Clint Murchison's Southern Union Company, Houston Oil was impelled by the discovery of gas to construct a pipeline to reach a market. The company's business of oil became the business of oil *and* natural gas.

Houston Oil was founded by John Henry Kirby just months after the world's largest oil field was discovered at Spindletop Knoll near Beaumont, Texas. Kirby, the seventh child of Thomas and Sarah Kirby, was born on a small Tyler County farm in East Texas on November 16, 1860. He was the state's "first great industrialist" and first "home-grown multi-millionaire." The parallels between John Henry Kirby and Ken Lay—three generations apart—are many and varied. Both went from the bottom to the top, from where their business, civic, and charitable largesse made them seem larger than life. Both suffered bankruptcies that stunned their city and made headlines near and far. Who would have guessed that the still-named Kirby Mansion at 2006 Smith Street would outlive the Enron Center at 1400 Smith in downtown Houston?[1]

"Without [Kirby's] bold enterprise, there might not have been a Houston Natural Gas Corporation," wrote company historian Kenneth Fellows. Without HNG, there might not have been Enron. But the story surely would have played out under different company names. Ken Lay and through him Jeff Skilling still

---

1. Also see Internet appendix 10.1, "John Henry Kirby and Ken Lay: Parallels" at www. politicalcapitalism.org/Book2/Chapter10/Appendix1.html.

373

would have had their shining moment—and fate of Icarus, who flew too close
to the sun.

"Father of Industrial Texas"

"The Greatest Banquet Ever Given in Texas," exclaimed a Houston newspaper
headline of November 13, 1901. The resplendent seven-course meal at the Rice
Hotel, attended by 300 local, state, and national dignitaries, ended at 4:30 AM
after many toasts, tributes, and after-dinner pleasantries. The $10,000 fete (about
$250,000 today) honored hometown hero John Henry Kirby, who just weeks
before had announced in New York City the $40 million capitalization of the
sister companies Houston Oil Company of Texas ($30 million) and Kirby
Lumber Company ($10 million).[2] By far the largest company ever chartered in
the state, Houston Oil would sell timber and extract crude oil from a million
acres in East Texas. Kirby Lumber would turn timber into lumber in the largest
milling operation in the South.

Lumber was the top industry in Texas, and petroleum was rapidly ascending. The two-company agreement required Kirby Lumber to turn 8 billion
feet of long-leaf yellow pine into commercial board in the next 20 years, with
the sales going to fund oil exploration and related activity by Houston Oil,
separately run by Patrick Calhoun from New York City. Was this the beginning of an empire? Could John Henry Kirby become the first Texan to join the
ranks of the great Northeastern industrialists?

Late into the banquet evening, the master of ceremonies stood to give his
speech, but the crowd shouted for Kirby. R. M. Johnson, the editor/owner of the
Houston Post, sat down, and Kirby rose with great anticipation and purpose. He
had to assuage fears that his joint enterprise was a trust as defined by the broad
Texas antitrust statute. He wanted to sell Texas as a promising place to do
business to the national press, and he sought to inspire Texans to follow his lead
and adopt a higher business calling. Launching his remarks, Kirby said of
mother Texas:

> She is rich beyond the dream of avarice in lumber, oils, iron ores, coal, clays,
> precious metals and other minerals—in agriculture and horticulture, and only
> needs industrial expansion in lines of manufacture. This need she expects her
> sons to supply. She lays these marvelous resources before us and says: Build
> factories and railroads and cities and give employment to my people. Distribute
> wealth and opportunity, and promote the prosperity of every household and the
> comfort of every human creature.

---

2. A $40 million capitalization in 1901 would be closer to a billion dollars today; deals of
this magnitude were unheard of in Texas or anywhere else outside of the Northeast financial
centers at the time.

Kirby credited the "Lucas gusher at Beaumont" for opening up a huge new industry in Texas. "The whole of East Texas from Shelby County to the Gulf was underlaid with oil bearing sands," said Kirby about the geologists' reports. "Here now was presented the opportunity I had long dreamed of," he continued, oil beneath and "splendid yellow pine forest" above.

Absinthe   Oysters
Astrakhan Caviar   Canape Lorenzo
Celery   Stuffed Olives
Green Turtle Soup (Clear)
Amontillado Sherry

Soft Shell Crabs   Sauce Tartar
Salted Almonds   Cheese Straws
Dressed Cucumbers
Hauté Sauterne

Small Pates, a là Financiere

Filets of Breast of Spring Chicken
(Peregord Style)
Châuteau La Rose
Diamond Back Terrapin
(Sam Ward's Manner)

Champagne Punch
Roast English Snipe with Cresses
Chamberlin

Artichokes with French Dressing
Lubec Asparagus

Charlotte Russe   Jelly in Oranges
Roederer Brut
Metropolitan Ice Cream
Assorted Cakes   Fruits

Roquefort Cheese   Camembert Cheese
Bent's Crackers
Cigars
Rice Hotel Brulo

Figure 10.1 The unprecedented "Industrial Awakening of Texas" banquet was held in 1901 at the Rice Hotel in Houston (left), featuring John Henry Kirby (upper inset). Patrick Calhoun (lower inset), the other principal of the company, could not attend. The menu celebrating the formation of Houston Oil Company and Kirby Lumber Company was the best money could buy.

Kirby spoke of "my especial pride," Kirby Lumber Company. There were many well-established lumber firms in the state (he named eight0, which precluded monopoly. But size had advantages, he explained. Large timber orders hitherto had to be subdivided between companies, "a thing difficult in achievement if not under Texas statutes unlawful."

No more! With a daily production capacity of a million board feet, Kirby Lumber "shall be able to inaugurate such economies of management, manufacture and distribution as to materially reduce the cost of the product and enable us to compete in nearly every market where yellow pine is sold." Any surplus would be sold as exports to capture foreign wealth for the native "toilers." Kirby ended his speech with exhortation:

> Men of Texas! It is the hour of Fate! Under the providence of God you are brought face to face with destiny! ... The eyes of the civilized world are upon us.... Let us rise to the importance and dignity of our matchless environment, and, in our efforts to improve the opportunities which God has presented to us, we shall have the hearty and earnest co-operation of the capital and the brains of all the world.

At the banquet Texas Governor Joseph Sayers gave Kirby a halo that would never leave his head: "the father of industrial Texas."[3] The entrepreneur who had already created several successful companies was ushering in a new era. The *Houston Post* described the man "whose achievements had been the triumph of a big mind, an indomitable will, and a tireless energy, and are an encouraging example to the youth of the land that merit can and will win!" Kirby had already won, it seemed, although the gun had just sounded on his biggest and boldest venture. Few knew that the dual enterprise was off to a troubling start.

⌁

John Henry Kirby, on the cusp of his forty-first birthday, sported a "million-dollar smile" to go with many other attributes. He was smart, energetic, and ambitious. He was singularly cheerful ("every day is like Christmas to me," he would say). Handsome, blue-eyed, and ruddy-cheeked, a Washington newspaper described the tall Texan as "a noble Roman in appearance who could play a senator in *Julius Caesar* without a make-up."

Kirby was perennially optimistic and fearless. He had a diplomat's "ability to calm irate callers and compromise difficulties." He had a "talent for drudgery" and genuine interest in books and learning. Kirby was destined to think grand thoughts and do big things, all the while being just about everyone's friend.

The lawyer-turned-entrepreneur had already had a successful career when he decided to engineer the deal of all deals. Houston's wealthiest citizen (he had moved from Woodville in 1890) had made his fortune buying and selling timberland in East Texas through two firms he founded: Texas Land and Lumber Company (1885) and Texas Pine Land Company (1890). In 1896, Kirby cofounded the Gulf, Beaumont, and Kansas City Railroad. The forward vertical integration—his wood needed transportation to market—created a profitable company that he sold four years later.

---

3. Another sobriquet given to Kirby was the "Moses of Texas," and he was called "the leading southern financier."

Kirby found himself in the oil business too. Texas Pine Land Company was signing leases with oil prospectors on its land, and Kirby was receiving a 40 percent return on his investment from Southwestern Oil Company of Houston, where he was president. Southwest was an expanding enterprise that Standard Oil had its eye on acquiring through its Texas agent.

"Business here is very good," Kirby wrote about Houston in 1899. "There are lots of good buildings going up and lots of them that are already completed. Very few idle men on the streets and a mechanic is hard to find when you want him."

But property values and rental rates were depressed, Kirby related, a situation that could be rectified if Houston upgraded Buffalo Bayou to allow shipping, a civic project that would soon come Kirby's way. Still, Houston was the right place at the right time for an organizer like Kirby. "Money is in abundant supply and interest rates are easy," he reported to one New York financier.

Winding up his railroad affairs, Kirby was now thinking about organizing a "mammoth lumber concern" capitalized at $10 million, an unheard of sum for those days. He foresaw "monopolizing absolutely the entire output of the Atchison, Topeka & Santa Fe [railroad] territory." His confidence was unbounded. "It will be a money earner from the very start and organized on a conservative and safe basis," he told potential investors.

Then something happened to make John Henry Kirby go in two directions at once. In January 1901, history's greatest oil well blew in just east of Houston. The size of the Lucas No. 1 well, soon to be known as Spindletop, was astounding. *More oil was spewing out of the discovery well than was being produced the world over.*

Within weeks, the center of the North American oil industry gravitated to Beaumont and nearby Houston as tens of thousands arrived for work and opportunity. Hundreds of oil-related companies were formed. Many failed or merged, but strong independents and integrated leaders, such as Texaco and Gulf Oil, would survive and become world-class companies.

John Henry Kirby saw gold in both wood and oil from the fertile soil of East Texas. The quality of the gusher's oil was fine, reported Kirby to his investors, refuting malicious rumors started by operators in other oil regions. The bounty from Spindletop, and East Texas oil in general, was a good lubricant that could be expected to "revolutionize the fuel situation in America." He explained:

> The demand for it for fuel is practically unlimited and being near the Gulf can be transported by sea at moderate cost. It is a tremendously big thing even as a fuel oil, and the big oil operations such as the Standard Oil Co. … and dozens of other big oil people of less prominence than those named have numerous representatives on the ground and are seeking leases and lands with great activity. No higher proof of its value need be cited.

While inundated with "20 or 30 different propositions ... for my consideration and co-operation," Kirby sought "a valuable permanent privilege," not "temporary financial advantage." That meant his large-scale timber/oil scheme. "My plan is to acquire a million acres of timber land at their value and then prospect them for oils," he wrote in one letter. "I expect people to fall over each other to get in. It's different from the ordinary oil speculation in that no man can lose a penny, and he stands ... to become a Rockefeller."

The lumber industry was primed for growth too. Labor and capital were migrating to the Gulf South's virgin forests from Michigan, Wisconsin, Minnesota, and other states with cut-over forests. Kirby, soon to earn the sobriquet *prince of the pines*, was in the right place at the right time on two counts.

One Plan, Two Companies

Kirby was wealthy, but many millions of dollars were needed to finance his acquisition of timberland—replete with mineral rights to any oil and gas below the surface—and his purchase of sawmills. He traveled to the financial center of the world and found his rainmaker in Patrick Calhoun, the grandson of John C. Calhoun, the former vice president of the United States. The prominent New York City attorney had invested in Texas's Corsicana field prior to Spindletop and embraced the idea of a two-company interlock to steer clear of Texas antitrust law.

Calhoun sent dozens of timber experts and accountants to Houston to audit the land and mills Kirby planned to purchase—and to investigate Kirby himself. The chief inspector was Charles Haskins of Haskins & Sells, which for more than a half century would audit the books of Houston Oil Company and, later, Houston Natural Gas.

Everything checked out. The acreage and sawmills that Kirby intended to buy could support a master agreement to turn trees into board, Calhoun was told. Kirby was described as a leading citizen with wealth and credentials. Although Kirby was "something of a plunger," he "had plunged very successfully ... in the acquisition of a large amount of timber lands, and in the sale of a railroad to Santa Fe."

Ambitious himself, Calhoun sold Kirby on a bigger version of the original proposal. A promoters' agreement was reached in April 1901 whereby Calhoun would lead the oil company, and Kirby would lead the timber company. Neither man was an officer or a director of the other's business. Soon, Houston Oil was in negotiations to purchase two oil companies to position itself for its own exploration and production.

Calhoun secured financing from the Maryland Trust Company of Baltimore, which had experience in Texas real estate. As trustee, Maryland Trust would take title to the contracts with first lien on the companies' assets. In return, Maryland Trust would issue interest-bearing "timber certificates" to the public. Timber revenues would flow to Maryland Trust for bond payments, with any profit accruing to Kirby, Calhoun, and the other investors.

Houston Oil Company was chartered as an integrated oil operation for the purpose of

> establishing and maintaining an oil company with the right and power to acquire—own and hold lands by lease or purchase for said business—and for the purpose of prospecting for—developing—saving—transporting—refining and marketing minerals of whatever kind—coal—petroleum—final oils—illuminating oils—also the right to erect—build and own all necessary oil tanks—cars and pipes necessary for the handling and transportation of all the oil produced by this company and the operation of its business.

Natural gas went unmentioned. At the time, *gas* meant manufactured gas from coal; natural gas was not yet a marketable commodity except in unusual circumstances. Better pipelines would change this in the 1920s, but that was a long way off for Houston Oil Company.

Houston Oil controlled the acreage and stumpage contract between Houston Oil and Kirby Lumber. The 20-year, $38 million agreement required Kirby Lumber to cut, clear, transport, and mill 8 billion board feet of timber from its 14 to 16 sawmills. The first year's 350 million feet, for which Kirby Lumber would pay Houston Oil $3 per thousand feet, would generate revenue from an expected sale price of more than $10 per thousand feet to support the semi-annual payments due to Maryland Trust. That was the plan, anyway.

Figure 10.2 The $40 million idea of John Henry Kirby combined the towering pines of East Texas with the oil wealth awakened by the Spindletop oil gusher.

Problems

Unbeknownst to the banquet revelers and press, Kirby and Calhoun's grand arrangement was springing leaks—not good with the first semiannual payment only two months away. Kirby had not executed final agreements for a quarter of his promised acreage, and the price of land that included mineral rights had oil fever.

Kirby had even greater problems on the manufacturing side, where he was inexperienced. His targeted mills had raised their asking price, partially in response to publicity of the lavish banquet, although to Kirby, the "most whole-some" evening had achieved its aim of charming investors and the public. Kirby found himself searching for new mills to buy. The new acquisitions would be cheaper, but operational problems and assumed indebtedness, some unknown, would prove problematic.

Working capital was inadequate, especially after the second major lender to the project, Brown Brothers and Company of New York City, trimmed its loan by several million dollars because of Kirby's acreage shortfall. The hurried legal agreements failed to spell out clear lines of authority between Kirby as chief of Kirby Lumber in Houston, and Calhoun as head of Houston Oil in New York City. With the two offices days away in train time, there were coordination problems working by telegraph and special-delivery letters. Texas was home to the companies' business.[4] Kirby was in the action; Calhoun was where he wanted to be.

Kirby and Calhoun each began working behind the other's back. Kirby complained about "tramping in the dark" and fussed when Calhoun spent money on oil properties ("a problematic speculation") when every dollar was needed to upgrade the purchased sawmills to meet the stumpage contract. Timber-centric Kirby privately complained about his counterpart:

> Mr. Calhoun thought that there was more money in oils than in timber. I simply want to say to you that I don't share in that opinion for a minute. The oils are underground, and the volume is a matter of mere speculation. The trees are on top of ground and can be calculated with certainty. I never put a penny into a piece of land in my life that had pine trees on it that I did not make big money.[5]

Kirby was also nonplussed about oil's price: two cents a barrel. "We Texans are bringing in so confounded much oil that I see nothing ahead but utter demoralization unless we can find ... a sufficiently large bunch of money to

---

4. Kirby's letters to investors complained about informational discrepancies. Said one letter: "The statements which [Brown Brothers] are furnishing Calhoun are so utterly at variance with what this man says to me here that I am incapable of forming any clear opinion as to what his final action is going to be."

5. Kirby described the timber side of the company as "a dead sure winner" and better than "a gold mine."

build pipe lines and refineries and engage tank ship and tank cars," he complained. Calhoun, meanwhile, fussed about Kirby's saddling Houston Oil with obligations without his consent.

The accounting system of the companies was in disarray. Kirby originally hired William Fuqua as general auditor at Kirby Lumber to implement "a purely modern system of accounting." But Calhoun insisted on Haskins & Sells, the New York accounting firm that had done the due diligence on Kirby. So a team from Hawkins & Sells came to Houston to implement a new accounting system. Problems developed, and a new boss came down from New York—and then another. Finally, it was back to Fuqua.

"It is the most provoking, most exasperating, and most humiliating condition," Kirby wrote in 1902. "Here we are in large need of funds, and trying to close an underwriting for a large amount of our securities, and yet we can't go to the bank or to an individual with a statement and say 'This is our condition, and reflects our progress.'" As it turned out, Maryland Trust would generate the financial reports out of Baltimore, creating a third center for the one company.

Another difficulty was an antitrust suit filed in late 1901 against Kirby Lumber by the district attorney of Travis County (Texas) at the urging of a former Travis County judge, D. A. McFall. Described by Kirby as "a very ordinary gutter snipe and black-mailer," McFall had ambitions of running for attorney general of Texas. And under state law, McFall stood to collect part of any financial settlement.

"The pendency of the suit is hurting like the devil because people in New York, Boston, Philadelphia and other financial centers who have money to invest will not risk a penny of it in a litigated case," Kirby complained. "These people have the whole world in which to pick their investments and they don't have to come to Texas or go into any other locality."

The suit was dismissed, reinstituted, and dismissed again. Publicity about the case in the Northeast was to Kirby a plot to "keep investments out of Texas." Who could have done this, Kirby asked, "for certainly no set of people on earth have any financial interest in injuring me or my enterprise except for the Standard Oil crowd."

The Houston banquet was intended to insulate against such populism. But Texas law was too broad and too tempting for opportunists, leading Kirby to warn: "Enterprise is always retarded where there is uncertainty as to the Statutes which may affect business conditions." Texas needed a legal environment to complement its home riches, he stressed.[6]

◇

---

6. McFall would strike again three years later when a Travis County grand jury indicted Kirby on a bribery charge. The "blackmailing job" against Kirby would be once again dismissed from a lack of evidence, but it was another distraction both before and during the receivership of Kirby Lumber Company.

The sawmills—a new collection that Kirby ended up purchasing—were not able to meet the stumpage requirement, even after adding a night shift. Upgrades were needed to increase capacity, but capital was scarce. A lack of rail car (trackage) capacity created bottlenecks. Mills began falling behind on their payroll in summer 1903, creating labor problems. Kirby Lumber could not be rescued by Houston Oil, given that crude oil prices had fallen to pennies a barrel, less than the cost of a cup of fresh water. There was just too much oil production post-Spindletop, some of it coming from Houston Oil's own properties.

The dual-company operation did not reach full production before January 1902 and struggled to break even. Houston Oil borrowed money to make its first payments to Maryland Trust, and partial payments followed when new loans could not be secured. Time ran out in early 1904 with $210,000 on hand to pay a $700,000 obligation to Maryland Trust. The operation was more than $3 million past due, and Kirby was desperately trying to mortgage properties that were already being used as collateral. The underlying problem was simple: the 477 million board feet of lumber cut through December 1903 was 55 percent of the 875 million contractually required.

The grand one-in-two arrangement, which had been intended to take advantage of economies of scale, instead brought mismanagement and head-aches. "What was everybody's business was, as usual, nobody's business," one observer concluded. A *transaction cost* problem existed between two companies that should have been one entity or two separate companies—but not two heads on one body.[7]

Bankruptcy

On February 1, 1904, Maryland Trust asked that both Houston Oil and Kirby Lumber be placed into receivership. Bankruptcy was granted, and all assets were placed under the direction of the United States Court for the Southern District of Texas. The news caused a run on Kirby's Planters and Mechanics National Bank in Houston, and the fallen man himself broke the news to those acquaintance-investors who could least afford to bear it.

Board member B. F. Bonner of Beaumont was appointed receiver. Kirby was out at his namesake company, although he would remain very much informed about its business. Bonner would shutter seven mills in hopes that wages would fall at the remaining ten.

Kirby reacted emotionally, calling the bankruptcy action a "Wall Street plot." He lambasted Calhoun as evil, incompetent, and a thief—a complete reversal of Kirby's earlier characterization of his partner as a "sagacious and safe man of

---

7. Transaction costs and business form are discussed in *Capitalism at Work*, pp. 113–17.

affairs." At the heart of Kirby's complaint was that the $2.5 million in Houston Oil stock Calhoun received in 1901 was intended to be returned to Kirby Lumber for working capital when Kirby secured the sawmills and acreage. But Calhoun pledged the stock to meet his own capital needs, leading Kirby to remark, "I furnished the properties and Mr. Calhoun furnished the wind."

Kirby's offer to sell out to Calhoun for $1.5 million was not enough to avoid litigation. With a reputation as "an aggressive, ruthless lawyer perhaps given to sharp practices to gain his ends," Calhoun was the last man any reorganization needed. Kirby turned things over to Andrews, Ball, and Streetman for a long fight.

Kirby told the *New York Times* about his plan to have the Texas Legislature "place wholesome restrictions on the power of irresponsible foreign [out of state] trust companies to embarrass Texas citizens and corporations." The state had thrown out Standard Oil's Texas affiliate in 1897, and Kirby let it be known that he had much better relations in Austin than did his out-of-state financiers. This, however, was bush league and McFall-like.

Kirby spun the situation to his liking. "Both corporations," he told the *New York Times*, "are thoroughly solvent." The blame lay elsewhere: "The sole cause of the present trouble lies in the fact that securities issued by the Houston Oil Company have not been marketable." Taking it up a notch, Kirby Lumber countersued both Maryland Trust and Houston Oil Company. Kirby even argued that he had not been authorized to execute the contract that the lumber company violated, leading a director of Houston Oil to complain, "There never was a more flagrant plea of the 'baby act' than Kirby's claiming that he was not authorized to act for the Kirby Lumber Company."

In a reply lawsuit, lawyers for Maryland Trust and Houston Oil accused John Henry Kirby of willful misrepresentation of the timber properties and sawmills on the original purchase list. The fact that he had stacked the board of Kirby Lumber with cronies, including his father and brother, was brought out. What would in the end be a four-year legal fight was presided over by a Special Master in Chancery, Joseph Sayers, the former governor who had lionized Kirby five years prior as the Father of Industrial Texas. An army of lawyers, including Houston's finest from the firms now known as Andrews & Kurth and Baker & Botts, was engaged.

Fight, not remorse, was embedded in Kirby's persona. "Those Wall Street sharks have affected my reputation as a business success in some degree, but they cannot result in the loss of my fortune," Kirby wrote to a relative. "I shall whip the fight and whatever business prestige I have lost, I shall regain." A letter the same day was meant to assure his father that his son was still on the top of his game. "You would have been proud of your boy if you could have been there [in St. Louis for my speech]," Kirby wrote. "I held the crowd from the time I uttered the first word until the last, a crowd of 3,000 or more, which is more than any of the speakers were able to do."

John Henry Kirby, after all, excelled in everything and apologized to no one. Had he not been the fiddle champ at the square dances, the boomer at church gatherings, and victor at card games ("he could make two deuces win," said a friend)? Was it not Kirby who crammed years of formal study into mere months before teaching a class at the Peach Tree village school until a real instructor arrived? And had he not learned law while profitably buying and selling timberland?

It was Kirby-the-doer whom the Houston city fathers sent to Washington to persuade Congress to unblock the project that became the Houston Ship Channel ("Kirby Hauls Down the Chain!" a newspaper headlined proclaimed). It was he who traveled East where a New York banker, forewarned that the Texan did not have collateral but only a million-dollar smile, remarked, "You were right, that young fellow, Kirby, smiled me out of a million." Kirby had never failed or thought he could. But now he was in the middle of the biggest bankruptcy case in America.

It could have been different. What if Kirby had quietly secured the timberlands and sawmills and forgone the headline-grabbing celebration? The folks on Kirby's buy list might not have upped their price. What if Kirby had scaled back his operation to obtain the best acreage and mills and built up his business from there? What if the two companies had been governed by a more flexible, market-conforming contract? What if the legal agreements had more carefully defined the duties and relationship between Kirby and Calhoun?

Caution aside, Kirby rushed into his dream for Texas—a monument characterized as the business equivalent of Sam Houston's military exploits.[8] Kirby's feat with eastern capital had opened the door for industrial Texas, but subsequent out-of-state capital was surely frightened by Kirby's virulent reaction toward his creditors when bankruptcy struck.

The lawyers would be the only winners in the five-year skirmish. Kirby had the better case, but Calhoun had deep pockets, proximity to Kirby's investors, and lots of animosity and cunning to fight. "Calhoun is so much smarter than all of you put together that all he had got to do is to ring a bell and every one of you think that the chimes of Trinity church are turned loose," Kirby complained to one investor whom Calhoun had impressed at the expense of Kirby. "None of you ever take the pains to ascertain that this arch Machiavelli, this wonderful prestidigitator, this superlative incarnation of infernalism, is making a mere Punch and Judy show of you."

The Calhoun-Kirby fight went on, with one year turning into the next. "The enemy has been talking for three years," Kirby said in November 1906. "In fact they have been talking for four years having begun one year prior to the

---

8. Sam Houston Oil Company was the company's original name, but the first name was dropped for convenience.

Figure 10.3 Kirby Lumber Company was involved in all stages of converting the trees of East Texas into lumber for houses and other structures in Texas and the South. The sales slip for Kirby Lumber was issued (in 1905) during the company's receivership.

receivership, but up to this good day they have not submitted a proposition." But this changed when the opposing lawyers met face to face for the first time and John Henry Kirby himself made his case. After his two-day oratory, no doubt impressive, settlement was in the air.

Kirby Lumber, meanwhile, operated at partial capacity in the face of low margins and from bottlenecks, such as from a 1906/1907 railcar shortage that stranded stacks of lumber. Dividends, which had never been paid by Kirby Lumber, remained out of the question. Finally, in January 1908, a settlement was reached. Six months later, the Special Master in Chancery made the decree final. Never had the country seen as contested a bankruptcy filing as this.

Resurrection

The formal receivership lasted five years and five months—the time it took John Henry Kirby to buy back Kirby Lumber and become its largest stockholder. Kirby borrowed against the asset value of the 14 sawmills for part of the financing, but his own dollars—earned from East Texas timber deals and Houston real estate—made the difference. A million dollars came from parceling his 168-acre farm into the tract that would become downtown Houston. "I cut Main Street through it, cut it up into lots and peddled it out," Kirby later recalled.

Kirby and Patrick Calhoun fought to a draw in their personal lawsuits and emerged with valuable stock positions in the two companies they originally ran. "Peace is better than war even though that peace is more expensive than justice or fairness could demand," an exhausted Kirby wrote to Calhoun as the settlement decree was being finalized.

The decree of July 28, 1909, substituted a new stumpage contract between Kirby Lumber and Houston Oil at 80 percent of its former requirement (6.4 billion of 8 billion feet). Kirby had wanted a more realistic agreement since 1903, and this agreement would survive into the 1940s. As before, Maryland Trust Company as trustee had the right to take possession of and operate the railroad, sawmills, and other equipment of the company in the event that Kirby Lumber did not make its regular payments.

Debt halved, governed by a more realistic stumpage contract, and now able to evict "squatters and shyster lawyers" from the land, Kirby Lumber and Houston Oil were financially healthy when they emerged from bankruptcy in 1908.[9] Kirby Lumber, down to one active mill amid a surfeit of supply relative to demand, had nowhere to go but up.

Kirby personally had everything in Kirby Lumber and was unable to borrow or spend otherwise. "The bulk of my fortune went into the Kirby Lumber Company seven years ago, and from that time to this I have not had one cent income and during the past four and one-half years I have not even had a salary," he confessed. The other investors, too, had never received a dime of dividends.

Kirby greeted his new/old company with resolve:

> We are going to turn out a product as cheaply as skill and industry will do it. Whether we make any money or not will depend on the market. We are not making any money now but I hope to be able to get some increase in the average price we receive for our output and some decrease in the average cost of the product.

Wholesale changes were not necessary, and Kirby resisted suggestions to decentralize from Houston to such locals as Beaumont and Silsbee. Otherwise, "there would be inconvenience of communications and useless delay and more or less demoralization for that department of the work located at a distance." The mistakes of 1901 would not be repeated; Kirby Lumber was now a truly autonomous company with one leader: John Henry Kirby. Better yet, relations with Houston Oil Company, now in Houston, were "very agreeable." And all emphasis and resources was on the core business, not litigation.

---

9. Better management improved forest care. See Internet appendix 10.2, "Timber Conservation Practices," at www.politicalcapitalism.org/Book2/Chapter10/Appendix2.html.

Figure 10.4 John Henry Kirby, shown here in his Houston office, was back in the saddle running Kirby Lumber Company after the receivership ended in 1909.

Although the hum of 6,300 men cutting and logging to supply 12 mills was not a reality as once expected, Kirby Lumber would profitably participate in the state's "golden decade" of lumbering. One active mill would reach eight in the postreceivership period: better yet, without debt, the operation was profitable and earnings retained.

⌒

The new head of Houston Oil Company was Samuel Fordyce, a successful businessman from St. Louis, home to the company's largest stockholders. Kirby would have no direct involvement with Houston Oil and would form his own oil concern in 1920. By that time, Houston Oil had become a bona fide oil exploration and production company, owing to a successful joint venture with Joseph Cullinan's Republic Production Company.

Kirby Lumber remained bound to Houston Oil with a cut-or-pay contract, obligating Kirby Lumber to pay a minimum monthly fee to Houston Oil whether or not the trees were felled. Kirby was able to expand to 18 mills by 1911 and to stay ahead of the stumpage minimums. But margins were slim in an industry in which forests abounded, and newer, better-equipment mills seemed always to be springing up. Foregoing dividends to retire obligations, John Henry Kirby by the early 1920s owned "the most valuable empire of timber that any man has ever possessed, free of debt."

Kirby became busy on another front. In 1920, despite "not being myself a practical oil man," he formed Kirby Petroleum Company by consolidating the small oil ventures he had helped finance over the years. This company would remain with Kirby for the rest of his life; post-Kirby, the majority stockowners would be George and Herman Brown of Texas Eastern Corporation fame and then Clint Murchison of Delhi Oil and Florida Gas Transmission renown.[10] Houston Oil Company, too, would have a big future, being sold for $243 million in 1956 (about $1.8 billion today) to Atlantic Richfield Company.

The Great Man

Kirby was a multifaceted doer. He founded and led local, state, multi-state, and national groups and lobbied fervently for his causes. He was the friend of nine presidents: Grover Cleveland through Herbert Hoover. His varied, numerous positions over several decades gave him an unrivaled stature in the lumber industry as well as national esteem. All this was what he called his *"pro bono publico"* work:

- President, Houston Baseball Association (1895)
- King, Houston Cotton Festival (1900)
- Texas representative, National Association of Manufacturers (1902)
- President, Texas World's Fair Commission (1903)
- President, Trans-Mississippi Commercial Congress (1904)
- Organizer and president, Texas Five Million Club (1905–8)
- Legislator, Texas House of Representatives (1913–14, 1927–28)
- Founder and president, Southern Pine Association (1916, 1922)
- Delegate, Democratic National Convention (1916)
- Member, Raw Materials Committee, Council of National Defense (1917)
- President, National Lumber Manufacturers' Association (1917–21)
- Southern Lumber Administrator, United States Shipping Board, Emergency Fleet Corporation, War Industries Board (1918)
- Founder and president, Southern Tariff Association (1920–30)
- Member, Federal Unemployment Commission (1921)
- Commissioner, Brazilian Centennial Exposition (1922)

----

10. Murchison sold the company to Continental Oil Company in 1953 but retained the undeveloped acreage to form a new company, Kirby Oil and Gas, which was renamed Kirby Petroleum in 1957, Kirby Industries in 1967, and Kirby Exploration in 1974. The company sold its oil and gas assets in 1988 to leave its other businesses, notably marine transportation, as the publicly traded Kirby Corporation.

- Cofounder, American Anti-Klan Association (1922)
- President, National Council of State Legislatures (1927)
- Cofounder, Southern Committee to Uphold the Constitution (1933)

Kirby had other associations with the Federation of Construction Industries (Philadelphia), Merchant Marine Association (Washington), Mississippi Valley Association (New Orleans), National Economic League (Boston), and United States Chamber of Commerce (Washington). Attending meetings in the nation's capital and elsewhere took days by train, but Kirby traveled, read, and sent and received wires at each stop. Kirby was also active with public boards and commissions in Texas, sometimes serving as chair. His social organizations were also many, for he loved to fraternize with old schoolmates and new business associates. In addition, there was Kirby's spellbinding oratory, invoking an eclectic philosophy that mixed rugged self-help wisdom with biblical commandments of charity and benevolence.[11]

How could one man do all these things in his day and age? Kirby seemed everywhere, but he was actually scarce where it mattered most: at his business core. Indeed, in 1920, his sixtieth birthday near, he admitted to "getting to be an old man, with less ambition than I once had in an industrial sense and without any plan or purpose to expand." That would have consequences for a man depending on live income to meet his sizeable, if not extravagant, expenses and philanthropy.

Kirby was as close as a man could be to a *private-sector politician*. If not for a one-vote loss in a run for the Texas legislature in 1886, Kirby might have been at age 26 a real politician, first in Austin and then Washington. He had the background and personality to be a great populist, for few could rival his charisma when he had a cause or a message.

From 1901 until about 1930, Kirby rode high as a go-to philanthropist and as, along with the emerging Jesse Jones, *Mr. Houston*. Even with his company tied up in receivership between 1904 and 1908, John Henry Kirby's personal worth made him Houston's wealthiest citizen, or nearly so. He rehabilitated his fortune during his exile from Kirby Lumber and accumulated wealth all the way through the Roaring Twenties. He became a multimillionaire at a time when very few were in the South.[12]

For Kirby it was always "big things in a big way." His mansion, Inglenook, had no peer in Houston or even Texas and was the center of the elite social scene in Houston. He befriended thousands. He contributed generously to schools

---

11. See Internet appendix 10.3, "Kirby's Philosophy," at www.politicalcapitalism.org/Book2/Chapter10/Appendix3.html.

12. Ornate Inglenook is described in Internet appendix 10.4, "Conspicuous Consumption," at www. politicalcapitalism.org/Book2/Chapter10/Appendix4.html.

Figure 10.5 Purchased by Kirby in 1896, Inglenook (upper left) was remodeled and significantly expanded with a conservatory and greenhouse (upper right). The servants' quarters and horse stables (middle) was a grand structure in itself. Amenities of the mansion included an upstairs ballroom (lower left) and a downstairs swimming pool (lower right).

and churches and had a page full of students he was putting through college. Whether it was the Hood's Texas Brigade (a Civil War troop of which his father had been a member) or the Young Men's Christian Association, Kirby could be counted on.

Newspapers in Houston, Dallas, Beaumont, and many points in between sang the praises of John Henry Kirby after and between major events held in his honor, often on his birthdays. His sixty-third birthday was the occasion of a testimonial banquet held at the Rice Hotel for 700, reminiscent of the grand banquet of November 1901 but bigger. His seventieth and seventy-fifth birthdays were also grand, front-page events at the Rice Hotel and the Lamar Hotel, respectively.

The *Beaumont Journal*, the newspaper for "the first lumber capital of Texas," an area rich with Kirby Lumber sawmills, listed ten faces of Kirby's persona: "'governor,' counselor-at-law, counselor in neighborhood, giver of gifts, school builder, financier-of-students, builder of jobs, artisan of lumber, defender of the Constitution and servant of God." He also would be remembered as "lawyer, orator, lumberman, railroad builder, statesman, and philanthropist."

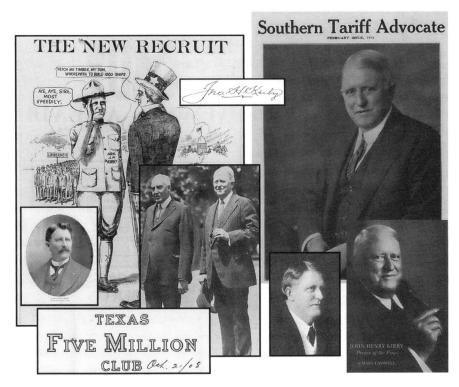

Figure 10.6 The bustling John Henry Kirby left his imprint on many causes, including the state's booster organization, the Texas Five Million Club. The go-to lumberman for the federal government in World War I was also a friend of presidents (shown here with Warren G. Harding) and instrumental in the Southern Tariff Association. Mary Lasswell's biography of Kirby appeared in 1967.

Patriot and Protectionist

Kirby pledged allegiance to the U.S. Constitution and the Holy Bible. His politics combined state's rights, America first, paternalism, and the gospel of wealth. He was nominally a Democrat but voted for the candidate, not the party. Kirby ardently opposed communism, socialism, and labor unionism, all of which he saw as interconnected. He lambasted FDR's New Deal, nominally rejecting a middle way between capitalism and socialism. He warned:

> We hear vaporings of a finer welding of human interest with the government, of social face-lifting and benevolent adjustments. But bureaucracy is colder than pagan charity. It cannot be moved by a heart-beat or touched with a tear. In its metallic grasp it crushes hope and liberty.

Kirby's worldview, forged by personal experience, was pragmatic. The heavy hand of government gave him much to dislike, even hate. Nationalized railroads (1917–20) did a poor job of transporting lumber. An increase in the corporate tax from 1 percent to 12 percent between 1909 and 1918 reduced Kirby Lumber's ability to reinvest earnings. (The company did not pay dividends in good times or bad.) During World War I, Kirby—both as president of the National Lumber Manufacturers' Association and as Lumber Administrator in Washington—found himself at odds with a price-fixing plan for yellow-pine timber proposed by the War Industries Board. The Code of Fair Competition pursuant to the National Recovery Act of 1933 (NRA) violated Kirby's sense of propriety. The NRA code regulated labor hours and pay, set maximum prices, and prohibited a variety of so-called unfair practices for lumber, as other NRA codes did for their industries.

Kirby defiantly refused to obligate Kirby Lumber to the NRA code. "Shall we proceed under conditions which we think are certain to confiscate our property," he asked, "or shall we close down our mills and cease all operations, or shall we assert our Constitutional rights and take these usurpers at Washington into the Courts?" He would finally sign the Lumber Code, but few were happier than he when the Supreme Court invalidated the NRA and its codes of fair competition in May 1935.

Antitrust law was another sore spot. Kirby Lumber and Houston Oil had a skirmish with the Austin district attorney in the early years, and a state antitrust suit against Houston Oil in 1917 occupied Kirby before it was dismissed. In February 1921, the Department of Justice alleged monopolization against the Southern Pine Association, a trade group founded by Kirby several years before. Kirby knew that competition was intense in the lumber and oil industries and that antitrust was more a play for votes than for consumer welfare. In his eyes, antitrust activism was just bad government.

A point of extreme sensitivity for Kirby was trade unionism, which at the time was not far removed from socialist and Marxist doctrines. There was violence, not only work stoppages, and Kirby felt personally violated with the unions' every intrusion. Kirby worked hard to give his workers the best deal he could ("I am paying every cent the business will stand"), while using every means at his disposal to stymie unionists wanting to organize labor on his property.[13] Kirby warned his workers, "We will close down our mills and retire from activity before we will destroy the peace, safety, order and tranquility of the communities in which we do business."

---

13. Kirby's positions have been the subject of study by American historians, but their pro-union slant has created as much heat as light. See Internet appendix 10.5, "Labor Issues," at www.politicalcapitalism.org/Book2/Chapter10/Appendix5.html.

Kirby passionately opposed many government interventions, particularly those that directly disadvantaged his business interests. But he supported a wide range of government interventions that he deemed good for business and society. He was a *political capitalist*, not a free-market capitalist, and philosophically was a pliable middle-of-the-roader.

Kirby was a tariff advocate—a universal tariff advocate. When Nebraska's fireball senator William Jennings Bryan accused Kirby Lumber in 1909 of working "so hard" for a lumber tariff, Kirby answered in a six-page letter that his company was not politically active in the area. As Kirby explained, lumber imports from Canada had their own northern U.S. market with or without a tariff, due to the high shipping costs from Texas. "Certainly the placing of lumber on the free list [in place of a $1.25 per thousand feet tariff] would not have deprived the Kirby Lumber Co. of a market for a single car." Kirby Lumber's 12 mills, competing against more than 400 in Texas and more than 4,000 in the United States, "does a strictly legitimate business on a strictly competitive basis."

"I am not a protectionist," Kirby wrote in a later exchange with Bryan, claiming differentiation by favoring comprehensive import levies "on all industries alike without favor or discrimination toward any" as a substitute for the income tax and other federal levies. As one of the "tariff-for-revenue Democrats," he opposed both "the new philosophy … of free raw materials" and targeted tariff protection championed by Republicans.

Kirby's international trade position took on a protectionist, xenophobic tone as he eloquently and tirelessly promoted tariffs on sugar, rice, cotton, wool, beef, peanuts, and other Southern products. "Nationalism has made American great," Kirby preached. Foreigners were the enemy because they were exporting their lower standard of living along with their cheaper goods.[14] Kirby was alarmist: "Is any man blind enough not to know and not to see that [free trade] means the soup house and the bread line and an army of tramps—that it means idleness, sinfulness, unhappiness, tears, heartaches, and suffering?"

The Panic of 1907 was blamed in part on President Theodore Roosevelt's low-tariff policy. "We paid in sorrow and distress for the folly of opening our ports to the products of the Orient," Kirby said. "The Southern farmer, with a high civilization to maintain, was compelled to feed and clothe his family on such an allowance as satisfied the Mongol tribesmen of Asia."

In 1920, Kirby founded the Southern Tariff Association (STA), which would swell to include more than 50 organizations lobbying for higher tariffs and removing goods from the free list. Lumber was not targeted. Kirby, as father of the organization, was reluctant to tie the STA to his special interest, and he could

---

14. Although a xenophile in this matter, the characterization of Kirby as a racist is debatable if not unfounded. See Internet appendix 10.6, "Kirby and Bigotry," at www.politicalcapitalism. org/Book2/Chapter10/Appendix6.html.

afford this neutrality because his industry *exported* as much forest product as it imported. A tariff would not appreciably affect prices—Kirby stated as much—but would only complicate patterns of trade. Only after World War II would forestry exports be outpaced by imports, mostly Canadian timber supplying northern markets.

In his role as president of STA, Kirby gave speeches across the South and traveled to Washington to participate in tariff debates. He tied the Founding Fathers to the doctrine of protectionism and justified duties on the theory "that a man should pay taxes in accordance with the amount of protection or security that his government gives him." To those unschooled in classical economics and to those whose business fortunes were threatened by imports, Kirby was convincing.[15]

⌐∾·

Kirby's protectionism went from the international border to the corner store. As in other states, the Texas legislature in 1930 debated placing an occupation tax on chain stores to help the mom-and-pop individual proprietorships. The greater the number of commonly owned stores, the higher the tax per store, a measure designed to negate the new retailers' economies of scale.[16]

Kirby asked legislators to exempt Kirby Lumber's commissaries—general stores that served workers in the small timber towns. Otherwise, he supported the tax as helping the little guy and gal. As he wrote to one legislator:

> Very probably there should be some legislation on the subject of Chain Stores. My objection to the system is that it tends to diminish the opportunities of our young men and young women who have an ambition to be merchants because the system of Chain Stores is monopolistic in effect.... If all the stores were owned by the Chain people then all of the boys and girls will be reduced to the position of clerks without the opportunity to develop into merchants upon their own account.

Parsing the issues, he added, "It is the economic effect of the Chain Store system rather than the convenience and cheapness of distribution to which I object."

Another Kirby deviation from limited government was titanic. As an anti-Depression measure, he advocated a *$50 billion* bond issue by the federal government to buy and improve land for sale to citizens at a subsidized interest rate. "Having played Big Brother to the people abroad," Kirby asked rhetorically in March 1932, "is it not time that we showed some concern for the great American people who furnished this money?" Newspapers across the country

---

15. Also see Internet appendix 10.7, "Kirby and Protectionism," at www.politicalcapitalism. org/Book2/Chapter10/Appendix7.html.

16. Eighteen states passed such taxes between 1927 and 1934, but not Texas.

had fun with the 72-year-old's back-to-the-land proposal. One noted that this sum was greater than the nation's total bank deposits!

Bankruptcy, Again

Kirby's personal and philanthropic habits made him fond of debt, and debt turned into a very bad thing with the advent of the Great Depression and deflation. In the Roaring Twenties, his personal net worth had been about $22 million ($30 million in assets minus $8 million in liabilities), buoyed by a 75 percent ownership of Kirby Lumber.

Suddenly, it was gone. With Kirby Lumber operating only 3 of 12 mills, with oil prices depressed, with a failed timber investment on the Pacific Coast, and in arrears on his taxes, John Henry Kirby filed for personal bankruptcy on May 9, 1933, blaming FDR:

> Personally this debacle, sometimes called the depression, wrecked me and many other good citizens, because when the government went down in credit by repudiating its obligations, public confidence was destroyed and only the strong could survive. In my case I borrowed too much money to lend to my friends who were unable to return it to enable me to be classed among the strong ones. I turned over to my creditors all of the property I had accumulated during fifty years of business activity.

The incurable optimist, now 75, spoke bravely. "I face the future with confidence, and with the restoration of our precious government which the patriotic forefathers established for us, I can come back."

Houston, faring much better than the most of country, owing to a petroleum industry built around the great oil wealth of East Texas and an emerging natural gas business, was shocked by Kirby's filing. There were rumors, but no one thought it would come to this. Wasn't John Henry Kirby invincible?

Kirby Lumber Company declared bankruptcy in January 1934, eight months after Kirby's personal filing. The company was recapitalized and given a new name, Kirby Lumber Corporation. McDonald Meachum was appointed receiver and head of the company. With hundreds of interventions in the case, Andrews & Kurth, attorneys for Kirby Lumber, together with many other legal scavengers, would do very well.

Samuel Insull went bust in 1932 and lived abroad on the cash his son could ferry to him. Kirby was spared Insull's predicament through the charity of his companies. Kirby Lumber gave its namesake an honorary title—chairman of the board—and a $15,000 salary (more than $200,000 per annum today). Kirby also received $5,000 per annum as head of Kirby Petroleum. He retained his mansion and furnishings by law, and his lifetime railroad passes could take him most anywhere in the country. All this was enough for him to remain active and champion his causes, although his days as a philanthropist were all but over.

Just shy of his eightieth birthday, having gone from the backwoods to the highest station in life, having endured bankruptcies nearly 30 years apart, John Henry Kirby died at his Houston mansion. On November 9, 1940, the person was gone. But his name lived on with the Kirby Building and Kirby Mansion in downtown Houston; Kirby Drive running through the River Oaks subdivision, the future home of Ray Fish, Jack Bowen, Robert Herring, Jeff Skilling, and Ken Lay; Kirbyville and John Henry Kirby State Forest in East Texas; and his namesake companies. John Henry Kirby had other markers, such as the towns he named after family and friends.[17] A thousand stories survived, as well as a saying that would ring through East Texas for decades, "I'm feeling pretty good, thank the Lord and John Henry Kirby."

Kirby died with little to offset $2.5 million in debt. Most estates, even bankrupt ones, could be liquidated and closed in a year, but not his. Litigation erupted, and the estate's mineral rights would blossom into assets as new drilling found enough oil and gas to pay the lawyers and postpone a final liquidation.

It was *the estate that would not die*, as if John Henry Kirby was working from the grave. Six receivers presided over the estate, and the IRS began taxing the estate as an ongoing concern. Final disbursements in the mid-1960s allowed the creditors to get their principal back, although depreciated dollars (as a result of inflation) were received, and no interest payments were received.

John Henry Kirby Reconsidered

John Henry Kirby, the happy-go-lucky prince of the pines, was extremely intelligent and likable. To know him was to come under his spell. Even today, his charming, erudite correspondence makes it difficult for the chronicler to be anything but sympathetic.

Kirby was a passionate man with countless good deeds to his credit. Yet his personality had downside. Kirby was at the center of the greatest business debacle of his day, and his largesse came at the expense of his creditors, whose interests surely came first.

Kirby's political philosophy was hardly the principled capitalism that was advertised by him or many interpreters. His thinking on some of the most important issues of the day was superficial, not learned, and damaging to the very economic system he professed to honor.

---

17. Houston writer Leon Hale remarked: "Kirby was maybe the town-namingest Texan that ever lived. He named Bessmay for Bessmay Kirby, and Votaw for the assistant land commissioner of his lumber company, and Evadale for a music teacher at Jasper, and Kirbyville for himself. And he hung names on who knows how many of his lumber camps, some of which developed into towns and some of which faded away."

Unquenchable Optimist

In his personal and public lives, John Henry Kirby was much like Ken Lay of Enron infamy. Both were incurable business optimists who counted success after success before hitting the shoals of shipwreck. Kirby's pronouncements before his early receivership were not unlike Ken Lay's assurances about righting a tottering Enron a century later.

"Houston Oil Company ... is going to have a market value second to no oil stock in the country," Kirby told one investor. "Kirby Lumber Company ... is one of the most meritorious enterprises ever organized," he opined to another. "[I]t is going to pay good money and take care of itself amply."

In mid-1903 Kirby wrote: "The financial condition of the Kirby Lumber Company will be as strong as any institution in this country, and I have confidence that we shall be able to make a record with it that will place it among the leading industrial organization[s] of America." But he also admitted "the iron facts" that "after eighteen months of the hardest work and the greatest anxiety of my life, and after turning over to our friends East a business opportunity that I had created after fifteen years of slavery, my fortune is a great deal smaller than it would have been had I never touched this enterprise." In fact, both companies would never get off the ground and entered into receivership in early 1904.

In later life, Kirby's communications incessantly indicated a running battle between cash flow and his obligations. But his philanthropy continued.

"Lord Bountiful"

John Henry Kirby gave away an estimated $8 million in his lifetime—a figure that would be a dozen times more in contemporary dollars. Frank Andrews, Kirby's attorney and a principal of the firm today known as Andrews & Kurth, spoke for many at Kirby's seventy-fifth birthday celebration when he said: "This man has loved more people, helped more people and done good to more people to his own hurt than any man who ever lived." Another concluded: "No man ever lived who found it harder to say no, when he was asked for help." The *Houston Post* asked, "When again shall the elements of genius in the material realm, of rare intelligence, of iron integrity, of love of country, of loyalty to conviction, of native generosity and of winsome personality be so merged in one man, as that we shall have his like again?"

Kirby's time was also donated generously. "He never dodged a civic job," stated Jack Dionne, "and never failed to put his best efforts behind each one." "Lord Bountiful," another wrote, "appears to have operated on the theory that it is better to be taken in by ninety-nine frauds than to refuse one deserving person."

But the populist businessman-philanthropist was the creditors' foe, for creditors lost what the recipients of Kirby's largesse gained. Kirby gave until he was broke—and past broke. Typical was a letter to a student in need: "Creditors can wait; your education cannot. Enclosed you will find a check." Politics could not wait either, as when Kirby donated $15,000 to the Democratic Party during the Great Depression, a time when his second bankruptcy loomed.

Kirby's munificence explains how he remained so popular despite his financial setbacks. Never has a multibankrupted man been so universally loved and acclaimed. Still, Kirby was effectively committing theft by providing charity with dollars that were not his. True philanthropists do not borrow to give and then default. *"The munificent charity of an insolvent estate appears to me ghastly,"* moralist Samuel Smiles once said. Adam Smith, who blessed his country's harsh laws against bankruptcy, would no doubt agree.[18]

The man with a "social conscience" also had a proclivity for running his mills at a loss to keep his beloved laborers afloat. It is fiscally prudent to keep a unit running if variable costs are met and a contribution made to fixed costs such as debt. But running operations only to benefit labor is a transfer of wealth from investors and creditors, and it is unsustainable.

Kirby sometimes crossed this line from investor to welfare provider. "Long after the lumber market justified," one tribute to Kirby surmised, "he continued to run his mills that his employees might have food, clothing, and shelter." The desperate times of the Great Depression, when new businesses were less able to pick up the pieces of failed ones, thanks to unprecedented government intervention in the economy, mitigates a harsh judgment of Kirby's folly. But selling products at a loss destroys wealth that could have been put to productive and profitable use once unproductive plants were closed and unprofitable workers were dispersed.

Kirby was bankrupt but unbowed. "I would infinitely prefer that posterity should say of me that I have won and held the confidence and friendship of men than that I had earned and saved great wealth," he declared. "I would infinitely prefer that it be said of me that I was a good citizen; that I loved the United States; that I supported its constitution; that I obeyed its laws; that I respected its flag and that I defended it against its enemies, than to be applauded throughout all the generations as a great financier or a great captain of industry."

So be it. But dissipated wealth from bad business practices is not charity; it is the opposite. And spending past solvency to leave creditors holding the bag is robbing Peter to pay Paul. It is also, if Smiles is right, *moral* bankruptcy.

Business failure happens in a free market. But two bankruptcies are a pattern, and the rights and welfare of creditors—the capital of capitalism—come first.

Capitalism à la Carte
John Henry Kirby was fond of quoting a dictum of Thomas Jefferson—"That government is best which governs least"—and adding, "We've got to get

---

18. See *Capitalism at Work*, pp. 27–29, 51–53.

entirely away from the idea that it is the duty of the government to support the people." According to his biographer, Kirby "was always violently opposed to Federal invasion of personal and private rights."

Kirby in action, however, advocated and sought government favor at many turns. Didn't Kirby champion economic isolationism from foreign products, as well as discriminatory taxation to hurt scale retailers and help mom-and-pop stores? Wasn't this the man who proposed such a large government welfare program that even the New Dealers laughed? And didn't he support Prohibition, one of America's most unworkable social experiments?

Like many before and since, John Henry Kirby could talk a good game about life, liberty, and the pursuit of happiness. But walking the talk was another thing, especially in times of business need. Kirby professed his opposition to antitrust law but rattled the antitrust saber after his creditors placed his companies into receivership in 1904. This political capitalist welcomed the prospect of state regulation to increase crude oil prices in the 1930s. Yes, Kirby liked to appear above the fray when it came to the protection of lumber. But given the prevailing terms of trade, he could afford to. Had his timber income been depressed by imports, Kirby undoubtedly would have added lumber to the 1920s wish list of the Southern Tariff Association.

Kirby loved books and learning. "I am never happier than when in my own library reading," he once said. Among his 3,000 volumes was surely the bible of capitalism, *The Wealth of Nations*, which refuted the economic argument for protectionism. The wealth of nations came from increasing specialization in an international division of labor, Adam Smith explained.[19] Labor was never more productive than in an open international market, although workers had to be willing to change jobs to exploit their comparative advantage.[20] Universal tariffs would protect not only the least efficient businesses but also all but invite the efficient to become less so behind a wall of protection.

Kirby was for exports and against imports, yet imports gave foreigners American dollars to buy American goods (exports) or to invest in American financial institutions. (Exports would include Southwest lumber, including Kirby's.) International trade improved cross-border relations; protectionism invited retaliation. Herbert Hoover's Hawley-Smoot Tariff Act of 1932 led to retaliatory protectionism, which contributed to America's general economic

---

19. See *Capitalism at Work*, pp. 32–33.

20. David Ricardo (1772–1823), the most famous economist in the period after Adam Smith, discovered the law of comparative advantage, which said that even if a nation is better than another nation at producing everything, it is to the advantage of all for each country to produce what it is *relatively* better at producing, and then trade.

malaise, which—ironically—contributed to the bankruptcy of John Henry Kirby and Kirby Lumber Corporation.

Kirby's endorsement of chain store taxes was based on a romantic, the-way-it-has-always-been past. Business change in a free market is about better service to consumers with better pricing, more convenience, and greater variety—which chain stores offered. Kirby's idealistic naïveté was also manifested in his proposed $50 billion back-to-the-land palliative during the Great Depression, a crying gasp from an old man about to enter into personal bankruptcy. Desperate times lead men to say and do desperate things.

⌒

Nice guys can finish last in a free-market world of creative destruction. But John Henry Kirby wasn't just a nice guy who benefitted many but failed through factors beyond his control. His "unshakeable faith" in his business ventures and his unfunded charity directly created victims, mostly silent, invisible, and unknown. The same would be true of another Great Man who was far too aggressive, optimistic, and showy—Ken Lay, the central figure of the final bankruptcy associated with the Kirby story: that of Enron Corp.

11

Robert Herring and Ray Fish

THE PREVIOUS CHAPTER SHOWED how Jack Bowen was the link between first-generation natural gas pipeliner Clint Murchison and third-generation pipeliner Ken Lay. This chapter documents the mentorship between first-generation pipeliner Ray Fish and second-generation pipeliner Robert Herring. Thus, Herring and Bowen were leaders of the second generation: Herring atop the premier intrastate, Houston Natural Gas Corporation; Bowen, as head of the nation's biggest interstate gas carrier, Transco Energy. In different ways, both men are part of the prehistory of the company that for most of the 1980s and 1990s was the largest pipeline operator in America, Enron Corporation.

"Pretty Boy"—Robert Herring

The news spread fast in the small West Texas town of Ranger one January day in 1923. The local paper reported that the son, not quite two, of Lonnie and Clara Herring "captured almost everything in sight" at the bicounty Better Baby Show. Of the 17 finalists, Robert Ray won first prize, grand prize, and the silver loving cup. Another newspaper asked whether the pretty boy had "accumulated enough fame on which to retire." Robert Herring (1921–81) would never retire. Therein lies a key part of the Enron prehistory.[1]

The haloed baby wasn't born with a silver spoon in his mouth. Very few were in rural America, particularly during the Great Depression, which began

---

1. Robert Herring was born in Childress, Texas on February 11, 1921, and died in Houston, Texas, on October 11, 1981, age 60. He spent his entire life in Texas except for his World War II military service.

in late 1929 and stubbornly persisted through the 1930s. The good news was that Lonnie had a steady job as chief engineer of a gas-liquids plant owned by Lone Star Gas Company of Dallas, Texas. Stripping BTUs out of methane to make natural gasoline was very competitive in the hydrocarbon belt, and Papa Herring's job was to make sure that all the equipment was running efficiently.

Robert's mother, Clara, was a school teacher. She was also the family disciplinarian, all the more so because of her husband's gregarious and carefree manner.

The Herring house was one of several in Camp 101, a compound owned by the Delhi Oil Company two miles outside of Ranger.[2] Robert's basic necessities were taken care of, but any luxuries would have to wait. The greatest luxury of his youth—indoor plumbing—came when Robert was well into high school. Such conditions were shared by many families. There wasn't much to envy in rural West Texas in those days.

Robert showed great promise from the get-go. Legend has it that his mother had to reprimand him only once—a swat on the hand when the six-month-old invaded a freshly baked cake. (Clara, not easily impressed, would later call Robert "a near marvel.") Robert was a good student and popular with his teachers and classmates. He participated in speech and debate and, with the help of his father, became an Eagle Scout.

Robert's work life began early as a soda jerk at the local drugstore and then with jobs at the picture show. Ranger had two theaters—the Shoot 'em Up and Love 'em Up. Like the other theater hands, Robert graduated from the former to work at the latter. The only known bad experience during these years was not his fault. One day while walking home alone on the railroad tracks after work, Robert was roughed up and robbed.

Robert skipped a grade at Ranger High School and, at age 16, entered John Tarleton State Junior College, a military school in Stephenville, Texas. Never did he look so handsome as in his army cadet uniform, which he proudly wore around campus. He majored in chemical engineering as his father wished and got a taste of politics when he was elected senior representative to the student council. His good looks and popularity earned him the campus nickname, "Pretty Boy."

After graduating from Tarleton, Herring enrolled at Texas A&M University. He was interested in the social sciences and decided to major in economics rather than engineering. Social science offered a much broader view of the world, which he liked. In spring 1941, the 20-year-old received his bachelor of science in economics.

---

2. Clint Murchison's Delhi Oil was the company that hired Jack Bowen as junior engineer in 1949. Bowen and Herring both went through the military but got to know each other only through business in the 1960s.

HERE ARE PRIZE WINNERS
IN RANGER BABY CONTEST

ROBERT R. HERRING
BRECKENRIDGE, TEXAS
CANDIDATE FOR CONGRESS
FROM THE
17TH DISTRICT OF TEXAS

Figure 11.1 A young Robert Herring in the newspaper; Herring in uniform at Tarleton State; and Herring in Air Force uniform as a candidate for Congress.

"A World Beyond"

After graduation, what to do? Robert was interested in pursuing a graduate degree to learn more about business and government and perhaps enter the diplomatic corps. Politics seemed interesting. Military fever was rising on the troubling news from Europe. What better place to be positioned than in Washington, D.C.! Robert could not afford to do just anything, but he convinced his parents of the opportunities there. Lonnie and Clara reached deep and bought him a one-way bus ticket to the nation's capital to let him try.

Robert almost lost his chance. The bus caught fire even before it reached Ft. Worth. Everyone was stranded, their possessions destroyed. Among the losses was the lone draft of a novel he was writing, "A World Beyond." But the industrious young man from Ranger did what came naturally to him. He sprang into action, writing down the name of each passenger, cataloguing their lost possessions, and helping arrange alternative transportation. The appreciative bus company reissued Robert his ticket and gave him a bit of spending money to complete the trip. Returning to Ranger never crossed his mind.

In Washington, Herring found entry-level work at the Department of Agriculture and enrolled in night school at Georgetown University, pursuing a master's degree in government, economics, and international law. Then, just a few months later, everything changed with Japan's attack on Pearl Harbor. Planning to enlist in the army, Herring happened upon a retired military man on a park bench. "No, no," said the man upon hearing of Herring's intention. "You want to get into the Air Corps, into intelligence."

The two talked at length, after which the gentleman gave Herring a place to stay until he enlisted. As luck would have it, Herring had found a mentor in a desperate hour, a man whom he would forever credit with setting him on a new course that would help build the skill set he would need in his future career.

In March 1942, Herring embellished his age by a year and enlisted in the U.S. Air Force. He was just in time for the first class of the intelligence school at Harrisburg, Pennsylvania. After graduation, the second lieutenant, Intelligence Corps, was sent to New Guinea. Three months later, Herring began a 45-month tour of duty in the Pacific where he served as a leading intelligence officer on the staffs of General George C. Kenney and General Douglas MacArthur in campaigns that included the Battle of the Bismarck Sea.

Robert proved proficient in the service. Lonnie and Clara received a letter from a fellow intelligence officer praising Robert's "uncanny predictions" and his ability to "keep more information and figures in his head than I could keep in a notebook." The letter told the proud parents that Robert had integrated intelligence protocol between different Air Force sections, generals were bidding for Herring's services, and those in the know wanted Robert grounded from air combat to concentrate on intelligence work.

But Herring flew missions and completed intelligence assignments, and by the end of the war, 63 bombing runs and 465 hours of air combat duty had earned him a Silver Star, 13 Battle Stars, 2 Legion of Merit badges, and the rank of Lieutenant Colonel. He was involved in the planning of the atomic bomb's drop on Japan.[3] Herring stayed through the initial occupations of Japan and Korea before returning to civilian life, at age 24, a decorated war hero.

Herring endured some harrowing events in his four years of duty, including plane crashes. But something else was perilous as far as his future was concerned. It seemed harmless at the time. A random assignment in New Guinea had him guarding a covered mound of supplies. His nerves were tested by intermittent bombings punctuated by utter stillness and boredom. Curious, Herring looked under the flap to discover stacks of cigarette cartons. He opened a pack and lit up.

He enjoyed smoking, lighting one cigarette right after the other. Clara had kept her children away from cigarettes for a reason. She believed that the death of her brother-in-law from cancer was due to smoking, and her mother's boarding house was burned down by a smoker. When Clara opened a wartime letter that included a photo of Robert holding a cigarette, she muttered, "Oh, no."

---

3. See Internet appendix 11.1, "Herring at Ground Zero," at www.politicalcapitalism.org/Book2/Chapter11/Appendix2.html.

Back to Texas

Herring's first move in civilian life occurred before he left the South Pacific when he married Sylvia Grant, an attractive Australian of Scottish-Irish descent, whom he had met during the war on a blind date in her native town of Sydney, Australia, where he was sent to recuperate from a jungle disease. It was love at first sight, and the two stayed in touch. On his last "mission," Herring and 35 crewmen flew in a warplane from Tokyo to Sydney for the wedding ceremony.

The newlyweds began life together in Breckenridge, Texas, a small town about 100 miles west of Fort Worth, where Lonnie managed a gas plant. Lonnie, Clara, and Robert's younger sister and brother lived on the local compound.

Figure 11.2 Wife Sylvia Grant was Robert Herring's gift from World War II. Her death in 1971 left him with their three children.

Political ambitions were foremost on Robert's mind. He had credentials and confidence as a college-degreed, decorated war veteran. He also had strategic experience and a knack for all things interpersonal. Robert committed his only $1,000, saved up during the war, to run for U.S. Congress from the 17th District of Texas.

His campaign letterhead included the slogan: "The democratic principles of individual freedom, free enterprise, and state rights free from bureaucratic controls are inherent as the basis of our life; that they be preserved in strong and true form is my promise for service." Robert and Sylvia campaigned hard, but he came in second out of a field of eight in the Democratic primary. The victor, Omar Burleson, won the general election in 1946 handily, as Democrats regularly did in Texas, and would go on to hold this seat for 32 years.

Politics out of his system, Robert turned to selling a product the war had popularized for servicemen and their families—life insurance. Although he could not fully grasp it at the time, these policies provided the capital needed to finance the capital-intensive, long-lived natural gas pipeline industry. Individual investors, with a short time horizon, were not a good match for gas pipeline bonds. But the insurance industry was ideal for financing the gas industry's 20- and 30-year notes.

When Herring began his practice, life insurance companies provided several hundred million dollars of capital to the industry; by 1955, the insurance industry held nearly $2 billion of gas pipeline notes, 65 percent of the industry's total indebtedness.[4] Herring and many other life insurance agents substituted, as it were, for utility holding companies that had once capitalized pipelines. Such multistate holding companies had been disbanded by a 1935 federal law, the Public Utility Holding Company Act, enacted in the wake of the collapse of Samuel Insull's utility empire in 1932.[5]

⟜⟍

Herring's selling skills caught the attention of Milton Daniel, a Breckinridge businessman. The two talked, and Herring was hired to manage oil and gas properties that Daniel and 22 others owned in partnership. Milton also helped the youngster with the winsome personality and lovely wife be elected mayor of Breckenridge, a part-time office Robert held from 1946 to 1949.

A negotiation on behalf of Daniel in Houston would put Herring in a new business orbit. The meeting was with Ray Fish, founder and head of Fish Engineering Corporation, a builder of gas pipelines and other energy infrastructure.

Fish wanted Daniel's gas for an interstate project. Herring, not getting the favorable terms he wanted, broke off negotiations and returned to Breckenridge. For Herring, that was the end of that. But Ray Fish was soon in Breckenridge finding out everything he could about the resolute young man. The gas deal suddenly became secondary when Fish asked Herring to join his three-year-old company as vice president and his personal assistant.

Herring demurred, but Sylvia insisted that he take the job and that they move to Houston. The year was 1950. The United States was in a postwar

---

4. Restated in today's dollars, insurance companies were responsible for more than $13 billion of the pipeline industry's total $21 billion debt capitalization.

5. The Public Utility Holding Company Act of 1935 is discussed in chapter 5, pp. 218–19.

economic boom, and natural gas was coming into its own as a household and boiler fuel.

Herring had found his second mentor in Milton Daniel. But it was Ray Fish who would prove to be the most lasting and special. "Whatever ability I have in the gas business, it is due to Ray Fish," Herring would say decades later. "He was one of the great pioneers in this industry, and he was blessed with more vision than anyone else in the field."

"Mr. Pipeliner"—Ray Fish

Ray Fish (1902–62) was unique in the history of the twentieth-century U.S. natural gas industry. He was not a great wildcatter like Sid Richardson and some others. He did not create and run a large publicly held gas-transmission company like Paul Kayser of El Paso Natural Gas, Gardiner Symonds of Tennessee Gas Transmission, Reginald Hargrove of Texas Eastern Gas Transmission, or Claude Williams of Transcontinental Gas Pipe Line. Nor was Fish an integrated gas operator or venture capitalist like Clint Murchison.

Ray Fish was the century's most accomplished designer and builder of gas-transmission systems, both before and after he founded Fish Engineering Corporation in 1946. His "idea to operation" oeuvre began with engineering and construction. Then came a full range of services for the industry: procuring gas supply, executing gas-sales contracts, designing transmission rates, setting up accounting systems, preparing applications for regulatory approval, negotiating financing, and training personnel for postconstruction operations. The Fish Engineering Corporation, and no other, offered *total project outsourcing* to the midstream gas industry.

∾

Ray Clinton Fish was born March 6, 1902, in Tiverton, Rhode Island, a quaint seventeenth-century town of Revolutionary War fame, located on an inlet of the Atlantic Ocean. As the son of a commercial fisherman and grandson of a sea captain who sailed the South Pacific, Ray grew up hearing about the wonders of California and Texas. These states were larger than life, far-away places few townsfolk had visited. Some stories, and a few tall tales, concerned the romance of the petroleum industry. From his early childhood, Fish began to dream "beyond the horizon" (not unlike Herring's "A World Beyond"), a motif he would use to characterize his 40-year professional life.

The bright-eyed youngster excelled in grammar school in Tiverton and high school in nearby Fall River, Massachusetts, after which he enrolled in and took his first business course at Roger Williams College in Providence. Fish was more interested in working in the local textile mills, however, where he discovered his proficiency in solving engineering problems. Wanting more, and taking a risk even he could not completely understand, the 21-year-old packed a few possessions and journeyed far in search of opportunity in the energy business.

He journeyed first all the way to Utah, his first stop, to work at a coal mine. But California is where he wanted to be. Soon, he was in Long Beach, working as a roughneck at the Signal Hill field—the hottest oil play in the country.

Discovered in 1921, Signal Hill's feverish lease speculation, town-lot drilling, and loads of oil made it "the richest oil field per acre in all history" by the time Fish arrived in 1924. Not since the Spindletop strike near Beaumont, Texas in 1901 had there been such a flurry of excitement and movement of men and materials in the petroleum industry.

Unlike his coworkers, Fish did not spend his nights carousing. He saw his job as a beginning, a means, not a lifestyle or end. Evenings were for self-education, reading practical books about industry, men, and events that would stir the imagination and help him rise in the world. Moralist Samuel Smiles (of Book 1) could not have picked better.

Earning enough money, Fish resumed his college studies, this time at the University of Southern California. But his real passion lay outside the window, so he left USC after three semesters for a full-time position at the Los Angeles refinery of General Petroleum Corporation. On-the-job training made him an engineer, degree or not, like many others of his generation, including Clint Murchison.

Fish did well at General Petroleum and in 1926 boldly invested his earnings in three small area refineries. It seemed the beginning of something grand—at least until the notorious gasoline price wars in the Los Angeles Basin ruined his plans. There was just too much supply relative to demand, and margins suffered. Industry leaders Signal Oil and Gas Company and Standard Oil of California (later Chevron) were making gasoline from natural gas at the wellhead. A flood of crude oil had to be turned into products and sold in a limited geographical area because the topography of the region made transportation to other markets for better prices difficult.

Unlike integrated oil companies, refiners like Fish couldn't recoup their losses at the wellhead. Refinery margins were more volatile than in any other phase of the industry.[6] Fish had once seen a healthy spread between crude oil and gasoline; now it had evaporated. Fish lost his entire investment.

The technically gifted young man learned a lesson. From now on, he would concentrate on engineering and construction projects under contract with strong companies. Commodity-price risk would be borne by others.

⌁

---

6. "The fluctuations in the refining margin were characteristically more violent than at any other level of the industry," a Harvard Business School study would later explain. For integrated majors, it was more like business as usual, because "in gaining protection against wide fluctuations in its profit position, an integrated company not only avoids large, short-term losses but also foregoes the opportunity for large, short-term gains."

The road back began in 1927 with the Los Angeles firm of J. A. Campbell, where Fish supervised construction of gas-liquids plants and oil refineries. After three years in the Golden State, the 26-year-old was loaned out to manage the construction of a natural gas processing plant in Alto, Louisiana. The call had come from Denver-based Stearns-Roger Manufacturing Company, which was behind schedule and facing performance penalties on the project. Lou Weiss, an executive for Stearns-Roger, was good enough friends with Julian Campbell to borrow one of his best young men.

Weiss was at the train station at nearby Monroe to greet his new troubleshooter. Before long, Fish turned things around at the plant, and an ahead-of-schedule finish earned a significant and welcome bonus from the client.

Weiss, seeing a rare talent, hired Fish to become operating manager of Stearns-Roger's entire oil and gas division, which was focused on a variety of construction projects in the prolific Monroe gas field.

Northeast Louisiana was a mecca for the fledgling natural gas industry. Two of the nation's longest pipelines had been built from Monroe to Houston and Beaumont in the mid-1920s. Three new lines were underway from Monroe to St. Louis, Atlanta, and Memphis. Only the Hugoton gas field in the Texas Panhandle could rival the activity that Fish found. The man who would become known as Mr. Pipeliner was right where he needed to be.

After Louisiana, it was to Moore County, Texas, where Fish designed and built gas-liquids plants for Stearns-Roger client Shamrock Oil and Gas Company between 1933 and 1937. Gas formerly flared was piped into the plant, where products such as natural gasoline (then worth a nickel per gallon) were produced. Market conservation was at work.

A history of Stearns-Roger described a man "constantly on the go":

> [Ray Fish] eventually became one of the most prolific salesmen Stearns-Roger had ever seen. He was very personable, and clients and fellow employees alike placed great faith and confidence in him. He was extremely ambitious, hard working, and impatient to a fault. Nothing ever was finished quickly enough to suit Ray.

Stearns-Roger, founded in 1885 and continuously operated out of Denver, was an industry leader in the design and manufacture of industrial projects, including natural gas pipelines. Good projects came Fish's way. The biggest and most challenging was a job in the late 1930s to design a large-diameter line to bring gas from the Texas Gulf to New York City. The project was sponsored by a paper company owned by Hope Natural Gas Company (Jersey Standard) and a Chicago corporation, Reserve Gas Pipeline Company.

Gas-supply commitments were lined up, but the necessary sales contracts proved elusive. Consolidated Edison, Brooklyn Union, and other Northeast utilities were hesitant to execute agreements that would require them to write off their extensive coal-gas facilities. Negotiations ceased with the advent of World War II.

Ray Fish and Stearns-Roger came back into the interstate pipeline picture several years later when the Federal Power Commission (FPC) certificated a proposal to bring natural gas from the Texas Gulf to Appalachia, a center of wartime manufacture.[7] A coveted steel allocation was awarded by the War Production Board. Tennessee Gas and Transmission Company (Tennessee Gas), headed by a 40-year-old Harvard MBA, Gardiner Symonds, turned to the young man who had scoped the Reserves Gas line several years before.

At Symonds's insistence, Fish took a leave of absence from Stearns-Roger to join Tennessee Gas in October 1943 as vice president and director with responsibilities for design, engineering, and construction.[8] His colleagues back at Stearns-Roger would do all the compressor work, but Ray would be wearing the client's hat for a while. Fish then chose the rest of the team. Bechtel-Dempsey-Price, the primary contractor, subcontracted with Williams Brothers and a company that would later make its own name in the interstate gas transmission industry: Brown & Root.[9]

The 1,265-mile line was completed in less than a year, supplying 200 MMcf/d to defense plants and other users in and around Pittsburgh, Youngstown, and Wheeling. The Tennessee Gas Transmission project not only broke a decade-long dry spell in the long-line gas-transmission industry, but also was the start of the postwar boom in interstate pipelines.

The first annual report of Tennessee Gas Transmission announced that first-year deliveries exceeded design capacity, "demonstrat[ing] that the pipe line system is well designed and constructed." Ray Fish and his contractors had successfully incorporated the latest technology to set a new standard.

Mission accomplished, Fish returned to Stearns-Roger in 1945 as head of its natural gas pipeline division. But something bugged him upon his triumphant return. His bosses gave him only a $5,000 promoter's check (bonus) for the huge project he had brought to the company. Ray thought, "I can do this myself." And just then, Fish zeroed in on an opportunity to build a second major interstate line—and not for his employer. It was time once again to think beyond the horizon.

---

7. Under the Natural Gas Act of 1938, interstate gas lines had to receive a certificate of public convenience and necessity from the Federal Power Commission to build and commence service. A 1942 revision tightened the certification requirement and put the burden of proof on new entrants into occupied areas.

8. "Gardiner [Symonds] and I were the first two employees of Tennessee Gas ... at the same hour and same minute of the same day. Dick Wagner substantially turned it over to us and said 'Go build it'."

9. This entry by Brown & Root would lead to George and Herman Brown's participation in a consortium that would win an auction for the Big Inch and Little Inch oil pipelines in 1947, which were subsequently converted to natural gas. See chapter 9, pp. 315–17.

Ray Fish foresaw a breakout in the natural gas business. Reserves were rapidly expanding in the triangle between New Mexico, Kansas, and Louisiana. Welding technology was making the seams stronger than the pipe itself. Markets were abandoning coal gas for cheaper, cleaner natural gas. Pipeline systems operating in one state (such as Houston Pipe Line Company in Texas), unregulated and market responsive, were booming. Louisiana, where Fish had cut his teeth in gas transmission, was becoming spaghetti-like too. And new players—independents and start-ups—were stepping in where, preregulation, the major oil companies with all the gas reserves had dominated.[10]

The federally regulated interstate gas market benefitted from all the intrastate activity. Under the Natural Gas Act, incumbents gained an advantage. New projects faced hearings on why a new line was needed rather than an expansion by the existing provider. Public-utility regulation did have risks, as the gas industry would later find out. But pipelines could be a so-called cash cow if their rate base could be maintained or expanded and company expenses did not run afoul of the FPC's just-and-reasonable standard.[11]

The initial cost of construction set the rate base. This meant that a somewhat higher cost here or there—say, for premium or superpremium quality—accrued to the benefit of the contractor *and* the owners. Cost-plus contracts worked well as long as the resulting rates enticed buyers to leave manufactured gas for natural gas. This was easier than the unregulated intrastate market, where gas-on-gas competition was more pronounced. And it was a far cry from the commodity-price risk that got the best of Fish back in California as an asset owner.

Fish Engineering Corporation

In April 1946, Fish left Stearns-Roger to form Fish Engineering Corporation in Houston, already the nation's energy capital.[12] He brought with him four seasoned Stearns-Roger colleagues, each to manage a division: pipelines, oil refineries, gas

---

10. Fish supported the passage of the Natural Gas Act of 1938, citing the prior "abuse" by the majors in deciding what cities to serve or not serve ("they skimmed the cream"), since they controlled the gas reserves. "It was the abuses of the Insull crowds ... the Cities Service group of companies, and all the rest that were in the gas business."

11. Public-utility regulation, as Samuel Insull had discovered earlier with electricity (see pp. 125–26), was a double-edged sword. The natural gas industry found this out when regulatory creep expanded cost-based rates from interstate pipelines to gas production dedicated to interstate commerce. The result was gas shortages in the 1970s, which promoted hyperaggressive supply contracting and gas surpluses in the 1980s, as discussed in chapter 9.

12. Houston was the natural home for an industry engineering firm. The interstate gas-transmission industry was Houston based, Fish noted, and "helped to bring prosperity to this whole area" that had once been a "cow town."

liquids facilities, and chemical/petrochemical plants.[13] The five pooled $60,000 (over a half million in today's dollars) to capitalize the closely held company. This corporate structure tied them to collective success. This ownership approach would also allow them to attract cream-of-the-crop talent from other leading companies in the field, such as Fluor, Texaco, and Dow Chemical.[14]

The company started with a few desks, chairs, and typewriters in 1,600 square feet of office space. In short order, the bank credit line reached a million dollars on the strength of signed contracts. One of Fish Engineering's early plums was consulting work for the just-incorporated Trans-Continental Gas Pipe Line Corporation, destined to become the third and largest interstate serving the Northeast.

Trans-Continental had been formed to buy and convert the federal government's wartime Big Inch and Little Inch pipelines to natural gas. After narrowly losing the bid to Texas Eastern Transmission Corporation in 1946, the pipeline's organizers forged ahead with plans to build their own line from the Gulf Coast to the Mid-Atlantic seaboard and up to New York City.

The FPC certificated the renamed Transcontinental Gas Pipe Line (later Transco) in May 1948. Four months later, Fish Engineering finalized a contract to design, engineer, build, and test the line. The personal investment of Fish and his partners in the paper project was decisive in winning the project. So was their idea-to-completion (turnkey) service, which included setting up a uniform accounting system for regulatory scrutiny and calculating rates per customer class within the total revenue requirement, as determined by regulators.

The 20-month construction process included new techniques to improve efficiency and durability, such as reengineering pipe-welding processes to be done on site rather than at the factory. That first would lead an interviewer to ask Fish to name other breakthroughs, to which he replied many years later: "No, I can't [because] … we have done so many firsts since then."

The 1,840-mile pipeline Transcontinental Gas Pipe Line project—the world's longest—delivered 340 MMcf/d from the Rio Grand Valley of south Texas to 134th Street in New York City beginning in early 1951. Expansions would soon be necessary for the lone pipeline serving what was now the world's largest natural gas market.[15]

〜

---

13. At least initially, Richard Ricketts was over pipelines, C. B. Ames over chemical/petrochemical, A. J. L. Hutchinson over process engineering (from Fluor), and O. L. Mullen over construction.

14. Top Fish Engineering executives Hutchison and Tom Tabbert came from Fluor, Robert Imber from Texaco, and Don Simecheck from Dow Chemical.

15. The early history of Transcontinental Gas Pipe Line is described in chapter 9, pp. 314–321.

Fish Engineering boasted a wide array of "idea to operation" projects in its first years. The company advertised a can-do spirit and cited engineering achievements "from Canada to Argentina, from Oregon to Iraq" with a client list that included Chicago Corporation, Humble Oil & Refining, Northern Natural Gas Company, Panhandle Eastern Pipe Line Company, among other industry leaders. Revenue in 1956 of $290 million (a multibillion-dollar sum today) included a Honolulu oil refinery, carbon black plant in Oklahoma, dehydration plant in Louisiana, desulfurization plant in West Texas, and barge-mounted compressor station near New Orleans, in addition to gas pipelines.

Fish Engineering quietly became one of the larger privately held companies in the country, with employment as high as 1,250. The company's cost-plus contracts were structured for profitability, not risk, with the work done within budget and on time. Ray Fish and his bankers rode on the strong credit of the clients, and the infrastructure they built provided strong collateral for their sizeable working-capital needs.

Another plum for Fish Engineering in its early years was a 1,140-mile, 374 MMcf/d gas pipeline from the Texas Gulf to Chicago, sponsored by Peoples Natural Gas Light & Coke Co, a subsidiary of Natural Gas Pipeline of America (NGPL) of Chicago. NGPL had built the nation's first major interstate gas pipeline in 1931, running from the Texas Panhandle to Chicago, an $80 million project of Samuel Insull, one of his last before his insolvency. Peoples engaged Fish to incorporate the latest in project design for the Texas-Illinois Natural Gas Pipeline. The $130 million project (about $1 billion today) received its FPC certificate in mid-1950 and entered service in November 1951 after 14 months of construction.

Fish was a company builder no less than Murchison, Kayser, Symonds, and Hargrove. But he did not continue in pipeline-company management. Fish Engineering was closely held, not a publicly traded corporation. Ray Fish began by persuading a handful of top men to leave satisfactory, stable jobs to aim a little higher. With contracts came hundreds of new positions where Ray set a tone of excitement and challenge. "We are trying not to deliver routine jobs," he said, but "jobs where creativity and a thorough understanding of risk and rewards can turn what is in the imagination into reality."

And not only the principals but also the managers shared in the profits on a project-by-project basis by personally receiving promoter stock. Such issues had a nominal cost—say $2 per share—which could be exercised when the project or company went public at a price of $13 or $16 per share, in many cases.

Fish lived up to what he told clients: "I never start a project that doesn't justify the investment of my own money," he would later reminisce, "and once I know that all risks have been removed, everybody in my office has an opportunity to invest and profit." The dapper pencil-mustached New Englander was a born cheerleader seeking to make every employee like himself—energetic, optimistic, and proficient. He reveled in a good story, even tale. "If you can't tell a story better than you heard it, you're not a good storyteller," he would say.

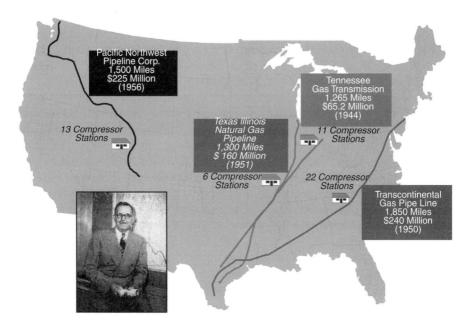

Figure 11.3 Ray Fish earned the moniker Mr. Pipeliner by building Tennessee Gas Transmission (completed 1944), Trans-Continental Pipe Lines (1950), Texas-Illinois Natural Gas (1951), and Pacific Northwest Pipeline (1956). The cost of these projects in today's dollars would be between $4 and $5 billion.

Ray Fish built a strong corporate culture. This resulted from his unique, energetic personality within a self-created privately held company where he was the largest stockholder. The ownership positions of Fish's top lieutenants reinforced what was coming from the top. The overlap between owners and managers avoided the *principal/agent problem* that economists from Adam Smith onward have recognized as a weakness of publicly held companies.[16]

Ray Fish was a self-described creator and builder. But business had to continually come in the door. That required a culture of selling, which inspired a New Year's Day 1960 letter from Fish to his employees. Salesmanship," Fish explained, "is the foundation of our Fish companies." Everyone is born a salesman "from the office boy to the president," he explained, but many become too "impressed with their professional knowledge" to reach their potential. (Post-Enron, this would be called the *smartest-guys-in-the-room* problem.) This is a great loss, Fish asserted, because successful communication and accomplishment are

---

16. See *Capitalism at Work*, pp. 30–31, 315n9.

vital to "a successful life of love, marriage, religion, business, and politics"—indeed, to a "zest for living" and good health.

Amid Fish's sales pointers was his value system. "Be understanding of the desires and requirements of others," he wrote. Be "creative," "imaginative," and "aggressive," but also be "appreciative," "humble," and "considerate." He advised his staff to be "modestly egotistical," *not* "loud or gaudy." Lots of Samuel Smiles, some Adam Smith, and bits of Ayn Rand were implicit in his common sense.

Fish might have wanted each employee to be just like him. But he was realistic enough to apply the message to "the [area] we are really interested in"—business life. "The employee sells his boss, his fellow employees, his business contacts. It means a raise, a better position." He exhorted his many employees to think big.

> Each and every one of you has the ability and can make a major contribution in increasing not only our business volume but also our performance many times over.... You have no limits. And in using your unlimited abilities, you will not only improve yourselves financially, but experience the real pleasure of accomplishment.

And Ray Fish was natural gas's greatest salesman. "Our product is a clean, safe, economical, and convenient fuel," he stressed, giving kudos to what was the nation's sixth-largest industry. After all, Mr. Pipeliner was about as close as anyone was to also being Mr. Natural Gas.

Pacific Northwest Pipeline
As assistant to the president, Robert Herring was Ray Fish's alter ego and point person for special projects, even very big ones. Herring's first project could not have been more challenging or, in the end, more financially rewarding.

In 1949, Fish conceived of an interstate project transporting gas from the New Mexico's San Juan Basin to the Pacific Northwest. The Pacific Northwest Pipeline project promised gas to a vast new market, providing competition to Paul Kayser's El Paso Natural Gas for the new market, at least on the supply end.[17] To Fish, it was all in the mind's eye. There was waiting gas demand at the terminus, waiting gas supply at the source, and "the middle will take care of itself." That middle was what he had grandly done in the East and was now ready to do in the West. But never had he tried to do the *whole* project.

Herring was put in charge of the entire project: designing and constructing the pipeline and compressor stations, executing supply and sales contracts for gas, defending the project before regulatory bodies, and arranging for short- and long-term financing. Herring became president of Pacific Northwest on a moment's notice when Ray Fish, on the phone with his lawyer in Washington,

---

17. The Kayser/El Paso Natural Gas story is told in chapter 6, pp. 240–42.

was told that he had to name the project's chief officer to complete an FPC form. "Ray looked up, saw me, and told the lawyer!" Herring remembered.

The "Scenic Inch" (a play off World War II's Big Inch and Little Inch pipelines) was a gamble for Fish Engineering. If the pipeline was not built, all the design and promotion costs would be unrecoverable. Gas reserves had to be developed in the field to match what consumers committed to in the final markets.

The pressure on, it was back to army-style intelligence work for Herring. He made initial market surveys of gas demand and worked to establish new distribution companies in Washington State, Oregon, and Idaho, all of which had expensive manufactured (coal) gas—or no gas at all. Herring testified before state public-utility commissions and the FPC on feasibility, rates, and finance. He was as adroit at understanding engineering limits as he was financial economics and regulatory rules. The handsome, personable, quick-minded young man possessed a world of potential—something that man in the Washington park, Milton Daniel, and Ray Fish had all seen.

The target market was one of the very last major U.S. territories not supplied with natural gas, so the coal interests—coal companies, labor, and related railroads—threw everything they had against the project. Twelve months of continuous hearings produced 28,000 pages of testimony and 650 exhibits before Pacific Northwest Pipeline received its FPC certificate in mid-1954.

Leon Payne, an attorney with the Houston law firm of Andrews, Kurth, Campbell, and Bradley (now Andrews & Kurth), was instrumental in the $221 million project. His success working on Pacific Northwest would lead to another interstate gas transmission certification project, this one from Texas to the Florida peninsula, the last major market not served by natural gas (subject of chapter 8).

Ray Fish encountered Payne, one of the most distinguished pipeline lawyers in FPC history, in an unusual way. Fish purchased a mansion in Houston's River Oaks subdivision only to encounter a squatter. To gain possession of 939 Kirby Drive,[18] Fish hired his neighbor, a bright young lawyer with one of Houston's top firms. A forcible entry and detainer action evicted the squatter, and Fish then asked Leon Payne to handle some legal chores at Fish Engineering. All were expertly done.

When the Pacific Northwest project began, the young attorney asked Ray whether he needed help in the certification process. Fish did, and Payne got up to speed quickly. When the project's lead lawyer had a heart attack during the FPC hearings, Payne was suddenly thrust into the first chair.

Aided by seasoned Washington attorneys, Payne navigated the process and was a bona fide gas pipeline attorney by the time the project was certificated.

---

18. Kirby Drive, a prominent street in Houston's most storied residential neighborhood, was named after John Henry Kirby.

The Fish account would prove vital to Andrews & Kurth, "lay[ing] the foundation of the Firm's rapid rise as a leading law firm in the energy field." Florida
Gas, then Transco, and then later El Paso, were in the firm's future.

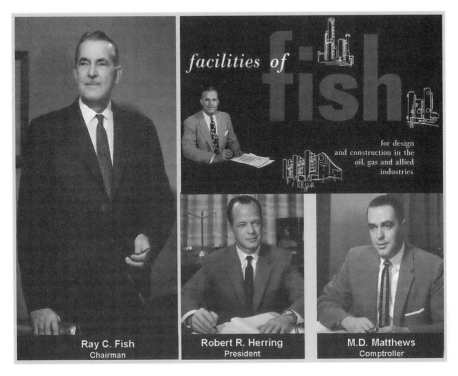

facilities of

for design
and construction in the
oil, gas and allied
industries

Ray C. Fish
Chairman

Robert R. Herring
President

M.D. Matthews
Comptroller

Figure 11.4 Fish Service Corporation was led by Ray Fish and Robert Herring. Herring
would go on to become CEO of Houston Natural Gas, where his successor there would
be his old colleague M. D. Matthews.

Within three years, Herring was promoted to president of Fish Service Corporation, a wholly owned subsidiary of Fish Engineering, a position he would
hold for six years. It was in this capacity that Herring put all the pieces together
to certificate and construct the Northwest project, which entered into service in
late 1956.

No sooner did gas begin to flow in late 1956 than cost overruns and low
demand put Northwest Pipeline in difficulty. But Fish and Herring had secured
a beachhead in one of the nation's leading supply regions and end-user markets.
The line had great potential, and competitor El Paso Natural Gas provided the
proof. Paul Kayser had fought hard against the project's certification at the FPC.

Now, he wanted to buy it. Kayser wanted the same gas reserves and worried about such a formidable competitor within reach of his market area.

In early 1957, just weeks after the line became fully operational, El Paso purchased Pacific Northwest for $152 million and the assumption of debt. El Paso secured gas reserves from San Juan, as well as from Alberta via Westcoast Transmission, to serve rapidly growing markets in California and the Northwest hitherto served by coal gas or fuel oil. The purchase of Pacific Northwest's 2,500-mile system also ended the threat that a branch line from Northwest would bring Canadian gas to California.

Business Week characterized the merger as "Everybody Wins." El Paso Natural Gas positioned itself for "phenomenal growth" in the West, while the Fish investors saw their stock almost double.

One problem lurked for Paul Kayser, nearing 70 years old and now running the nation's leading pipeline network of 10,000 miles. California Governor Edmund G. "Pat" Brown interested the Justice Department in challenging the merger on antitrust grounds, a challenge that ultimately prevailed. This was a huge piece of business for Leon Payne and Andrews & Kurth. The case, one of the longest in U.S. history, would last nearly 16 years and reach the Supreme Court five times.

In just ten years, Fish and associates had turned a $60,000 investment into a world-class engineering/construction company with a one-third interest in El Paso Natural Gas. For the principals, including Robert Herring, the El Paso stock swap generated a $37.5 million gain for seven years' work. The privately held company was doing just what Ray Fish wanted it to do—make its top people wealthy for a job well done.

Losing a Protégé

Herring's next projects at Fish Service Company—a gas pipeline in Mexico and chemical facility in Argentina—were successful but anticlimactic. International travel was more difficult now that he and Sylvia had children. The upstream side of the gas business—exploration and production—interested him more than the downstream.

The continent was Fish's oyster. But Herring knew that there were plenty of good projects in Texas. Just as Ray Fish had concluded in 1946, Herring now decided that it was time for *his* own show. Ray Fish was supportive, even putting up part of the capital Robert needed to start his own energy company.

It had been an exciting and lucrative nine years. Herring would look back with great respect and affection for Ray Fish. "He kept me running all over the world, and gave me as great an exposure as I could have possibly gotten," Herring would later say of "my mentor."

Robert Herring had an excellent reputation when he went into business for himself in 1958. He pooled his own capital with majority investor Ray Fish and

Figure 11.5 International travel for Fish Service Company grew tiresome, so Robert Herring (shown here late in his Fish career) decided to venture out on his own and start a South Texas gas production and gathering company in 1958.

Fish Engineering to form Valley Gas Production, Inc., to own and operate oil and gas wells and (small) gathering lines to feed the gas into major pipeline systems. Two divisions were created: Valley Gas Transmission, a wholly owned gas-gathering line serving mainly interstate pipelines, and Valley Pipe Lines, a subsidiary 50 percent owned with Pan American Gas Company selling gas to industrial users.

By the time of its sale to Houston Natural Gas Corporation five years later, Valley Gas owned interests in 156 oil and gas wells, 24 gathering systems carrying 200 MMcf/d of gas, and 6 liquid-extraction plants in 22 counties in Texas and 1 Louisiana parish. Herring did well for himself and his investors, and no one more than Ray Fish.[19] Herring also got something else in the deal: a vice presidency at Houston Natural Gas Corporation running the nation's largest intrastate natural gas transmission network.

---

19. The sale of Valley Gas to Houston Natural Gas is discussed in chapter 12, pp. 440–41.

Fish Engineering, meanwhile, continued to forge ahead domestically and internationally. Different divisions were designing and constructing pipelines, compressor stations, power plants, petroleum processing units, and petrochemical facilities. New processes were engineered, and patents were developed that were the marks of a company not only following the tried and true but also innovating to win contracts and earn performance bonuses.

Fish Engineering advertised that "nothing was too difficult or too far." Perhaps the most ambitious project of all was the engineering and construction of twin 1,100-mile gas pipelines and a 900-mile petroleum-products line from the Bolivia/Argentine border southwest to population and industrial centers near Buenos Aires. The 41-month, $220 million project, completed in 1960, involved such complexities as working with a state-owned bureaucracy (Yacimientos Petroliferos Fiscales), integrating equipment with different national specifications, and working with the currency and credit of eight countries. The reward for the developing region was replacing the imported energy used to build and run factories with less-expensive supply.

The Campo Duran Pipelines project was a technical success, but the rigors of public-sector-side work did not leave a good impression on Fish. "It takes private enterprise to do things fast," Fish stated. "Governments are too slow." Fish noted how his domestic pipeline projects were privately financed on the strength of customer contracts alone—unlike the government-guaranteed projects of the New Deal and World War II. Still, infrastructure projects in government-run countries offered a "world full . . . of opportunities" to help developing countries advance. But the wealth gap between home and abroad was unmistakable. That gulf between free and unfree countries was one reason the Ray C. Fish Foundation (launched in 1959) decided to promote private enterprise.

⌘·

The consummate salesman and hands-on developer shuttled between projects in one of his many corporate planes. The pace of international travel was hectic, although he found time to enjoy his Miami Beach winter home and his 65-foot yacht with his wife, Mirtha Galvez, a native of Havana. Houston was home, but in some months, he might be there for only a day or two.

There was much to do. Fish Engineering had a full book of business in just about every area of energy, from pipelines to refineries to power plants. Then there was Ray's latest idea: building a pipeline to move gas from Africa's French Sahara (holding an estimated 35 trillion cubic feet of gas reserves) to Spain, France, and across the English Channel to Britain.

This and others dreams were not to be. On December 7, 1962, Fish died suddenly of heart failure four months shy of his 61st birthday. It was his second heart attack. It was hard to believe a man so energetic and full of life was felled so abruptly.

Fish Engineering lost its founder, head, and 55 percent owner. Richard Ricketts cashed out his 17 percent interest. The remaining owners—C. B. Ames,

Robert Imber, Tom Tabbert, and Don Simecheck—retained their interests and let Imber manage what was now an investment company. Meanwhile, a new company, Fish Engineering and Construction Corporation, was formed with Ames as president, Tabbert and Simecheck as vice presidents, and Byron Smith as treasurer. Department heads and key employees were allowed, as Ray Fish would have it, to become stockholders as well.[20]

Among the stunned and saddened by Fish's death was Robert Herring. A director of the Ray C. Fish Foundation, he started a philanthropic mission to tackle heart disease in memory of his friend and mentor.

---

20. Fish Engineering and Construction continued under the new team, with Simecheck becoming president and CEO in 1972. Jim Boyd, formerly of Brown & Root, became president in 1987 and managed through tough times. In 1995, Fish sold out to a German company, Mannesmann, a holding company that also owned a California boiler company, Kinetic Technology International (KTI). KTI and Fish operated together in Houston and were sold by Mannesmann in 1999 to Technip, a large French company with the operation still in Houston today.

12

Formation and Maturation

H OUSTON NATURAL GAS CORPORATION (HNG), the company that
hired Ken Lay as CEO in 1984 and would become, through acquisition
and merger, Enron Corporation two years later, grew up alongside
Houston, Texas. HNG was founded in 1925 as a sister company to Houston
Pipe Line Company (HPL), a wholly owned division of Houston Oil Company
of Texas. Houston Oil, formed in 1901 by John Henry Kirby as part of an oil and
lumber play in East Texas, was actively finding oil when it hit large quantities
of gas. HPL was created to pipe the gas to the Houston city limits, and HNG
was created as a separate company (because of Texas's antitrust law) to buy gas
from HPL for resale to residential and commercial customers. But in 1957, with
the anti-integration law removed, and facing a new owner as counterparty, the
sister companies merged into one, Houston Natural Gas.

The history of HNG, from its founding until Robert Herring became CEO in
1967, is the subject of this chapter. The subsequent remaking of Houston Natural
Gas into a diversified natural gas major is described in chapter 13.

Houston Oil Company Breaks Out

The formation of the $30 million Houston Oil Company of Texas in 1901 set
high expectations. The size of the company was practically unknown outside of
major financial regions of the country and was certainly unknown in backwater
Houston. The company's capitalization (about $800 million today) was well
beyond that of any other business in the Lone Star State.

The *Houston Daily Post* welcomed the prospect of this mineral-rights
colossus:

> It means more for the State, perhaps, than any ten or twenty enterprises hereto-
> fore launched in Texas.... It signifies more than may be seen on the surface, for it

> is assurance that no one trust or corporation, not even the Standard Oil Company, can control the Texas oil fields![1]

Yet for the next 15 years, 5 of which were spent in bankruptcy, Houston Oil never lived up to its promise. It was a heavily indebted land company, collecting stumpage income from Kirby Lumber Company (separately capitalized at $10 million) under an intercompany agreement. Houston Oil had little to show for its exclusive mineral rights to 800,000 acres.

That changed in 1916 when Samuel Fordyce of Houston Oil created Southwest Settlement and Development Company to house the company's mineral interests and entered into a 50–50 production agreement with the Republic Production Company of Joseph Cullinan. Fordyce, who ran Houston Oil from 1904 until shortly before his death in 1919, was no oilman, but he certainly found one in "Buckskin Joe" Cullinan.

Cullinan (1880–1937) was the dean of the burgeoning Texas petroleum industry. He founded the Texas Company, a Spindletop baby that grew to become Texaco (now part of Chevron Corporation). A Standard Oil Company protégé, Cullinan had left Pennsylvania for Texas in 1899 to bring order to the Corsicana field, Texas's largest, by constructing storage and refinery facilities. He then applied his vertical-integration model to the Spindletop oil region in 1901, forming Texas Fuel Company to build the facilities necessary to turn the wave of crude oil into finished products. It was this company that became Texas's leading integrated oil company and, later, national and international oil major.

Cullinan saw enormous potential in developing the "Kirby million acres" (actually about 800,000 acres). In 1902, he offered Texas Company stock for the right to drill on Houston Oil's land but was rebuffed by the company's then-president, Patrick Calhoun. But Calhoun, John Henry Kirby's partner, was fired after Houston Oil declared insolvency in 1904. So Cullinan tried again in 1907, only to find that he could do nothing while Houston Oil was in bankruptcy.

In 1916, however, three years after leaving the Texas Company in a management dispute,[2] Cullinan inked a deal that proved to be "a boon to both

---

1. Political discrimination against Standard Oil in Texas is discussed in Internet appendix 12.1, "Standard Oil and Texas Politics," at www.politicalcapitalism.org/Book2/Chapter12/Appendix1.html.

2. Cullinan built the Texas Company into a profitable, integrated entity. But his aggressive, even "unbridled," expansion initiatives, sometimes at the expense of current-year profits, alarmed his East Coast majority investors. The battle between "Texas ideas" and "New York ideas" was a conflict between an independent-minded president and his board's executive committee. Cullinan was also a notable proponent of government intervention in the oil industry, at least until the New Deal soured him on political capitalism. See Internet appendix 12.2, "Joseph Cullinan as a Political Capitalist," at www.politicalcapitalism.org/Book2/Chapter12/Appendix2.html.

companies." Industry historian Charles Warner went further, calling the deal "one of the great 'horse trades' of Texas petroleum history."

In return for a half interest in any oil and gas found and produced, Cullinan's Republic Production Company obtained exclusive rights to drill on Houston Oil's acreage. Republic would absorb all drilling and production costs, which could not be less than $250,000 annually in the first four years. Houston Oil would passively receive the other half interest from oil and gas sales, supplementing its timber revenue from Kirby Lumber.

In July 1918, Cullinan struck a 1,200-barrel-per-day well on Houston Oil land 60 miles east of Houston. The press in Saint Louis, Missouri—the home of Fordyce and other prominent Houston Oil investors—reported that a "mystery well" had sent the stock price up sixfold, a bonanza for the company's long-suffering investors. Millions of barrels would be produced from Liberty County's Hull field in the next decade, providing Houston Oil with the capital for its own drilling and discoveries in neighboring Hardin and Tyler counties. John Henry Kirby's early optimism about oil being beneath the pines of East Texas was finally vindicated.

New Companies for Natural Gas

Texas was a coal and lignite state until the 1890s, when the Corsicana field put the state in the oil business. The field's owners set out "to educate the state on [fuel oil's] clean, cheap qualities" compared to solid fuel. Another fuel, coal gas, was manufactured by plants such as one built in 1866 by the Houston Gas Light Company, the city's first.[3] "It was a happy day," stated Kenneth Fellows, "when Houston's ultra-modern homemakers and homeowners were able to forsake the chores of carrying in wood and coal for cooking and heating and, conversely, no longer had to carry out the ashes."

Texas recorded its first natural gas usage in 1910 when a rancher substituted on-site methane for wood and coal. But natural gas was found mostly in remote spots where people were not, and the norm was to cap gas wells or flare gas associated with oil wells for safety. One exception was the city of Corsicana, which stopped making coal gas in 1899 in order to utilize nearby natural gas. It was Joseph Cullinan who secured a franchise to serve the city with the superior substitute.

The proximity of gas wells to major markets also proved to be a business proposition for the Lone Star Gas Company, which supplied Dallas and Fort Worth from the adjacent Petrolia field. But for the most part, economical

---

3. Houston Gas Light Company became Houston Gas and Fuel Company before being renamed United Gas Company (1936) and then Entex, Inc. (1974). In 1976, Entex purchased the distribution assets of Houston Natural Gas Corporation, which left HNG in wholesale gas transmission and sales.

transmission to towns and cities from more distant fields awaited improvement in pipeline technology. Another clean-fuel campaign was also needed to encourage consumers to leave fuel oil and coal gas for a cleaner, cheaper alternative.

Cash-rich Houston Oil was now drilling its own wells, not only receiving royalties from Cullinan. In 1925, two major gas finds in south Texas sparked a debate: *Should a natural gas pipeline be built to Houston a hundred miles away?* It was not an automatic decision. Natural gas was a different business from oil, and Houston Oil's charter did not mention those two words. In a March 1925 decision that caused 4 of the company's 13 directors to resign, Houston Oil created a wholly owned subsidiary, Houston Pipe Line Company (HPL), to build to Houston.

With its business charter filed in the state capital of Austin, HPL entered into material and labor contracts, negotiated with landowners, and began laying pipe. (Regulatory permissions were not needed in those early days.) Nine months later, two lines stood completed: a 54-mile branch line serving Texas Gulf Sulphur (a large industrial that signed a five-year contract for gas), and a 96-mile, 80 MMcf/d mainline intended to serve Houston. However, just as the mainline neared completion, HPL lost out on an expected wholesale contract with the city's only franchised gas distributor, Houston Gas and Fuel Company (HGF), the successor of Houston Gas Light Company. HGF, poised to convert its 30,000 customers from manufactured gas, contracted instead with another natural gas upstart, Houston Gulf Coast Company. Houston Gulf won out because it was willing, unlike HPL, to enter into a noncompete clause that would leave the city in the monopolist's hands.

Without a contract, HPL found much of its $3.6 million investment stranded at Houston's city limits. Quickly, the company decided to get into the gas-distribution business—a forward integration from wholesale to retail. Yet a wholly new company had to be created to steer clear of Texas's antitrust law, a statute that cast a shadow on firms performing more than one function.

Houston Natural Gas Company (HNG) was incorporated on November 20, 1925, to sell gas to residential, commercial, and industrial users. The new entity had much of the same staff and management as Houston Oil's Houston Pipe Line, and many of its owners also owned stock in HPL. But HNG was separately capitalized. Houston Oil president E. H. Buckner, who had taken the same title with HPL upon its formation, was named president of HNG as well.

HPL had reached the outskirts of Houston in time for a gas-cooked New Year's Day feast for employees at the home of president Buckner. But sister company HNG could not lay gas mains in city streets without a franchise, which left only service to the suburbs. In the next two years, HNG built a network of small-diameter gas lines that formed "a highly effective encircling of the City of Houston." With its first meter installed on Bellaire Boulevard on March 27, 1926, HNG went on to become the natural gas supplier to Bellaire, Galena Park, Meadowbrook, Monticello, Pasadena, Rice Court, River Oaks, South Houston,

Figure 12.1 Houston Pipe Line Company reached Houston's outskirts only to lose its expected wholesale customer, which led to the decision to form a retail company, Houston Natural Gas. The companies had largely overlapping ownership. E. H. Buckner (left inset) was president of both companies.

Southside Place, and West University Place. HNG's rates were identical to those of Houston Gas: a usage fee of $0.65 per thousand cubic feet (Mcf) and a monthly meter charge of $0.50 (the 65/50 rate).

Mayor Oscar Holcombe and the Houston City Council were prohibited under Texas law from awarding an exclusive franchise to a utility. But Houston Gas and Fuel, with 605 miles of distribution line and 47,000 customers, had an effective monopoly until a second authorization was granted. The company, and its president, Captain James A. Baker—described as "a power in politics and business and general affairs extending from Houston to Washington"—dominated City Hall.[4]

Local politics, however, could work both ways. Just four months after converting Houston to natural gas, HGF petitioned the city council to increase rates by approximately one-third. The company had made new investments and

---

4. Captain Baker's grandson, James A. Baker III, the former secretary of state under President George H. W. Bush, would have involvement with Enron, as discussed in Book 3.

wanted an 8 percent return on all its plant, equipment, and property. The request was badly timed. With city elections just three weeks away, Mayor Holcombe demeaned Baker's bunch with the words: "Your company is the poorest managed, most inefficient public service corporation with which any city anywhere in the world was ever afflicted."

Of course, it was just politics. Six months later, HGF reapplied and received 80/75 rates, a 28 percent increase, which was still cheaper than the manufactured gas that had sold for $1.05/Mcf just several years before.

The rushed increase did not escape public notice, however. Just ten days prior, on May 14, 1927, HNG had filed for a franchise to serve Houston and compete head to head with HGF. The upstart proposed a fixed, ten-year 65/50 rate, the same rate charged in the suburbs—and the very rate that HGF said it could no longer afford to receive.

Enter M. E. "Mefo" Foster, writer of the *Houston Chronicle*'s "Our City" column and an opponent of the Mayor's gas-monopoly policy. Mefo shared some disconcerting facts about HGF: The company served half as many customers as the city's electricity provider, Houston Lighting and Power Company, and its gas-leakage rate of 26 percent was made to look bad by Dallas's 10 percent and an achievable 5–7 percent using new materials.

Mefo editorialized repeatedly against HGF's rate increase and jabbed hard at the Mayor and City Council:

> We have the beautiful spectacle of ten suburbs of Houston getting gas for 65¢ and only a 50¢ service charge, while 36,000 customers within the city pay 80¢ and 75¢…. Why not do something to bring to the city that fuel that will add factories, that will mean more labor employed and millions of more dollars spent here?… We must show the Mayor and our city commissioners the error of their ways wholly from the standpoint of Houston's welfare.

Unmoved, Mayor Holcombe argued that gas-on-gas competition was redundant, would inconvenience Houstonians by tearing up the streets, and would eventually end up in consolidation with one supplier. Such was the textbook view of public utility regulation that Samuel Insull had helped to popularize several decades before.[5] But Houston's most influential journalist retorted:

> Why worry so much about the streets being torn up, Mr. Mayor, if you can save Houston gas consumers half a million dollars annually? If we get more and better gas, we will not object to a little activity on or alongside our streets and sidewalks…. Far better to tear up a small part of the streets for the purpose of laying gas mains than to let one company tear the money from our pocketbooks.

---

5. See chapter 2, pp. 86–88 and chapter 3, pp. 121–25. For a critical view of monopoly theory, see the Epilogue, pp. 509–511.

Mefo also challenged fears of destructive competition by means of an example:

> If you are really worrying about our streets, take a look at River Oaks and be comforted. That addition got natural gas after all the streets were beautifully paved. Did you see anything torn up while the work was being done? The mains were placed [underground] along the side between the streets and sidewalks. Not one bit of paving was destroyed nor was one tree or shrub disturbed.

Houston Gas and Fuel, now on the defensive, responded with a public education campaign to justify its newly implemented rates. But after three weeks of escalating controversy, the City of Houston rescinded HGF's rate increase. Mefo had lit the fire, but the real force for change was led by Houston's housewives, organized as the City Federation of Women's Clubs and the Women's Democratic Club. They held mass meetings and collected signatures for a referendum to repeal the recent rate ordinance and award a second franchise to HNG. The homemakers, using gas to cook meals and clean clothes, and in many cases paying the utility bills, overcame the "conspicuously silent" Houston Chamber of Commerce, whose leaders were not going to cross Captain Baker. Mefo noted the irony: "The women turned on the searchlight; the men hid from the public!"

Total victory for gas competition followed quickly. On July 28, 1927, 19 months after encountering "the blockade of Houston," HNG received permission to lay gas mains in the city of Houston. The "Battle of the Gas Franchise" was over, and the "Battle for Gas Business" was joined.

Competition Makes a Company

Under its franchise, HNG could lay a gas main only if more than half of the residents signed up for its service, which occasionally required bringing carloads of customers to City Hall for verification. Some disaffected residents, preferring monopoly to construction, or just out of loyalty to the incumbent, filed petitions and injunctions against HNG. Still, the resulting competition "was a free-for-all and no holds were barred!" as Kenneth Fellows wrote in his history of HNG, published on the company's fiftieth anniversary in 1975.

The "furious, street-by-street warfare" lasted two years. The end came in 1929 with market saturation and the onset of the Great Depression. But what a rivalry it had been! HNG's 78 solicitors went door to door to sign up new customers and persuade others to switch suppliers; HGF's 125 solicitors worked to protect its turf and enlist new customers. Construction crews laid gas mains 'round the clock, sometimes just to beat an injunction order. Fistfights broke out between rival crews whose supervisors would say, "Don't report back to work if you ever get licked!" Even petty vandalism occurred when meter setters hid the other company's disconnected equipment.

HNG was the people's choice against the dethroned monopolist, whose rates had been recently beaten back by public outcry. But HNG could not waste a dollar when rates were frozen, and every penny pinched accrued to the bottom line. There was no rate-base mentality. This was not cost-of-service regulation, under which a monopolist could add an allowed margin to its permissible cost. In the Houston market at least, waste was checked by gas-on-gas competition and the full incentive to keep costs as far below the charged rate as possible. Consumers, meanwhile, got plenty of attention from two eager gas distributors—and lower gas rates by competition.[6]

At the four-year mark (1929), HNG's 650-mile distribution network, fed by HPL deliveries from 11 fields, served 20,000 gas meters. Many thousands were inside Houston, a considerable achievement considering HGF's head start. But most of HNG's growth had come from the introduction of new gas service in locales within reach of the mainline. Those connections had begun in April 1926 with Stafford and Missouri City in Fort Bend County; by 1930, some 40 major communities were receiving natural gas for the first time.

Operationally, four divisions were established under a Delaware holding company, Houston Natural Gas Corporation (HNG): Houston Natural Gas Company, serving the city of Houston and surrounding areas; Gulf Cities Natural Gas Company, serving coastal towns, such as Baytown, Texas City, and Galveston; Tex-Mex Natural Gas Company, serving the border towns; and Texas Natural Gas Utilities, serving areas in Fort Bend, Wharton, and surrounding counties.

Eighty-five percent of revenue came from industrial sales, with the balance from small users (households and commercial establishments), making HNG the largest industrial gas seller anywhere. A quarter of gas sales were in Houston, where competition was fierce; the rest were in areas where the company was the sole franchised distributor. The corporation's $7 million capitalization from its founding in 1925 was eventually exhausted and supplemented by a $600,000 bond issue floated in late 1928. Growth and recapitalization would be the story from here on out.

The Great Depression forced layoffs for the first time in HNG's history. Sixteen service crews were pared to one, and the solicitor department was chopped down to ten men. A $2.50 reconnection fee was initiated to discourage deadbeats from switching to HNG from HGF. The Depression's price deflation increased gas rates in real terms for the company and its suppliers, but this was limited consolation given stagnant demand and growing problems with accounts receivable.

---

6. The gains from competition challenge the rationale for natural-monopoly regulation, as discussed in Internet appendix 12.3, "'Natural Monopoly' and Gas Regulation in Houston, Texas," at www.politicalcapitalism.org/Book2/Chapter12/Appendix3.html.

Tough conditions led the parent of HGF, United Gas Corporation, to propose either to buy HNG or to be sold to the same—or to combine their properties for sale to a third party. HNG responded that such a sale to United would have to include HNG's distribution assets outside of Houston, but the asking price was too rich for United. The negotiations of 1930/31 ceased without further action.

The Frank Smith Era (1933–55)

When E. H. Buckner was beset by health and family problems in 1930, HNG's day-to-day management went to W. B. "Tex" Trammell. "Bright, brash and husky," the former field hand had begun his career at HPL and joined HNG as vice president and general manager.

Trammel knew the gas business from the ground up and had done well in the Houston gas wars of 1927–29. Buckner recommended him to the board, and Trammel became acting president in early 1932. But Tex was no polished big-company executive. Soon after he was elected president of HNG in 1933, problems set in. Setting out to diversify HNG away from its sole supplier and half-sister, HPL, Trammell strong-armed the board into approving a gas-supply contract with the little-known Balcones Company. Meanwhile, missing a monthly payment from HNG and having operated at a loss for several years, HPL was in a cash crunch.

This was no small problem. Investigation by HNG's board confirmed its worst suspicions: Balcones was a paper company that, if brought to life, would threaten the viability of Houston Pipe Line, while not appreciably benefitting HNG.

In an unregulated market, Tex's play would have made sense. Some large gas discoveries in Conroe and Tomball by Humble Oil and Refining offered a nearby, cheaper gas source for Houston and neighboring areas. But HPL/HNG and HGF had saturated the market with gas sold at rates approved by state and local authorities. Lower gas costs would be passed through, not pocketed, if state and local authorities had their way. But Tex, married to the daughter of one of Humble Oil's founders, Walter Fondren, and thus serving a second master, had the Houston law firm of Fulbright, Crooker, and Freeman (now Fulbright and Jaworski) charter a new pipeline company (Balcones) that would sell Humble's gas at a significant discount to HNG. The new system, much shorter than HPL, would cost about $500,000, well below the depreciated cost of multi-million-dollar HPL. HPL would have no choice but to match the competition, ruining its return on investment.

HNG's board designated its newest member, Frank C. Smith (1892–1971), to address the threat. Smith was a former mortgage banker whose company, Houston Land and Trust Company, had been waylaid by the Great Depression. He had grown up in Kentucky, got his first job at age 15 as a lumber company timekeeper, and attended Vanderbilt University before leaving to fight in World War I, achieving the rank of first lieutenant.

After the war, he moved to Houston and began a banking career. David Hannah, a major HNG stockholder, as well as board director, got to know Smith during this period. What he saw in the man nearly 30 years his junior was an uncommon combination of smarts, diligence, judgment, and style. In March 1932, six months shy of his fortieth birthday, Smith was elected to HNG's board per Hannah's recommendation. It was a good move; Smith would soon be dedicating all his time to resolving the Trammel/Balcones imbroglio.

Smith and the majority of his fellow directors acted quickly when problems surfaced in summer 1933. The first move was to expand the board to dilute Trammel's hold. The reconstituted board fired Trammel "for cause, in that among other things, he has defied and set at naught the expressed direction of the stockholders of this Company, and has acted, and threatens to continue to act, in disregard of sound business principles and the best interests of this Company."[7] Given the regulatory environment, HNG had little to gain from a substitution that would cause a reduction in its retail rates and strand HPL's investment. For HPL, HNG's abandonment would be akin to the moment eight years earlier when its line reached Houston only to find no gas buyer.[8]

For his efforts, Frank Smith was elected head of Houston Natural Gas Corporation on November 13, 1933. It was the beginning of a 22-year presidency that saw the company survive the Great Depression, expand during World War II, and prosper thereafter by internal growth and by acquisition. Smith would always marvel about his first day at HNG as president when he knew so little about gas. "I wouldn't have known a BTU if I had encountered one on the street," he would say.

Smith's "first class citizenship" came to HNG at a crucial time. The Great Depression had halted system expansions. Discipline and professionalism were needed. Smith put the field personnel in uniform and launched an advertising campaign documenting how much money Houstonians had saved from HNG's gas rate, which had forced down HGF's rate back in 1927.

This was well and good, but the biggest challenge was to increase sales and better utilize the existing system—and not spend a lot of scarce capital doing so. "Gas is of no value whatsoever just sitting in our lines," Smith stressed. "It needs to be used in more and more ways and sold through more and more outlets."

---

7. The enigmatic Tex Trammell survived this episode and went on to have a successful career as an independent oilman before becoming active in Houston politics.

8. The full story of Balcones may never be known. The embarrassing situation led HNG employee Kenneth Fellows to describe the incident only in the broadest terms, and many in the know would not discuss it afterward, because of the prominence of the Trammel/Fondren families in Houston.

Figure 12.2 Frank Smith, whose first day at HNG was as president, would lead the company in this capacity for 22 years (1933–55), before continuing full time as chairman for 12 years (1955–67) and retiring as honorary chairman in 1971. He is shown (bottom right) with his successor at HNG, Bus Wimberly.

HNG studied the residential market and confirmed that there were few gas appliances per home and that those few did not get very high marks. Rather than go into the merchandizing business, as did many other gas utilities, HNG in 1934 began a load-building initiative by subsidizing dealers selling gas-fired cooking, heating, and washing appliances. Under the motto "close cooperation and non-competition," HNG donated advertising, offered inexpensive gas hook-ups, and sponsored equipment demonstrations described as "civic happenings." Frank Smith extolled the benefits of gas in presentations throughout the community. To push improvements in gas-using equipment, he co-founded the Institute of Gas Technology in Chicago in 1941 and became its first chairman.

The dealer program was successful. Millions of dollars of new gas appliances increased gas demand enough for HNG to call its subsidy program "self-sustaining." Further, much goodwill was generated for a company whose trademark would become "A Texas Gulf Coast Service Institution."

A reorganization in 1940 eliminated HNG's 12-year-old holding company structure. The Public Utility Holding Company Act of 1935, a federal law enacted after the collapse of Samuel Insull's holding companies, cast doubt on the legality of HNG's Delaware incorporation, given that the company's operations were in Texas. So HNG repositioned itself as a Texas corporation, and all four divisions—with over 50,000 meters in 70 cities, towns, and villages in 20 South Texas counties—were collapsed into the parent, Houston Natural Gas Corporation. The reorganization retained Smith as president and elected L. S. Zimmerman to the new position of chairman of the board of directors, which made him, in effect, Smith's boss. Zimmerman operated out of Baltimore, the city where he grew up and, at age 33, had become president of Maryland Trust Company. He continued in his HNG role until his death in 1954.

◌⁘

World War II was a time of great uncertainty, and HNG, like other businesses, labored under a federal income tax that included additional levies on so-called excess profits.[9] Still, HNG was selling an essential product in a market brimming with national defense manufacturing. "Natural gas has thoroughly lived up to its designation as the perfect fuel," HNG's *1942 Annual Report* stated: By the war's end, gas sales had tripled to 15 Bcf thanks to growing attached gas reserves and system expansions (HNG qualified for steel rations). Gas curtailments did not occur in HNG's area as they did in many states distant from gas production. Gas rates were lowered in 1940, 1943, and 1945 from indirect regulation and politics,[10] but the company was profitable and growing. In its growth mode, HNG created a Production Engineering Department in 1943 and, with postwar demand in mind, a Department of Gas Utilization in 1945.

Most economists and business analysts predicted a postwar recession, even a deep one. The thinking was that the contraction of the defense industry would bring down the national economy. Such pessimism was not held by HNG, however, which heralded the Texas Gulf Coast as "The Nation's No. 1 Opportunity."

And so it came to be. One business publication reported in early 1946: "Houston, often referred to as the depression-proof city because it has never experienced a recession of business, is adjudged to have superior prospects of retaining the wartime growth it enjoyed between the years of 1940 and 1945." *Fortune, Life,* and the *Saturday Evening Post* noted how the city did not seem to

---

9. HNG's federal tax payments between fiscal years 1942 and 1946 averaged 65 percent of the company's net income, the combination of a regular tax rate and an excess-profits tax.

10. The 1943 decrease was ordered by the city of Houston in response to a reduction in HNG's gas-purchase cost from an interstate supplier, which itself resulted from an order from the Federal Power Commission.

Figure 12.3 HNG's service territory covered most of the Texas Gulf Coast by 1945. The 22-story Petroleum Building (inset) was the home of HNG from 1927 until 1967.

miss a beat after V-J day. The whole Texas Gulf Coast was thriving, a trend only nicked by the April 1947 Texas City chemical explosion that left hundreds dead, thousands injured, and numerous industrial facilities destroyed—the worst industrial accident in U.S. history.

HNG reached 100,000 meters in 1947, the result of double-digit annual growth since the company's inception. The cooperation program with gas-appliance dealers, suspended during the war, was humming again. Competition for workers and general economic prosperity led the company to increase wages, shorten the work week (from 54 to 48 hours in the field; from 43 to 40 hours in the Houston office), extend vacation time, and introduce an employee retirement plan "entirely independent of, and in addition to, those provided under social security." Perks, such as an employee award program were also launched amid the postwar prosperity.

When HNG celebrated its silver anniversary in 1950, it was a company marked by evolutionary, internal growth. Annual net income was consistently over the half-million dollar mark, and plant and property values exceeded $20 million. There were 755 employees and 2,000 stockholders. HNG's pipeline network was huge—stretched in a straight line, it would reach from Houston to Alaska.

The company's philosophy was continuous improvement, or in Frank Smith's words, "a vision of ever greater service to the public, who are truly the 'keepers of the flame.'" HNG had practiced Schumpeter's creative destruction by helping eviscerate manufactured gas, but there was no rival fuel threatening the same to HNG's 135,000 customers.

The 1950s would be "generally good living" in HNG's service area. The city of Houston recorded its millionth citizen in 1954, and the suburbs and entire

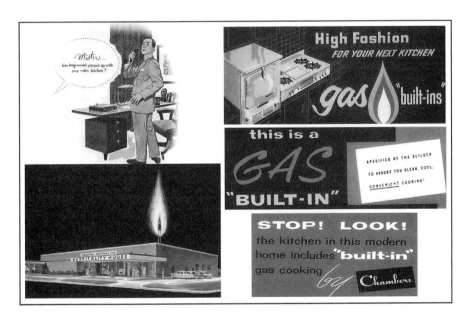

Figure 12.4 Load building was the name of the game during a period when profit margins were falling on each unit of sales and spare capacity existed in the gas system.

Gulf Coast were expanding rapidly. Increasing gas sales and good margins caused the company's stock to appreciate again and again. Huge new industries, such as oil refining and petrochemicals, looked to natural gas to fuel operations. HNG's physical plant *quadrupled* in the first decade after World War II.

HNG's reputation shined too. There would be no major controversies in the Frank Smith era. The company leader was well respected by his employees and by the gas industry at large, as evidenced by his election as president of the American Gas Association in 1952. HNG's gas rates were stable, and the company's political and community relations were strong. (Despite inflationary conditions, the company's first rate increase did not come until 1952.)

It was fun too. Appliance shows at the company's Hospitality House were a hit. Employees, called the "HNGang," enjoyed free coffee during 15-minute morning and afternoon breaks in the Coffee Corral, a large room in the Petroleum Building. *Safety Valve*, HNG's company magazine, calculated the perk's cost at 59 cents a cup, a figure that included, somewhat facetiously, lost labor time—as if the breaks did not improve employee productivity and morale. Even so, this high-loaded estimate made news in the *Wall Street Journal* and evoked a few murmurs from company stockholders.

But Frank Smith did not have to be told to watch his pennies. Nothing was extravagant, certainly not the annual board meeting held in Smith's office in hastily assembled, cramped, mismatched chairs—a practice that continued for 24 years (1933–57). "He wanted no visitor to his office, particularly a customer or stockholder, to go away feeling that the head of the gas company was basking in luxurious surroundings at the expense of the public," Kenneth Fellows explained.

In 1953, Houston Natural Gas created its first subsidiary, the Houston Natural Gas Production Company. (HPL was still unaffiliated with HNG.) This backward integration was encouraged by rising gas prices, the need for greater supply, and a desire to diversify into a nonregulated core business.

HNG Production had little success drilling in its early years. But it put itself on the map in 1957 by acquiring McCarthy Oil and Gas Corporation out of bankruptcy for $6.6 million. The legendary wildcatter Glenn McCarthy had rolled the dice too many times, and now his 40 employees, 110 producing wells, and 7,800 acres of undeveloped leases—all situated within 100 miles of Houston—were part of HNG. It was a pure production play with "a good deal of romance" of development upside. But it was not system supply for the pipelines or company customers.[11]

◌⋅

---

11. HNG would rework a number of the McCarthy wells to increase production and increase the extraction of gas liquids from the gas stream. On the oil side, an eight-day allowable under Texas's market-demand proration rules limited each well's output to one-fourth of maximum capacity.

Populist-driven government activism was HNG's chief hindrance and threat in these go-go years, and the company practiced defensive politics to counter the threat.[12] A reimposed excess-profits tax during the Korean War saw HNG's federal liability reach 87 percent of net income, higher than that during the World War II years and a far cry from the 1 percent business tax introduced by the Revenue Act of 1909. HNG never liked the tax surcharge, once stating in an annual report: "Your company stands ready, as always, to do its full part in support of the government's military requirements, but will actively resist inequitable excess profits tax legislation; since in regulated public utilities, such as ours, there normally is not such thing as 'excess profits.'"

Another headache during the period came from municipalization drives in the company's service territory. In several elections between 1949 and 1954, voters decided bond issues that would have financed either a buy-out of HNG's facilities or authorized construction of a duplicate gas system. Not even 20- and 30-year franchises held by HNG were enough to avoid the issue from time to time, particularly when a big gas well was found near a community. "Our business is NOT for sale!" HNG declared, fearing that one small loss within its system could lead to other battles.

The company defeated most initiatives, but doing so was expensive and time consuming. Thus, HNG executives developed strong, negative feelings toward "evidences of the socialistic economy which advocates more government in business."

The John H. "Bus" Wimberly Era (1955–67)

E. H. Buckner had roiled both HNG and HPL by choosing Tex Trammell as his replacement back in the early 1930s. The ever-careful Frank Smith spent many years grooming his successor—John H. "Bus" Wimberly.

A native Houstonian, Wimberly joined HNG in 1928 as chief clerk in the secretary/treasurer department after receiving a business degree from the University of Texas. He proved to be a "comer," working his way up in the finance department and joining the board of directors in 1940. In 1946, he was promoted to vice president and secretary; and two years later, he was named executive vice president. In June 1955, at age 50 and in his twenty-seventh year with the company, Wimberly became president, with Frank Smith, age 62, becoming chairman, the title previously held by L. S. Zimmerman, who had died the previous December. The Smith-Wimberly operating team was now Wimberly-Smith.

---

12. Defensive politics, by moving the system toward free-market capitalism, works against political capitalism. The opposite is true of business support for existing or new intervention, called rent-seeking by economists. See *Capitalism at Work*, pp. 120–21, 332–33.

Wimberly was a tall man with great presence. Although reserved, he was competitive and highly able. He also had big shoes to fill. Frank Smith, during his long tenure, had brought the company "a new kind of leadership," combining a "magnetic personality" with intellect and propriety. David Hannah had done very well in bringing a great leader and disciplinarian to Houston Natural Gas, and Hannah's legacy would continue with Smith's hand-picked successor.

Purchasing Houston Pipe Line Company

In mid-1956, Atlantic Refining Company (later Atlantic Richfield) purchased Houston Oil Company for $198.5 million (about $1.5 billion today). The transaction was one of the most intricate in the history of the oil industry, involving assets whose combined surface area was larger than the state of Rhode Island.

A new owner had special significance given HPL and HNG's monopoly/monopsony relationship. The pricing of gas sales between the two companies had become difficult.[13] The range of indeterminacy was wide. It had been a "rich-kid, poor-kid" relationship from the beginning, with HNG as Cinderella. The conditions for a vertical integration were certainly present.

HNG launched a preemptive offer as soon as Atlantic Refining indicated intent to bid out its natural gas properties. "Our operations and those of Pipe Line's have been so intertwined throughout the years that no other company knows Houston Pipe Line as well as we do," Wimberly argued to his Atlantic Refining counterparts. "Nor can anyone else effect a merger or acquisition with less confusion or difficulty for all involved," he added. The offer was 13 times earnings, or $26 million, to purchase the company's stock. Debt of $11.7 million would also be assumed.

After a tense wait, Atlantic Refining accepted HNG's offer. So in just his second year as president, Wimberly had doubled his company's assets. It was, to company historian Kenneth Fellows, "the greatest step forward, physically and financially, in Houston Natural's history."

The $38 million purchase (about $300 million today), effective November 1956, provided HNG with 408 miles of gathering line and 350 miles of mainline, anchored by production contracts from 82 producing fields with an estimated 1.5 Tcf of gas reserves. About 300 MMcf/d of HPL's system capacity of 375 MMcf/d was moving to HNG.

---

13. Stated Fellows: "As the years progressed, price negotiations [between HPL and HNG] became increasingly difficult, with both companies showing reluctance to yield to the other's point of view in attempts to adjust contracts as a means of correcting existing and future inequities."

HNG praised the acquisition for providing "increased flexibility, greater stability, and the opportunity for achieving the full benefits of completely [vertically] integrated operations." Bookkeeping entries by a single firm were far more reliable and manageable than those subject to the vagaries of an arm's-length transaction.

The good news was conveyed simultaneously by Bus Wimberly at headquarters and Frank Smith in the field. "I would not have traded places at that instant with any man alive, and I am certain that Mr. Smith felt a like emotion," Wimberly recalled.

After three months of arduous financial and legal work, consummated by a November 1 signing in the stately board room of Chase Manhattan Bank in New York City, Houston Natural Gas Corporation became one of the, if not *the*, premier integrated natural gas companies in America.

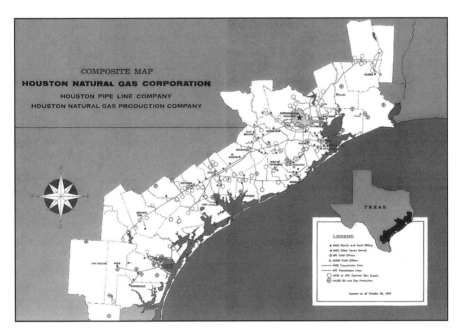

Figure 12.5 The purchase of Houston Pipe Line Company doubled the size of HNG and provided the security of wholesale/retail integration. The $38 million transaction was consummated by 50 individuals representing 31 parties—attorneys, bond and debenture purchasers, corporate officers and directors, trustees, bankers, and underwriters.

HNG's *1957 Annual Report* reported the very good news: "The consummation of the transaction finds your company's assets nearly doubled, and although only nine months have elapsed since the acquisition became effective, there is indication that the company's newly combined production, transmission, and distribution facilities will receive the enlarged benefits to be derived from completely integrated operations." The full extent of the home run was buried in the financial reports. HNG had more than doubled its debt to acquire HPL, but its debt-to-capital ratio had hardly budged, increasing to 67 percent from 64 percent. The tape-measure shot was in the equity account, which almost doubled, to $24.8 million. The stock market loved the purchase.

Wall Street was cluing in to a company that was virtually in a class by itself. The new HNG had size—$100 million in gas assets, a fourfold increase from that recorded at the silver anniversary ten years before. It was vertically integrated from the wellhead to burner tip—unlike the interstate gas pipelines that had shed their distribution properties because of a 1935 federal law and had disposed of production properties because of regulatory disincentives under the Natural Gas Act.[14]

HNG was benefitting from light-handed regulation by the Texas Railroad Commission on one side and by local officials on the other. In some ways, HNG became America's most attractive, stable gas-company investment. Standard & Poor called HNG's outlook "promising." Another investor organ blessed "the benefits of completely integrated operations," operations that "are wholly intrastate, free of Federal Power Commission regulation." HNG could claim to be a *natural gas major,* at least in the mighty gas-producing and gas-consuming state of Texas.[15]

Purchasing Valley Gas Production, Inc.

As an integrated company, HNG looked first to itself in obtaining natural gas. "The company recognizes that a foremost requisite for future growth is the maintenance of a sound gas reserve position," HNG's *1961 Annual Report* explained. Without an adequate, stable gas supply, indeed, the company's midstream and downstream operations would be idled, and the goodwill built up with regulators and consumers over the decades would evaporate.

HNG was hungry for new gas supplies, but it was also in the market for something else. The company needed a top-notch pipeline executive, perhaps even someone who could rise to the top of the whole corporation. Robert Dabney, the head of HPL, was approaching retirement. In the eyes of Bus Wimberly, no heir apparent had emerged. The job was obviously one of the most important at the company.

HNG found its man in a medium-sized gas production, extraction, and transmission company operating in 22 South Texas counties and 1 Louisiana

---

14. See Internet appendix 12.4, "Federal Regulation and Gas-Industry Disintegration," at www.politicalcapitalism.org/Book2/Chapter12/Appendix4.html.

15. Enron in the mid-1990s set out to become *the world's first natural gas major,* as discussed in Book 3.

parish. Valley Gas Production Company sported interests in more than 150 oil and gas wells and in two dozen gathering systems moving 200 MMcf/d, as well as in a half-dozen liquid-extraction plants. The profitable company had been founded in 1958 by Robert Herring, who had left a successful career with Fish Engineering Corporation to concentrate on South Texas gas opportunities.

When HNG purchased Valley Gas in September 1963, Herring and his investors received more than one million dollars, and the operation was recapitalized. As part of the deal, all employees moved over to the new company. The 42-year-old Herring's new title was vice president and general manager of transmission at Houston Pipe Line, with responsibilities for HPL, Valley Gas Transmission (a gas gatherer selling to interstate pipelines), and Valley Pipe Lines (an intrastate gatherer selling gas to industrial users). Before long, Bus Wimberly knew he had found his successor. "[Valley Gas] was a good buy,' Wimberly would reminisce, "but the greatest asset we acquired in the transaction, by far, was Bob Herring."[16]

The New Company

Herring's crown jewel, HPL, had doubled its volume and tripled its earnings in its first eight years as an HNG subsidiary. Several million dollars were being invested in the system annually, notably in a 60 MMcf/d expansion in 1964. HPL managed 400 industrial contracts, which while a speck compared to HNG's customer list of 285,000, was dominant volumetrically. Industrial sales and transportation accounted for two-thirds of the corporation's total deliveries of 900 MMcf/d, led by a contract to supply Shell's refinery and petrochemical facilities (55 MMcf/d, which would reach 200 MMcf/d).

In 1965, the expansion of HPL's mainline to meet demand growth was complemented by the purchase of the Bammel gas storage field, located just 20 miles north of downtown Houston. A depleted oil and gas storage reservoir, Bammel was ideally suited for cycling gas, whether by the day or the season. By injecting gas during low-demand summer months, for withdrawal during the winter peak, existing pipeline capacity was better utilized. Thus, HPL's 1 Bcf/d system could deliver close to 1.5 Bcf/d—and did so in early 1966 with the help of Bammel.[17]

The sizeable storage cavern "operated very much like a bank," noted Kenneth Fellows, with gas moving in and out according to temperature-driven gas

---

16. Other talent came with the acquisition, including M. D. Matthews, who began as assistant to the president (Herring) and was promoted to vice president and assistant treasurer a year later.

17. HNG first laid a gas line and entered into a contract with Bammel owners in 1951 to withdraw up to 125 MMcf/d. The 7,000-acre facility was purchased by HNG on October 5, 1965. Bammel storage would also be involved in a controversial deal with a company owned by Mark Lay, the son of Ken Lay, in the mid-1990s, discussed in Book 3.

demand. Two decades later, Jeff Skilling would unveil a new concept of a *gas bank*, moving from physical supply to a guaranteed long-term price for supply. But ensured physical supply on short notice was a prerequisite.

◇

Gas processing soon became a major business line for the company, signified by the 1967 creation of a $28 million subsidiary, HNG Petrochemicals. Taking liquid products out of high-BTU gas had long been a staple of the Texas gas industry: Robert's father, Lonnie Herring, was doing it for Lone Star Gas Company back in the 1920s. In 1963, Robert Herring's Valley Gas supplied HNG with a portfolio of gas-processing plants. Four years later, HNG created its own subsidiary in Alvin, Texas, to operate a huge 1 Bcf/d gas-processing plant that was 35 percent owned by HNG and capable of producing a million gallons of liquids a day.[18] "The Company's entry into this new, but related, field," explained the *1967 Annual Report*, "became feasible as a result of the recent growth of its transmission and storage operations, both of which have provided the major gas streams required, and of the continued expansion and diversification of the Texas Gulf Coast petrochemical industry."

◇

The residential/commercial market, averaging 2.5 percent annual growth, was the easy side of the business—so long as state and local authorities allowed the company to adjust rates in tandem with its wholesale costs. (HNG shared the greater Houston market evenly with United Gas.) Industrial load was the tougher side of the business, given that plants generally had multiple hookups from suppliers. But HNG had a competitive niche and favorable regulatory environment. As the company explained (with Bammel's vital contribution embedded):

> The Texas Gulf Coast industrial sales market is extremely competitive and involves a number of pipelines and producers. Historically, the Texas Railroad Commission never has attempted to fix industrial gas prices and has permitted the market to find its own level.
>
> As evidenced by the annual growth in deliveries and revenues, the Company has more than held its own in this atmosphere of free competition in which price and the ability to do a good job are controlling. A key factor is location of facilities. The transmission subsidiaries now cover more of the Texas Gulf Coast than any other pipeline system. New industrial load can be added in many instances without substantial new investment in facilities. This advantage also applies to the acquisition of reserves as discoveries occur.

---

18. Gas liquids processed out of the gas stream include ethane, propane, butane, isobutane, and heavier hydrocarbons, including natural gasoline. The balance of the project, 65 percent, was owned by British Petroleum.

HNG had a simple, sound business model combining a winning fuel, a winning market, and scale economies.[19] A do-no-harm regulatory policy by the state of Texas allowed free-markets forces dominant leeway. Good execution, disciplined by gas-on-gas competition, was also integral to the mix.

Other Developments

Still, governmental challenges loomed over the company's oft-reported "substantial progress." There were always taxation issues—local, state, and federal. General inflation from expansionary monetary policy required rate increases: Texas Railroad Commission hearings in Austin to increase the wholesale charge between HPL and HNG, and meetings with municipal officials in almost 50 locales to increase retail charges between HNG and residential/commercial customers. (Industrial rates were not regulated, reflecting gas-on-gas competition.)

HNG's first rate increase in 1952 was followed by increases in 1959 and 1962. Then there was the municipalization of gas service, what HNG called "the threat of creeping socialism," which company officials warned could engulf the retailers of other products if allowed with natural gas.

Wimberly's biggest socialism problem concerned the city of Corpus Christi. HNG won election skirmishes in Corpus in 1949 and 1959, but defeats in the early 1960s forced the company to sell its distribution properties to the city. "A decision to sell any part of our system is always distasteful if it involves municipal ownership," Wimberly wrote. But Corpus Christi was a unique situation, the all-employee memo continued, and the sale was in the best interests of stockholders, given the circumstances.

⟨∾⟩

In 1967, HNG broke the $10 million net income threshold (nearly $60 million today). Enduring changes also came in this year. HNG Petrochemicals was created as the fourth division of the company. Houston-based employees, scattered in four downtown buildings, were consolidated in the new 28-story Houston Natural Gas Building. Houston's sixth-largest structure wasn't as fancy as Jack Bowen's Florida Gas Building in Winter Park completed three years later, but it was a stately addition to the Houston skyline. What both buildings had in common, however, was a gas-fired total energy system in the basement, doing everything from boiling water to generating electricity. Natural gas was technically capable of doing it all, but the economics of doing so was another matter—at least for buildings that did not have a gas marketing message to sell.

---

19. Houston and the Texas Gulf Coast generally were winning markets. See Internet appendix 12.5, "'Houston Milestones," at www.politicalcapitalism.org/Book2/Chapter12/Appendix5.html.

Figure 12.6 HNG headquarters were in the Scanlan Building (1925–27), Petroleum Building (1927–67), and Houston Natural Gas Building (1967–). Some 550 HNG employees moved over Labor Day weekend 1967 to the brand new $13 million structure (right) bounded by Travis, Polk, Milam, and Dallas streets. A sketch of Houston (left) goes from the Ship Channel (bottom) to downtown (top) where HNG resided.

Bus Wimberly, like Frank Smith several decades before, was a respected member of his profession. Wimberly was elected president of the American Gas Association in 1966, championing a platform of *Action, Acceleration, and Accomplishment*. This was incrementalism, not revolution, something that business guru Peter Drucker was warning might no longer be enough. A new *Age of Discontinuity*, Drucker posited, meant that businesses could be "aiming too low" with business as usual. The Schumpeterian-school strategist longed for "truly productive … men who set out to create something new."

Perhaps Smith and Wimberly were old school, or old economy as the top Enron brass would later term it. But there could be no question that little had gone wrong for the company, or the industry, in its formative decades. And now, a new-age executive—Robert R. Herring—was on his way to lead Houston Natural Gas.

13

Robert Herring and After

HOUSTON NATURAL GAS CORPORATION (HNG) was chartered in 1926, a quarter century after John Henry Kirby founded its parent, Houston Oil Company. HNG became a major gas-transmission and distribution company under the leadership of Frank Smith (1933–55) and John "Bus" Wimberly (1955–67). The cautious, old-school company would be transformed and reach its apex during the reign of Robert Herring (1967–81). A post-Herring HNG period was little more than a transition from caretaker M. D. Matthews to change-maker Ken Lay.[1]

HNG's growth paralleled that of its hometown, as well as that of the broader Texas Gulf Coast. The company became a grand dame of energy-capital Houston, so it was a proud time when Herring extended HNG's reach across the nation and into 28 foreign countries. Ken Lay would inherit not just a company but also a Houston institution, albeit one whose markets and margins were under severe competitive pressure in the face of industry overcapacity and falling energy prices.

The Robert Herring Era (1967–81)

Robert Ray Herring rose like a rocket after joining HNG in 1963. With Valley Gas Production Company, Bus Wimberly was buying not only physical assets

---

1. As told in Book 3, Lay would sell HNG's non-oil-and-gas assets and acquire two interstate natural gas pipelines, one being Florida Gas Transmission, the major asset of a company he had formerly headed. The new Houston Natural Gas would then merge with Omaha-based InterNorth to form HNG/InterNorth in 1985, a company renamed Enron Corporation the next year.

but also the man appointed vice president over Houston Pipe Line, which housed most of the company's assets. In just his second year, Herring was made senior vice president of HNG and elected to the board.

Effective December 8, 1967, Herring was named president and chief executive officer, with Wimberly (like Frank Smith before him) becoming board chairman. Smith retired to the status of honorary chairman of the board, a moniker he would retain for the last three years of his life. Herring's promotion to the top spot was only the third such change at HNG since 1933, the year Smith replaced Tex Trammel.[2]

Another appointment several months later would prove central to HNG's future: the election to the board of John Duncan, head of Gulf & Western Industries. It would be Duncan, as chairman of the executive committee, who would choose M. D. "Bill" Matthews to replace the late Robert Herring in October 1981. It would also be Duncan who less than three years later would replace Matthews with Ken Lay before leading the company through a 16-year ride of peaks and valleys that culminated in Enron's demise.

HNG's board had always been strong. Some of the directors were major stockholders, which put the incentives in the right place. There was also a nice mix of Houston and Baltimore investors who were not beholden to each other.

The first generation of directors joined between 1926 and 1933; a second generation came aboard in 1939/40, and a third group emerged in the 1950s as the company expanded by acquisition. In the third group was V. F. "Doc" Neuhaus, who was elected in 1961. A South Texas institution, with wide interests in banking and oil and gas, Doc was also on the boards of Kirby Petroleum Company and Florida Gas Company. It was a small world as far as hydrocarbon-rich South Texas was concerned.

A Fast Start

Herring introduced himself as president and CEO in an all-employee memorandum, in which he outlined his business philosophy:

> These days, one has to run very hard and very fast just to stay even, and so I would expect that a good part of our company's future growth must come from better, faster, more efficient and more economical ways of conducting our business. The gas business is neither so old nor so well understood that all of the good ideas are in its past....
>
> Mr. Smith and Mr. Wimberly ... said ... that we never would aspire to grow just for the sake of getting big ... that we would have to make growth work for us. I'm a staunch believer in that philosophy too, and I know that you will join

---

2. The other front runner for the presidency, Jackson Hinds, a protégé of Frank Smith, joined HNG in 1956. Hinds ran gas distribution and Herring the pipelines, making them rivals for the top job at HNG. Herring got the nod, and Hinds left the company in 1969 to head HNG's distribution rival, Entex, Inc., where he remained chairman and CEO until 1987.

with me and others in our management team in making the years ahead as fruitful as those of the past.

HNG proved strong even before the great energy boom commenced in 1973. After a respectable fiscal year (FY) 1968 marked by record revenue in excess of $100 million, earnings in FY 1969 surged 25 percent to $13.4 million.[3] Gas deliveries averaged 1.4 Bcf/d for the year, and customers notified the company that another 900 MMcf/d would be needed by 1975.

Figure 13.1 Chairman John "Bus" Wimberly and President Robert Herring present a silver Revere bowl to honorary chairman Frank Smith on behalf of company officers, directors, and employees at HNG's 1968 management conference.

Such growth was doable. Although national reserve additions were discouraged by federal price controls on wellhead gas dedicated in interstate commerce, HNG was adding a Tcf per year to its system by paying higher prices for

---

3. All references to annual financial results in this chapter refer to HNG's fiscal year, which ran from August through July. Thus, some differences exist with calendar-year information. HNG went from fiscal-year to calendar-year reporting in 1984 after Ken Lay became CEO.

unregulated intrastate supply.[4] It would not be long until gas-needy industry began relocating to the Gulf Coast from gas-short states, which compounded the benefit for HNG from misguided federal natural gas policy.

⌒

Gas demand was soaring; reserve replacement was lagging. Robert Herring was concerned. So, in addition to hunting for gas, HNG embarked on a new strategy "to broaden the base of the company in related fields."

In early 1969, Houston Natural Gas Corporation was transformed by the purchase of Liquid Carbonic Corporation (LCC), a world-class producer and marketer of industrial gases and a maker and supplier of beverage, food, and medical services; food processing; welding and cutting equipment; and flavorings and extracts.[5] Most notably, Liquid Carbonic was the world's leading supplier of carbon dioxide (CO_2) in gaseous, liquid, and solid form. It took five pages in HNG's *1969 Annual Report* to describe what the company did—and another page to list, in the smallest of type, 89 Liquid Carbonic production locations in 16 countries outside North America. The $100 million acquisition extended HNG from Texas to many parts of the Western Hemisphere and Spain[6]—and turned a large company into a very large one with 4,700 employees (from 1,500) and 38,000 stockholders (from 6,700).

Herring's move was a bold, unprecedented diversification for HNG, although the new business was related broadly to petrochemicals. HNG's strong cash flow made the move possible, and the company's stock—newly listed on the New York Stock Exchange as *HNG*—was a growth, not yield, investment. This meant that rather than concentrate on distributing earnings to shareholders, HNG would reinvest most of its income in order to increase future earnings and thereby increase the stock price over time.

Strategically, HNG saw opportunities for cost reduction in the industrial gas business, as well as "exciting growth potential" from "the rapid development of new techniques in the use of industrial gases in the fields of oceanography, aerospace and chemical processing." Increasing linkages of industrial gases to

---

4. The price premium for intrastate gas producers began at 15–20 percent in 1969/70 and rose several times higher in 1973/74.

5. Liquid Carbonic Acid Manufacturing Company was founded in 1888 in Terre Haute, Indiana, to produce CO_2 for soda carbonation and began manufacturing in Chicago the next year. The genesis of the sale to HNG came from a divestiture order from the Justice Department to General Dynamics Corporation to sell Liquid Carbonic. HNG, one of 60 interested buyers, engaged Arthur D. Little to evaluate the company and recommend a purchase price, which proved to be the winner.

6. Liquid Carbonic's foreign subsidiaries were joint ventures, lessening the political risk for HNG stockholders.

natural gas were also foreseen. Herring himself learned the complicated new business on the fly, but it turned out to be good enough.[7]

HNG was not only wise but also lucky with this purchase. The closing was postponed because of unexpected delays with the federal tax rulings needed to consummate the transaction, during which time the industrial gas market weakened. Renegotiations reduced the original $120 million purchase price not once but twice, saving HNG $20 million at the end. The new price left HNG's debt ratio virtually unchanged—and ensured that the acquisition would be accretive to earnings from the start.

Houston Natural Gas began its first-ever national advertising campaign after the purchase of Liquid Carbonic. "What's Houston Natural Gas Doing in Canada?" read one full-page spread. HNG was in all sorts of places—from Canada to Argentina to Spain to Hawaii—the ad continued, and "it's only the beginning."

The Roaring 1970s

Houston Natural Gas was one of America's top corporate performers for the decade ending in 1981 as revenue and net income surged from $277 million to $2.9 billion, and $21 million to $239 million, respectively. In today's dollars, the 1981 results would be $6 billion in sales and $500 million in net income, numbers that HNG's successor, Enron, rarely achieved in its 16-year active life. True, the Herring era was fortuitously timed with an energy price boom, but it also reflected successful diversification, timely attention to company challenges, and effective capital redeployment.

Much was going right for the company that nearly doubled net income between FY 1968 and FY 1972. A 25 percent earnings jump in FY 1973 led to a two-for-one stock split, the first of this size at HNG since 1958. Energy markets were strong across the board, and Liquid Carbonic, responsible for one-third of company revenue, was expanding rapidly.

The best news was a solid start for HNG's new gas-supply strategy, a diversification from the Gulf Coast ("the most-developed oil and gas region in the world") to West Texas. Back in 1969, Herring had announced plans for HNG to develop deep-zone gas in West Texas and purchase neighboring supply for shipment through a new 479-mile, 1.1 Bcf/d pipeline to Katy, Texas, just west of

---

7. Recalled one HNG executive: "I'll never forget a trip to Chicago in 1969 ... to acquaint ourselves with the management of Liquid Carbonic Corporation, a company we had just acquired. [We] were generally unfamiliar with the company's technical operations.... We arrived in Chicago in late afternoon and Bob suggested we go to a nearby book store. Bill [Matthews] and I bought light reading—Bob emerged with a textbook on cryogenics [meaning low-temperature chemistry, not suspended animation]. At the next morning's meeting, he literally floored the assembled executives with his freshly acquired knowledge of their industry.... He was a real pro."

Houston.[8] The $140 million Intratex Gas Company project (about $750 million today)—involving gas production, purchasing, gathering, treating, and transportation—was undertaken at a time when gas prices were low and capital for exploration and production tight. But Herring knew that his customers would pay a profitable price for the needed gas and that gas supply would tighten and prices rise. An unprecedented negative statistic for 1969, new gas reserves failing to offset production (negative reserve replacement), a consequence of federal wellhead price controls, had a lot to do with his thinking.

In July 1971, some major assets of Intratex were merged into a new corporation, Oasis Pipe Line Company. HNG took half of the $60 million project, Dow Chemical 30 percent, and Tenngasco 20 percent.

Another key step in the West Texas play was acquiring Roden Oil Company, a Midland oil and gas producer, which was renamed HNG Oil Company in 1971.[9] Such gas would be part of the supply brought to the Gulf Coast.

In August 1972, Oasis Pipe Line, the longest intrastate line in the United States, began moving gas from West Texas to near Houston, and the line was soon running at full capacity. This gas—more and more of which would be self-produced rather than purchased from others—maintained a 12- to 13-year reserve life for HNG's wholesale and retail customers. This market-determined cushion compared to the regulated FPC requirement for pipelines to have a ratio of 20-year gas reserve to consumption ratio.

The rising price of natural gas at the wellhead in 1972/73 was good news for HNG Oil but less so for HPL, which had long-term fixed-priced contracts with industrial users that were suddenly out of the money. Contract renegotiations began, and an accounting reserve was created for anticipated losses. The problem was not nearly as bad as the take-or-pay problem was for interstate pipelines,[10] however, and end users agreed to renegotiate their contracts in return for up-front payments of several million dollars.

Lesson learned, HNG's future gas contracts would be priced flexibly so that future cost increases could be automatically passed through. Further, following an industry trend, the terms of its commitments were shortened. Such action would contribute to making HPL the most profitable gas pipeline in the country during the next decade.

---

8. The Delaware Basin in West Texas, which HNG targeted, contained an estimated 100 trillion cubic feet of reserves, making it a premier lower-48 production frontier.

9. HNG Oil drilled 126 wells in 1972 (compared to 33 in 1970 and 26 in 1971), indicative of its ramped-up activity. Another wholly owned subsidiary, HNG Fossil Fuels Company, would be formed in 1973 to explore, for the first time, outside of Texas and offshore.

10. Transcontinental Gas Pipe Line's take-or-pay problem plagued the company in the 1980s and early 1990s, whereas Florida Gas, under Selby Sullivan, who overruled Ken Lay on the use of such provisions, avoided most of the problem. See chapter 8, pp. 306n31, 450, and chapter 9, pp. 337, 338, 354, 359.

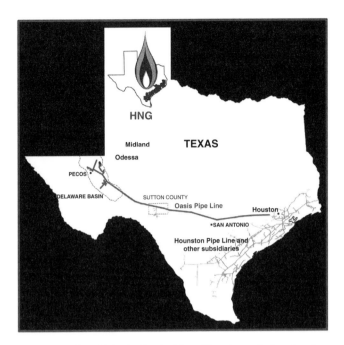

Figure 13.2 The 500-mile, 36-inch Oasis Pipe Line imported natural gas from West Texas to HNG's Gulf Coast service area beginning in 1972. This timely addition allowed Houston Pipe Line to keep up with growing customer demand and made HNG's pipeline network one of the largest in the country.

On the regulatory front, HPL persuaded the Texas Railroad Commission (TRC) to institute new procedures to expedite requests to pass through increased gas costs at wholesale for residential and commercial users; on that basis, local authorities allowed passthrough at retail without major challenge. Wholesale represented 5 percent of the company's total throughput, with 95 percent being for industrial users.

The municipalization threat quieted, making the company's overall government exposure minimal compared to federally regulated gas companies. HNG's strategy of avoiding federal jurisdiction, even offshore, had benefits. In fact, the avoided federal regulation that was hurting interstate pipelines was indirectly *helping* Texas-specific HPL.[11]

---

11. See Internet appendix 13.1, "Intrastate Regulation by the Texas Railroad Commission," at www.politicalcapitalism.org/Book2/Chapter13/Appendix1.html. Price regulation under President Nixon's wage-and-price-control program was avoided by state jurisdiction exercised by the Texas Railroad Commission.

HNG was committed to "full development of the natural gas potential in Texas, which we expect will provide a viable business for a number of years to come." But Herring had broader horizons. In late 1973, HNG purchased Zeigler Coal Company for $30 million, calling it "a timely investment in a major energy resource for the future." Zeigler's four underground mines in Illinois and one in western Kentucky, containing over a billion tons of high-sulfur coal, came with 1,500 unionized employees.

Herring's timing with this purchase was exquisite. Reserves purchased at $7.60 per ton were worth twice as much within two years. The new economics would have meant an acquisition price of $150 million, five times what HNG had paid for Zeigler, Herring estimated. Energy in the 1970s was a good business to be in—and nowhere more so than on the commodity side.

"A significant part of our future," Herring declared, "will relate to coal." Elsewhere, Herring labeled coal "the brightest new source of fossil fuel in this country." Similar thoughts were heard from Jack Bowen and Ken Lay at Transco Energy, an interstate natural gas transmission company headquartered in Houston five miles from HNG. Both companies, however, would overplay their energy-diversification hands on a belief that natural gas was a wasting asset. The problem with natural gas was *regulatory*. Shortages resulted from wellhead price controls, not a tiring resource base. Coal would bring its own problems, and Ken Lay, once ensconced at HNG, turned against coal with a vengeance.

❧

By the mid-1970s, business analysts described HNG as a *diversified energy supplier*. Oil exploration, coal production, uranium mining, specialty gases—these were the new frontiers where the "aggressive opportunist" Robert Herring was leading the company. "I'm an energy man," he explained when asked about his move into uranium production. HNG Production Company began looking for the nuclear power feedstock on 170,000 acres in northern New Mexico in 1970; several years later, HNG, in a joint venture with Ranchers Exploration & Development Company, opened a $12 million uranium mine in New Mexico. This side of the business, however, would prove problematic and be deemphasized amid the company's much bigger operations elsewhere.

In FY 1976, revenues reached a billion dollars, and a second two-for-one stock split was announced. The annual report thanked "an economic system which still permits realization of some degree of reward for innovation, commitment of private capital, fiscal responsibility and efficiency," while lambasting national energy policies "being shaped far more on fancy than on fact." Actually, federal intervention was helping HNG in myriad ways, the latest example of which was allowing gas-rich intrastate pipelines to make emergency sales to gas-short interstates—a lucrative business that came at the expense of producers that would have otherwise made the sale.[12]

HNG's angst toward federal energy policy and populist President Jimmy Carter pertained to the coal side of its business. The company increased its coal bet in 1976 with the $27.5 million purchase of Empire Energy Corporation of Colorado, but environmental restrictions were inhibiting the production and burning of coal. In a special personal message from the chairman that fronted the *1976 Annual Report*, Herring called for a 50 percent increase in national coal production to offset oil imports and improve the balance of trade. Similar rhetoric would come from Ken Lay a decade later regarding the ability of natural gas to displace oil imports.

By FY 1975, HNG's three new businesses—Liquid Carbonic, HNG Oil, and Zeigler Coal—were contributing 50 percent of HNG's consolidated income, supplementing the mainstay of natural gas transmission and sales. But Herring was not through. A fifth major business line—marine transportation, services, and construction—was established with the 1977 purchase of Pott Industries for $165 million. The acquisition was in keeping with Herring's strategy of investing in new energy-related businesses. Employing 3,000 people, Pott manufactured ships and owned and operated the Gulf Fleet: 80 tugboats, ships, and barges moving oil and coal and servicing the offshore energy industry.

Coal transportation was part of Herring's vertical-integration plan with regard to America's most plentiful fuel. "As the national momentum builds toward coal conversion for utilities and industries, particularly in the South and Midwest," the *1977 Annual Report* explained, "the barge lines are in a favorable position to participate in the required transportation of the coal."

But there was another impetus for the purchase, although the reason was not mentioned in press releases or annual reports. Pott was in the middle of a major government maritime subsidy program. Taxpayer-backed loan guarantees and cash payments for construction and operating costs began back in 1936. In the 1970s, barges, crew boats, and offshore rig service vessels got into the act. It was sweet for incumbents, but longer term, the subsidies would result in an overbuilt, unprofitable business, as HNG would find out.

·◇·

HNG's reinvention included the sale of one of its oldest business lines, gas distribution, to rival Entex for $64 million in March 1976. The division was valued slightly above its depreciated book value, allowing a straightforward transaction to overcome the sentiment in selling a major division just after its fiftieth anniversary.

---

12. This peculiar wealth transfer is examined in Internet appendix 13.2, "HNG and Federal Gas Regulation," at www.politicalcapitalism.org/Book2/Chapter13/Appendix2.html.

The sale was spurred by regulation. The Texas Railroad Commission had initiated a policy allowing only 65 percent recovery of increased gas costs between HPL and HNG as affiliates, a liability that did not apply to arm's length transaction between separate companies. As a result, distribution had lost $8 million the year before the sale, whereas public-utility regulation was supposed to guarantee a profit!

Instrumental in the transaction was a 20-year contract between HPL and Entex whereby the former locked in a $0.15/Mcf margin and was assured full recovery of increased gas costs. As an HNG executive explained, distribution was "taking about 40% of our time and producing about 10% of our revenues." Now, HNG would no longer have to deal with the minutiae of 360,000 gas accounts and a host of regulatory matters at the local and state levels. Entex, on the other hand, led by former HNG executive Jackson Hinds, expanded its primary business and economically spread its fixed costs over more sales.

Asset acquisitions were outpacing divestitures, but record cash flow made the growth easily digestible. HNG reported in FY 1977 that its debt-to-capital ratio was down to a new low of 38 percent. These were heady times, with record income, earnings, stock splits, and ever-rising share prices.[13]

HNG's meteoric pace then slowed. Gas sales fell 6 percent in FY 1978 as industrial users conserved or switched to oil in response to record high gas prices (the beginning of the long-lived gas bubble). Texas gas prices actually began to erode in late 1977, falling below $2 per Mcf. The pricing provisions of the Natural Gas Policy Act of 1978 (NGPA), combined with the emergence of a surplus of gas relative to demand, exposed the high-cost position of HPL and other intrastates that had paid premiums to get gas when the interstates could not.

Federal energy policy was also pushing for coal to replace natural gas as a boiler fuel to generate electricity, which culminated in the Powerplant and Industrial Fuel Use Act of 1978 (Fuel Use Act). Herring bought into this view, looking at gas as the bridge fuel to a coal future. "We now are entering a new era in the gas business," the company's *1978 Annual Report* opined.[14]

Two of the company's major new business lines were having problems. Beginning in December 1977, Zeigler Coal was hit with a 112-day strike by the United Mine Workers of America, and Pott Industries was suffering from a

13. HNG did not begin reporting its stock price in the annual report until 1974, nearly a half century after the company began.

14. For Herring's view of coal relative to gas reserves, see Internet appendix 13.3, "HNG: Transitioning from Natural Gas to Coal," at www.politicalcapitalism.org/Book2/Chapter13/Appendix3.html.

stagnant market. Still, HNG was a very strong and profitable company with a debt-to-capital ratio that Enron would never achieve.

∾

In FY 1980, HNG got back on the fast track when net income increased more than 40 percent on revenues of $2.4 billion. Behind the surge was a gangbuster gas market. HPL's sales increased 25 percent from the previous fiscal year, thanks in part to a jump in world oil prices, which ended fuel switching away from gas. Federal decontrol of gas-liquid prices benefitted HNG Petrochemicals. Liquid Carbonic attained another earnings record—as it had every year since its purchase in 1969.

A flat performance at Zeigler Coal was about the only negative—the year in which Herring and HNG made their last major acquisition. The purchase of Houston-based Alamo Barge Company in August 1980, announced as "in excess of $50 million," added 79 towboats and barges transporting petroleum and chemical products to the vessels of Pott Industries purchased three years before. It also made Edgar "Ed" Smith, Alamo's owner, the largest stockholder of HNG and newest board member. Herring described the purchase as adding "a new dimension" to HNG's "increasing role as a major producer and transporter of energy and energy-related materials." To critics, however, including Joe Foy, HNG's former president who left the company because of concern over Herring's coal/marine strategy, Herring was throwing good money after bad.

The new HNG was a diversified natural gas powerhouse. By the late 1970s its gas business stood at 2.5 Bcf/d, representing 5 percent of national consumption. This was four times the volume handled by Florida Gas Transmission (0.7 Bcf/d) and nearly that of Transcontinental Gas Pipe Line (3 Bcf/d). The decade ended strongly as the stock soared from a low of $20 per share in early 1979 to past $60 by the end of 1980.

Natural gas was a great business, and Wall Street applauded Herring's diversification efforts. "Herring always seems to be thinking about 10 years ahead," one analyst said in *Financial World*. "He's got Houston Natural Gas positioned for a much longer term than other natural gas executives." Being touted as the industry visionary was heady stuff and a bit of an affront to those on the interstate pipeline side of the gas business, including Jack Bowen at Transco Companies and Ken Lay at Continental Resources Company.

Fiscal year 1981 was the last hurrah for Herring—and one of the last great years for HNG. Stricken with cancer, Herring was working on company matters from his bed. His chairman's letter, written shortly before the end, reported much good news. Records were set with revenues of $2.9 billion and earnings of $239 million. Income from the marine division almost doubled with the acquisition of Alamo Barge and favorable market conditions. Natural gas was strong across the board. Bammel, one of the premier gas-storage fields in the country, with a withdrawal capacity of a billion cubic feet a day, increased the

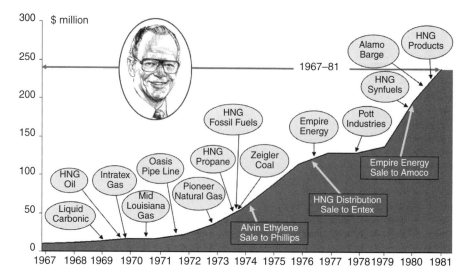

Figure 13.3 The 14-year reign of Robert Herring as CEO of Houston Natural Gas Corporation produced many more acquisitions than divestitures amid increasing earnings and cash flow. The Herring era was one of the great runs in the history of the natural gas industry. HNG's diversifications helped net earnings as well.

company's annual throughput by better matching purchases (injections) in flat periods with sales (withdrawals) in peak periods. Given Bammel's ability to take or supply gas on short notice, innovative contracts with higher margins were being executed with industrials.

In fact, although never publically stated, HPL was *the* most profitable pipeline in the country, even registering *triple-digit* rates of return.[15] HNG Fossil Fuels Company was actively exploring for oil and gas outside of the company's traditional areas, drilling more than 150 wells in FY 1981 alone.

"The coal business has developed more slowly than was anticipated when HNG acquired Zeigler," Herring reported. But he was not discouraged. "Planning is going forward for the day when the market may require a versatile substitute fuel for natural gas." Indeed, "HNG's engineers are keeping abreast of developments in synthetic fuels, while monitoring market potentials," he added. Such was part of HNG's "master plan" of

> an integrated system of Zeigler coal moving through our Cora Coal Terminal into Federal barges for transportation to Gulf Coast power-steam plants, wholly

---

15. "There were some years when if you backed into the rate of return by covering your gas cost, covering your cost of service," remembered an HNG rate analyst, "[HPL's] return on equity ... exceeded three digits."

or partly owned by HNG. Revenues to HNG would be generated by each phase of the project.

But this strategy was already in trouble and would not again appear in an HNG annual report.

Herring's final stockholders' letter ended with a statement that would ring loudest two decades later, though nobody would hear it then.

> It has been popular recently for critics to accuse American business of seeking short term profits to the detriment of the unwise investor. I hope this letter will allay any fear in that regard concerning HNG. Our management, with the dedicated support of its more than 12,000 loyal employees, is achieving increased profits year to year, while devoting attention to planning, investing and preparing for the future. To do otherwise would violate the trust placed in us by the Company's stockholders.

Energy Politics

"We have a ready ear in Washington for the first time in a long time," Robert Herring remarked in 1971, a year in which federal oil-price regulation joined long-standing natural gas controls. He urged the gas industry to show "more statesmanship than we have shown in the past"—a theme Ken Lay also stressed in his ghost-written book for Humble Oil & Refining Company chairman Mike Wright several years before.[16] Federal gas policy was affecting HNG's intrastate market in unforeseen ways. And Washington would only grow in importance with HNG's 1974 major entrance into coal, a fuel that was in the crosshairs of federal environmental policy.

Federal gas regulation affected HNG, although the company was subject only to state regulation. "We need an end to [federal] controls which create artificial pricing," Herring declared in HNG's *1976 Annual Report*. "We need a return to a free market." But HNG's position was less straightforward—and less free-market—than advertised. The next annual report, written in the heat of the debate over federal gas legislation, stated: "HNG has consistently opposed full and immediate deregulation but does strongly advocate a phase-out of price controls over a three to five year period." This was exactly the time period the company expected the gas surplus to persist and then end.

Herring's point man on gas politics was his president and chief operating officer, Joe Foy, a lifelong Democrat whose introduction to energy came as a city attorney challenging gas rate increases by the very company he later joined. Foy endeared the Carter administration with his opposition to immediate wellhead gas decontrol, a position that put HNG at odds with just about the entire oil- and gas-producing industry. "The heretic," as *Texas Monthly* described Foy, could not hide behind a vague call for an eventual return to a free market, such

---

16. See *Capitalism at Work*, pp. 172–74.

as Herring had made earlier.[17] Joe Foy, in fact, responding to an emergency phone call from James Schlesinger, President Carter's secretary of energy, persuaded Rep. Charlie Wilson (D-TX) to vote out of conference the bill that became the Natural Gas Policy Act of 1978 (NGPA).[18]

Full deregulation would have been water thrown in the face of HPL, given higher prices for the gas purchased for resale—prices that were higher than the gas acquired by interstate pipelines. Intrastate gas was already selling for almost $2/Mcf, whereas price-controlled interstate gas averaged around $0.80/Mcf. If HPL's gas cost rose further, its volumes and margins would be jeopardized, for industrial users and power-plant customers were poised to switch to another fuel or to another gas supplier—or to just reduce demand altogether.

This was ironic. The profitable gas strategy followed earlier in the decade now put HNG in a competitive pickle once the regulatory playing field had been evened, and supply turned from not enough to too much.

Interstate pipelines were better positioned for the new surplus-supply environment. Their sales were mostly for resale to residential and commercial customers, whose demand was less sensitive to price, and that gave the interstates an ability to pay top dollar for new supply. The interstates' gas portfolio also had large quantities of low-price-controlled gas, allowing them to aggressively bid for new supply. They would not lose market share or margins from higher gas costs and rates as would the intrastates. Even if HPL did not buy any new gas, its gas cost would increase if nearby purchases by an interstate triggered HPL's most-favored-nation clause with producers.[19]

HNG did the math, determining that the price rise from full decontrol would benefit the company less as a gas producer (HNG Oil, HNG Fossil Fuels) than it would hurt by squeezing its industrial contracts. Interstate pipelines, in fact, with lower gas prices, might even capture HPL's load. Despite Herring's grand words praising the free market and criticizing government intervention, his company needed Big Brother to protect its wholesale gas division. Like Foy, Herring was a political capitalist, and Houston Natural Gas Corporation was advancing the system of political capitalism.

Indeed, Robert Herring was not a principled free-market capitalist. Like so many before and after him, he *generally* supported the American ideals of private property and limited government. But he failed to get beyond a good-for-business, good-for-society view of government in the economy. He did not

---

17. Herring's free-market rhetoric became more pronounced in the troubled 1970s, a time when he was married to his second wife, Joanne, profiled later in this chapter.

18. The "bitterly debated" NGPA, as one historian described it, "came close to defeat at virtually every stage of its existence."

19. This situation was also a catalyst in the formation of Florida Gas Transmission, as discussed in chapter 8, p. 272.

recognize how government intervention fostered by business—as that fostered by antibusiness interests—can have unintended consequences and should be avoided.

In Herring's thinking, there was no ideal state, in which both allegedly good and allegedly bad intervention are demoted in favor of self-help alternatives, including simple rules of a complex world.[20] Thus in 1972, when energy shortages resulted from pervasive federal regulation, Herring called for "a new national energy policy" that would comprehensively include "all sources of energy" to meet "the needs of our people and industry with due consideration of the environment and of cost." Such was not unlike what Jack Bowen at Transco advocated in the troubled decade.[21]

But by the end of the decade, even the political capitalist had had enough. This was not industry enlightened regulation—it was "federal ... 'go it alone' [regulation]." Federal regulation was "excessive and oftimes ridiculous"—even "whimsical."

But HNG welcomed taxpayer support for its energy reaches. In the early 1970s, the company announced its participation in a three-year coal-gasification project between the gas industry ($10 million per year) and federal government ($20 million per year).

Later in the decade, HNG got more directly involved. "We are actively engaged in investigating new technology—such as gasification—for the use of our coal resources," Herring reported in 1979. But this interest was more than the company would do on its own. Nor would a bank finance such a project on a nonrecourse (stand-alone) basis. HNG's gasification play—housed in its new subsidiary, HNG Synfuels Company—necessitated a $3.6 million Department of Energy (DOE) grant, jointly awarded to HNG and Texaco, to study the feasibility of producing gas and methanol from coal.

DOE's grant, and the $500,000 that HNG and Texaco each invested in the project, did not bear commercial fruit. HNG Synfuels was dissolved in 1984.[22] Transco's Great Plains Coal Gasification Project, as discussed in chapter 9, would become commercial with a lot of government support and after both taxpayers and stockholders lost their investment.

---

20. For elucidation of the common-law alternative to government regulation, see *Capitalism at Work*, pp. 295–99.

21. See chapter 9, pp. 342–45.

22. HNG vice president Norman Callner was a candidate to join the U.S. Synthetic Fuels Corporation (1980–85) in its last year of its existence, a potential appointment that was complicated by HNG's pending interest in new grants. "Many people were involved or talking about being involved because it was a great big Federal grab bag," remembered Joe Hillings of HNG's Washington office.

Some of Herring's other esoteric ventures did not reach the construction phase either. Years of negotiations with Saudi Arabia to process flared waste gas associated with crude oil into methanol were finally called off. Plans to enter the oil-shale and coal-slurry-pipeline businesses went unfulfilled, although the latter would bear fruit through an antitrust settlement several years later.

~

Herring traveled to Washington regularly for something other than natural gas policy in the 1970s: federal environmental policy. Coal usage, which had been stagnant for many years before HNG purchased Zeigler, surged when supplies became inadequate for oil and gas, coal's competitors in electric generation. With higher usage came rising emissions of sulfur dioxide (SO_2), linked to acid rain, which prompted a drive to amend the Clean Air Act of 1970.

The Clean Air Act Amendments of 1977 required coal-fired power plants to install scrubbers to reduce emissions. This particular approach, supported by HNG, as well as the United Mine Workers of America, advantaged high-sulfur coal in the Midwest and East, where Zeigler was located, relative to low-sulfur Western coal deposits. Thus, Herring and others got their wish to redirect the cost of emissions reduction from the mine to the smokestack, thereby removing the incentive for power plants to meet their emission reductions by importing low-sulfur coal from the West as an alternative to scrubbing. This negatively affected coal from HNG's Empire Energy, but that Colorado operation was so much smaller than Zeigler's as to not determine HNG's overall policy.[23]

~

One of Robert Herring's assets on the national and international stage was his attractive, intelligent, worldly, ambitious wife, the former Joanne King (later of *Charlie Wilson's War* fame). Robert's first wife, Sylvia Grant Herring, died in a swimming pool accident in 1971. Two years later, after only five dates, Robert and Joanne married.

Meeting Robert's parents, Joanne, then a Houston television personality, promised to take good care of her husband-to-be—and to be an asset in his business life as well. Joanne proved to be that and more. She was a hit on the Washington social scene, and before the company had a Washington office, she did by evening what visiting HNG executives could not do by day. She was well briefed and astute enough to understand the issues. The new Mrs. Herring did

---

23. About 90 percent of HNG's coal was high-sulfur, and it became all high sulfur when Empire Energy was sold to Amoco Minerals in early 1980. (The $53 million sale netted $10.3 million for HNG, a nice return for an asset held for less than four years.) For more discussion about the 1977 law and HNG's coal portfolio, see Internet appendix 13.4, "HNG and High-Sulfur Coal," at www.politicalcapitalism.org/Book2/Chapter13/Appendix4.html.

Figure 13.4 During the politically charged 1970s, Robert Herring and his second wife, Joanne, became a notable couple, not just in Houston but also in Washington and foreign capitals.

well back in Houston too, as Houston's honorary consul to Morocco and Pakistan (titles that Robert first declined).

In the 1978 article "The Black-Tie Executive—Pleasure? Or Business?" *Forbes* profiled the lobbying/social activity of the Herrings: "Bob Herring goes to lots of parties in Washington, D.C.," the subtitle read, "but the Houston Natural Gas boss doesn't go just for the hors d'oeuvres." The article detailed how the Herrings had been regulars in the nation's capital for the last two years and quoted Robert as saying: "I do far more good at these parties than I do trying to go up on the Hill with that damn staff sitting there."[24] The dynamic duo effectively worked both sides of the political aisle, making positive impressions not only on friendly oil-state legislators but also with such gas-industry critics as John Dingell (D-MI), Bob Eckhart (D-TX), and Jacob Javits (R-NY).

24. Joanne King Herring's Houston and Washington activity is further described in Internet appendix 13.5, "Joanne King Herring," at www.politicalcapitalism.org/Book2/Chapter13/Appendix5.html. Robert Herring's statement notwithstanding, Joe Foy was HNG's secret weapon to work the other side of the political aisle.

A World Beyond

Robert Herring devoted as much as a third of his time to civic and charitable activities. As president of the Houston Chamber of Commerce (now the Greater Houston Partnership) in 1970, he addressed three of Houston's most pressing problems: pollution, transportation, and downtown street construction. Taking on a range of activities, prominently including medicine and education, Herring became a virtual Mr. Houston, a title that John Henry Kirby had held earlier in the century and one that Ken Lay could claim for the 1990s.[25]

A *Houston Chronicle* profile of Herring published shortly after he became HNG's CEO described the man who had everything: money, power, family, friends, and wide respect. The exasperated reporter wrote how he had made "too many" phone calls looking for a negative angle without avail. Herring must be different from most everyone else, he wrote, and anyway, being the holiday season, "this is that time of year for Noble Thoughts and Belief in Man."

No civic matter was more important to Herring than the Texas Heart Institute (THI). In 1962, a heart attack felled his beloved mentor, Ray Fish, age 60. As a trustee of the Ray C. Fish Foundation, Herring founded THI with a $5 million donation and became its president in 1967. THI's star-in-residence was Dr. Denton Cooley, a heart surgeon on his way to world renown.

Rice University became Herring's second major civic interest. Through a close friendship with Rice president Norman Hackerman, Herring joined Rice's Board of Governors in 1972 and became its chairman in the last year of his life. Herring also was trustee of the University of Houston Foundation and a benefactor of his two alma maters, Tarleton State and Texas A&M University.

⌒

Houston soared alongside HNG in the 1970s. While high oil and gas prices were hurting most cities, none more so than Detroit, home of the big-three automakers, the opposite was true for the oil and gas capital of the world. Houston surpassed Detroit as the nation's fifth-largest city, and Philadelphia, at number four, was in sight. Such landmarks as the Galleria (home of Transco Energy) and Greenway Plaza (home of HNG rival Coastal Corporation) created cities within a city. Youth, newness, and enthusiasm abounded. A visiting *New York Times* architectural critic described the "extraordinary, unlimited vitality" of what she called "*the* city of the second half of the 20th century." *Fortune* magazine announced: "Houston has achieved the status of a leading international business center" and was "well along the path of finding a position among the major cities of the world."

----

25. Robert Herring's extracurricular activities and awards are listed in Internet appendix 13.6, "Robert Herring: Civic and Professional Associations and Awards," at www.political-capitalism.org/Book2/Chapter13/Appendix6.html.

Houston was described as a place where new people, new ideas, and new businesses were welcomed. "Free enterprise was the gospel," *Business Week* reported, and "a minimum of red tape," such as the absence of zoning, helped make it so. A "stampede" of international banks were locating to Houston, and international heads of state were making the city a "must stop." Half a dozen languages could be heard in Houston's hot spots, no place more so than the Petroleum Club atop the 44-story Exxon building.

Many visiting dignitaries, *Fortune* noted, were being entertained at the home of Robert and Joanne King Herring, one of Houston's and Washington's most talked about couples. Indeed, their 23-room River Oaks mansion hosted King Hussein of Jordan, King Carl Gustaf of Sweden, and Prince Saud al Faisal of Saudi Arabia, among other international dignitaries. Often filled with foreign guests, the "Herring Hilton" on Inwood Drive would become the future home of Ken and Linda Lay after Ken Lay became CEO of Houston Natural Gas.

The rarified orbit of Robert Herring made an impression on those who knew him best. Diane Herring remembers thinking, upon learning that her father and stepmother were flying to New York City to attend Henry Kissinger's birthday party: *Is this really my dad?* But all this, while unplanned, was a natural progression for Robert Herring, just another chapter in his real-life story, "A World Beyond."[26]

⌀

Robert Herring had one problem—and it could not be graver. In the fall of 1979, while watching a football game at home, Herring felt a sharp pain in his chest. Fearing a heart attack, his sons Robert Jr. and Randy summoned their neighbor and close friend, Denton Cooley. All rushed to the hospital. The boys knew that the news was bad when Dr. Cooley fingered the lung area of an X-ray and noticed a spot. It was lung cancer, the result of several decades of smoking two or three packs of cigarettes a day.

Herring had smoked his last cigarette. Treatments followed in earnest. Determined and optimistic, Herring kept up his work schedule as much as was humanly possible. His secretary drove him to his civic and board meetings when he could no longer drive. HNG established the Robert R. Herring Professorship in Clinical Research at the University of Texas M. D. Anderson Cancer Center, and Herring's physician, Charles A. "Mickey" LeMaistre, president of the University of Texas System Cancer Center in Houston, became an HNG director.

On October 11, 1981, Robert Herring died at age 60, the same age as did his mentor Ray Fish. Herring's final days were spent in the Texas Heart Institute at

---

26. The title of a manuscript Herring was writing after college, lost in a bus fire during his trip from hometown Ranger, Texas, to Washington, D.C. See chapter 11, p. 403.

Houston's St. Luke's Episcopal Hospital in the wing established by the Ray C. Fish Foundation. It had been a two-year struggle. Robert had tried everything, from state-of-the-art treatment at Houston's world-renowned medical center to laetrile treatments in Mexico. His caregivers admired his courage, and Herring never wavered from his belief that he would recover and lead HNG in the 1980s.

But the mind could not beat the body. No doubt, if he had had any inkling of what the outcome would be, Herring might have resisted the temptation to smoke, taken up during a grueling military assignment 36 years before.

Herring's passing was front-page news in Houston's two daily newspapers and was noted in the *New York Times*. "Houston is a better place because of Robert R. Herring," the *Houston Post* editorialized. "Seldom is a community blessed with such a well-rounded leader." The overflow crowd at St. John the Divine Episcopal Church included pallbearers Ben Love of Texas Commerce Bank, John Duncan of HNG's board, Mike Wright of Exxon USA, Norman Hackerman of Rice, and Robert Mosbacher of Mosbacher Production.

Herring left a legacy. In his 14 years as CEO (1967–81), total revenues at Houston Natural Gas grew from $86 million to $2.9 billion; profit, from $10 million to $239 million. Herring's ambitious goal of 15 percent annual growth actually ended up averaging an astounding 25 percent during his reign. He had turned a Texas Gulf Coast natural gas company into a diversified energy company well known on Wall Street.

Fundraising in his memory endowed the Herring professorship at M. D. Anderson Cancer Center and underwrote the construction of the new home of Rice University's graduate school of business: the $7 million Robert R. Herring Hall, designed by Cesar Pelli and Associates.

The M. D. Matthews Era (1981–84)

Houston Natural Gas's storied past now faced a cloudy future. The energy boom was ending. A national recession was reducing oil, gas, and coal prices, as well as the tonnage and rates received from marine energy carriers. Shipyards building these vessels were also being negatively impacted. HNG was in all these businesses and feeling the pinch. The new CEO would have a bigger job than anyone knew.

A New CEO

Frank Smith had Bus Wimberly, and Wimberly had Robert Herring—a clear one and two. Both Smith and Wimberly seamlessly took the chairman's title to let a well-groomed president become the top executive.

When 70-year-old Bus Wimberly relinquished his chairman's title in 1973, Herring, age 53, became chairman, president, and CEO. In 1976, Herring filled out the executive suite with himself as chairman and CEO, Joe Foy as president and COO, and Bill Matthews as vice chairman and chairman of the executive committee of the board of directors. But who was number two?

Foy and Matthews were given coequal authority and paid to the same dollar. Each could feel like the number two, depending on their relative assignments. But Herring really remained as one and two in this arrangement. Herring played no favorites and refused to get personally close to any particular HNG executive or even board member. Cronyism, needless to say, did not exist at the top.

Still, because of his versatility, Foy was arguably the real number two at HNG behind Herring. A lawyer by training, Foy could handle almost any corporate situation in his no-nonsense, efficient way. Matthews knew the numbers and acted the part, but he was not one to send to a fire.

Foy, five years his boss's junior, was the best in-house candidate to succeed Herring. But Foy's end came—prematurely, in retrospect—just months before Herring was diagnosed with cancer. The genesis of the split concerned the company's business strategy. Foy was a natural gas man and saw the future in gas, not coal. Herring was partial to an integrated coal/marine strategy, what he called HNG's "master plan." Herring was not alone in his vision that coal gas would supplement, and eventually overtake, natural gas. Federal energy planners thought the same, as did none other than the trade group of gas distributors, the American Gas Association.

On the eve of the May 1979 board meeting, Herring told Foy, somewhat curtly, of a reorganization that reduced Foy's responsibilities. J. A. Edwards of Liquid Carbonic and Richard Conerly of Pott Industries, previously reporting to Foy, were being promoted to vice chairmen reporting to Herring. In no uncertain terms, Foy expressed his surprise and disappointment at the decision.

The two men had rarely disagreed. Herring, loyalty to his chief lieutenant returning, invited Joe to consider his options. "You have done so much for this company that I feel you are entitled to anything that you want," Herring said. Foy then went back to his office to begin work on a severance agreement with the company that he had joined almost 15 years before as vice president and general counsel.

Effective February 1, 1980, Foy left the company under a five-year consulting agreement. He remained an HNG board director and would handle company matters as senior partner of Bracewell & Patterson (now Bracewell & Giuliani). It seemed the best of both worlds given where HNG was going— except nobody knew that Herring had less than two years to live.

Foy traded his pension for a lucrative consulting contract. Herring reclaimed the president title, with Matthews remaining vice chairman. Herring was chairman, CEO, and president—and right at the time of his 59th birthday.

Herring had chosen not to choose between the two candidates prior to Foy's departure. Herring, while remaining chairman, could not give Foy his CEO title without demoting Matthews. Neither did Herring want to bring in a person from the outside to risk demoralization. This was one reason Herring resisted

Figure 13.5 Robert Herring made his two top lieutenants coequal in title, authority, and compensation. Joe Foy, president and COO, departed HNG in early 1980; Bill Matthews, vice chairman, would stay and succeed Robert Herring as CEO in 1981. The HNG and Enron stories might have played out differently if Foy had remained at HNG and succeeded Herring.

overtures to leave HNG for a top job elsewhere—a concern that his entrance could result in a lack of cooperation from holdovers of the new company.[27]

Believing that his cancer would go into remission, Herring thought that he and the company had more time than would turn out to be the case. The board, meanwhile, did not force the issue with their Great Man.

That left M. D. "Bill" Matthews, age 60, a solid finance man who had been by Herring's side at Fish Engineering, Valley Gas, and Houston Natural Gas.

27. Herring turned down opportunities at Conoco as L. F. "Mac" McCollum's successor and at Transco Companies as Montgomery "Monty" Mitchell's replacement. In both instances, Herring wanted his suitor to buy HNG whole to get him—HNG's modus operandi for getting him when purchasing Valley Gas in 1963.

Before joining Fish in 1955, six years after Herring, Matthews was chief accountant of Texas Gas Transmission Corporation.

For 35 years in industry, Bill crunched more numbers than just about anyone else in a variety of accounting, tax, cost control, and feasibility studies. He did well in his supervisory roles, including that of regulatory compliance.

Matthews was honest, dependable, and likable enough. He worked well with Herring and Foy. But Matthews was no Herring or Foy. He was a custodian, not an innovator, builder, or motivator. "Bill was the kind of guy a lot of people would pick as the good bank trust officer," remembered John Duncan of HNG's board.

But needing to act quickly, and with little other choice, Matthews was named chairman, CEO, and president just two days after Herring's death. John Duncan led the board in the unanimous decision. It seemed to be a safe choice, given that the company had good business lines and was profitable, and Herring had left no indications to the board to act otherwise.

Matthews had never envisioned himself as CEO.[28] He was comfortable with finance and had gone far in that capacity. When life without Herring loomed, Matthews let the board know that he stood ready to serve as interim CEO—but maybe not much more beyond that.

But once Matthews became ensconced, he found that he liked it—immensely. There were good people around him, and he was confident in his ability to keep the company financially sound.

Still, it was a huge step for a bachelor numbers man who shunned public life. This company man gave at the office and disappeared. Proud and protective, Matthews never appointed a number two, although James Walzel, a 15-year company veteran, was elected in mid-1983 to be executive vice president of the parent company in addition to his role as president of HPL.

At the same time as Walzel's promotion, three new corporate officers were named. Terence Thorn was elected vice president - government relations, giving him control of the Washington office, which he had joined in 1981. Robert Hermann, a CPA with a law degree, was elected vice president - corporate taxes. Both Thorn and Hermann would have long, consequential careers at HNG's successor, Enron Corporation. A third vice president, Thomas Richard, was given a new responsibility that reflected a new industry trend: special mergers and acquisitions.

Operating Results

Matthews had good news to report for FY 1982. Revenues and earnings hit a record $3.2 billion and $263 million, respectively. Total assets were north of

---

28. Matthews's situation closely paralleled that of George Slocum, who unexpectedly became CEO of Transco Energy when Ken Lay left Transco to replace Matthews as head of HNG. Matthews and Slocum were both finance men who did not, in retrospect, have the suite of skills needed to be the chief executive officer. See chapter 9, pp. 358–61.

$2.6 billion, and shareholder equity stood at $1.3 billion (double that in today's dollars). But the market was not cooperating; HNG's stock price was off by almost half from its early-1981 peak.

Weak demand was affecting just about all of HNG's businesses, so Matthews did what he knew how to do: cut costs. Capital spending was pared by a fourth, and the head count was reduced by one thousand, or 8 percent. Synthetic-fuel development, a Herring bet for the 1980s, was tabled. The new debt-to-equity ratio, Matthews proudly reported, was 25 percent, down from 42 percent five years before. HNG was going to keep its pockets full under Bill Matthews.

The gas surplus was expected to be temporary, so spending was directed toward exploration and production, as well as connecting HPL's West Texas hub to gas reserves in Oklahoma, New Mexico, and the Texas Panhandle. The 475-mile Llano Pipeline, one-fourth owned by HNG, delivered gas from New Mexico to another pipeline for redelivery to HNG in West Texas. The 360-mile, $150 million Red River Pipeline project (also jointly owned) entered into service in 1982, linking gas wells in the Anadarko Basin in the Texas Panhandle to HNG's West Texas pipeline.

"We're going to continue to move ahead in profitability in this difficult period," stated HPL president Jim Walzel in *HNG Magazine*. "That's only partially because we're smart and work hard, and partially because of where we're located and what we can do."

HPL was, after all, the largest and most-respected Texas gas pipeline, serving the biggest and best, such as Shell Oil and Chemical Complex, ARCO's largest refinery, Monsanto's chemical facilities, and Houston Lighting & Power's generating plants. HNG's record of never having curtailed a customer was a great marketing tool, one that reflected good management, the great versatility of the Bammel storage field, and light-handed regulation by the Texas Railroad Commission.

Still, gas sales were very difficult to maintain in a buyers' market. In congressional testimony, Walzel estimated a national gas surplus of 2.5 Bcf/d, or about 5 percent of total deliverability, most of it intrastate and most of that in Texas. Delhi Gas Pipeline, Lone Star Gas Company, United Gas Transmission Company, Valero Transmission, Westar Transmission, and other area lines created gas-on-gas competition in the most gas-rich, pipeline-networked state in the nation.

Interstate gas pipelines, also with more gas under contract than they could sell, were releasing their gas for the short-term spot market, offering end users a cheaper option than HPL's long-term contracts. HPL was also competing against residual fuel oil in an estimated 10 to 20 percent of its market. For these reasons, the Texas Railroad Commission blessed voluntarily negotiated rates as just and reasonable, quite unlike federal policy under the Natural Gas Act administered by the Federal Energy Regulatory Commission.

⌒

CEO Matthews's second annual report told a story quite unlike any in the Herring era. "Fiscal 1983 was a challenging year for Houston Natural Gas Corporation," he wrote. "The effects of one of the most severe environments in recent history were felt, in varying degrees, by each of the company's lines of business." Net income fell $72 million, or 27 percent from FY 1982—the first yearly decline in earnings per share in more than two decades.

Natural gas, accounting for 80 percent of company revenues, was holding up reasonably well. Liquid Carbonic remained a pillar of earnings. But coal was losing money, and marine transportation was adding almost nothing to earnings. Moreover, as an indicator of where the market thought the company was going, the stock price was down one-quarter from the year before, continuing the decline.

HNG was still profitable, earning $190 million and increasing its dividend to pace inflation. The debt-to-equity ratio remained at a lean 25 percent, thanks to Matthews's spending cuts, including an 11 percent workforce reduction in the year. The company did not have a take-or-pay problem with producers, as interstate pipelines did. On the contrary, the market-out clauses in its contracts allowed HPL to lower purchase costs if end-user prices declined (a practice begun in 1975) and were keeping gas prices competitive in end-use markets. Higher margins on gas sales offset most of the volume decline, but the gas-supply bubble was expected to last for two or three more years.

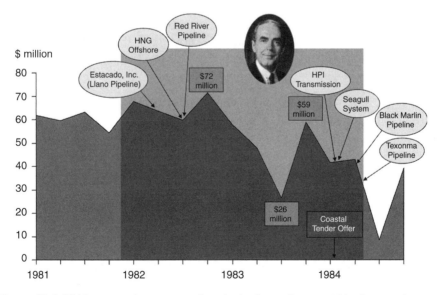

Figure 13.6 HNG reported strong earnings in the immediate post-Herring era, but market conditions overtook the company and the conservative approach of Bill Matthews, leading to his replacement by Ken Lay in mid-1984.

The annual report said nothing about what could and probably should have been the grand news of the year—an acquisition with a major interstate pipeline system. In 1982, El Paso Natural Gas Company approached HNG about merging. But Matthews and his financial chief Michael Pieri did not want to take on new debt. Their knee-jerk rejection caused consternation among some HNG officials. After all, El Paso was one of the nation's premier pipeline systems, serving two of the best gas markets in the country: northern and southern California. Matthews didn't raise the matter with his board outside of a lunch with Joe Foy, who recommended the purchase.

El Paso was feeling vulnerable and rightly saw synergies with HPL. Surely Robert Herring would have jumped at the idea of creating an interstate pipeline division at HNG and called the board into session. But Bill Matthews disliked the idea of leverage to remake the company. He stood pat, making incremental improvements with the intention of riding out the energy recession. As it turned out, Burlington Northern bought El Paso in 1983.

"Houston Natural Gas moves into 1984 with confidence," Matthews wrote near the end of the FY 1983 letter to stockholders. Little did he know that it would be his last such letter.

A Tender from Coastal Corporation

In late 1983, rumors began to fly that some company was accumulating HNG shares with the intent to purchase the company. HNG's stock price was languishing, even to the point of pricing the company below its liquidation value. Matthews was sitting on a lot of "lazy dollars," as Duncan recalled. Still, the company had the most profitable gas pipeline in the country, and Liquid Carbonic was an industry leader and marketable in a corporate revamp. HNG's stock price started edging up. Someone big was buying.

On Friday, January 27, 1984, tombstone advertisements in national publications announced an offer to acquire up to 18.75 million shares of HNG's common stock at $68 per share, a $1.3 billion proposition that valued HNG at roughly twice book value. The buyer was Colorado Interstate Corporation, a wholly owned subsidiary of Houston-based Coastal Corporation.[29] Coastal had quietly accumulated two million shares, about 5 percent of HNG; the

---

29. Oscar Wyatt's Coastal States Gas Producing Company purchased Colorado Interstate Corp. in 1972 for $182 million, which led to a name change to Coastal States Gas Corporation. In 1983, Coastal Corporation fell short in a $550 million hostile offer to buy Texas Gas Transmission Corporation. Coastal went on to acquire American Natural Resources Company (ANR) for $2.5 billion in March 1985, making it the nation's second-largest gas pipeline company, in terms of revenue, between Tenneco and third-place InterNorth (an Enron predecessor company that would buy HNG in 1985).

tender would give Coastal a bare majority control of Houston Natural Gas Corporation.[30]

Two events were behind Coastal's offer. First, this company had been forced to divest its own intrastate gas pipeline several years before (an issue discussed later). Second, just seven months earlier, Coastal had netted $26 million and valuable experience in its failed hostile takeover of Texas Gas Transmission Company. HNG was seen by Coastal as owning complementary, undervalued assets, which, if combined, would create a "financially sound, well-balanced company."

HNG's share price, which had been in the $20s just several months before, reached the $40s on speculation. Coastal's offer was a 25 percent premium over the previous day's close. HNG's stock price reached $63 per share on the take-over news, double the price of the previous year and nearly reaching its 1981 peak. Coastal's stock rose 10 percent the day of the announcement, indicating that more bidding could follow.

Despite Coastal's rescue of its rival's stock price, something HNG's own management had failed to accomplish, there was no celebration at 1200 Travis Street. The proffered reason was that Coastal's offer made no provision for the remaining 49.5 percent of HNG's common stock. The bigger reason was a clash of corporate cultures. It was one man, in particular, who caused near pandemonium that Friday at HNG.

Coastal, founded in 1955, was still run by founder Oscar Wyatt, an industry renegade whom *Texas Monthly* described as "meaner than a junkyard dog." Wyatt, whose first industry venture was named Hardly Able Oil Company, did things his way. His aggressive style put him into corners that resulted in a lot of bad feeling and name calling, if not litigation. "My stockholders do not pay me to run a popularity contest—they pay me to make money," Wyatt said, to which J. Howard Marshall II, the chairman of the board of his executive committee, responded: "Yes, Oscar, and you are the largest stockholder of the company."

Oscar Wyatt had few friends in the industry. But one of them had been Robert Herring, a fellow Texas A&M University alumnus. Wyatt and Herring respected each other and had private lunches together. They had a brotherhood as graduates of Texas A&M. Still, Herring let Joe Foy deal with his mercurial friend at times.

Wyatt was a major competitor to HNG, whether it was supplying gas to the city of Corpus Christi or transporting gas in southern or central Texas. A few times Coastal and HNG were venture partners, as in a transportation agreement

---

30. Among the surprised was the Federal Trade Commission, which Coastal failed to notify pursuant to the Hart-Scott-Rodino Act of 1976, a statute requiring involved companies to notify the FTC and Justice Department of contemplated mergers and acquisitions. Coastal would pay a $230,000 penalty, the first under this law.

in the early 1970s to move HNG gas from West Texas to Houston when Oasis Pipe Line was under construction. But there were no Coastal advocates at HNG. Wyatt knew this. The takeover attempt was hostile, coming without any prior warning or negotiation.

The next day, a Saturday, Matthews and fellow directors Ed Smith and Mickey LeMaistre met Wyatt's team at the Remington Hotel (now the St. Regis), located near Wyatt's River Oaks home. A Coastal lawyer began by summarizing the proposal. Breaking in, LeMaistre asked Coastal about its intentions with the proposed acquisition. Wyatt took over but spoke only to the technicalities of the offer. This time Smith interrupted, asking Wyatt to share his strategy. After more of the same, the HNG side adjourned.

Early the next week, HNG's board unanimously rejected the $1.3 billion offer and instructed management to "take all appropriate actions to prevent Coastal from taking control of HNG." White-knight discussions were held with Transco's Ken Lay. Then a counterattack came to Coastal's "coercive and destructive" offer: a $42 per share offer to Coastal stockholders whereby HNG would be the surviving company.

HNG's $924 million offer (the so-called Pac-Man defense) represented roughly a 20 percent premium for Wyatt's shareholders, which Coastal rejected as "clearly inadequate." HNG also began a buyback program of its own shares at $69 per share, a dollar above the Coastal offer. Coastal responded with an offer to buy the rest of HNG's stock with securities worth about $55 per share to join the $68 offered for the first 18.75 million shares.

HNG then upped its acquisition price for Coastal stock to $50 per share, or $1.1 billion. Coastal again rejected the offer. "So far they haven't unearthed a white knight or they wouldn't be struggling with me so much," Wyatt told a *New York Times* reporter covering the action. Indeed, white knights, such as Transco and InterNorth, were not ready or willing, at least yet, to better Coastal's offer.

All this dueling occurred in less than two weeks. Something had to give.

Matthews was nominally in charge, but the board was doing the real work. Joe Foy was the man to go one-on-one with Wyatt, but the board member did not want to upstage his CEO. Nonetheless, Foy saved the day. Reviewing a 1979 court agreement Coastal made to settle a contract breach between its wholly owned subsidiary Lo-Vaca Gas Gathering Company and gas customers in central and south-central Texas, Foy found a legal basis for challenging Coastal's offer.

⌁

Wyatt's trouble concerned a firm (that is, noninterruptible) long-term gas-sales agreement between Lo-Vaca, an intrastate line transporting gas from producers in South Texas to Austin and San Antonio, among other points. Most, if not all, of the wellhead gas was under long-term fixed rates to lock in a profit on

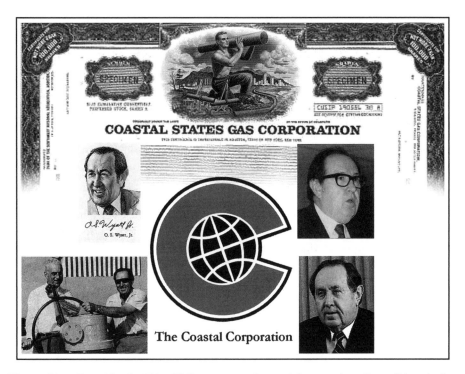

Figure 13.7 From Hardly Able Oil Company to Coastal Corporation, Oscar Wyatt built a company that grew from its Texas roots to a national energy company. Coastal had assets in interstate gas transmission, as well as interests in exploration and production and domestic and international oil refining.

Lo-Vaca's sales—a standard industry practice to avoid performance risk. But Lo-Vaca entered into new gas-sale contracts not backed by such assurance. Coastal had chosen, at great risk, to play the spot market, potentially making more money—or losing it.

When wellhead gas prices took off in 1973, Wyatt got into double trouble. First, Lo-Vaca could no longer profitably buy spot gas to cover some of his set-price sales. Second, he began making "extraordinary transactions," using some of the gas previously dedicated to Lo-Vaca customers, to get higher margins. On both counts, the Lo-Vaca customers lost so-called firm gas. Curtailments began in 1973, and Coastal petitioned the Texas Railroad Commission to allow a rate increase above the contractual level.

The traditionally staid TRC rejected the request as "preposterous." "A more arrogant position under the facts of this case is hard to imagine," the commissioners ruled. Without enough gas, and paying more for gas than specified under the contract, Lo-Vaca's customers sued—and won.

As part of a TRC settlement and court judgment, Wyatt and Coastal were required to divest Lo-Vaca (which was placed into receivership and then spun off as the renamed Valero Corporation), refund $1.6 billion to aggrieved ratepayers, and spend several hundred million dollars developing new reserves to sell at discounted rates to the injured customers.

By Foy's reckoning, the verdict was about more than restitution for wronged customers. It was about making sure that Coastal was not in a position to repeat the offense. HNG was a large gas supplier to Valero and even owned stock in the company. A takeover of HNG would put Coastal right back in the saddle—and on a bigger horse.

◦

Foy went straight to his friend Jim Mattox, the Texas attorney general. Mattox liked what his fellow Democrat had to say. Here was HNG, which had never curtailed a customer, in danger of being bought by Coastal, the perpetrator of the biggest gas fiasco in the state's history.

Citing Coastal's "long history of irresponsible and gross disregard for the public interest," Mattox, using the very language Foy drafted, filed suit on behalf of the state of Texas to enjoin the takeover attempt. The legal argument was that the takeover attempt breached its 1979 settlement because Coastal's obligations to Valero would be compromised. "Defendants have once again disrupted the stability and integrity of the natural gas supply system in Texas and threaten to impair Houston Natural's financial ability to continue responsible implementation of its public obligation," the brief thundered. It would be risking "grievous public injury" to lose HNG to Oscar Wyatt.

On February 10, 1984, the Austin District Court issued a temporary restraining order against Coastal, siding with Mattox as well as with a brief submitted by the Lower Colorado River Authority, the central and south-central Texas municipal gas distributor that had been victimized by Lo-Vaca. Foy, who had helped shape the NGPA to HNG's specifications, had done it again. For his part, Mattox's press release crowed, "Fighting for the rights of consumers is one of my main reasons for being in office."

Three days later, an agreement was reached whereby Houston Natural Gas purchased Coastal's HNG stock for $60 per share (versus the then-market price of $52.50 per share) and paid $15 million in so-called greenmail, ostensibly to cover Coastal's costs in the aborted takeover attempt. A $22 million after-tax charge was taken against FY 1984 earnings. The two companies entered into a standstill agreement, promising not to purchase stock in the other or otherwise try to influence each other's business for five years.

It was a come-from-behind victory for HNG management. "This is a very significant development," stated one leading investment banker, "because very few companies which get attacked remain independent."

HNG was a shaken winner. With the end of the takeover offer, HNG's stock fell to $47 a share, a 25 percent fall from the share price in late January when Coastal made its offer. With the status quo no longer an option if the company sought to remain independent, HNG announced a major restructuring plan to focus on natural gas transmission and sales, gas liquids, and oil and gas exploration and production. Liquid Carbonic, Zeigler Coal, and marine assets Pott Industries and Alamo Barge—deemed noncore—were put up for sale. The company announced its intent to make one major acquisition in its core area and to begin a stock-buyback plan.

The idea was to get the stock price back to merger-talk levels. "If they succeed," stated John Olson, an analyst at the Houston office of Drexel Burnham Lambert, "it will be one of the most interesting equities in the industry. If not, they will be a takeover candidate again."

The core would remain natural gas. Capital was directed toward finding and connecting gas, particularly offshore supply that was no longer the exclusive domain of interstate pipelines. The 52-mile Seagull Shoreline Pipeline, 25 percent owned by HNG, became operational in early 1984, and Black Marlin Pipeline, a 54-mile pipeline from the Gulf to Texas City, was purchased from Union Carbide Corporation for $17 million. The biggest deal was the $120 million purchase of the 457-mile Texoma crude-oil pipeline, extending from Nederland, Texas, to Cushing, Oklahoma, for conversion to natural gas.

∾

HNG's new path needed some new blood, an executive with brainpower and expertise in acquisitions and mergers. The man Bill Matthews and Jim Walzel found for the new position of vice president, corporate development, was John M. "Mick" Seidl.

Seidl, an easy-going intellect, sported a Ph.D. in political economy from Harvard and had a decade of operational experience at Natomas Company, where he had started its corporate development division. Natomas had been bought out by Diamond Shamrock Corporation, and Seidl, head of its North American operations since 1981, left in late 1983 with a seven-figure severance. He was looking for new opportunities in Houston and liked the challenge at HNG. But with a long-standing family vacation planned, Mick began his new job midsummer 1984.

New Leadership: Ken Lay

The Coastal scare did not endear Bill Matthews to the board. It was Foy who led the countercharge and saved the day as far as HNG's remaining an independent company. Matthews was exposed as a weak CEO in an increasingly demanding business. With the stock price still languishing despite the announced restructuring and the completion of a five-million share buyback, some 13 percent of the total stock outstanding, HNG was still in peril of being restructured on someone else's terms. Further, the board faced lawsuits for rejecting both an allegedly reasonable offer from Coastal and a white-knight overture from Transco.

The March restructuring plan, formulated with the help of First Boston Corp., was well and good. But the board asked Matthews for more specifics about HNG's future plans given a revamped base. The board presentation that followed concluded that the company could glow again, but it would take a few years to work through the gas bubble.

HNG did not have the luxury of time, board director John Duncan thought. He polled his fellow directors. Almost instantly they came to agreement: *New leadership was required*. It had been a long two and a half years since the passing of Robert Herring, and there was no more time to wait.

A candidate to replace Bill Matthews quickly emerged. He was youthful and dynamic. He possessed one of the best reputations in the natural gas industry. Duncan knew and respected him from the work they did together on a YMCA fundraising project. Other board members knew him from some white-knight talks with Transco during the Coastal ordeal. But before contacting Ken Lay, the 42-year-old president of Transco, Duncan called his close friend Jack Bowen, Transco's chairman, to ask for permission.

"We are in desperate shape over at Houston Natural Gas. We need a man, and our committee says we need your man—Ken Lay. But Jack, I will not call on Ken unless you give me permission."

"Why should I give you permission?" Jack responded

"Because I think you are going to be at Transco for some time to come. I think we will pay Ken more than you would pay him, and I think you are smart enough to run Transco without him, and we are not smart enough to run HNG without him."

"Well, let me call you back."

Later the same day, Bowen released his president to talk to HNG, telling Duncan that Ken Lay was a fine man and fully capable of running a large company such as HNG.

John Duncan and Ed Smith visited with Ken. Duncan got to the point. "We want you to be CEO of Houston Natural Gas Corporation. It is the same size as Transco. You can start immediately." Surprised, Lay responded, "Let me talk to Linda."

Ken talked to his confidante. He then talked to Bowen to make sure that there was no new urgency in keeping him at Transco. Jack Bowen, who planned to stay on as CEO until he turned 65 in the middle of 1987, said that the company hated to lose him but that HNG was a bird in the hand.

Bowen's cavalier reaction surprised Lay. Was his stellar work at Transco and esteemed stature in the gas industry (chapter 9) a bit disconcerting to the Boss? Was Jack disappointed that HNG had not come to him instead?

Ken dropped by John Duncan's home after work to find out more. "What's wrong with the company?" Ken asked. "Everything," Duncan replied. "That's why we need you." A truth session followed. The company didn't have a good plan to add shareholder value, and three lawsuits had been filed against HNG and the board of directors for not acting in the shareholders' best interest.

This challenge, thought Lay, was certainly no greater than Transco's contractual problems with producers that needed a reversal of gas prices, and soon. HNG needed to refocus on gas by following through on its noncore asset–divestiture plan, but HPL was a great base from which to refocus the company. Lay was plenty optimistic that, as CEO, he could attract new talent to capitalize on the new opportunities emerging with natural gas.

The evening ended with Ken saying he needed to talk to Linda again. Lay called Duncan the next day and asked that they meet with his attorney, Evans Atwell, managing partner of Vinson & Elkins and well known to Duncan. Duncan offered HNG's terms as both men scribbled on their yellow pads. Before the evening was over, Duncan affixed his signature to a contract prepared by Atwell. The five-year employment contract had a base compensation value of approximately $225,000 per year, subject to cancellation in the event of gross negligence or willful misconduct, or if Lay voluntarily left the company. But if there were a change in control—for instance, if HNG were purchased by another firm—Lay would receive a minimum of $510,000 per year for the balance of his contract.

Stock options provided upside to the base package; almost 150,000 shares granted for the balance of 1984 at the then-going share price of $50 per share. This meant that, after a vesting period, for every dollar the stock rose over that amount in the future, Lay would earn $150,000. Lay would continue under five-year contracts henceforth at the company that would become known as Enron.

Duncan went back to the board with the final terms of Ken's agreement. The next job was to inform Bill Matthews. Duncan arrived at Matthews's office with Bryan Wimberly, who was the eldest son of HNG's longtime former CEO, the late Bus Wimberly. Bryan was also the newest board member who had been appointed by Matthews himself.

"What's this meeting about?" asked Matthews. "Bill," Duncan said, "I am here because the independents on your board have selected a new CEO." Stunned, Matthews declared, "You can't come into my office and do that. The board has to do that." "Well," Duncan replied, "if you want me to, I can get them all on a conference call right now."

Bill Matthews looked down. The meeting was all but over. Wednesday, June 6, 1984, was his last day at the company he had joined alongside Robert Herring more than 20 years before.

The board was elated. "[We wanted] good, aggressive management, and we think we've found it now," Ed Smith told the *New York Times*. The board had traded up, getting, in its estimation, a new, young Robert Herring. In fact, Lay was the same age as Herring had been when he joined HNG in 1963.[31] "We didn't dream it would be such a significant upgrade," Duncan related in an interview before Enron's collapse, "but we knew it was better." Duncan went on to exude:

> [Ken Lay's] resume is a storybook. He was 14 years old before he had indoor plumbing. When he was writing speeches for Exxon, he was working all day in a little office and going to school at night to get his doctorate in economics.... There was motivation and education. It was Horatio Alger.

Ken Lay, in fact, had never failed in the business world. He had only achieved—and overachieved. From tending lawns, baling hay, and delivering newspapers before he was a teen to managing large corporations by age 40; earning the full complement of educational degrees; working at high government levels in various capacities; and serving in a variety of nonprofit roles, Ken Lay was Horatio Alger fiction turned fact. But John Duncan, and many, many others, would be shocked before 2001 was out at the lack of business acumen and poor personal judgment of Kenneth L. Lay.

---

31. Also see Internet Appendix 13.8, "Robert Herring and Ken Lay: Parallels" at www.politicalcapitalism.org/Book2/Chapter13/Appendix8.html.

Market Order, Political Challenges

C*APITALISM AT WORK* (Book 1) contrasted the market's natural moral and economic order with government interference in business, a process that "feeds on itself" and promotes "politicking in which the worst can gain advantage and get on top." The example of examples is Enron, but case studies in *Edison to Enron* (Book 2) too differentiate market capitalism from political capitalism.

The U.S. energy market has resulted primarily from the invisible hand of private-property rights and profit-and-loss entrepreneurship, not the visible hand of government ownership and command. True, public-utility regulation of both natural gas and electricity was pervasive enough to allow a political operator such as Ken Lay to reach the top.[1] But market forces shaped these nascent industries before their business leaders—prominently including Samuel Insull—successfully lobbied for the regulatory covenant of cost-based (maximum) rates in return for franchise protection (territorial monopolies).

This epilogue revisits the political economy of two of America's largest industries to grasp the wider implications of markets versus government and to describe the environment in which Ken Lay incubated Enron in the mid-1980s. Lay's once-grand creation was all but finished by 2002. But the post-Enron world has been marked by Enron-like failures of both business and public policy, the subject of *Enron and Ken Lay: An American Tragedy* (Book 3).

Market Ordering

"Trade tries character perhaps more severely than any other pursuit in life," Samuel Smiles wrote in *Self-Help* 150 years ago. "It puts to the severest tests

---

1. See *Capitalism at Work*, pp. 3–6.

honesty, self-denial, justice, and truthfulness; and men of business who pass through such trials unstained are, perhaps, worthy of as great honor as soldiers who prove their courage amidst the fire and perils of battle." Smiles's Capitalist Man was characterized by *self-respect, cleanliness, chastity, reverence, honesty, thrift, sobriety, politeness, courtesy, generosity, forethought, economy,* and most of all, *perseverance.*[2]

Smilesian virtue has been codified into a "science of success," whereby employees integrate "urgency, discipline, accountability, judgment, initiative, economic and critical thinking skills, and risk-taking mentality" to create "real value in society while always acting lawfully and with integrity." *Real value* does not mean profits gained through special government favor, a defining business strategy at Enron and at a large number of post-Enron companies. Political profit making does not create wealth but instead redistributes and destroys it. Value creation comes from profitability as determined by consumers in a free market where, ipso facto, business outputs (revenue) exceed business inputs (cost). Real profit is the "economic means" to success.

Book 1's epilogue explained how free-market profit seeking within a framework of ethical norms and integrity, codified as "principled entrepreneurship"™, creates the "heroic enterprise" and, in the aggregate, "heroic capitalism."[3] The parallel between the free and prosperous commonwealth and the market-driven enterprise has been emphasized by libertarian entrepreneur Charles Koch:

> In a market economy, the combination of well-defined and protected property rights, the right culture, useful knowledge, and incentives from prices and profit and loss spontaneously lead to a network of relationships that maximizes value and creates prosperity and progress. In a company, the combination of a well-designed decision rights process, good values, knowledge sharing, measures, and incentives brings about a spontaneous order that maximizes value creation and growth.

Adam Smith and Samuel Smiles, a century apart, discovered how self-reliant individuals working within a framework of simple rules and ethical norms prosper personally and socially. Modern management theory has translated the *science of liberty* into the *science of success.*

·◇·

Market order is the collective result of innumerable invisible-hand outcomes. This has been true in the U.S. energy market since its inception. As documented in such books as the present author's *Oil, Gas, and Government: The U.S. Experience,*

---

2. For the timeless, insightful worldview of Samuel Smiles, in light of the rise and fall of Enron, see *Capitalism at Work*, pp. 37–57.

3. See *Capitalism at Work*, pp. 314–19.

private-property entrepreneurship, without central direction, resulted in a well-coordinated, growing oil and gas industry. The U.S. petroleum industry also led the way internationally with exports of capital, equipment, technology, and managerial expertise to father the petroleum sectors of Brazil (beginning in 1887), Mexico (1900), Venezuela (1913), Canada (1914), Bolivia (1926), Iraq (1927), Hungary (1937), Saudi Arabia and Kuwait (1939), Chile (1945), and Libya (1956), among others. The fact that these countries did not privatize their oil and gas resources to democratize wealth and depoliticize development—colossal mistakes all—cannot be associated with market-driven human ingenuity that otherwise has advanced the world hydrocarbon market.

Still, government intervention in U.S. energy markets is noteworthy. Price and allocation regulation with oil and natural gas created physical shortages and collateral chaos during World War I, World War II, and the peacetime 1970s. Outside of these periods, consumers were well served, and the market's coordination and economic growth imparted rising expectations to the masses. Still, a plethora of less-intrusive government intervention created inefficiencies that market forces had to overcome in order to meet consumer demand.[4]

In electricity, inventor Thomas Edison and businessman Samuel Insull fathered a new industry that they would still recognize today. Their complementary genius was unique: Edison was foremost in his field, and Insull's deft development and implementation of the central-station/massing model rivaled John D. Rockefeller's rationalization of the petroleum industry. Electricity came in one brand and oil products many, but both men seized upon scale economies and other managerial innovations to reduce costs and expand markets to benefit the masses.

Electricity stood apart. As transformed, or secondary, energy, electrical current could do more things more easily than could the primary fuels of oil, gas, and coal. In terms of divisibility, controllability, transportability, and versatility, electricity could power innumerable devices at the flip of a switch. "Electricity resparked the Industrial Revolution, found new worlds to conquer, and accelerated the process of mechanization not only of manufacture and transport, but of agriculture as well," noted resource economist Erich Zimmermann in 1951. "It set in motion a new wave of inventions which reduced and continues to reduce the cost of inanimate energy and thus encourages the further spread of its use." A half century later, energy polymath Vaclav Smil described the most utilitarian energy: "Electricity is the preferred form of energy because of its high efficiency, instant and effortless access, perfect and easily adjustable flow, cleanliness, and silence at the point of use."

---

4. This conclusion is supported in *Oil, Gas, and Government*'s 2,000-page, 6,600-footnote, 15,000-reference review of local, state, and federal intervention from the nineteenth century through the mid-1980s.

Lord Macaulay (1800–59) identified the alphabet and the printing press as civilization's most important inventions. "I think if [Macaulay] were living today," Insull noted, "he would have had in mind among the inventions which have abridged distance not only the telegraph and telephone, but he would add inventions that have enabled us to carry energy for the use of men at remote distances, in small towns and country districts." Still more, electricity *enabled* the telegraph and telephone industries, confirming energy as the master resource and electricity as the *master* form of the master resource.

Electricity's utilitarian applications and worldwide reach would have certainly occurred without Thomas Edison and Samuel Insull. But without these two progenitors, its introduction and utilization would have been far less timely, less complete, and less efficient.

More from Less—and Less to More

Coal launched the modern energy era. W. S. Jevons was the first to systematically explain the sea change in not so much energy but rather the ability to do work. *"Civilization … is the economy of power*, and our power is coal," he wrote in his 1865 treatise, *The Coal Question.* "It is the very economy of the use of coal that makes our industry what it is, and the more we render it efficient and economical, the more will our industry thrive, and our works of civilization grow."

But as such economy increased, resulting in less usage per application for the desired work, total usage did not decline. *"It is wholly a confusion of ideas to suppose that the economical use of fuel is equivalent to a diminished consumption. The very contrary is the truth,"* he explained. "As a rule, new modes of economy will lead to an increase of consumption, according to a principle recognized in many parallel instances."

Jevons documented the less-to-more phenomenon, which came to be called the Jevons Paradox: *"The reduction of the consumption of coal, per ton of iron, to less than one-third of its former amount, has been followed, in Scotland, by a ten-fold total consumption,* not to speak of the indirect effects of cheap iron in accelerating other coal-consuming branches of industry."

The story of electricity and natural gas under market entrepreneurship (as with petroleum) has been about getting more from less—and using more for proportionally more. Greater supply, falling costs and prices, greater efficiency, expanded reach, and less environmental impact have resulted from profit-and-loss economics.

Energy efficiency and energy conservation have not been confined to government edicts amid wartime scarcity or during the 1970s energy crisis.[5]

---

5. For the contrast between self-interested conservation and government-mandated *conservationism*, see *Capitalism at Work*, pp. 187, 245, 251, 284.

Less input per unit output is competitively required in an open economy in which income-constrained consumers choose between rival energies.

The ecology of business did not go unnoticed. "Today the conservation movement is led by sober business men and is based on the cold calculations of the engineers," observed Erich Zimmermann in 1933. "Conservation, no longer viewed as a political issue, has become a business proposition." Energy conservation was part of a grander phenomenon. "Numerous studies of efficiency of material use over time have convincingly demonstrated that, in a market economy, scarcity-induced price increases dissuade any long-term inefficient use of resources, encouraging reductions in the quantity of inputs needed to maintain, or even increase, output," one recent literature review concludes.

Energy historian Jesse Ausubel has noted how "the wheels of history" have long been "rolling in the direction of prudent, clean use of resources." He explained:

> Three-hundred years have increased the efficiency of [electric] generators from one percent to about 50 percent of their apparent limit, the latter achieved by today's best gas turbines, made by General Electric.... The United States has averaged about one percent less energy to produce a good or service each year since about 1800.... A grand substitution of leading energy sources has taken place over the past century and a half ... from wood and hay, to coal, to oil, and now to natural gas [with] ... each new leading fuel ... superior from an environmental point of view.

Enter Samuel Insull, whose business model was all about inducing more from less to service his "24 hours a day and 365 days a year" debt while profiting investors. At Commonwealth Edison Company, generation advances spearheaded cost reductions per kilowatt-hour (kWh) that reached consumers. Adams Street Station, which opened in 1888, required 12 pounds of coal per kWh. Harrison Street (1894) averaged 6 pounds, Fisk Street (1903) 2.5 pounds, Calumet Station (1921) 1.8 pounds, and Crawford Station (1924) 1.5 pounds. By 1930, the industry's best new steam turbines required but a half pound of coal to generate a kilowatt-hour.

New technology and economies of scale were at work. Ever bigger steam turbines (turbogenerators) replaced the belt-connected dynamos of Adams Street (160 kilowatts each) and Harrison Street (400 kilowatts), beginning with Fisk Street's 5 MW units and continuing with Calumet's 30 MW and Crawford's 50 MW units.

Market-driven efficiency made pleas by government officials and social reformers superfluous, if not disingenuous. "While a great many of our well intentioned friends have been shouting about the conservation of natural resources," Insull stated in 1916, "the steam-turbine inventors and the designing engineers of the great power companies using steam as a prime source of power have probably done more to conserve the natural resources of this country, in so far as fuel is concerned, than has been done by all the agitation that has taken place upon the general subject of conservation."

To Insull, such economies not only lowered current rates but also promised cheaper electricity in the distant future from forestalled depletion of a mineral resource. "Every effort should be made to conserve such resources as coal for the use of future generations," he concluded from his simplistic fixity-depletion view.

Upstream economies were enhanced by downstream improvements in transmission and in transregional coordination. "[The] creation of so-called super-power systems is going on from day to day by private enterprise as a matter of economy and as a matter of increased safety in operation," Insull noted. He gave an example from 1923 of how a plant outage led to a transsystem shipment of replacement power over high-voltage lines such that "properties two hundred and fifty miles away came to the help of the territory where the plant was destroyed."[6] Such substitution meant that less generation capacity was needed overall, and a higher capacity factor of individual systems benefitted all.

Consumers were paying less and getting more. Between 1902 and peak-year 1929, U.S. power consumption increased 19-fold, while rates fell by 60 percent. Chicago led the way. Between 1892 and 1931, exactly the Insull era, Commonwealth Edison Company (CEC) increased sales 690-fold, while rates fell approximately 80 percent. Rates changed 14 times—all down. Never did Commonwealth Edison file for increased rates, and never did regulators calculate a necessary rate reduction.

◦❧◦

Natural gas was once an unwanted byproduct of oil exploration and production. Gas was originally flared at the wellhead to remove the hazard of explosion, but technological advances and infrastructure investment allowed gas to be collected and piped for home heating, cooking, and other uses, displacing manufactured (coal) gas. Intrastate and then interstate gas-transmission systems, one by one, brought the new fuel to markets throughout North America.

Beginning in the 1920s, Houston Pipe Line Company and Houston Natural Gas Company accomplished as much in Texas. Ray Fish did the same in Louisiana, building pipelines to take gas from producers and constructing gas-processing plants to extract liquids for sale.

---

6. Eight decades later, Enron pronounced a new era of network economies around a regulatory transformation: mandatory open access of interstate gas and electricity transmission. The self-styled new-economy logistics company, however, was not the master it purported itself to be of the energy grid.

Robert Herring, longtime CEO of Houston Natural Gas and a central figure in Part III of this book, explained the progression of the intrastate industry by 1970:

> As products became available from the refineries and liquid was stripped from natural gas, we found building blocks for the petrochemical industry. The by-product of one plant would become the feedstock of another plant. The movement of products by pipelines between plants from Beaumont to Corpus Christi created flow systems which have been termed "the spaghetti bowl." Today, 40% of the basic petrochemicals produced in the United States is produced on the Texas Gulf Coast. And 80% of the synthetic rubber produced in the United States is produced on the Texas Gulf Coast.

Some of this industrial concentration was the result of federal price regulation of natural gas flowing in interstate commerce, which gave an artificial advantage to in-state markets where the gas was produced. Industries thrived in Texas and moved there from states that did not have enough native gas. Louisiana also benefitted in this (artificial) way.

Longer interstates also turned a waste product into premium energy for America, displacing manufactured gas in city after city, town after town. "Considerable of the gas supply for [Transcontinental Gas Pipe Line] will be 'flare gas' which will be put to useful use,' reported the *Texas Oil Journal* in 1949. "This new project thus becomes another rung in the ladder of conservation." Robert Herring explained the transformation generally:

> Natural gas, which still was a "waste" product in many places in the early years of World War II, began to move to market through high-pressure steel pipelines. At the beginning of our growth period, natural gas was supplying less than 6% of the total energy requirements of the United States, and last year [1969], despite the amazing growth in our energy requirements in this country, the natural gas percentage increased to more than 30%.

Today, natural gas holds a quarter share of the U.S. energy market, compared to 15 percent in the post–World War II period. Gas is second only to petroleum's 37 percent market share, with coal in third place (21 percent) followed by nuclear (9 percent) and renewables (8 percent, mostly hydroelectricity).

Creative Destruction

The best businesses rise to the top in consumer-driven markets. Less competitive firms contract and even disappear. *Creative destruction* is the process whereby the bad is eliminated, the better replaces the good, and past performance gives way to new strategies and victors. No firm is forever, and financial *loss* is a characteristic of capitalism, as is the more used term *profit*.[7]

---

7. Introduced by Joseph Schumpeter in 1942, *creative destruction* is, after Adam Smith's *invisible hand*, the second-most famous term in the lexicon of economics.

Incumbent firms in an open economy confront would-be or actual rivals, unlike under public-utility regulation where a certification process discourages entry, or an exclusive franchise prohibits rivalry. Firms must also confront the prospect or reality of cheaper imports, where international borders are free of tariffs and quotas. Without political protection, firms must innovate and improve as gauged by profit and loss. Such firms shape their businesses around underlying market demand, quite unlike their political counterparts, which rely on special government favor to supplant consumer verdicts.

Competitive toil brings reward outside of specific monetary gain. More efficient resource allocation within an existing means/ends framework and wholly new means and ends from entrepreneurial discovery give society new and more goods and services. Another benefit is the discipline and pride of constructive business achievement, as celebrated by Samuel Smiles and Samuel Insull.

Economic coordination and growth allow profits to exceed losses in the aggregate—the opposite of a no-growth, zero-sum economy, in which every win (profit) must be offset by a loss. Adam Smith contrasted the three tempos of economic life: "The progressive state is in reality the cheerful and hearty state to all the different orders of the society. The stationary is dull; the declining melancholy."

᠊ᢙ᠊

Energy is the story of creative destruction. Coal gas and later coal oil replaced a variety of animal and vegetable oils, including whale oil, camphene oil, and stearin oil. Crude (mineral) oil then displaced manufactured (coal) oil, just as later natural gas would displace manufactured (coal) gas.

Coal itself displaced primitive biomass (burned plants and wood) and other forms of renewable energy, such as falling water and wind. Fossil fuel was a concentrated, continuous-burn *industrial-grade* energy. W. S. Jevons explained how coal (and by implication, gas and oil) were uniquely suited for—and indeed, prerequisites for—the machine age. The intensive energy mass of fossil energy can be understood as a *stock* of the sun's work over the ages, not a *dilute flow* from the sun (solar, wind) or a *low-density mass* from limited years of sunshine (biomass). "The ancient resource pattern depends primarily on animate energy and hence on current solar radiation," Erich Zimmermann explained. "The modern resource pattern is built around stored-up solar radiation."

"[T]he economy of power … consists in withdrawing and using our small fraction of force in a happy mode and moment," said the father of modern energy thought. Given fossil fuels, the unreliability of wind power and water flow were overcome. "The first great requisite of motive power is, that *it shall be wholly at our command, to be exerted when, and where, and in what degree we desire,*" Jevons explained. "The wind, for instance, as a direct motive power, is wholly inapplicable to a system of machine labour, for during a calm season the whole business of the country would be thrown out of gear."

But even if wind were consistent and storable, it was still too little from too much. Jevons explained:

> No possible concentration of windmills ... would supply the force required in large factories or iron works. An ordinary windmill has the power of about thirty-four men, or at most seven horses. Many ordinary factories would therefore require ten windmills to drive them, and the great Dowlais Ironworks, employing a total engine power of 7,308 horses, would require no less than 1,000 large windmills!

Biomass was no escape. "We cannot revert to timber fuel, for 'nearly the entire surface of our island would be required to grow timber sufficient for the consumption of the iron manufacture alone.'" And on geothermal: "The internal heat of the earth ... presents an immense store of force, but, being manifested only in the hot-spring, the volcano, or the warm mine, it is evidently not available."

Water power had reliability problems compared to coal and locational issues as well. Explained Jevons:

> When an abundant natural fall of water is at hand, nothing can be cheaper or better than water power. But everything depends upon local circumstances. The occasional mountain torrent is simply destructive. Many streams and rivers only contain sufficient water half the year round and costly reservoirs alone could keep up the summer supply. In flat countries no engineering art could procure any considerable supply of natural water power, and in very few places do we find water power free from occasional failure by drought.

Furthermore,

> The necessity ... of carrying the work to the power, not the power to the work, is a disadvantage in water power, and wholly prevents that concentration of works in one neighbourhood which is highly advantageous to the perfection of our mechanical system. Even the cost of conveying materials often overbalances the cheapness of water power.

In reference to California's 1920s energy picture, Samuel Insull explained how so-called white coal (hydroelectricity) required steam-plant backup for reliability. And so it came to be in Enron's time, when a bad water year in that state triggered an electricity crisis in light of government retail price ceilings, setting the stage for the company to game the wholesale market. Steam plants, Insull added, could be situated near the load, unlike hydro production, which was at the river.

Jevons's energy-by-energy analysis is as true today as it was when penned in 1865. Coal could be burned continuously and evenly, avoiding the intermittency of wind or sunshine. Coal did not depend on the season or on a weather condition, as did water flow. Coal was storable and transportable. Coal production and combustion needed far less surface area than would a similar amount of renewables. In short, there could not be a return to the chancy, inflexible, dilute energies of the past—which were, ironically, all renewable from a physical viewpoint.[8] Seizing upon this point, Jevons was the first intellectual to question the ability of renewables to serve as primary energies for industrial society.

"Coal, in truth, stands not beside but entirely above all other commodities," Jevons concluded. "It is the material energy of the country—the universal aid—the factor in everything we do. With coal almost any feat is possible or easy; without it we are thrown back in the laborious poverty of early times." As the "source of fire ... of mechanical motion and of chemical change," coal was "the Mainspring of Modern Material Civilization."

This wonder fuel, Jevons added, was "the chief agent in almost every improvement or discovery in the arts which the present age brings forth." The *iron age* was really the *age of coal,* since "coal alone can command in sufficient abundance either the iron or the steam." Substitute carbon-based energy for coal—add oil and gas to coal—and Jevons's conclusion is clear and correct for today.

·♾·

Coal creatively destroyed renewables as primary energy. The carbon-based energy era introduced creative destruction between coal, manufactured gas (coal gas), manufactured oil (coal oil), crude oil, and natural gas.

Thomas Edison's electricity rocked the manufactured-gas industry across an ocean, as witnessed in London by a young Samuel Insull. It was coal versus coal once removed, with gas distilled from coal competing against coal-generated electricity. Later, natural gas would go head to head with coal to generate steam for producing electricity, a rivalry that reached a crescendo in the era of Enron and Ken Lay and continues today.[9]

In transportation, creative destruction encompassed the gasoline-powered internal-combustion engine knock electricity off its perch (see chapter 2). Try as they might, Edison, Insull, and even Henry Ford could not make electric vehicles viable against petroleum-powered cars and trucks. Batteries were heavy, costly, and slow to recharge compared to the energy from on-board motors. Neither could electricity break into the railroad market, despite the entreaties of Samuel Insull. Wood, then coal, then diesel burned on board was simply too economical for rural locomotion, as opposed to urban street locomotion.

Samuel Insull's standards of excellence made him an agent of creative destruction. The "creative rearranger" improved his industry over multiple decades. Early in his Chicago career, Insull persuaded manufacturers, retailers,

---

8. Also see *Capitalism at Work*, pp. 194–98.

9. Enron's first (and most successful) business plan centered on natural gas as a superior alternative to coal and fuel oil in stationary markets (electricity, industrial boiler, home heating).

traction companies, and farm villages to stop generating their own power and to buy instead his cheaper, more reliable supply. Insull's new-and-improved electricity reached across the energy market, pressuring both kerosene and coal gas in the illumination market to improve or perish.

Chicago's man of electricity was also public enemy number one to hometown Peoples Gas Light and Coke Company—at least until he went to work for them also (see chapters 3 and 4). And Insull's progressive corporate culture rattled the cages of competitors inside and outside of energy.

But Insull's best efforts could not make electricity competitive for transportation outside of streetcars, and his battery packs at power plants proved to be a very expensive, limited option to serve peak demand (see chapter 2). Electricity had to be consumed the moment it was produced, creating a different set of economics that *über*-entrepreneur Insull addressed via two-part rates and other strategies.

Natural gas tried to beat electricity at its own game (see chapter 8). In the 1960s, Florida Gas Company experimented with gas-powered fuel cells in a joint venture with Walt Disney World. Low-emission electricity was the prize, but sour economics made the venture little more than a photo opportunity. Another experiment in Jack Bowen's time, natural gas air conditioning, fell short but not for a lack of effort.

～

Creative destruction results from market verdicts at the intersection of supply and demand. Innovation and expected profit drive supply; price, availability, and quality (including reliability) attract demand.

Outside of the free market, energy hopes and legislative votes have created a *political market,* a subindustry whose activity results from special tax favors, government grants, and/or mandates. Uneconomic energies are a form of postmodernism under which market-rejected, politically correct offerings spring to life—liabilities parading as assets. Today, government-dependent alternative energies comprise 6 to 7 percent of total U.S. production. Political energy includes virtually all wind power, biomass, and ethanol, as well as the large majority of solar—or just about all nonhydro renewables. (Off-grid solar has a market niche.)

The market's creative destruction has created triumph and tragedy as the rags-to-riches-to-rags life of Samuel Insull (chapters 1–5) attests. John Henry Kirby (chapter 10) went through the feast-and-famine cycle more than once. The boom-bust cycle in natural gas spun the fortunes of one of the top industry executives of his generation, Jack Bowen (chapter 9).

Still other company builders described in various other chapters—Ray Fish, Robert Herring, and, for the most part, Clint Murchison—built well and left the scene in full regalia. But it was topsy-turvy for most under a combination of the market's gales of creative destruction, political risk, and political capitalism's business cycle. All this was before Ken Lay and Enron.

Sustainable Energy

The market order encompasses the concept of *sustainability*, which has been defined as "development that meets the needs of the present without compromising the ability of future generations to meet their own needs."[10] In a sustainable energy market, the quantity, quality, and utility of energy improve over time. Sustainable energy becomes more available, affordable, usable, and reliable. Energy consumers do not borrow from the future; they subsidize their progeny by enabling the expansion of technology and upgraded infrastructure.

The catchphrase *sustainable energy* encompasses the goals of security and reliability, energy availability, and environmental progress. Critics of industrial modernism censure fossil fuels, beginning with coal and continuing with oil. Relatively cleaner-burning natural gas is preferred of the three, but sometimes only as the transition fuel to an envisioned posthydrocarbon economy.

Market failure is alleged where private benefits from producing and using carbon-based energies create net social costs (more costs than benefits). It is the invisible hand in reverse, whereby self-interested action creates a so-called negative externality. But is this the case?

Statistics support the conclusion of *increasing* energy sustainability, not its opposite, whether measured in terms of air emissions or resource development.[11] Regarding the latter, the natural science concept of mineral fixity—and thus depletion with every extraction—is contradicted by the business and social science reality of replenished supply and net reserve additions from entrepreneurship, or in this case, *resourceship*.

Feared mineral depletion and the false allure of renewables have colored energy economics and public policy from the beginning. W. S. Jevons pessimistically calculated the coming end of Britain's coal abundance. Samuel Insull, a resource pessimist, feared the decline of coal supplies and saw natural gas as but a fleeting respite from the past and future of gasified coal.

In 1981, leaders of the natural gas industry voiced their pessimism about future supply and prices. "Domestic oil and gas will never be in an oversupply position," said Jack Bowen of Transco. "Planning is going forward for the day when the market may require a versatile substitute fuel for natural gas," stated Robert Herring of Houston Natural Gas. Both gentlemen would be proved wrong within a year.

---

10. Also see the discussion of energy optimism versus pessimism in *Capitalism at Work*, pp. 186–88.

11. Rising energy-related emissions of carbon dioxide (CO_2), a greenhouse (global warming) gas, is the exception to this trend. But CO_2 is not a pollutant and has distinct environmental goods, not only environmental bads, to make it an externality of uncertain sign.

The paradox of growing exhaustible or depleting minerals—such as oil, nat-ural gas, and coal—can be explained in terms of improving knowledge and expanding capital. "Knowledge is truly the mother of all resources," Erich Zimmermann concluded. Julian Simon called human ingenuity the "ultimate resource," a nondepletable, expansive resource. "Discoveries, like resources, may well be infinite: the more we discover, the more we are able to discover," Simon said. This was the opposite of a "closed system," Simon found, allowing "human beings ... [to] create more than they destroy."

Minerals cannot be synthetically reproduced in human time frames. But in the world of human action, neither crude oil, nor natural gas, nor coal exists in one, total, known form to start a depletion clock. Erich Zimmermann warned against the fallacy of importing the physical science concept of fixity to the real-world process of mineral development. "If petroleum resources were in their entirety available from the beginning and could not increase but only decrease through use, it might be correct to advocate "sparing use so as to delay inevitable exhaustion'," He explained. "But if petroleum resources are dynamic entities that are unfolded only gradually in response to human efforts and cultural impacts, it would seem that the living might do more for posterity by creating a climate in which these resource-making forces thrive and, thriving, permit the full unfolding of petroleum reserves than by urging premature restraint in use long before the resources have been fully developed."

Human ingenuity in market settings explains why age-old predictions of energy famine have failed to come to pass. Joining dire forecasts of prior decades, the chief geologist of the United States Geological Service stated in 1919: "The peak of [U.S.] production will soon be passed—possibly within three years." Erich Zimmermann, whose functional theory of resources pointed to open-ended resource development, waxed pessimistic when comparing the alternatives to coal: "Oil and natural gas are forging ahead rapidly, but because their total reserves are much smaller than those of coal they are bound to lose in relative importance in the not too distant future."[12]

Energy czar James Schlesinger, the first secretary of the Department of Energy, created in 1977 legislation signed by President Jimmy Carter, similarly warned about "a classic Malthusian case of exponential growth against a finite source." He quantified the supply problem:

> Since World War II, we have had a phenomenal rate of malusage so that in each decade—the '50s and the '60s—the world consumed more than had been used up in all previous human history. Oil production should peak out around the world in the early 1990s. The world, which is now consuming about 60 million bbl. a day,

---

12. For further explanation of Zimmermann's expansionist versus depletionist views, see *Capitalism at Work*, pp. 185–88, 208–14.

faces a limit on production somewhere around 75 million or 80 million bbl. a day. That means in five years' time we may have chewed up most of the possibility of further expansion of oil production.

World oil production reached and then exceeded Schlesinger's maximum range in 1997 and 2004, respectively. Supply today is limited by demand, not a physical limitation on production. Higher prices from higher demand, in other words, would elicit greater petroleum production not only from crude oil but also from the heavier oils that can be expected to gain market share within the hydrocarbon family.

The exaggerated demise of carbon-based energies has been joined by errant predictions of the growing market share of renewables. "The range of energy possibilities grouped under the heading 'solar' could meet one-fifth of U.S. energy needs within two decades," wrote Robert Stobaugh and Daniel Yergin in 1979. Compared to about 8 percent at the time of their prediction, the year-2000 actual was less than 9 percent versus the predicted 20 percent. In 2009—and only because of massive government subsidy for nonhydro renewables—the percentage was still less than 11 percent. The carbon-based energy age has not waned.

The increasing sustainability of conventional energy in market settings does not mean that market-based energy is problem-free. Worst-case events—such as coal-mine accidents, major oil spills, or pipeline explosions—occur. Such setbacks are part of an industrial society in which operations are not perfect. But improvement can be expected. In fact, such problems *advance* sustainability over the longer term by allowing learning and inspiring reform. Problems are not ends in themselves but part of the improvement process, as Julian Simon has explained.

Problems of energy sustainability involve *energy statism*, not depletion, pollution, or climate change. Whereas affordable, plentiful, reliable energy is a natural byproduct of market capitalism, government intervention has historically disrupted coordination and progress, disadvantaging consumers and creating a government-dependent business class. Available resources, particularly those that are owned and controlled by government, reflect a political and cultural, not only physical/scientific, dimension. "Laws, political attitudes, and government policies, along with basic geological and geographical facts," stated Erich Zimmermann, "become the strategic factors in determining which oil fields will be converted by foreign capital from useless 'neutral stuff' into the most coveted resource of modern times."[14] And so it is with natural gas and coal deposits. Because such factors have more often than not discouraged development, supply is being transferred from the present to the future.

Questions of sustainable energy went to the core of Ken Lay and Enron's business model, as described in Book 1. Book 3 will chronicle the evolution of this political economy strategy in light of the legislative climate and push by special-interest environmental groups.

Government Intervention

The perils of political capitalism for the American experiment have long been recognized. "The sober people of America are weary of ... sudden changes and legislative interferences [that] become jobs in the hands of enterprising and influential speculators, and snares to the more-industrious and less-informed part of the community," founding father James Madison wrote in 1788. "They have seen, too, that one legislative interference is but the first link of a long chain of repetitions, every subsequent interference being naturally produced by the effects of the preceding."

Madison's lament captured the counterproductive, often unintended, effects of government intervention, from opportunism and gaming in business to the propensity of politicians to add new interference to bad. Applied political economy has filled in the specifics ever since.[13]

A real-world *process theory* of interventionism illuminates the U.S. experience in the realm of manufactured gas and natural gas and in the realm of electricity, two foci of this book. Public-utility regulation began in the nineteenth century as an industry-led revolt against a combination of open entry (pure competition) and burdensome rate edicts, went statewide in the next decades, and became federalized in the 1930s. After a half century of regulatory promiscuity and bureaucratic bungling, a new approach unbundled the commodity from transmission services: the former for deregulation, and the latter for traditional (cost-of-service) public-utility regulation. But short of a free-market, the new rules required owners of interstate transmission assets to offer transportation services to outside parties under prescribed conditions.

Beginning in the mid-1980s, the *mandatory open-access era* created a new industry segment: natural gas and electricity marketing (the buying and selling of methane and electrons apart from transmission). This was the new competitive space, the new industry segment, which propelled Ken Lay's company to the top of the energy field.

Typology of Interventionism

Regulation, taxes, and subsidies can be categorized and linked to show how government activism unfolds over time, across jurisdictions, and among business functions. This typology is inspired by, but broader than, the *Mises interventionist thesis*, which, similar to Madison's lament, recognizes the propensity

---

13. For other warnings against political capitalism from Adam Smith forward, see *Capitalism at Work*, pp. 122–24.

of government activity to expand from its own shortcomings in the elusive quest to achieve economic rationality and political calm.[14]

Three classifications compose an interventionist typology (Figure E.1). The first identifies a government action as either dormant or causal. *Dormant intervention* does not meaningfully affect market activity, because it is a dead letter (an irrelevant law still on the books), superfluous (not market-impacting but enforceable), or not respected and unenforced. *Causal intervention* affects market activity—or more precisely, the motivations and actions of market participants.

The great majority of real-world intervention is causal, because legislators and regulators take action intended to have certain outcomes and/or the intervention has unintended effects. Either way, market outcomes are altered from what they would have been in the absence of the regulation, subsidy, or tax. Dormant intervention is thus the exception to the rule.

A second categorization differentiates between initiating and noninitiating action. *Initiating intervention* leads to further government involvement and is active and generative, creating an interventionist process. *Noninitiating intervention*, on the other hand, is causal but sterile—an end in itself—and for that moment, at least, does not lead to subsequent intervention. However, a noninitiating intervention can become initiating should a new interpretation of the statute or regulation trigger an interventionist process.

A third distinction describes the *cumulative process*, whereby an *initiating* intervention produces *consequent* intervention, wherein sequential phases can be segregated and described. Changes in cumulative intervention can be *expansionary*, *contractionary*, or *amendatory* (mixed). Expansion is the most common, although the historical record contains examples of a contractionary process that falls short of total, immediate deregulation. An amendatory change is not predominately expansionary or contractionary but still represents a distinct revision or phased change—as subjectively perceived by the economic actors.

A particular legislative action can be part of a lineage of interventions, some of which are expansive and other parts of which are contractionary. The common denominator may regard energy, for example, but the potpourri must be analyzed in its parts and in the whole before its consequences can be understood for a historical linkage.

An interventionist dynamic can span political jurisdictions and geographical regions. The process can be intermittent (nonsequential), with prior intervention relating to later intervention after an elapsed period. Also, the

---

14. Economist Ludwig von Mises (1881–1973) explained how most intervention is theoretically at odds with well-intended purposes and how intervention in practice typically becomes more comprehensive and problematic, not less.

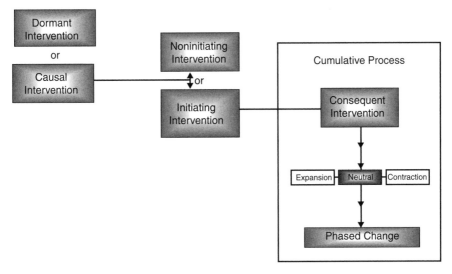

Figure E.1 The categories of interventionism and applied political economy, trace real-world regulation, subsidies, and taxes.

microeconomics of major intervention can impact the macroeconomy (e.g., engender a general business downturn).

Experience can lead legislators or regulators to front-load a particular intervention with what otherwise might have been a future intervention in a cumulative process. Maximum price controls can include allocation regulations to address anticipated shortages. Such inclusiveness can make the initial regulation, tax, or subsidy edict more complex than it otherwise would be—all in the expectation of preventing future distortions or preplugging regulatory gaps to try to avert entrepreneurial gaming.[15] Modern regulation, both enacted and proposed, has become increasingly complex, with hundreds of pages of text attempting to anticipate actions and reactions by the regulated. As the antithesis of "simple rules for a complex world" for social order, fine-print intervention ensures gaming at best and illegality at worst—as was the case with Enron and Ken Lay—for social disorder.

A real-world theory of political economy can be employed to understand government involvement in a variety of industries. In our case, the economics and politics of government intervention with gas and electricity explain the environment inherited and manipulated by Enron, the subject of Book 3.

---

15. Regulatory gaming by entrepreneurs is described in *Capitalism at Work*, pp. 89, 112, 260–62, 292, 298, 303.

Interventionist Dynamics

The U.S. energy experience is replete with strings of interventions unfolding over time from a variety of reasons and with a variety of results, many humbling to their proponents.[16] The dynamics of intervention result from the fact that government activism fails to solve perceived problems and instead creates new, even unanticipated, ones. Such excursions tend to either reinstate market conditions or bring the government deeper into the particular industry. But more often than not, ironically, government involvement tends to expand; authorities attempt to rescue prior intervention rather than uproot it (Figure E.2). Regulation, in any case, is rarely unchanged, given the shifting political sands and unstable economics of the middle way between competitive markets and government planning. Regulation itself, in other words, creates the economic conditions that light the fires for political reform.

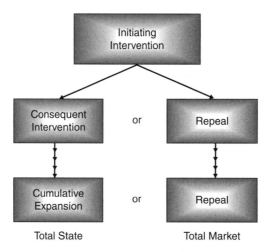

Figure E.2 The so-called Mises interventionist thesis identifies the propensity of government involvement to expand as a response to its own shortcomings. In any case, the unstable middle way gives way to either more or less intervention in the elusive quest for stability.

Economist James McKie used the term "'tar baby effect'" to describe the plight of regulators who find partial regulation frustrated by profit-maximizing behavior within the prescribed constraints. The mirage of effective regulation is always a regulation away, because each constraint creates "compensatory variations" by entrepreneurs. Like an entanglement with a statue of tar, the more one tries, the more enmeshed one becomes in a bad situation.

---

16. Also see *Capitalism at Work*, pp. 137–140.

Fellow economist Paul Joskow applied the tar baby effect to U.S. regulation. "A regulatory agency may attempt to implement some policy using a particular regulatory instrument," he explains, "but the effect is not what is expected or is undesirable in terms of some other objective of the regulatory commission." Rather than give up its mission, "the agency then tries to correct its initial inadequacy or mistake by extending its regulations to other aspects of firm or industry behavior or even to other industries." But like plugging a leaky dike, "regulation plugs up one hole only to find that a leak springs up somewhere else." Joskow concludes: "Regulation in the U. S. often seems to be at least one leak behind."

Once an interventionist process is under way, the competitive positions of affected firms become defined to accentuate lobbying efforts. Regulators, meanwhile, have the self-interested propensity to try again with intervention rather than give up, so to speak, with deregulation. It is not coincidental that major regulatory episodes have become more politicized—that is, further removed from original purposes and less focused—the longer they have been in effect.

This propensity is explained by insights from the public-choice school of economics. Legislators and regulators are not selfless public servants who recognize failure and make midcourse corrections, as entrepreneurs must under a profit-and-loss system. So-called public servants value the employment, wealth, and prestige they command. They want more, not less, to do in their taxpayer-funded sphere. This is the "politics without romance" of the real world.

Unintended Consequences

The history of U.S. energy politics is replete with unintended consequences. Price controls on natural gas not only created physical shortages but also inspired business strategies creating secondary problems. The experience of Jack Bowen at Transco (1974–92) is a case in point. While not allowed by federal law to bid up prices paid to natural gas producers, Transco entered into liberal take-or-pay contracts to attract more supply to end curtailments to its wholesale customers. Unregulated non-price terms, in other words, substituted for regulated price terms. Those panic-inspired contracts, however, overcommitted Transco to take natural gas, which (along with other problems detailed in chapter 9) almost sank the company.

There was a golden period for Transco stockholders between its shortage and surplus periods, but the regulation-induced predicament caused Bowen to overaccelerate from one ditch only to land in the other. Such was the supply cycle for much of the interstate gas market, which was hardly anticipated by the architects of natural gas regulation.

Unintended consequences spilled over from economics to the environment. Natural gas shortages in the 1970s increased the usage of (more polluting) oil and particularly coal. Synthetic, or coal, gas, an obsolete industry brought back to life by price-control distortions on natural gas, added wholly unnecessary manufacturing processes to a more benign alternative.

Extraneous profit opportunities are an unintended consequence of government intervention in the economy. The highly energy-regulated 1970s spawned superfluous entrepreneurship (gaming) that became obsolete in the less regulated 1980s. Although midstream companies, such as Transco, were victimized for the most part, other segments of the industry thrived. Oil and natural gas prices reached record levels in the face of regulation designed (ironically) to keep energy prices down in order to protect consumers. The end of regulatory boom led one industry executive to confess in the *Wall Street Journal* about longing for

> a politician … who would be more blatantly anti-oil, pro-consumer. In short I'd like to vote for a politician who would truly set out to do me in…. While screaming "don't throw me in that briar patch," I will be studying his proposed new regulations carefully, looking for the loopholes that will allow me once again to prosper in the oil and gas business.

Unintended economic and environmental consequences explain why price ceilings on energy have fallen out of favor as a policy alternative. In a victory for economic rationality (and economic education, once removed), neither major political party, nor any major special-interest group, is pushing for a repeat of price controls. Yet such was the law of the land for oil and gas just several decades ago.

"Bootleggers and Baptists"

In times past, unopposed political activism by business often resulted in the desired regulation, tax provision, or public grant. Such rent-seeking was not illegal or considered morally repugnant, which left the particular firm or trade association free to amorally calculate costs versus benefits in order to guide its public-sector strategy.

But the rent-seeking environment has become much more competitive and pluralistic in recent decades. In 1967, a 29-year-old Ken Lay (ghost) wrote in *The Business of Business* about the growing reach of political decision making—and the requirement that business interests make their public-policy case plain and compelling.[17] In the political 1970s, and nowhere more than in the energy industries, self-interest groups proliferated. A variety of nonprofits emerged to stand toe-to-toe against for-profits, and even within business, splits occurred between segments.

Public and voter opinion was necessary more than ever before to get politicians to acquiesce to business favor. But how does business land government intervention (such as protectionism) when the public welfare is compromised,

---

17. See *Capitalism at Work*, pp. 173–74.

as it typically is? How does business portray itself, when virtually all know that money making is primary?

The answer, in short, is that business needs help to get across the finish line. Legislators need help too in selling intervention to the public. The narrow-interested need the public-interested, the do-gooder(s), to get its work done—just as the bootleggers needed the Baptists to retain Prohibition.

Bootleggers and Baptists has become an aphorism for understanding political capitalism in action. Clemson economist Bruce Yandle coined the term after a 1970s stint at the Federal Trade Commission, where he found himself surprised by how often business lobbyists favored rather than opposed regulation. "I asked myself, what do industry and labor want from the regulators?" His answer: "They want protection from competition, from technological change, and from losses that threaten profits and jobs."

But camouflage was needed in order for rent-seeking to appear to serve the wider good. Yandle saw a modus operandi: "A carefully constructed regulation can accomplish all kinds of anticompetitive goals of this sort, while giving the citizenry the impression that the only goal is to serve the public interest." Thus, the history of twentieth-century government intervention was increasingly the saga of bootleggers recruiting the Baptists, and, increasingly, the Baptists recruiting the bootleggers.

A century ago, Samuel Insull donned the public-interest mantle in a deter-mined quest for statewide public-utility regulation. Through unsigned newspa-per editorials, textbooks, and civic presentations, the case for entry regulation, coupled with cost-of-service rate ceilings, came with Insull's direct or indirect sponsorship. Historian Marvin Olasky detailed the sophisticated methods:

- Sending press releases on regular, factual material to win the confidence of newspaper editors and then issuing more subjective press releases on political themes (such as favored public-utility regulation)

- Buying advertising for goodwill with print-media owners and editorial-page staff

- Paying civic leaders for the use of their names with utility-written articles

- Working with authors of economics and government textbooks to reverse their position against franchised monopoly

The Salem, Oregon, public relations firm E. Hofer & Sons, on retainer from the National Electric Light Association, issued as many of 13,000 articles annually in this regard. Olasky provided one striking example of how well the bootleg-gers co-opted the Baptists:

> In 1925, the Alabama Power Company received a silver cup for public relations accomplishments from *Forbes* magazine. *Forbes*, noting that 90% of Alabama newspapers were editorializing favorably about the company, presented a list of

company accomplishments that had improved its popularity. Perhaps the improvement was real, but the measurement was faulty: The editorials were canned and shipped from Oregon by Hofer. The newspapers were paid for running them.

Professors and colleges were persuaded to join the fold too. In 1925, the director of the Nebraska Committee on Public Utility Information reported on what had gone into its victory: "We have been at it for more than two years here … first selling the idea to the agricultural college folk and letting them take the spotlight and assume all the leadership…. The college can say things that we can not say and be believed."

Insull and NELA member companies also perfected the practice of buying civic memberships and having utility employees become active in them. Groups need speakers, and the right speaker for the company message went to work.

Ken Lay's political capitalism had Enron ride the backs of the Left environmental movement, while such environmentalists courted Enron. It was pragmatism over principle. "If there is one thing I have been impressed with over the last decades, it is that when the environmental community defines a number one priority, something happens," Lay allowed. "Not always something good—but something."

Public-Utility Regulation: Manufactured/Natural Gas

"A fascinating theme that runs through the long, convoluted history of natural gas regulation is the seemingly inexorable expansion of government intervention," Arlon Tussing and Connie Barlow wrote in 1982. "Regulation seems to have spawned further regulation; soon after one regulatory gap was filled, another appeared." Two years later, the authors noted: "Federal regulation of the gas industry is coming to look more like a tar baby. The ink barely dries on a new law or a new rule when it becomes obvious that the intended solution gives rise to altogether new headaches."

The roots of gas industry problems did not begin in the crisis 1970s or even in the 1950s with pervasive federal regulation of wellhead prices. It did not begin with federal regulation of gas pipelines during the New Deal. What is arguably the longest—and most regretted—cumulative interventionist episode in history began in the late nineteenth century and evolved, six stanzas later, into a regulatory regime (mandatory open access) that Enron inherited, capitalized on, and advanced.

Beginnings

At the industry's dawn, private companies manufactured and piped gas to nearby users. Although not formally regulated, firms under corporate charters worked in a quasi-public environment. Such permits, which sometimes provided franchise protection to induce the initial entry, put local government in an

oversight role. Municipal lighting agreements also gave local government officials contractual power over firms. In some places, municipal (government-
owned and -operated) enterprises acted as so-called yardstick enterprises
whose rates and general operation could be compared to that of private firms.
The specter of municipalization, indeed, was a club-in-the-closet for local officials should the firm reach an impasse with customers, prominently including
city fathers in charge of street-lighting contracts.

There was never quite a laissez-faire era of the gas industry, although private firms certainly were less regulated than they would be later. Restated, the
early gas industry was not, for the most part, entry and rate regulated. Rates
were set by supply and demand (including by municipal contract), and new
entry was possible in many locales. "There was no demand for regulation,"
observed John Gray in the *Quarterly Journal of Economics* in 1900. "Both the public and companies were inclined to let well enough alone and to jog along as
they have been doing for so long a time."

Call for Regulation
In the 1880s, the industry began to embrace formal rate regulation as the quid
pro quo for protection against new entrants, many of them utilizing new,
superior technologies for manufacturing gas. Price wars and financial uncertainty, exacerbated by growing competition from electricity and kerosene,
became commonplace. "The question before had been how to prevent state
interference," noted Gray. "It now became how to stimulate, direct, and control state interference so as to protect investments." He explained the sea
change:

> The more far-seeing members of the [gas] associations recognized that the days
> of high charges and high profits ... were gone forever, and that ... they must ...
> claim protection for "honest investments." They realized, also, that a request for
> protection would raise the cry of monopoly, which could be safely met only by
> an acknowledgement of the state's right to regulate the monopoly in the public
> interest.... The question now became simply how much of their previous claims
> the companies could afford to give up for the sake of state protection against
> rivals.

The 1890 presidential address by Emerson McMillin before the American
Gas Light Association (now American Gas Association) captured the changing
mood of the industry. "Raiders are still abroad in the land," McMillin complained (Figure E.3). He continued:

> The men with processes that can make gas for almost nothing, and still have a
> valuable residual, do not seem to despair in their efforts to get a standing in cities
> already well supplied. If they were only modest enough to go to small towns not
> now supplied with gas, and demonstrate the value of the process there, they
> would merit the everlasting gratitude of existing companies.

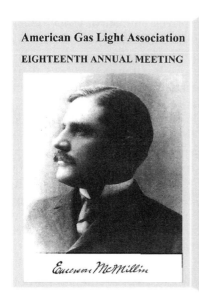

American Gas Light Association

EIGHTEENTH ANNUAL MEETING

Eucenvn McMillin

"Raiders are still abroad in the land. The men with processes that can make gas for almost nothing, and still have a valuable residual, do not seem to despair in their efforts to get a standing in cities already well supplied. If they were only modest enough to go to small towns not now supplied with gas, and demonstrate the value of the process there, they would merit the everlasting gratitude of existing companies."

– Emerson McMillin (1890)

Figure E.3 In the late nineteenth century, Emerson McMillin personified the manufactured-gas industry's preference for public-utility regulation, effectively trading undesired rate regulation for desired franchise protection with the political class.

McMillin and other harried industry leaders sought the public-utility covenant whereby cost-based rate regulation would come with entry regulation. Prescribed rate maximums would allow each company, in theory at least, to recover its prudently incurred costs and earn a reasonable rate of return on invested capital. A certificate of public convenience and necessity would place the burden of proof on an aspiring entrant to show cause (in a formal hearings process) in order to receive permission to enter into a serviced market.

Statewide Regulation

McMillin saw the future in Massachusetts, which in 1885 became the first state to enact a comprehensive gas law. *An Act to Create a Board of Gas Commissioners*, authored by the Boston Gas Company, was hardly an end, however. A vigorous cat-and-mouse game between the regulators and the regulated resulted in approximately 90 new laws passed between 1885 and 1900 to make the statute more effective.

The chief reason for Massachusetts's "wide-reaching inquisitorial powers" was to uncover and redress opportunistic business strategies to maximize profits under regulatory constraints. Monopoly firms were typically in a position to charge higher rates to their captive customers and to increase total revenue, so their incentive was to maximize the rate base upon which their regulated profit was applied. The strategy was to avoid writedowns or writeoffs of obsolete assets while aggressively purchasing assets that were rich in book value or had an extra goodwill valuation, whether a building, equipment, or patents (in-house or purchased). So-called overcapitalization, or stock-watering strategies, countered what otherwise could be a shrinking rate base from depreciation charges under cost-of-service maximum-rate regulation.

Massachusetts's law was followed by legislation establishing continuous-control state public-utility commissions in New York (1905) and Wisconsin (1907). By 1927, 48 states had followed suit with manufactured gas, which over time would morph into natural gas imported from the Southwest for the most part.

Statewide regulation replaced home-rule franchises that sometimes involved back-room deals between city fathers and the captains of industry. In such cases, the company got a valuable, protective franchise, and politicians got cold cash or campaign contributions. In contrast, statewide regulation by full-time officials was considered scientific, not political. Such formalized regulation in place of ad hoc local edicts constituted the second phase of gas-industry regulation.

Federal Regulation: Interstate Pipelines

Opportunistic strategies by firms toward state regulation—first in Massachusetts and then across the country—became secondary to a new regulatory gap that emerged in the 1920s when interstate pipelines carrying natural gas began displacing coal gas. The gap involved the U.S. Constitution's commerce clause, which left state regulators powerless to control the purchase of out-of-state gas by local distributors. Nor could state officials block a distribution company with an interstate transmission affiliate from using a transfer price to receive at wholesale what public-utility rate making might disallow at retail. So long as final users would still buy enough gas at a higher price to increase total revenue (and under exclusive franchises, demand was less sensitive to price than it otherwise would have been), the integrated company was well positioned to circumvent regulatory constraints.

This so-called breakdown of regulation led Congress to pass the Natural Gas Act of 1938, which subjected interstate gas transmission companies to public-utility regulation of entry, rates, and terms of service by the Federal Power Commission (FPC). The targeted pipelines were originally ambivalent toward what state regulators and New Deal Washingtonians were pushing. "Possibly State regulation should be supplemented by Federal control of interstate activities," said Floyd Brown of Natural Gas Pipeline of America, the line Insull had built just years before as Chicago's new gas supply. But when a strong certification requirement for new entry in occupied areas was added to the draft—Section 7(c)—the to-be-regulated industry changed its tone. "We have no objection to the bill," said a lawyer representing four interstates. He added: "We think that generally it is sound regulation. It follows the lines of regulation in many of the states. Frankly, I think about the only result that will occur is increased costs both to the Federal Government ... and to the competition."

Cost-inflating, time-consuming hearing processes, which would involve hundreds of FPC staffers and outside attorneys, would indeed give incumbents a leg up. This expensive quid pro quo for cost-of-service rate ceilings would also mean less competition at wholesale and service delays for millions of gas consumers in the years and decades ahead.

In the space of a half century, local intervention had graduated to statewide public-utility regulation of gas-distribution companies and then to federal public-utility regulation of interstate gas transmission. The city-gate market (whereby gas was sold by interstate pipelines to local distribution companies) was now federally regulated at wholesale to complement state regulation at retail.

This left one part of the gas-industry chain—wellhead production—unregulated. Sans regulation, (upstream) natural gas producers were positioned to receive, in theory if not in practice, the economic rent that federal regulators denied to (midstream) pipelines and that state regulators denied to (downstream) distribution companies but that captive consumers had to pay. This regulatory gap was also present for municipal gas companies that received gas that was not regulated at the wellhead.

Under the just-and-reasonable pricing provision of the Natural Gas Act, the FPC administratively responded in 1940 by imposing cost-based price ceilings on affiliated sales between the production subsidiary and the pipeline division. So-called field orders were punitive to the involved integrated companies, which responded by selling their production properties on nonregulated terms to nonintegrated producers to escape per unit price controls for market value.

The regulatory gap now remained for producers and interstate pipelines engaged in arm's length transactions. In 1954, the Supreme Court ruled that all gas sales for resale (wholesale transactions) in interstate markets came under the jurisdiction of the Natural Gas Act to "plug the 'gap' in regulation . . . [for] protection of consumers against exploitation."

For the first time, the upstream interstate market was comprehensively regulated to join midstream and downstream regulation. The intrastate market, where gas was sold by producers to pipelines or to distribution companies within the same state, was not reachable by federal price regulation, just by the supervision of state utility commissions (such as the Texas Railroad Commission).

Figure E.4 shows the cumulative process that began in the nineteenth-century with the initiating intervention of government street ownership and corporate charter policy. This beachhead led to gas-company charters and municipal lighting contracts—the opening stanza of government involvement in the gas industry. Home-rule charters specified rates for street lighting and sometimes contained special provisions restricting new entry. Phase 1's consequent intervention led to statewide public-utility regulation (Phase 2), which in turn led to federal regulation of interstate pipelines (Phase 3) and like regulation of wellhead transactions (Phase 4).

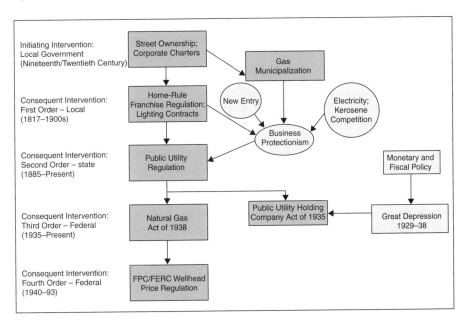

Figure E.4 Intervention in the gas industry began on the local level, expanded state-wide in the next decades, and was federalized for interstate pipelines in 1938. Federal regulation reached producers selling gas in interstate commerce soon thereafter.

A national network of municipal gas companies served as initiating intervention for private-side regulation, since industry leaders rallied toward public-utility regulation in part to quell the threat of municipalization. The Great Depression, itself consequent to government intervention into money and banking, contributed to industry instability that engendered demand for regulatory protection, not to mention a federal law prohibiting common ownership of multiple distribution systems. The Public Utility Holding Company Act of 1935, one of several responses to the collapse of the Insull empire, led to divestitures whereby commonly held gas and electric divisions, as well as interstate transmission and distribution affiliates, were separated and sold.

Federal Regulation: Production
FPC regulation of gas producers in the 1940s began a tar baby exercise that would endure for a half century. The wellhead market hardly had the natural monopoly characteristics ascribed to interstate gas pipelines and distribution

companies. Few, if any, textbooks claimed it did. But regulators like to regulate, and prior regulation had sprung a leak. Yet good intentions are not enough, and cost-based regulation went from problematic to unworkable for multiple reasons, including assigning a well's costs between associated flows of unregulated oil and regulated natural gas.

The FPC, under its newfound authority, would implement four successive wellhead pricing regimes in the next three decades, with the problems of each leading to the next. Each stanza represented a *cumulative process within a cumulative process*. FPC activities grew as hearings became more politicized and new areas of regulation were assumed. The initial volume of FPC matters from 1931 through mid-1939, totaled fewer than 1,000 pages. Volume 2 was more than 1,000 pages and covered mid-1939 through 1941. In the mid-1940s, weighty volumes were published yearly and by the mid-1950s became semiannual. Natural gas issues were responsible for most of this growth, but interstate electricity and waterway issues also occupied the commission's attention.

The first (of three) FPC wellhead-gas-pricing methodologies was *individual-producer* price regulation (1954–60), which treated some 5,000 gas-production companies selling gas in interstate commerce as public utilities subject to federal control. The result was administrative chaos, or what President Kennedy's Landis Commission called "the outstanding example in the federal government of the breakdown of the administrative process," as firms pancaked rate request after rate request, while regulators grappled with determining cost-based maximum price assignments.

Area price regulation (1960–73) divided the U.S. natural gas map into 23 regions for "in-line" pricing for "new gas" contracts, and slightly lower prices for "old gas" contracts. Consumerist, redistributive pricing by President Kennedy's new slate of FPC commissioners rolled back prices in many instances—with the unintended but predictable consequence of critical gas shortages in the winter of 1970/71 in many interstate markets. At the same time, gas was plentiful, even oversupplied, in (unregulated) intrastate markets.

National price regulation (1974–78) set a single cost-based price ceiling to reduce the complexity introduced by the area approach. But the price liberalization necessary to attract gas interstate required regulators to jettison cost-based rate making for a new methodology based on "the price of competitive fuels, the impact upon supply and demand, inflationary pressures, the nation's natural gas shortage and conservation factors."

But prices were still below market-clearing levels. Interstate gas shortages were experienced for the second time in the winter of 1976/77 and were relatively worse. But gas-state consumers (such as those of Houston Natural Gas) basked in gas surpluses as production stayed in unregulated home markets. In addition, gas-consuming industries began relocating to gas states to take advantage of secure, competitively priced supply. This plenty-amid-crisis resulted in the Natural Gas Policy Act of 1978 (NGPA), the fifth stanza of FPC (now Federal

Energy Regulatory Commission, or FERC) regulation, which set maximum intrastate gas prices for the first time in exchange for higher permitted prices elsewhere.

Figure E.5 illustrates the cumulative dynamics of gas interventionism at the wellhead. The initiating and enabling intervention was the Natural Gas Act of 1938, which the FPC and then the U.S. Supreme Court interpreted as extending just-and-reasonable pricing to natural gas at the wellhead. The figure shows how the five phases of consequent regulation—the second expansionary, the third and fourth amendatory, and the fifth both expansionary and contractionary—are linked.

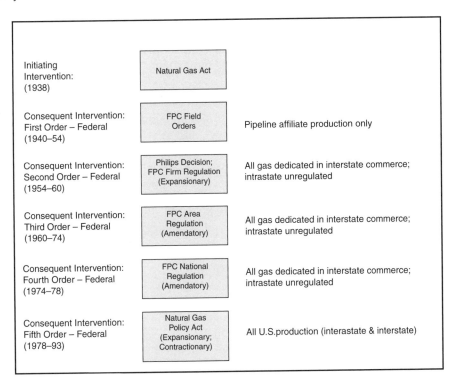

Figure E.5 The cumulative regulatory process with natural gas went from distribution to interstate transmission and then to the wellhead. Wellhead regulation—with five distinct phases—was an interventionist process working within an interventionist process.

The NGPA set some 20 categories for wellhead pricing, depending on the age and location of the gas find. Some categories were targeted for immediate or prospective decontrol, whereas old-gas categories remained under NGA price ceilings. Intrastate gas was regulated for the first time, the quid pro quo for wellhead price increases and deregulation elsewhere.

The perversity of the NGPA's tiers, or vintages, was demonstrated when one driller struck gas but redrilled the well from a nearby hill to exceed the 15,000-foot depth for unregulated pricing. This redrill was an act of superfluous entrepreneurship, defined by Israel Kirzner as regulatory-induced "pure profit opportunities that would otherwise have been absent."

Revamped Federal Regulation

The NGPA was part of the five-part National Energy Act of 1978 (NEA), which was passed in response to the natural gas crisis of the winter of 1976/77. Already, the Emergency Gas Act of 1977 gave special powers to the FPC, soon to be the FERC, to expedite gas transfers between companies and imports from Canada. The five major pieces of legislation were:

- *NGPA*, which in addition to regulating producer prices, relaxed interstate transmission regulation to facilitate the movement of gas from surplus to shortage areas;

- *Powerplant and Industrial Fuel Use Act*, which prohibited natural gas burning in such facilities to reserve supply for residential and commercial usage;

- *Public Utility Regulatory Policies Act*, which, among other provisions, subsidized the construction of new gas-fired combined-cycle power plants by non-utility owners;

- *National Energy Conservation Policy Act*, which mandated energy-efficiency standards and subsidized conservation programs to reduce energy demand;

- *Energy Tax Act*, which implemented a raft of tax breaks for energy efficiency.

These interventions were intended to *construct* equilibrium within a price-control framework by either increasing supply or reducing demand—a policy described above as gapism.

Figure E.6 shows the various government-intervention linkages either triggering or exacerbating natural gas shortages, including the secondary cause of petroleum price regulation that created fuel-oil shortages that shifted demand to gas, as well as consequent intervention intended to address the shortages. These laws represented expansive intervention, although some liberalization was present in the complicated, concocted political stew.

Despite its complexity, the NGPA achieved one goal by ending natural gas shortages. Yet the regulatory framework replaced one crisis with another, as described in reference to Jack Bowen's career.

The "gas bubble" led to administrative regulation by the FERC to substitute cheaper spot-market (short-term) gas for more expensive gas under long-term contracts and to allow pipelines to offer short-term transportation. This cumulative process within a cumulative process deconstructed traditional public-utility regulation; now interstate gas pipelines no longer bought and sold gas but unbundled their service by transporting supply for third parties for a

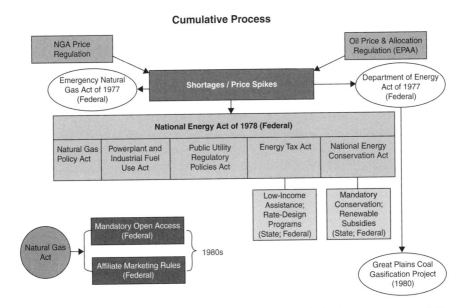

Figure E.6 Wellhead price regulation in the 1970s created shortages, more regulation, and complicated partial decontrol. The new regime benefitted interstate Transco Energy (Jack Bowen) at the expense of intrastate Houston Natural Gas (Robert Herring). Ken Lay would emerge from this tumult as an industry star.

carriage fee. The mandatory open-access era (contract carriage era) was largely complete by the 50th anniversary of the Natural Gas Act of 1938.

Two other interventionist legacies refused to die after markets turned from shortages to surpluses in the 1980s: conservationism and alternative-energy subsidies. Reduced natural gas usage became an end in itself, fostering a variety of government interventions from appliance-efficiency mandates to conservation programs funded by utility ratepayers or taxpayers. A variety of subsidies for wind power and other favored renewables (solar, geothermal, and biomass but not hydroelectricity) were enacted at the state and federal levels. Gas shortages also sparked interest in synthetics, which resulted in the federal loan guarantees authorized in 1977 legislation, that were behind such builds as Transco's Great Plains Coal Gasification Project.[18]

Why Regulation?
Regulation of manufactured gas and natural gas is premised on the impracticality of gas-to-gas competition in retail markets. Consumers, especially

---

18. Great Plains would default on its $2 billion federal loan in 1986 amid falling natural gas prices; the federal Synthetic Fuels Corporation was terminated in 1985 after a five-year life.

households, are captive to one gas supplier, the textbooks explain. Therefore, there should be cost-of-service regulation in return for an exclusive right to serve, a monopoly franchise for the gas- utility company.

But a counterexample exists in our story, as told in chapter 11. In the 1920s and 1930s, competition between Houston Natural Gas and Houston Gas and Fuel (HGF) occurred subdivision by subdivision, street by street, and house by house. In this case, *natural monopoly* was not natural, and there were gains from actual and potential competition.[19]

It was not until 1976, after a half century of rivalry, that HNG's distribution division merged with the successor company to HGF, Entex Corp. Even then, the consolidation was because of regulation that discriminated against any company (HNG) integrated between wholesale and retail, as discussed in chapter 13.

The case for regulation is not textbook clear, for alongside market imperfections exist government imperfections. Experts, even if they are the smartest guys in the room, must answer hard questions to implement the right solution, such as: What costs are prudent for passthrough in a one-firm-only world? What is a reasonable rate of return? The economist must ask: What is foregone without the prospect, the mere possibility, of new entry to serve even a part of the monopolist's territory? Samuel Insull himself grappled with these questions for electricity, but they also apply to gas.

What are the costs, both to the firm and to taxpayers, for the regulatory process? What regulatory gaps will result in expanded intervention and the unintended consequences thereof? Could private contracting protect users without government formalism, particularly if organized consumers created a monopsony situation?

Competitive fatigue within the gas industry, not ideology within or outside of the industry, was a driving force behind public-utility regulation. The industry led, not followed. But a rationale for policy reform was needed. That rationale, however self-serving and however static for a real-world dynamic economy, would rule the textbooks and expand the halls of government. Reconsideration is long overdue, however, as argued by Richard Posner in his resurrected classic, *Natural Monopoly and Its Regulation.* "The practical difficulties of constraining a monopolist's pricing," Posner argued, "is more likely to produce distortions than to bring about a reasonable simulacrum of competitive pricing and output." Both informational problems (because regulators are not god-like) and incentive problems (because regulators are all too human) create the regulatory failures that had to be considered alongside alleged market failures.

---

19. Also see Internet appendix 12.3, "'Natural Monopoly' and Gas Regulation in Houston, Texas," at www.politicalcapitalism.org/Book2/Chapter12/Appendix3.html.

Similarly, Jerry Ellig and Joseph Kalt spoke to "a new, emerging consensus among professional economists about government regulation in general" on four principles.

- Government regulation is imperfect.
- Entry conditions are crucial.
- Entrepreneurship and dynamic efficiency are critical.
- Private negotiation can substitute for regulation.

All point toward a model different from statewide public-utility regulation, which is so old and so entrenched that fundamental questions of its *why* are too often forgotten.

Public-Utility Regulation: Electricity

Samuel Insull's crusade for statewide public-utility regulation, launched in 1898 before the National Electric Light Association (now Edison Electric Institute), bore fruit. "All now seem to assent to the proposition that municipal utilities must be regulated," wrote one economist in 1914, with only "the point of difference [being] as to the method and extent of regulation." Twenty-eight states would establish statewide public-utility commissions between 1910 and 1915 alone, including Illinois in 1914.

What Emerson McMillin et al. got for gas, Samuel Insull and his followers secured for electricity with a slight lag. Political capitalism, not laissez-faire, was alive and well in the gas and electricity industries—as it was in other major sectors of the U.S. economy, such as banking and railroads.

State public-utility regulation of electricity began a long-lived cumulative process. As on the gas side, state commissions found themselves reaching deeper and deeper into managerial decision making to make the regulation of power generation and distribution more effective. "There has been a steady growth in commission jurisdiction over more types of utilities, and greater authority over the managerial affairs of the utilities," wrote C. O. Ruggles in 1937. "Increased attention was focused especially on such matters as the power to change contract rates, to issue terminable or indeterminate permits, to control depreciation rates, to approve consolidation and mergers, and to authorize the construction of electric transmission lines."

As on the gas side, early electricity municipalization was cumulative to the initiating and enabling intervention of municipal street ownership. Municipalization was also resultant from home-rule regulation whereby, in some cases, the government firm was organized in response to politicized franchise awards. Richard Ely and other economists made this argument for municipalization in the 1880s; politicians made the argument in their respective locales. Detroit, for example, established an electric municipality in 1895 after political corruption surrounding the franchises was uncovered.

Statewide regulation with power, as with gas, was not the panacea that advocates had hoped. Opportunistic strategies by firms to maximize profits in the face of regulatory constraints diluted hoped-for captive ratepayer gains. "After a twenty-year struggle with rate regulation the public authorities today are scarcely in a better position than when they started," two economists found. They explained:

> During these two decades they have conducted endless investigations, caused the expenditure of hundreds of millions of dollars, piled up mountains of records and opinions; and mostly have not reduced rates when fairly justified, nor advanced them when reasonably needed. They are all but helpless before the huge task of prescribing rates for the many utilities operating under greatly vary-ing conditions, rapidly shifting prices and tremendous transitions in industrial organization—unless principles and policies of regulation are definitely estab-lished and exact methods prescribed.

With Samuel Insull in his gun sights, Franklin D. Roosevelt, then governor of New York, complained:

> The condition of over-capitalization by the issuance of watered stock has come about under the regulation of public utilities by public service commissions, so that the policy has failed to maintain that degree of protection for the public, which was contemplated at the outset. It appears to me that the policy of public service commission regulation has broken down and proved itself ineffectual for the purposes originally intended.

·◇·

The fall of the House of Insull in 1932 piqued congressional interest for major reform. The first Insull-related law was the Securities Act of 1933, which was followed by the Securities and Exchange Act of 1934. Two energy laws were then enacted in 1935. "It is no exaggeration to see in the legislative innovations of the New Deal a phoenix arising from the ashes of the Insull empire," two historians wrote.

The Federal Power Act of 1935 regulated entry and rates for electricity sold between utilities under a broad interpretation of interstate commerce. The familiar term plugging regulatory gaps applied. Explained one study:

> The FPC was given jurisdiction over electricity in interstate commerce in order to close a gap in regulation. A considerable quantity of electricity is transmitted in interstate commerce and sold at wholesale to companies engaged in distribution to ultimate consumers. Since the wholesale rate is an interstate rate, a state com-mission does not control it, yet it has an important effect on the costs of a com-pany whose rates to ultimate consumers are subject to state commission control. Obviously, regulation of the rates to ultimate consumers could not be effective or

intelligent unless the state commission investigates the reasonableness of the wholesale rate, but this was beyond its control.

The second law regulated utility holding companies, which were at the center of many regulatory controversies. The Public Utility Holding Company Act of 1935 addressed a "lack of effective public regulation" that created "abuses … injurious to investors, consumers, and the general public." By breaking up multistate, multisystem holding companies, the law sought to eliminate a variety of opportunistic company practices whereby profit making could be transferred from regulated to unregulated divisions. Henceforth, only one integrated system could be owned by a company to remove the complex interstate "financial legerdemain" that was "not susceptible of effective control by any State."

Those federal extensions were consequent to the failures of previous regulation, on close inspection. Accounting historian George May noted how gaming financial statements was sport in the regulated public utilities, not unregulated firms. "The grant to a regulatory commission of power over accounting in unregulated industries was not and could not have been supported by a claim that abuses had developed in that field which did not exist where accounting was regulated," he explained.

> On the contrary, the practices which had become discredited were more general in the regulated industries (and among the utility holding companies) and had spread from those fields to unregulated industry to only a minor extent where they had spread at all. This is true of the non-acceptance of the cost amortization concept of depreciation; of reappraisal and improper charges against capital surpluses resulting therefrom; of pyramiding of holding companies; of periodical stock dividends improperly accounted for; and of the practice of charging to surplus items which more properly belong in the income account.

May ended: "These together constitute the major defects of accounting that had developed in the prosperous period that ended in 1929 and in the depression that followed."

The long history of electricity regulation is illustrated in Figure E.7. Government power policy paralleled the experience with gas, with the major difference being passage of the Federal Power Act three years before the Natural Gas Act—although both were originally part of the same bill. Only with the interstate gas shortages in the 1970s would the federal path for gas and electricity diverge.

The cumulative process of government intervention into electricity markets slowed in the 1940–70 period, notwithstanding the rise of nuclear power, an industry that would not have come into being without accident-liability limits enacted in the Price-Anderson Act of 1957. Electricity rates fell in real terms with technology improvements and steady energy input prices. Life was serene inside the franchised monopolies, where every pound of engineering required only an ounce of entrepreneurship.

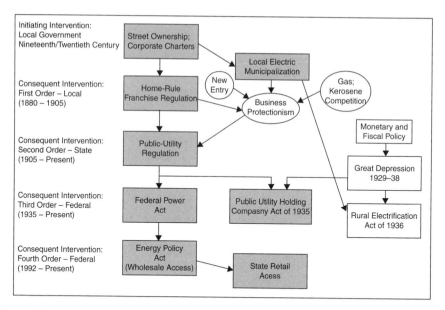

Figure E.7 The cumulative process of U.S. electricity regulation began on the local level, spread to the state level, and became federalized during the New Deal. A new stanza of federal power regulation began in 1992 with Enron's fingerprints, the mandatory open-access era.

This radically changed in the 1970s, when turmoil in oil and gas markets impacted the production and distribution of electric power. The Public Utility Regulatory Policies Act of 1978 was enacted to motivate the entry of independent (nonutility) power producers to compete, for the first time, with integrated power utilities as well as with municipalities. This meant requiring utilities to purchase power from the upstarts under specified conditions.

Not until the 1990s would fundamental changes begin to occur for electricity as had occurred for gas more than a decade before. An Enron-sponsored provision in the Energy Policy Act of 1992 set into motion a new regulatory regime whereby owners of interstate transmission had to open up their systems to outside parties (mandatory open access) to move power. For the first time, independent producers or traders could step between utilities or municipalities—the wholesale market—and buy, sell, and transmit power.

Gaining access to utility wires to serve end users was a state matter. States began to implement mandatory open access at retail, but the momentum stopped when California's half-slave, half-free deregulation effort produced electricity shortages in 2000–2001. The state's crisis was the result of its own multi-decade cumulative interventionist process with electricity. "Each stage, and in fact the whole process" of California electricity regulation, one economist concluded, "should be seen not as a random set of disconnected events but rather as a continuing sequence in which choices were made."

The Rent-Seeking Mentality

"The rich and powerful too often bend the acts of government to their selfish purposes," Andrew Jackson complained in 1830. "[They] have not been content with equal protection and equal benefits, but have besought us to make them richer by acts of Congress." Milton Friedman 150 years later identified corporations, along with "my fellow intellectuals," as the major foes of free-market capitalism. In the post-Enron era, two scholars concluded: "Capitalism's biggest political enemies are not the firebrand trade unionists spewing vitriol against the system but the executives in pin-striped suits extolling the virtues of competitive markets with every breath while attempting to extinguish them with every action." Such was the case at Ken Lay's Transco and Robert Herring's Houston Natural Gas.

One does not have to look far for examples in and around the Enron orbit. Reminiscent of Samuel Insull's effort a century before to secure public-utility regulation for his industry, James E. "Jim" Rogers, CEO of Duke Energy, persuaded his fellow executives in the Edison Electric Institute to endorse cap-and-trade regulation of carbon dioxide (CO_2) emissions for power plants. A protégé of Ken Lay at Enron before entering the electric-utility business, Rogers took Lay's climate alarmism and get-to-the-table-first lobbying strategy with him— but only to fall short in a grand political play in 2010.

T. Boone Pickens, who came to national prominence as the founding CEO of Mesa Petroleum and went on to make (and also lose) billions of dollars in energy trading, personally spent more than $60 million to promote government-forced energy transformation. The Pickens Plan proposed to displace natural gas with wind generation in the electricity sector, whereupon the freed natural gas would substitute for petroleum in the transportation sector. T. Boone scaled back his plan and failed, like Jim Rogers, in the very political year of 2010.

Then there is Jeffrey Immelt, the successor to Jack Welch at General Electric, the company that Thomas Edison and Insull relinquished in 1892. In 2002, GE purchased Enron Wind Corporation as part of its "eco-imagination" campaign predicated on climate alarmism and government-directed energy transformation. In a sense, Immelt took over where Lay left off. Enron never turned a profit on wind power, and GE's experience with the same has been uneven, if not problematic, reflecting the vagaries of a government-dependent investment.

Business has been anything but an advocate and protector of capitalism proper in the history of the U.S. energy market. All too often, profit seeking has turned into rent-seeking under the pressure of profit and loss. New Deal petroleum regulator J. Howard Marshall II relished the irony:

> Many big shots in the business, who later denied it, literally prayed for us ama-teurs in government "to save us else we perish." A few years later, when most of them, for one reason or another, found salvation, few sinners remembered their prayers. Such is human nature.

Four decades later, amid a peacetime energy crisis, with natural gas and oil in shortage, a cry for national economic planning came from the CEO of ARCO (Atlantic Richfield Company), the seventh-largest oil company in the United States at the time. In "My Case for National Planning" published in *Fortune* magazine, Thornton Bradshaw argued for government-set prices and output for petroleum and national gas. The former Harvard professor and member of President Jimmy Carter's energy task force built his case on an alleged long-standing failure of petroleum production under private ownership and free-market incentives.

In response, Koch Industries CEO Charles Koch argued that energy woes, past and present, were government related and that national planning would only make things worse. In "Let's Try a Free Market in Energy," Koch reinter-preted the New Deal past and the energy crisis present to conclude that free markets were not the problem but the unappreciated solution. He brought in the history of political capitalism to turn the tables on Bradshaw:

> The majority of businessmen prefer power and government-guaranteed profits to philosophical consistency; they are more than willing to trade off market prin-ciples for a system that promises less competition and more security.... Almost every major piece of interventionist legislation since 1887 has had important business support, and certainly regulation in the oil and gas industry is no exception.

Koch then lowered the boom:

> Economic planning by its very nature is *people* planning. It is part of a misguided policy that would return us to the dark ages of political economy where the State controlled the entire economy and society in its own political interests. To return to that system is to finally abandon the American experiment and the American dream.

Such free-market thinking from a leading CEO was rare in 1977 and is still exceptional today.

·<small>∽</small>·

Political pragmatism and amoralism have colored the central characters of the previous chapters. John Henry Kirby was a Jekyll and Hyde of political philoso-phy. In the first third of the twentieth century, the Texas titan intensely fought government activism when it thwarted his profit making, whether it concerned nationalized railroads, corporate taxation, antitrust suits, or New Deal price controls. But government intervention was welcomed, even championed. The founder of the Southern Tariff Association was a universal tariff advocate (all goods, not some), believing that U.S. living standards would otherwise decline to those of the rest of the world. Still, Kirby would declare, "I am not a protectionist."

In his seventy-third year, Kirby advocated a $50 billion federal bond issue to subsidize the sale of land to citizens to help bring back the good times (see chapter 10). His quixotic anti-Depression proposal was laughed out of court. But it was emblematic of Kirby's populism, which trumped limited government and included a push for progressive chain-store taxation to protect small stores (see chapter 10). The self-described Constitutionalist was a philosophically pliable middle-of-the-roader.

Clint Murchison also knew how to play the government game (see chapter 6). He ingeniously produced "hot oil" (oil above the assigned government quota) in the early 1930s in East Texas. He drilled wells for free, courtesy of a provision in the World War II excess-profits tax under which all his costs, even for dry holes, were deductible from his tax liability. Murchison's Dallas taxicab business was predicated on an exclusive franchise from City Hall. But all that was small potatoes when it came to his ego-driven Trans-Canada Pipe Lines project, a six-year by-hook-or-by-crook saga that resulted in the construction of an all-Canadian pipeline instead of cheaper, market-ready intercontinental pipeline networks.

Of course, Clint was hardly the only one who played the political game for business gain. So too did his contemporary and business partner, Paul Kayser. Kayser saved El Paso Natural Gas Company from probable receivership by working to secure a copper tariff for his smelter customers in Herbert Hoover's Internal Revenue Act of 1932 (see chapter 6). Buoyed copper prices kept the gas on and El Paso's debt serviced.

Kayser struck again the next year when he leaned on his former legal client, Jesse Jones, head of the Reconstruction Finance Corporation, for a $2.2 million loan for a pipeline expansion. The loan required that pipeline trenching be done with picks and shovels, not machinery, to create more local jobs. Such was the economic thinking, or really the *un*economic thinking, of Hoover and then FDR, that prolonged the Great Depression.

Jack Bowen was an engineer by training and outlook, as was energy-crisis President Jimmy Carter. Given price controls and other government constraints, Bowen was all for government-fixing-government via gapism. Government-created shortages, in other words, needed to be addressed by new government intervention to reduce demand and/or augment supply. Hence directives in Carter's National Energy Plan of 1977 were embraced by Bowen as "something the nation must do."

Predicting $7 per Mcf gas for the mid-1980s, Transco and several industry partners (including Peoples Gas Company, once run by Samuel Insull) erected the Great Plains Coal Gasification Project (see chapter 9). The Reagan administration approved a $2.02 billion federal loan guarantee to produce pipeline-quality coal gas. But with spot-gas prices at half the cost of synthetic gas, the so-called Great Pains project was immediately in trouble. The project was turned back to the government in 1985 after the sponsors failed to secure new taxpayer or ratepayer subsidies.

Bowen routinely sought political fixes for company challenges (see chapter 9). Transco asked federal authorities to abrogate its out-of-the-money natural gas contracts with producers. In the 1980s, Transco also lobbied Congress to enact a tariff on petroleum to help natural gas fend off competition from fuel oil.

Also in the Reagan era, as discussed in chapter 9, Bowen pushed for federal legislation to expedite (fast-track) permission for major non-nuclear energy projects. A cabinet-level Council on Energy Mobilization, the centerpiece of the proposed Energy Mobilization Act of 1981, would determine qualifying projects. The Transco-backed initiative—intended to aid synthetic gas projects—died in committee.

Robert Herring of Houston Natural Gas, who generally thought of himself as a free-enterpriser ("I am greatly concerned … about heavy-handed regulation from Washington, D.C.") was also thinking politically. In 1972, when energy shortages were disrupting the country, Herring endorsed *a new national energy policy* in this context:

> While we have always acknowledged the need for federal guidance of this country's basic energy policy through an effective regulatory system, the current situation demands much more. We must establish a new national energy policy, one which considers all sources of energy—a comprehensive plan which will supply with assurance the needs of our people and industry with due consideration of the environment and of cost.

Herring's interest in such a comprehensive approach reflected a sympathetic view of government's role in America's development. He praised early government subsidies for railroads, as well as more recent "public welfare" initiatives. "Monopolistic tendencies had to be curtailed, the banking industry and utility rates required regulation, working standards and the rights of the worker had to be protected," he explained in a 1970 speech on business responsibility. And, like Bowen at Transco, Herring of HNG participated in a government-enabled synthetic-fuel project. HNG, too, helped get the NGPA over the top.

Bowen and Herring were not outliers in their belief that diminishing oil and gas resources gave government a special role in energy markets. In 1977, the 75th anniversary issue of the *Oil & Gas Journal* featured a stream of industry leaders prognosticating about a new era of synthetic fuels and renewables. Maurice Granville, CEO of Texaco and chairman of the American Petroleum Institute, declared "the era of 'cheap energy' has ended," seconding "President Carter's call upon the Congress to support a program calling for a lower energy growth rate and higher energy costs." In the same issue, George Lawrence, head of the American Gas Association, saw the future in "a whole new spectrum of solar-assisted gas-fired equipment" and a growing market share of synthetic (coal) gas.

·ᛩ·

Samuel Insull's view of business and government, developed in the 1890s and operative through the 1920s, was several parts pragmatic for every part idealistic. His cerebral, nuanced view was a high-wire act between what was seen as too much market on one side and bad government on the other. In the end, the results-getter got the distinct regime he wanted—or even more than he wanted, as discussed in chapter 4.

Insull's program was defense-first against ad hoc regulation by "the demagogue or the politician with some axe to grind (usually at the expense of the public) or the rabid reformer, misinformed on the true economics of the business." Local regulation by city fathers--with immediate popularity and votes trumping economics and abstract notions of fairness and efficiency–was dangerous indeed. There were few constraints on destructive political opportunism, whether concerning a punitive rate ceiling or a municipalization drive, as Insull knew personally, as well as from industry experience.

Although Insull was slow to reject municipalization per se, he came to dislike utility socialism more and more. "The result of municipal ownership is usually, I would say almost universally, a waste of the taxpayers' money," Insull opined in 1913. Municipalization "lacks the incentive that goes with the desire for personal achievement, personal improvement, position and wealth," he explained in 1916. Public money to build isolated plants was particularly censured. Insull warned of municipalization if punitive regulation prevailed, a reasoned speculation given that resultant unprofitability would erode service to the public and light the fires for a takeover.

The specter of municipalization helped Insull build support for his proposal to bypass local politics with statewide public-utility regulation. His program was sought for self-interested reasons ("In the long run, regulation means protection"), but the wider gain was lower capital costs from such protection to lower rates for consumers.

Insull came to realize that his preferred form of regulation had its own set of problems, as discussed in chapter 3. Regulation *is* political and thus subject to what Insull otherwise recognized as the "poison" of politics. Commissioners are elected or appointed by the elected, and regulators as human beings have personal goals, agendas, and fallibilities. Indeed, while seeing the implementation of statewide regulation as "the greatest event ... in the last ten or fifteen years in the local public utility business," Insull confided: "Laws are getting more strict, and regulation is becoming closer; and that has its advantages and disadvantages."

But what about free-market competition as an alternative to regulation, given that regulation cannot be anything but political outside, perhaps, of a honeymoon period? Why not open entry and unregulated pricing and terms of service, as determined by self-interested consumers and producers?

Insull summarily rejected free-market competition as "ruinous." He decried "the raiding promoter" who dared enter into occupied territories, declaring himself above the practice. Insull argued that "the disadvantage of the interference with our liberty of action is not bad," regulation being a form of "the discipline and chastening that many of us need."

But as discussed in chapter 3, the logic and results of Insull's central-station model suggested that the efficacy of natural monopoly was not time-limited.[20] Insull himself wrote the book on consolidating the companies and plants of his competitors for economies of scale. Who was to say that the competitive process was over at any point in time? According to Insull, lower rates were the key to expansion and profitability, and market saturation was not in sight.

Neither did large consumers need regulation. "A large consumer is well able to regulate his own price because the price has to come to a point where it will compete with his own plant," Insull observed.

The *real* reason Insull rigidly rejected market outcomes was that he did not believe that such an argument would carry the day. Regulation was required to beat regulation in the public-policy field, he stressed. This is where pragmatism bested idealism, if, indeed, Insull was open to realizing that his own practices were Exhibit A against the textbook view of natural-monopoly market failure.

In this sense, Insull's case for middle-way regulation was cumulative to the initiating intervention of local regulation or municipalization. Given politics, in other words, regulation had to be right rather than absent. But this did not make for a textbook case of market failure correctable by government intervention.

Insull supported good government, even "proper" local regulation. But he saw harm in governmental reaches. One warning came in 1921 before the Commerce Club of the University of Chicago. "You cannot create wealth by legislation; you cannot create wealth by the issue of paper money of any description," he intoned. "You can run a printing press to issue pieces of paper which you call worth a certain value, but there is relatively little difference between the credit of a nation and the credit of an individual." Given such downside of expansive government, Insull added:

> One of the greatest possible benefits to business would be for most of the legislative bodies of the country to shut up and go home and leave business alone, and I am not a man who does not believe in proper regulation of all classes of business.

---

20. Commonwealth Edison, for example, was described by Insull as "a company whose rates have never been regulated, whose reductions have always been made of its own free will."

But what I think is, they need a rest, and they need the legislators to go home and take off their coats and help create the wealth that is necessary to straighten out not only this country, but the rest of the world.

Good regulation in place of bad, Insull philosophized. But if it were only so easy! Politics invades the textbook ideal, creates unintended consequences, and triggers a cumulative interventionist process. Good intentions cannot overcome real-world results.

In the same talk, Insull identified the socialists of the chair—the academics—who *knew* and educated that public ownership was better than private. "I receive a great many letters from [college] students telling me they want to write a thesis on municipal ownership, and they always want me to tell them the points in their favor; it is seldom they want me to tell them the points in favor of private ownership," Insull related.

> But it is hardly necessary for me to discuss municipal ownership. We have had a really fine specimen of government ownership in this country, the taking over of the railroads and then finally handing them back to the owners in such poor condition. The country is suffering from a tragedy in governmental ownership today that should convince everybody that the function of government is to do as little as possible beyond the maintenance of order and see to it that everybody has a square deal.[21]

All said, the Great Man did economic freedom no favors by employing his considerable talents to implement comprehensive regulation as a middle way between market capitalism and socialism. There were tensions in both his case for regulation and the results of the real-world regulation that he, more than anyone else, championed and fathered in electricity. Decades later (as described in Book 3), his public-utility regulation would become a Christmas tree for pet interventionist schemes, for worse, not better.

The Open Door for Ken Lay—and Enron

The politicization of natural gas and electricity in the United States over a century's time reached a crescendo in the 1980s, when the shortage era gave way to surplus. This cycle, the legacy of government intervention, required new business strategies and called upon new skills from that of consumer-driven markets. Washington ability was important, not to mention ability in state capitals, where the public-utility commission and the legislature might reside. A government-affairs office in Washington, D.C., not only at headquarters (such

---

21. To Insull, the ills of private industry were more the result of unwise regulation than company mismanagement, and the "the fallacy of the so-called reformer's theory" for municipalization is looking at the negatives and not the positives of private ownership and operation.

as established by Transco in 1975), became par. At such companies, the public-affairs department almost became adjunct to government affairs.

Political energy required big thinking from the smartest guys in the room. Ph.D. economist James Schlesinger came from the government side as the inaugural head of the Department of Energy. The twelfth DOE head, Nobel laureate (in physics) Steven Chu, part of the "green dream team" appointed by President Obama, continues the search for silver bullets to transition to a schemed postcarbon-energy economy.

But this is hardly new. In the Carter era, Keynesian economist Paul Samuelson set Chu's agenda. "What we plainly need is a big Manhattan Project—like the one that gave us the atomic bomb but not like the one that narrowly missed finding a cure for cancer," the Nobel laureate in economics stated. But game-changing breakthoughs have been elusive for politically correct energies; in fact, technological change has continued to bless consumer-driven energies, one salient example being the recent shale-gas revolution. The carbon-energy era is still young, and consumers qua voters are instructing politicians to keep it that way in the United States and Canada, if not elsewhere.

The smartest guys in the room emerged on the private side in the political energy market also. The Thornton Bradshaw of the 1970s is the T. Boone Pickens, Jim Rogers, and Jeffrey Immelt today. The greater the mixed economy, the more the politics in energy, and the more company figures with politically correct messaging.

Between Bradshaw and Pickens, Rogers, and Immelt came Ken Lay, a big-picture Ph.D. economist who left a very political Transco Energy in 1984 for his own show. Houston Natural Gas Corporation was not federally regulated, but Lay would soon change that through acquisition and merger. By 1985/86, the old Houston Natural Gas received the biggest makeover in its 50-year life. The new company was a regulated colossus. Such was the beginning of a political corporation, a paragon of political capitalism, whose rise and fall would be for the ages.

Bibliography

Expanded chapter bibliographies are online at www.politicalcapitalism.org/
book2/fullbibliography/.

"Administrative Changes." *Transgas*, November–December 1971, 4.

Aitken, Hugh. "Government and Business in Canada: An Interpretation." *Business History Review* 38, no. 1 (Spring, 1964): 4–21.

Allen, Frederick. *The Great Pierpont Morgan*. New York: Dorset Press, 1948.

American Gas Association. *Gas Facts 1985*. Arlington, VA: AGA, 1986.

"Annual Meeting: Transco Doing Well." *HotTap*, May 31, 1984, 1.

Ash, Clarke. "How Miami Rates on Natural Gas." *Miami News*, September 6, 1959.

Ausubel, Jesse. "The Environment for Future Business: Efficiency Will Win." *Pollution Prevention Review* 8, no. 1 (Winter 1998): 39–52. Also available at http://phe.rockefeller .edu/future_ business/.

"Awarding of the Franklin Medal." *Science,* May 28, 1915, 785.

Baker, Charles. *Monopolies and the People*. New York: G. P. Putnam's Sons, 1889.

Baldwin, Neil. *Edison: Inventing the Century*. Chicago: University of Chicago Press, 1995, 2001.

Barton, Robert. "Transco Suffers FERC Setback, Faces Refund of $50 Million." *Natural Gas Week*, September 30, 1991, 3–4.

"Battling the Decontrol Maze." *HotTap,* October 1982, 2–5.

Bauer, John, and Peter Costello. *Public Organization of Electric Power*. New York: Harper & Brothers, 1949.

Beahler, John. "Pinkney [Walker] Sends His Best." *Mizzou*, Summer 2001, 20–23.

Bethell, Tom. "The Gas Price Fixers." *Harper's*, June 1979, 37–44, 104–105.

Bischoff, Susan. "Transco Chief's Artistic Bent Influences Firm." *Houston Chronicle*, March 11, 1984.

Black, Conrad. *Franklin Roosevelt: Champion of Freedom*. New York: PublicAffairs, 2005.

"The Black-Tie Executive—Pleasure? Or Business?" *Forbes*, June 12, 1978, 35–36.

Blühm, Andreas, and Louise Lippincott. *Light! The Industrial Age 1750–1900: Art & Science, Technology & Society*. New York: Thames & Hudson, 2001.

Boehnke, Karen. "Transco Turns 40." *The Energizer*, October 31, 1988, 1–10.

Bothwell, Robert, and William Kilbourn. *C. D. Howe: A Biography*. Toronto: McClelland and Stewart, 1979.

Bourne, Randolph S. *Youth and Life*. Boston: Houghton Mifflin, 1913.

Bowen, Jack. "Gas Industry—Year 2000." Transco Companies, 1977. (Copy in author's possession.)
———. "Presentation before the New York Society of Security Analysts." Houston, TX: Transco Investor Relations, September 15, 1981.
———. "President's Letter." *HotTap*, November 15, 1975, 3.
———. "Tightening Gas Supply." Reprinted in *Transgas*, July–August 1970, 23–25.
———. "To the Board of Directors." July 2, 1975, 1–4. (Copy in author's possession.)
———. "To the Board of Directors." October 16, 1975, 1–3. (Copy in author's possession.)
———, with Eric Fredrickson. *An American Life in the Twentieth Century: The Autobiography of Jack Bowen*. Houston, TX: privately printed, 2007.
"Bowen Is Elected Chairman, Sullivan President, Wilhite Pipeline President." *Gaslite News*, November–December 1973, 1.
"Bowen Named Top Executive." *HotTap*, February 1978, 1.
"The Bowen Ticket to Relaxation." *HotTap*, February 1982, 15.
Bradley, Robert L., Jr. *Capitalism at Work: Business, Government, and Energy*. Salem, MA: M & M Scrivener Press, 2009.
———. *Climate Alarmism Reconsidered*. London: Institute for Economic Affairs, 2003.
———. "The Distortions and Dynamics of Gas Regulation." In *New Horizons in Natural Gas Deregulation*, edited by Jerry Ellig and Joseph Kalt, 1–29. Westport, CT: Praeger, 1996.
———. "Interventionist Dynamics in the U.S. Energy Industry." In *The Dynamics of Intervention: Regulation and Redistribution in the Mixed Economy*, edited by Peter Kurrild-Klitgaard, 301–333. New York: Elsevier, 2005.
———. *The Mirage of Oil Protection*. Lanham, MD: University Press of America, 1989.
———. *Oil, Gas and Government: The U.S. Experience*. 2 vols. Lanham, MD: Rowman & Littlefield, 1996.
———. "The Origins of Political Electricity: Market Failure or Political Opportunism?" *Energy Law Journal* 17, no. 1 (1996): 59–102.
———. "A Typology of Interventionist Dynamics." In *Economics, Philosophy, and Information Technology: Essays in Honor of Don Lavoie*, edited by Jack High, 64–85. Northampton, MA: Edward Elgar, 2006.
Bradshaw, Thornton. "My Case for National Planning." *Fortune*, February 1977, 100–104.
Bright, Arthur, Jr. *The Electric-Lamp Industry: Technological Change and Economic Development from 1800 to 1947*. New York: Macmillan, 1949.
Broch, Nathan. "Backward Areas Must Be Helped, Says Ray C. Fish." *Houston Post*, July 27, 1959.
Brown, George. *The Gas Light Company of Baltimore: A Study of Natural Monopoly*. Baltimore: Johns Hopkins University Press, 1936.
Bryce, Robert. *Pipe Dreams: Greed, Ego, and the Death of Enron*. New York: PublicAffairs, 2002.
Buchanan, James. "Politics without Romance: A Sketch of Positive Public Choice Theory and Its Normative Implications." In *The Theory of Public Choice II*, edited by James Buchanan and Robert Tollison, 11–22. Ann Arbor: University of Michigan Press, 1984.

Buchanan, Norman. "The Origin and Development of the Public Utility Holding Company." *Journal of Political Economy* 44, no. 1 (February 1936): 31–53.

"Bulk of Testimony Favors Lease Sale." *Oil and Gas Journal*, August 27, 1973, 36–38.

Burka, Paul. "The Heretic." *Texas Monthly*, September 1977, 144–48, 193.

Burrough, Bryan. *The Big Rich*. New York: Penguin Press, 2009.

———. "Houston Natural Gas Chairman Quits; Transco Energy President Is Successor." *Wall Street Journal*, June 7, 1984.

Busch, Francis. *Guilty or Not Guilty? An Account of the Trials of the Leo Frank Case, the D.C. Stephenson Case, the Samuel Insull Case, the Alger Hiss Case.* New York: Bobbs-Merrill, 1952.

Butterfield, Herbert. *The Reconstruction of an Historical Episode: The History of the Enquiry into the Origins of the Seven Years' War*. Glasgow: Jackson, 1951.

"Call Automobile Ban Folly." *Chicago Record*, June 16, 1899.

"Canada: The Indispensable Ally." *Time*, February 4, 1952, 26–30.

Canadian-American Committee. "Wanted: A Working Environment More Conducive to Canadian-American Trade in Natural Gas." November 1959.

"Can Houston Natural Gas Be Its Own White Knight?" *Business Week*, March 26, 1984, 113.

Cannan, James. "The Campo Duran Pipelines." Presentation before the Petroleum Mechanical Engineering Conference, New Orleans, September 1960. Reprinted by Fish International Corporation. (Copy in author's possession.)

Carlson, W. Bernard. *Innovation as a Social Process: Elihu Thomson and the Rise of General Electric, 1870–1900*. Cambridge: Cambridge University Press, 1991.

Casey, Robert J., and W. A. S. Douglas. *The Midwesterner*. New York: Wilcox & Follett, 1948.

Castenada, Christopher. *Invisible Fuel: Manufactured and Natural Gas in America, 1800–2000*. New York: Twayne Publishers, 1999.

———. *Regulated Enterprise: Natural Gas Pipelines and Northeastern Markets, 1938–1954*. Columbus: Ohio State University Press, 1993.

Castaneda, Christopher, and Joseph Pratt. *From Texas to the East: A Strategic History of Texas Eastern Corporation*. College Station: Texas A&M University Press, 1993.

"Central Unit Set Up for Spot Gas Sales." *Oil & Gas Journal*, June 25, 1984, 32–33.

Chandler, Alfred. *The Visible Hand: The Managerial Revolution in American Business*. Cambridge, MA: Harvard University Press, Belknap Press, 1977.

"Charges Ickes Behind Move to Oust Wilkerson." *Chicago Tribune*, May 25, 1934.

Chernow, Ron. *The House of Morgan: An American Banking Dynasty*. New York: Atlantic Monthly Press, 1990.

Chesnutt, N. P. *Southern Union*. El Paso, TX: Mangan Books, 1979.

Chesterton, G. K. "On St. George Revivified." *All I Survey*. London: Metheun, 1934.

"Chicago Millionaire to Wed Gladys Wallis." *New York Evening World*, May 20, 1899.

Cicero, Marcus Tullius. *On the Ideal Orator*. Translated by James M. May and Jakob Wisse. New York: Oxford University Press, 2001.

"Civic Leader Robert R. Herring Dies." *Houston Chronicle*, October 12, 1981.

Clark, James, and Michel Halbouty. *Spindletop: The True Story of the Oil Discovery that Changed the World*. Houston, TX: Gulf Publishing, 1952.

"Coastal in Houston Gas Bid." *New York Times*, January 27, 1984.

"Coastal to Pay Fine to Settle Charges." *New York Times*, August 31, 1984.

"Coastal States Gas, Colorado Interstate Agree to Combine." *Wall Street Journal*, September 22, 1972.

Cochrane, J. L. "Carter Energy Policies and the Ninety-fifth Congress." In *Energy Policy in Perspective: Today's Problems, Yesterday's Solutions*, edited by Craufurd Goodwin, 547–600. Washington, DC: Brookings Institution, 1981.

"C of C Electee Lists '70 Goals." *Houston Post*, December 10, 1969.

Cole, Robert. "Coastal and A.N.R. Near Pact." *New York Times*, March 14, 1985.

———. "Coastal Rejects Offer for Houston Gas." *New York Times*, February 9, 1984.

———. "Houston Gas Raises Coastal Bid." *New York Times*, February 6, 1984.

———. "Houston Is Seeking Coastal." *New York Times*, February 1, 1984.

Coleman, Charles. *P.G. & E. of California: 1852–1952*. New York: McGraw-Hill, 1952.

Collins, Albert. "Gasifying of Coal Is Seen by Late 1974." *Houston Chronicle*, January 20, 1971, sec. 7.

———. "New Transco President Plans Oil Exploration." *Houston Chronicle*, October 10, 1974.

———. "Texas Natural Gas Needs Will Be Met." *Houston Chronicle*, March 1, 1970.

Collins, Theresa, and Lisa Gitelman. *Thomas Edison and Modern America*. New York: Bedford/St. Martin's, 2002.

"Colossus!" *Transgas*, February 1952, 21–30.

"Company Announces New Dividend Policy." *HotTap*, July 1984, 14.

"Company Joins Continental Group: Becomes Continental Resources Company." *Energetic People*, Fall 1979, 2–3.

"Company Seeks Action for Billion Feet SNG/LNG." *HotTap*, February 15, 1972, 1.

Connors, John. "City Blocks Houston Gas Expansion." *Miami Herald*, February 4, 1960.

———. "City Lifts Its Ban on Gas Extension." *Miami Herald*, March 17, 1960.

Conot, Robert. *Thomas A. Edison: A Streak of Luck*. New York: Da Capo, 1979.

Continental Group. Annual report, various years.

"Continental Group Inc. Buys Florida Gas Co. for $350 Million Total." *Wall Street Journal*, August 29, 1979.

Cook, James. "The Old-Fashioned Way." *Forbes*, September 10, 1984, 54, 56–57.

Crandall, Robert. "Air Pollution, Environmentalists, and the Coal Lobby." In *The Political Economy of Deregulation*, edited by Roger Noll and Bruce Owen, 84–96. Washington, DC: American Enterprise Institute, 1983.

"Crime: Receipt Given." *Time*, April 23, 1934. http://205.188.238.109/time/magazine/article/ 0,9171,747352,00.html.

Cudahy, Richard, and William Henderson. "From Insull to Enron: Corporate (Re)Regulation after the Rise and Fall of Two Energy Icons." *Energy Law Journal* 26, no. 1 (2005): 35–110.

DeGraff, Leonard. "Corporate Liberalism and Electric Power System Planning in the 1920s." *Business History Review* 64, no. 1 (Spring, 1990), 1–31.

Desrochers, Pierre, and Colleen Haight. "Squandered Profit Opportunities? Some Historical Perspective on Industrial Waste and the Porter Hypothesis." *Journal of Institutional Economics* (forthcoming).

Devine, Edward. *Coal*. Bloomington, IL: American Review Service Press, 1925.

Dewing, Arthur. *The Financial Policy of Corporations*. New York: Ronald Press, 1953.

Dionne, Jack. *A Brief Story of the Life of John Henry Kirby*. Houston, TX: Kirby Lumber Corporation, 1951.

———. "The Passing of John Henry Kirby." *Gulf Coast Lumberman*, November 15, 1940, 12–16.

Doern, G. Bruce, and Glen Toner. *The Politics of Energy: The Development and Implementation of the NEP*. Toronto: Methuen, 1985.

Downes, Larry, and Chunka Mui. *Unleashing the Killer App*. Boston: Harvard Business School Press, 1998.

Drucker, Peter. *The Age of Discontinuity*. New York: Harper & Row, 1968.

Dyer, Frank, and Thomas Martin. *Edison: His Life and Inventions*. New York: Harper & Brothers, 1910.

Ebdon, J. Fred. "The Scenic Inch: The Pacific Northwest Story." *GAS*, October 1955, 3–40.

Eichenwald, Kurt. *Conspiracy of Fools*. New York: Broadway Books, 2005.

"El Paso Gas Pushes the New Frontier." *Business Week*, January 26, 1957, 76–85.

Ellig, Jerry. "Intrastate Pipeline Regulation: Lessons from the Texas Experience." In *New Horizons in Natural Gas Regulation*, edited by Jerry Ellig and Joseph Kalt, 159–73. Westport, CT: Praeger, 1996.

Ellig, Jerry, and Joseph Kalt, eds. Introduction to *New Horizons in Natural Gas Deregulation*, xi–xxvi. Westport, CT: Praeger, 1996.

"Employees Honor Jack Bowen." *Transcogram*, June 15, 1987, 1–2.

"Energy Industry Says Carter Plan Neglects Need for Increased Supplies." *HotTap*, April 1977, 1, 4.

Energy Information Administration. *Annual Energy Review 1983*. Washington, DC: U.S. Department of Energy, 1984.

———. *Annual Energy Review 2001*. Washington, DC: U.S. Department of Energy, 2002.

———. *Annual Energy Review 2003*. Washington, DC: U.S. Department of Energy, 2004.

———. *Annual Energy Review 2009*. Washington, DC: Department of Energy. www.eia.doe.gov/emeu/aer/pdf/aer.pdf.

———. *Historical Monthly Energy Review 1973–88*. Washington, DC: U.S. Department of Energy, 1991.

Enron Corp. Annual report, 1990, 1991, 2000.

Epstein, Alex. "Energy at the Speed of Thought: The Original Alternative Energy Market." *The Objective Standard*, Summer 2009, 47–66.

Epstein, Richard. *Simple Rules for a Complex World*. Cambridge, MA: Harvard University Press, 1995.

Executive Office of the President, Energy Policy and Planning. *The National Energy Plan*. Washington, DC: Government Printing Office, 1977.

"The Faithful Service of John H. Kirby." *Southern Tariff Advocate*, February 1930, 1–6.

Feagin, Joe. *Free Enterprise City: Houston in Political and Economic Perspective*. New Brunswick, NJ: Rutgers University Press, 1988.

Federal Energy Regulatory Commission. Various decisions, 1989.

Federal Power Commission. "In the Matter of Columbia Fuel Corp." 1940. In 2 *Federal Power Commission Reports (FPC)* 200. Washington, DC: Government Printing Office, 1940.

———. "In the Matter of El Paso Natural Gas Company, *et al.*" May 31, 1946. In 5 *FPC* 115–29. Washington, DC: Government Printing Office, 1946.

———. "In the Matter of Houston Texas Gas & Oil Corporation and Coastal Transmission Corporation." December 28, 1956. In 16 *FPC* 118–51. Washington, DC: Government Printing Office, 1956.

———. "In the Matter of Northwest Natural Gas Company, *et al.*" 13 *FPC* 221–41, June 18, 1954.

———. "In the Matter of Pacific Northwest Pipeline Corporation, *et al.*" 14 *FPC* 157–85, November 25, 1955.

———. "In the Matter of Pacific Northwest Pipeline Corporation, *et al.* 22 *FPC* 1091, December 23, 1959.

———. "In the Matter of Trans-Continental Pipe Line Company, Inc." In 7 *FPC* 24. Washington, DC: Government Printing Office, 1948.

———. Letter from the Chairman of the Federal Power Commission in response to Senate Resolution 329, 69th Congress, 2nd Session, 1927.

———. Opinion No. 598, 46 *FPC* 86–189. July 16, 1971.

———. Opinion No. 622, 47 *FPC* 1624–1729. June 28, 1971.

———. Opinion No. 622-A, 48 *FPC* 723–40. October 5, 1972.

"Federal Prosecutor Charges All Insull's Aides Knew of Vast Frauds," *Chicago Tribune*, October 5, 1934.

Federal Trade Commission. *Summary Report of the Federal Trade Commission to the Senate of the United States Pursuant to Senate Resolution No. 88*, 70th Congress, 1st Session. Economic, Financial, and Corporate Phases of Holding and Operating Companies of Electric and Gas Utilities No. 72-A, at 43. Washington, DC: Government Printing Office, 1935.

Fellows, Kenneth. *Houston Natural Gas Corporation: Its First Fifty Years, 1925–1975.* Houston, TX: Houston Natural Gas, 1976.

"FERC Rejection a Disappointment." *The Energizer*, July 31, 1989, 1.

Fiftieth Anniversary Commemoration (Samuel Insull, 1881–1931), bound booklet of proceedings, Chicago, 1931. (Copy in author's possession.)

"Financial Analysts Query Henderson after Speech." *HotTap*, November 15, 1971, 1–2.

Fire Prevention and Engineering Bureau of Texas and the National Board of Fire Underwriters. *Texas City, Texas, Disaster: April 16–17, 1947.* www.local1259iaff.org/report.htm.

Fish, Ray. "… and the Story of the Builders [of Transcontinental]." *Oil and Gas Journal*, May 4, 1950, 84–85.

———. "Free Enterprise Brings New Energy to the Booming Pacific Northwest." *Petroleum Engineer*, October 1956, 2–3.

———. "Remarks to Washington-Oregon Chamber Managers and Officers, Portland, Oregon. February 7, 1956.

———. "Salesmanship: Letter to the Employees of the Fish and Affiliated Companies," January 1, 1960. (Copy in author's possession.)

Fish Engineering Corporation. *Facilities of Fish for Design and Construction in the Oil, Gas and Allied Industries.* Houston, TX: circa 1951.

———. *Fish Service Corporation.* Houston, TX: circa 1956.

———. *Progress Report.* Houston, TX: circa 1955.

Fish Foundation. *Ray C. Fish Foundation*. Kerrville, TX: Braswell Printing Company, 1996.

Florida Gas Company. "Agreement of Merger." In "Notice of Special Meeting of Shareholders to be Held on August 28, 1979," August 2, 1979.

———. Annual report, various years.

———. *Second Quarter 1978 Interim Report*, August 11, 1978.

———. *Statistical Summary: 1972–1976*, undated. (Copy in author's possession.)

"Florida's First Fuel Cell Powerplant Tested." *Gaslite News*, December 1972, 5.

Flynn, John. "J. Pierpont Morgan: The Promoter." In Flynn, *Men of Wealth*, 452–513. New York: Simon and Schuster, 1941.

Franks, Zarko. "The Industry Marveled at Herring, But Success Didn't Surprise Him." *Houston Chronicle*, December 21, 1969.

"Frank Smith Heads National Gas Group." *Houston Press*, October 30, 1952.

Fredrickson, Eric. *Andrews & Kurth L.L.P.: The First Hundred Years of Excellence*. Houston, TX: Andrews & Kurth, 2002.

Friedel, Robert, and Paul Israel. *Edison's Electric Light: Biography of an Invention*. New Brunswick, NJ: Rutgers University Press, 1986.

Friedman, Milton. "Which Way for Capitalism?" *Reason*, May 1977, 18–21, 61.

"Gas Industry Organizes Research Institute." *HotTap*, August 1976, 4.

Gas Pipeline Mergers. Hearing before the Subcommittee on Fossil and Synthetic Fuels of the Committee on Energy and Commerce, House of Representatives, 98th Cong., 2nd sess., 1984, 44–59.

"The Gas Pipelines: A New Set of Rules? *Forbes*, September 1, 1963, 20–23.

Gaworowski, Joanna. "Combined Admission History and Discharge Summary: Judith Diane Ayers Lay," Highland Hospital, Ashville, NC. September 1981. (Copy in author's possession.)

———. "Records from Divorce Proceedings between Kenneth L. Lay and Judith A. Lay," Civil Action No. 81–4125, Ninth Judicial Circuit in and for Orange County, Florida.

"Gladys Wallis to Wed." *San Francisco Bulletin*, May 20, 1899.

Gleisser, Marcus. *The World of Cyrus Eaton*, rev. ed. Kent, OH: Kent State University Press, 2005.

Goldberger, Paul. "Philip Johnson Is Dead at 98; Architecture's Restless Intellect." *New York Times*, January 27, 2005.

Gooch, Gordon. "Current Developments in FPC and Natural Gas Matters." In *23 Oil and Gas Institute*, 1972, 99–109.

Gordon, John Steele. *An Empire of Wealth: The Epic of American Economic Power*. New York: HarperCollins, 2004.

Granville, Maurice. "Petroleum's Role from Now to the End of the Century." *Petroleum/2000: Seventy-fifth Anniversary Issue*, August 1977, 57–62.

Gray, John. "Competition and Capitalization, as Controlled by the Massachusetts Gas Commission." *Quarterly Journal of Economics*, February 1901, 254–76.

———. "The Gas Commission of Massachusetts." *Quarterly Journal of Economics*, August 1900, 509–36.

Gray, Steve. "Changing of the Guard." *HotTap*, July 1984, 2–3.

———. "A Decade of Leadership." *HotTap*, October 1984, 16–18.

———. "A Diplomat for Our Times." *HotTap*, June 1987, 2–5.

"Great Plains Goes!" *Transcogram*, August 31, 1981, 1–2.

"The Great Plains Saga." *HotTap*, September 1981, 8–13.

"Greece: Ideal Justice." *Time*, November 13, 1933. www.time.com/time/magazine/article/0,9171,746302,00.html.

"Greece: Popp & Xeros' Client." *Time*, March 26, 1934. www.time.com/time/magazine/ article/0,9171,747234,00.html.

Groner, Alex. *The History of American Business and Industry*. New York: American Heritage, 1972.

Gross, Bertram. *The Legislative Struggle: A Study in Social Combat*. New York, McGraw-Hill, 1953.

Guennewig, Vicki. "DesBarres Leading Transco to a New Frontier." *The Energizer*, October 15, 1991, 1–2.

Gunderson, Gerald. *The Wealth Creators: An Entrepreneurial History of the United States*. New York: Truman Talley, 1989.

Hale, Karen. "Bowen: 'Progress is Being Made.'" *The Energizer*, April 30, 1991, 1.

———. "DesBarres Leading Transco to a New Frontier." *The Energizer*, October 15, 1991, 1–3.

———. "Slocum: 'Time to Make a Change.'" *The Energizer*, March 28, 1991, 1.

———. "Slocum: 'Transco's 1990 Operating Results Show Promise.'" *The Energizer*, March 15, 1991, 1–2.

Hale, Leon. "John Henry Kirby Was a Great One for Naming Towns." *Houston Post*, May 19, 1960.

———. "Thank God and John Henry Kirby." *Houston Post*, September 4, 1979.

Hall, J. W. "Double Jointing for Transcontinental Project." *Oil and Gas Journal*, May 4, 1950, 94–96.

Hammond, John. *Men and Volts: The Story of General Electric*. New York: J. B. Lippincott, 1941.

Hansard, Sara. "FERC Rips Transco Settlement, Threatens Marketing Divestiture." *Natural Gas Week*, July 17, 1989, 1, 5, 11.

———. "FERC Scrambles Transco; Customers Eye $50 Million Cost." *Natural Gas Week*, July 24, 1989, 1, 6–7.

———. "FERC Slaps Record Penalty on Transco for Violating Rules." *Natural Gas Week*, June 3, 1991, 1, 9–10.

Hanson, Eric. *Dynamic Decade*. Toronto: McClelland & Steward Limited, 1958.

Hayes, Thomas. "Gas Pipelines Seen as Merger Targets." *New York Times*, January 13, 1986.

———. "Recruiting Via Acquisitions." *New York Times*, November 30, 1979.

Heady, Kenneth. "Gas Producer Regulation in a New Environment." *Proceedings of the Institute on Oil and Gas Law* 24 (1973): 1–23.

"Here Are Prize Winners in Ranger Baby Contest." *Fort Worth Star-Telegram*, January 28, 1923.

Herring, Robert Ray. Speeches, 1957–80. Woodson Research Center, Fondren Library, Rice University.

Higgs, Robert. "Regime Uncertainty: Why the Great Depression Lasted so Long and Why Prosperity Resumed after the War." *Independent Review*, I, no. 4 (Spring 1997): 561–90.

High, Jack. "Regulation as a Process: On the Theory, History, and Doctrine of Government Regulation." In *Austrian Economics: Perspectives on the Past and Prospects for the Future,* edited by Richard Ebeling, 261–79. Hillsdale, MI: Hillsdale College Press, 1991.

"HNG Acquires Alamo." *Houston Chronicle,* June 20, 1980.

HNG/InterNorth. "America's Premier Energy Company," 1985.

Hodge, Shelby. "At Home: Joanne King Herring." *Houston Post,* August 11, 1979.

Hogan, John. *A Spirit Capable: The Story of Commonwealth Edison.* Chicago: Mobium Press, 1986.

Holmes, Ann. "Herring-do: New Rice U. Building Blends New, Old with Wit and Grace." *Houston Chronicle,* August 12, 1984.

Hoover, Herbert. "Letter to Judge James H. Wilkerson Accepting His Request Not to Resubmit His Nomination to the Seventh Circuit Court of Appeals," December 6, 1932. The American Presidency Project, http://www.presidency.ucsb.edu/ws/index.php?pid=23375#axzz1JtTWvg1o.

"Hoover Names Wilkerson to Appeal Court." *Chicago Tribune,* January 13, 1932.

"HotTap Reviews Journal's Interview of Mitchell." *HotTap,* April 15, 1972, 3.

"Houston: A City Coming of Age." *Fortune,* January 30, 1978, 24, 27–28, 30, 36, 40, 43, 45.

The Houston Corporation. Annual reports, various years.

"Houston Corp. Picks President, Revises Debt, Maps Expansion." *New York Times,* December 2, 1960.

"Houston Gas Corp. Sets Acquisition." *New York Times,* June 20, 1980.

Houston Natural Gas Corporation. Annual report, various years.

———. *Form 10-K for the Five Months Ending December 31, 1984.*

———. *Form S-1 Registration Statement to the Securities and Exchange Commission,* July 22, 1958.

———. *Natural Gas for Florida.* St. Petersburg, FL: Houston Corporation, 1959.

———. "Natural Gas Has Anniversary Here," press release, June 9, 1960.

———. Press releases, May 27, 1960; July 11, 1960.

———. Remarks [by several executives] before the New York Society of Security Analysts, July 20, 1977, New York City.

———. *The Safety Valve,* June 1953.

"Houston Natural to Buy CO_2 Maker." *Oil and Gas Journal,* February 10, 1968, 84.

Houston Oil Company of Texas. "Prospectus." 1911. Kirby Lumber Company, East Texas Research Center, Stephen F. Austin State University, Records, Box 173.

Howe, C. D. "Address to the Canadian Institute of Mining and Metallurgy." Calgary, Alberta, November 29, 1955.

———. Correspondence with Clint Murchison, 1951–1960. (Copies in author's possession.)

Howell, Paul, and Ira Hart. "The Promoting and Financing of Transcontinental Gas Pipe Line Corporation. *Journal of Finance* 6, no. 3 (September 1951): 311–24.

Hughes, Thomas. *Networks of Power: Electrification in Western Society, 1880–1930.* Baltimore: Johns Hopkins University Press, 1983.

Hunt, E. T. E; F. G. Tryon; and Joseph H. Willits. *What the Coal Commission Found: An Authoritative Summary by the Staff.* Baltimore: Williams & Wilkins, 1925.

"Industrialist Ray Fish Dies at Miami Beach." *Houston Chronicle*, December 8, 1962.

Insull, Samuel. "Broad Questions of Public Policy." Remarks to the public-policy committee of the National Electric Light Association, Chicago, June 4, 1913. Reprinted in *Central-Station Electric Service*, 405–413.

———. "Can a Ten-Thousand-Dollar Man Be Made?" Address to the annual meeting of the Commonwealth Edison Company Section of the National Electric Light Association, Chicago, November 10, 1915. In Insull, *Public Utilities in Modern Life*, 33–39.

———. "Careers of Two Electrical Men." Remarks to the Commonwealth Edison Company Section of the National Electric Light Association, Chicago, December 5, 1911. Greater part reprinted in Insull, *Central-Station Electric Service*, 241–42.

———. "Centralization of Energy Supply." Lecture to the Finance Forum of the Young Men's Christian Association, New York, April 20, 1914. Reprinted in Insull, *Central-Station Electric Service*, 445–75.

———. *Central-Station Electric Service: Its Commercial Development and Economic Significance as Set Forth in the Public Addresses (1897–1914) of Samuel Insull*. Chicago: privately printed, 1915.

———. "A Certain Hostility to Public-Service Corporations." Lecture to the Commercial Club of Chicago, December 9, 1911. Reprinted in Insull, *Central-Station Electric Service*, 243–48.

———. "Chicago Central-Station Development—1892–1922 and Thereafter." Lecture to the Western Society of Engineers, Chicago, February 1, 1923. Reprinted in Insull, *Public Utilities in Modern Life*, 368–84.

———. "City Club Discussion of the 21,000-Kilowatt Contract with the Chicago City Railway Company." Discussion at the City Club of Chicago, October 19, 1908. Portions of a report on the discussion printed in Insull, *Central-Station Electric Service*, 65–72.

———. "Co-Operative Societies of Employees." Lecture to the Annual Joint Conference under Employees' Representation Plan of the Peoples Gas Light and Coke Company, Chicago, February 23, 1922. Reprinted in Insull, *Public Utilities in Modern Life*, 316–18.

———. "The Development of the Central Station." Lecture to the Electrical Engineering Department of Purdue University, Lafayette, IN, May 17, 1898. Reprinted in Insull, *Central-Station Electric Service*, 8–33.

———. "Developments in Electric Utility Operating." Lecture to the Pittsfield (MA) Section of the American Institute of Electrical Engineers, March 14, 1917. Condensed version printed in Insull, *Public Utilities in Modern Life*, 108–132.

———. "Economic Significance of Electricity Supply." Lecture at a dinner for the National Association of Railway Commissioners, San Francisco, October 13, 1915. Reprinted in Insull, *Public Utilities in Modern Life*, 26–32.

———. "The Electrical Industry and the War." Lecture to the Electrical Development League, San Francisco, March 27, 1918. Reprinted in Insull, *Public Utilities in Modern Life*, 145–51.

———. "Electrical Securities." Lecture to the convention of the Investment Bankers' Association of America, Chicago, October 13, 1913. Condensed version printed in Insull, *Central-Station Electric Service*, 427–44.

———. "Elucidation of Electric-Service Rates for Business Men." Remarks delivered at a luncheon at the City Club of Chicago, March 7, 1908. Condensed report printed in Insull, *Central-Station Electric Service*, 54–64.

———. "Employees and Management." Speech at the Annual Joint Conference under Employees' Representation Plan of the People Gas Light and Coke Company, February 23, 1922. Printed in Insull, *Public Utilities in Modern Life*, 319–21.

———. "Employees Urged to Study Economic Questions." Lecture to the Commonwealth Edison Company Section of the National Electric Light Association, Chicago, November 1, 1910. Reprinted in Insull, *Central-Station Electric Service*, 158–66.

———. "The Engineer's Influence in Public Utilities." Lecture to the Western Society of Engineers, Chicago, April 2, 1920. Reprinted in Insull, *Public Utilities in Modern Life*, 207–15.

———. "The Final Test of Welfare Work." Remarks to the public-policy committee of the National Electric Light Association, New York City, May 31, 1911. Reprinted in Insull, *Central-Station Electric Service*, 193–96.

———. "Future Expansion in the Use of Central-Station Power." Lecture to the annual convention of the National Electric Light Association, Chicago, June 1, 1921. Condensed version printed in Insull, *Public Utilities in Modern Life*, 240–49.

———. "The Gas Industry's Biggest Task." Lecture to the annual convention of the American Gas Association, Chicago, November 11, 1921. Reprinted in Insull, *Public Utilities in Modern Life*, 252–62.

———. "Illinois in the War." Lecture to the Commercial Club of Chicago, January 18, 1919. Reprinted in Insull, *Public Utilities in Modern Life*, 166–77.

———. "Influence of Engineering on Modern Civilization." Lecture for the dedication of the Transportation Building and the Locomotive and Mining Laboratories of the University of Illinois, Urbana, IL, May 8, 1913. Reprinted in Insull, *Central-Station Electric Service*, 392–98.

———. "Just as One Friend to Another." Lecture to the annual meeting of the Peoples Gas Club, Chicago, December 6, 1923. Condensed version printed in Insull, *Public Utilities in Modern Life*, 396–403.

———. "The Larger Aspects of Making and Selling Electrical Energy." Lecture to the Association of Edison Illuminating Companies, September 1, 1909. Reprinted in Insull, *Central-Station Electric Service*, 73–96.

———. Letter to J. E. Kingsbury, May 1, 1881. Reprinted in Insull, *Central-Station Electric Service*, xxxvi–xxxix.

———. "Looking Backward." Lecture to the Public Service Company of Northern Illinois Section of the National Electric Light Association (second division), Chicago, October 24, 1919. Reprinted in Insull, *Public Utilities in Modern Life*, 184–98.

———. "Massing of Energy Production an Economic Necessity." Lecture to a General Electric Company dinner, Boston, February 25, 1910. Reprinted in Insull, *Central-Station Electric Service*, 127–43.

———. *The Memoirs of Samuel Insull*. Polo, IL: Transportation Trails, 1934, 1992.

———. "My Business Is Your Business." Lecture to the Peoria, IL, Chamber of Commerce, March 11, 1921. Reprinted in Insull, *Public Utilities in Modern Life*, 224–39.

———. "The Necessity of the Appraisal of Public-Utility Properties." Remarks to the National Electric Light Association, New York City, June 2, 1911. Reprinted in Insull, *Central-Station Electric Service*, 197–98.

———. "'The Obligation of Monopoly Must Be Accepted." Lecture to H. M. Byllesby & Co. and affiliated companies, January 7, 1910. Condensed version printed in Insull, *Central-Station Electric Service*, 118–22.

———. "Opportunity for Advancement." Lecture to the Commonwealth Edison Company Section of the National Electric Light Association, Chicago, November 1, 1911. Reprinted in Insull, *Central-Station Electric Service*, 234–40.

———. "Outlook for Technical Education." Lecture to the Department of Superintendence of the National Education Association of the United States, Chicago, February 27, 1922. Reprinted in Insull, *Public Utilities in Modern Life*, 322–29.

———. Papers, 1799–1970. Loyola University Chicago Archives and Special Collections.

———. Papers, Addendum 2, 1899–1960. Loyola University Chicago Archives and Special Collections.

———. "Possibilities of Unified Electricity Supply in the State of Illinois." Lecture to the Commonwealth Edison Company Section of the National Electric Light Association, Chicago, May 15, 1913. Reprinted in Insull, *Central-Station Electric Service*, 399–404.

———. "Present and Future Distribution of Electrical Energy." Lecture to the Cooperation Conference, Association Island, Lake Ontario, NY, September 4, 1913. Reprinted in *Central-Station Electric Service*, 414–26.

———. Presentation of the Edison Medal to Elihu Thomson, February 24, 1910. In Insull, *Central-Station Electric Service*, 123–26.

———. "Present-Day Problems of Public Utilities." Lecture to the Illinois Gas Association, Chicago, March 19, 1919. Reprinted in Insull, *Public Utilities in Modern Life*, 178–83.

———. "Problems of the Edison Central-Station Companies in 1897." Reprinted in Insull, *Central-Station Electric Service*, 1–7.

———. "Production and Distribution of Electric Energy in the Central Portion of the Mississippi Valley." The Cyrus Fogg Brackett Lecture in Applied Engineering Technology, Princeton, NJ, December 1, 1921. Reprinted in Insull, *Public Utilities in Modern Life*, 263–303.

———. "The Production and Distribution of Energy." Lecture to the Franklin Institute, Philadelphia, March 19, 1913. Reprinted in Insull, *Central-Station Electric Service*, 357–91.

———. "Production and Sales of Electrical Energy in Chicago." Lecture to the Electric Club of Chicago, October 20, 1909. A major portion printed in Insull, *Central-Station Electric Service*, 97–102.

———. "Progress of Economic Power Generation and Distribution." Lecture to the joint meeting of the New Haven sections of the Civil, Electrical, Mining, and Mechanical Engineering societies, New Haven, April 5, 1916. Reprinted in Insull, *Public Utilities in Modern Life*, 40–53.

———. *Public Control and Private Operation of Public Service Industries: Municipal Ownership.* Chicago: Other Side Publishing, 1899.

———. *Public Utilities in Modern Life: Selected Speeches (1914–1923).* Chicago: privately printed, 1924.

———. "Public-Utility Commissions and Their Relations with Public-Utility Companies. Address to a joint session of the Iowa Section of the National Electric Light Association, the Iowa Street and Railway Association, and the Iowa District Gas Association. Condensed version printed in Insull, *Public Utilities in Modern Life*, 54–68.

———. "A Quarter Century Anniversary." Speech to the Commonwealth Edison Company, Chicago, June 25, 1917. Reprinted in Insull, *Public Utilities in Modern Life*, 133–37.

———. "A Quarter-Century Central-Station Anniversary Celebration in Chicago—1887–1912." Lecture to the Commonwealth Edison Company Section of the National Electric Light Association, Chicago, April 29, 1912. Condensed version printed in Insull, *Central-Station Electric Service*, 316–37.

———. "The Relation of Central-Station Generation to Railroad Electrification." Lecture to the American Institute of Electrical Engineers, New York City, April 5, 1912. Reprinted in Insull, *Central-Station Electric Service*, 255–307.

———. "Relations of the Public to the Public-Service Corporations." Lecture to the Chicago Engineers' Club, January 24, 1911. Reprinted in Insull, *Central-Station Electric Service*, 182–88.

———. "Rise and Development of the Electric Central Station." Address at a dinner honoring Thomas Alva Edison, New York City, September 11, 1922. In Insull, *Public Utilities in Modern Life*, 330–40.

———. "'Satisfy Your Customer.'" Lecture to a banquet of H. M. Byllesby & Co. and affiliated companies, Chicago, January 20, 1911. Condensed version printed in Insull, *Central-Station Electric Service*, 174–81.

———. "Selling of Electricity in London and Chicago Compared." Lecture to a convention of H. M. Byllesby & Co. and affiliated companies, Chicago, January 18, 1911. Reprinted in Insull, *Central-Station Electric Service*, 167–73.

———. "'Sell Your Product at a Price Which Will Enable You to Get a Monopoly." Lecture to H. M. Byllesby & Company and affiliated companies, Chicago, January 6, 1910. A portion reprinted in Insull, *Central-Station Electric Service*, 116–17.

———. "Service." Lecture to students of the Chicago Central Station Institute, May 7, 1915. Reprinted in Insull, *Public Utilities in Modern Life*, 7–25.

———. "Some Advantages of Monopoly." Address to the Engineers' Club, Dayton, OH, October 6, 1914. Condensed version printed in Insull, *Public Utilities in Modern Life*, 1–6.

———. "Some Comments on the Gas Industry." Address to the American Gas Association, 9th Annual Convention, Chicago, October 12, 1927. (Copy in author's possession.)

———. "Some Remarks on Diversity and Rate Making." Lecture to the National Commercial Gas Association, Atlantic City, NJ, November 14, 1916. Reprinted in Insull, *Public Utilities in Modern Life*, 69–107.

———. "Some Reminiscences of Business." Address to a joint meeting of the Kentucky Association of Public Utilities and the faculty and students of the University of Kentucky, Lexington, KY, December 12, 1922. Condensed report of the address reprinted in Insull, *Public Utilities in Modern Life*, 362–67.

———. "Standardization, Cost System of Rates, and Public Control." Lecture delivered to the National Electric Light Association, Chicago, June 7, 1898. Reprinted in Insull, *Central-Station Electric Service*, 34–47.

———. "Stepping Stones of Central-Station Development through Three Decades." Lecture to the Brooklyn Edison Company Section of the National Electric Light Association, June 26, 1912. Condensed version printed in Insull, *Central-Station Electric Service*, 342–56.

———. "Supplying the Energy Requirements of the Community." Lecture to the City Club of Chicago, May 23, 1912. Reprinted in part in Insull, *Central-Station Electric Service*, 338–41.

———. "Thirty Years of Chicago Central-Station History." Lecture to the University Club, Chicago, September 20, 1922. Condensed version printed in Insull, *Public Utilities in Modern Life*, 341–52.

———. "Thirty Years of Electrical Development—1879–1909." Lecture delivered to the annual meeting of the Electrical Trades Association of Chicago, Chicago, November 12, 1909. Reprinted in Insull, *Central-Station Electric Service*, 103–115.

———. "Twenty-five Years of Central-Station Commercial Development." Lecture delivered at the convention of the National Electric Light Association, St. Louis, MO, May 25, 1910. Reprinted in Insull, *Central-Station Electric Service*, 144–57.

———. "Utilities in Wartime—A Note of Assurance." Lecture to the National Electric Light Association, Atlantic City, NJ, June 13, 1918. Condensed version printed in Insull, *Public Utilities in Modern Life*, 152–59.

———. "'We Have Come Out of a Terrible Night'." Lecture to the Commonwealth Edison Company Section of the National Electric Light Association, Chicago, November 20, 1918. Condensed version printed in Insull, *Public Utilities in Modern Life*, 160–65.

———. "What Preparedness Meant in Wartime Utility Service." Lecture to the Commonwealth Edison Company Section of the National Electric Light Association, Chicago, October 25, 1917. Condensed report printed in Insull, *Public Utilities in Modern Life*, 138–44.

———. "Why I Am in the Utility Business." Lecture to the Luncheon Club, Springfield, IL, January 25, 1922. Reprinted in Insull, *Public Utilities in Modern Life*, 304–15.

"Insull Faces Two More Trials to Win Vindication." *Chicago Tribune,* November 25, 1934.

"Insuring Gas Supply." *Transgas*, July–August 1971, 8.

"An Interview with Selby Sullivan," *Insight* (Continental Group), August–October 1979, 6–7.

"Iran: The Country and Its People." *Transgas*, November–December 1973, 3–6.

Israel, Paul. *Edison: A Life of Invention*. New York: John Wiley, 1998.

Jarboe, Jan. "Meaner than a Junkyard Dog." *Texas Monthly*, April 1991, 122, 124, 126–27, 154, 156–63.

Jehl, Francis. *Menlo Park Reminiscences*. Dearborn, MI: Edison Institute, 1937.

Jeter, Lynne. *Disconnected: Deceit and Betrayal at WorldCom*. New York: John Wiley, 2003.

Jevons, W. S. *The Coal Question: An Inquiry Concerning the Progress of the Nation and the Probable Exhaustion of our Coal Mines*. London: Macmillan, 1865; 2nd ed., 1866; 3rd ed., edited by A. W. Flux, 1906. Reprint, New York: Augustus M. Kelley, 1965.

"J. H. Kirby Is Paid Tribute." *Houston Post-Dispatch*, November 18, 1930, 1, 9.

"John Henry Kirby." *Beaumont Journal*, November 11, 1940.

"John Henry Kirby: Founder of Epoch in Texas Industry, State's Benefactor." *Houston Post*, November 11, 1940.

"John H. Kirby Addresses Mill Workers." *Southern Industrial and Lumber Review*, July 1912, 32–33.

"John H. Kirby Is Honored on His Birthday." *Houston Chronicle*, November 18, 1935, 6.

Jonnes, Jill. *Empires of Light: Edison, Tesla, Westinghouse, and the Race to Electrify the World*. New York: Random House, 2003.

Josephson, Matthew. *Edison: A Biography*. New York: McGraw-Hill, 1959.

———. *The Robber Barons: The Great American Capitalists, 1861–1901*. New York: Harcourt, Brace, 1934.

Joskow, Paul. "Regulatory Activities by Government Agencies." Cambridge, MA: Massachusetts Institute of Technology, Department of Economics Working Paper No. 171, 1975.

Judah, Melvin, and Donald Pugh. "Coastal Transmission Combines Proven Methods with Promising Advances." *Pipe Line Industry*, June 1959, 40–46.

"Ken Lay Elected Vice President of Transgulf Pipeline." *Gaslite News*, September–October 1974, 4.

Keynes, John Maynard. *The General Theory of Employment, Interest, and Money*. 1936. Reprint, New York: Prometheus Books, 1997.

Kilbourn, William. *The Making of the Nation: A Century of Challenge*. Toronto: Canadian Centennial Library, 1965.

———. *PipeLine*. Toronto: Clarke, Irwin & Company, 1970.

Kilman, Ed. "John Henry Kirby Truly Has Lived His Credo." *Houston Post*, December 12, 1937.

———. "Were You at That Rice Banquet, Eight Courses and Six Wines?" *Houston Post*, September 13, 1953.

King, Clyde. *The Regulation of Municipal Utilities*. New York: D. Appleton and Company, 1914.

King, John. *The Early History of the Houston Oil Company of Texas, 1901–1908*. Houston: Texas Gulf Coast Historical Association, 1959.

———. *Joseph Stephen Cullinan: A Study of Leadership in the Texas Petroleum Industry, 1901–1908*. Nashville, TN: Vanderbilt University Press, 1970.

Kinsley, Philip. *Chicago Tribune* Insull trial articles, 1934: October 2, 3, 11, 16, 19, 27, 30; November 1, 2, 3, 6, 20, 23, 24, 25.

Kirby, John Henry. Private Letters. East Texas Research Center, Stephen F. Austin State University.

Kirby Lumber Archive (Kirby Lumber Corporation 1901–85). Forest History Collection, East Texas Research Center, Stephen F. Austin State University.

Kirby Lumber Company. *John Henry Kirby*. Houston, TX: Kirby Lumber Company, 1951.

"Kirby Receiver Granted Bonus by Court Order." *Houston Press*, July 29, 1936, 9.

Kirsch, David. *The Electric Vehicle and the Burden of History*. New Brunswick, NJ: Rutgers University Press, 2000.

Kirzner, Israel. "The Perils of Regulation: A Market-Process Approach." In *Discovery and the Capitalist Process*, edited by Israel Kirzner, 119–49. Chicago: University of Chicago Press, 1985.

Klein, Maury. *The Power Makers: Steam, Electricity, and the Men Who Invented Modern America*. New York: Bloomsbury Press, 2008.

Knight, Carleton, III. "High-Tech Skin on a Form from an Earlier Era." *Architecture*, May 1985, 182–86.

Koch, Charles. "Let's Try a Free Market in Energy." *Libertarian Review*, August 1977, 34–37. Also available at www.masterresource.org/2010/10/koch-energy-policy-ii-1977/.

———. *The Science of Success*. Hoboken, NJ: John Wiley & Sons, 2007.

Lane, James, Jr. *Proud Journey: The History of Stearns-Roger*. Denver, CO: Colorado Historical Society, 1976.

Larson, Henrietta. *Guide to Business History: Materials for the Study of American Business History and Suggestions for their Use*. Boston: J. S. Canner & Company, 1948. Reprinted 1964.

Lasswell, Mary. *John Henry Kirby: Prince of the Pines*. Austin, TX: Encino Press, 1967.

Lavoie, Donald. "The Development of the Misesian Theory of Interventionism." In *Method, Process, and Austrian Economics*, edited by Israel Kirzner, 169–83. Lexington, MA: Lexington Books, 1982.

Lawrence, George. "Gas Industry Outlook Good for 2000." *Petroleum/2000: Seventy-fifth Anniversary Issue*, August 1977, 71–72.

Lay, Judith. "Answer and Counter Petition for Dissolution of Marriage including Partition of Real Property," IN RE: The Marriage of Kenneth L. Lay, Petitioner/ Husband, and Judith A. Lay, Respondent/Wife, Orlando, Florida, February 4, 1982. From "Records from Divorce Proceedings between Kenneth L. Lay and Judith A. Lay," Civil Action No. 81–4125, Ninth Judicial Circuit in and for Orange County, Florida.

Lay, Ken. "Coal Pipeline, Transgulf Projects Move Ahead in New Developments." *Energetic People*, Winter 1981, 1.

———. "Deposition IN RE: The Marriage of Kenneth L. Lay, Petitioner/Husband, and Judith A. Lay, Respondent/Wife, Orlando, Florida, February 4, 1982. From "Records from Divorce Proceedings between Kenneth L. Lay and Judith A. Lay," Civil Action No. 81–4125, Ninth Judicial Circuit in and for Orange County, Florida.

———. "The Energy Industry in the Next Century: Opportunities and Constraints." In *Energy after 2000*, edited by Irwin Stelzer, pp. 13–25. VIII Repsol-Harvard Seminar, June 1997.

———. "Letter to The Honorable Philip R. Sharp." January 12, 1983. Reprinted in *Natural Gas Contract Renegotiations and FERC Authorities*, Hearings before the Subcommittee on Fossil and Synthetic Fuels of the Committee on Energy and Commerce, United States House of Representatives, 98th Cong., 1st Sess., 1983, 458–61.

———. "Transco Energy Company." *HotTap*, March 1983, 3; April 1984, 3.

———. "Transcontinental Gas Pipe Line Corp." *HotTap*, March 1982, 4.

"Leo Hassenauer Reported in Line for Green's Post. Backed as U.S. Prosecutor by 3 New Deal Chiefs." *Chicago Tribune*, January 19, 1935.

Lewis, Pamela. "Fitting Right In: Pelli's Herring Hall Harmonious Addition to Rice Campus." *Houston Post*, April 12, 1983.

Lincoln, Freeman. "Big Wheeler-Dealer from Dallas." *Fortune*, January 1953, 117–20, 126, 130, 132, 134, 136, 139.

———. "Big Wheeler-Dealer from Dallas." *Fortune*, February 1953, 152–54, 226, 229, 231–33, 235–37.

"List 205 Insull 'Insiders.'" *Chicago Tribune*, September 23, 1932.

"LNG Purchase." *Transgas*, March–April 1972, 2.

Lollar, John. "Transco Exploration Company." *HotTap*, March 1983, 5.

Lueck, Thomas. "Fight Seen in Offer for Houston Gas." *New York Times*, January 28, 1984.

Machiavelli, Niccolò. "Discourses on Livy." *The Portable Machiavelli*. Edited and translated by Peter Bondanella and Mark Musa, 167–418. New York: Penguin, 1979.

Madison, James. "The Federalist No. 44" (1788). *The Federalist: A Commentary on the Constitution of the United States*, 289–97. New York: Modern Library, 1941.

Malik, Om. *Broadbandits: Inside the $750 Billion Telecom Heist*. Hoboken, NJ: Wiley, 2003.

"A Man for All Reasons." *Transgas*, September–October 1974, 3.

Mangan, Frank. *The Pipeliners: The Story of El Paso Natural Gas*. El Paso, TX: Guynes Press, 1977.

"The Many Wars of Gardiner Symonds." *Forbes*, May 15, 1957, 17–20.

Marshall, J. Howard, II. *Done in Oil*. College Station: Texas A&M University Press, 1994.

"Mattox Sues to Protect Natural Gas Consumers." Press release, February 10, 1984. Reprinted in *Gas Pipeline Mergers*. Hearing before the Subcommittee on Fossil and Synthetic Fuels of the Committee on Energy and Commerce, House of Representatives, 98th Cong., 2nd sess., 1984, 44–59.

Maurice, Beverly. "The Bob Herrings: Constant Hosts Have Charity Event Formula: Food, Fun and Fast." *Houston Chronicle*, December 5, 1979.

Maxwell, Robert, and Robert Baker. *Sawdust Empire: The Texas Lumber Industry, 1830–1940*. College Station: Texas A&M University Press, 1983.

May, George. "Accounting and Regulation." *Journal of Accountancy*, October 1943, 295–301.

McComb, David. *Houston: A History*. Austin: University of Texas, 1981.

McConn, Melinda. "The Acquisition of Florida Gas Company by the Continental Group." MBA thesis, University of Texas at Austin, May 1981.

McCormick, Blaine. *At Work with Thomas Edison*. Irvine, CA: McGraw-Hill/Entrepreneur Press, 2001.

McDonald, Forrest. *Insull*. Chicago: University of Chicago Press, 1962. Reprinted, Washington. DC: Beard Books, 2004.

———. *Recovering the Past*. Lawrence: University Press of Kansas, 1994.

———. "Samuel Insull and the Movement for State Utility Regulatory Commissions." *Business History Review* 32 (1958): 241–54.

McDonald, Stephen. "Erich Zimmermann, the Dynamics of Resourceship." In *Economic Mavericks: The Texas Institutionalists*, edited by Ronnie Phillips, 151–83. Greenwich, CT: JAI Press, 1995.

McGraw, E. Clyde. "First Mission Accomplished." *Transgas*, December 1952, 3, 46.

McKie, James. "Regulation and the Free Market: The Problem of Boundaries." *Bell Journal of Economics*, Spring 1970, 6–26.

McLean, Bethany, and Peter Elkind. "The Guiltiest Guys in the Room." CNNMoney.com, July 5, 2006, http://money.cnn.com/ 2006/05/29/news/ enron_guiltyest/ index.htm.

———. *The Smartest Guys in the Room*. New York: Portfolio, 2003.

McLean, John, and Robert Haigh. *The Growth of Integrated Oil Companies*. Boston: Harvard University Graduate School of Business Administration, 1954.

McNealy, Pat. "Romance of John Henry Kirby." *Houston Post-Dispatch*, November 16, 1930.

"Meet G. M. Mitchell." *Transgas*, July–August 1971, 3.

Mises, Ludwig von. *Human Action*. Chicago: Henry Regnery, 1966.

———. *Theory and History: An Interpretation of Social and Economic Evolution*. Auburn, AL: Ludwig von Mises Institute, 1985.

Mitchell, G. M. *President's Monthly Newsletter #245*, August 23, 1974. (Copy in author's possession.)

"Mitchell Tells Stockholders of Company Transition Plan." *HotTap*, April 15, 1973, 1.

Moffett, Matt. "Lay Doubles Houston Natural Gas's Size in Only 6 Months as Chairman and Chief." *Wall Street Journal*, December 4, 1984.

Mom, Gijs. *The Electric Vehicle: Technology and Expectations in the Automobile Age*. Baltimore: Johns Hopkins University Press, 2004.

Moody, Rush, and Allan Garten. "The Natural Gas Policy Act of 1978: Analysis and Overview." *Rocky Mountain Mineral Law Institute* 25, no. 2 (1979): 1–93.

"More Evidence on Insull Stock 'Rigging' Bared." *Chicago Tribune*, October 14, 1934.

Muller, Jerry. *The Mind and the Market: Capitalism in Modern European Thought*. New York: Anchor Books, 2002.

Munson, Richard. *From Edison to Enron: The Business of Power and What It Means for the Future of Electricity*. Westport, CT: Greenwood, 2005.

Murchison, Clint. Correspondence with C. D. Howe, 1951–1960. (Copies in author's possession.)

Myres, Samuel. *The Permian Basin: Petroleum Empire of the Southwest*. El Paso, TX: Permian Press, 1977.

"Name 318 in New Insull List." *Chicago Tribune*, September 30, 1932.

"Names of Favored Insull Stock Subscribers." *Chicago Tribune*, September 23, 1932.

"Natural Gas." *Forbes*, January 1, 1957, 62–66.

Natural Gas Clearinghouse. *A Decade of Excellence in Energy 1984–1994*. Houston, TX: NGC, 1994.

Natural Gas Legislation. Statement of James V. Walzel, President, Houston Pipe Line Co. Hearings before the Committee on Energy and Natural Resources, United States Senate, 98th Cong., 1st sess., 1983, 491–519.

"Natural Gas: The View from Transco." *Energy Daily*, October 22, 1982, 2–4.

Natural Gas Week. Various issues, 1987–92.

"The New Athenians." *Time*, May 24, 1954, 90–96.

"New Chapter in HPL's 58 Year Success Story." *HNG Magazine*, Winter 1983, 1–3.

"New Learjet Delivered to Houston." *Transcogram*, May 29, 1981, 1.

Newman, Peter. *Promise of the Pipeline*. Calgary: TransCanada PipeLines Limited, 1993.

"News in Review." *HotTap*, November 1982, 15.

"Newsmen Query President on Company's Future Plans." *HotTap*, May 15, 1972, 1–2.

Noble, Kenneth. "Washington Watch." *New York Times*, December 3, 1984.

"New Tower Will Have Water Wall." *Transcogram*, July 30, 1982, 1.

"The New Transco Tower." *HotTap*, July 1981, 2.

Oates, James. "The Story of the Texas Illinois Natural Gas Pipeline Co.: Its Over-All Purpose and Service Objective." *Oil and Gas Journal*, May 10, 1951, 1–2, 18.

Olasky, Marvin. *Corporate Public Relations: A New Historical Perspective*. Hillsdale, NJ: Lawrence Erlbaum, 1987.

O'Neill, Brian. Testimony on FERC Contract Carriage Proposal at hearings before the Subcommittee on Fossil and Synthetic Fuels of the Committee on Energy and Commerce, United States House of Representatives, 99th Cong., 1st Sess., 1985, 83–101, 161–63.

———. Testimony on Proposed Changes to Natural Gas Laws, at hearings before the Subcommittee on Fossil and Synthetic Fuels of the Committee on Energy and Commerce, United States House of Representatives, 98th Cong., 1st Sess., 1983, vol. 5, 227–42, 333–41.

"O'Neill, Miller Leave Transco; CEO Slocum Promotes Mackie." *Natural Gas Week*, November 23, 1987, 1, 7.

O'Reilly, Cary. "Transco Announces Major Cuts in Spending, Jobs, Assets." *Natural Gas Week*, November 4, 1991, 7.

Pacific Northwest Pipeline Corporation. *Pacific Northwest Pipes*. September 1955.

Paine, Thomas. *Age of Reason* (1795). New York: Wiley, 1942.

Parrish, Michael. *Securities Regulation and the New Deal*. New Haven, CT: Yale University Press, 1970.

Passer, Harold. *The Electrical Manufacturers, 1875–1900*. Cambridge, MA: Harvard University Press, 1953.

Peoples Gas Light & Coke Co. v. Chicago, 194 U.S. 1 (1904), at http://supreme.justia.com/us/194/1/case.html.

Phelan, Charlotte. "Kirby's Bankrupt Estate Will Be Liquidated Soon." *Houston Post*, July 26, 1964.

Phillips, Alan. "Who Will Win the Great Gas Pipeline Stakes?" *MacLean's Magazine*, October 1, 1953, 18–19, 81–86.

Phillips, Ed. *Guts & Guile: True Tales form the Backrooms of the Pipeline Industry*. Vancouver: Douglas & McIntyre, 1990.

"A Pipeliner Takes Over at Gas-Short Transco." *Business Week*, August 31, 1974, 22–23.

Pittman, Alfred. "The Thing That Will Count Most—If You Want to Be Promoted." *American Magazine*, March 1921. (Interview with Samuel Insull, reprint.)

Plachno, Larry. "Preface" in Insull, *The Memoirs of Samuel Insull*, pp. x–xvii.

Platt, Harold. *The Electric City: Energy and the Growth of the Chicago Area, 1880–1930*. Chicago: University of Chicago Press, 1991.

———. *A Treatise on the Law of Public Utilities*. Indianapolis: Bobbs-Merrill, 1933.

Pope, Kyle. "Transco Subsidiary to Exit Galleria Tower." *Houston Chronicle*, June 19, 1991.

Porter, Edward. "Are We Running Out of Oil?" American Petroleum Institute Discussion Paper 081, December 1995.

Posner, Richard. *Natural Monopoly and Its Regulation*. Washington, DC: Cato Institute, 1969, 1999.

"'Possibly Wrong, but Honest,' Is Opening Defense Plea for Insull." *Chicago Tribune*, November 1, 1934.

Pratt, Joseph. *A Managerial History of Consolidated Edison of New York*. New York: Consolidated Edison, 1988.

Pratt, Joseph, and Christopher Castaneda. *Builders: Herman and George R. Brown*. College Station: Texas A&M University Press, 1999.

Prendergast, William. *Public Utilities and the People*. New York: D. Appleton-Century, 1933.

"Presidency: Assistant President?" *Time*, November 12, 1934. www.time.com/time/magazine/article/0,9171,748062,00.html.

"The Presidency: Great Day." *Time*, April 2, 1934 http://205.188.238.109/time/magazine/ article/0,9171,747280,00.html.

""President Meets with News Media after Reporting to Stockholders." *HotTap*, May 15, 1971, 1–2.

President's Materials Policy Commission (Paley Commission). "The Outlook for Energy Sources. Vol. 1, *Resources for Freedom*. Washington, DC: U.S. Government Printing Office, 1952.

Prout, Henry. *A Life of George Westinghouse*. New York: American Society of Mechanical Engineers, 1921.

Raines, Franklin. "Don't Tar Us with an Enron Brush." *Wall Street Journal*, February 25, 2002.

Rajan, Raghuram, and Luigi Zingales. *Saving Capitalism from the Capitalists*. New York: Crown Business, 2003.

Ramsay, M. L. *Pyramids of Power: The Story of Roosevelt, Insull and the Utility Wars*. New York: Bobbs-Merrill, 1937.

"Ray C. Fish of Houston Dead at 60," *Houston Post*, December 8, 1962.

Raymond, James & Associates Institutional Research. *Florida Gas Company*, Report of November 29, 1974.

"Records Show Favored Buyers of Insull Stock." *Chicago Tribune*, September 21, 1932.

"Red Letter Day." *Transgas*, March 1951, 4–7.

Reed, Paul, and Gene Kinney. "The Florida Pipeline." *Oil and Gas Journal*, March 9, 1959, 108–116.

"Regret." *Detroit Free Press*, July 23, 1899.

Richardson, James, and Aaron Teller. "The Impact of Natural Gas on Florida." *Business Research Report Number 107*. Florida Development Commission: December 1957.

"Richberg Tries New Attack to Bar Wilkerson." *Chicago Tribune*, May 7, 1932.

Robbins, Lionel. *The Great Depression*. Auburn, AL: Ludwig von Mises Institute, 1934, 2007.

Rickey, Gail. "John H. Kirby: Generous Father of Industrial Texas." *Houston Business Journal*, June 3, 1985, 1, 10, 11B, 12B.

"Robert Herring Candidate for Congress." *Weekly Chronicle* (Eastland, TX), circa May 1946. (Copy in author's possession.)

"Robert R. Herring." *Houston Post*, October 14, 1981.

"Robert R. Herring: Community Service Remembered by Friends and Colleagues." Texas Heart Institute, *THI Today*, March 1982, 1–4.

"Robert R. Herring of Houston Natural Gas." *Financial World*, March 15, 1980, 28.

Roberts, Leslie. *The Life and Times of Clarence Decatur Howe*. Toronto: Clarke, Irwin & Company Limited, 1957.

Roosevelt, Franklin D. Commonwealth Club Address, September 23, 1932, available at http://webcache.googleusercontent.com/search?q=cache:30MMN8aHia8J:www.emersonkent.com/speeches/commonwealth_club_fdr.htm+FDR,+every+hand+versus+Insull&cd=3&hl=en&ct=clnk&gl=us&source=www.google.com.

Rothbard, Murray. *America's Great Depression*. 1963. Reprint, Los Angeles: Nash, 1972.

Rudolph, Richard, and Scott Ridley. *Power Struggle: The Hundred Year War Over Electricity*. New York: Harper & Row, 1986.

Ruggles, C. O. *Aspects of the Organization, Functions, and Financing of State Public Utility Commissions*. Boston: Harvard University Graduate School of Business Administration, 1937.

Runes, Dagobert, ed. *The Diary and Sundry Observations of Thomas Alva Edison*. New York: Philosophical Library, 1948.

———. "Autobiographical." In *The Diary and Sundry Observations of Thomas Alva Edison*, edited by Dagobert Runes, 43–59. New York: Philosophical Library, 1948.

———. "Education and Work." In *The Diary and Sundry Observations of Thomas Alva Edison*, edited by Dagobert Runes, 107–48. New York: Philosophical Library, 1948.

———. "The Philosophy of Paine." In *The Diary and Sundry Observations of Thomas Alva Edison*, edited by Dagobert Runes, 151–58. New York: Philosophical Library, 1948.

"Sales Activity." *Gaslite News*, August/September 1960, 5.

"Samuel Insull's Useful Life." *Sunday* [Chicago] *Chronicle*, May 28, 1899.

Samuelson, Paul. "Tragicomedy of the Energy Crisis." *Newsweek*, July 2, 1979, 62.

Satterlee, Herbert. *J. Pierpont Morgan: An Intimate Portrait*. New York: Macmillan, 1939.

Saunders, Barbara. "Arrival of Spot Market Clearinghouse Draws Cautious Reviews from Industry." *Natural Gas*, September 1984, 4–6.

Schlesinger, Arthur M., Jr. *The Crisis of the Old Order: The Age of Roosevelt*. New York: Houghton Mifflin, 1957, 1985.

———. *The Disuniting of America*. New York: W. W. Norton, 1998.

———. *The Politics of Upheaval: The Age of Roosevelt*. New York: Houghton Mifflin Company, 1960.

Schumpeter, Joseph. *Capitalism, Socialism and Democracy*. 1942; 3rd ed., 1950. Reprint, New York: Harper & Row, 1962.

Scott, Tom, and Barbara Shook. "Lay Move to HNG Sparks Top Reshuffling." *Houston Chronicle*, June 7, 1984.

"Selby Sullivan Elected to Board, Named Sec.'y, General Counsel." *Gaslite News*, August 1972, 3.

"Selby W. Sullivan Is Elected Vice President of Company." *Gaslite News*, December 1972, 4.

Sellers, Charles. *The Market Revolution: Jacksonian America 1815–1846*. New York: Oxford University Press, 1991.

"Senate to Begin Investigation of Insull Debacle." *Chicago Tribune*, September 24, 1932.

Shook, Barbara. "Takeovers Shape Coastal's History." *Houston Chronicle*, January 17, 1989.

Simon, Julian. *The Ultimate Resource*. Princeton, NJ: Princeton University Press, 1981.

———. *The Ultimate Resource 2*. Princeton, NJ: Princeton University Press, 1996.

Simonds, William. *Edison: His Life, His Work, His Genius*. New York: Blue Ribbon, 1940.

"$660,000 Gift Spurs Drive for Jobless Funds." *Chicago Daily News*, November 24, 1930.

Sloane, Leonard. "Houston, Coastal End Merger Battle." *New York Times*, February 14, 1984.

Sloat, Bill. "A Pipe Dream and a Nightmare." *South Magazine*, September 1978, 28–29.

Slocum, George. Testimony at hearings before the Subcommittee on Energy and Agricultural Taxation of the Committee on Finance, United States Senate, 99th Cong., 2nd Sess., 1986, 270–77, 359.

"Slocum Named President and Chief Operating Officer." *HotTap*, June 1984, 18.

Smil, Vaclav. "The Energy Question, Again." *Current History*, December 2000, 408–12.

Smiles, Samuel. *Duty*. New York: Harper & Brothers, 1881.

———. *Thrift*. New York: A. L. Burt, 1875.

Smith, Adam. *An Inquiry into the Nature and Causes of the Wealth of Nations*. 1776. 2 vols. Edited by R. H. Campbell and A. S. Skinner. Reprint, Indianapolis: Liberty Fund, 1981.

———. *The Theory of Moral Sentiments*. 1759. Edited by D. D. Raphael and A. L. Mcfie. Reprint, Indianapolis: LibertyPress, 1984.

Soapy Joe [pseud.]. "Depression Must Be Over, Soapy Says, as He Sees Gas Moguls in Battle." *Houston Chronicle*, November 9, 1933.

Sobel, Lester, ed. *Energy Crisis: Volume 1, 1969–73*. New York: Facts on File, 1974.

Stanley, Floyd. "Memorandum to All Employees," July 1, 1960. (Copy in author's possession.)

———. "Text of Dedication Address Commemorating the Introduction of Natural Gas Service to the Florida Market," Jacksonville, Florida, June 1, 1959. (Copy in author's possession.)

"The Steady, Swelling Stream." *Transgas*, January–February 1971, 13–20.

Stephenville (TX) Tribune, article circa January 28, 1923. (Copy in author's possession).

Stobaugh, Robert, and Daniel Yergin. "The End of Easy Oil." In *Energy Future: Report of the Energy Project of the Harvard Business School*, edited by Robert Stobaugh and Daniel Yergin, 3–15. New York: Random House, 1979.

Strouse, Jean. *Morgan: American Financier*. New York: Random House, 1999.

Stuart, Alexander. "Jim Bob Moffett Beats the Odds in Wildcatting." *Fortune*, May 5, 1980, 146–50.

Sullivan, Selby. "Initial Responsibilities of Ken Lay – Director of Corporate Planning." Memo of December 31, 1973. (Copy in author's possession.)

"Sullivan New Chief Executive Officer; Bowen Leaves for Transco." *Gaslite News*, September–October 1974, 1.

"Swanson Demands Arrest of Insulls." *Chicago Tribune*, October 5, 1932.

Swartz, Mimi, with Sherron Watkins. *Power Failure: The Inside Story of the Collapse of Enron*. New York: Doubleday, 2003.

Sweeney, James. *The California Electricity Crisis*. Stanford, CA: Hoover Institution Press, 1992.

Szmrecsanyi, Stephen. "InterNorth: The First Fifty Years" (unpublished official history). Omaha, NE: 1981.

Tate, Alfred. *Edison's Open Door*. New York: E. P. Dutton, 1938.

"Temperatures, Gas Supply Plunge as Arctic Air Grips Country." *HotTap*, January 1977, 2–3.

Tenneco Gas. *Fifty Years*. Houston, TX: Tenneco, 1993.

Tennessee Gas and Transmission Company. Annual reports, 1945, 1953–60.

"Testing a Free Market for Gas Pipelines." *Business Week*, May 25, 1981, 46–47.

Texas House of Representatives. *Resolutions on the Life of John Henry Kirby*, April 28, 1941.

"Texas Isn't Big Enough for HNG's Herring." *Business Week*, May 12, 1975, 103–04.

"Third Annual Energy Conference: Opening the Debate." *Time*, April 25, 1977. www.time.com/time/magazine/article/0,9171,918861,00.html.

Thompson, Carl. *Confessions of the Power Trust*. New York: E. P. Dutton & Co., 1932.

Thompson, Tommy. "Herring One of Industry's 'New Breed' in Management." *Houston Chronicle*, December 17, 1967.

"Three Corporate Vice Presidents Named." *HNG Magazine*, Winter 1983, 8.

Timber Resources of East Texas. Chicago: American Lumberman, 1902.

Tobey, Ronald. *Technology as Freedom*. Berkeley: University of California Press, 1996.

Tompkins, Walter. *Little Giant of Signal Hill: An Adventure in American Enterprise*. Englewood Cliffs, NJ: Prentice-Hall, 1964.

Tramdack, Ed. Letter to Mr. & Mrs. L. R. Herring, circa December 1944. (Copy in author's possession).

TransCanada PipeLines. *The Source*, June 2001, 4–5.

Trans-Canada Pipe Lines Limited. *1958 Annual Report*. Calgary, 1959.

"Transco Bails Out on E&P Unit, Blames Low Oil, Gas Prices." *Natural Gas Week*, January 30, 1989, 1, 11.

"Transco CEO Slocum Resigns; Bowen Takes Post Temporarily." *The Energizer*, March 25, 1991, 9.

Transco Companies. "Presentation before the New York Society of Security Analysts," September 15, 1981. Reprinted by Transco Investor Relations.

Transco Companies, Inc. (1974–81) and Transco Energy Company (1982–87) quarterly reports; annual reports (1982–93).

"Transco Cuts Dividend by 50%; Tries to Ease Financial Squeeze." *Natural Gas Week*, July 20, 1987, 7.

Transco Energy Company. *Form 10-K for the fiscal year ended December 31, 1975*.

———. Form 10-K for the period ending December 31, 1994, available at www.sec.gov/Archives/edgar/data/99231/0000950129-95-000242.txt.

———. *Our Legacy: Transco Energy Company*. Houston, TX: Transco, 1995.

———. "Presentation before the New York Society of Security Analysts," September 15, 1983. Reprinted by Transco Investor Relations.

———. *The Transco Tower: 1983*. Houston, TX: Transco Energy Company, 1983.

"Transco Energy: The Natural Gas Pipeliner That's Rewriting the Rules." *Business Week*, July 18, 1983, 126.

"Transco Is a Diversified Domestic Energy Company, Analysts Told." *HotTap*, October 1981, 18.

Transcontinental Gas Pipe Line Corporation. Annual reports (1969–73).

———. "A Status Report on Transco's Gas Supply and Market Situation," August 24, 1984. (Copy in author's possession.)

"Transco President Announces Replacement." *Transcogram*, April 15, 1981, 1.

"Transco's New President: Ken Lay." *HotTap*, June 1981, 2–3.

"Transco Studying Coal Gasification." *Transgas*, September–October 1973, 14.

"Transco Tower: The Tallest Building in Suburban Houston." *Transgas*, March–April 1971, 9–10.

"True Bill for Insulls Today." *Chicago Tribune*, October 4, 1932.

Tucker, John C. *Trial and Error: The Education of a Courtroom Lawyer*. New York: Basic Books, 2003.

Tullock, Gordon. "Public Choice." In *The New Palgrave: A Dictionary of Economics*, edited by John Eatwell *et al.*, 1040–44. New York: Palgrave, 1998.

Tussing, Arlon, and Connie Barlow. *The Natural Gas Industry*. Cambridge, MA: Ballinger, 1984.

———. "The Rise and Fall of Regulation in the Natural Gas Industry." *Public Utility Fortnightly*, March 4, 1982, 15–23.

Tussing, Arlon, and Bob Tippee. *The Natural Gas Industry*. Tulsa, OK: PennWell, 1995.

Twentieth Century Fund Report. *Electric Power and Government Policy*, 1948.

"Twin Oaks Feedstock Coming from Iran." *Transgas*, September–October 1973, 14.

"TXP Rejects Chalkley Bids; Transco Stock, Debt Rating Fall." *Natural Gas Week*, September 23, 1991, 6.

United States vs. Insull et al., Trial transcript (October/November 1934).

Urquhart, M. C., and K. A. Buckley. *Historical Statistics of Canada*. Toronto: Macmillan, 1965.

U.S. Bureau of the Census. *The Statistical History of the United States: From Colonial Times to the Present*. New York: Basic Books, 1976.

U.S. Department of Energy. *United States Energy Policy: 1980–1988*. Washington, DC: Department of Energy, 1988.

"U.S. Orders Insull Inquiry." *Chicago Tribune*, September 25, 1932.

Vadney, Thomas E. *The Wayward Liberal*. Lexington: University Press of Kentucky, 1970.

Valdez, William. "Transco Slams Carriage Door, Aims Message at Feds, Industry." *Natural Gas Week*, June 22, 1987, 1, 3–4.

Van Buren, Ernestine. *Clint: Clinton Williams Murchison*. Austin, TX: Eakin Press, 1986.

Vaughan, Christopher. "Interview with Robert Bradley." *Kaizen*, September 24, 2010. www.ethicsandentrepreneurship.org/20100924/interview-with-robert-bradley-jr/.

Wachhorst, Wyn. *Thomas Alva Edison: An American Myth*. Cambridge, MA: MIT Press, 1981.

"Walking the Marketing Tightrope." *HotTap*, May 1983, 2–9.

Wasik, John. *The Merchant of Power*. New York: Palgrave, 2006.

Wasserstein, Bruce. *Big Deal: Mergers and Acquisitions in the Digital Age*. New York: Warner, 1998.

Waters, L. L. *Energy to Move*. Owensboro, KY: Texas Gas Transmission Corporation, 1985.

Watson, Tracy. "Obama's 'Green Dream Team' Is Warmly Received." *USA Today*, December 12, 2008. www.usatoday.com/news/washington/environment/2008-12-11-greenteam_N.htm.

Wattenberg, Ben. *The Statistical History of the United States*. New York: Basic Books, 1976.

Weare, Eugene. "Depository of Power." *The Chicagoan*, September 28, 1929, 20, 22.

Weber, Max. *The Methodology of the Social Sciences*. Edited and translated by Edward Shils and Henry Finch. New York: Free Press, 1880, 1997.

"Wedding of Gladys Wallis and Samuel Insull the Latest in a Long Line of Alliances between Stage Favorites and Monied Men." *New York World*, June 11, 1899.

Wett, Tim. "Naphtha Supply, Controls Clouding Future of SNG." *Oil and Gas Journal*, July 31, 1972, 53–56.

Wheat, J. E. "The Life and Times of John Henry Kirby." *It's Dogwood Time in Tyler County*, March 1950, 9–29.

Wheatley, Richard. "Cost Competitive Fuels Seen Eroding Natural Gas Markets." *Oil & Gas Journal*, September 27, 1982, 329–30.

"'Whimsical' Energy Policies Cripple Nation, Gas Man Says." *Tulsa World*, January 31, 1979.

Wicks, Hattie. "Analysts Like Transco-CSX Deal but CNG Option Called Crucial." *Natural Gas Week*, January 2, 1989, 3–4.

Williams, Claude. "The Story of Transcontinental." *Oil and Gas Journal*, May 4, 1950, 81–83.

———. "Transcontinental 1952." *Transgas*, January 1952, 3, 42–43.

Williams, Richard. "Where Working Is a Gas." *Orlando Sentinel Florida Magazine*, January 31, 1971, 21–22.

Williams Companies, Inc. Annual reports, 1994–2000.

Winkler, John. *Morgan the Magnificent*. Garden City, NY: Garden City Publishing, 1930.

Wolfe, Jane. *The Murchisons: The Rise and Fall of a Texas Dynasty*. New York: St. Martin's Press, 1989.

Woodbury, David. *Elihu Thomson: Beloved Scientist*. Boston: Museum of Science, 1960.

Woolley, Edward. "Hunting Kilowatts for $100,000 a Year." *McClure's*, October 1914, 114–20.

World Commission on Environment and Development. *Our Common Future*. New York: Oxford University Press, 1987.

Yandle, Bruce. "Bootleggers and Baptists—The Education of a Regulatory Economist." *Regulation*, May/June 1983, 12–16.

Yergin, Daniel. *The Prize: The Epic Quest for Oil, Money & Power*. New York: Simon & Schuster, 1991.

Zimmermann, Erich. *Conservation in the Production of Petroleum*. New Haven, CT: Yale University Press, 1957.

———. *World Resources and Industries: A Functional Appraisal of the Availability of Agricultural and Industrial Resources*. New York: Harper & Brothers, 1933; 2nd ed., 1951.

Interviews (copies in author's possession)

Barnhart, Jim. Interview by Robert L. Bradley Jr. Houston, TX, July 31, 2002.

Bowen, Jack. First and second interviews by Robert L. Bradley Jr. and Joseph Pratt. Houston, TX, September 15, 2000.

———. Third Interview by Robert L. Bradley Jr. Houston, TX, July 11 and August 1, 2002.

———. Fourth Interview by Robert L. Bradley Jr. Houston, TX, August 19, 2005.

Fish, Ray. Transcription of a Taped Interview by Alan Dabney. Houston, TX, April 30, 1962. (Copy in author's possession.)

Hargrove, James. Interview by Robert L. Bradley Jr. Houston, TX, August 14, 2002.

Herring, Joanne King. Interview by Robert L. Bradley Jr. Houston, TX, May 5, 2003.

Horton, Stan. Interview by Robert L. Bradley Jr. Houston, TX, February 21, 2001.

Knorpp, Ron. Interview by Robert L. Bradley Jr. Houston, TX, October 5, 2006.

Lay, Ken. "Draft of Answers to Robert L. Bradley Jr.'s Questions." October 5, 2005.

———. Interview by Robert L. Bradley Jr. Houston, TX, April 28, 2005.

———. Interview by Robert L. Bradley Jr. Houston, TX, November 10, 2003.

O'Neill, Brian. Interview by Robert L. Bradley Jr. Houston, TX, June 10, 2005.

Sullivan, Selby. Interview by Robert L. Bradley Jr. Houston, TX, May 5, 2005.

Walker, Charls. Interview by Robert L. Bradley Jr. Potomac, MD, May 23, 2001.

Walker, Pinkney. Interview by Robert L. Bradley Jr. Fort Meyers, FL, March 15, 2001.

Illustration Credits

Figure I.1 *Bowen photograph*: Courtesy of Jack Bowen family. *Herring photograph*: Courtesy of Enron Corporation. *Murchison photograph:* Courtesy of Robert Murchison. *Fish photograph*: Courtesy of Ray Fish family. **Figure I.2** *Lay photograph*: Courtesy of Enron Corporation. *Herring, Matthews, Smith, and Wimberly photographs*: Courtesy of Enron Corporation. *Kirby photograph*: Courtesy of Stephen F. Austin State University, Forest History Collections. **Figure 1.1** *Photograph:* Courtesy of Loyola University Chicago Archives and Special Collections. **Figure 1.2** *Appliance renderings and early Edison photograph:* Courtesy of GE. *Edison illustration:* Courtesy of Henry Ford Museum. **Figure 1.3** *Edison etching and Edison proxy:* Courtesy of Edison Archives, Edison National Historic Site. *65 Fifth Avenue office building:* Courtesy of Henry Ford Museum. *Insull picture:* Courtesy of Loyola University Chicago Archives and Special Collections. **Figure 1.4** *Photographs and document:* Courtesy of Edison Archives, Edison National Historic Site. **Figure 1.5** *Morgan painting:* Frank Holl (1888), Courtesy of Morgan Library and Museum. *Early Wall Street:* Courtesy of Greenwich Publishing. *Charles Coffin photograph and Edison Building:* Courtesy of GE. **Figure 1.6** *Top:* Courtesy of Loyola University Chicago Archives and Special Collections. *Bottom:* Courtesy of GE. **Figure 1.7** *Edison buildings:* Courtesy of GE. *Insull photograph:* Courtesy of Loyola University Chicago Archives and Special Collections. **Figure 1.8** *Top left:* Courtesy of Rutgers University Press. *Bottom left:* Courtesy of Thames & Hudson. *Right:* Courtesy of Henry Ford Museum. **Figure 1.9** *Chart:* Courtesy of Macmillan. **Figure 1.10** *Top:* Courtesy of GE. *Bottom:* Courtesy of Loyola University Chicago Archives and Special Collections. **Figure 1.11** *Menu:* Courtesy of Loyola University Chicago Archives and Special Collections. **Figure 2.1** *Photographs:* Courtesy of Loyola University Chicago Archives and Special Collections. **Figure 2.3** *Photographs:* Courtesy of Commonwealth Edison Company (Exelon). **Figure 2.4** *Photograph and illustrations:* Courtesy of Loyola University Chicago Archives and Special Collections. **Figure 2.5** *Wedding announcement:* Courtesy of Loyola University Chicago Archives and Special Collections. **Figure 2.6** *Photograph:* Courtesy of Edison Electric Institute. **Figure 2.7** *Photographs:* Courtesy of Commonwealth Edison Company (Exelon). **Figure 2.8** *Photographs:* Courtesy of Peabody Energy. **Figure 3.1** *Photographs and map:* Courtesy of Commonwealth Edison Company (Exelon). **Figure 3.2** *Photographs:* Courtesy of Commonwealth Edison Company (Exelon). **Figure 3.3** *Photographs:* Courtesy of Commonwealth Edison Company (Exelon). **Figure 3.4** *Magazine cover:* Courtesy of Commonwealth Edison Company (Exelon). **Figure 3.5** *Left, portrait of Smiles:* National Portrait Gallery, London. *Right, photograph of Insull:* Courtesy of Loyola University Chicago Archives and Special Collections. **Figure 3.6** *Photographs and proclamation:* Courtesy of Loyola University

Chicago Archives and Special Collections. **Figure 4.1** *Left, map of Insull assets:* Courtesy of Commonwealth Edison Company (Exelon); *photograph of Gold Coast:* Courtesy of Chicago Historical Society. **Figure 4.2** *Photographs:* Courtesy of Commonwealth Edison Company (Exelon). **Figure 4.3** *Photographs and advertisement:* Courtesy of Commonwealth Edison Company (Exelon). **Figure 4.4** *Photographs and advertisement:* Courtesy of Commonwealth Edison Company (Exelon). **Figure 4.5** *Photographs and advertisements:* Courtesy of Loyola University Chicago Archives and Special Collections. **Figure 4.6** *Photographs and maps:* Courtesy of Loyola University Chicago Archives and Special Collections. **Figure 4.7** *Photographs, book covers, and graphs:* Courtesy of Loyola University Chicago Archives and Special Collections. **Figure 4.8** *Photographs, advertisement, and medallion:* Courtesy of Commonwealth Edison Company (Exelon).
Figure 4.9 *Caricature by John T. McCutcheon:* Courtesy of *Chicago Tribune.* **Figure 4.10** *Top left:* Courtesy of Loyola University Chicago Archives and Special Collections; *top right:* courtesy of *Chicago Tribune; office building:* courtesy of Chicago Historical Society. **Figure 5.1** *Photograph:* Courtesy of Loyola University Chicago Archives and Special Collections; *newspaper clippings:* Courtesy of *Chicago Tribune.* **Figure 5.2** *Maps:* Courtesy of Loyola University Chicago Archives and Special Collections. **Figure 5.3** *Advertisement:* Courtesy of Loyola University Chicago Archives and Special Collections. **Figure 5.4** *Commemorative brochure:* Courtesy of Loyola University Chicago Archives and Special Collections. **Figure 5.5** *Photograph and newspaper clippings:* Courtesy of Loyola University Chicago Archives and Special Collections. **Figure 5.6** *Magazine covers:* Courtesy of *Time.* **Figure 5.7** *Left:* Courtesy of *New York Daily News; right:* courtesy of *Chicago Tribune.* **Figure 5.8** *Upper left:* courtesy of *Chicago Tribune; upper right:* courtesy of Chicago Historical Society; *lower right:* courtesy of *Chicago Tribune; bottom center:* courtesy of *Chicago Tribune.* **Figure 6.1** *Photographs:* Courtesy of Jack Bowen family.
Figure 6.2 *Photographs of Clint and Frank Murchison:* Courtesy of Robert Murchison; *top center and lower photographs:* Courtesy of El Paso Corporation. **Figure 6.4** *Advertisement, photograph, and map:* Courtesy of El Paso Corporation. **Figure 7.1** *Magazine cover and map:* Courtesy of *Time.* **Figure 7.2** *Magazine cover of Howe:* courtesy of *Time. Murchison photograph:* Courtesy of Robert Murchison. **Figure 7.3** *Murchison photograph:* Courtesy of Robert Murchison. *Frost photograph:* http://deen.witran.org/wiki/Leslie_Frost. *Howe photograph:* Courtesy of Clarke, Irwin & Company. **Figure 7.4** *Maps:* Courtesy of *MacLean's Magazine.* **Figure 7.5** *Map, photograph, signature, and logo:* Courtesy of Enron Corporation. **Figure 7.6** *Photograph and logo:* Courtesy of El Paso Corporation. **Figure 7.7** *Newspaper clippings:* Courtesy of TransCanada Corporation. **Figure 7.8** *Left:* Courtesy of Robert Murchison; *upper right:* www.archaeolink.com/prime_13.gif; *lower right:* Courtesy of El Paso Corporation. **Figure 7.9** *Covers and illustration:* Courtesy of TransCanada Corporation. **Figure 8.1** *Logo, map, and photographs:* Courtesy of Jack Bowen family.
Figure 8.2 *Maps and photographs:* Courtesy of Jack Bowen family. **Figure 8.3** *Photographs and illustrations:* Courtesy of Jack Bowen family. **Figure 8.5** *Photographs:* Courtesy of Jack Bowen family. **Figure 8.6** *Photographs and maps:* Courtesy of Jack Bowen family. **Figure 8.7** *Photographs and logo:* Courtesy of Jack Bowen family. **Figure 8.8** *Photographs and documents:* Courtesy of Jack Bowen family. **Figure 8.9** *Photographs:* Courtesy of Jack Bowen family. **Figure 8.10** *Photographs of Wilheit and Lay:* Courtesy of Jack Bowen family. *Photograph of Morgan:* Courtesy of Enron Corporation. **Figure 8.11** *Photographs and chart:* Courtesy of Jack Bowen family. **Figure 9.1** *Covers, maps, and photograph:* Courtesy of Williams Companies, Inc. **Figure 9.2** *Photographs:* Courtesy of Williams Companies, Inc. **Figure 9.3** *Photographs:* Courtesy of Williams Companies, Inc. **Figure 9.4** *Photographs and logo:* Courtesy of Williams Companies, Inc. **Figure 9.5** *Photographs and map:* Courtesy of Williams Companies, Inc. **Figure 9.6** *Cover and photographs:* Courtesy of Williams Companies, Inc. **Figure 9.7** *Documents and photograph:* Courtesy of Williams Companies, Inc.

Figure 9.8 *Photographs:* Courtesy of Williams Companies, Inc. **Figure 9.9** *Photographs:* Courtesy of Williams Companies, Inc. **Figure 9.10** *Photographs and signature:* Courtesy of Williams Companies, Inc. **Figure 9.11** *Photographs:* Courtesy of Williams Companies, Inc. **Figure 9.12** *Document, photographs, and signatures:* Courtesy of Williams Companies, Inc. **Figure 9.13** *Map and photographs:* Courtesy of Williams Companies, Inc. **Figure 9.14** *Photographs and signatures:* Courtesy of Williams Companies, Inc. **Figure 9.15** *Magazine mastheads:* Courtesy of Williams Companies, Inc. **Figure 9.16** *Photographs:* Courtesy of Williams Companies, Inc. **Figure 9.17** *Map and photographs:* Courtesy of Williams Companies, Inc. **Figure 10.1** *Photograph of Rice Hotel:* Courtesy of George Fuermann City of Houston Collection, Special Collections, University of Houston Libraries. *Menu:* Courtesy of El Paso Corporation. *Kirby photograph:* Courtesy of Stephen F. Austin State University, Forest History Collections. *Calhoun photograph:* Courtesy Texas Gulf Historical Society. **Figure 10.2** *Left, photograph and map:* Courtesy of Stephen F. Austin State University, Forest History Collections. *Right, photograph of gusher:* http://upload.wikimedia.org/wikipedia/commons/d/d8/Lucas_gusher.jpg. **Figure 10.3** *Photographs and sales slip:* Courtesy of Stephen F. Austin State University, Forest History Collections. **Figure 10.4** *Photograph:* Courtesy of Stephen F. Austin State University, Forest History Collections. **Figure 10.5** *Documents and photographs:* Courtesy of Stephen F. Austin State University, Forest History Collections. **Figure 10.6** *Photographs:* Courtesy of Stephen F. Austin State University, Forest History Collections. **Figure 11.1** *Photographs and newspaper clipping:* Courtesy of Robert Herring family. **Figure 11.2** *Photograph:* Courtesy of Robert Herring family. **Figure 11.3** *Photograph:* Courtesy of Ray Fish family. **Figure 11.4** *Photographs and brochure:* Courtesy of Ray Fish family. **Figure 11.5** *Left, photograph of Fish:* Courtesy of Don Simecheck. *Right, photograph of Herring:* Courtesy of Robert Herring family. **Figure 12.1** *Graphic, photographs, and map:* Courtesy of Enron Corporation. **Figure 12.2** *Left, photograph and etching:* Courtesy of Frank C. Smith Jr.; *lower right:* Courtesy of Enron Corporation. **Figure 12.3** *Illustration:* Courtesy of Enron Corporation. **Figure 12.4** *Advertisements:* Courtesy of Enron Corporation. **Figure 12.5** *Map:* Courtesy of Enron Corporation. **Figure 12.6** *Drawing and photograph:* Courtesy of Enron Corporation. **Figure 13.1** *Photograph:* Courtesy of Enron Corporation. **Figure 13.2** *Map:* Courtesy of Enron Corporation. **Figure 13.3** *Etching:* Courtesy of Enron Corporation. **Figure 13.4** *Photographs:* Courtesy of Joanne King Herring. **Figure 13.5** *Photograph:* Courtesy of Enron Corporation. **Figure 13.6** *Photograph:* Courtesy of Enron Corporation. **Figure 13.7** *Document and photographs:* Courtesy of El Paso Corporation.

Name Index

Subject Index

Also of Interest

Still Available
Book 1 of Political Capitalism (A Trilogy)
From Amazon.com or www.scrivenerpublishing.com

Capitalism at Work
Business, Government, and Energy
2009, ISBN 978-0-9764041-7-0

By Robert L. Bradley Jr

Capitalism took the blame for Enron although the company was anything but a free-market enterprise, and company architect Ken Lay was hardly a principled capitalist. On the contrary, Enron was a politically dependent company and, in the end, a grotesque outcome of America's mixed economy.

That is the central finding of Robert L. Bradley's *Capitalism at Work*: The blame for Enron rests squarely with "political capitalism"—a system in which business firms routinely obtain government intervention to further their own interests at the expense of consumers, taxpayers, and competitors. Although Ken Lay professed allegiance to free markets, he was in fact a consummate politician. Only by manipulating the levers of government was he able to transform Enron from a $3 billion natural gas company to a $100 billion chimera, one that went in a matter of months from seventh place on *Fortune's* 500 list to bankruptcy.

But *Capitalism at Work* goes beyond unmasking Enron's sophisticated foray into political capitalism. Employing the timeless insights of Adam Smith, Samuel Smiles, and Ayn Rand, among others, Bradley shows how fashionable anti-capitalist doctrines set the stage for the ultimate business debacle.

Capitalism at Work's penetrating, multidisciplinary explanation of the demise of Enron breaks new ground regarding business history, business ethics, business best practices, and public policies toward business. As Bradley concludes: The fundamental lesson from Enron is this: Capitalism did not fail. The mixed economy failed.

Reviews

"Bradley's book is especially timely, and it raises fundamental questions about the business of competition. Given the author's documentation, a wide audience might be served by reading *Capitalism at Work*." **William A. Mogel,** *Energy Law Journal*

"Fascinating, comprehensive ... far surpassing my own history of political capitalism done in the 1960s." **Gabriel Kolko,** *Historian*

"He (Bradley) has succeeded in his effort to show that Enron was guided by faulty premises well-refuted in the economics literature. A definitive study." **Richard L. Gordon,** *Cato Journal*

"This book contains a treasure of information and insights that will delight and interest the reader." **Peter Lewin,** *Review of Austrian Economics*

"Recommended for public and academic library collections, lower-division undergraduate and up." *CHOICE*